BUILD, BABY

THE **SCIENCE** AND **ETHICS** OF **HOUSING REGULATION**

WRITTEN BY
BRYAN CAPLAN

ARTWORK BY
ADY BRANZEI

CATO
INSTITUTE

Published by the Cato Institute.
Cato Institute is a registered trademark.

Paperback: 978-1-952223-41-9
Ebook: 978-1-952223-42-6

Library of Congress Cataloging-in-Publication Data

Build, Baby, Build: The Science and Ethics of Housing /
Caplan, Bryan Douglas author. Branzei, Ady-Sebastian illustrator.
      p.   cm.
ISBN 9781952223419 (paperback) | 9781952223426 (ebook)
1. Housing policy—United States—Comic books, strips, etc. |
2. Housing—Prices—United States. | 3. Deregulation—United States.
HD7293 .C265   2024
363.5/5610973

Printed in Canada.

Cato Institute
1000 Massachusetts Ave. NW
Washington, DC 20001
www.cato.org

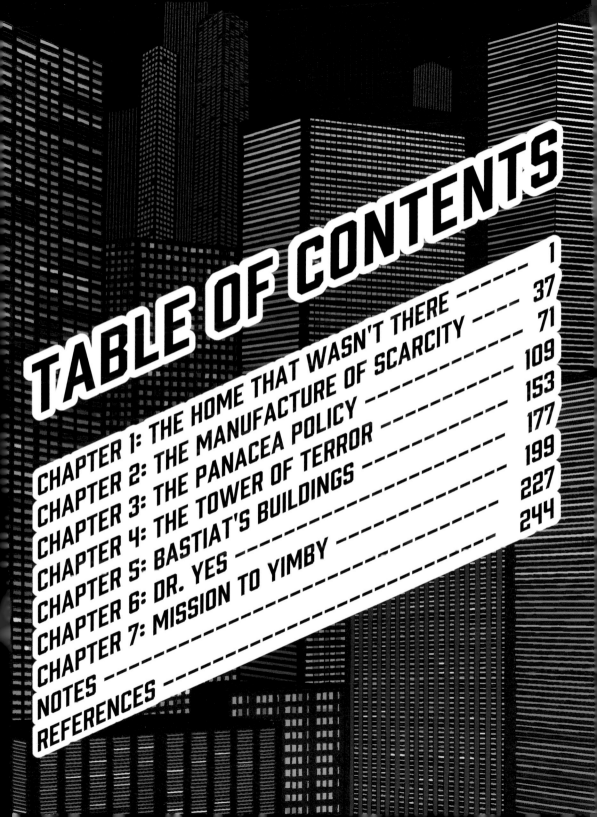

TABLE OF CONTENTS

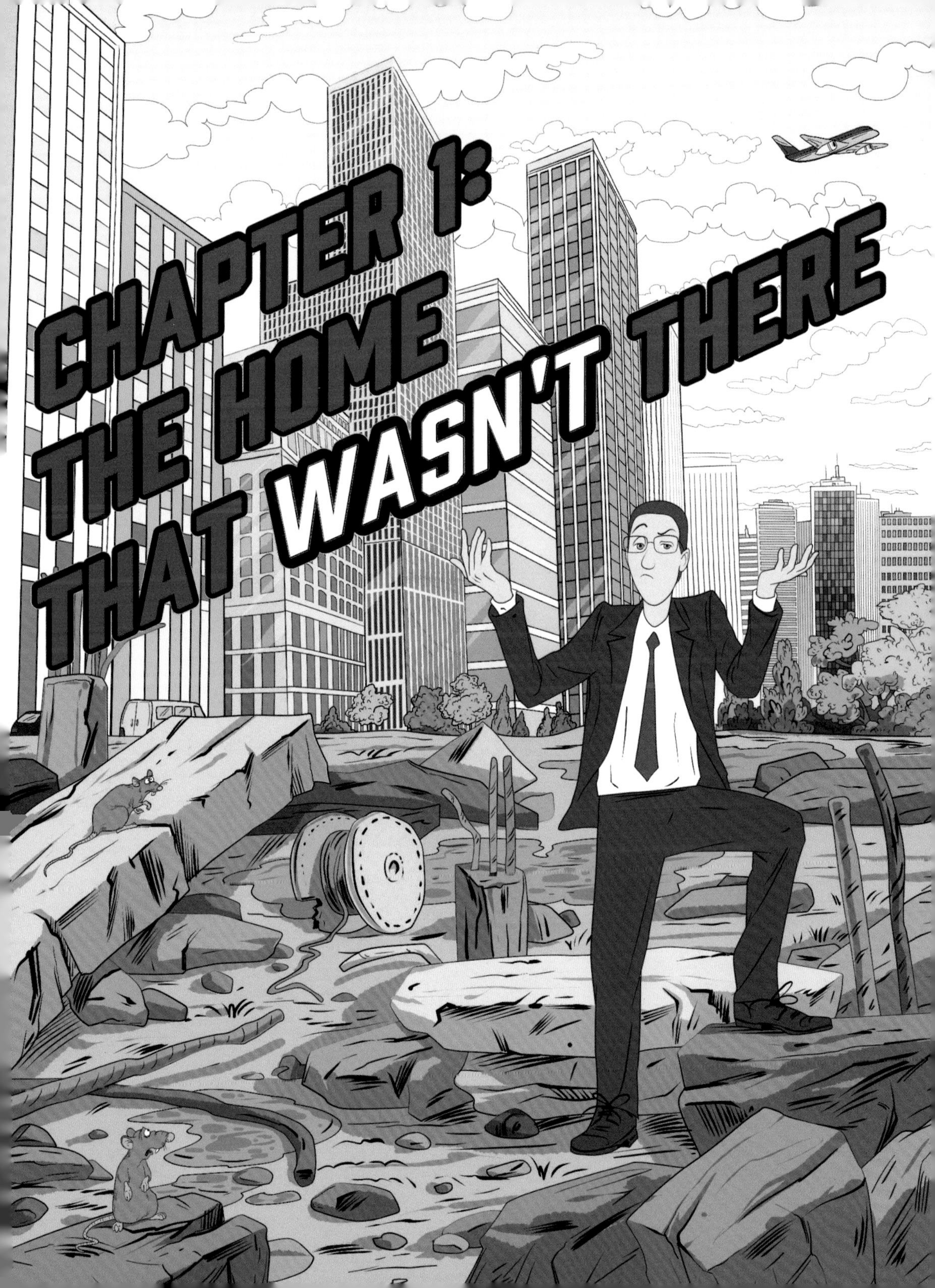
CHAPTER 1:
THE HOME
THAT WASN'T THERE

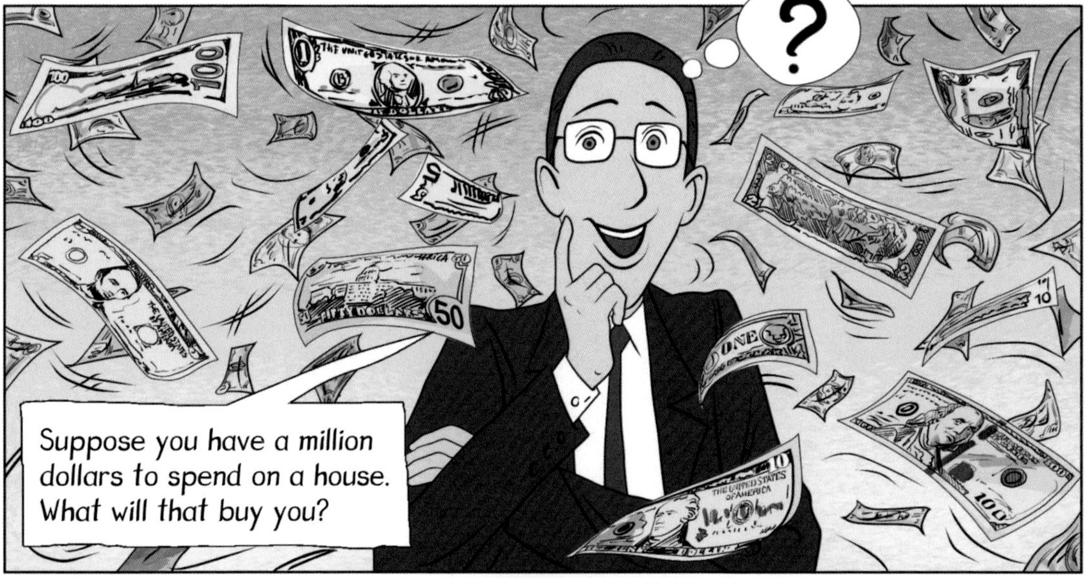
?
Suppose you have a million dollars to spend on a house. What will that buy you?

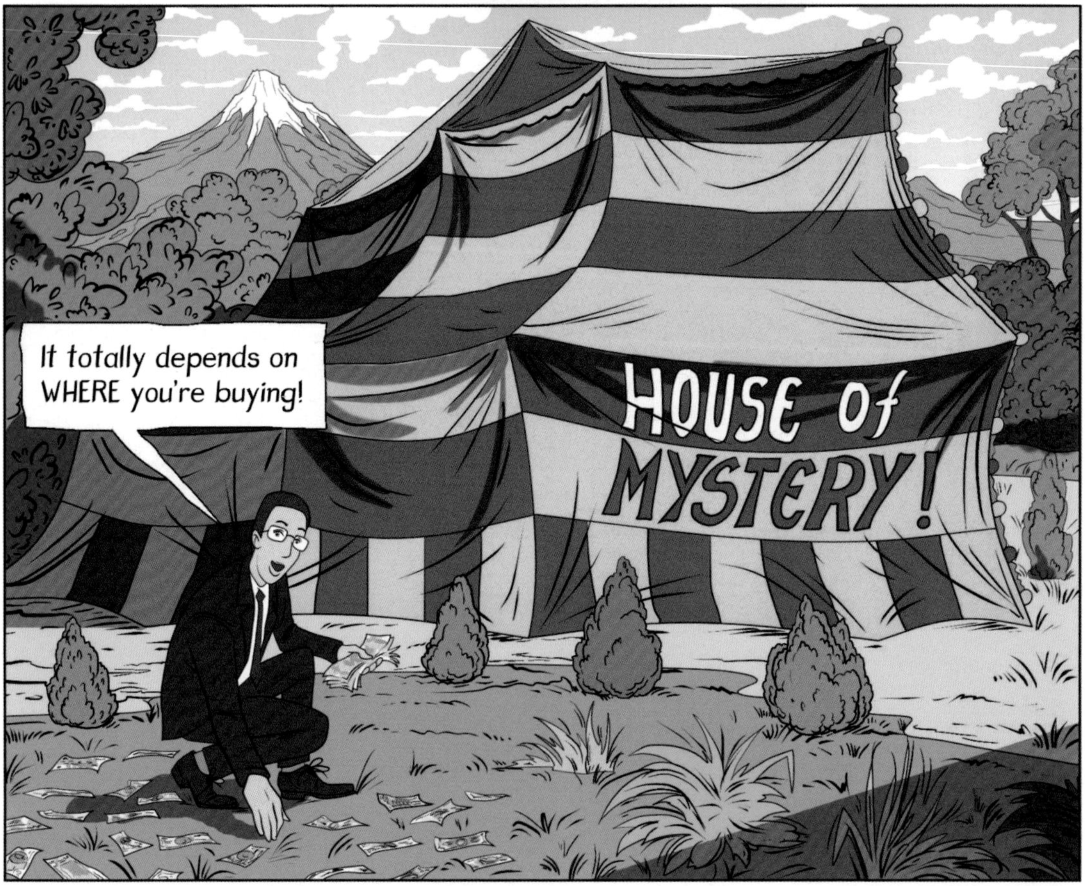
It totally depends on WHERE you're buying!
HOUSE of MYSTERY!

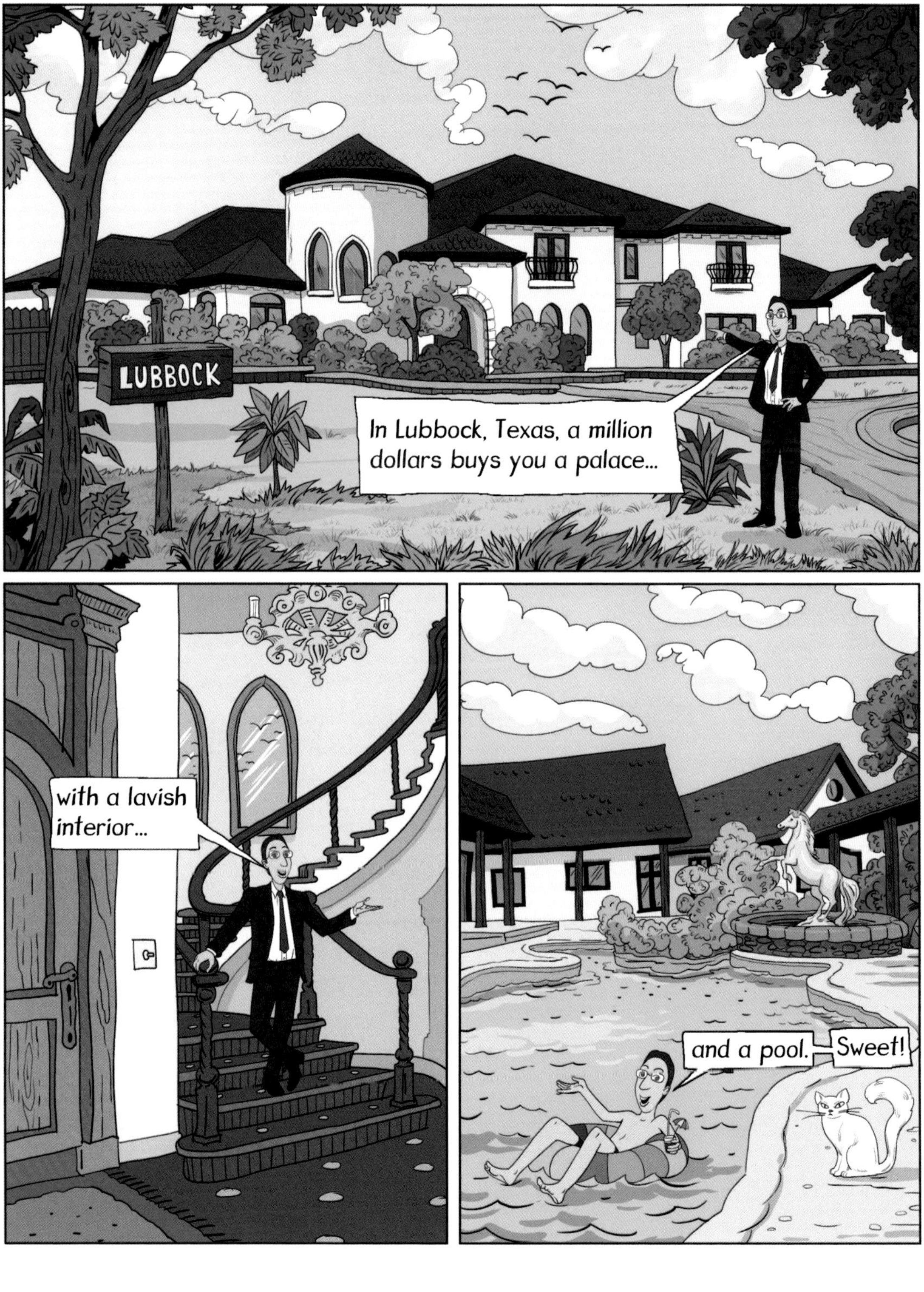
LUBBOCK
In Lubbock, Texas, a million dollars buys you a palace...
with a lavish interior...
and a pool.
Sweet!

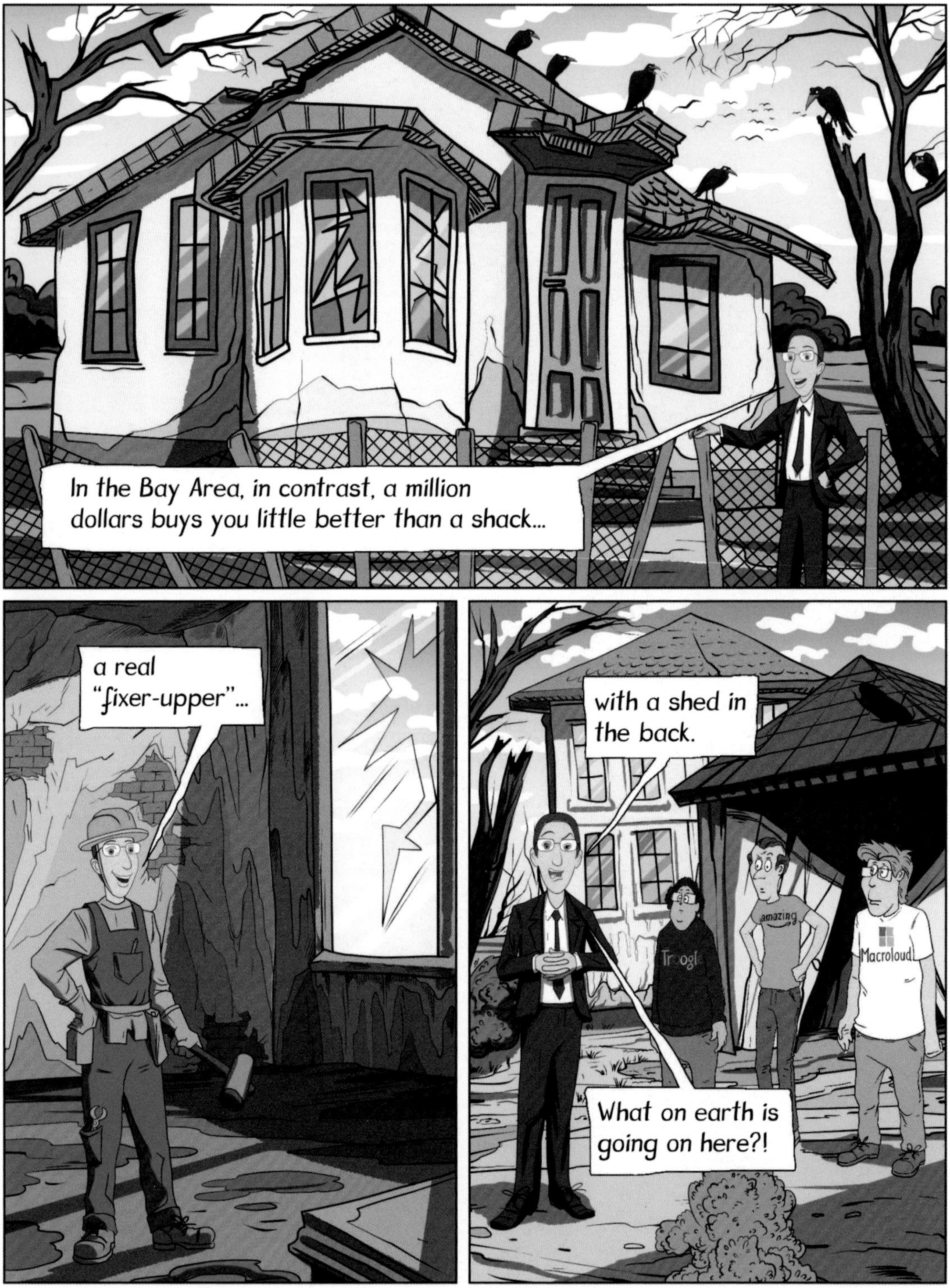
In the Bay Area, in contrast, a million dollars buys you little better than a shack...
a real "fixer-upper"...
with a shed in the back.
amazing
Macroloud
What on earth is going on here?!

Economists have a textbook answer:
"Supply and demand"!
Price
Equilibrium
Supply
S
P
Demand
D
Q
Quantity
COWEN TABARROK MODERN PRINCIPLES ECONOMICS
When demand is low and supply is high – as in Lubbock – housing is cheap.
Price
S_1
P_1
D_1
Q_1
Quantity
When demand is high and supply is low – as in the Bay Area – housing is expensive.
Price
S_2
P_2
D_2
Q_2
Quantity

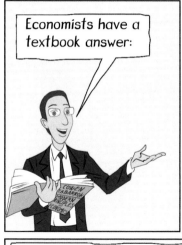

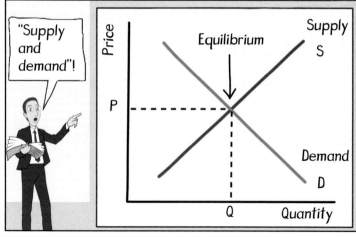

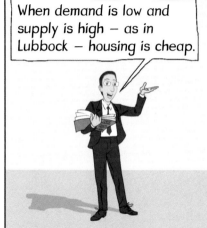

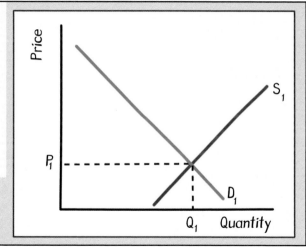

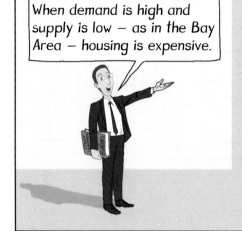

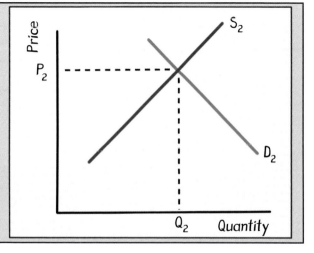

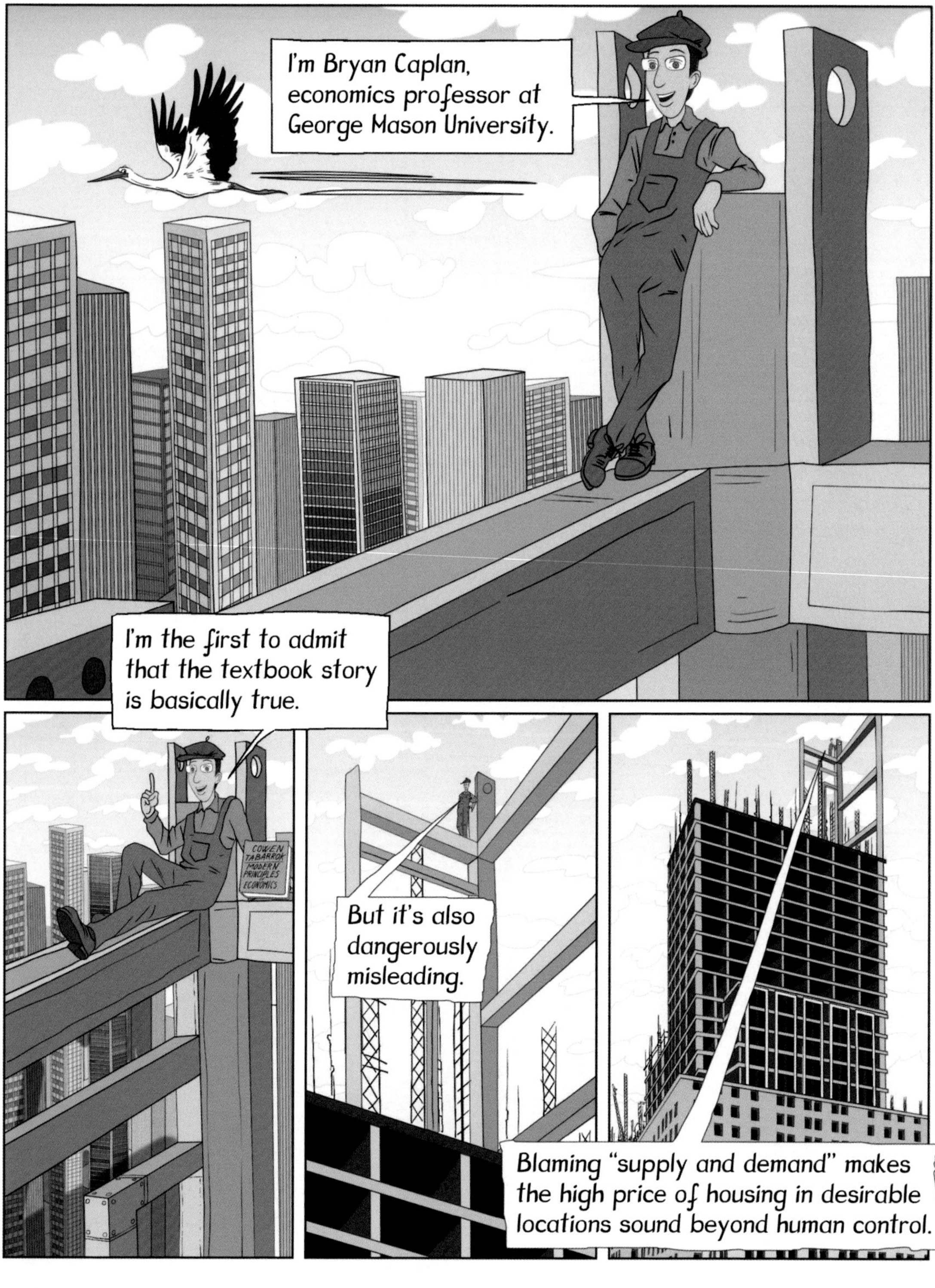
I'm Bryan Caplan, economics professor at George Mason University.
I'm the first to admit that the textbook story is basically true.
COWEN TABARROK MODERN PRINCIPLES ECONOMICS
But it's also dangerously misleading.
Blaming "supply and demand" makes the high price of housing in desirable locations sound beyond human control.

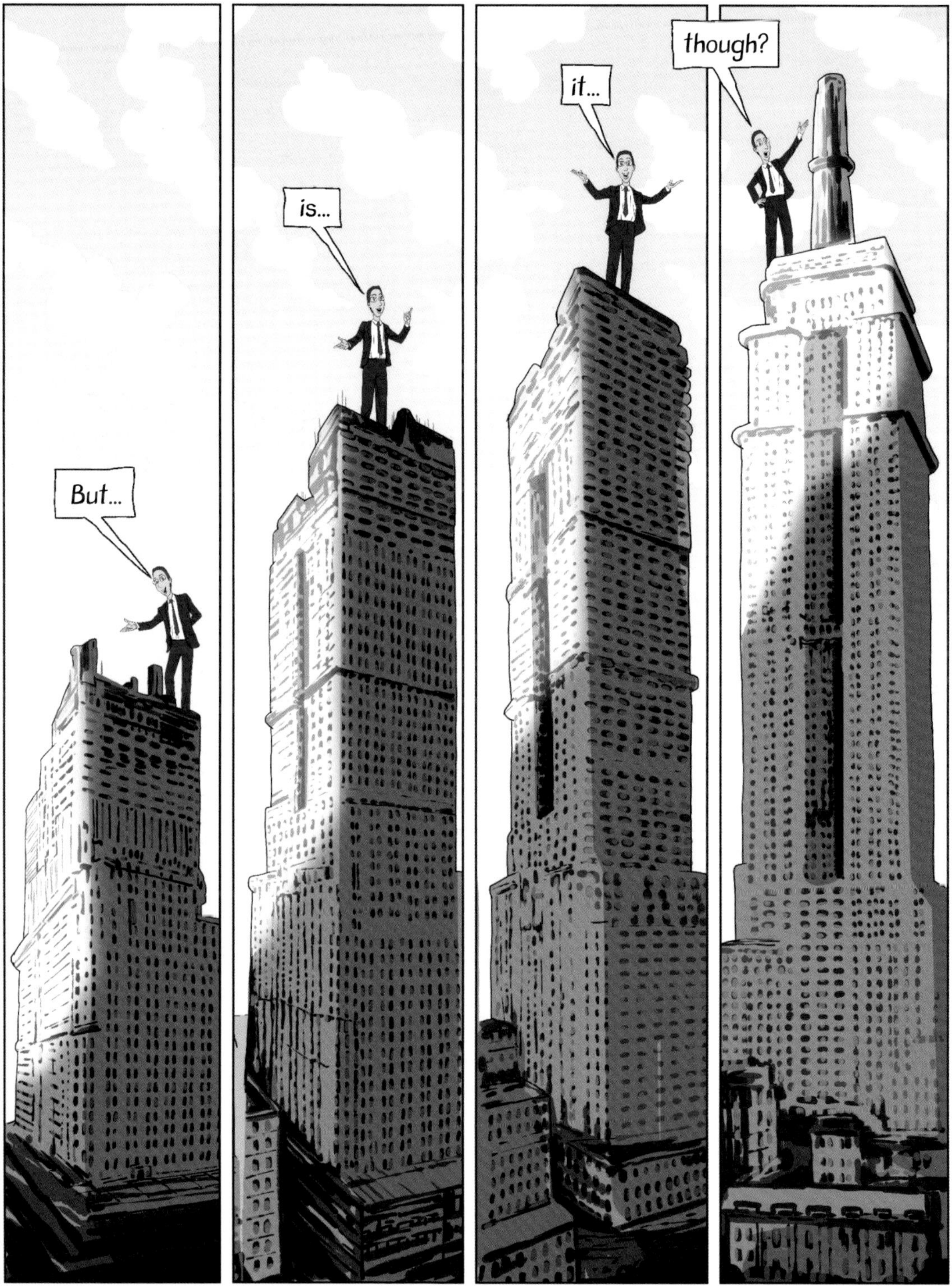
But...
is...
it...
though?

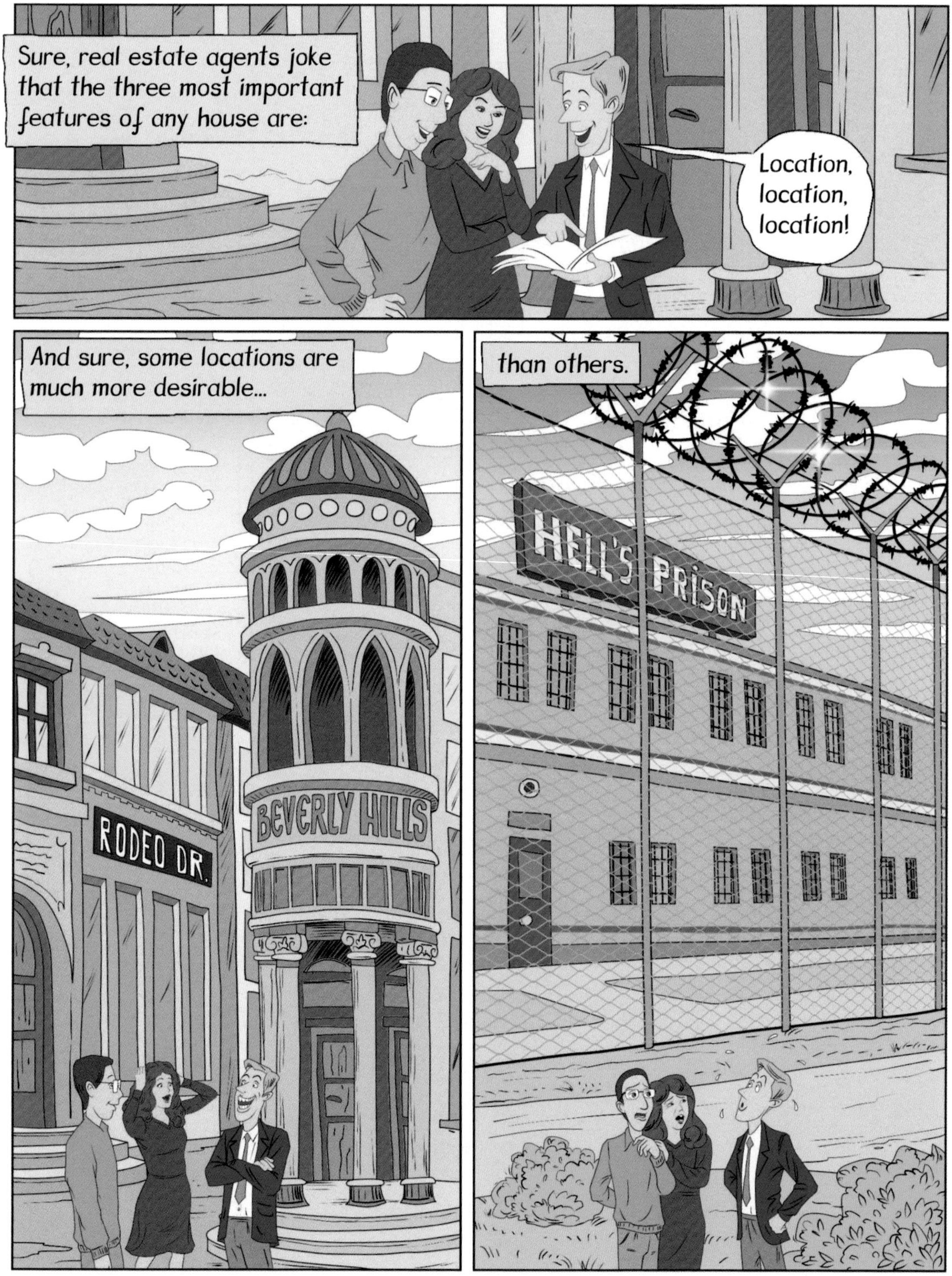
Sure, real estate agents joke that the three most important features of any house are:
Location, location, location!
And sure, some locations are much more desirable...
RODEO DR.
BEVERLY HILLS
than others.
HELL'S PRISON

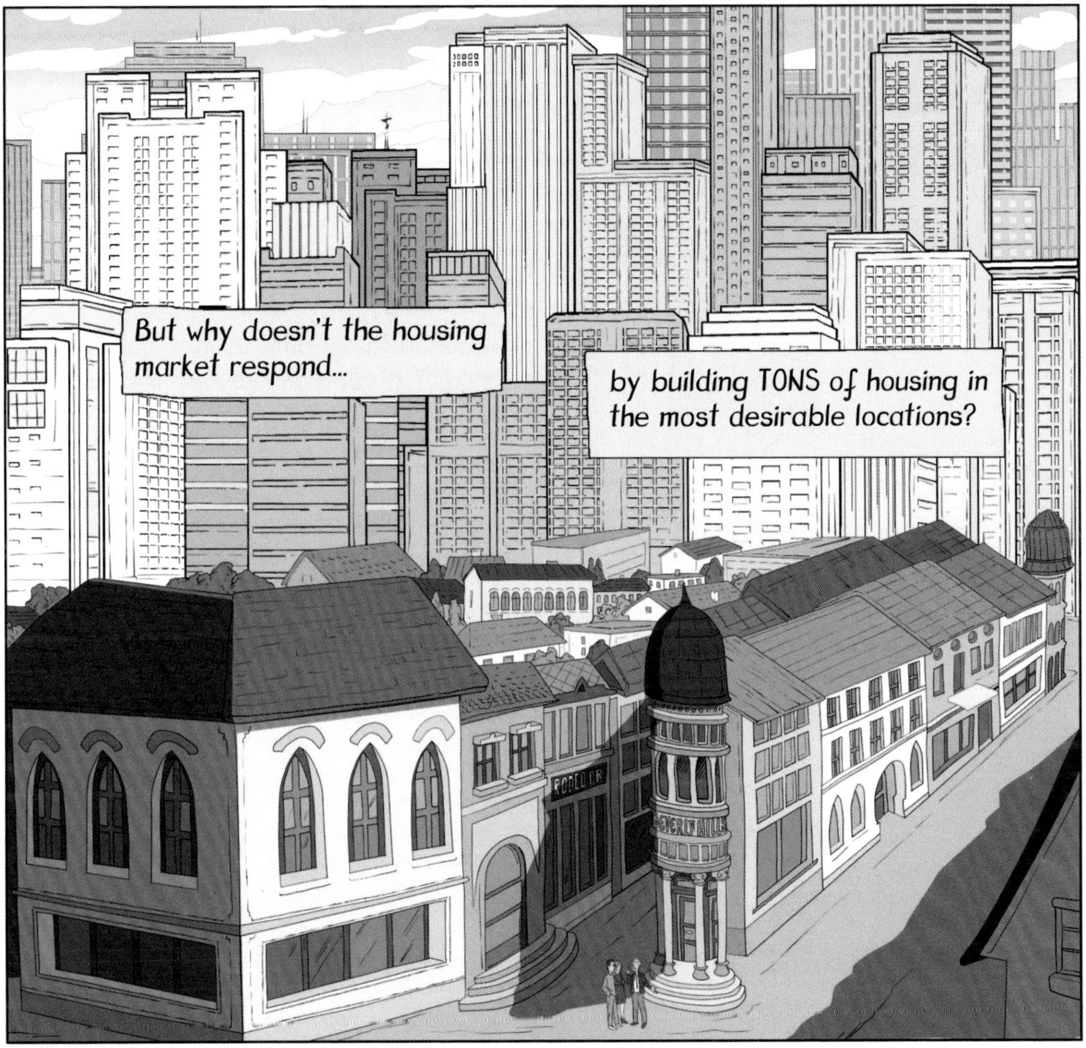
But why doesn't the housing market respond...
by building TONS of housing in the most desirable locations?
RODEO DR
BEVERLY HILLS

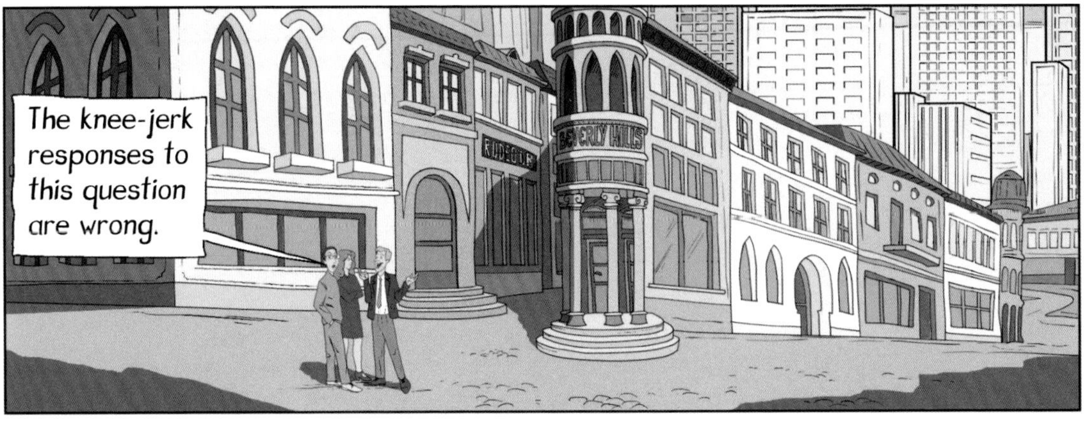
The knee-jerk responses to this question are wrong.
RODEO DR
BEVERLY HILLS

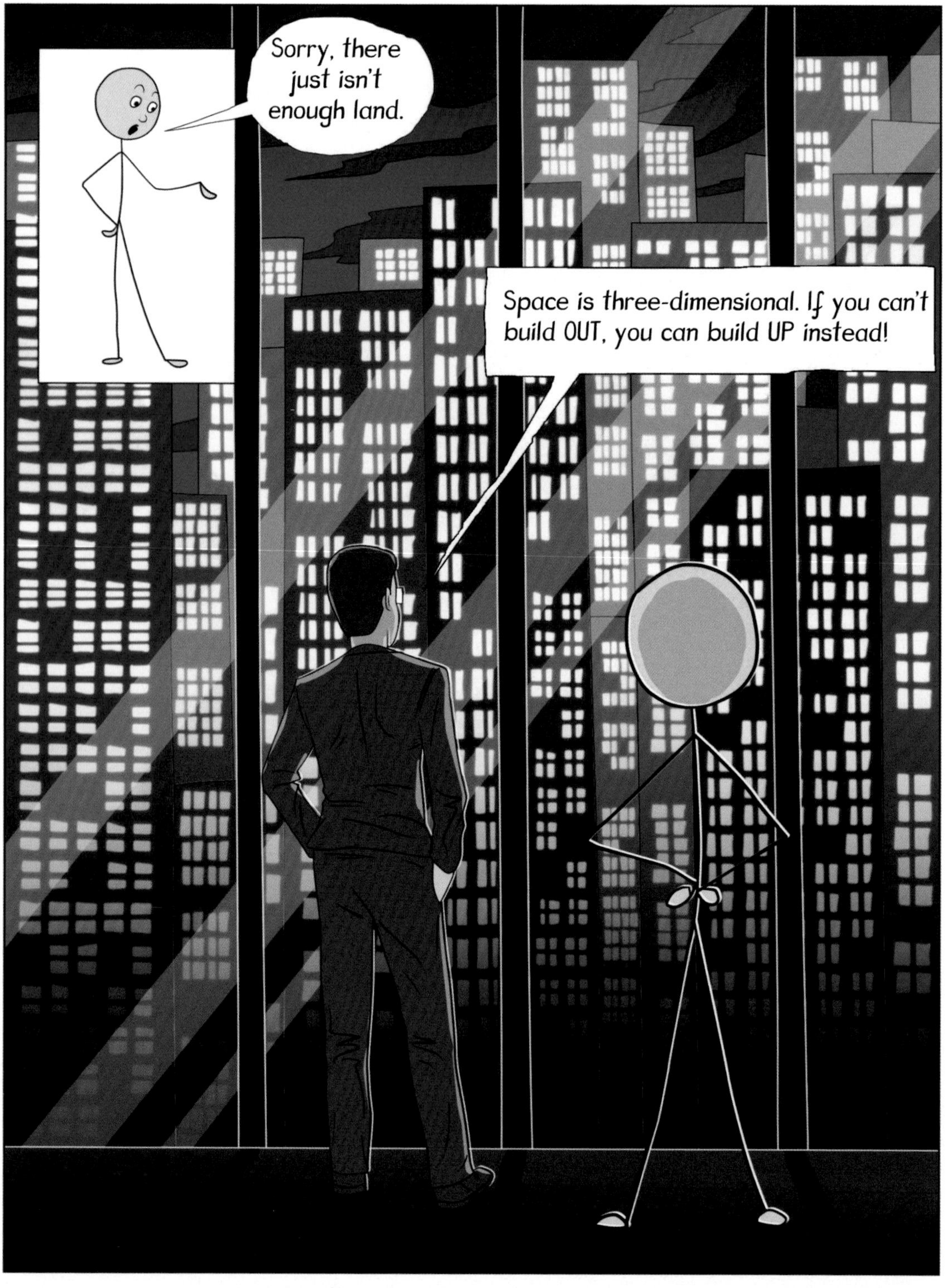
Sorry, there just isn't enough land.
Space is three-dimensional. If you can't build OUT, you can build UP instead!

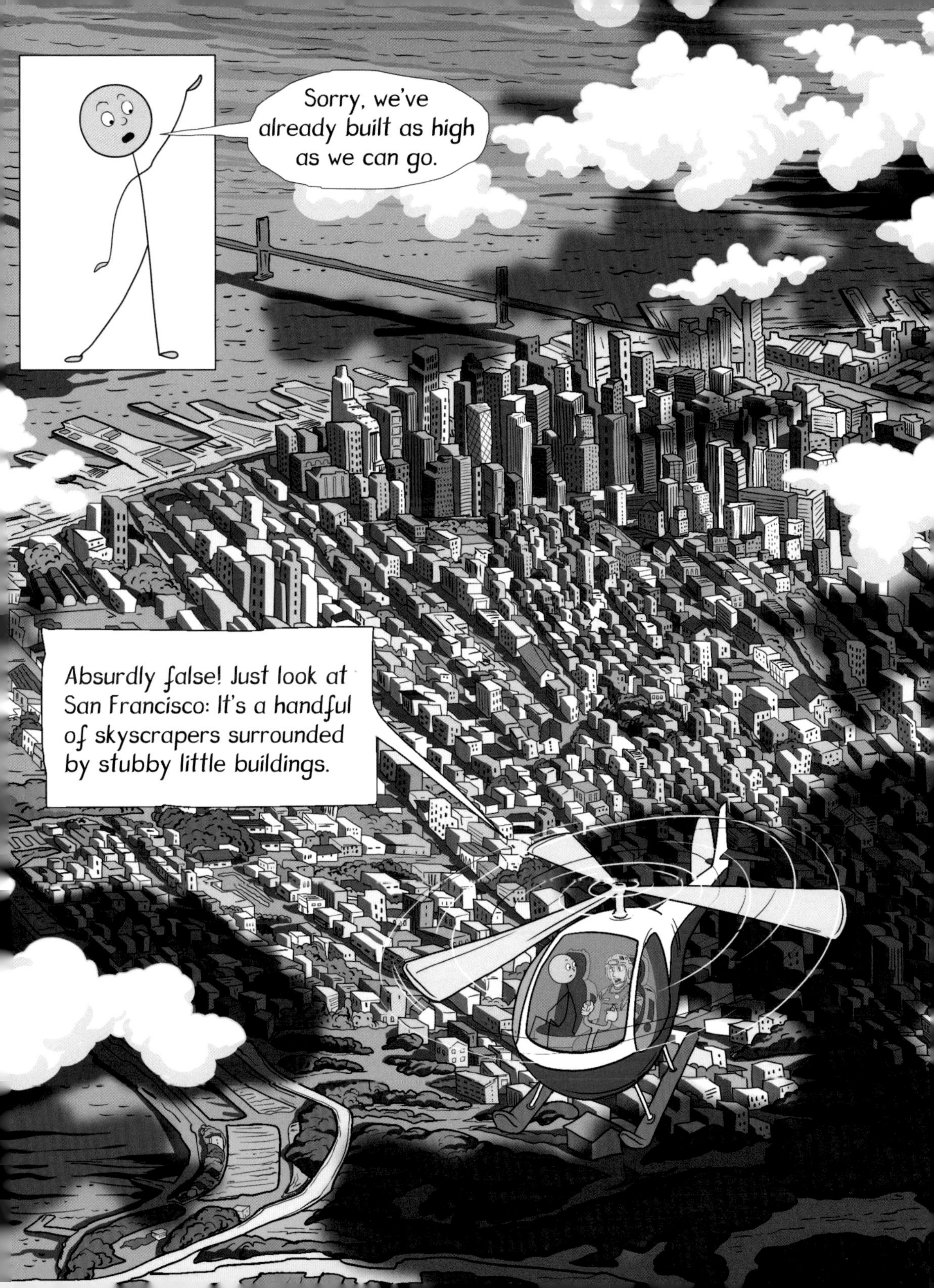
Sorry, we've already built as high as we can go.
Absurdly false! Just look at San Francisco: It's a handful of skyscrapers surrounded by stubby little buildings.

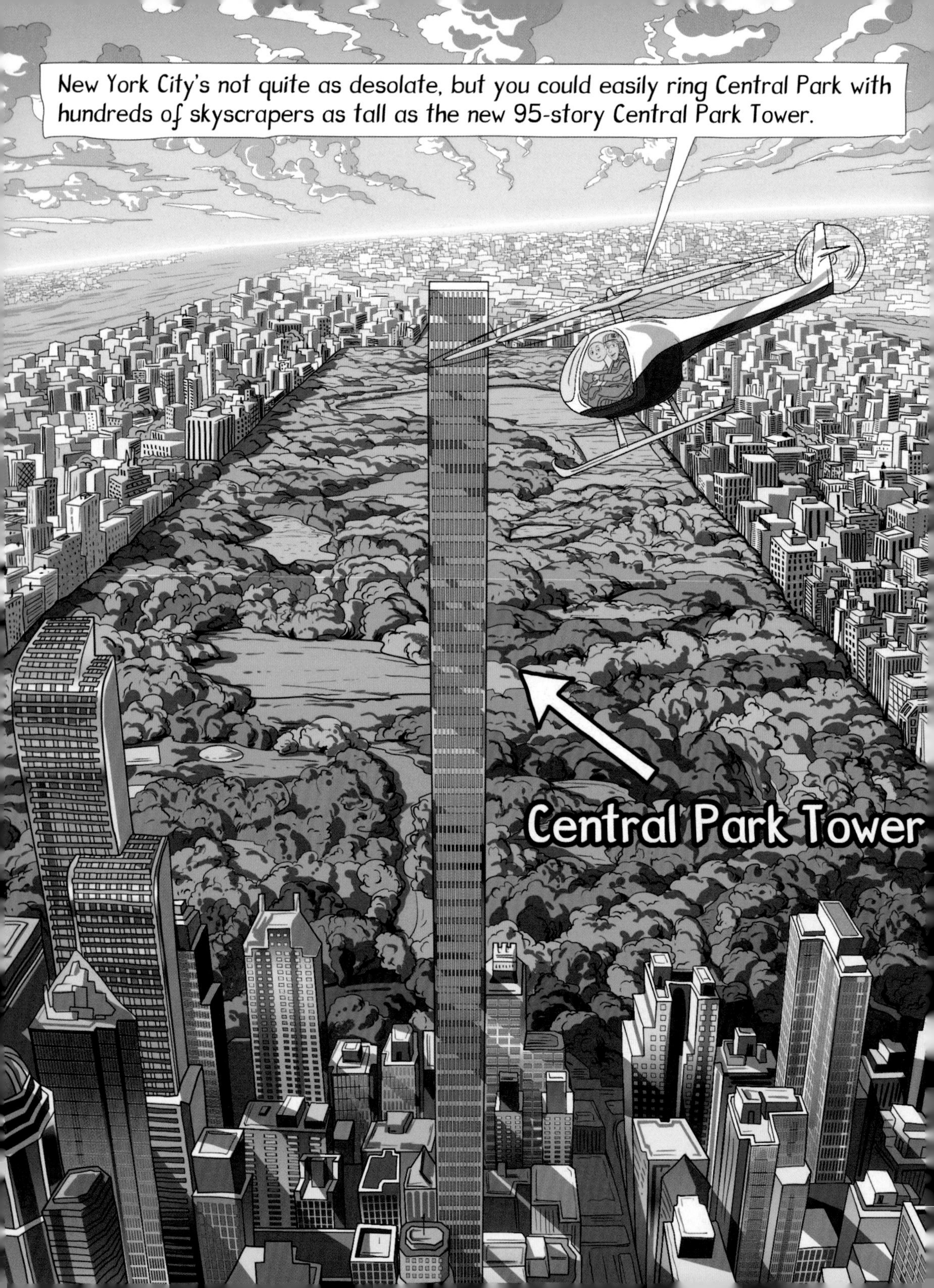
New York City's not quite as desolate, but you could easily ring Central Park with hundreds of skyscrapers as tall as the new 95-story Central Park Tower.
Central Park Tower

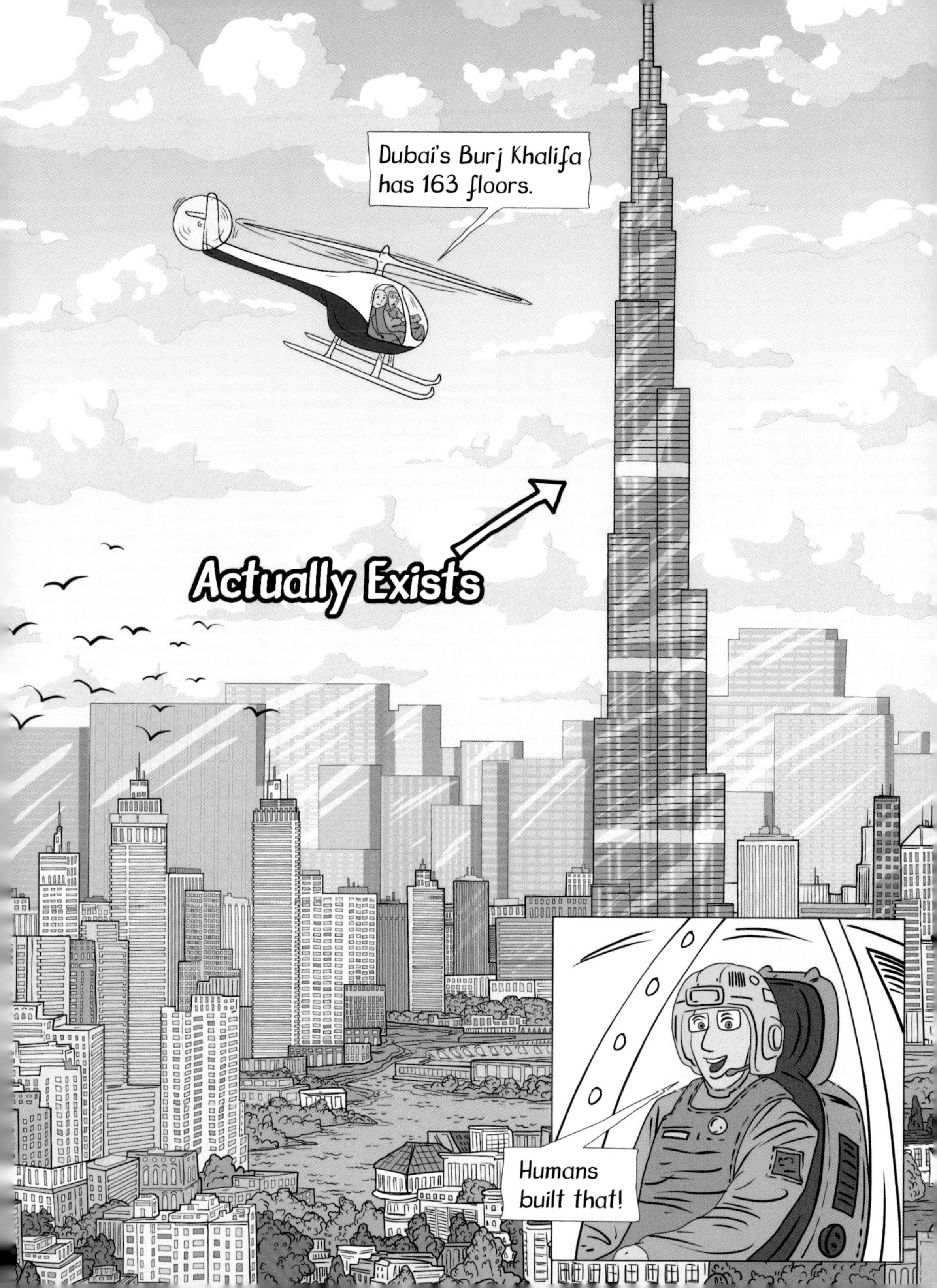
Dubai's Burj Khalifa has 163 floors.
Actually Exists
Humans built that!

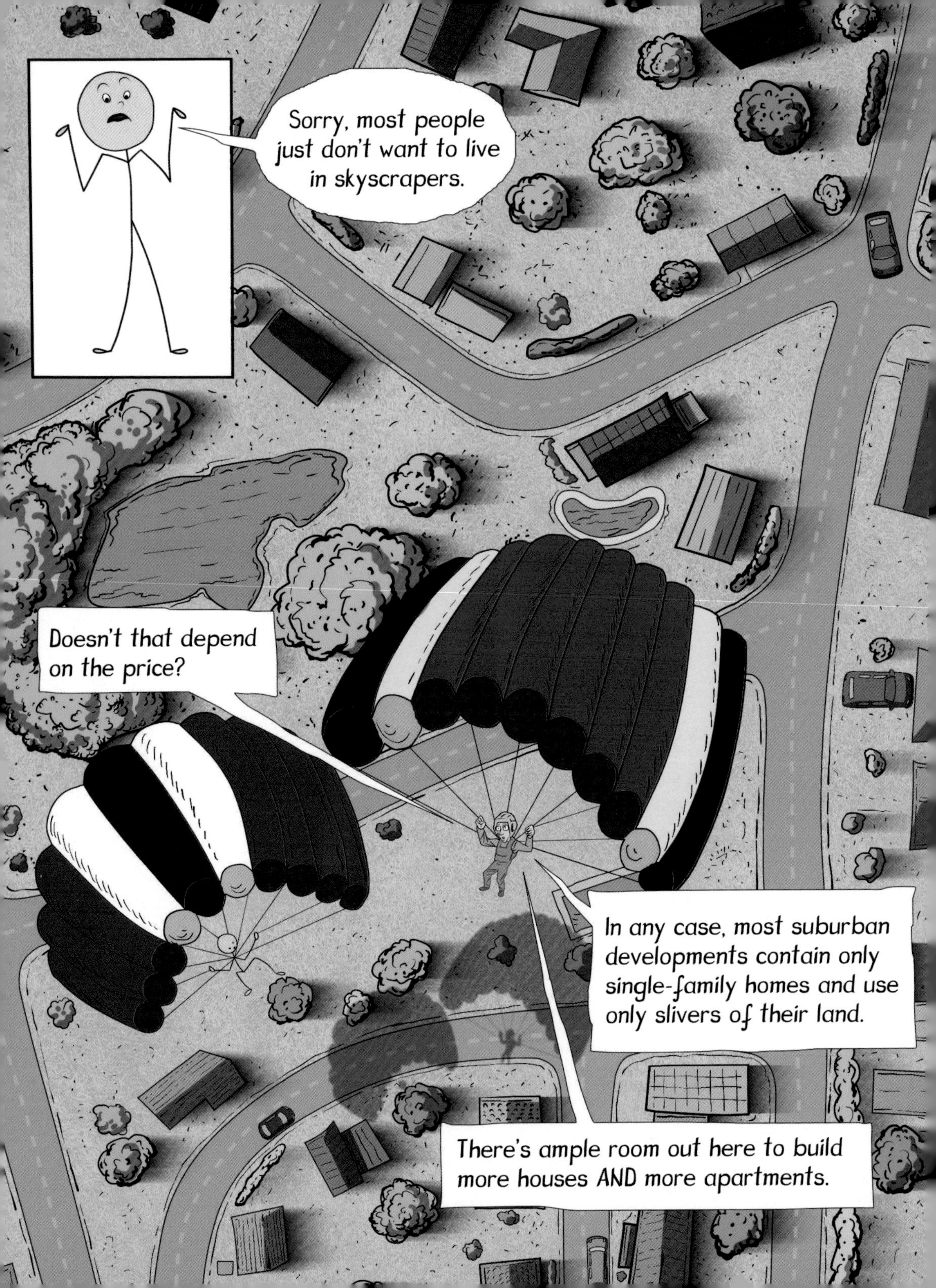
Sorry, most people just don't want to live in skyscrapers.
Doesn't that depend on the price?
In any case, most suburban developments contain only single-family homes and use only slivers of their land.
There's ample room out here to build more houses AND more apartments.

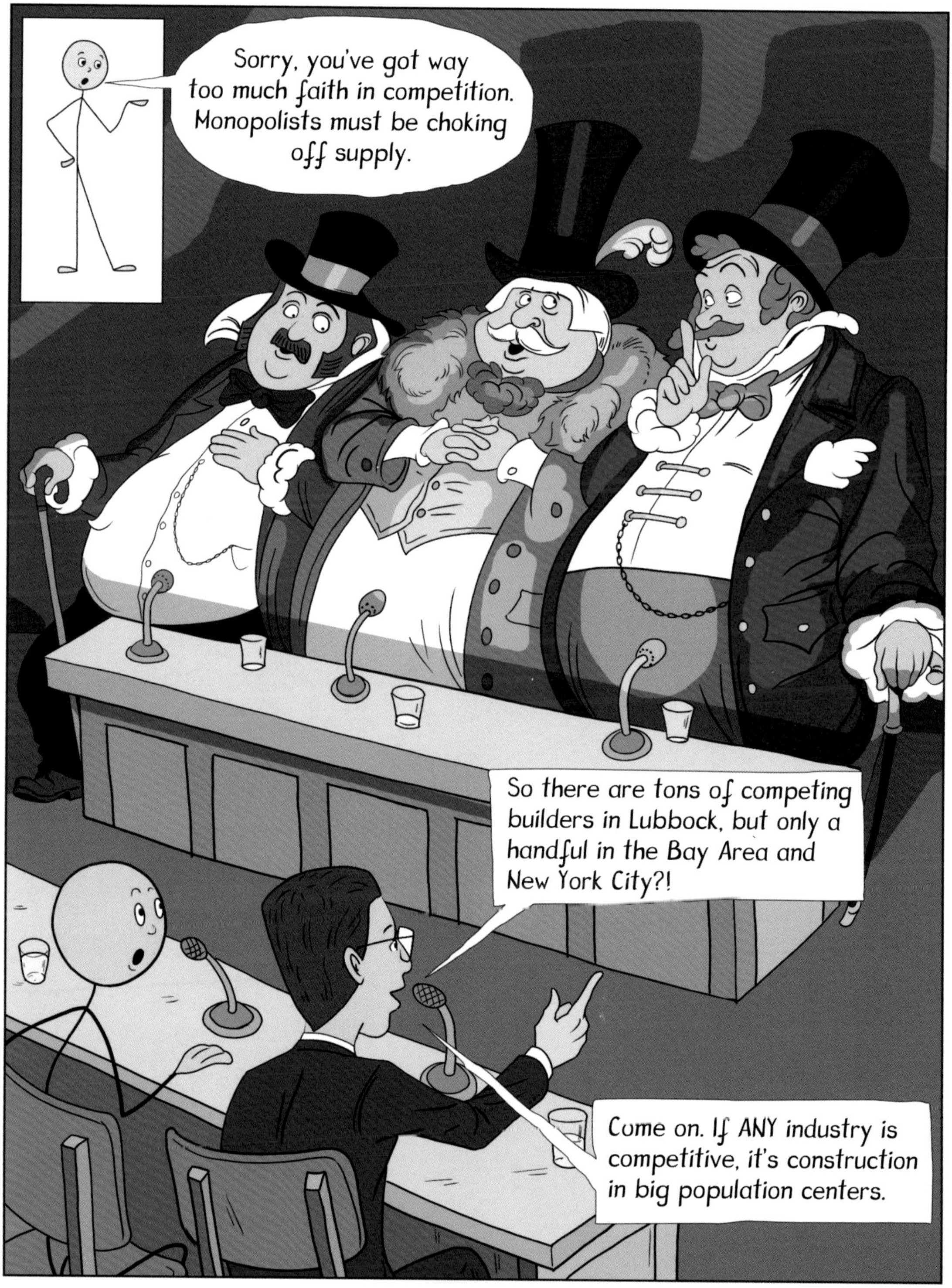
Sorry, you've got way too much faith in competition. Monopolists must be choking off supply.
So there are tons of competing builders in Lubbock, but only a handful in the Bay Area and New York City?!
Come on. If ANY industry is competitive, it's construction in big population centers.

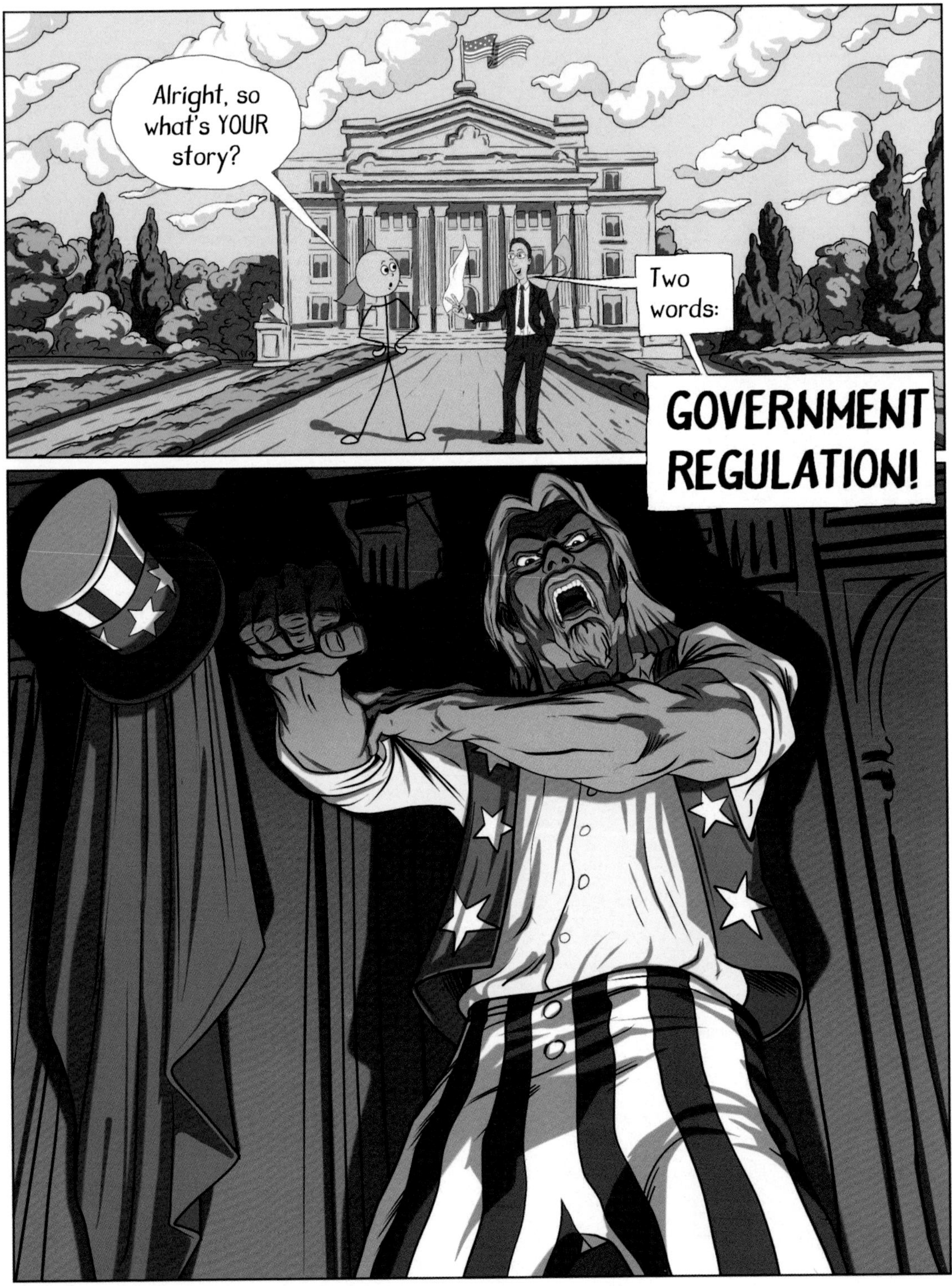
Alright, so what's YOUR story?
Two words:
GOVERNMENT REGULATION!

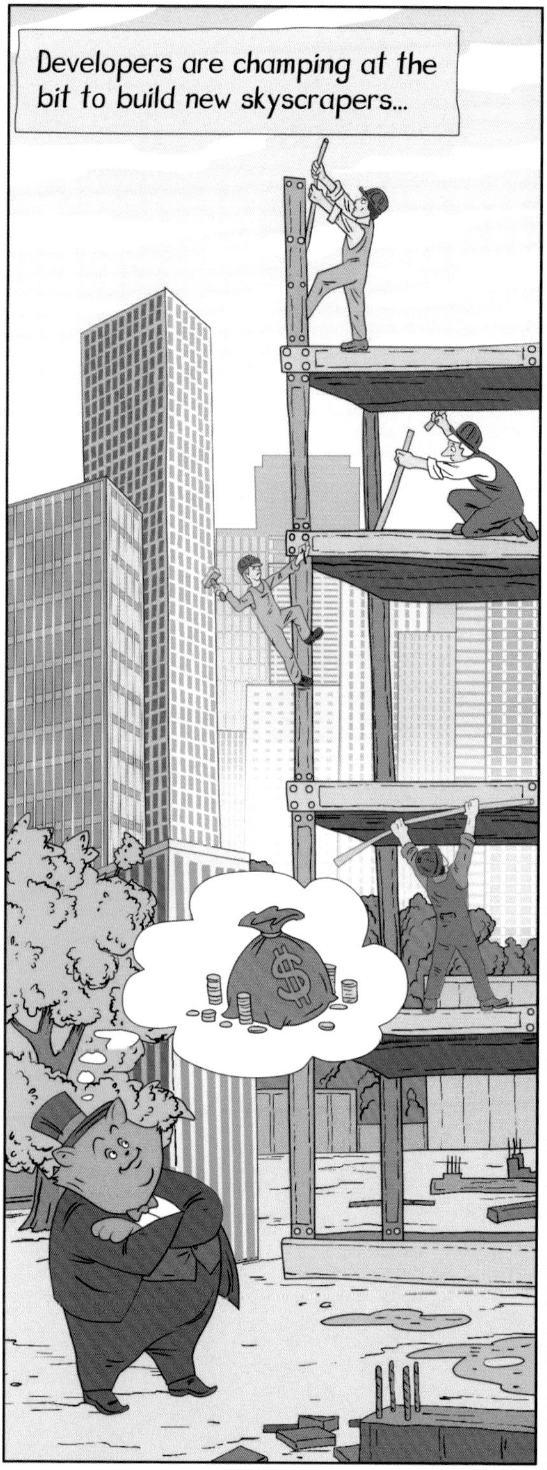
Developers are champing at the bit to build new skyscrapers...

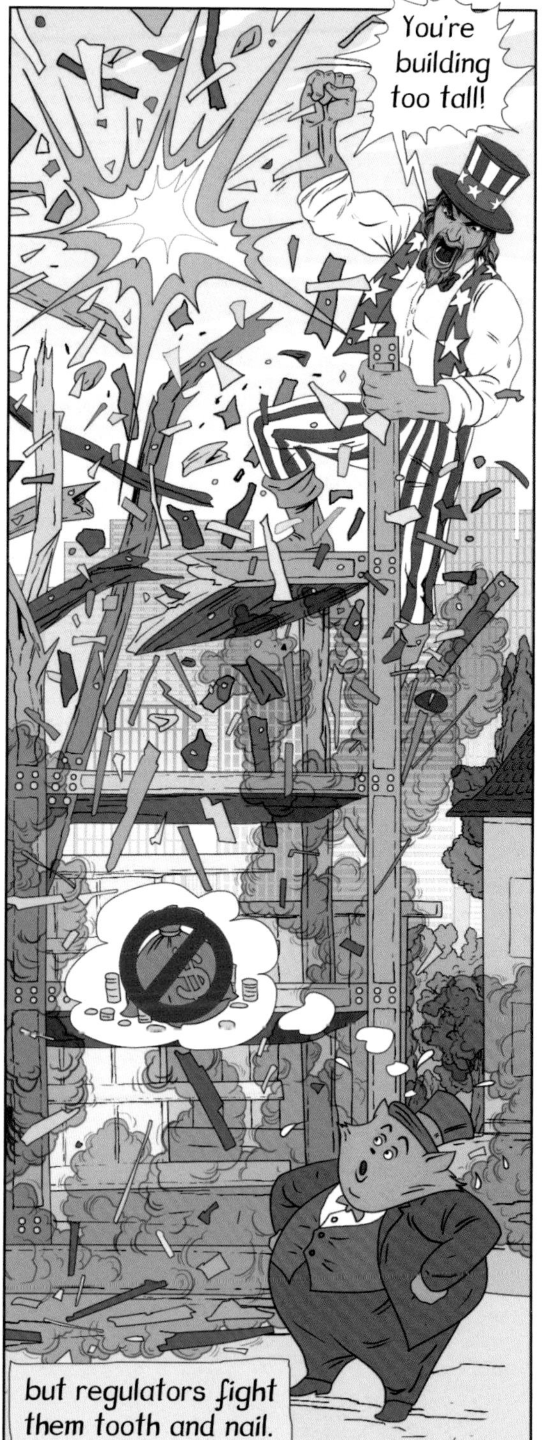
You're building too tall!
but regulators fight them tooth and nail.

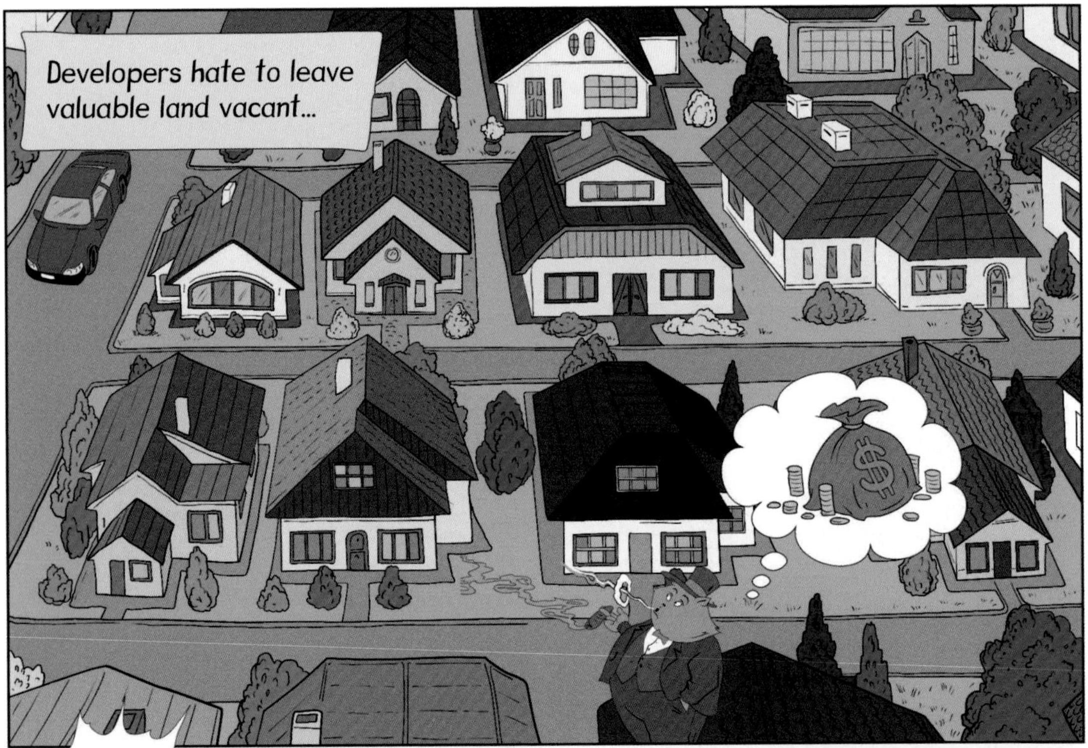
Developers hate to leave valuable land vacant...

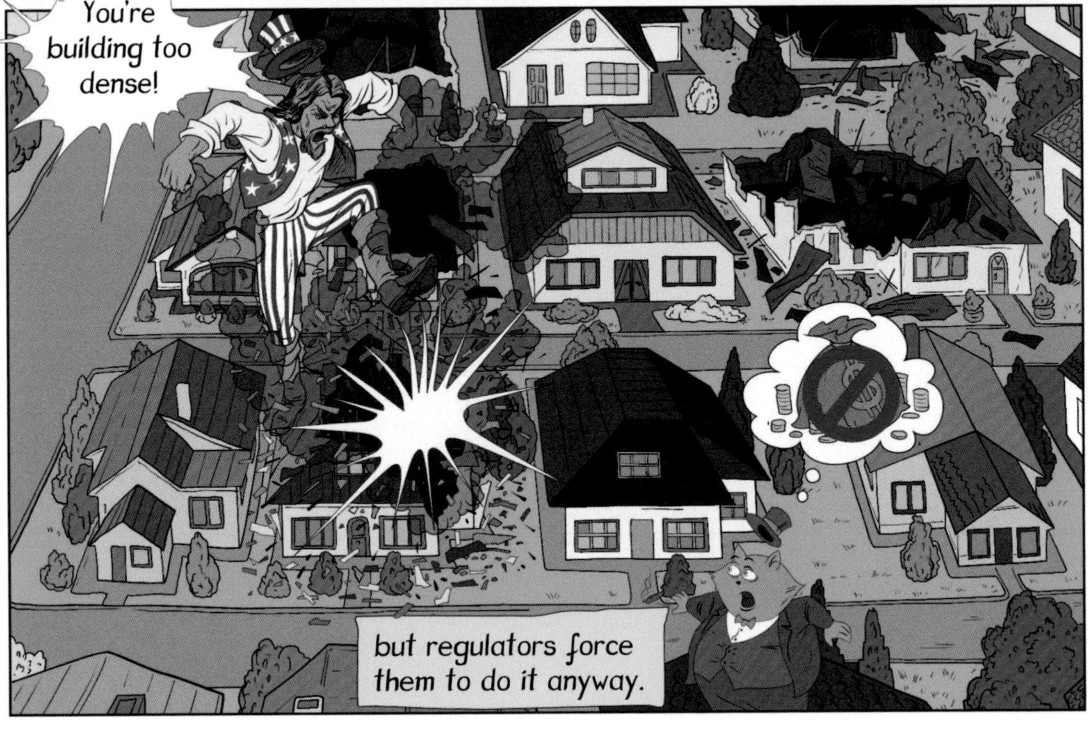
You're building too dense!
but regulators force them to do it anyway.

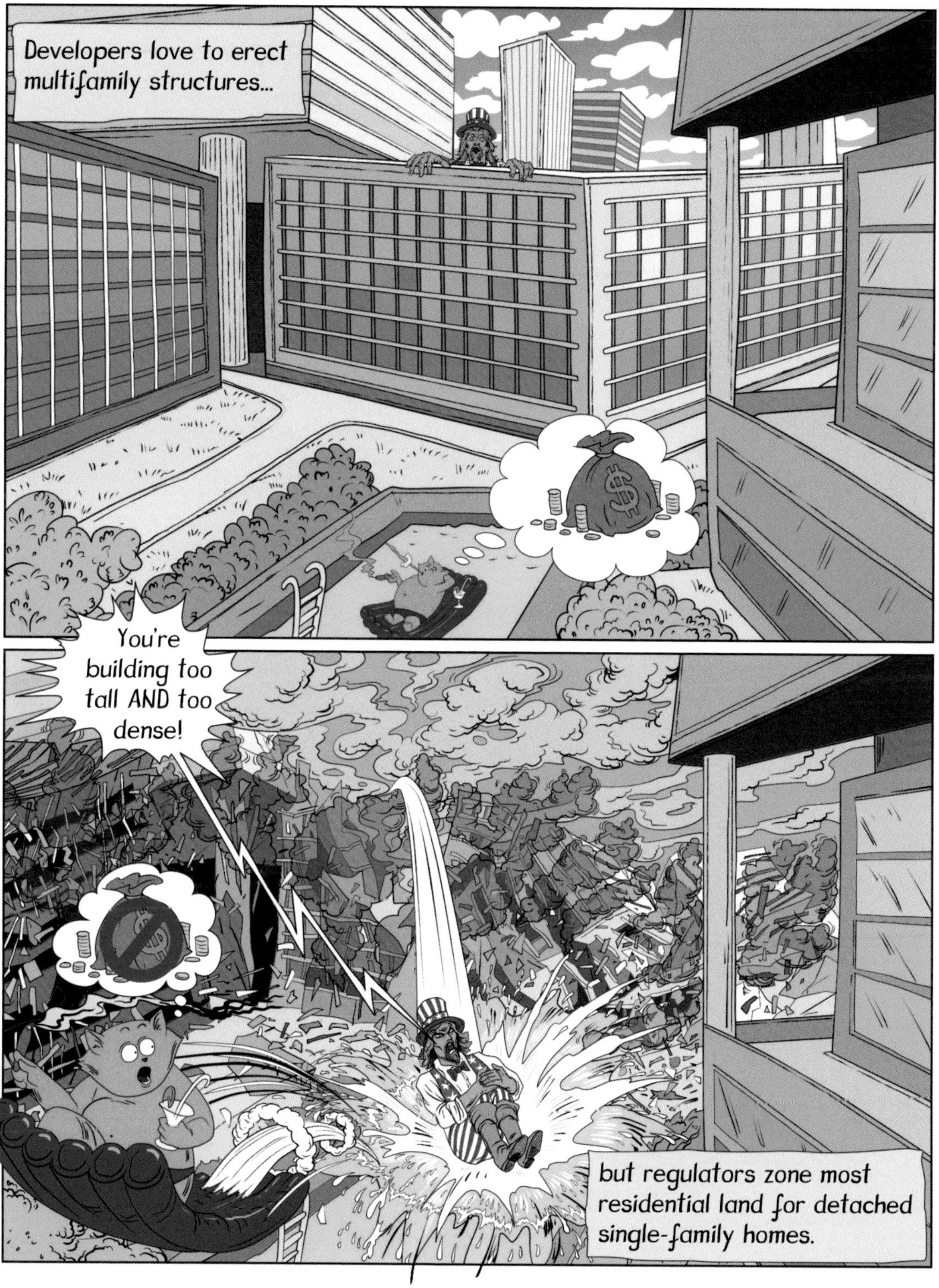
Developers love to erect multifamily structures...
You're building too tall AND too dense!
but regulators zone most residential land for detached single-family homes.

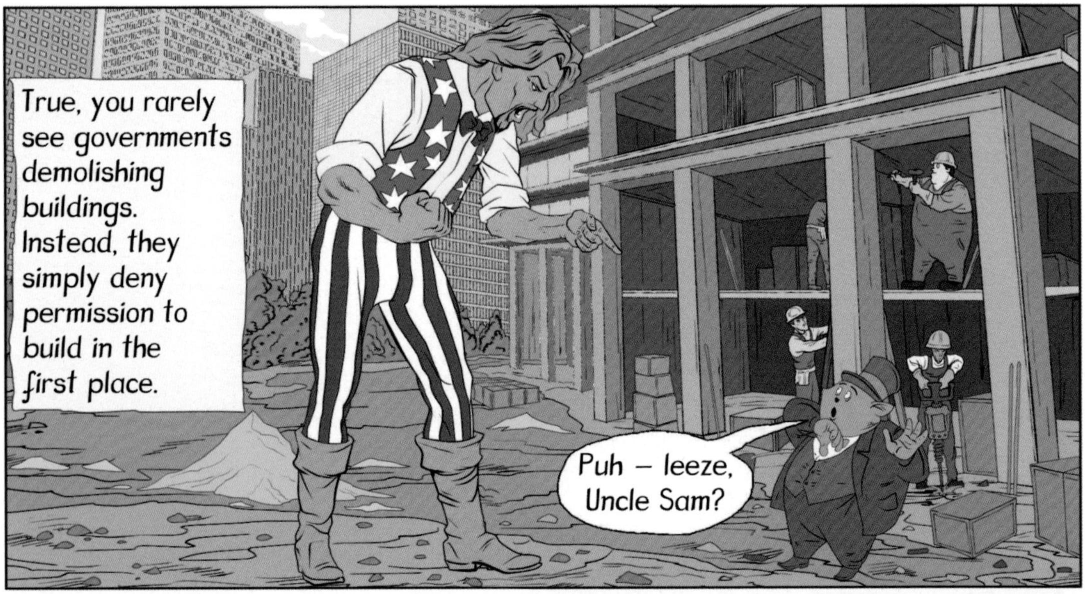
True, you rarely see governments demolishing buildings. Instead, they simply deny permission to build in the first place.
Puh – leeze, Uncle Sam?

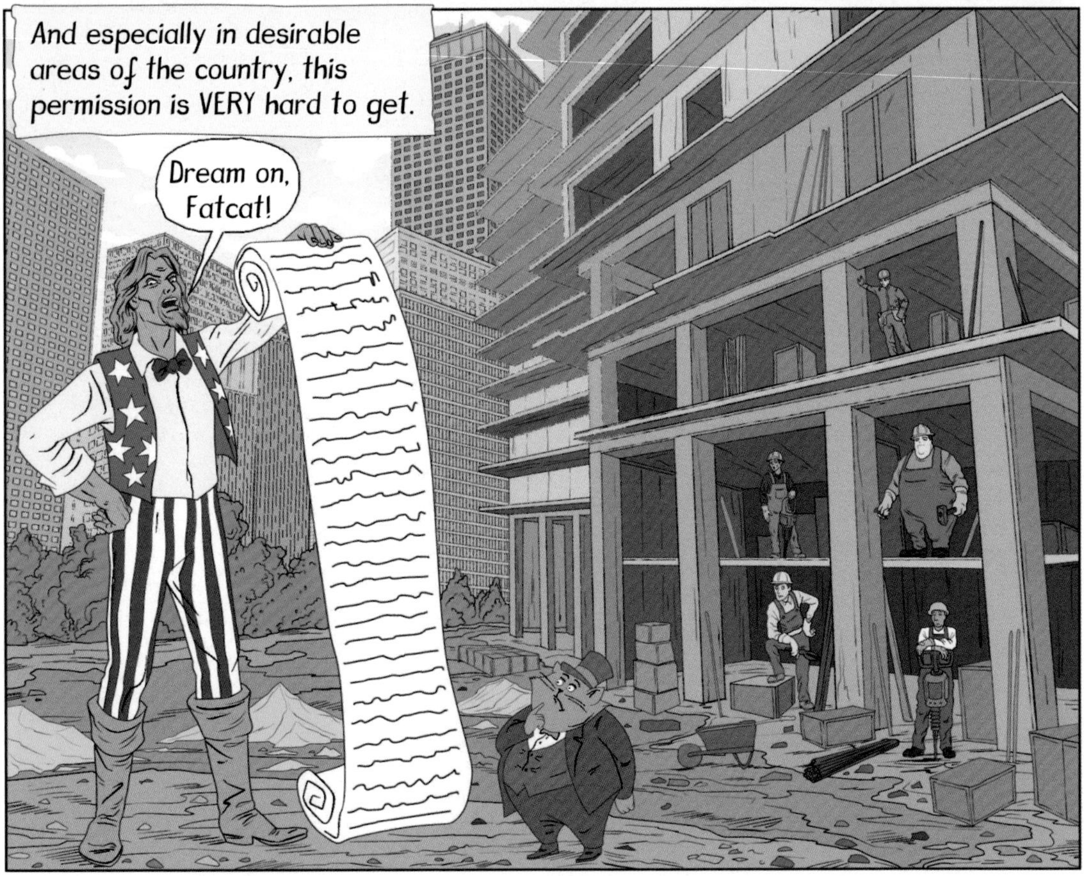
And especially in desirable areas of the country, this permission is VERY hard to get.
Dream on, Fatcat!

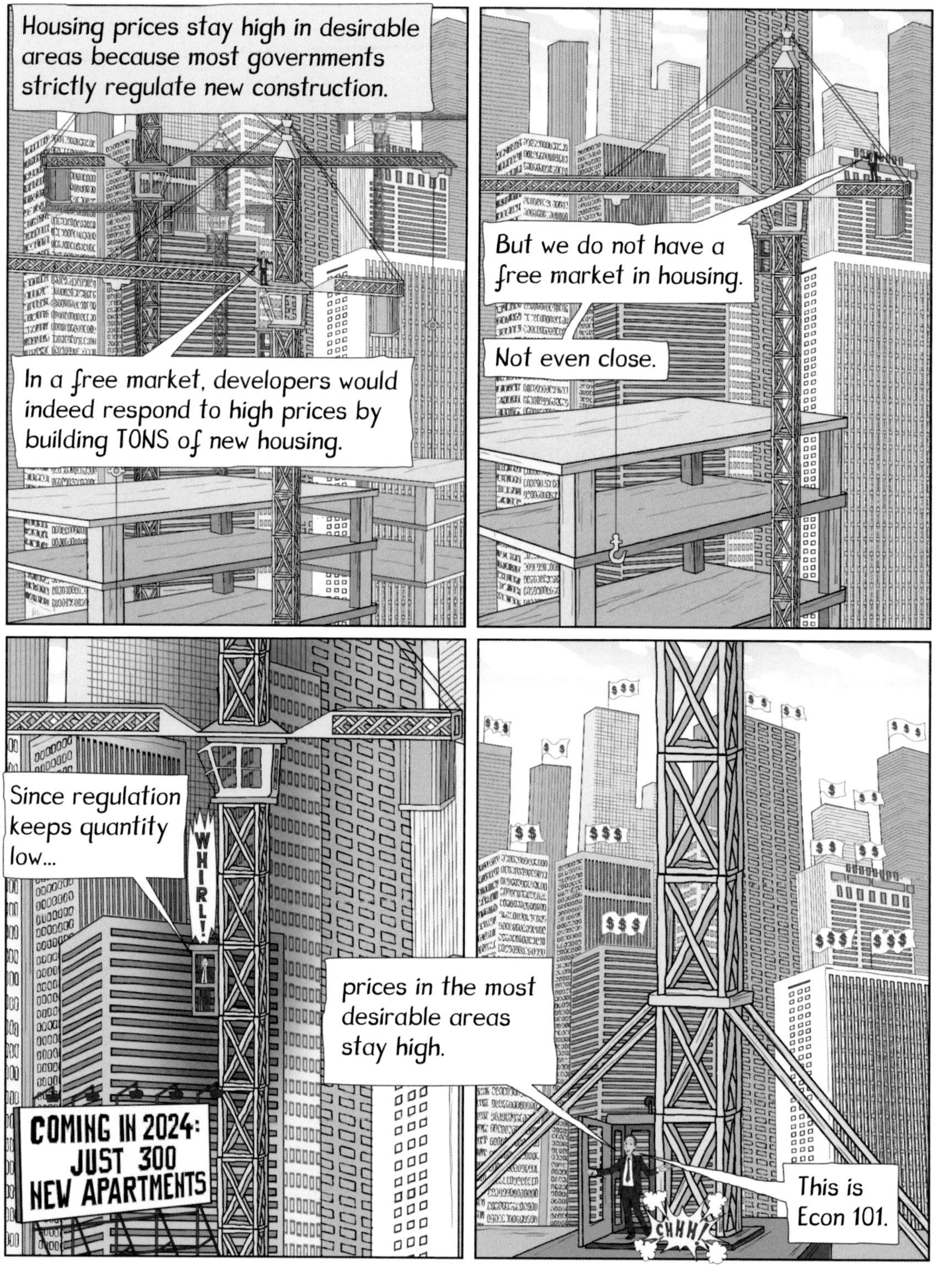
Housing prices stay high in desirable areas because most governments strictly regulate new construction.
In a free market, developers would indeed respond to high prices by building TONS of new housing.
But we do not have a free market in housing.
Not even close.
Since regulation keeps quantity low...
WHIRL!
COMING IN 2024: JUST 300 NEW APARTMENTS
prices in the most desirable areas stay high.
This is Econ 101.

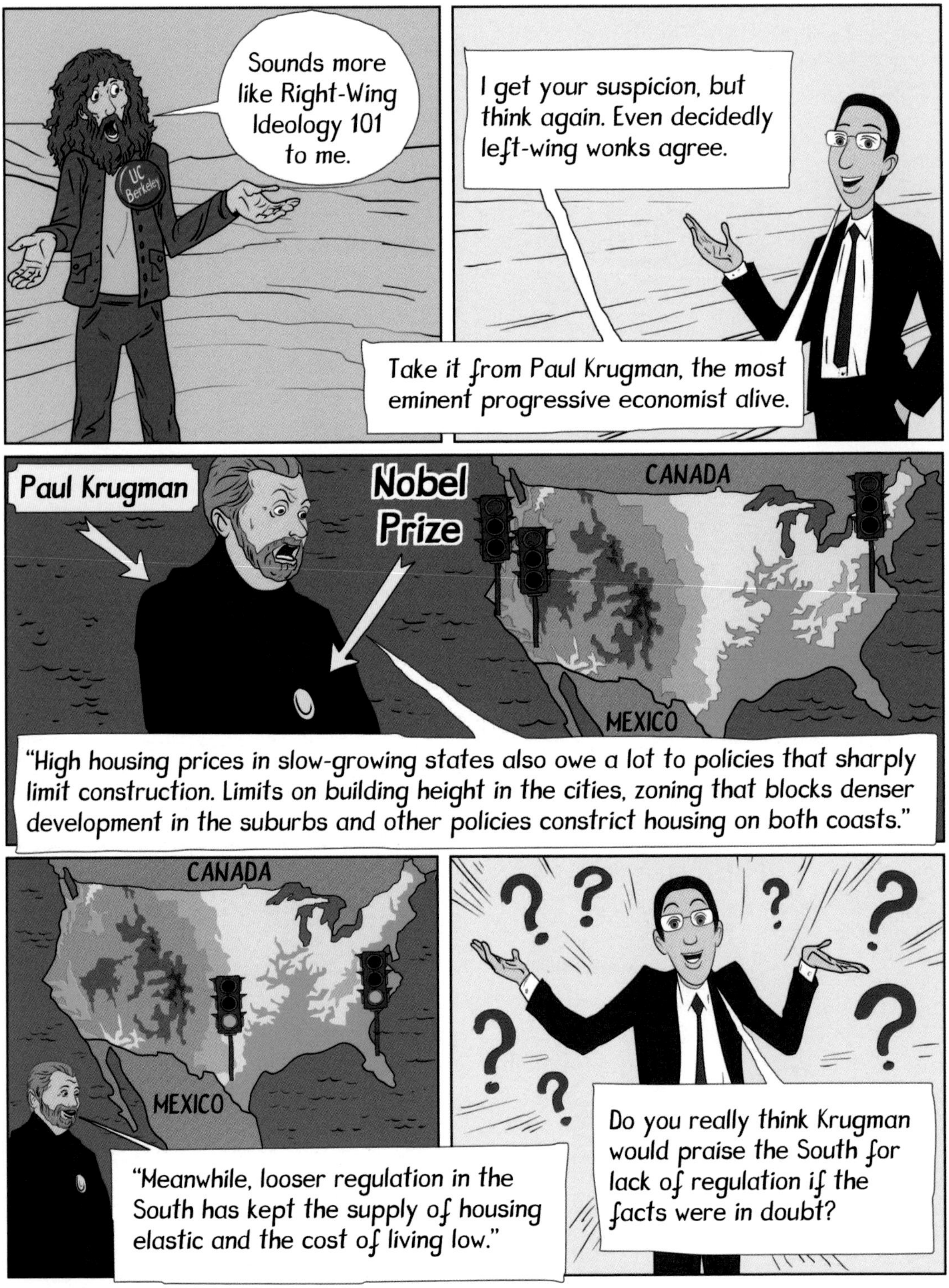
Sounds more like Right-Wing Ideology 101 to me.
UC Berkeley
I get your suspicion, but think again. Even decidedly left-wing wonks agree.
Take it from Paul Krugman, the most eminent progressive economist alive.
Paul Krugman
Nobel Prize
CANADA
MEXICO
"High housing prices in slow-growing states also owe a lot to policies that sharply limit construction. Limits on building height in the cities, zoning that blocks denser development in the suburbs and other policies constrict housing on both coasts."
CANADA
MEXICO
"Meanwhile, looser regulation in the South has kept the supply of housing elastic and the cost of living low."
Do you really think Krugman would praise the South for lack of regulation if the facts were in doubt?

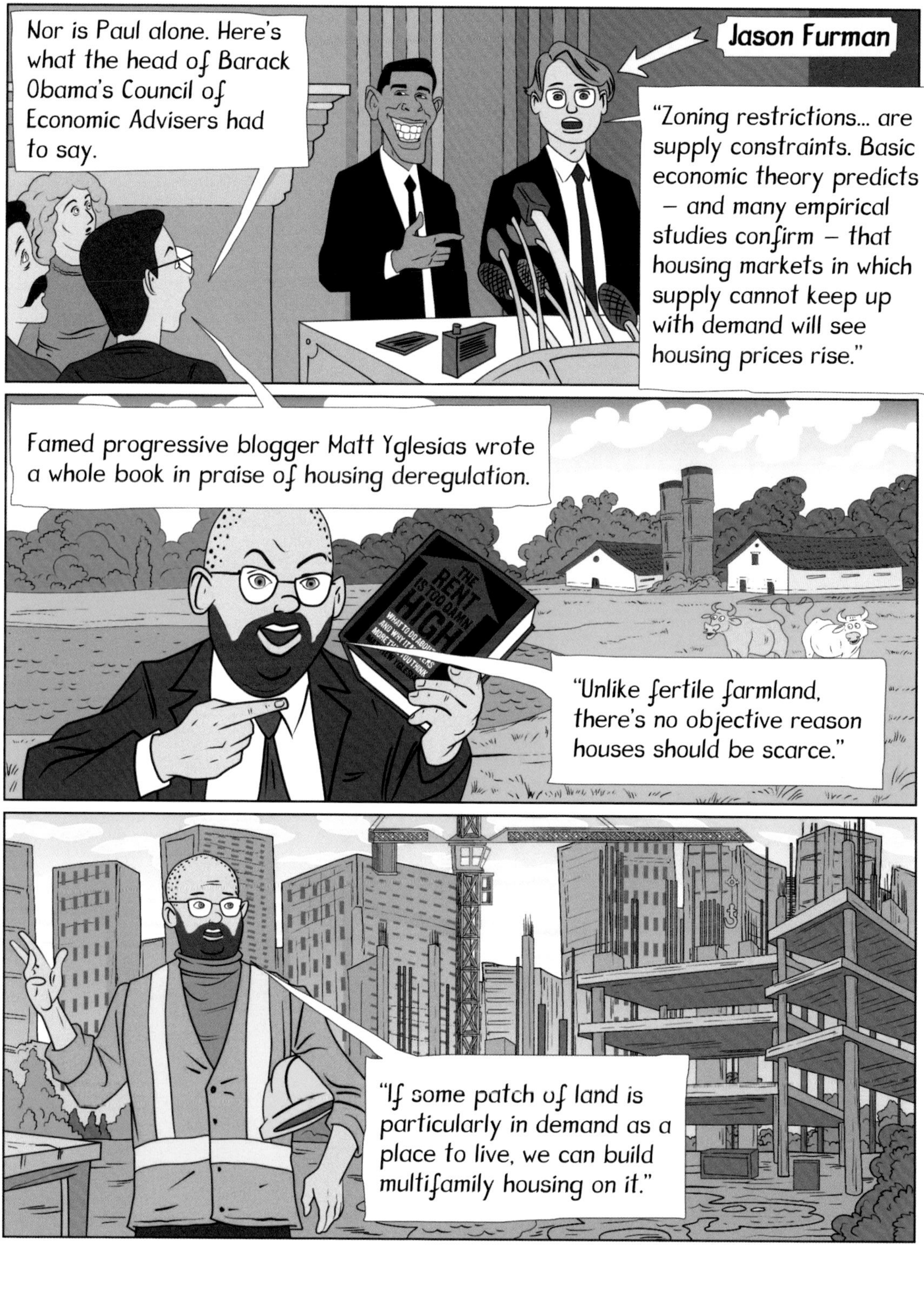
Nor is Paul alone. Here's what the head of Barack Obama's Council of Economic Advisers had to say.
Jason Furman
"Zoning restrictions... are supply constraints. Basic economic theory predicts – and many empirical studies confirm – that housing markets in which supply cannot keep up with demand will see housing prices rise."
Famed progressive blogger Matt Yglesias wrote a whole book in praise of housing deregulation.
THE RENT IS TOO DAMN HIGH
"Unlike fertile farmland, there's no objective reason houses should be scarce."
"If some patch of land is particularly in demand as a place to live, we can build multifamily housing on it."

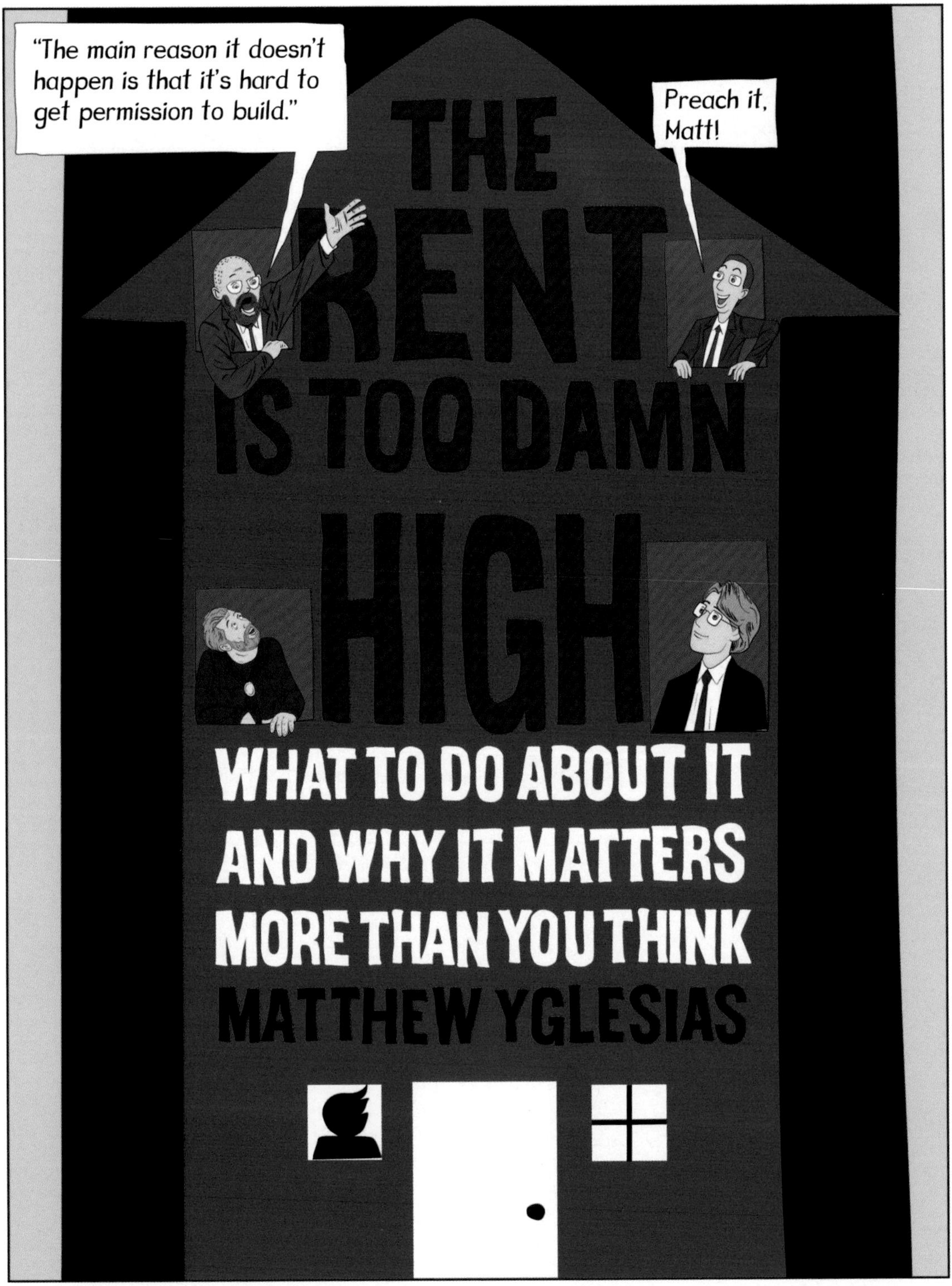
"The main reason it doesn't happen is that it's hard to get permission to build."
Preach it, Matt!
THE RENT IS TOO DAMN HIGH
WHAT TO DO ABOUT IT AND WHY IT MATTERS MORE THAN YOU THINK
MATTHEW YGLESIAS

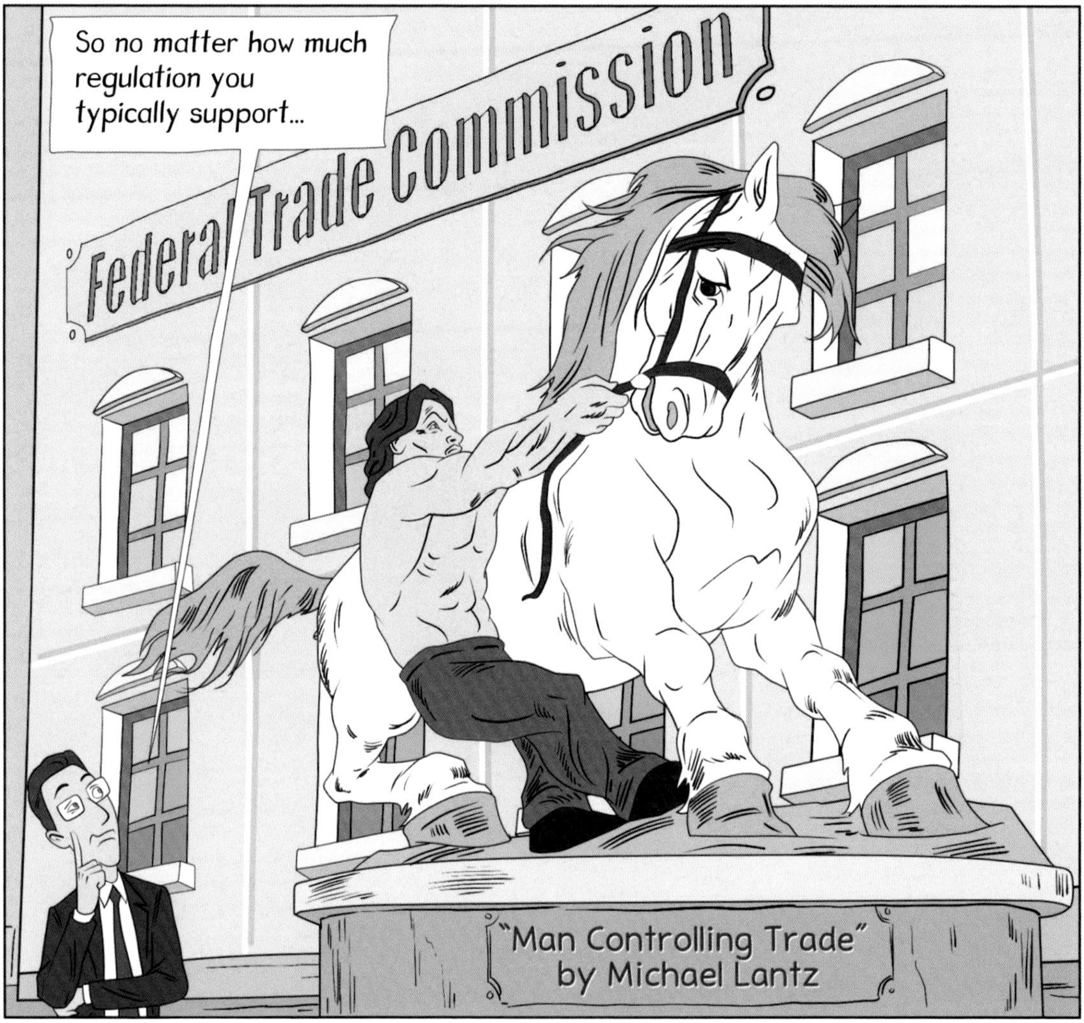
So no matter how much regulation you typically support...
Federal Trade Commission
"Man Controlling Trade" by Michael Lantz

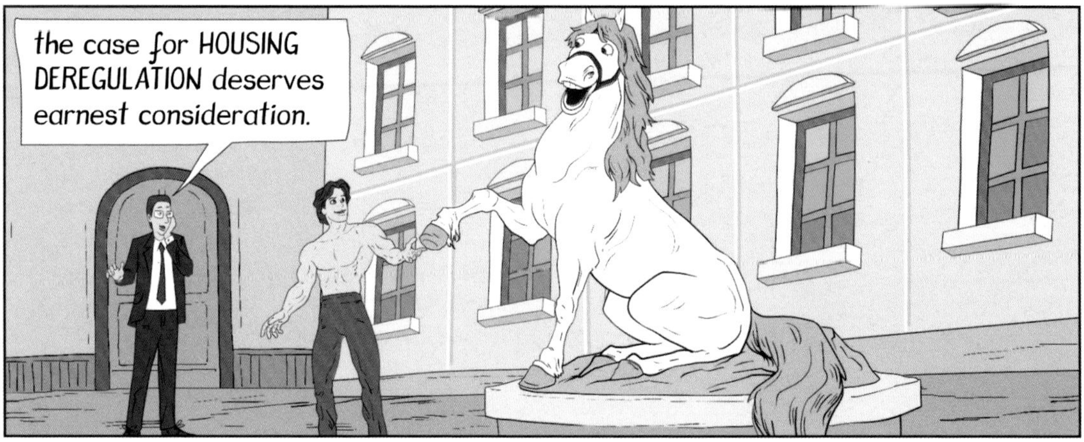
the case for HOUSING DEREGULATION deserves earnest consideration.

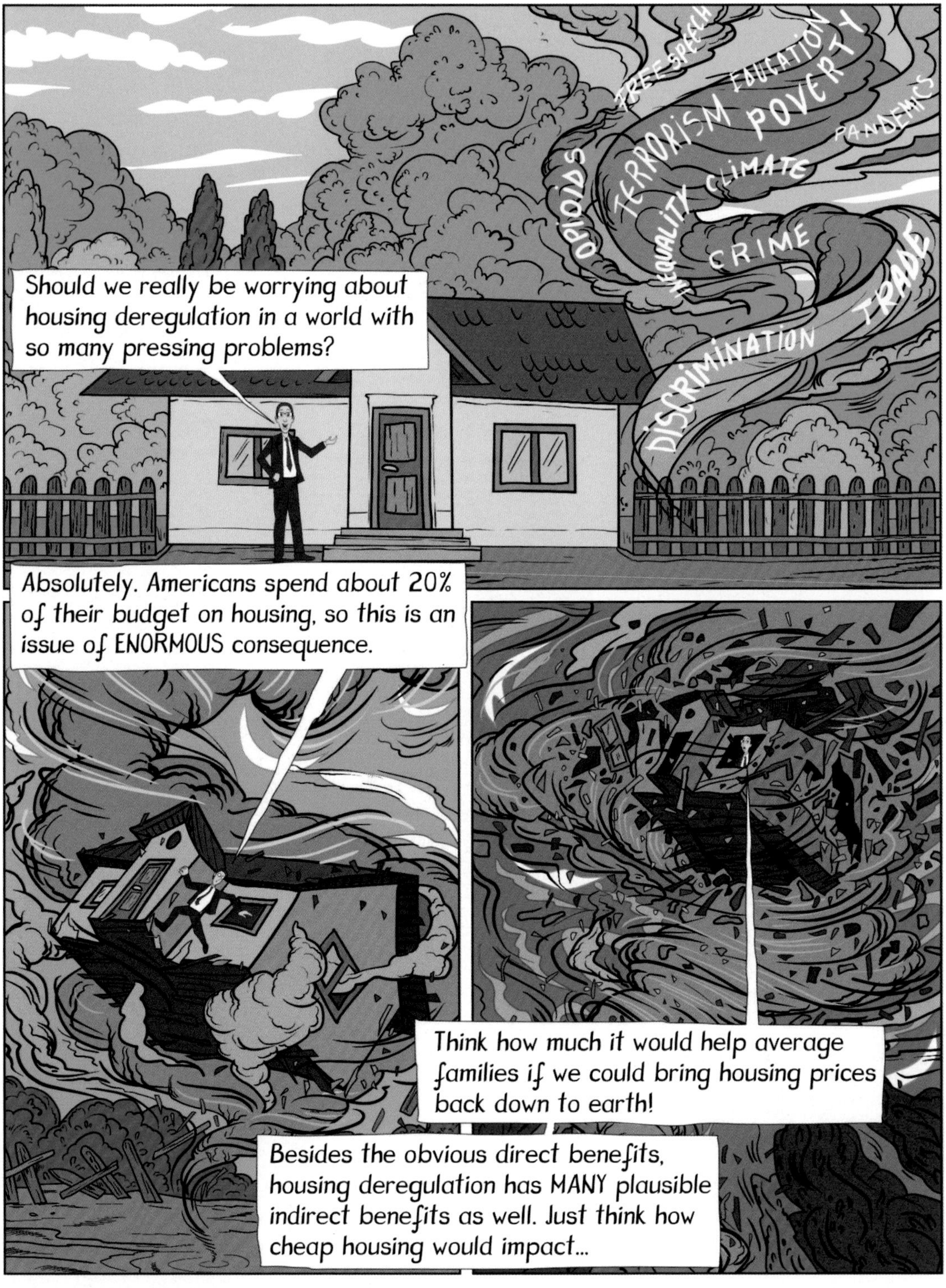
OPIOIDS
FREE SPEECH
TERRORISM
EDUCATION
POVERTY
PANDEMICS
INEQUALITY
CLIMATE
CRIME
TRADE
DISCRIMINATION
Should we really be worrying about housing deregulation in a world with so many pressing problems?
Absolutely. Americans spend about 20% of their budget on housing, so this is an issue of ENORMOUS consequence.
Think how much it would help average families if we could bring housing prices back down to earth!
Besides the obvious direct benefits, housing deregulation has MANY plausible indirect benefits as well. Just think how cheap housing would impact...

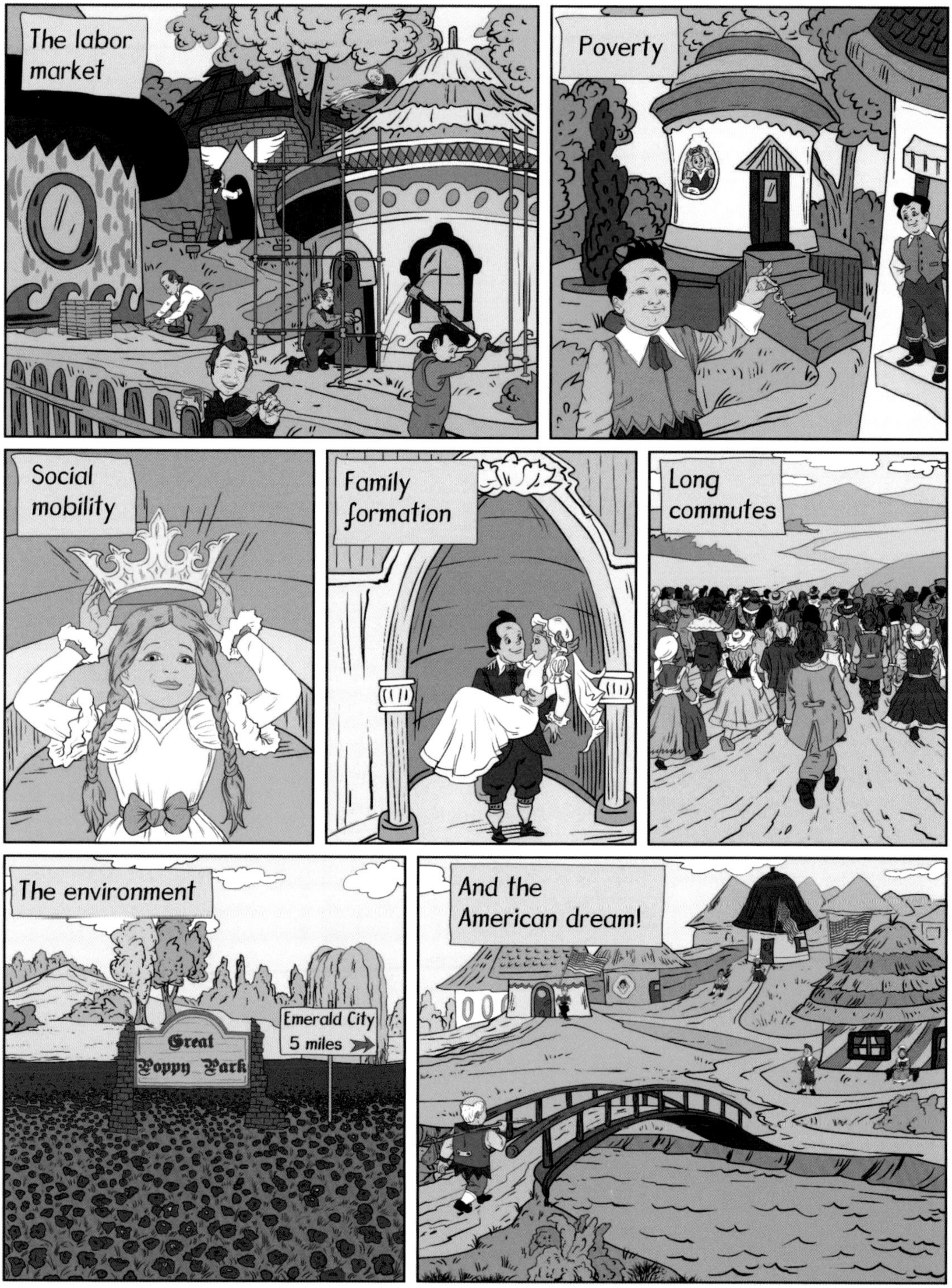
The labor market
Poverty
Social mobility
Family formation
Long commutes
The environment
Great Poppy Park
Emerald City 5 miles
And the American dream!

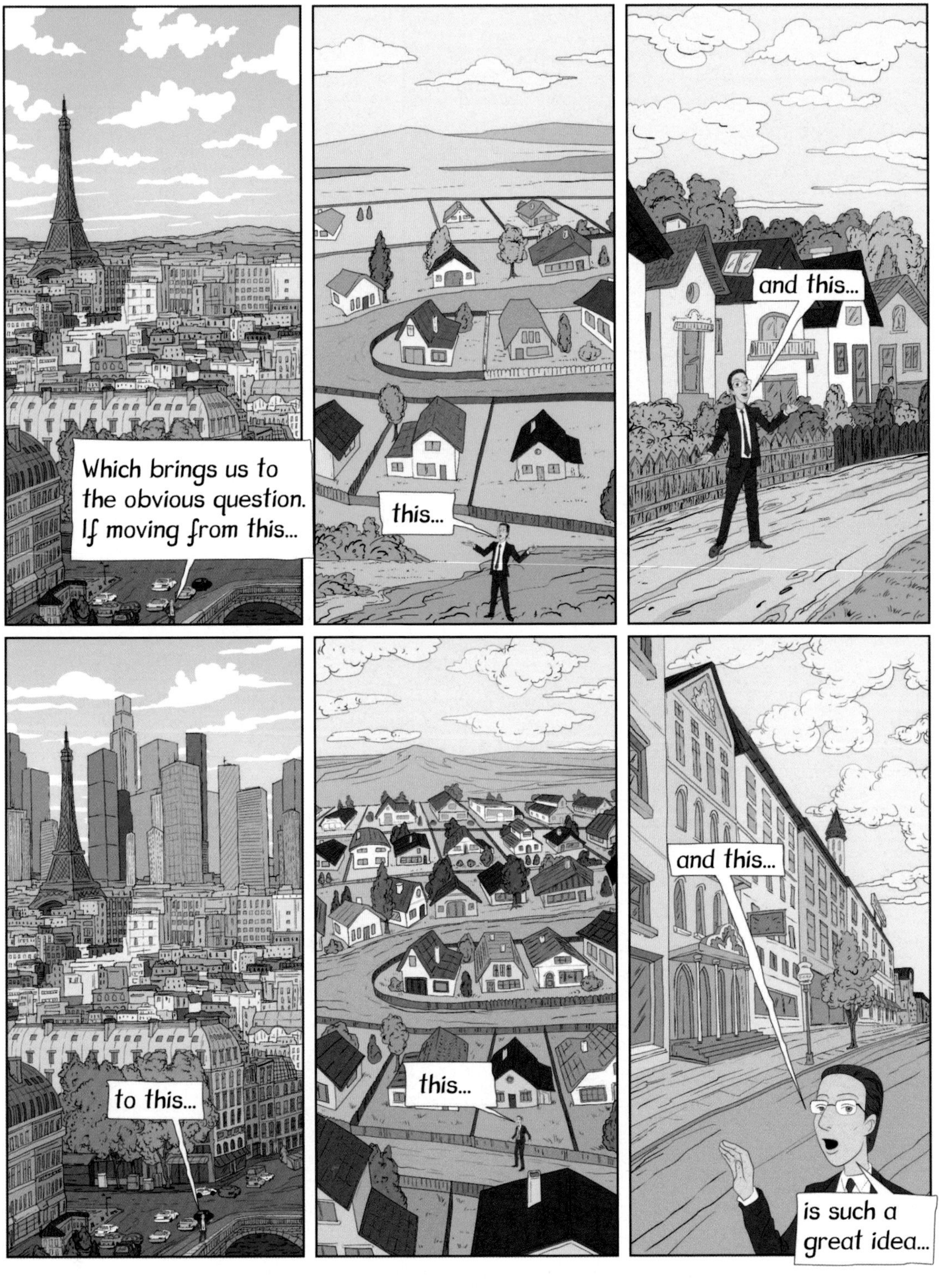
Which brings us to the obvious question. If moving from this...
this...
and this...
to this...
this...
and this...
is such a great idea...

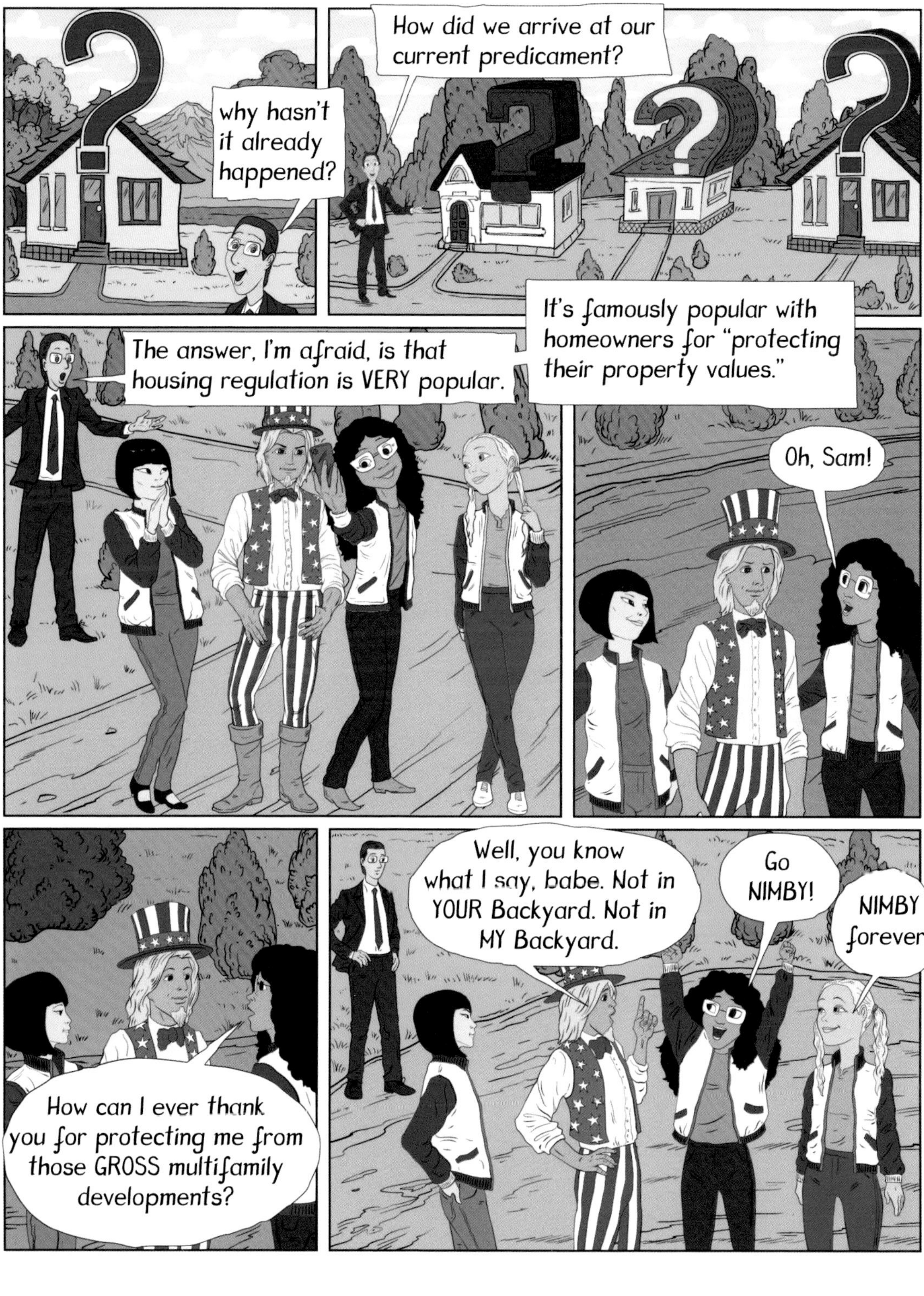
why hasn't it already happened?
How did we arrive at our current predicament?
The answer, I'm afraid, is that housing regulation is VERY popular.
It's famously popular with homeowners for "protecting their property values."
Oh, Sam!
How can I ever thank you for protecting me from those GROSS multifamily developments?
Well, you know what I say, babe. Not in YOUR Backyard. Not in MY Backyard.
Go NIMBY!
NIMBY forever!

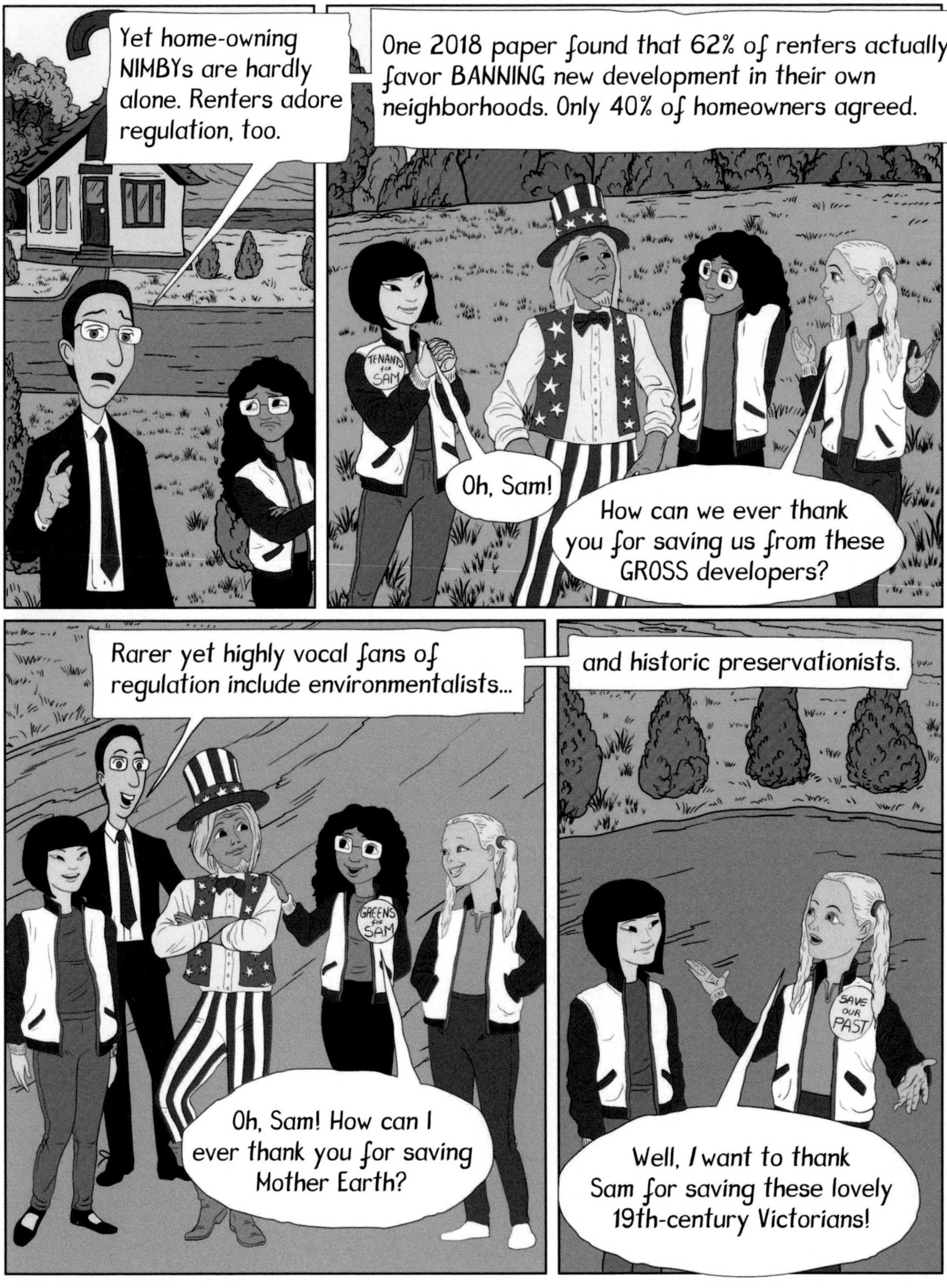
Yet home-owning NIMBYs are hardly alone. Renters adore regulation, too.
One 2018 paper found that 62% of renters actually favor BANNING new development in their own neighborhoods. Only 40% of homeowners agreed.
TENANTS for SAM
Oh, Sam!
How can we ever thank you for saving us from these GROSS developers?
Rarer yet highly vocal fans of regulation include environmentalists...
and historic preservationists.
GREENS for SAM
Oh, Sam! How can I ever thank you for saving Mother Earth?
SAVE OUR PAST
Well, I want to thank Sam for saving these lovely 19th-century Victorians!

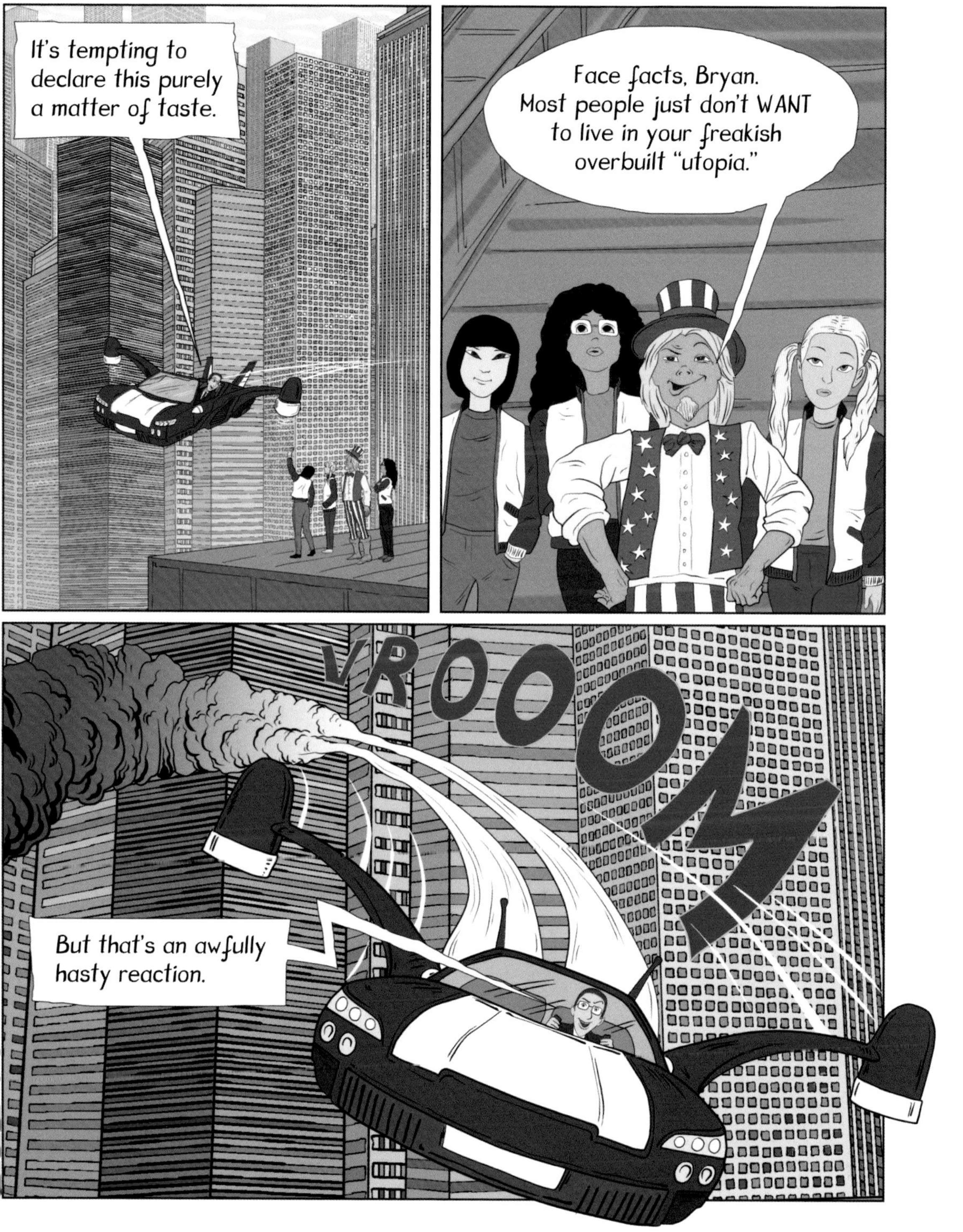
It's tempting to declare this purely a matter of taste.
Face facts, Bryan. Most people just don't WANT to live in your freakish overbuilt "utopia."
VROOOM
But that's an awfully hasty reaction.

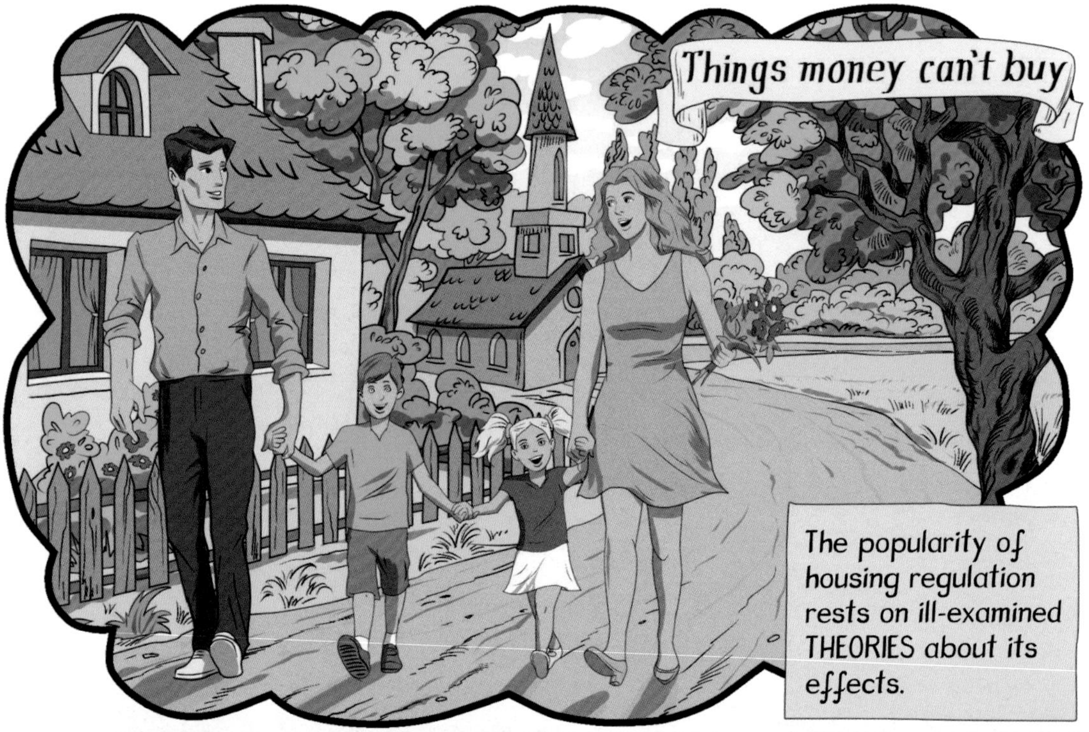
Things money can't buy
The popularity of housing regulation rests on ill-examined THEORIES about its effects.

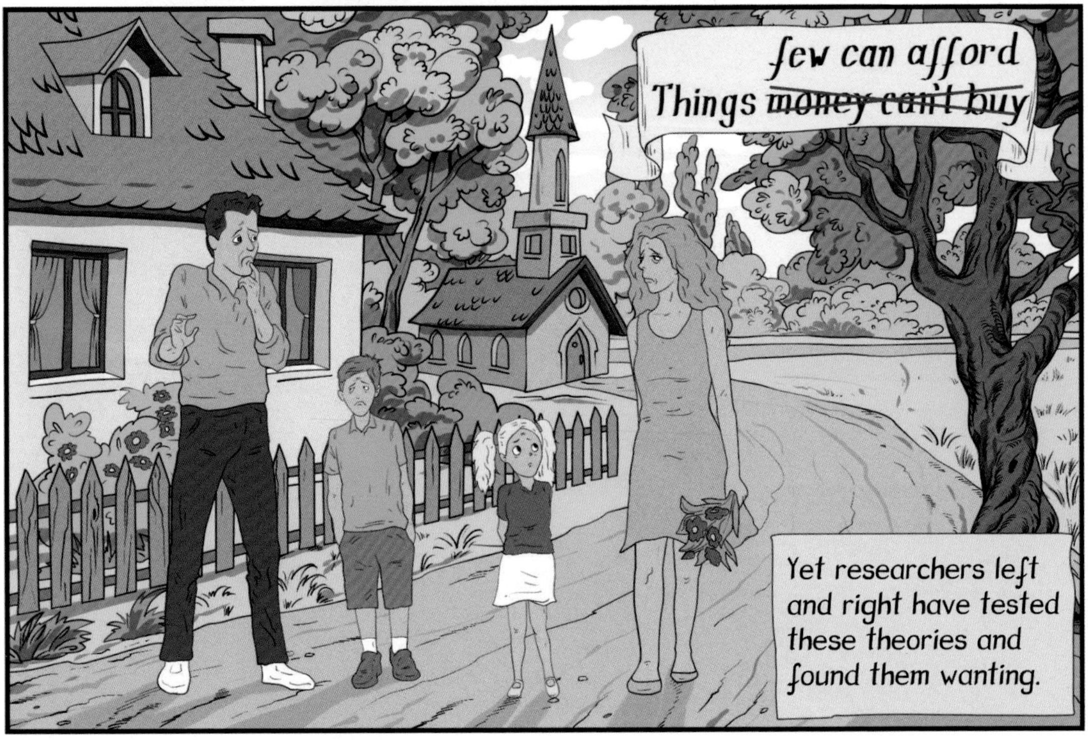
Things ~~money can't buy~~ few can afford
Yet researchers left and right have tested these theories and found them wanting.

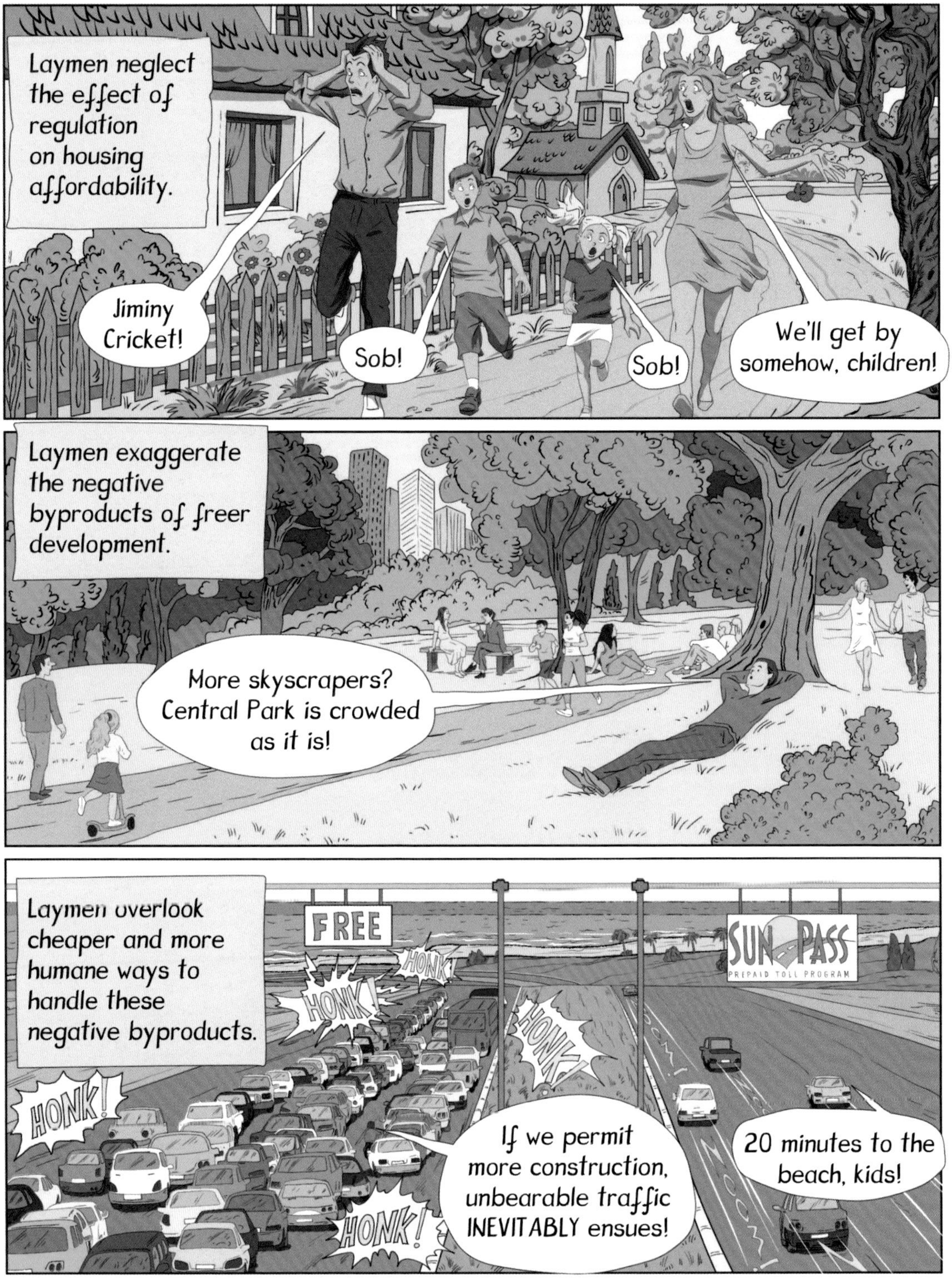
Laymen neglect the effect of regulation on housing affordability.
Jiminy Cricket!
Sob!
Sob!
We'll get by somehow, children!
Laymen exaggerate the negative byproducts of freer development.
More skyscrapers? Central Park is crowded as it is!
Laymen overlook cheaper and more humane ways to handle these negative byproducts.
FREE
HONK
HONK!
HONK!
SUN PASS
PREPAID TOLL PROGRAM
HONK!
HONK!
If we permit more construction, unbearable traffic INEVITABLY ensues!
20 minutes to the beach, kids!

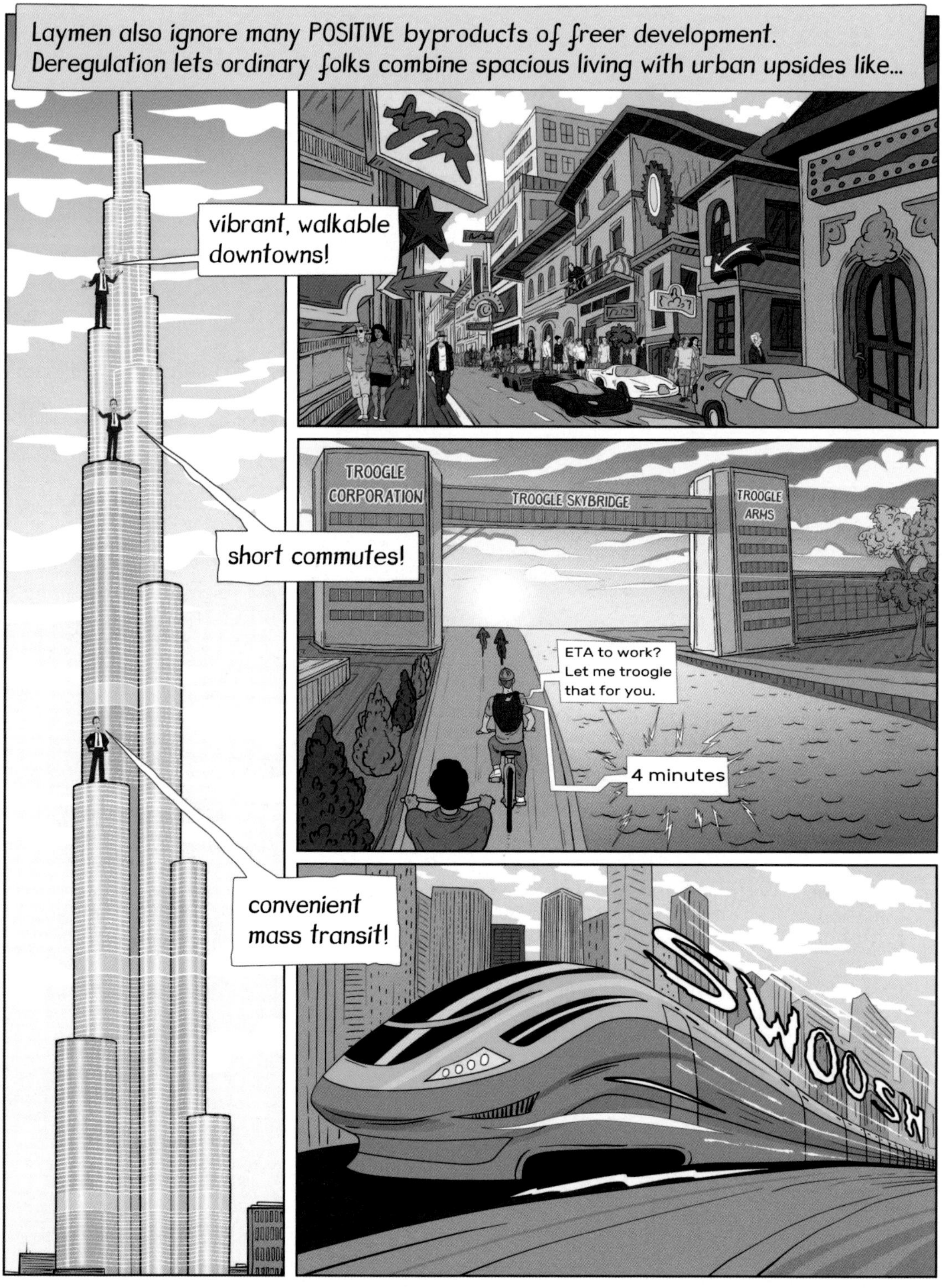
Laymen also ignore many POSITIVE byproducts of freer development. Deregulation lets ordinary folks combine spacious living with urban upsides like...
vibrant, walkable downtowns!
short commutes!
TROOGLE CORPORATION
TROOGLE SKYBRIDGE
TROOGLE ARMS
ETA to work? Let me troogle that for you.
4 minutes
convenient mass transit!
SWOOSH

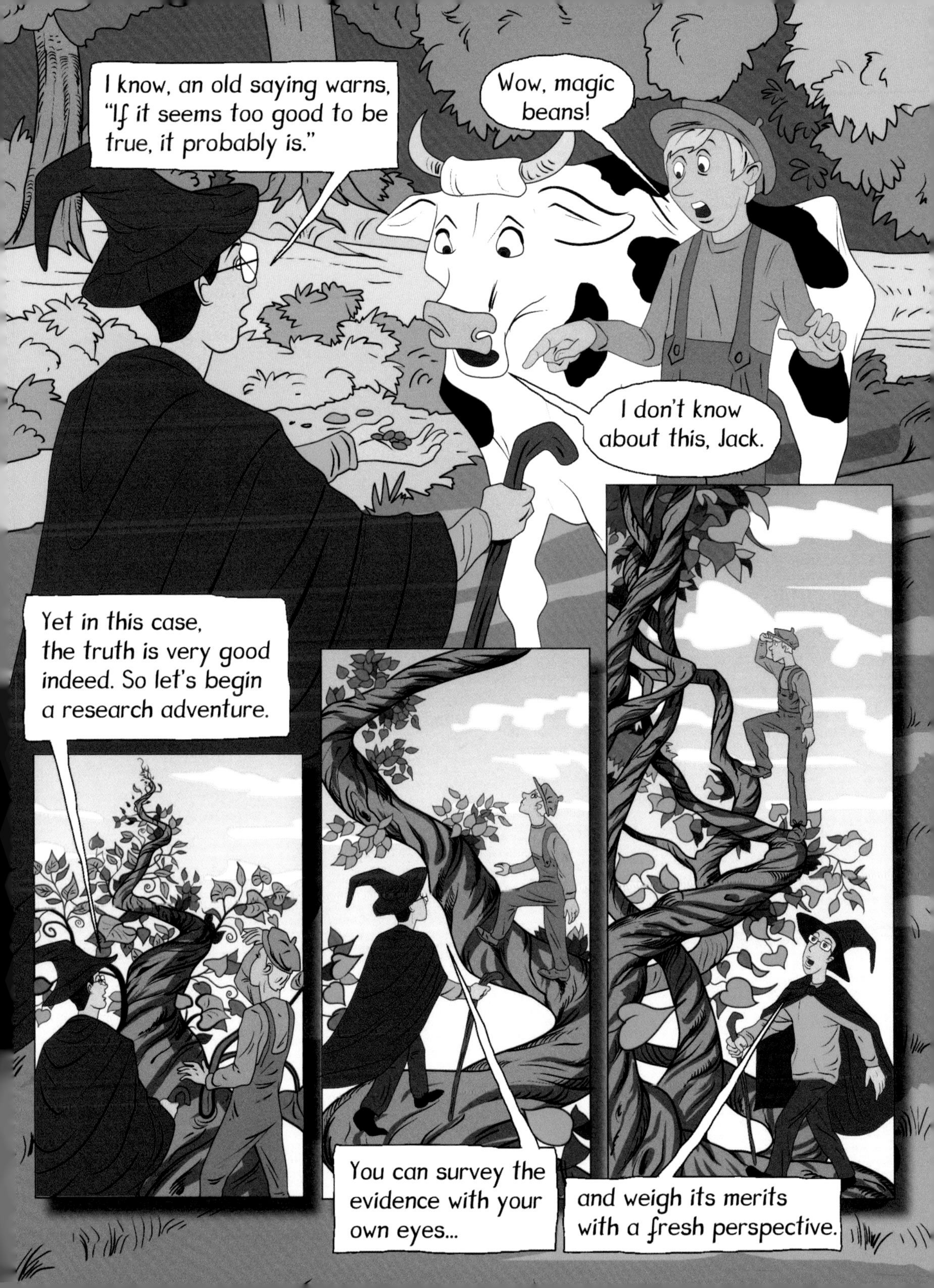
I know, an old saying warns, "If it seems too good to be true, it probably is."
Wow, magic beans!
I don't know about this, Jack.
Yet in this case, the truth is very good indeed. So let's begin a research adventure.
You can survey the evidence with your own eyes...
and weigh its merits with a fresh perspective.

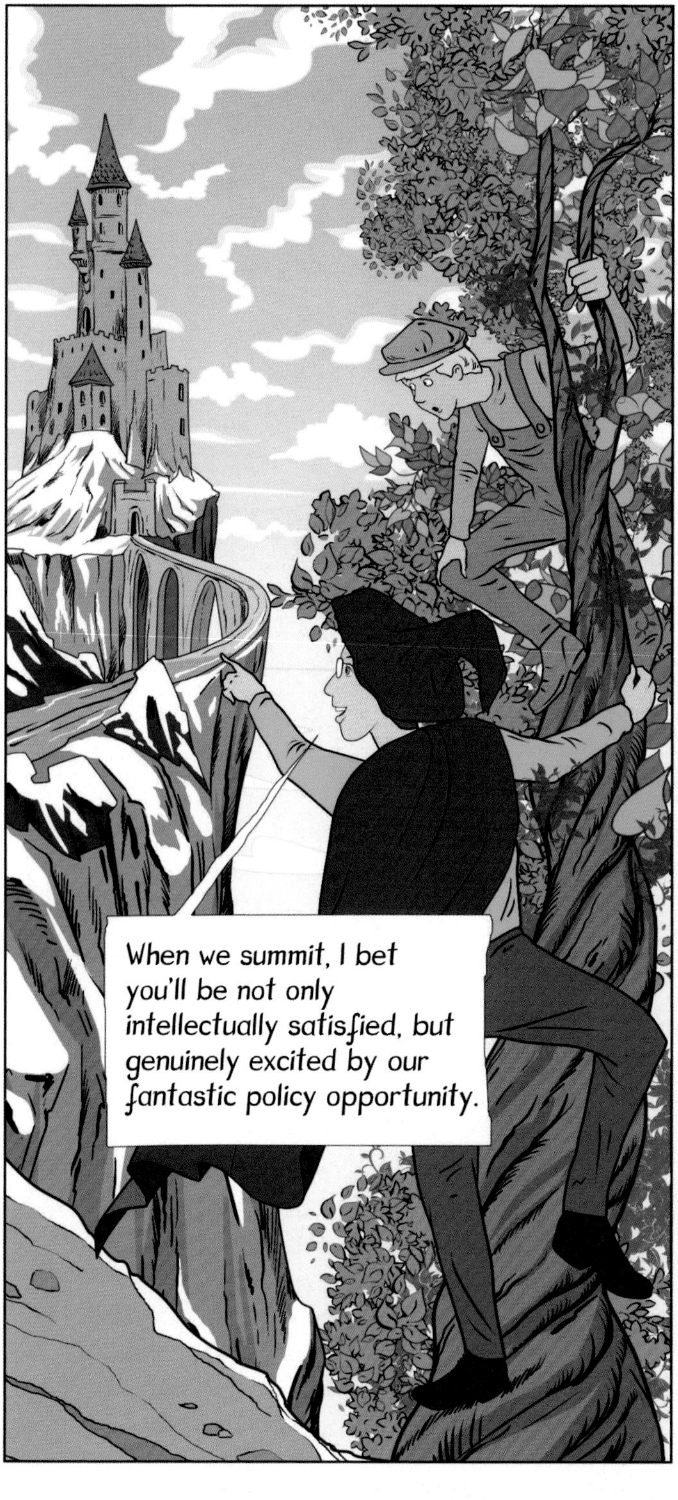
When we summit, I bet you'll be not only intellectually satisfied, but genuinely excited by our fantastic policy opportunity.

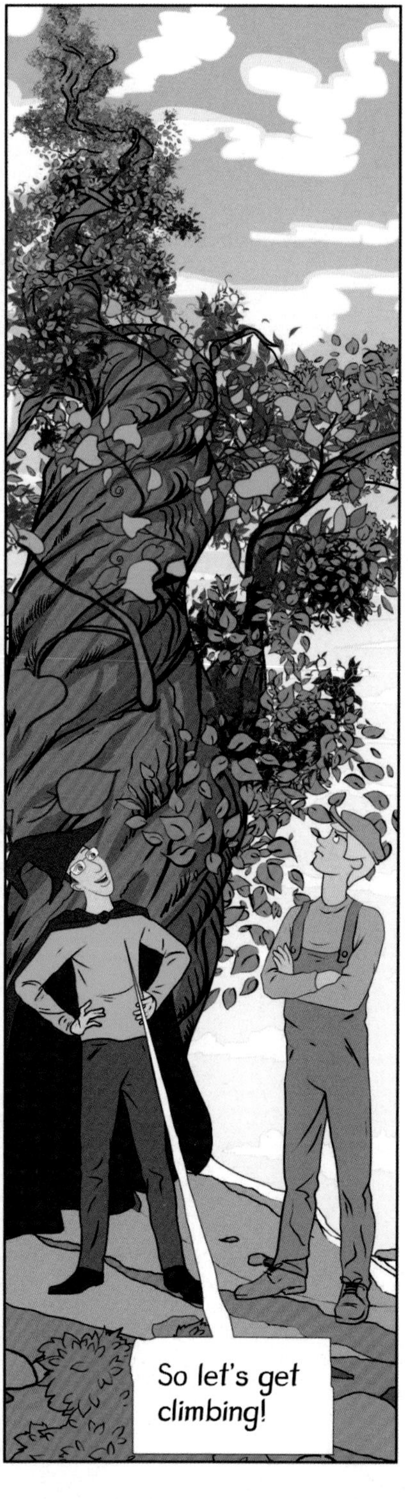
So let's get climbing!

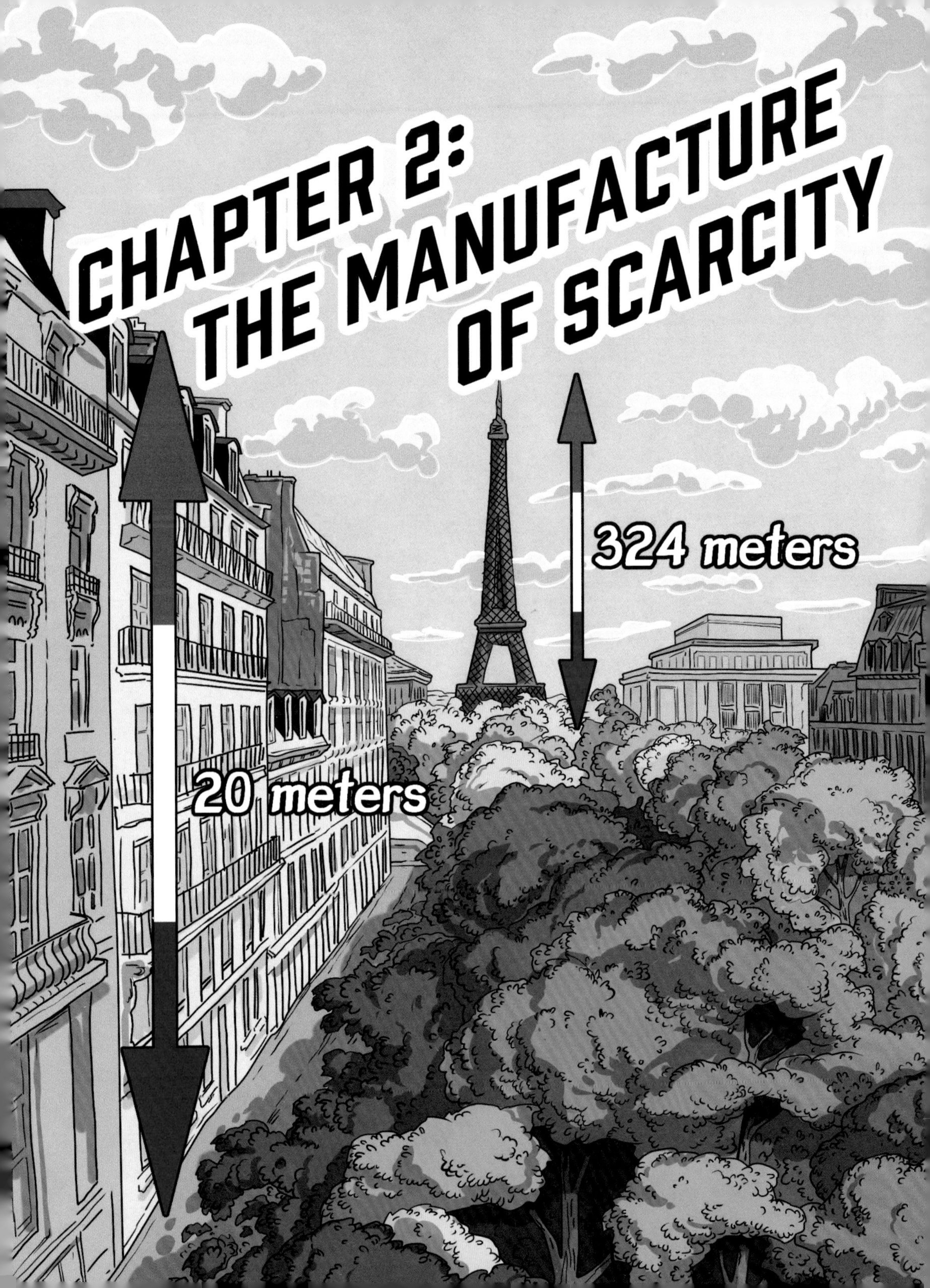
CHAPTER 2:
THE MANUFACTURE
OF SCARCITY
324 meters
20 meters

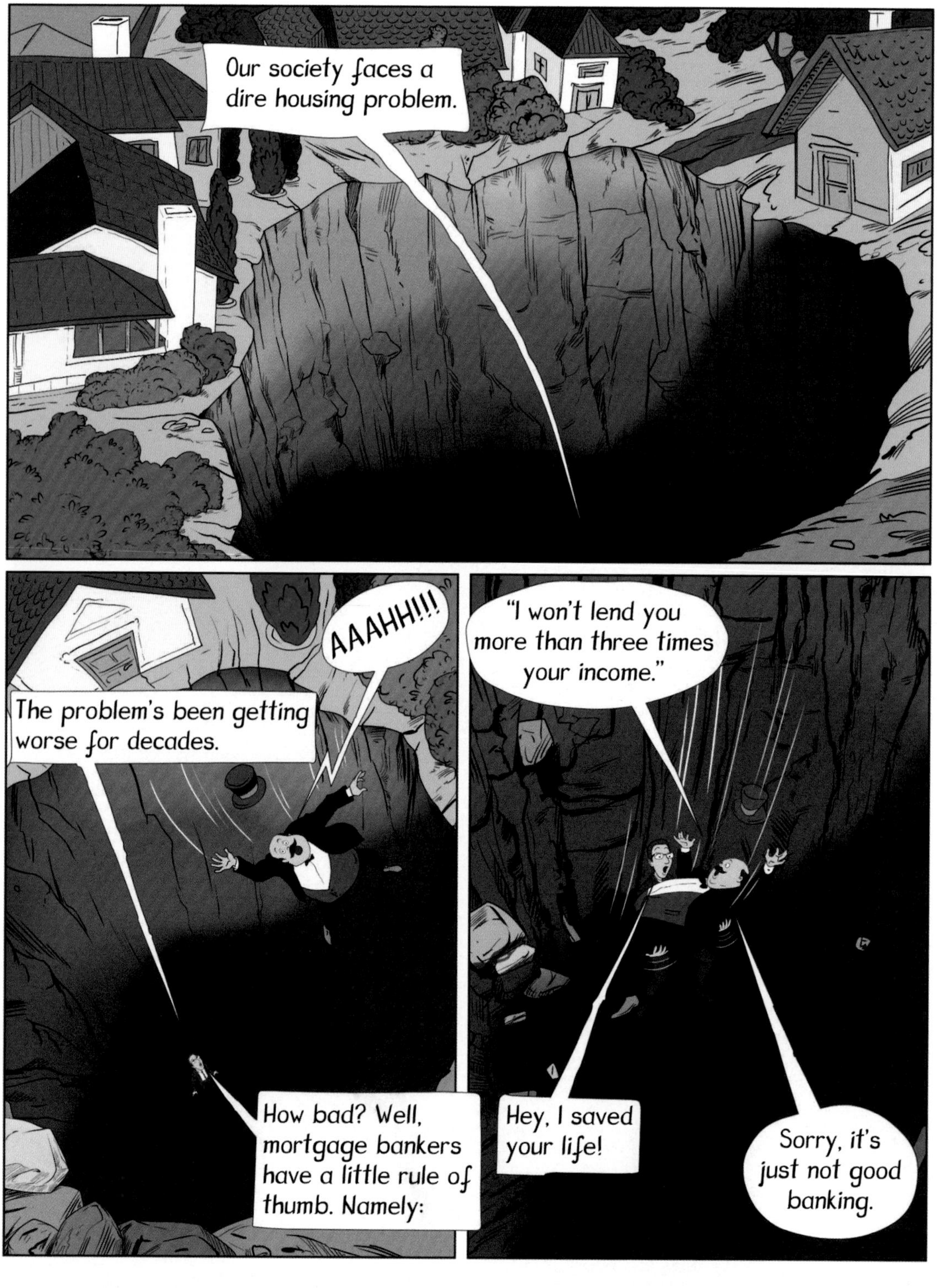
Our society faces a dire housing problem.
The problem's been getting worse for decades.
AAAHH!!!
How bad? Well, mortgage bankers have a little rule of thumb. Namely:
"I won't lend you more than three times your income."
Hey, I saved your life!
Sorry, it's just not good banking.

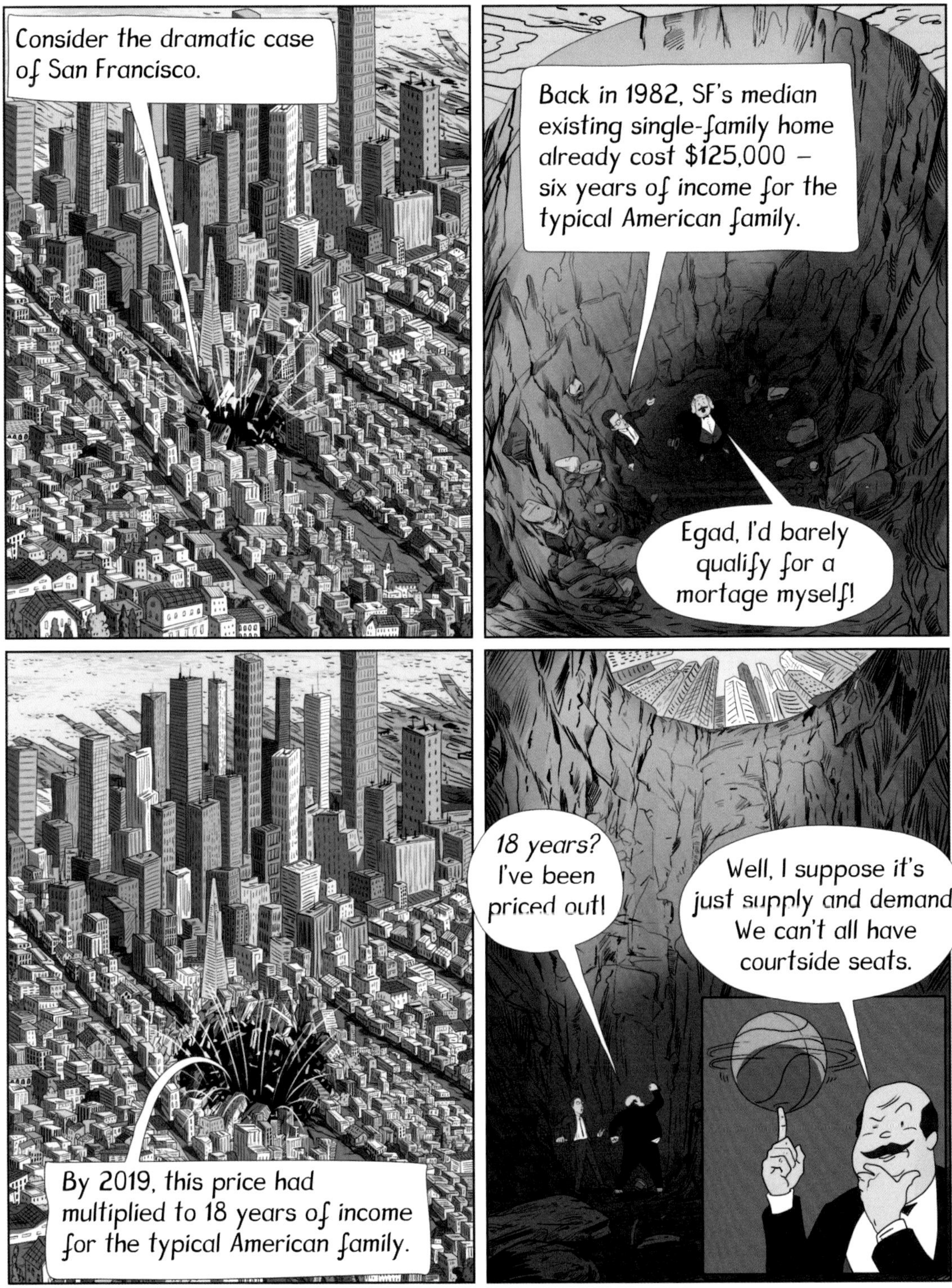
Consider the dramatic case of San Francisco.
Back in 1982, SF's median existing single-family home already cost $125,000 – six years of income for the typical American family.
Egad, I'd barely qualify for a mortage myself!
By 2019, this price had multiplied to 18 years of income for the typical American family.
18 years? I've been priced out!
Well, I suppose it's just supply and demand. We can't all have courtside seats.

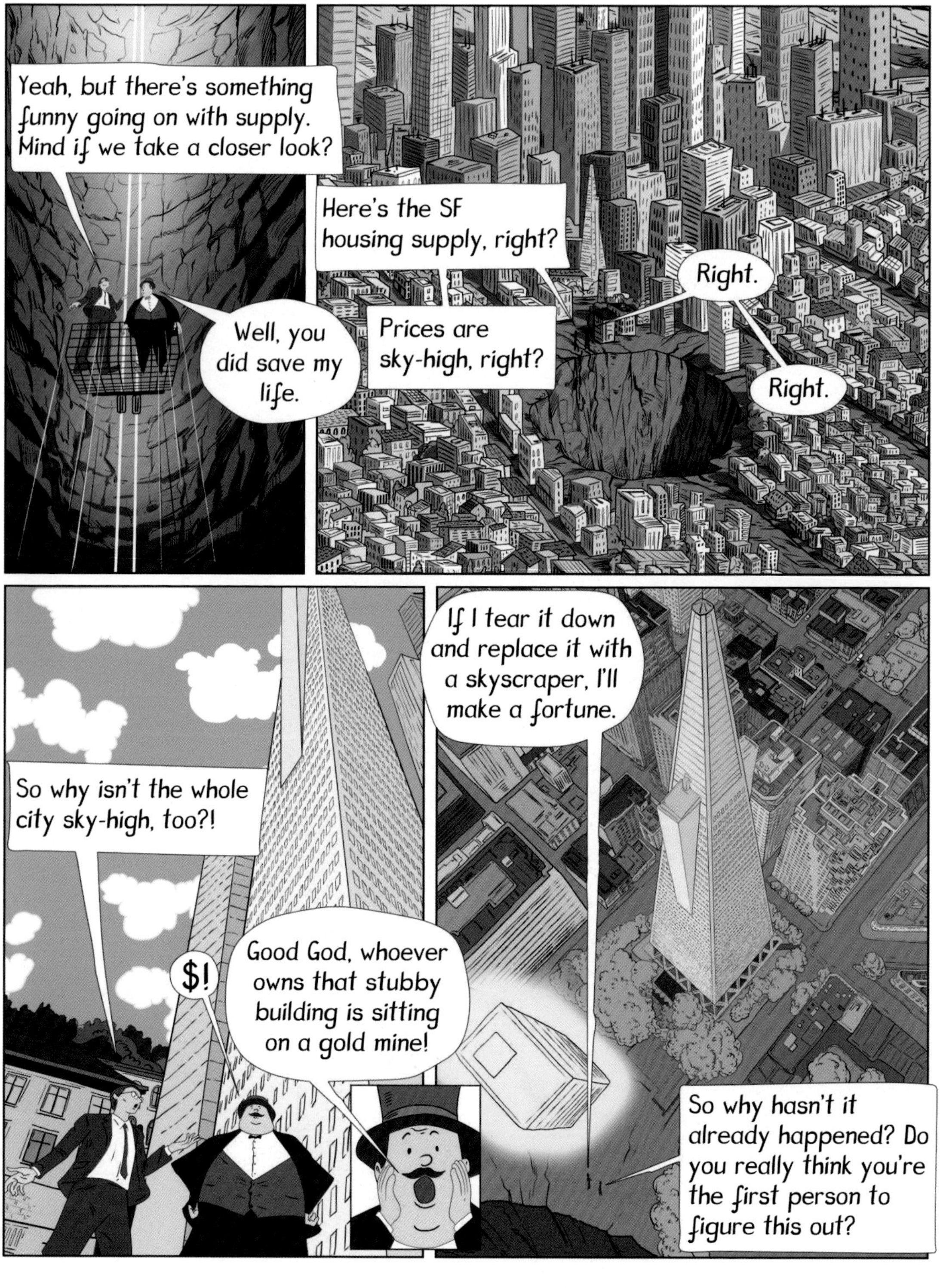

Yeah, but there's something funny going on with supply. Mind if we take a closer look?
Well, you did save my life.
Here's the SF housing supply, right?
Right.
Prices are sky-high, right?
Right.
So why isn't the whole city sky-high, too?!
$!
Good God, whoever owns that stubby building is sitting on a gold mine!
If I tear it down and replace it with a skyscraper, I'll make a fortune.
So why hasn't it already happened? Do you really think you're the first person to figure this out?

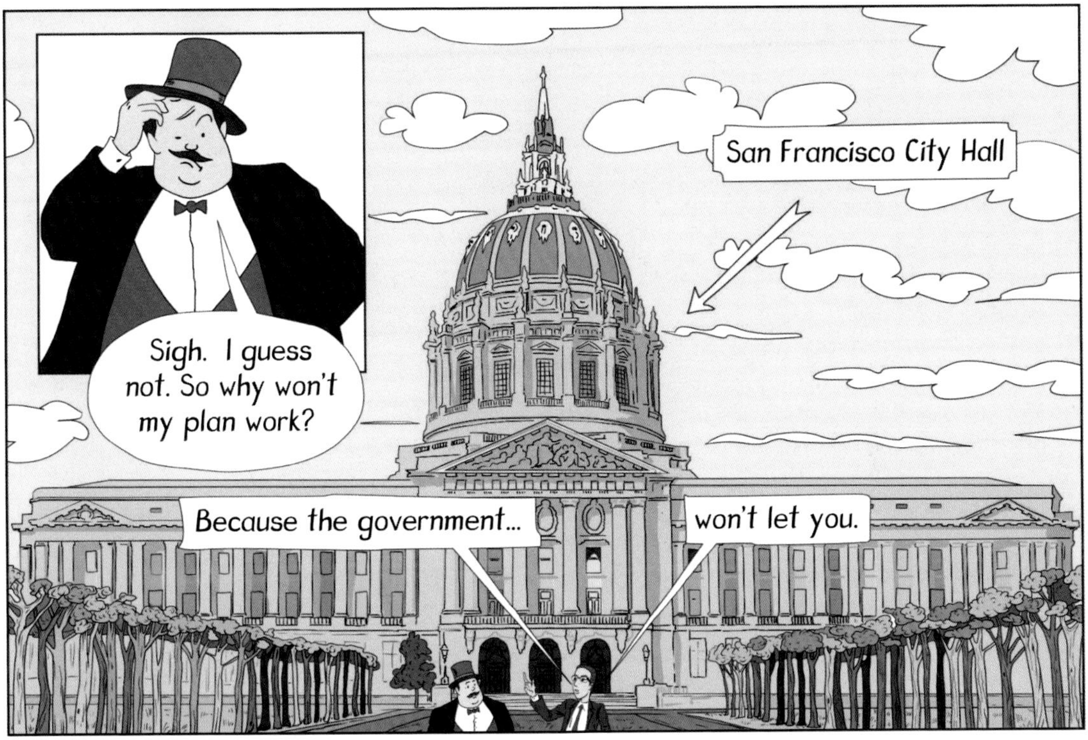
San Francisco City Hall
Sigh. I guess not. So why won't my plan work?
Because the government...
won't let you.

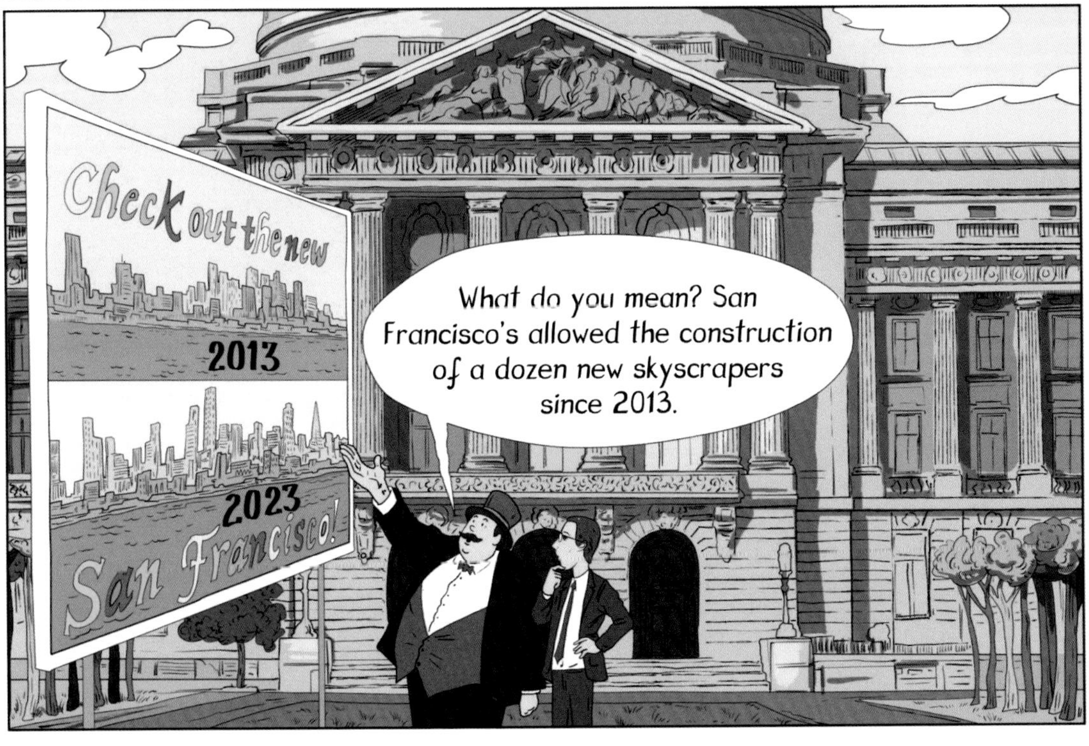
Check out the new
2013
2023
San Francisco!
What do you mean? San Francisco's allowed the construction of a dozen new skyscrapers since 2013.

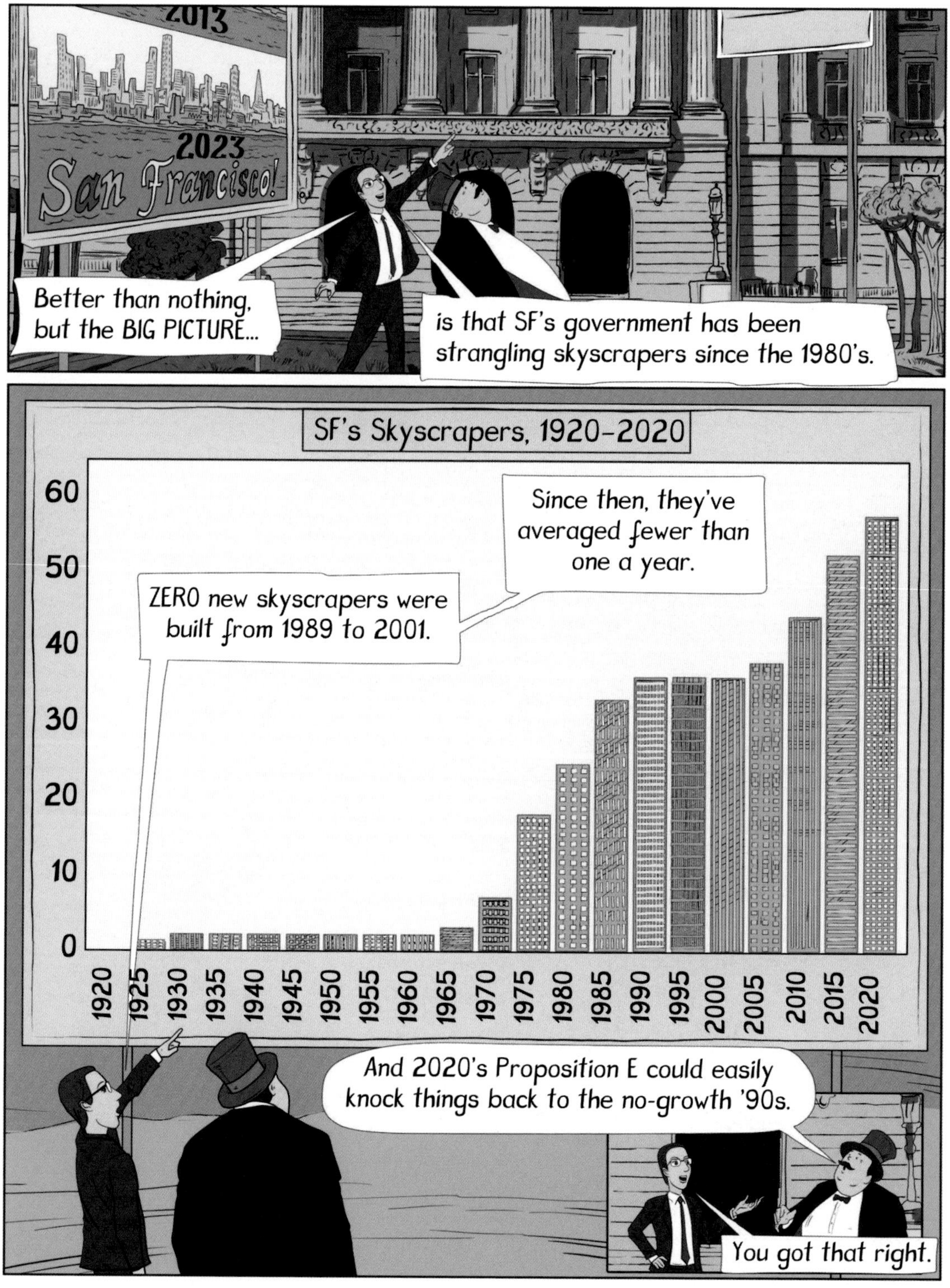
2013
2023
San Francisco!
Better than nothing, but the BIG PICTURE...
is that SF's government has been strangling skyscrapers since the 1980's.
SF's Skyscrapers, 1920-2020
60
50
40
30
20
10
0
1920 1925 1930 1935 1940 1945 1950 1955 1960 1965 1970 1975 1980 1985 1990 1995 2000 2005 2010 2015 2020
ZERO new skyscrapers were built from 1989 to 2001.
Since then, they've averaged fewer than one a year.
And 2020's Proposition E could easily knock things back to the no-growth '90s.
You got that right.

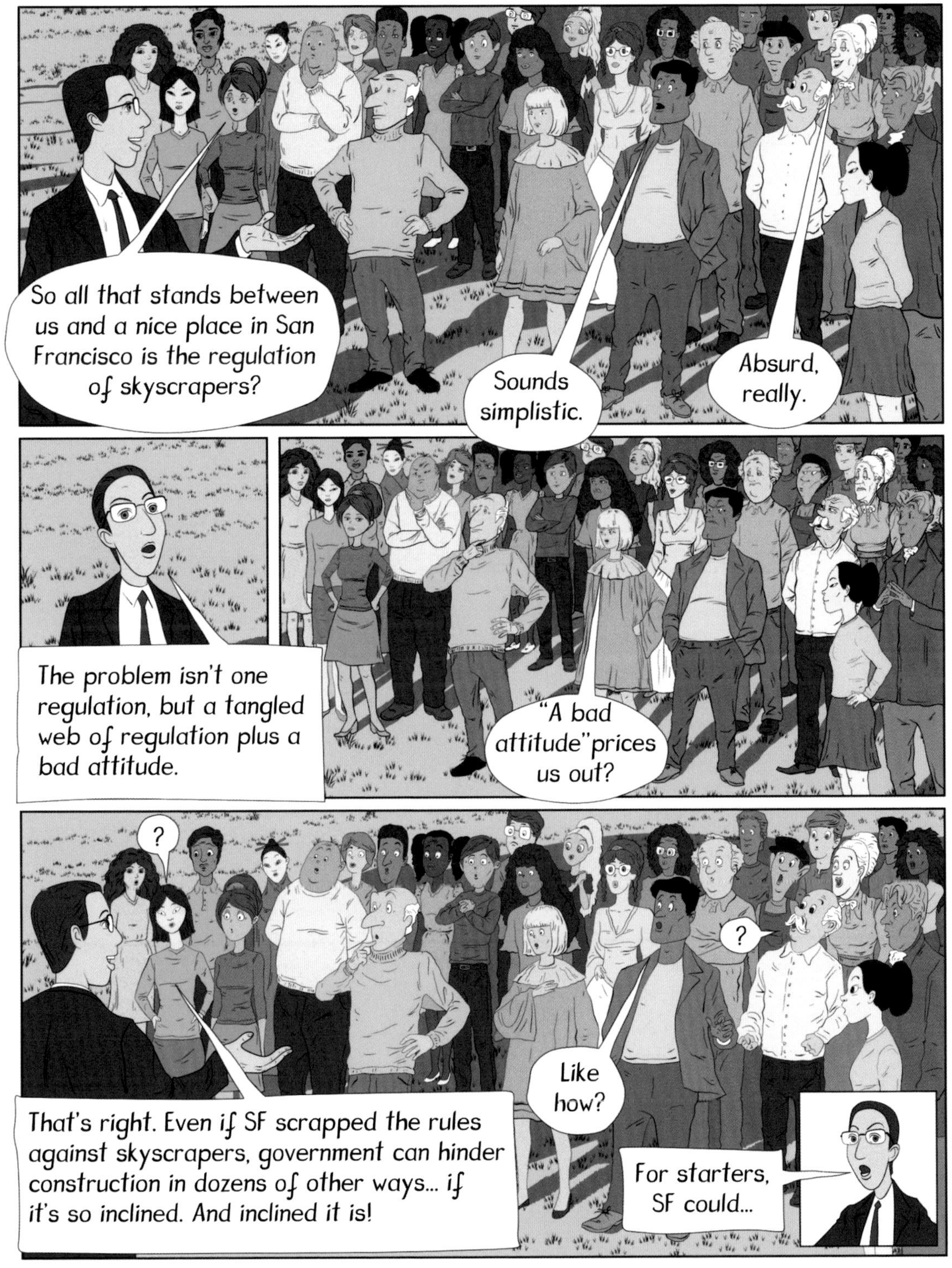
So all that stands between us and a nice place in San Francisco is the regulation of skyscrapers?
Sounds simplistic.
Absurd, really.
The problem isn't one regulation, but a tangled web of regulation plus a bad attitude.
"A bad attitude" prices us out?
?
?
Like how?
That's right. Even if SF scrapped the rules against skyscrapers, government can hinder construction in dozens of other ways... if it's so inclined. And inclined it is!
For starters, SF could...

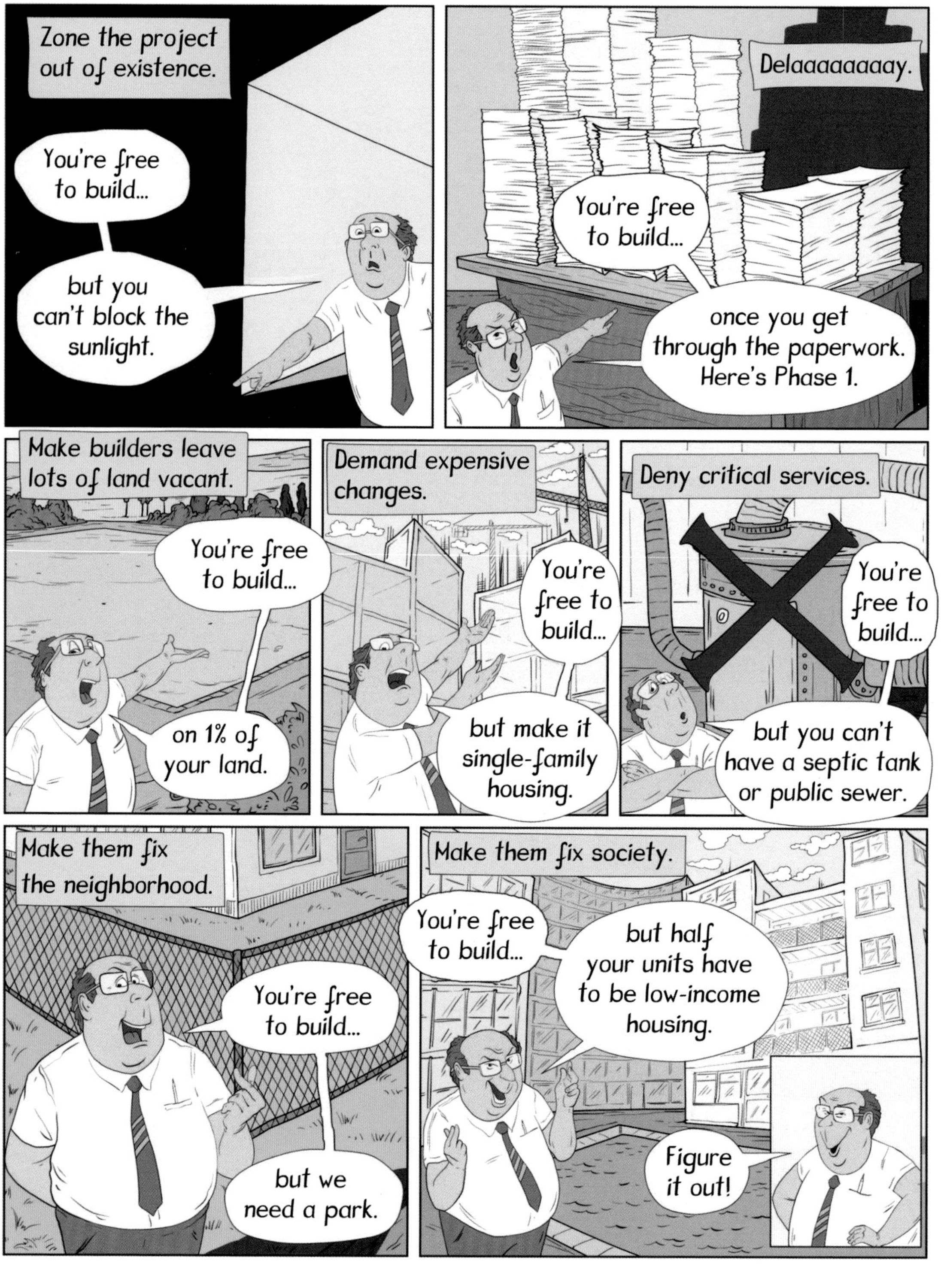
Zone the project out of existence.
You're free to build...
but you can't block the sunlight.
Delaaaaaaaay.
You're free to build...
once you get through the paperwork. Here's Phase 1.
Make builders leave lots of land vacant.
You're free to build...
on 1% of your land.
Demand expensive changes.
You're free to build...
but make it single-family housing.
Deny critical services.
You're free to build...
but you can't have a septic tank or public sewer.
Make them fix the neighborhood.
You're free to build...
but we need a park.
Make them fix society.
You're free to build...
but half your units have to be low-income housing.
Figure it out!

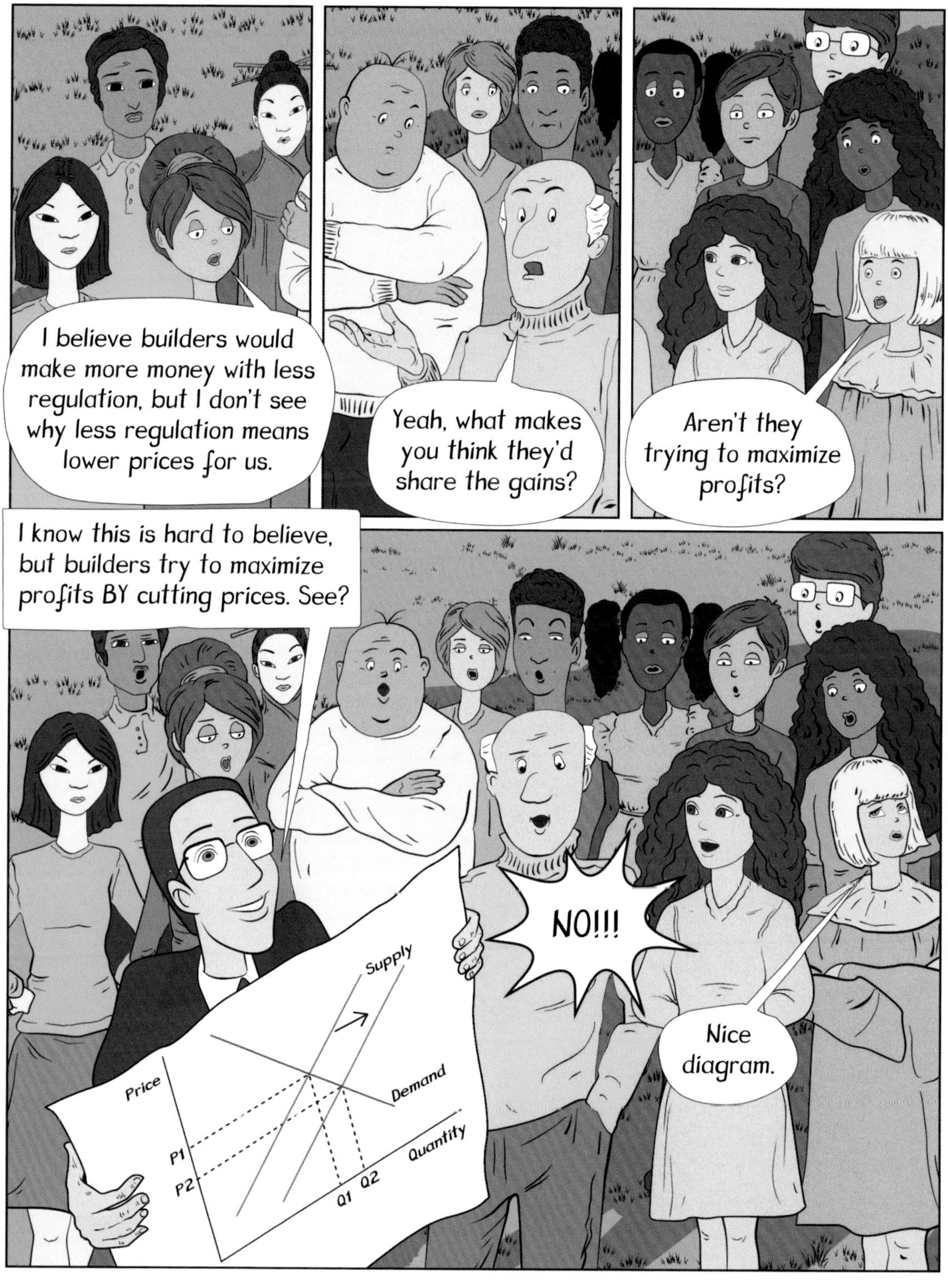
I believe builders would make more money with less regulation, but I don't see why less regulation means lower prices for us.
Yeah, what makes you think they'd share the gains?
Aren't they trying to maximize profits?
I know this is hard to believe, but builders try to maximize profits BY cutting prices. See?
Supply
Demand
Price
Quantity
P1
P2
Q1
Q2
NO!!!
Nice diagram.

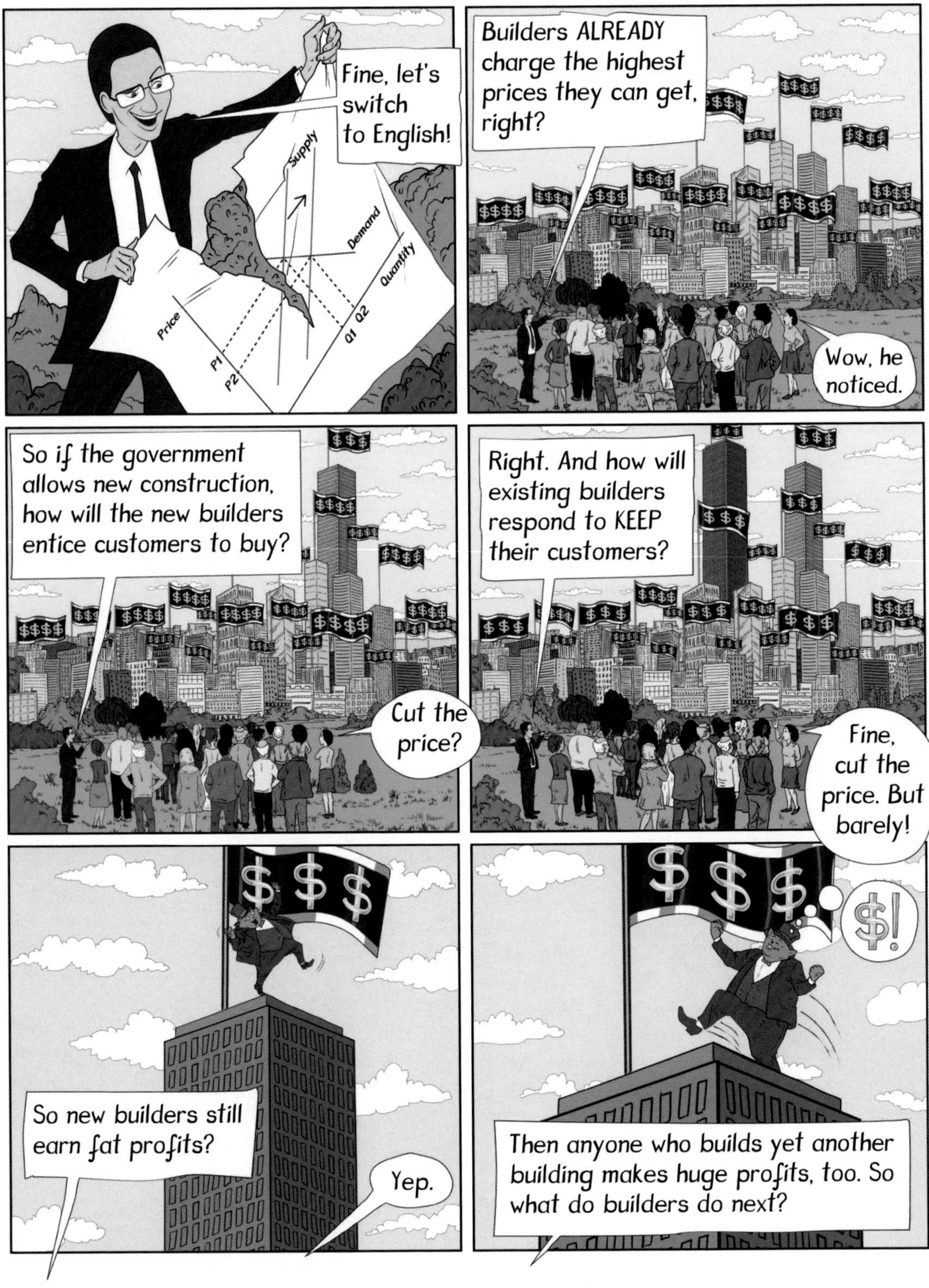
Fine, let's switch to English!
Supply
Demand
Quantity
Price
P1
P2
Q1
Q2
Builders ALREADY charge the highest prices they can get, right?
Wow, he noticed.
So if the government allows new construction, how will the new builders entice customers to buy?
Cut the price?
Right. And how will existing builders respond to KEEP their customers?
Fine, cut the price. But barely!
So new builders still earn fat profits?
Yep.
$!
Then anyone who builds yet another building makes huge profits, too. So what do builders do next?

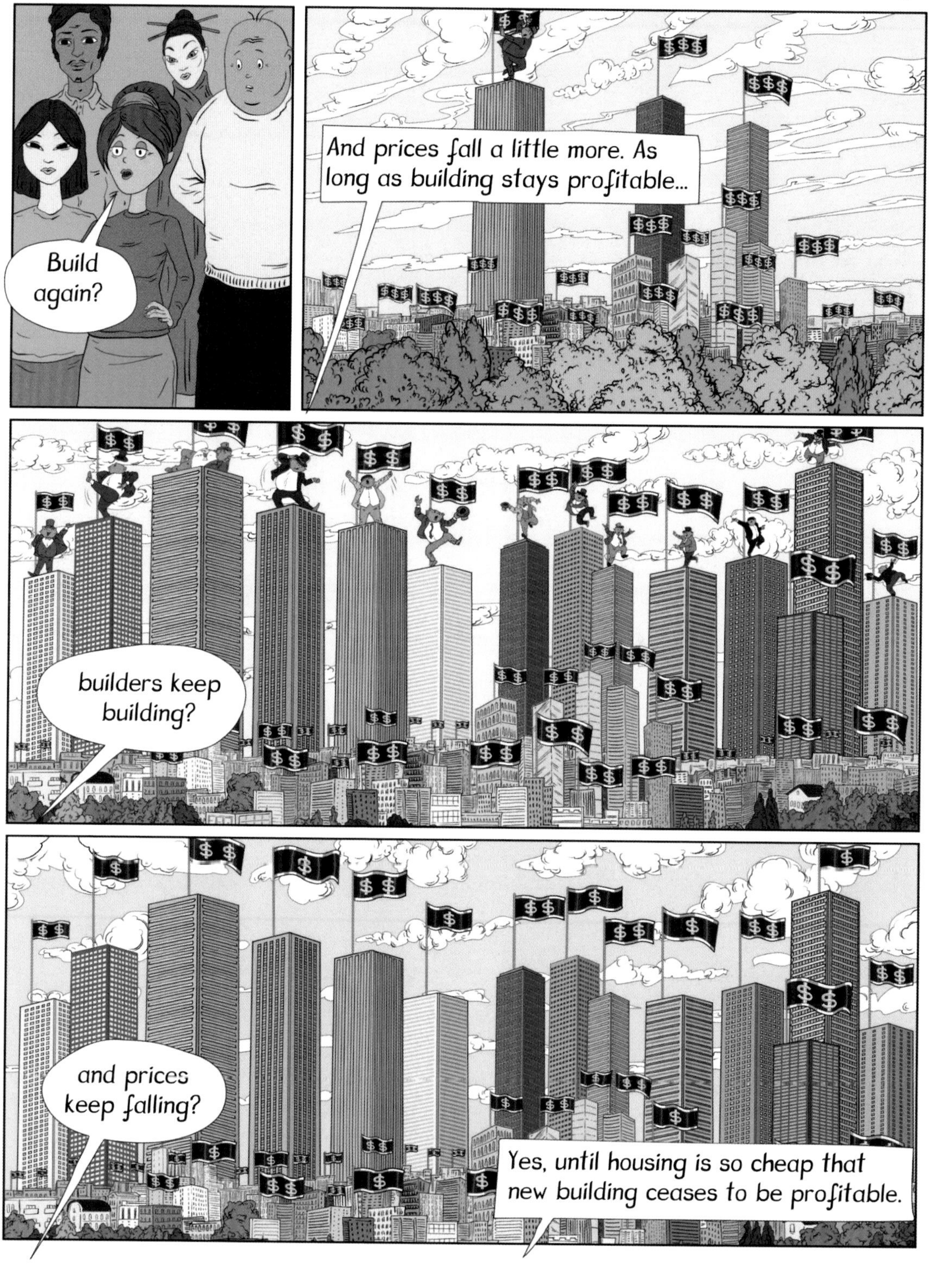
Build again?
And prices fall a little more. As long as building stays profitable...
builders keep building?
and prices keep falling?
Yes, until housing is so cheap that new building ceases to be profitable.

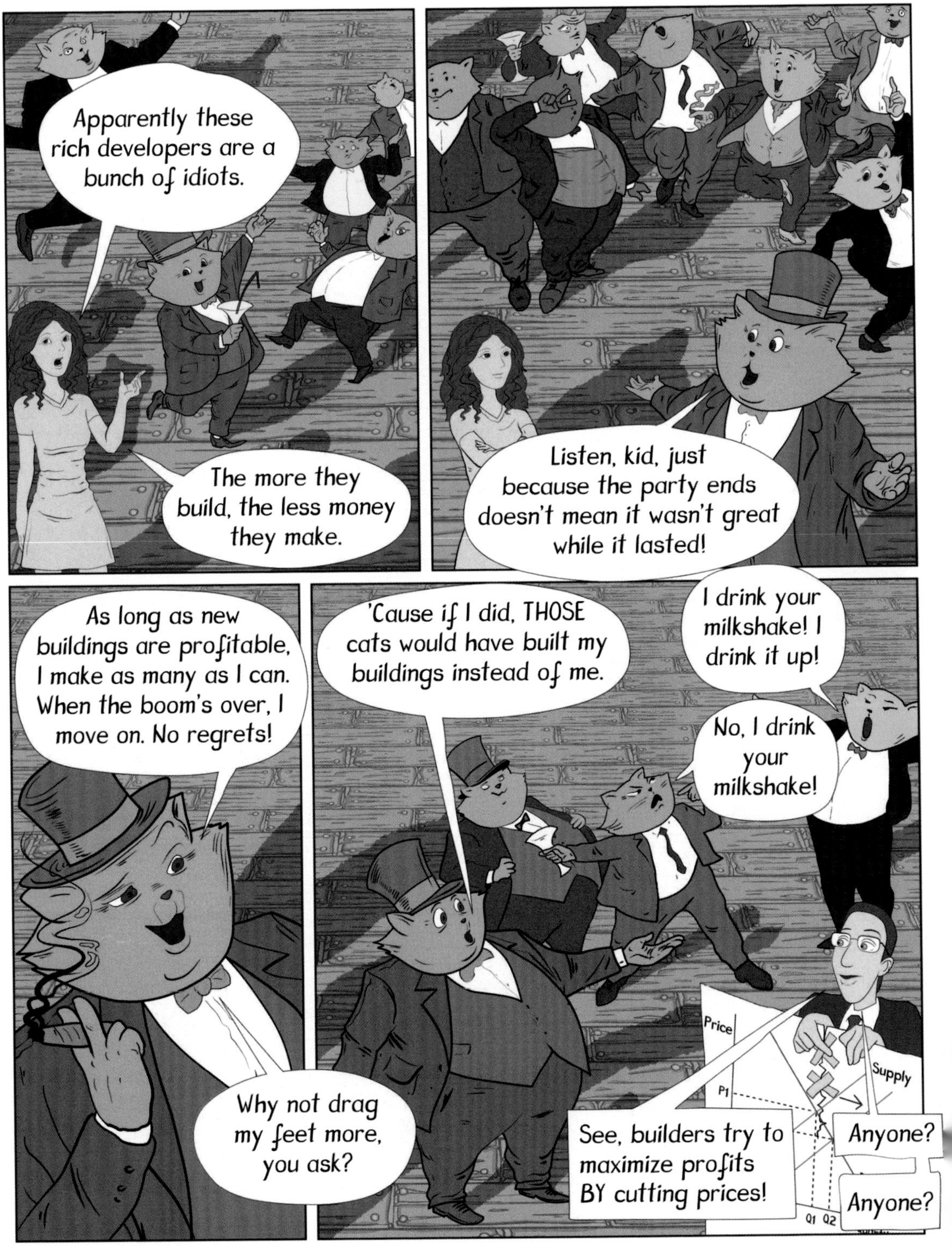
Apparently these rich developers are a bunch of idiots.
The more they build, the less money they make.
Listen, kid, just because the party ends doesn't mean it wasn't great while it lasted!
As long as new buildings are profitable, I make as many as I can. When the boom's over, I move on. No regrets!
Why not drag my feet more, you ask?
'Cause if I did, THOSE cats would have built my buildings instead of me.
I drink your milkshake! I drink it up!
No, I drink your milkshake!
Price
Supply
P1
Q1 Q2
See, builders try to maximize profits BY cutting prices!
Anyone?
Anyone?

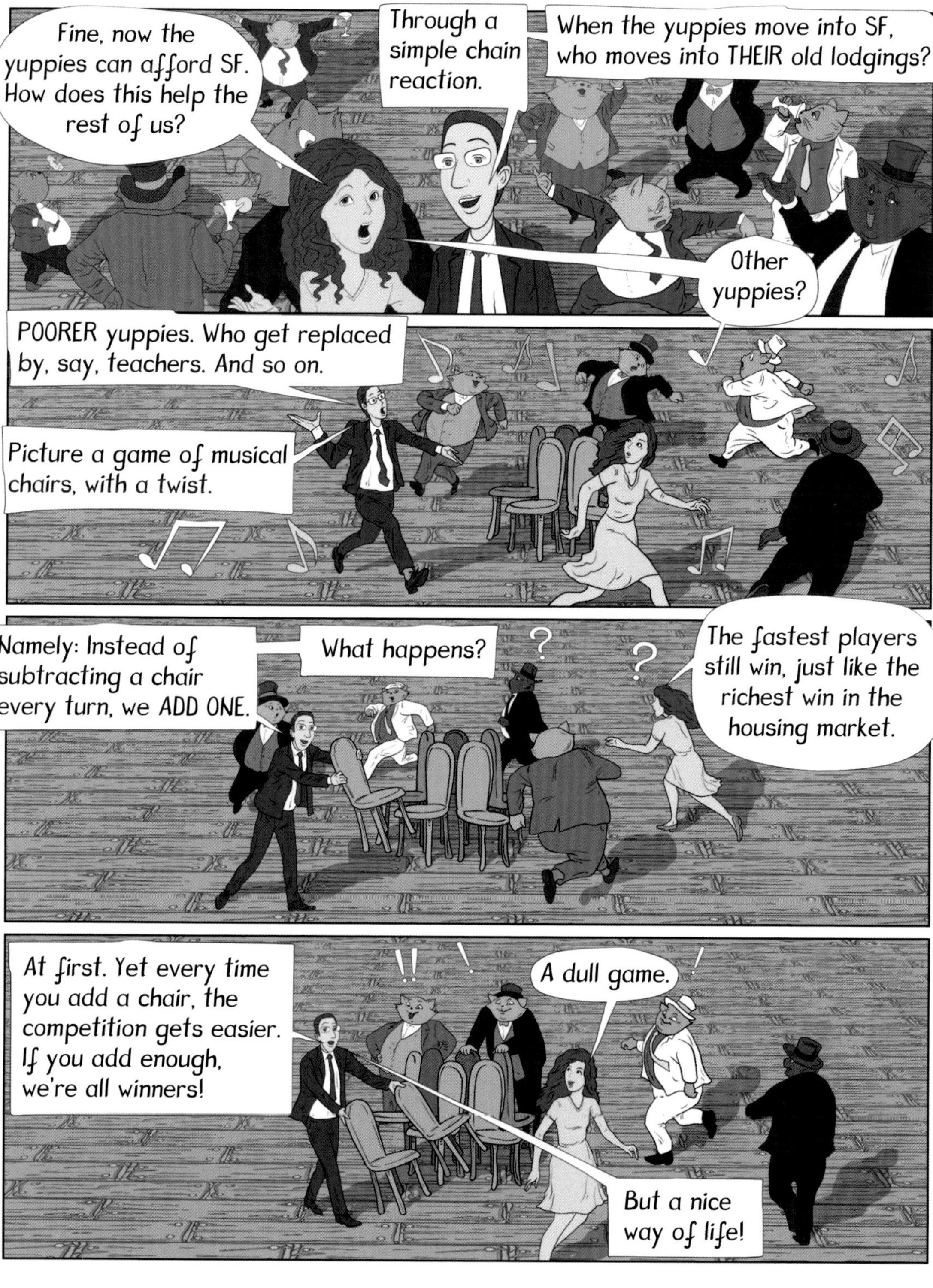
Fine, now the yuppies can afford SF. How does this help the rest of us?
Through a simple chain reaction.
When the yuppies move into SF, who moves into THEIR old lodgings?
Other yuppies?
POORER yuppies. Who get replaced by, say, teachers. And so on.
Picture a game of musical chairs, with a twist.
Namely: Instead of subtracting a chair every turn, we ADD ONE.
What happens?
The fastest players still win, just like the richest win in the housing market.
At first. Yet every time you add a chair, the competition gets easier. If you add enough, we're all winners!
A dull game.
But a nice way of life!

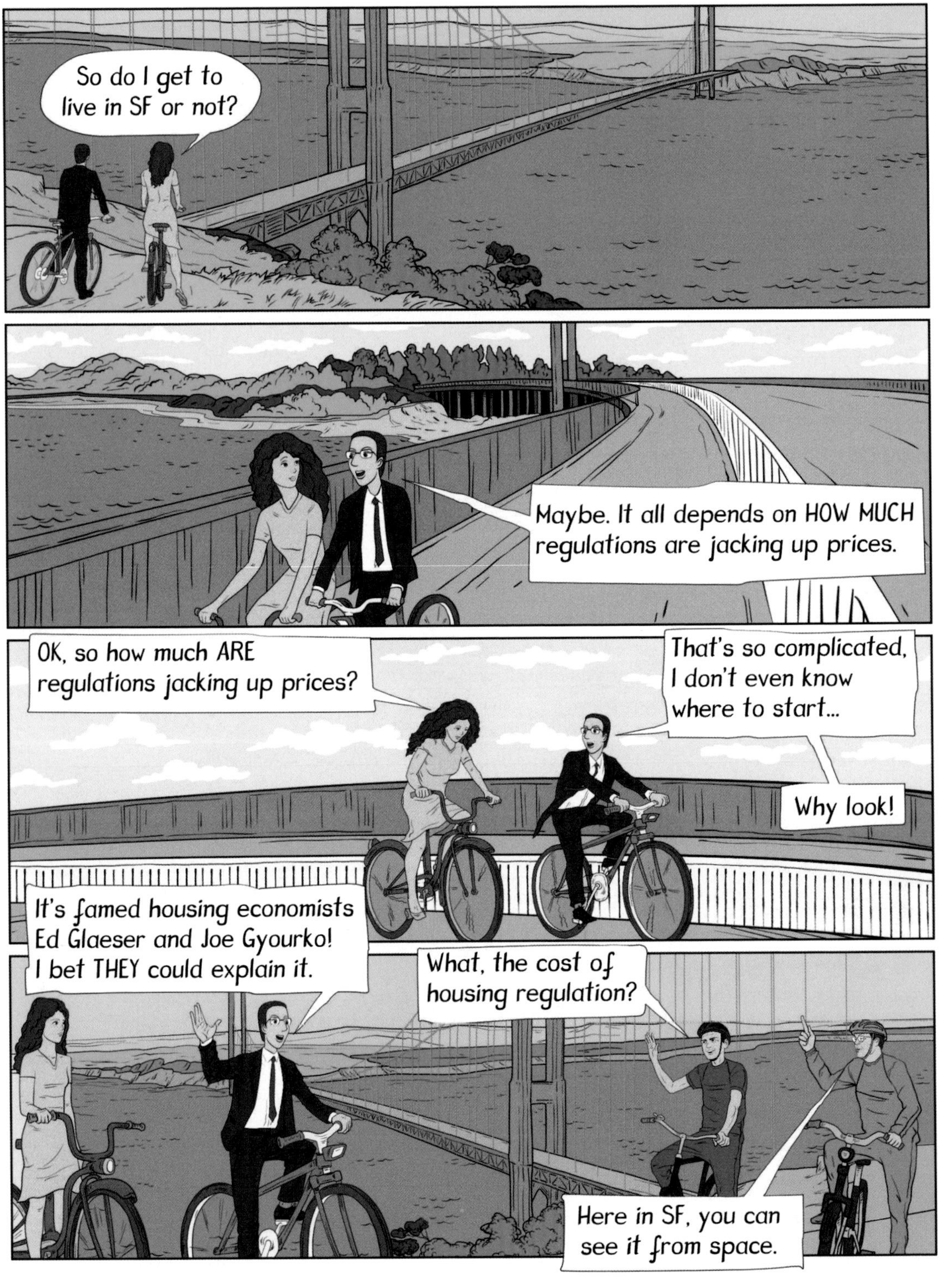
So do I get to live in SF or not?
Maybe. It all depends on HOW MUCH regulations are jacking up prices.
OK, so how much ARE regulations jacking up prices?
That's so complicated, I don't even know where to start...
Why look!
It's famed housing economists Ed Glaeser and Joe Gyourko! I bet THEY could explain it.
What, the cost of housing regulation?
Here in SF, you can see it from space.

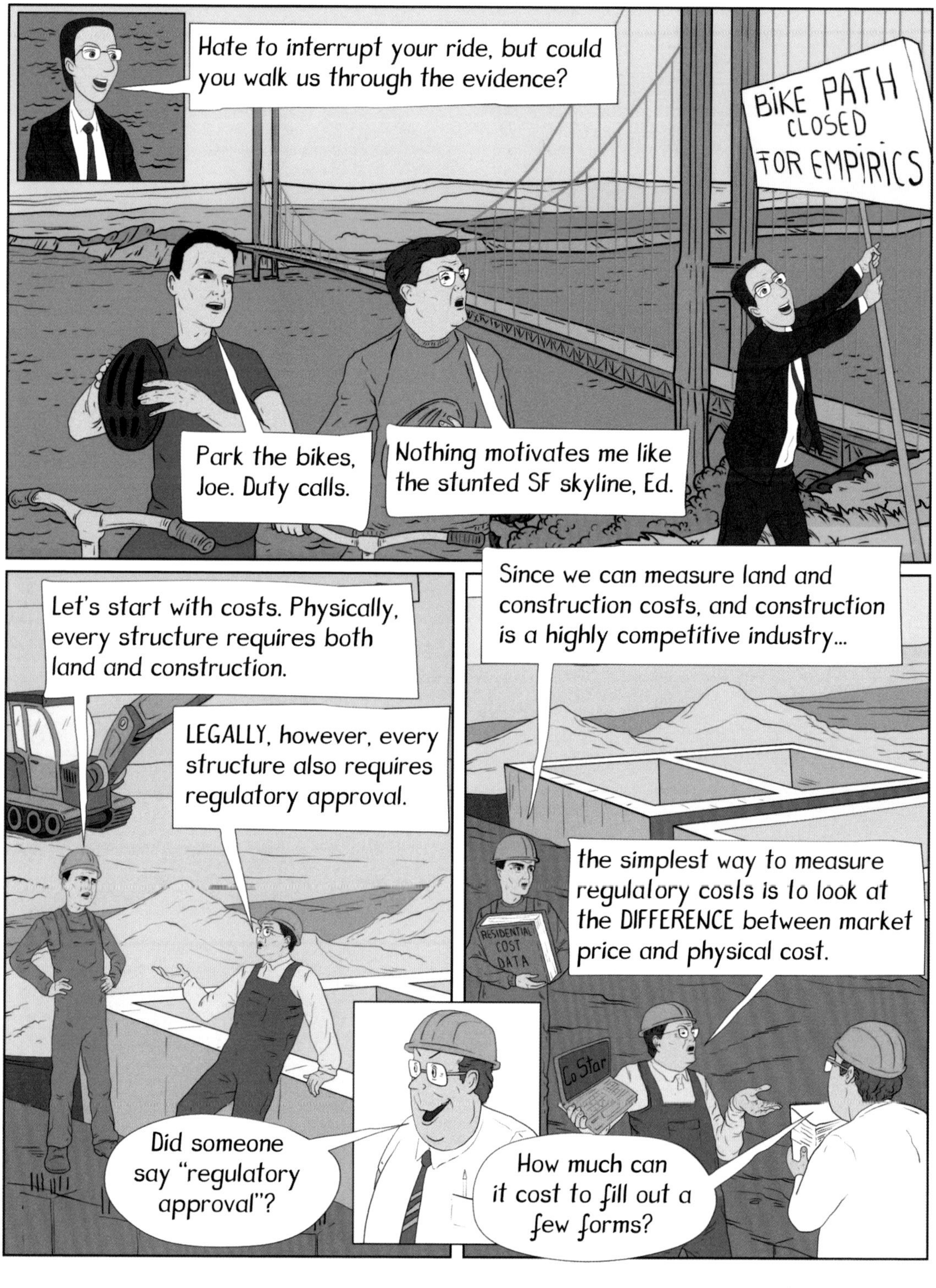
Hate to interrupt your ride, but could you walk us through the evidence?
BIKE PATH CLOSED FOR EMPIRICS
Park the bikes, Joe. Duty calls.
Nothing motivates me like the stunted SF skyline, Ed.
Let's start with costs. Physically, every structure requires both land and construction.
LEGALLY, however, every structure also requires regulatory approval.
Since we can measure land and construction costs, and construction is a highly competitive industry...
the simplest way to measure regulatory costs is to look at the DIFFERENCE between market price and physical cost.
RESIDENTIAL COST DATA
Co Star
Did someone say "regulatory approval"?
How much can it cost to fill out a few forms?

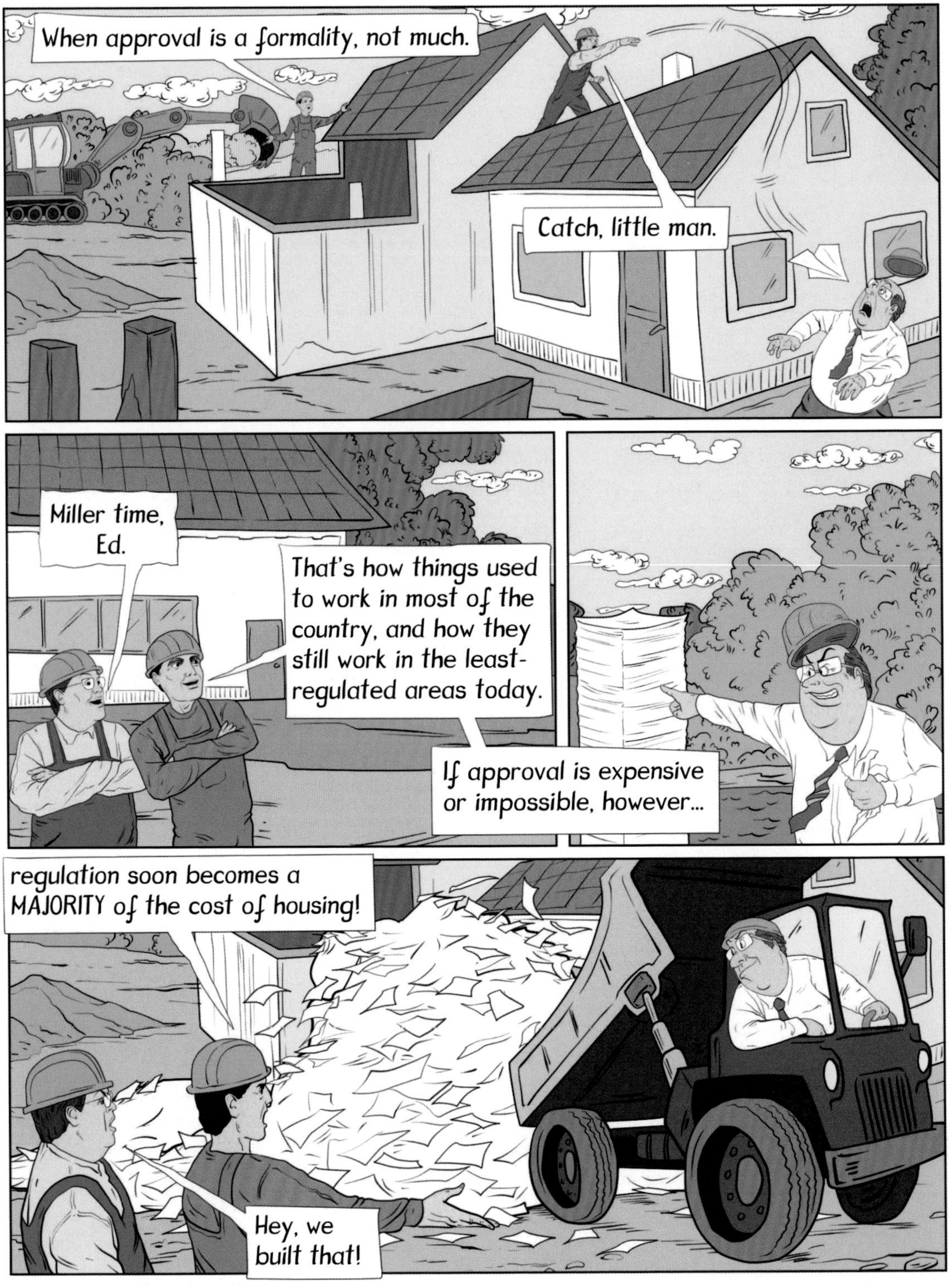
When approval is a formality, not much.
Catch, little man.
Miller time, Ed.
That's how things used to work in most of the country, and how they still work in the least-regulated areas today.
If approval is expensive or impossible, however...
regulation soon becomes a MAJORITY of the cost of housing!
Hey, we built that!

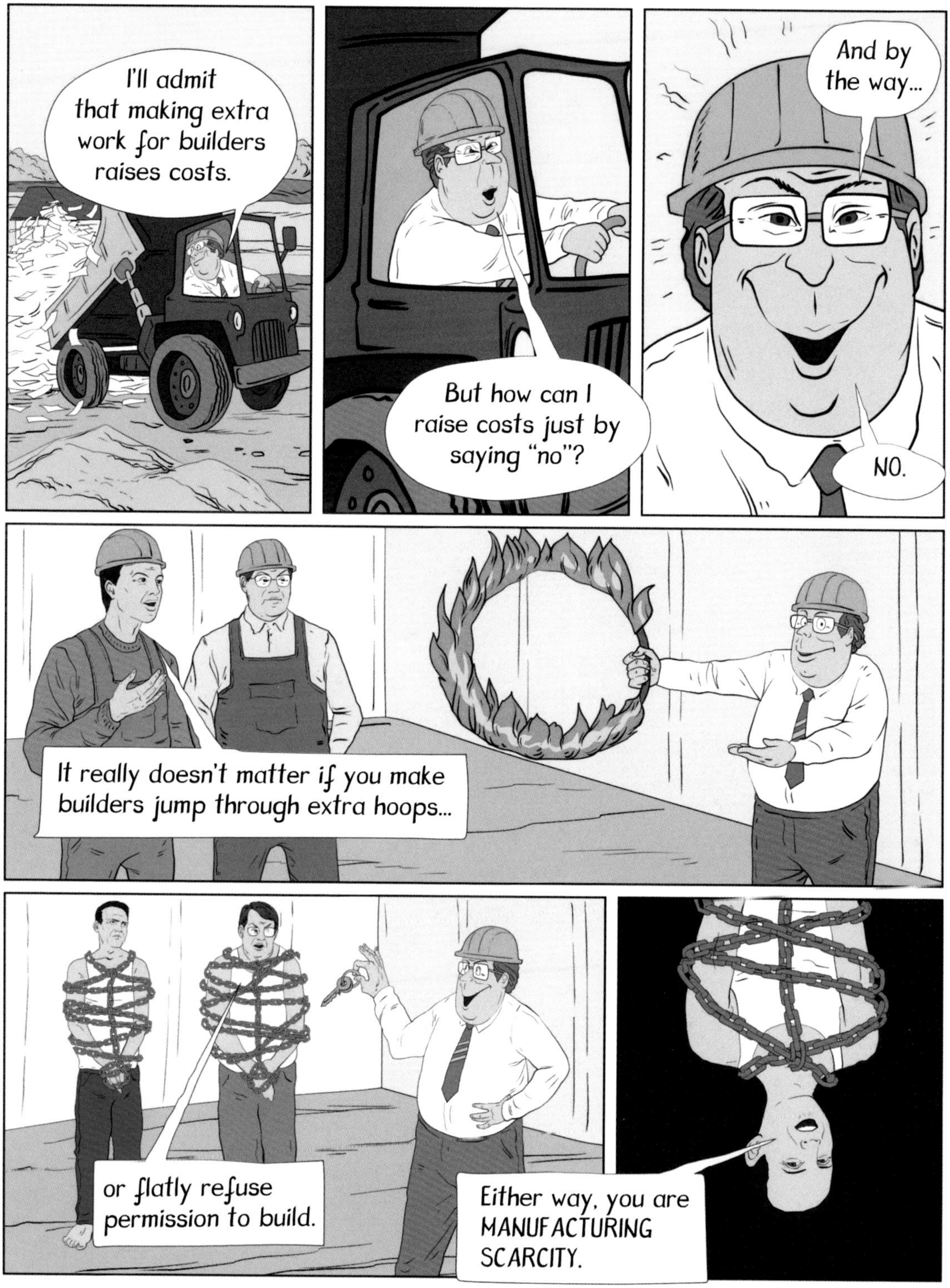
I'll admit that making extra work for builders raises costs.
But how can I raise costs just by saying "no"?
And by the way...
NO.
It really doesn't matter if you make builders jump through extra hoops...
or flatly refuse permission to build.
Either way, you are MANUFACTURING SCARCITY.

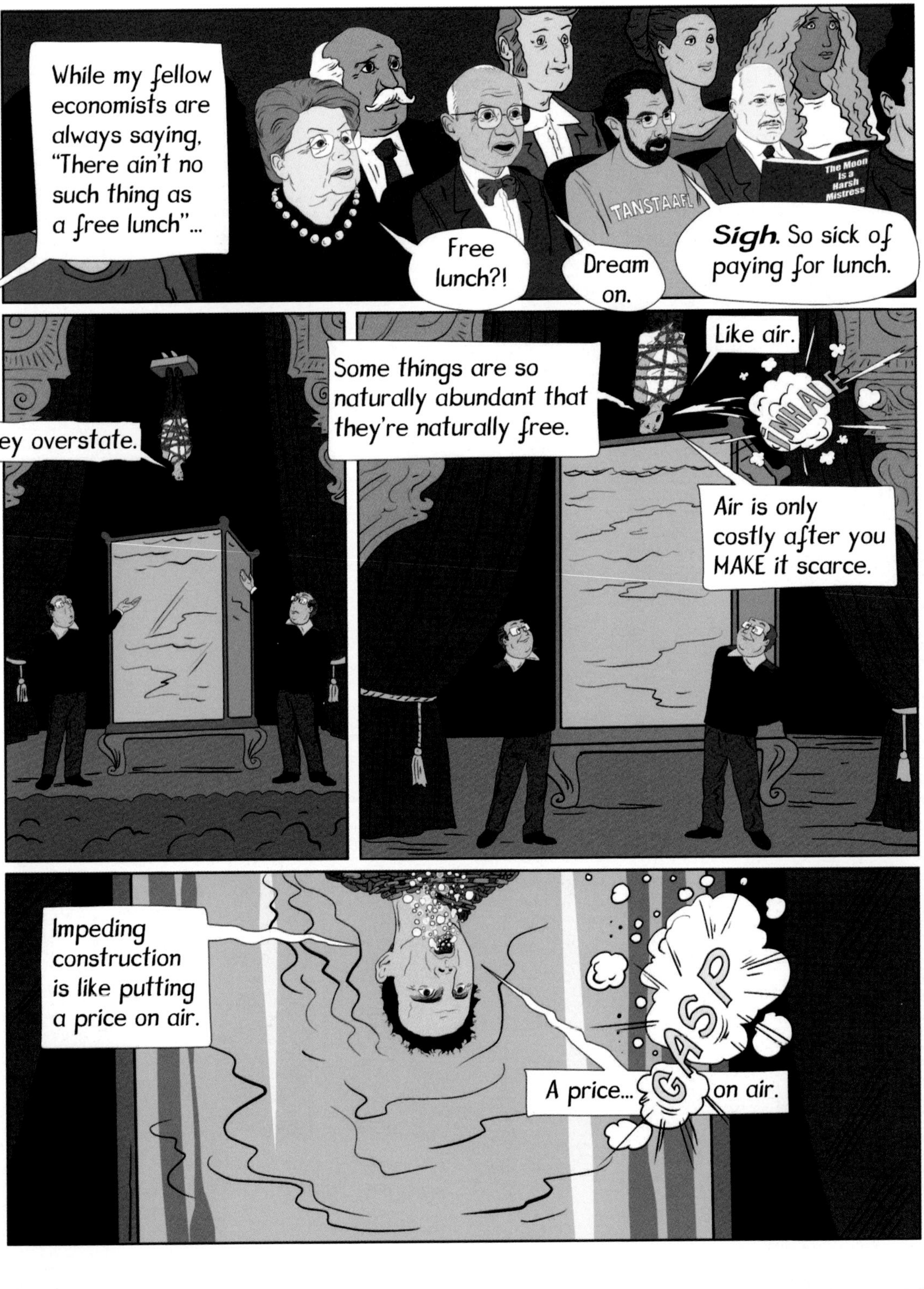
While my fellow economists are always saying, "There ain't no such thing as a free lunch"...
Free lunch?!
TANSTAAFL
Dream on.
The Moon Is a Harsh Mistress
Sigh. So sick of paying for lunch.
they overstate.
Some things are so naturally abundant that they're naturally free.
Like air.
INHALE
Air is only costly after you MAKE it scarce.
Impeding construction is like putting a price on air.
A price...
GASP
on air.

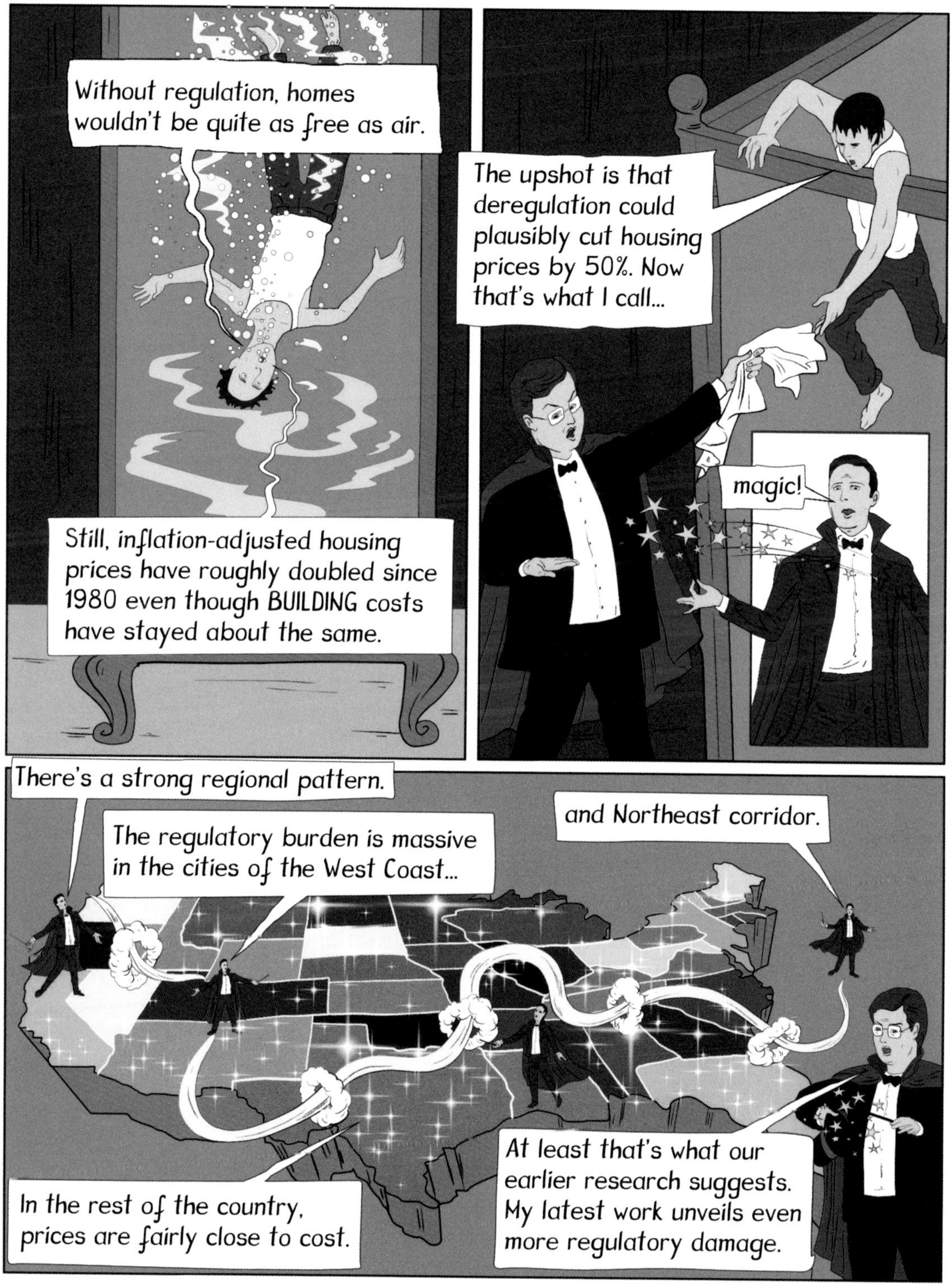
Without regulation, homes wouldn't be quite as free as air.
Still, inflation-adjusted housing prices have roughly doubled since 1980 even though BUILDING costs have stayed about the same.
The upshot is that deregulation could plausibly cut housing prices by 50%. Now that's what I call...
magic!
There's a strong regional pattern.
The regulatory burden is massive in the cities of the West Coast...
and Northeast corridor.
In the rest of the country, prices are fairly close to cost.
At least that's what our earlier research suggests. My latest work unveils even more regulatory damage.

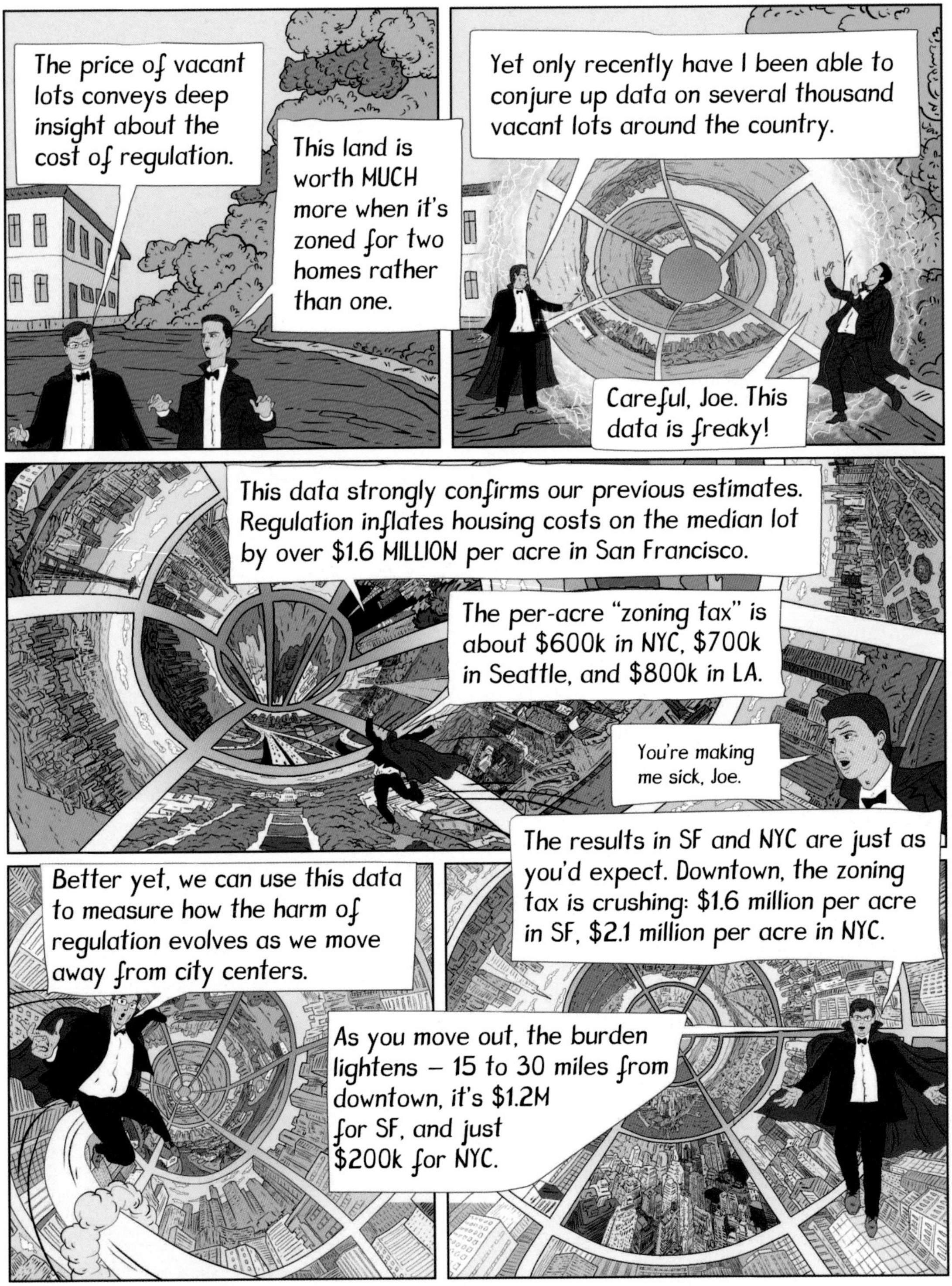
The price of vacant lots conveys deep insight about the cost of regulation.
This land is worth MUCH more when it's zoned for two homes rather than one.
Yet only recently have I been able to conjure up data on several thousand vacant lots around the country.
Careful, Joe. This data is freaky!
This data strongly confirms our previous estimates. Regulation inflates housing costs on the median lot by over $1.6 MILLION per acre in San Francisco.
The per-acre "zoning tax" is about $600k in NYC, $700k in Seattle, and $800k in LA.
You're making me sick, Joe.
Better yet, we can use this data to measure how the harm of regulation evolves as we move away from city centers.
The results in SF and NYC are just as you'd expect. Downtown, the zoning tax is crushing: $1.6 million per acre in SF, $2.1 million per acre in NYC.
As you move out, the burden lightens – 15 to 30 miles from downtown, it's $1.2M for SF, and just $200k for NYC.

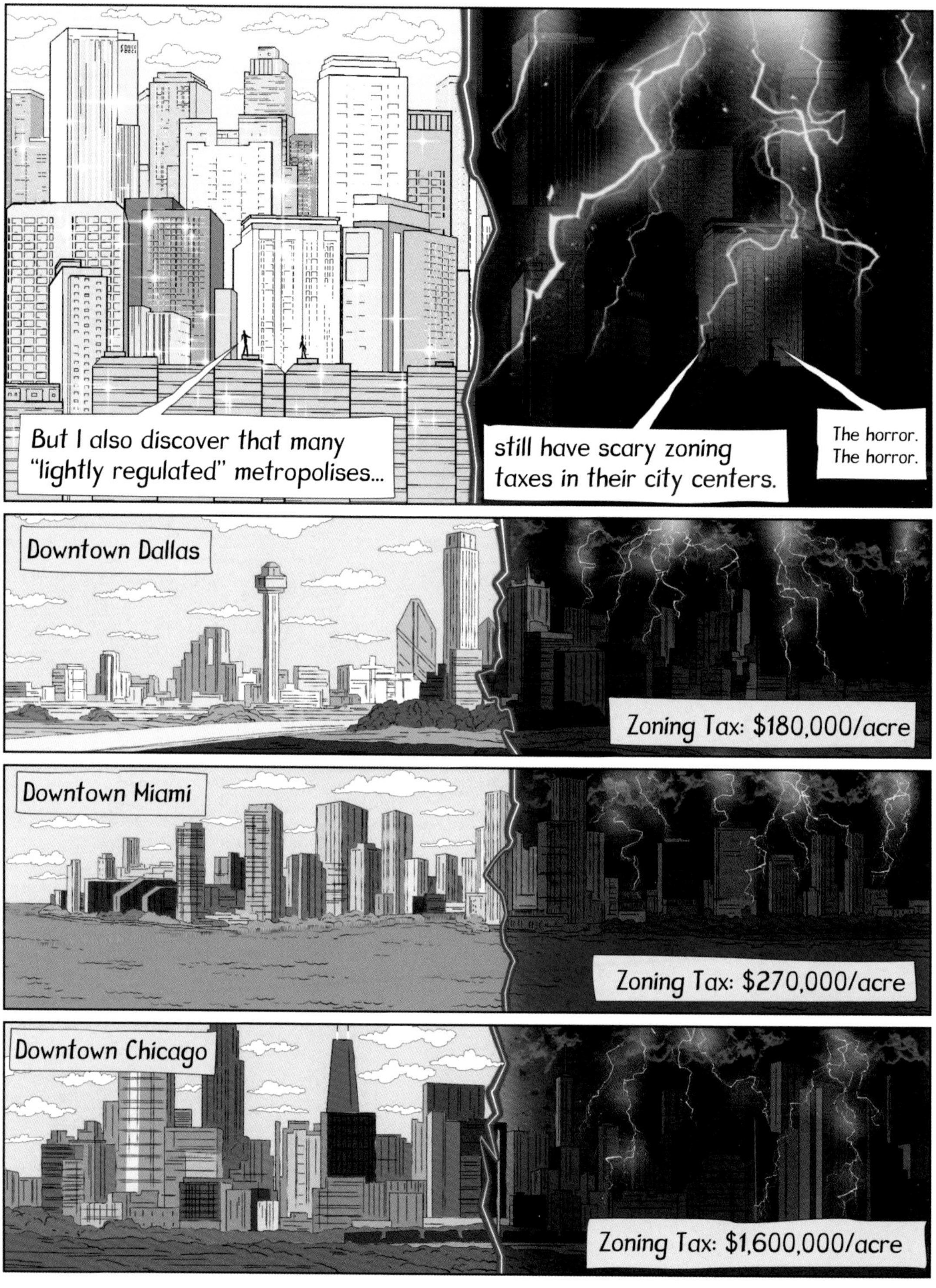

But I also discover that many "lightly regulated" metropolises...
still have scary zoning taxes in their city centers.
The horror. The horror.
Downtown Dallas
Zoning Tax: $180,000/acre
Downtown Miami
Zoning Tax: $270,000/acre
Downtown Chicago
Zoning Tax: $1,600,000/acre

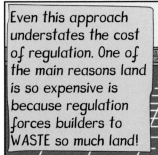

Even this approach understates the cost of regulation. One of the main reasons land is so expensive is because regulation forces builders to WASTE so much land!

Leading example: minimum parking requirements.

Hey, people need parking, people!

These regulations lead to so-called "egg" development: a "yolk" of buildings dwarfed by an "egg white" of parking spots.

Don't build here...

or here...

or here.

Here is OK.

This pushes up the price of land throughout the region.

Buy!

Buy!

We gotta buy!

Which means higher home prices...

New York's through the roof!

even in neighboring areas with less regulation!

Staten Island?!

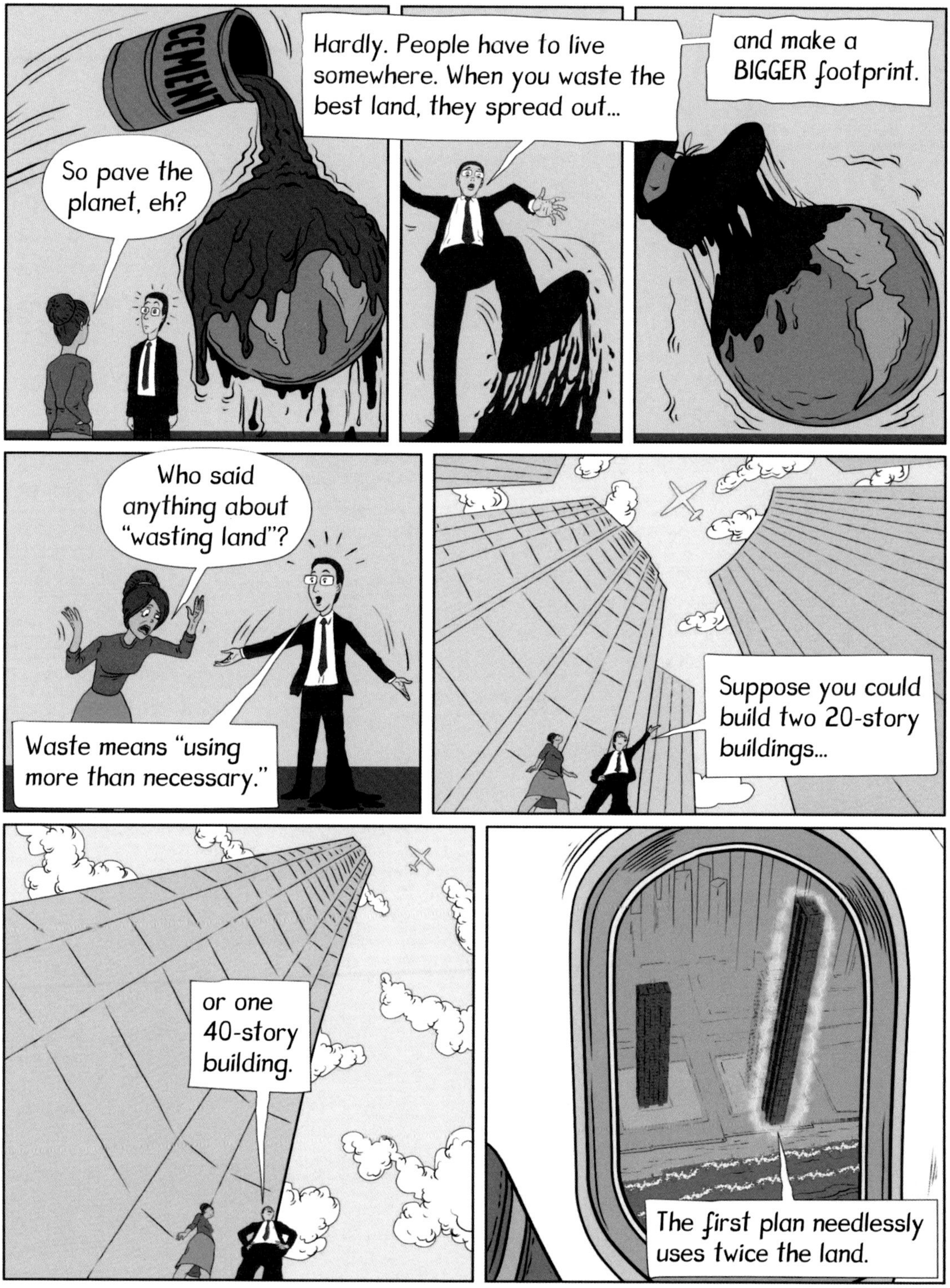

CEMENT
So pave the planet, eh?
Hardly. People have to live somewhere. When you waste the best land, they spread out...
and make a BIGGER footprint.
Who said anything about "wasting land"?
Waste means "using more than necessary."
Suppose you could build two 20-story buildings...
or one 40-story building.
The first plan needlessly uses twice the land.

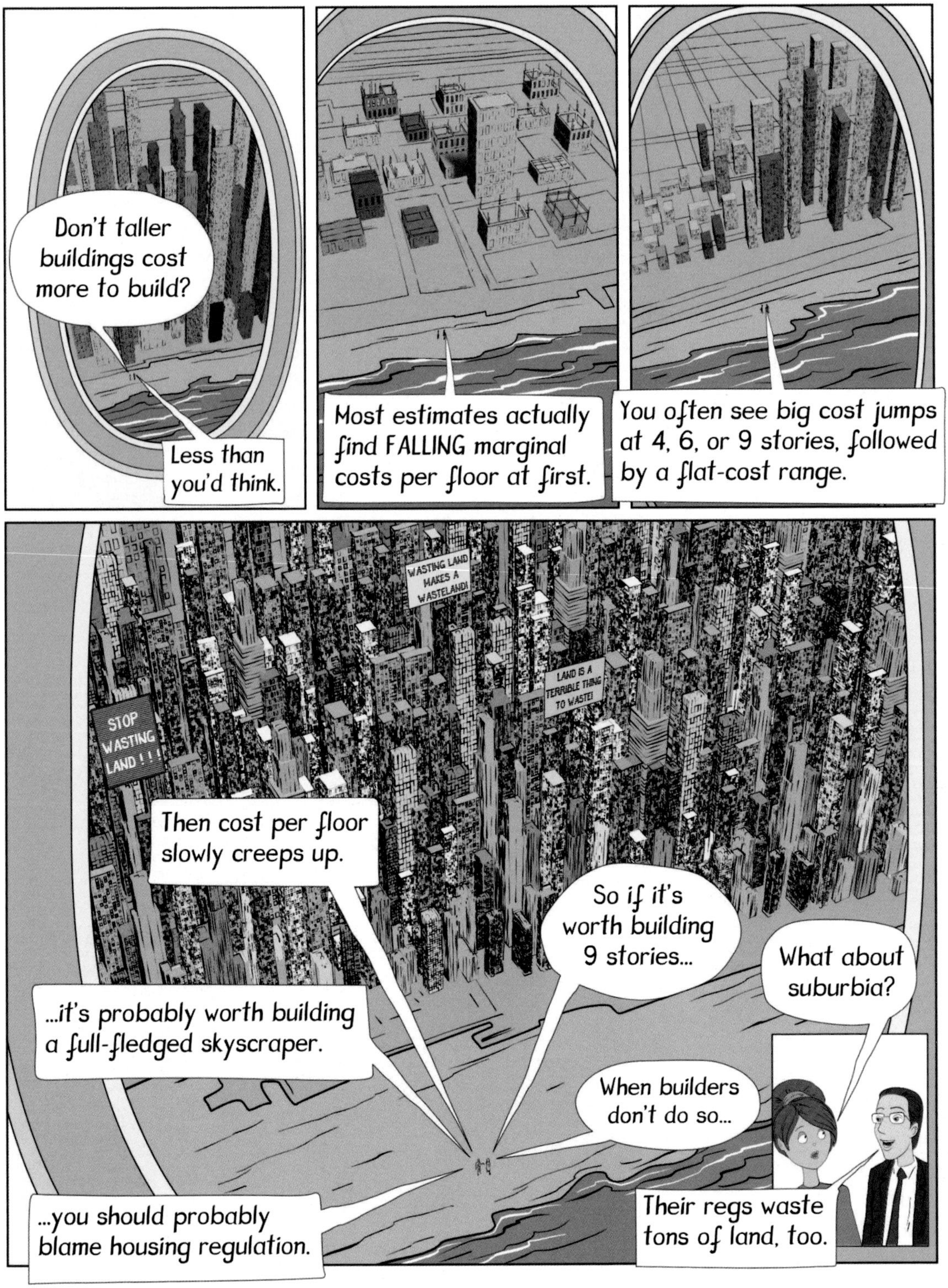
Don't taller buildings cost more to build?
Less than you'd think.
Most estimates actually find FALLING marginal costs per floor at first.
You often see big cost jumps at 4, 6, or 9 stories, followed by a flat-cost range.
WASTING LAND MAKES A WASTELAND!
LAND IS A TERRIBLE THING TO WASTE!
STOP WASTING LAND!!!
Then cost per floor slowly creeps up.
So if it's worth building 9 stories...
...it's probably worth building a full-fledged skyscraper.
What about suburbia?
When builders don't do so...
...you should probably blame housing regulation.
Their regs waste tons of land, too.

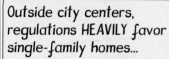
Outside city centers, regulations HEAVILY favor single-family homes...

so developers can't save land or construction costs...

by building apartments...

townhomes...

duplexes...

and so on!

Hobbit Hole

Multifamily regs do vary, but their overall strictness is shocking. Here's how things stood in 2019.

62

The share of residential land reserved for single-family homes is 75% in LA.

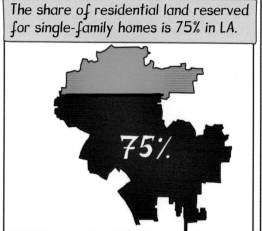

77% in Portland.

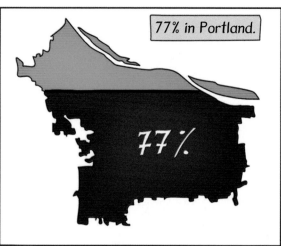

79% in Chicago.

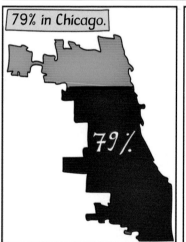

81% in Seattle.

84% in Charlotte.

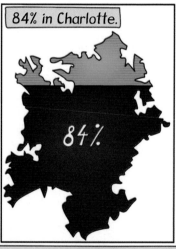

94% in San Jose!

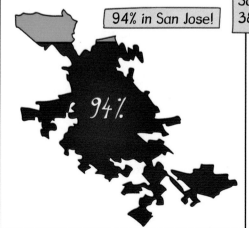

San Francisco, lax by comparison, still sets aside 38% of residential land for single-family homes.

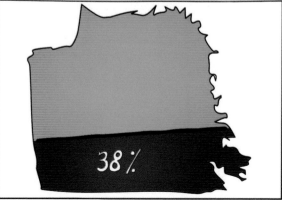

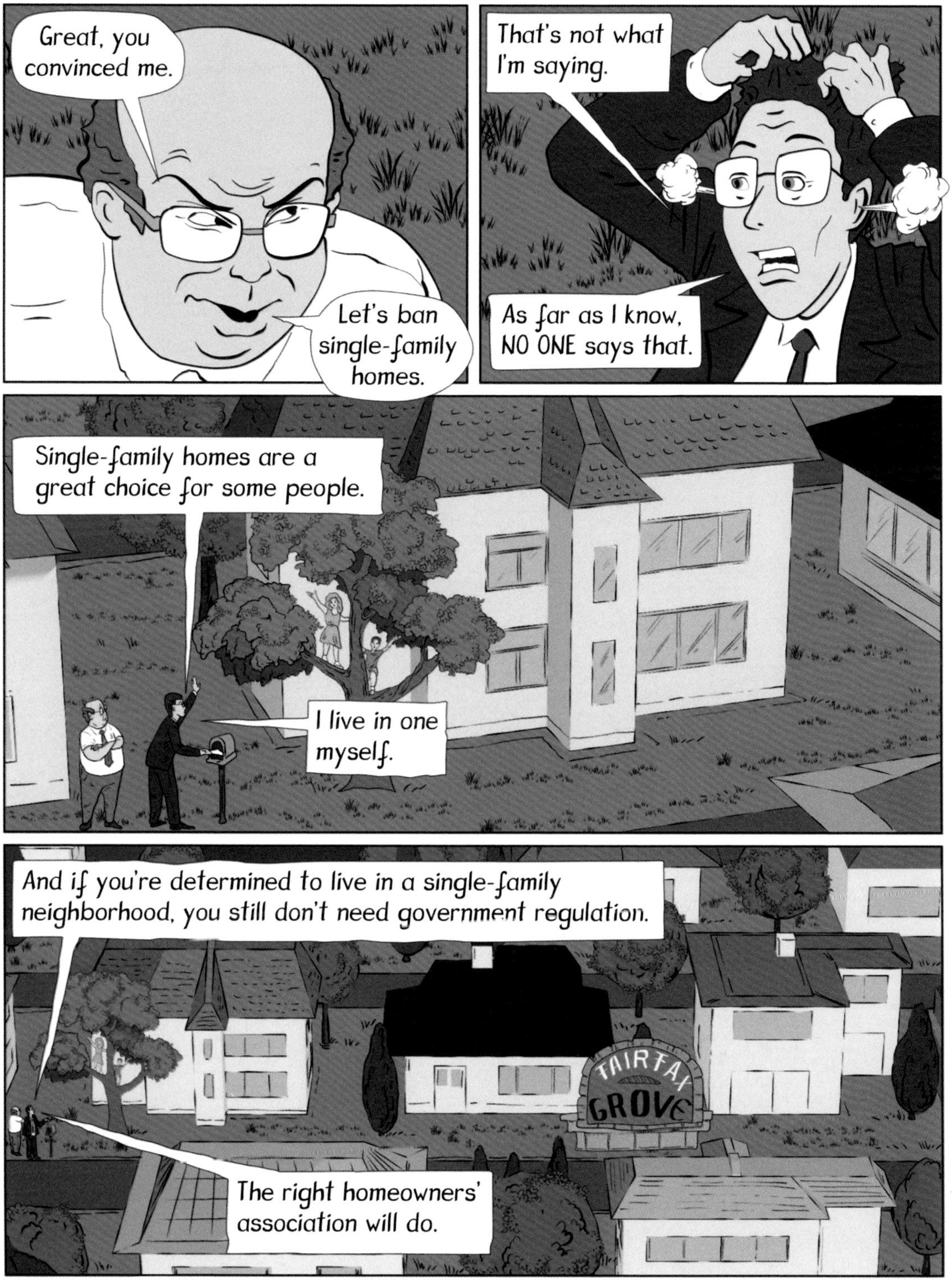
Great, you convinced me.
Let's ban single-family homes.
That's not what I'm saying.
As far as I know, NO ONE says that.
Single-family homes are a great choice for some people.
I live in one myself.
And if you're determined to live in a single-family neighborhood, you still don't need government regulation.
FAIRFAX GROVE
The right homeowners' association will do.

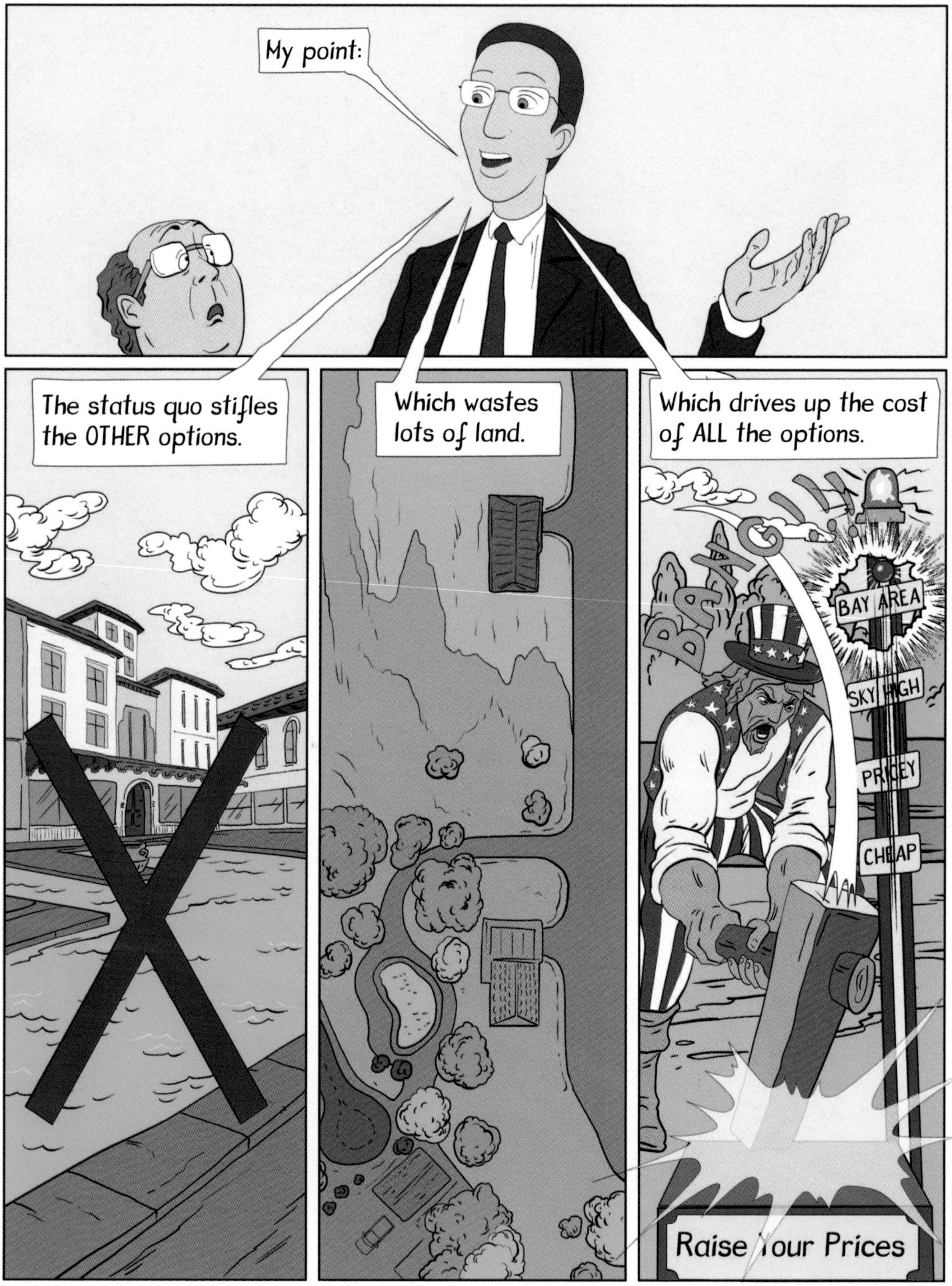
My point:
The status quo stifles the OTHER options.
Which wastes lots of land.
Which drives up the cost of ALL the options.
BANG!!!
BAY AREA
SKY HIGH
PRICEY
CHEAP
Raise Your Prices

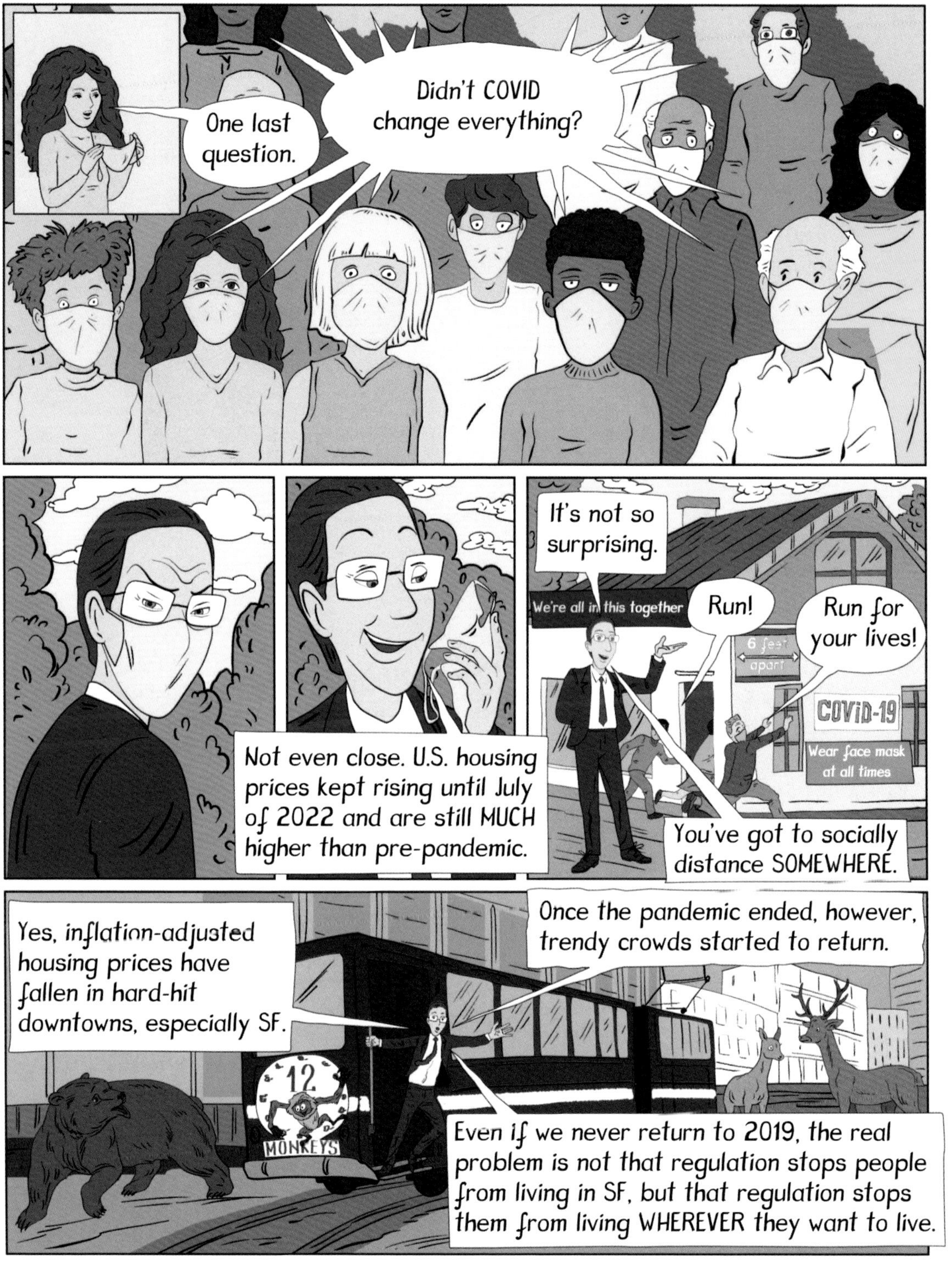
One last question.
Didn't COVID change everything?
Not even close. U.S. housing prices kept rising until July of 2022 and are still MUCH higher than pre-pandemic.
It's not so surprising.
We're all in this together
Run!
6 feet apart
Run for your lives!
COVID-19
Wear face mask at all times
You've got to socially distance SOMEWHERE.
Yes, inflation-adjusted housing prices have fallen in hard-hit downtowns, especially SF.
Once the pandemic ended, however, trendy crowds started to return.
12
MONKEYS
Even if we never return to 2019, the real problem is not that regulation stops people from living in SF, but that regulation stops them from living WHEREVER they want to live.

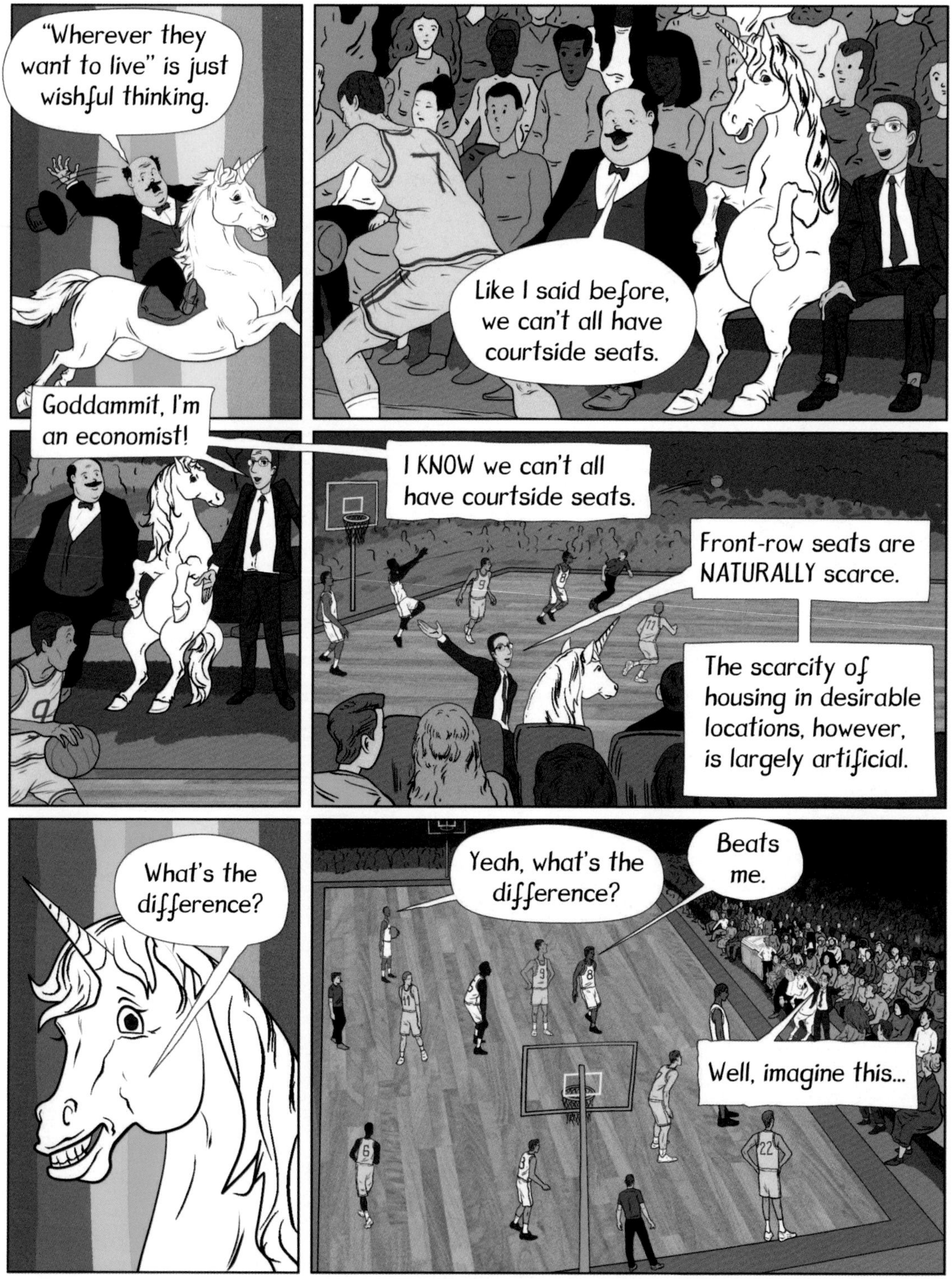
"Wherever they want to live" is just wishful thinking.
Like I said before, we can't all have courtside seats.
Goddammit, I'm an economist!
I KNOW we can't all have courtside seats.
Front-row seats are NATURALLY scarce.
The scarcity of housing in desirable locations, however, is largely artificial.
What's the difference?
Yeah, what's the difference?
Beats me.
Well, imagine this...

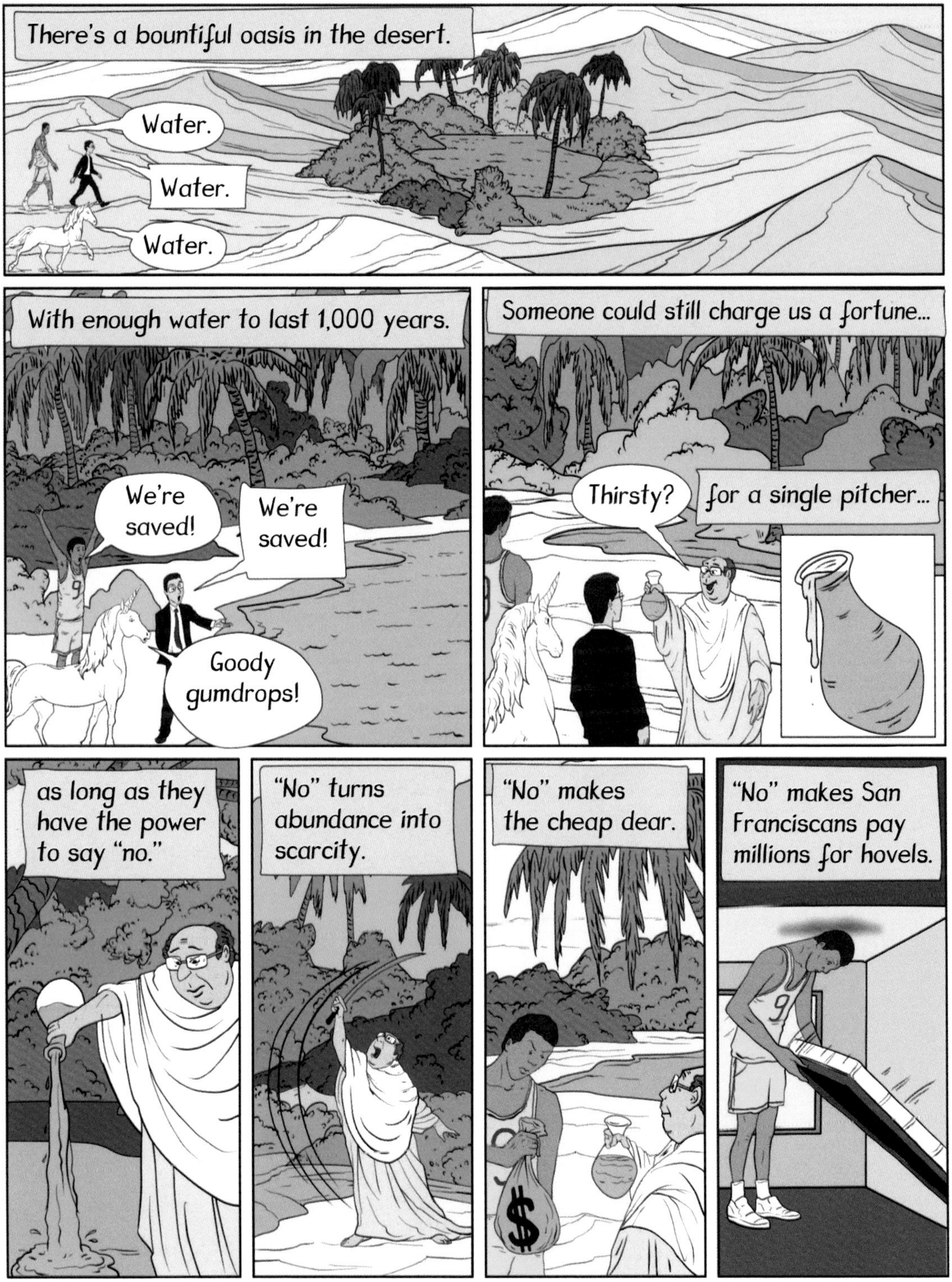
There's a bountiful oasis in the desert.
Water.
Water.
Water.
With enough water to last 1,000 years.
We're saved!
We're saved!
Goody gumdrops!
Someone could still charge us a fortune...
Thirsty?
for a single pitcher...
as long as they have the power to say "no."
"No" turns abundance into scarcity.
"No" makes the cheap dear.
"No" makes San Franciscans pay millions for hovels.

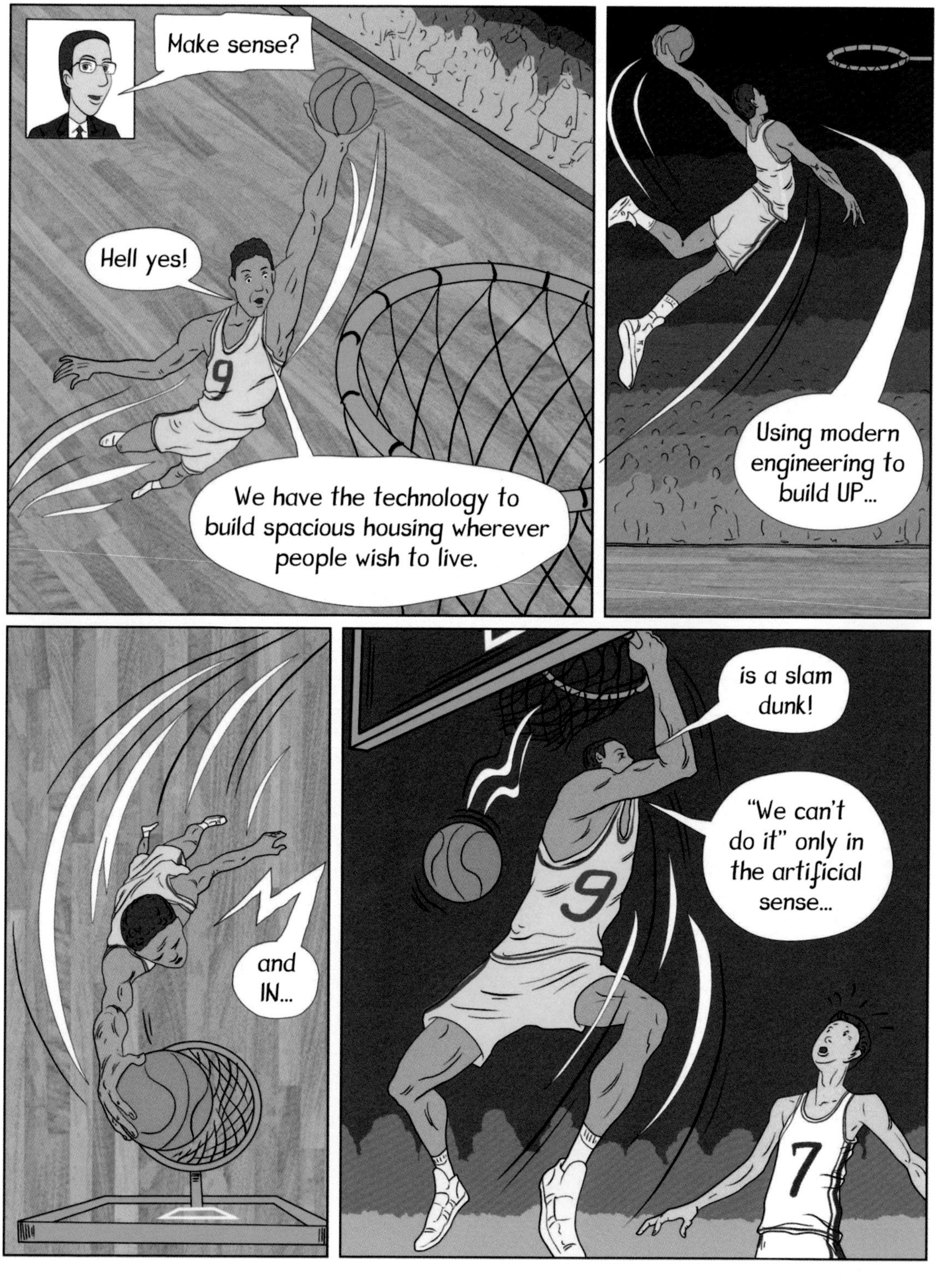
Make sense?
Hell yes!
We have the technology to build spacious housing wherever people wish to live.
Using modern engineering to build UP...
and IN...
is a slam dunk!
"We can't do it" only in the artificial sense...

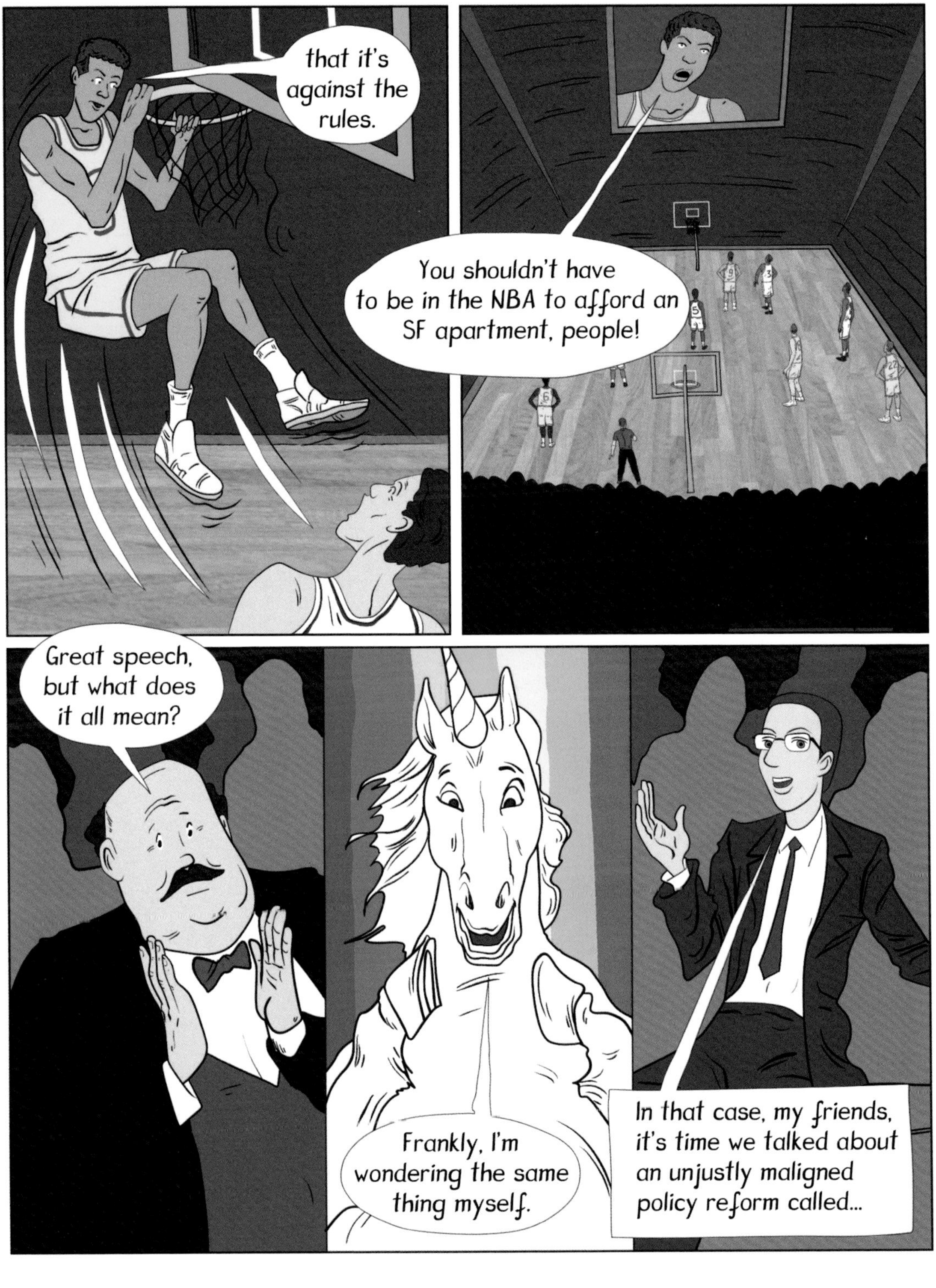
that it's against the rules.
You shouldn't have to be in the NBA to afford an SF apartment, people!
Great speech, but what does it all mean?
Frankly, I'm wondering the same thing myself.
In that case, my friends, it's time we talked about an unjustly maligned policy reform called...

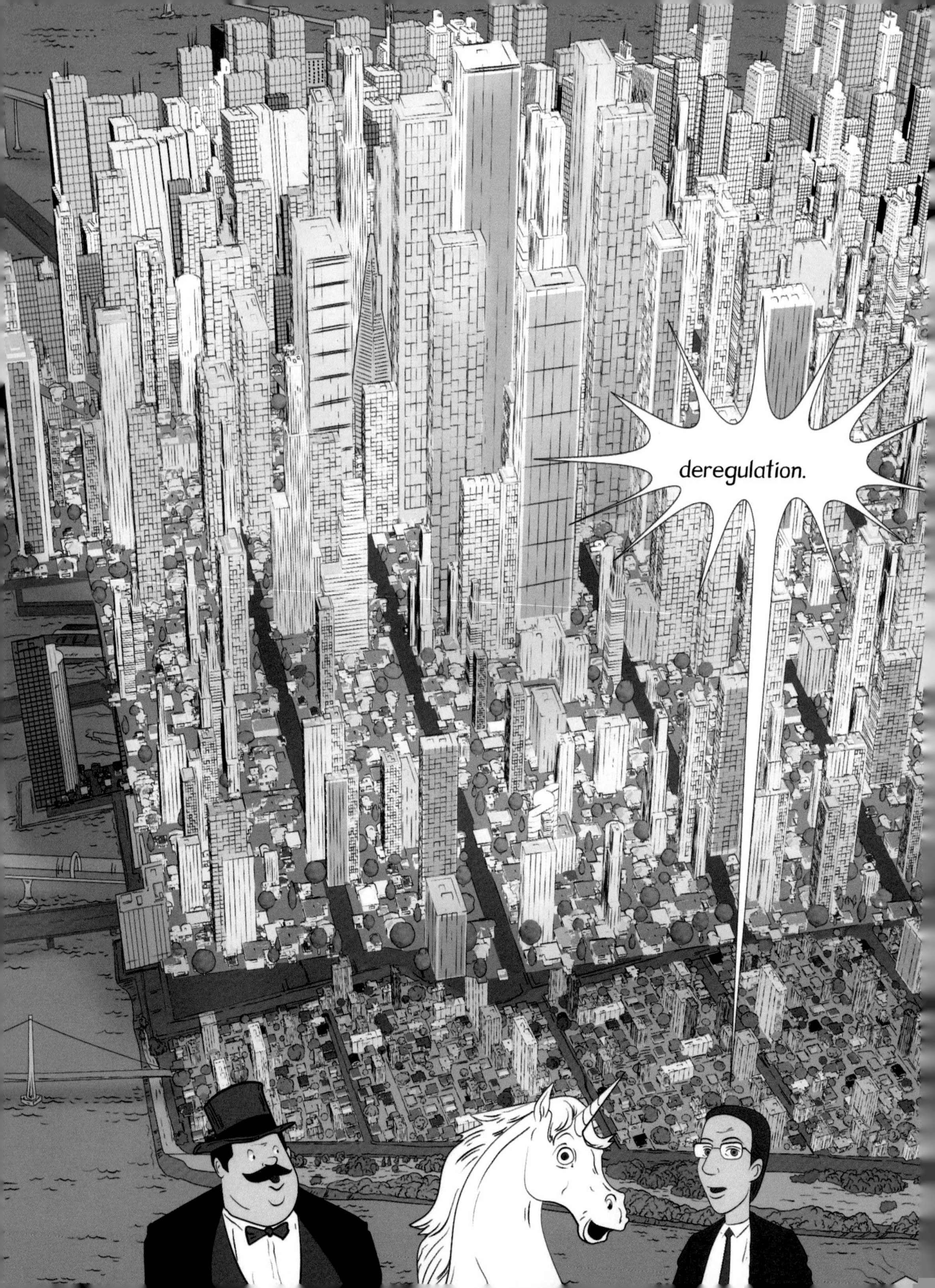
deregulation.

CHAPTER 3: THE PANACEA POLICY

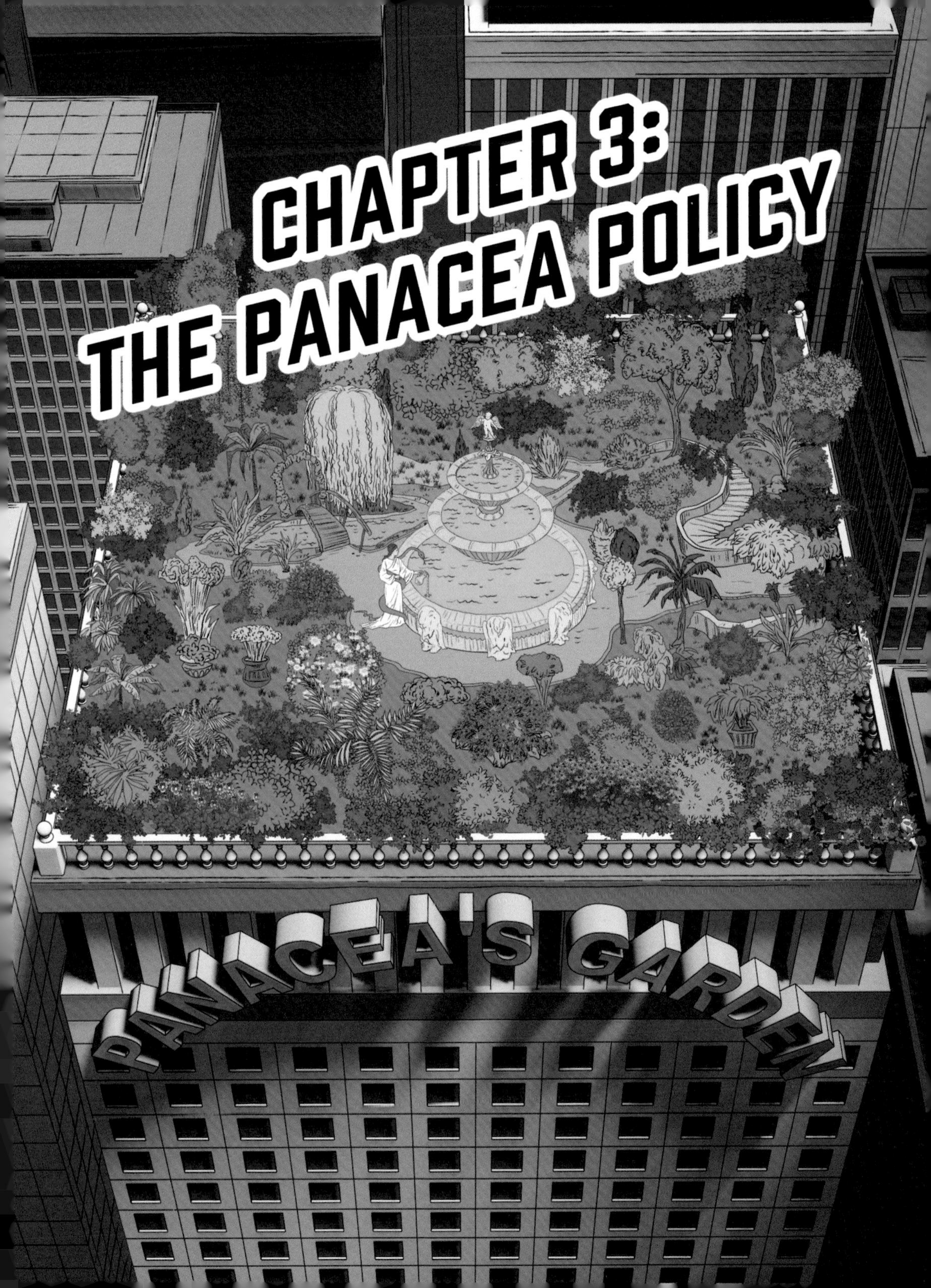
PANACEA'S GARDEN

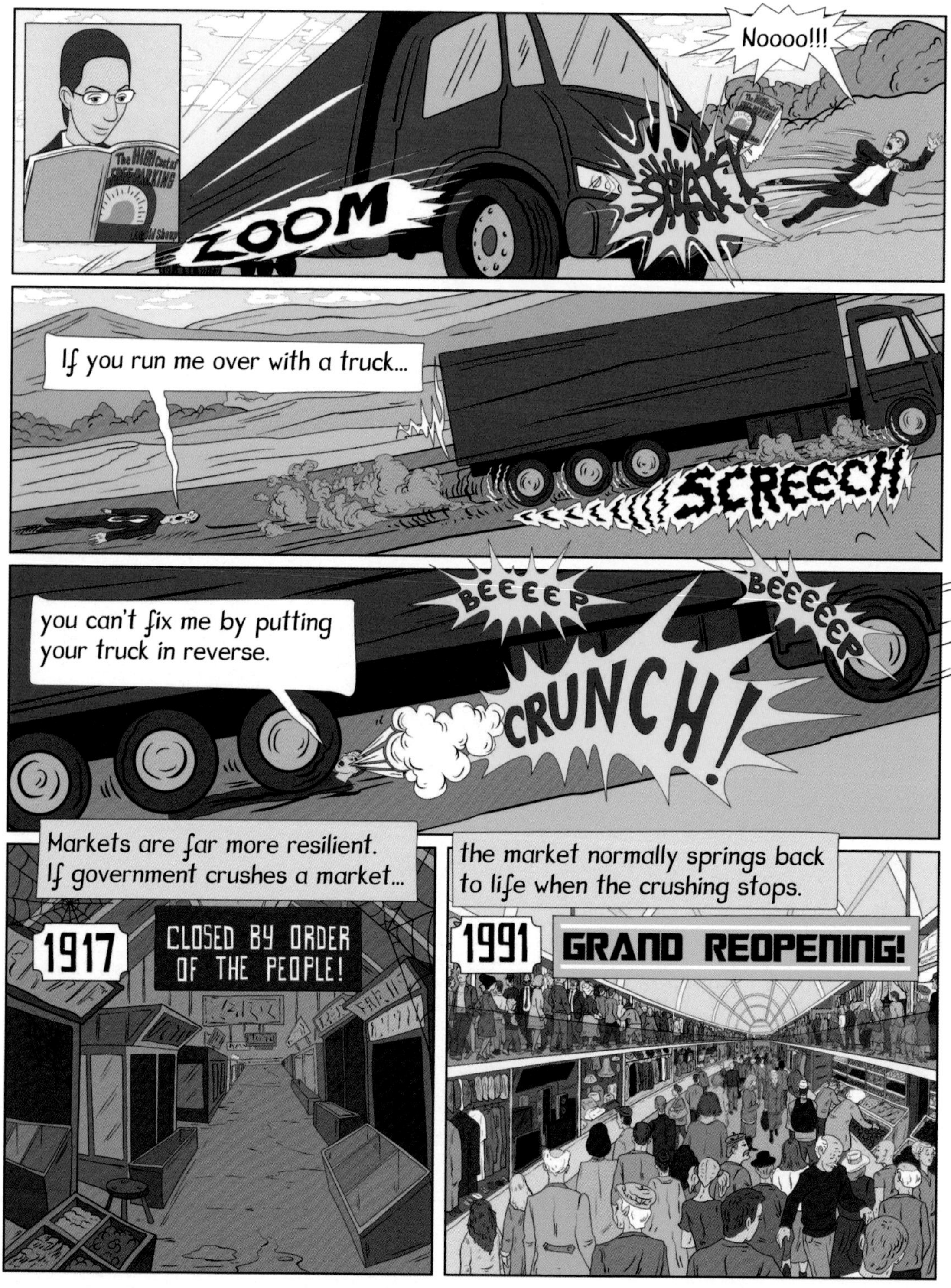
Noooo!!!
ZOOM
SPLAT
If you run me over with a truck...
SCREECH
BEEEEEP
BEEEEEEP
you can't fix me by putting your truck in reverse.
CRUNCH!
Markets are far more resilient. If government crushes a market...
1917
CLOSED BY ORDER OF THE PEOPLE!
the market normally springs back to life when the crushing stops.
1991
GRAND REOPENING!

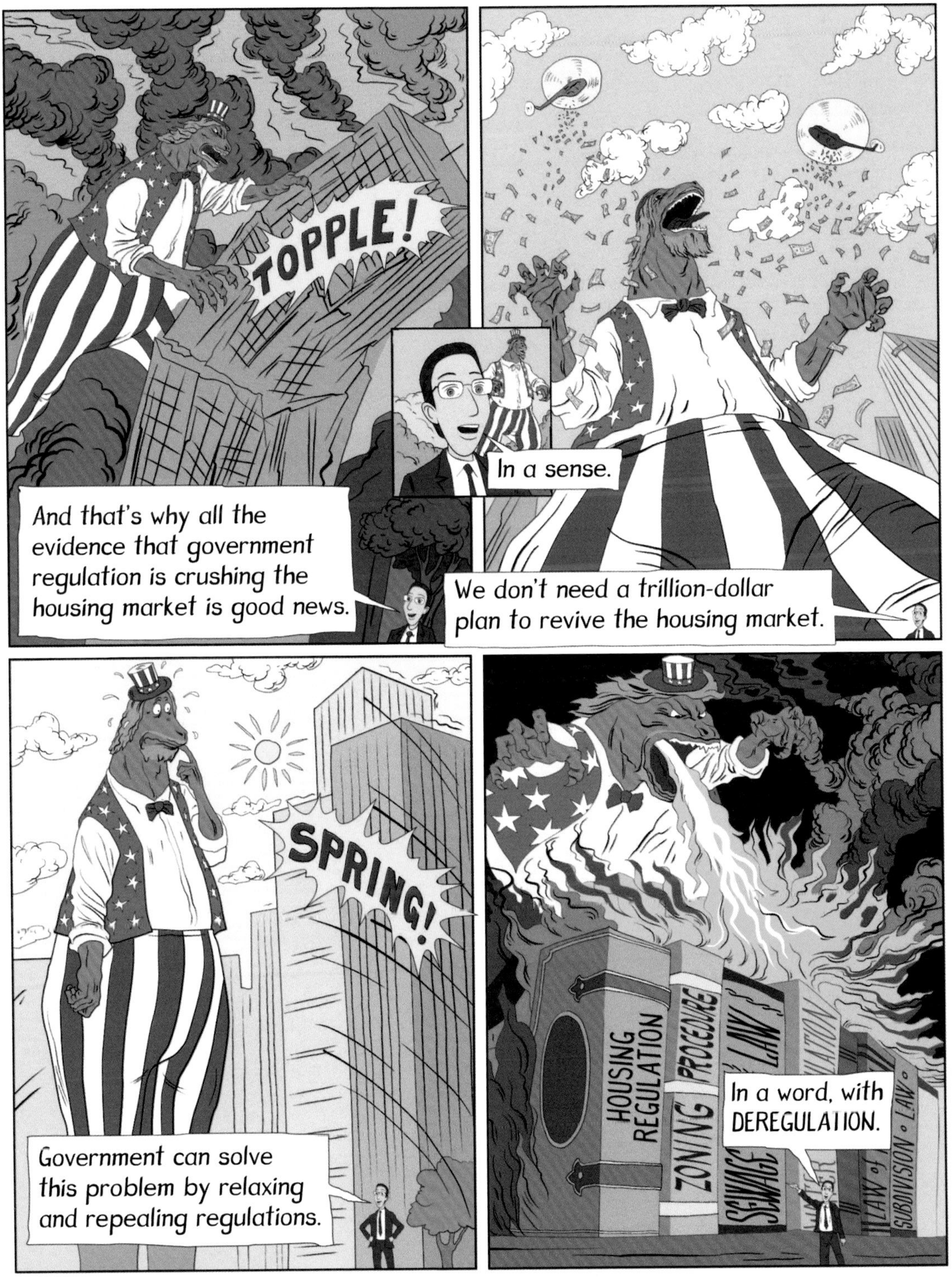
TOPPLE!
And that's why all the evidence that government regulation is crushing the housing market is good news.
In a sense.
We don't need a trillion-dollar plan to revive the housing market.
SPRING!
Government can solve this problem by relaxing and repealing regulations.
HOUSING REGULATION
ZONING
PROCEDURE
LAW
SUBDIVISION LAW
In a word, with DEREGULATION.

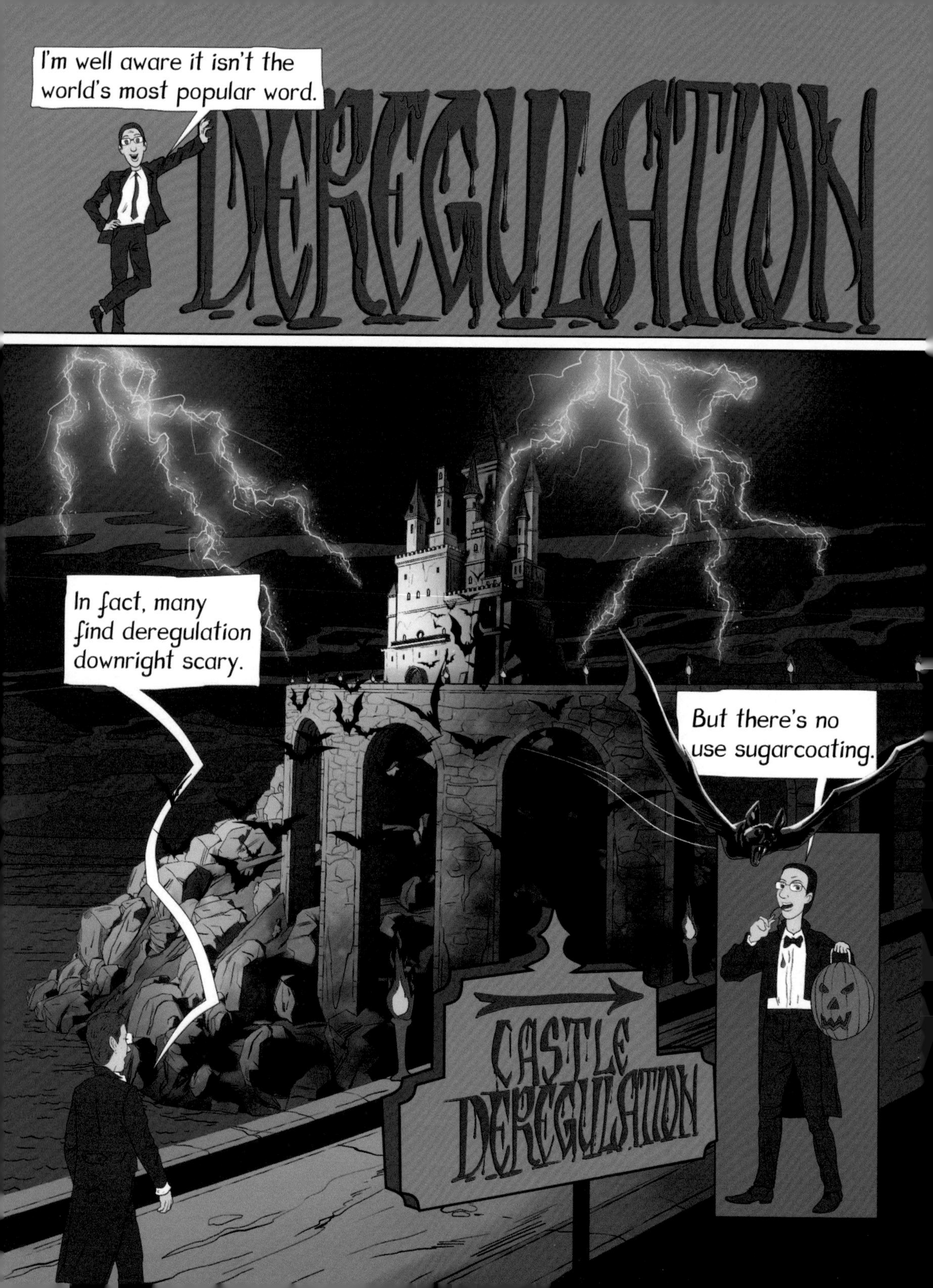
I'm well aware it isn't the world's most popular word.
DEREGULATION
In fact, many find deregulation downright scary.
But there's no use sugarcoating.
CASTLE DEREGULATION

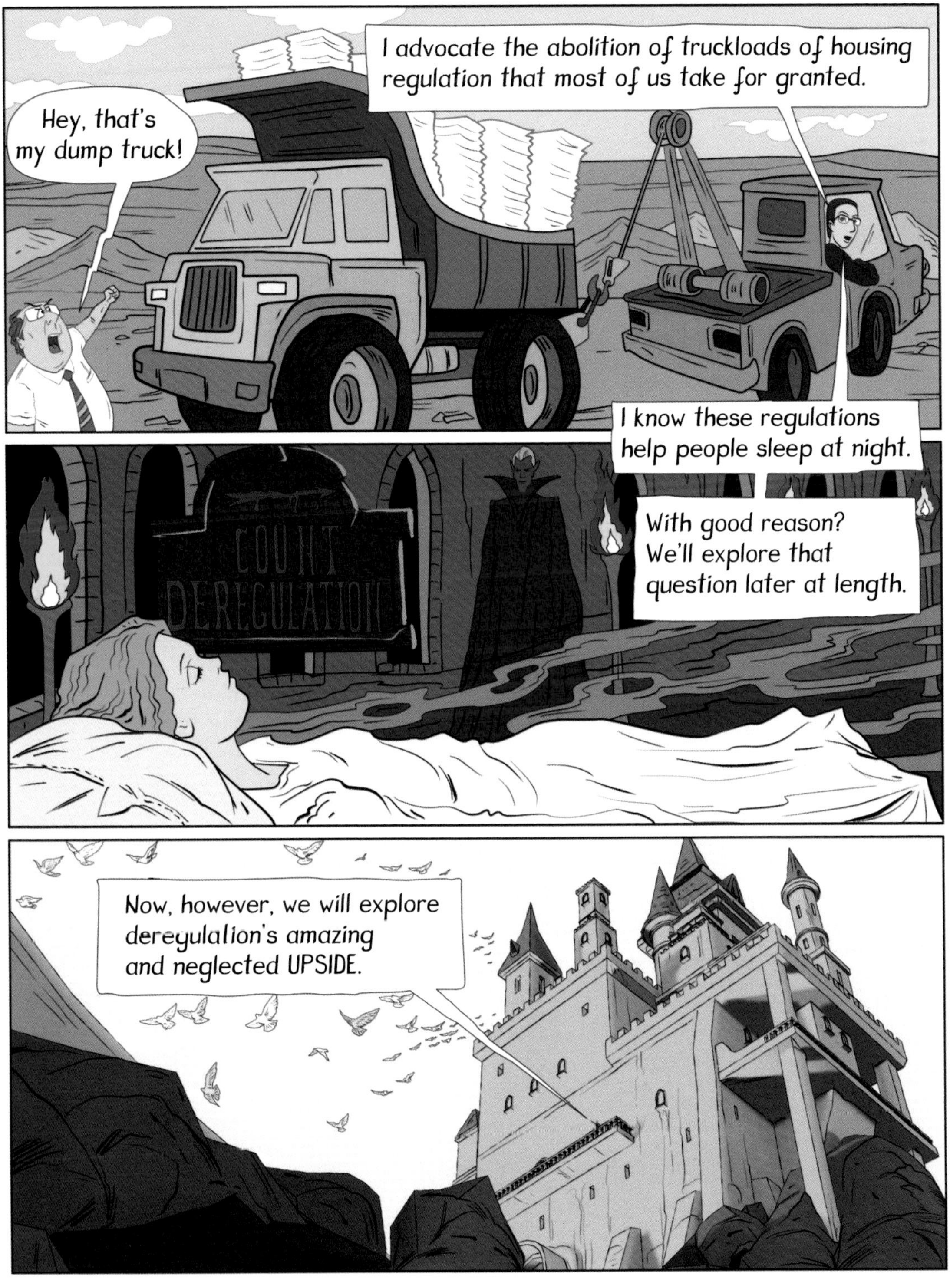
I advocate the abolition of truckloads of housing regulation that most of us take for granted.
Hey, that's my dump truck!
I know these regulations help people sleep at night.
COUNT DEREGULATION
With good reason? We'll explore that question later at length.
Now, however, we will explore deregulation's amazing and neglected UPSIDE.

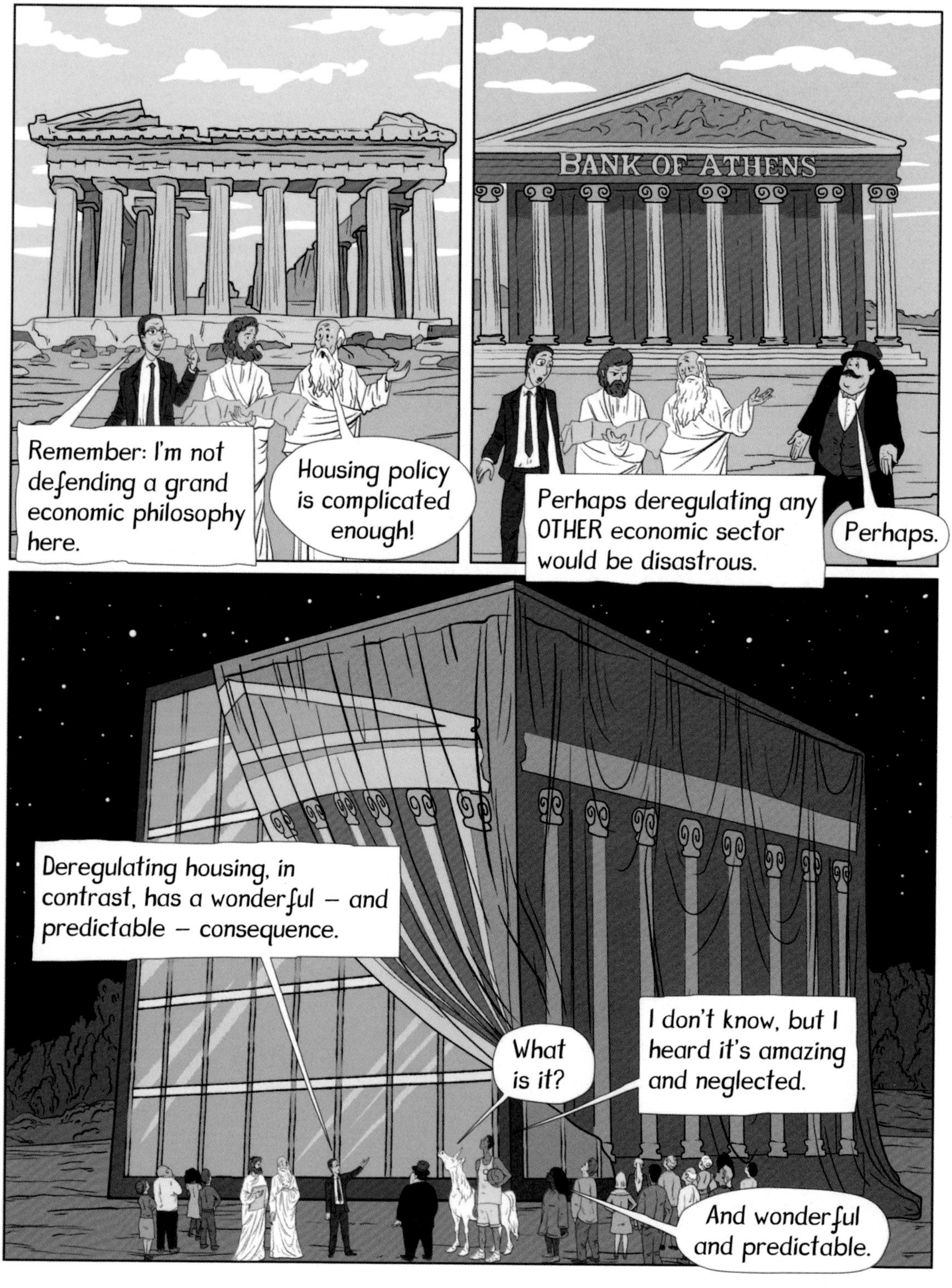

Remember: I'm not defending a grand economic philosophy here.
Housing policy is complicated enough!
BANK OF ATHENS
Perhaps deregulating any OTHER economic sector would be disastrous.
Perhaps.
Deregulating housing, in contrast, has a wonderful – and predictable – consequence.
What is it?
I don't know, but I heard it's amazing and neglected.
And wonderful and predictable.

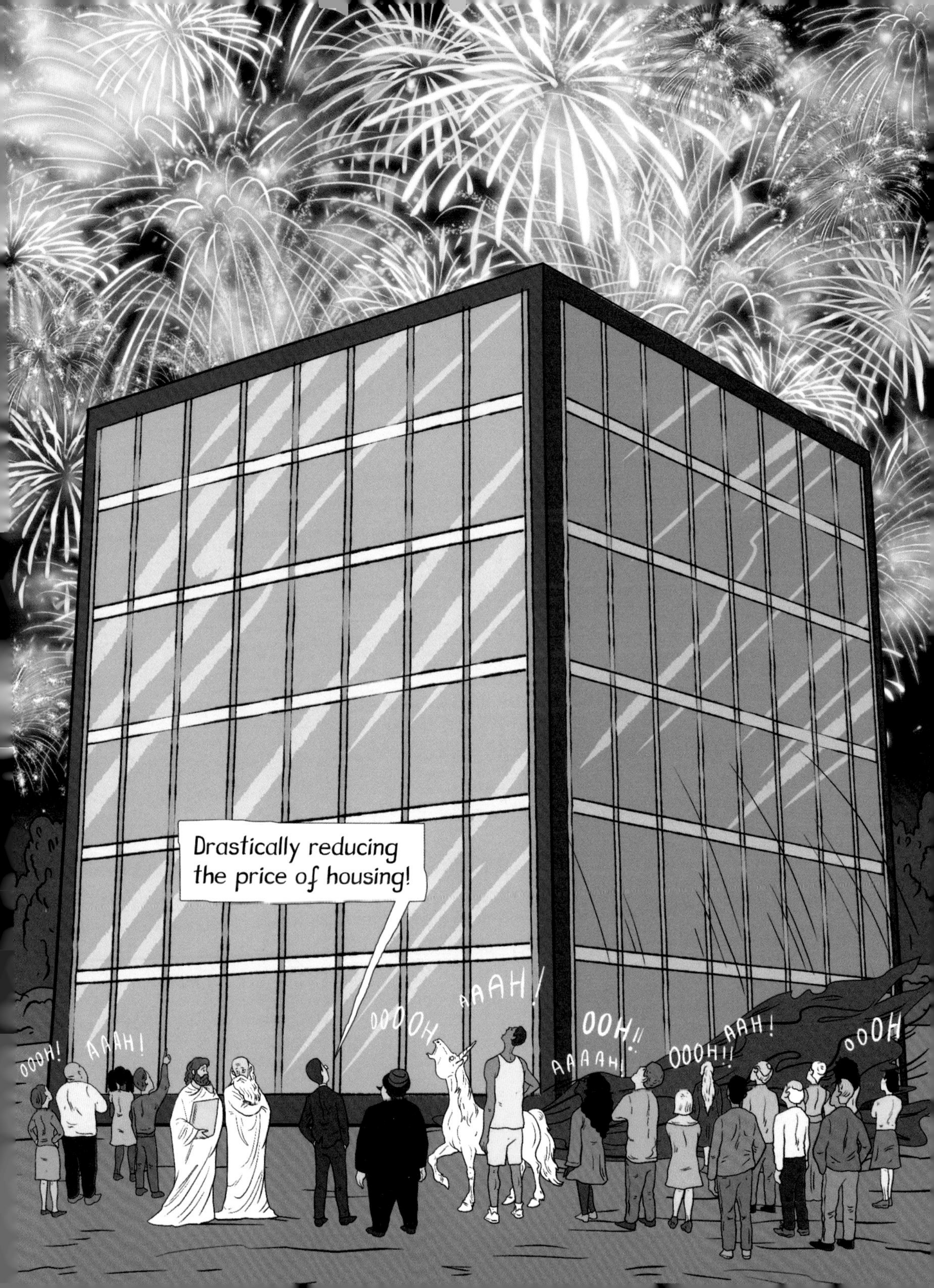
Drastically reducing the price of housing!
OOOH!
AAAH!
OOOOH
AAAH!
OOH!!
AAAAH!
OOOH!!
AAH!
OOOH

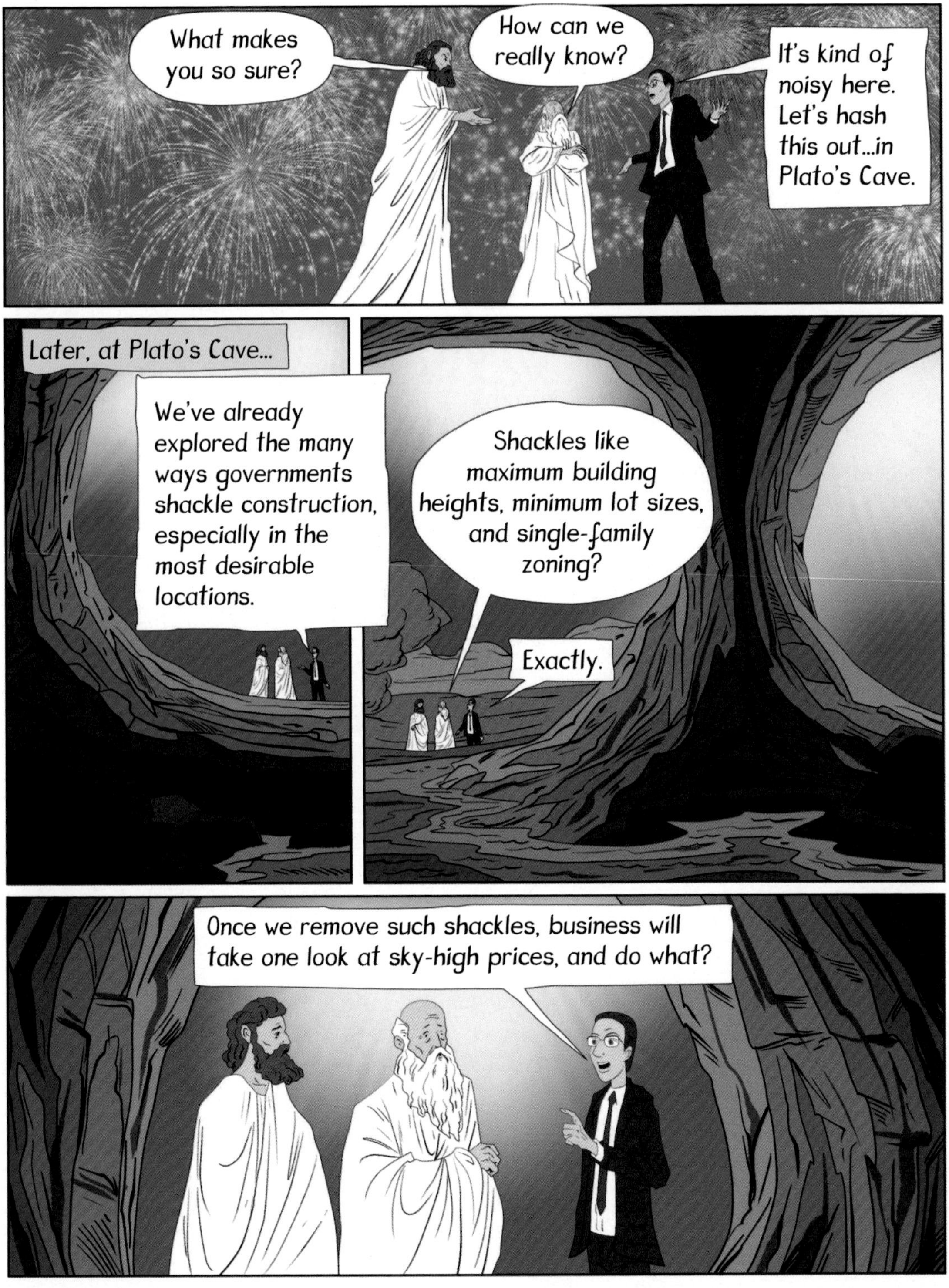
What makes you so sure?
How can we really know?
It's kind of noisy here. Let's hash this out...in Plato's Cave.
Later, at Plato's Cave...
We've already explored the many ways governments shackle construction, especially in the most desirable locations.
Shackles like maximum building heights, minimum lot sizes, and single-family zoning?
Exactly.
Once we remove such shackles, business will take one look at sky-high prices, and do what?

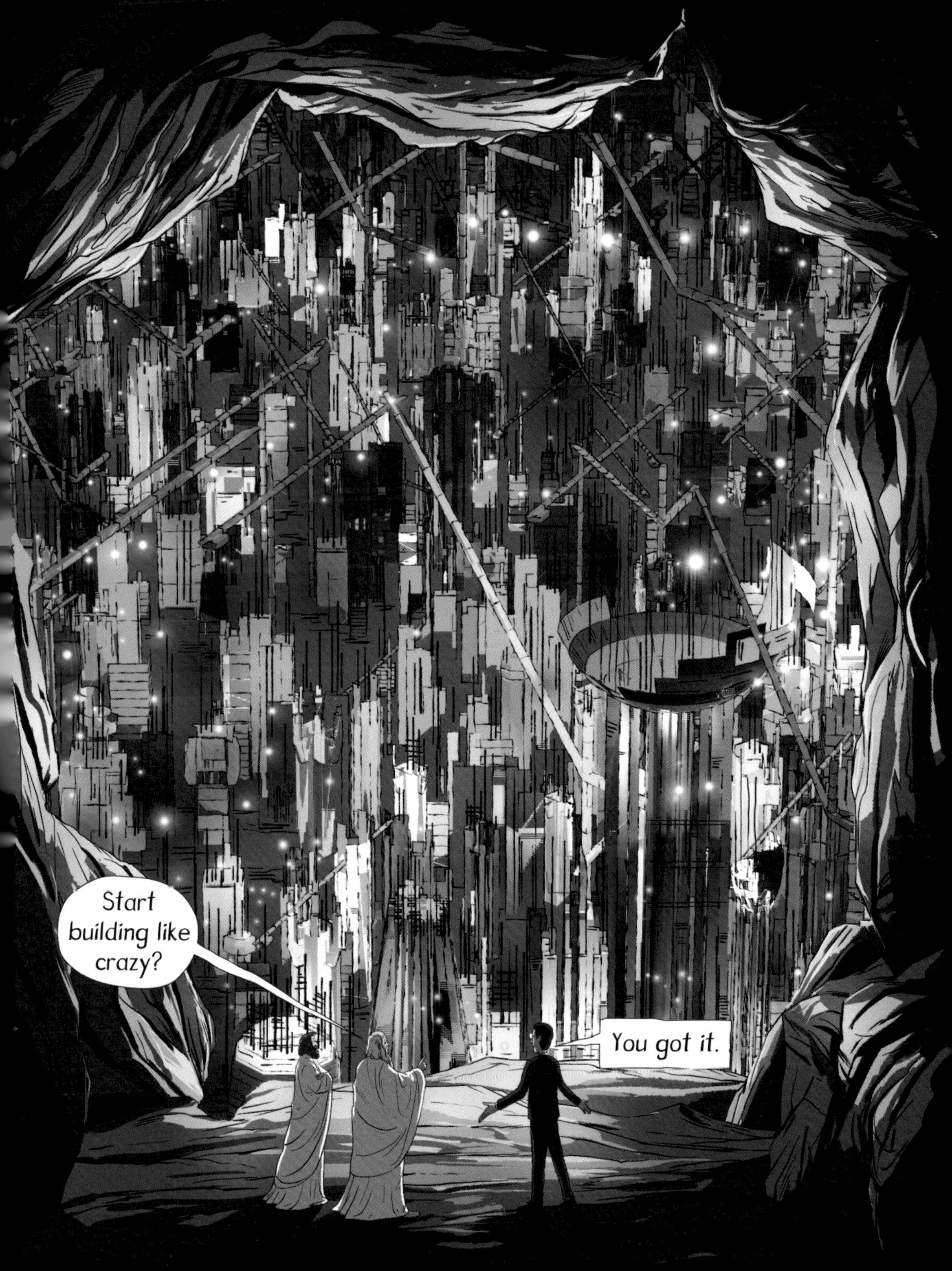
Start building like crazy?
You got it.

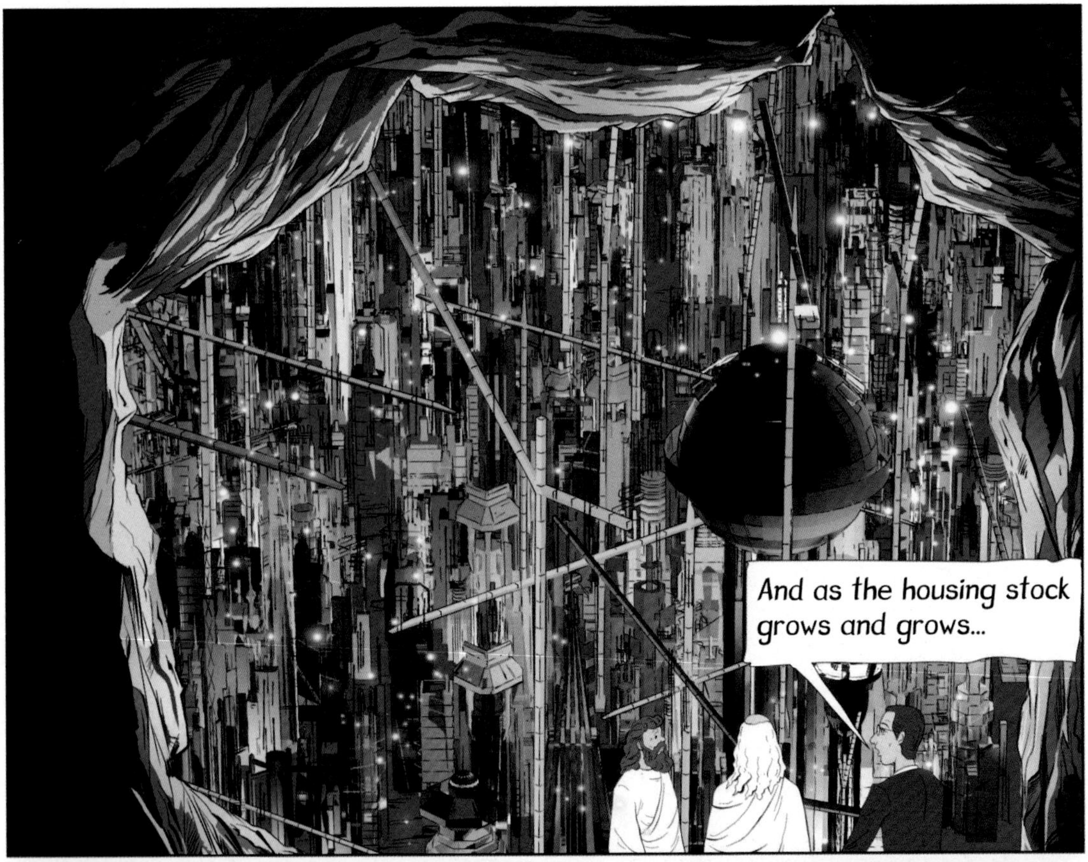
And as the housing stock grows and grows...

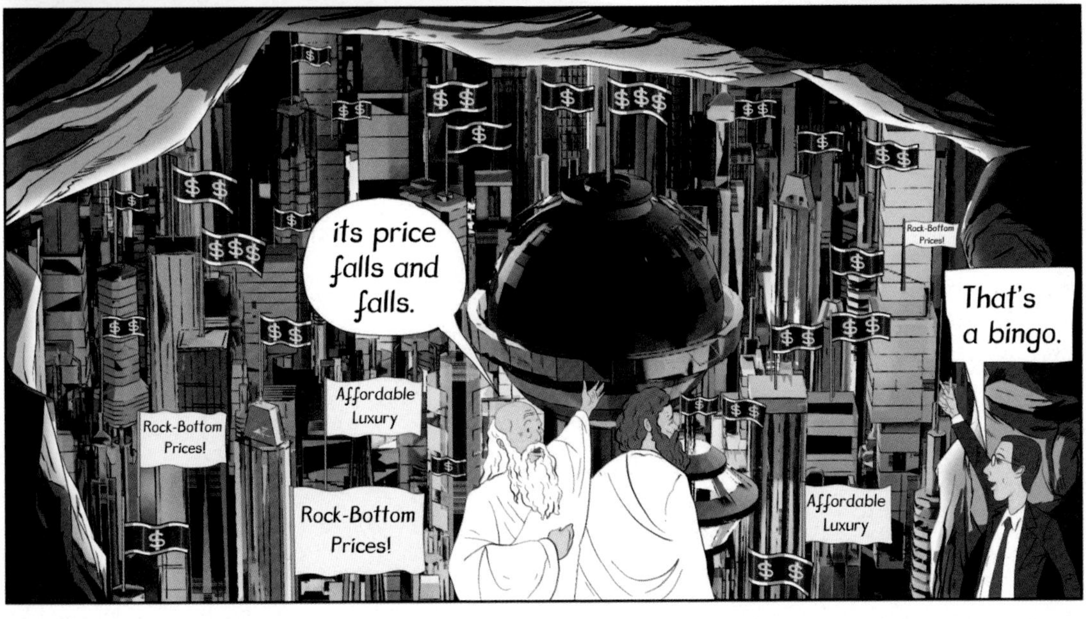
its price falls and falls.
That's a bingo.
Rock-Bottom Prices!
Affordable Luxury
Rock-Bottom Prices!
Affordable Luxury
Rock-Bottom Prices!

An old adage says, "If you're in a hole, stop digging."
But why stop there?
I say:
If you're in a hole, start building!

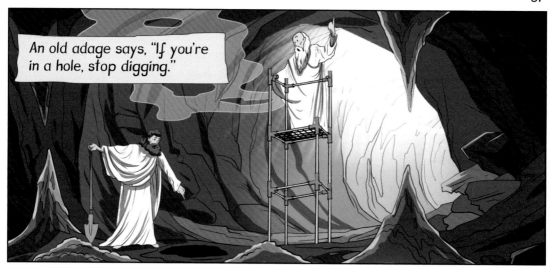

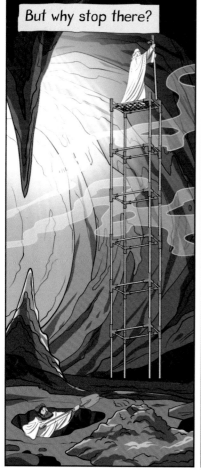

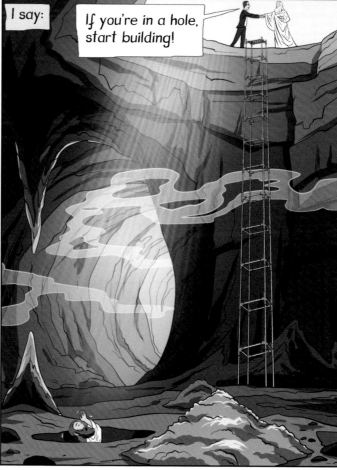

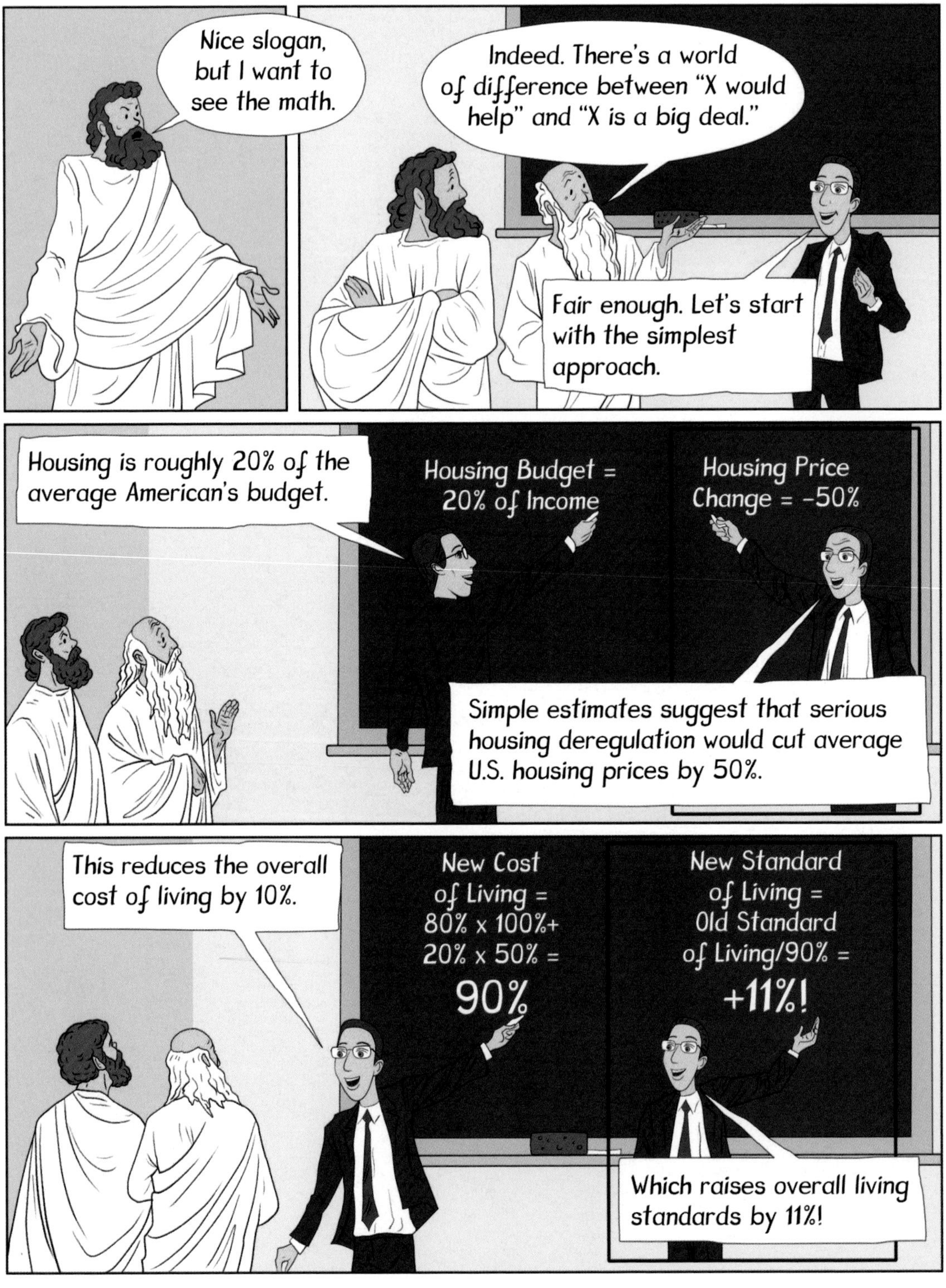
Nice slogan, but I want to see the math.
Indeed. There's a world of difference between "X would help" and "X is a big deal."
Fair enough. Let's start with the simplest approach.
Housing is roughly 20% of the average American's budget.
Housing Budget = 20% of Income
Housing Price Change = −50%
Simple estimates suggest that serious housing deregulation would cut average U.S. housing prices by 50%.
This reduces the overall cost of living by 10%.
New Cost of Living = 80% x 100%+ 20% x 50% = 90%
New Standard of Living = Old Standard of Living/90% = +11%!
Which raises overall living standards by 11%!

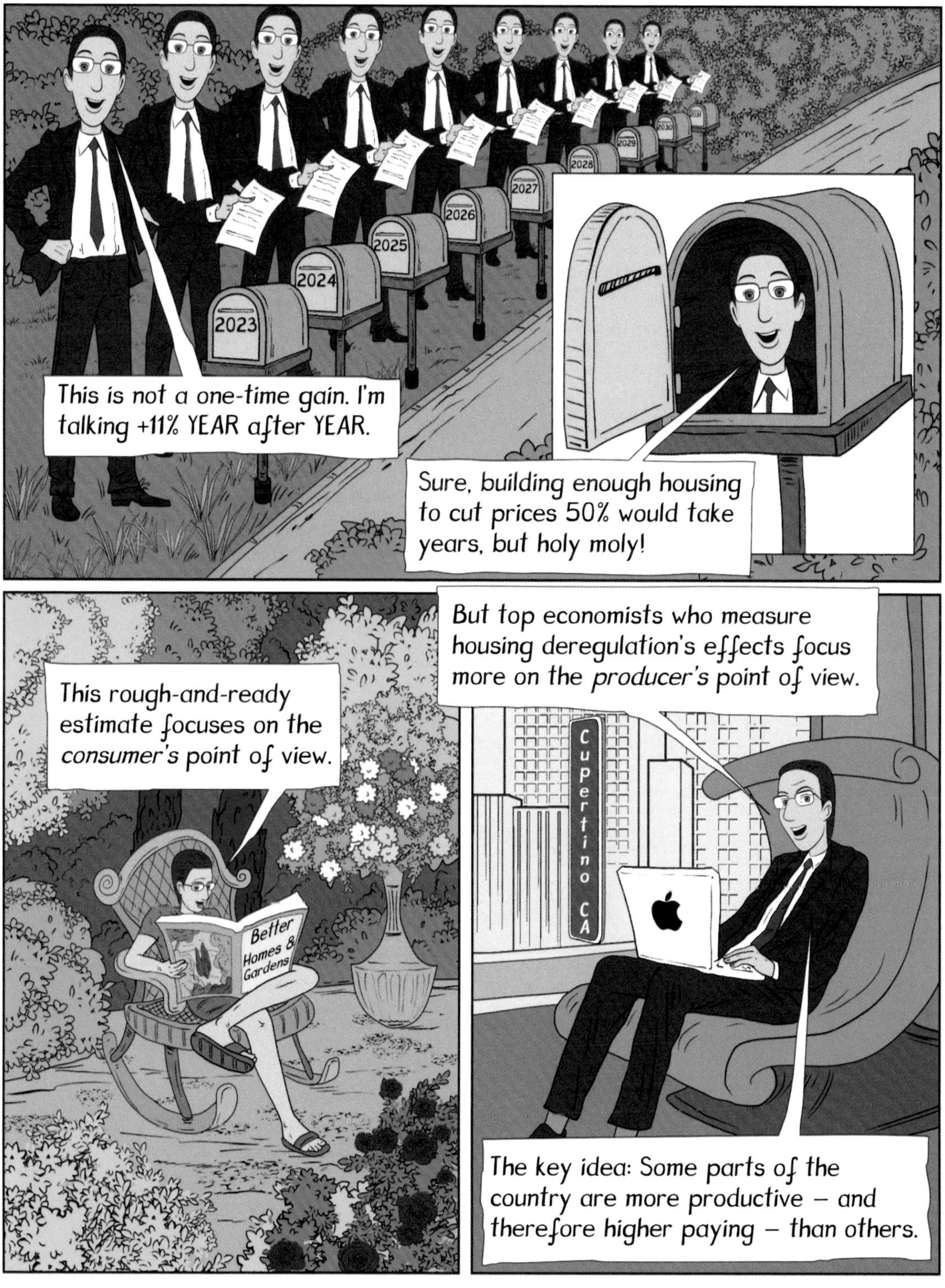
2023
2024
2025
2026
2027
2028
2029
2030
This is not a one-time gain. I'm talking +11% YEAR after YEAR.
Sure, building enough housing to cut prices 50% would take years, but holy moly!
This rough-and-ready estimate focuses on the *consumer's* point of view.
Better Homes & Gardens
But top economists who measure housing deregulation's effects focus more on the *producer's* point of view.
Cupertino CA
The key idea: Some parts of the country are more productive – and therefore higher paying – than others.

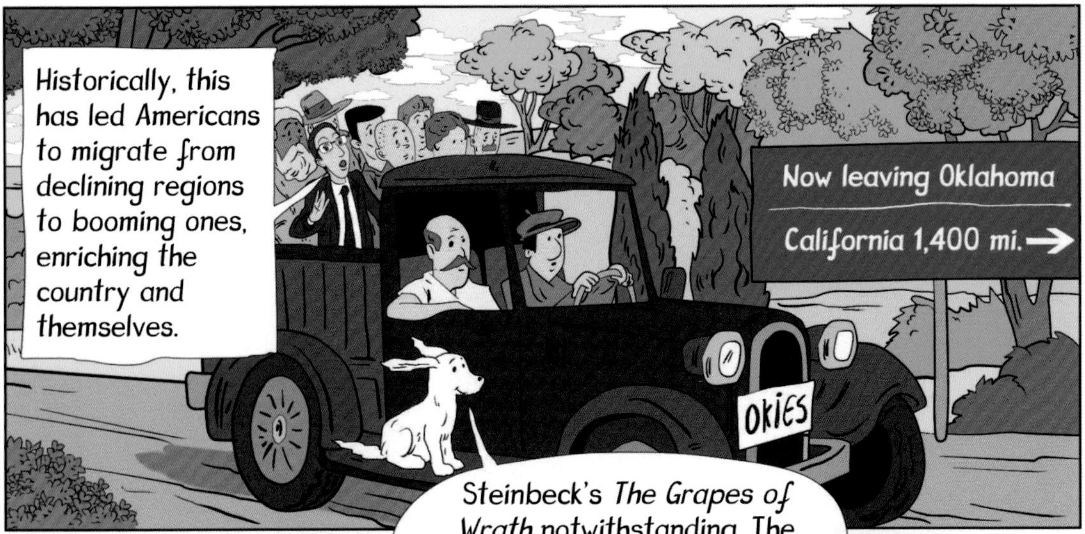
Historically, this has led Americans to migrate from declining regions to booming ones, enriching the country and themselves.
Now leaving Oklahoma
California 1,400 mi.
OKIES
Steinbeck's *The Grapes of Wrath* notwithstanding. The man wrote fiction, people!

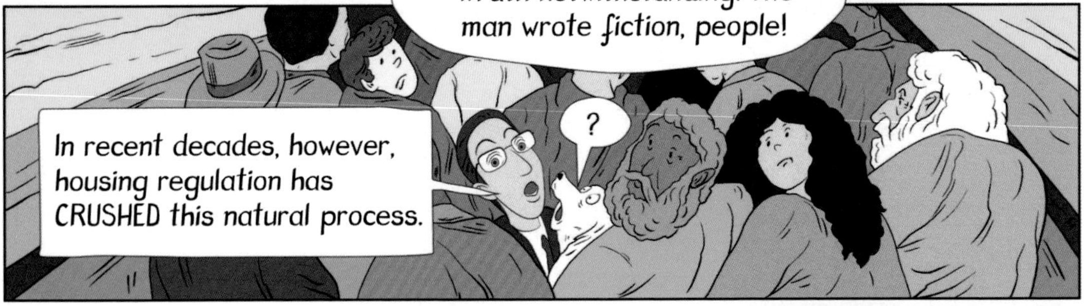
In recent decades, however, housing regulation has CRUSHED this natural process.
?

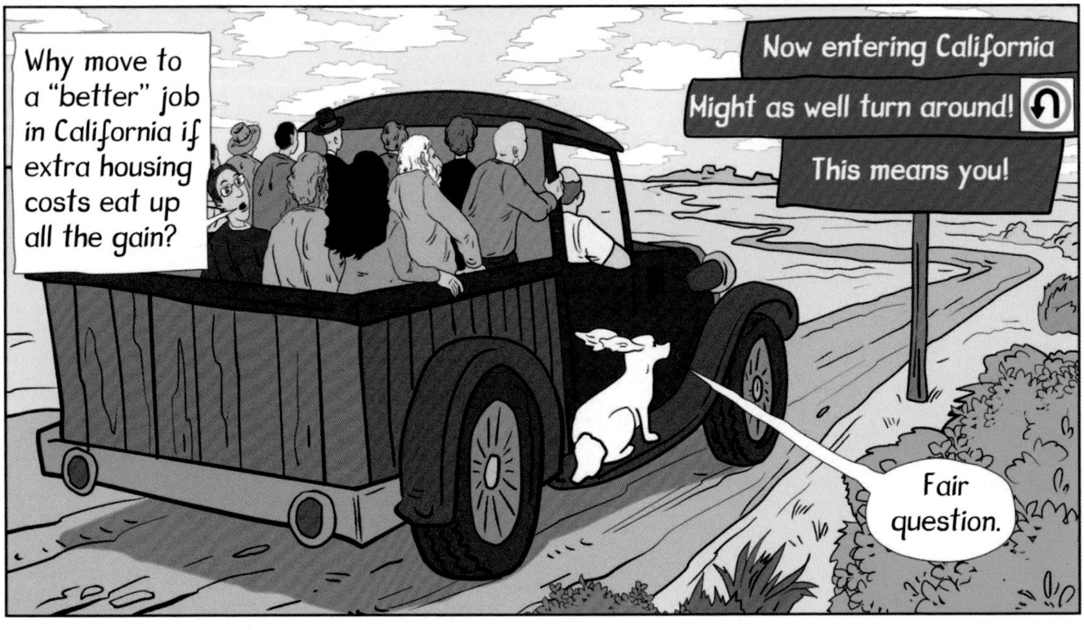
Why move to a "better" job in California if extra housing costs eat up all the gain?
Now entering California
Might as well turn around!
This means you!
Fair question.

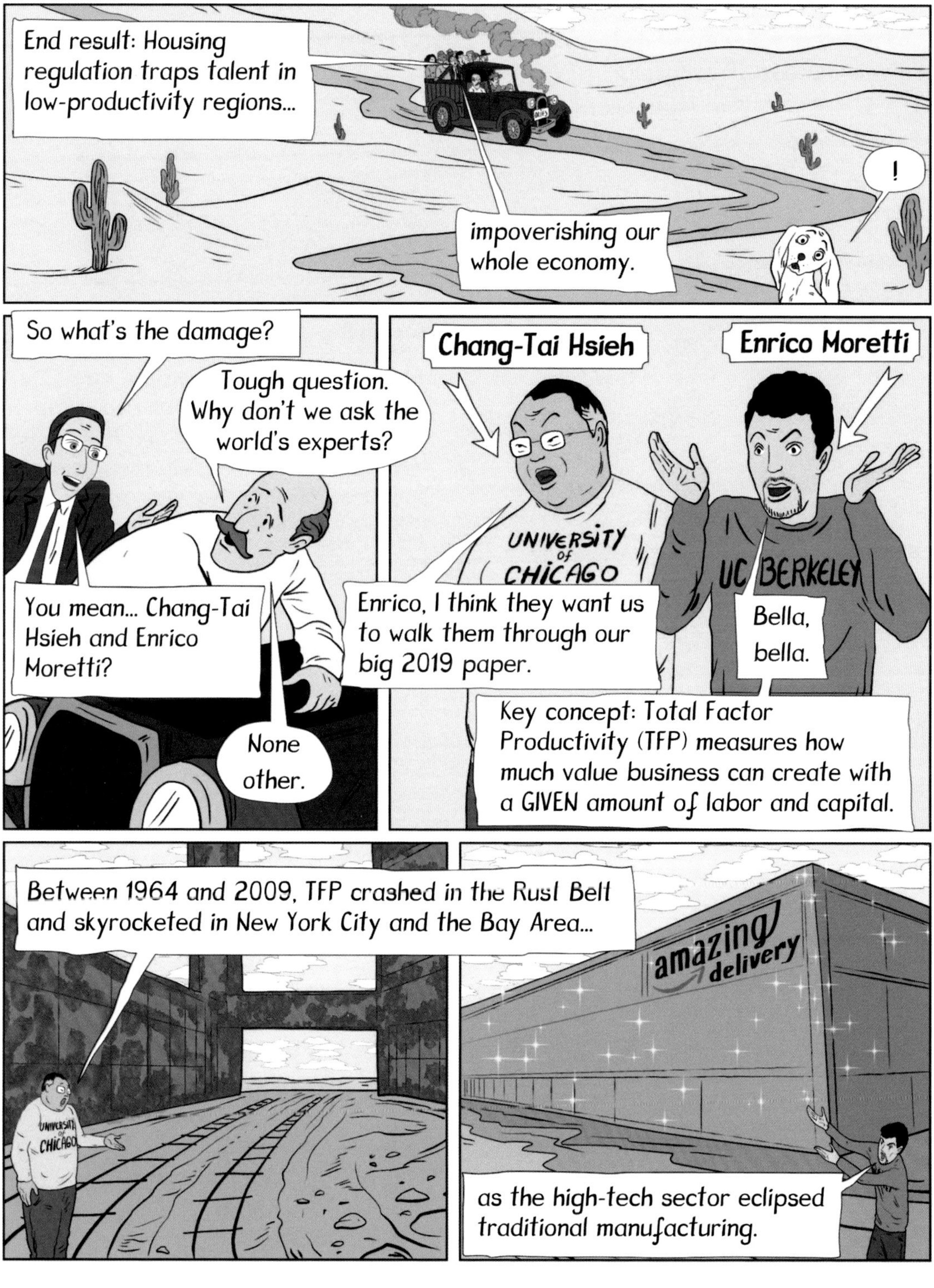
End result: Housing regulation traps talent in low-productivity regions...
impoverishing our whole economy.
!
So what's the damage?
Tough question. Why don't we ask the world's experts?
You mean... Chang-Tai Hsieh and Enrico Moretti?
None other.
Chang-Tai Hsieh
Enrico Moretti
UNIVERSITY of CHICAGO
UC BERKELEY
Enrico, I think they want us to walk them through our big 2019 paper.
Bella, bella.
Key concept: Total Factor Productivity (TFP) measures how much value business can create with a GIVEN amount of labor and capital.
Between 1964 and 2009, TFP crashed in the Rust Belt and skyrocketed in New York City and the Bay Area...
UNIVERSITY of CHICAGO
amazing delivery
as the high-tech sector eclipsed traditional manufacturing.

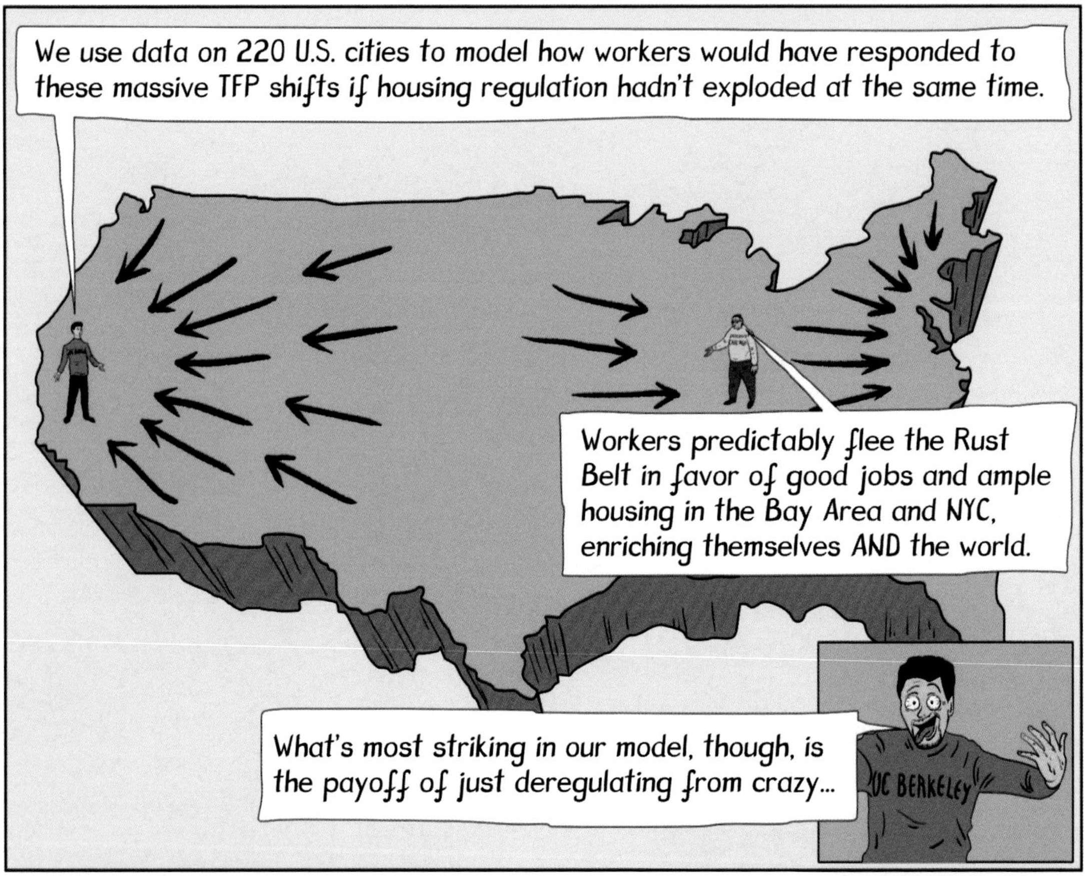
We use data on 220 U.S. cities to model how workers would have responded to these massive TFP shifts if housing regulation hadn't exploded at the same time.
Workers predictably flee the Rust Belt in favor of good jobs and ample housing in the Bay Area and NYC, enriching themselves AND the world.
What's most striking in our model, though, is the payoff of just deregulating from crazy...
UC BERKELEY

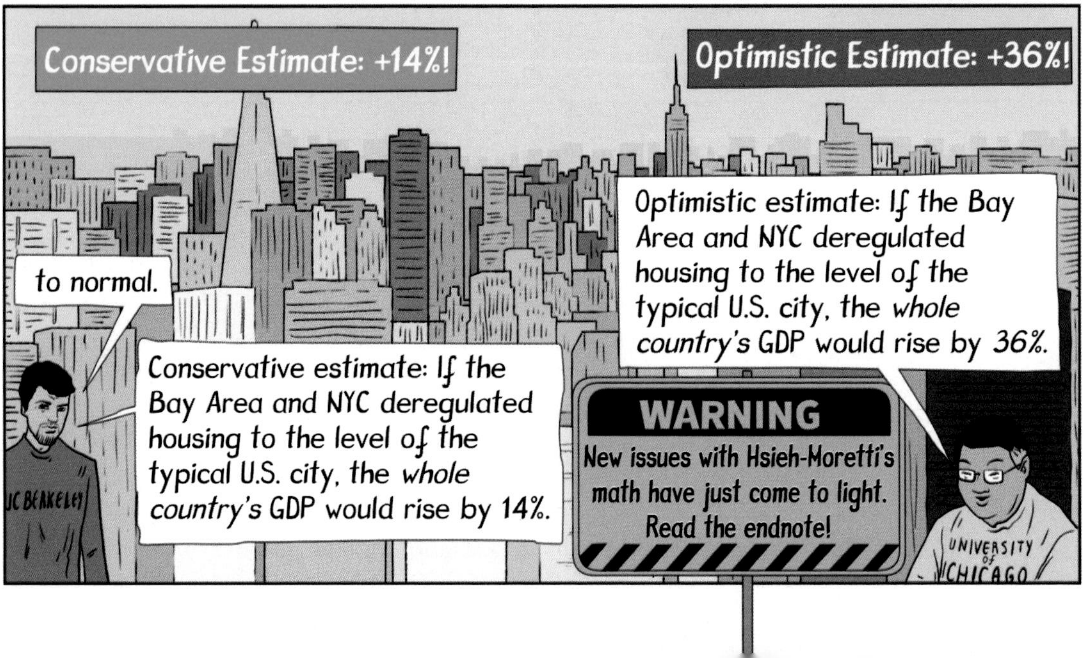
Conservative Estimate: +14%!
Optimistic Estimate: +36%!
to normal.
Conservative estimate: If the Bay Area and NYC deregulated housing to the level of the typical U.S. city, the *whole country's* GDP would rise by 14%.
Optimistic estimate: If the Bay Area and NYC deregulated housing to the level of the typical U.S. city, the *whole country's* GDP would rise by *36%*.
WARNING
New issues with Hsieh-Moretti's math have just come to light. Read the endnote!
UC BERKELEY
UNIVERSITY OF CHICAGO

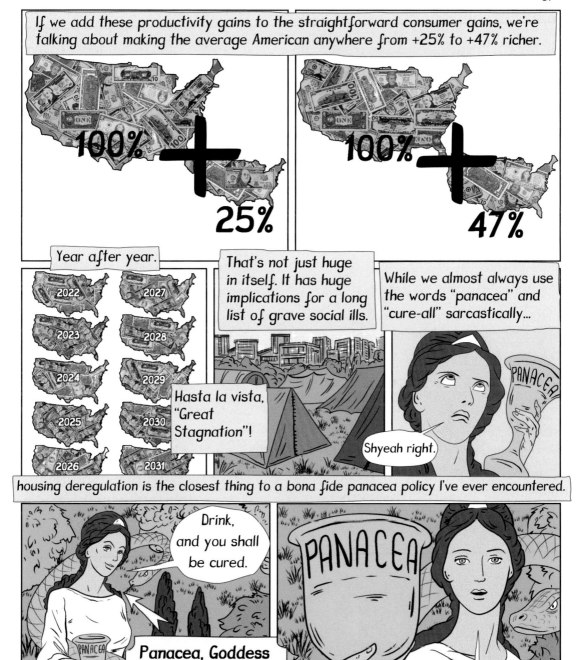

If we add these productivity gains to the straightforward consumer gains, we're talking about making the average American anywhere from +25% to +47% richer.

100% + 25%

100% + 47%

Year after year.

2022 2027
2023 2028
2024 2029
2025 2030
2026 2031

That's not just huge in itself. It has huge implications for a long list of grave social ills.

Hasta la vista, "Great Stagnation"!

While we almost always use the words "panacea" and "cure-all" sarcastically...

Shyeah right.

housing deregulation is the closest thing to a bona fide panacea policy I've ever encountered.

Drink, and you shall be cured.

Panacea, Goddess of Universal Remedy

PANACEA

Of all that ails you.

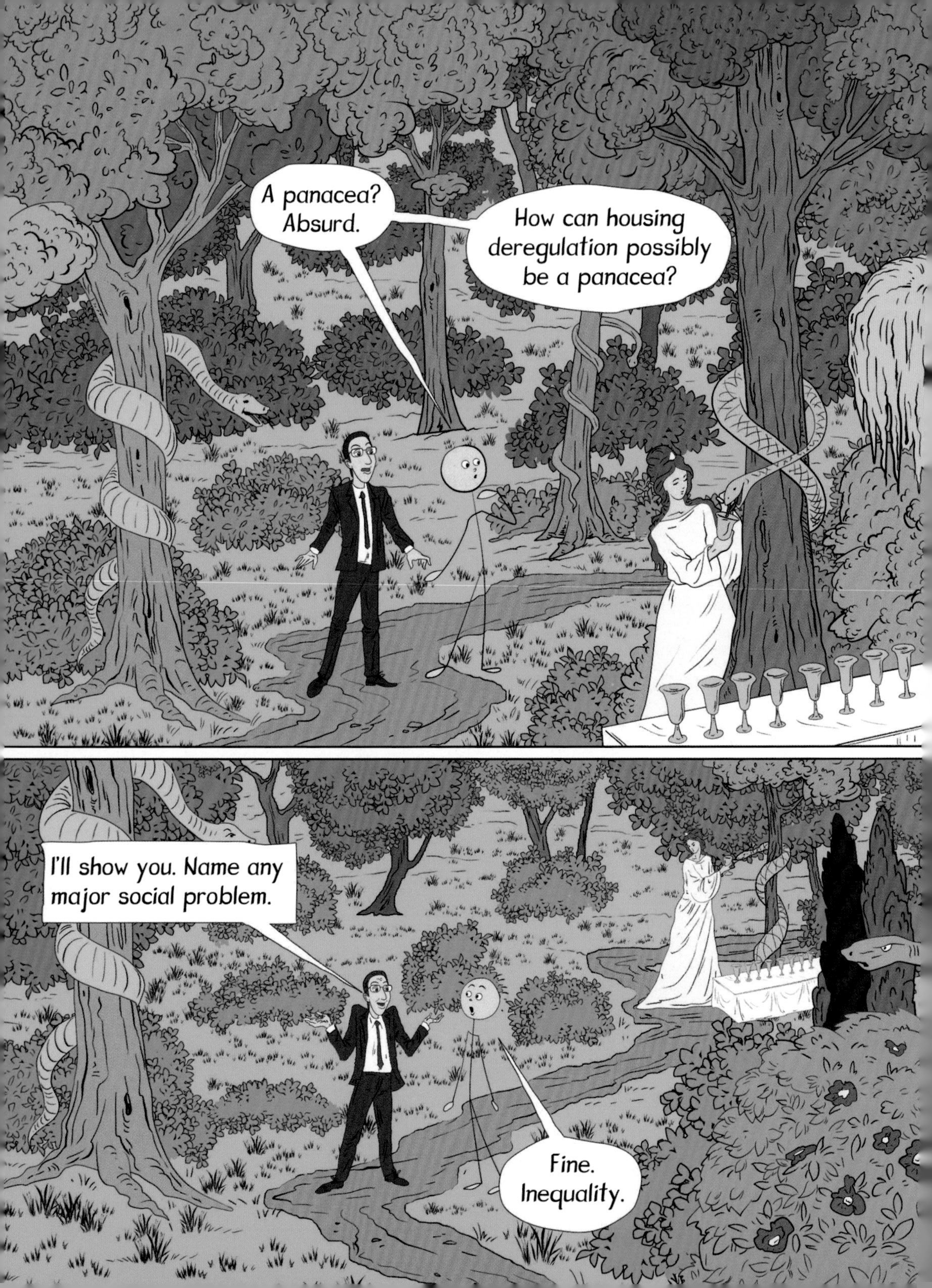

A panacea? Absurd.
How can housing deregulation possibly be a panacea?
I'll show you. Name any major social problem.
Fine. Inequality.

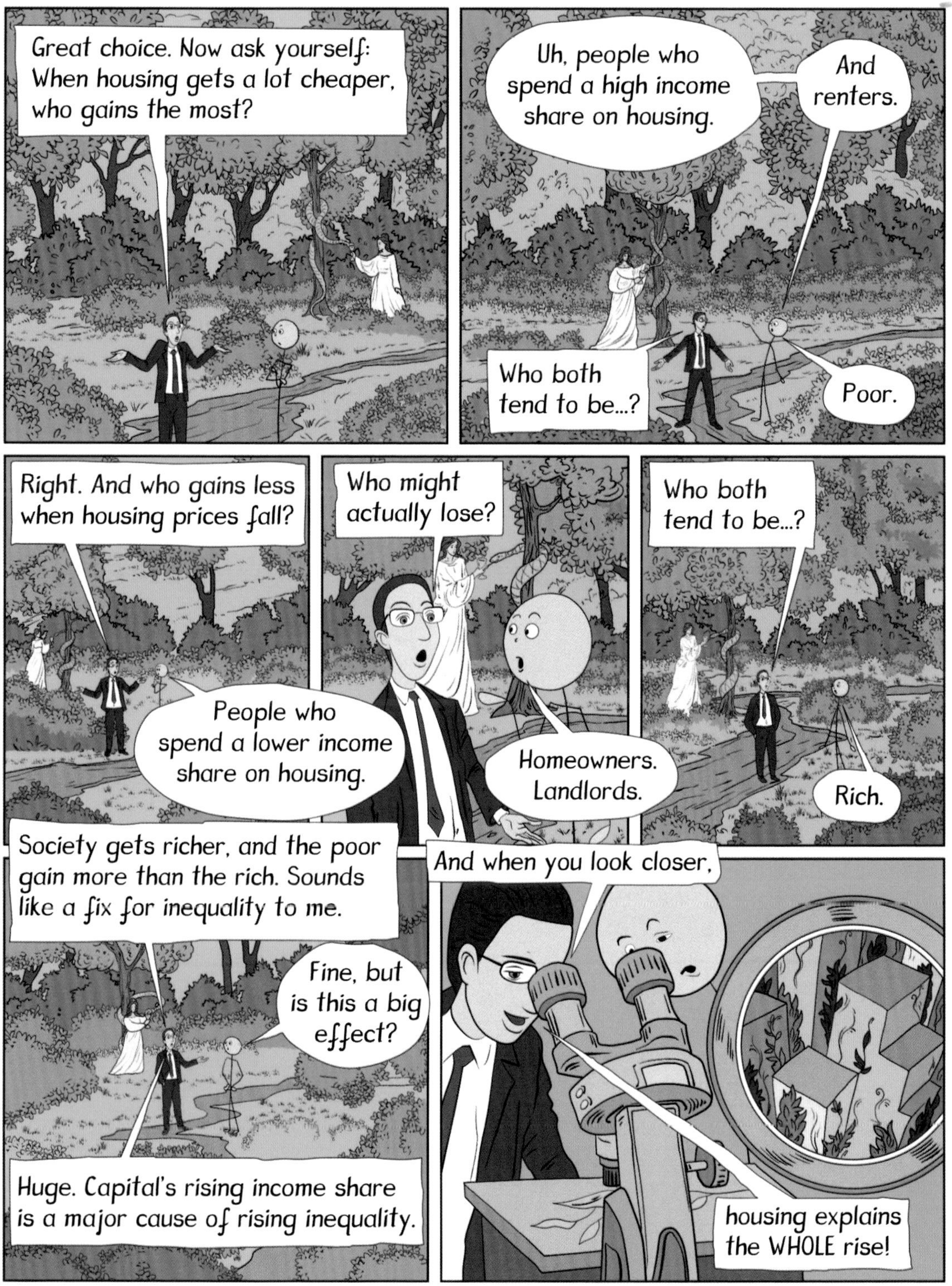
Great choice. Now ask yourself: When housing gets a lot cheaper, who gains the most?
Uh, people who spend a high income share on housing.
And renters.
Who both tend to be...?
Poor.
Right. And who gains less when housing prices fall?
People who spend a lower income share on housing.
Who might actually lose?
Homeowners. Landlords.
Who both tend to be...?
Rich.
Society gets richer, and the poor gain more than the rich. Sounds like a fix for inequality to me.
Fine, but is this a big effect?
Huge. Capital's rising income share is a major cause of rising inequality.
And when you look closer,
housing explains the WHOLE rise!

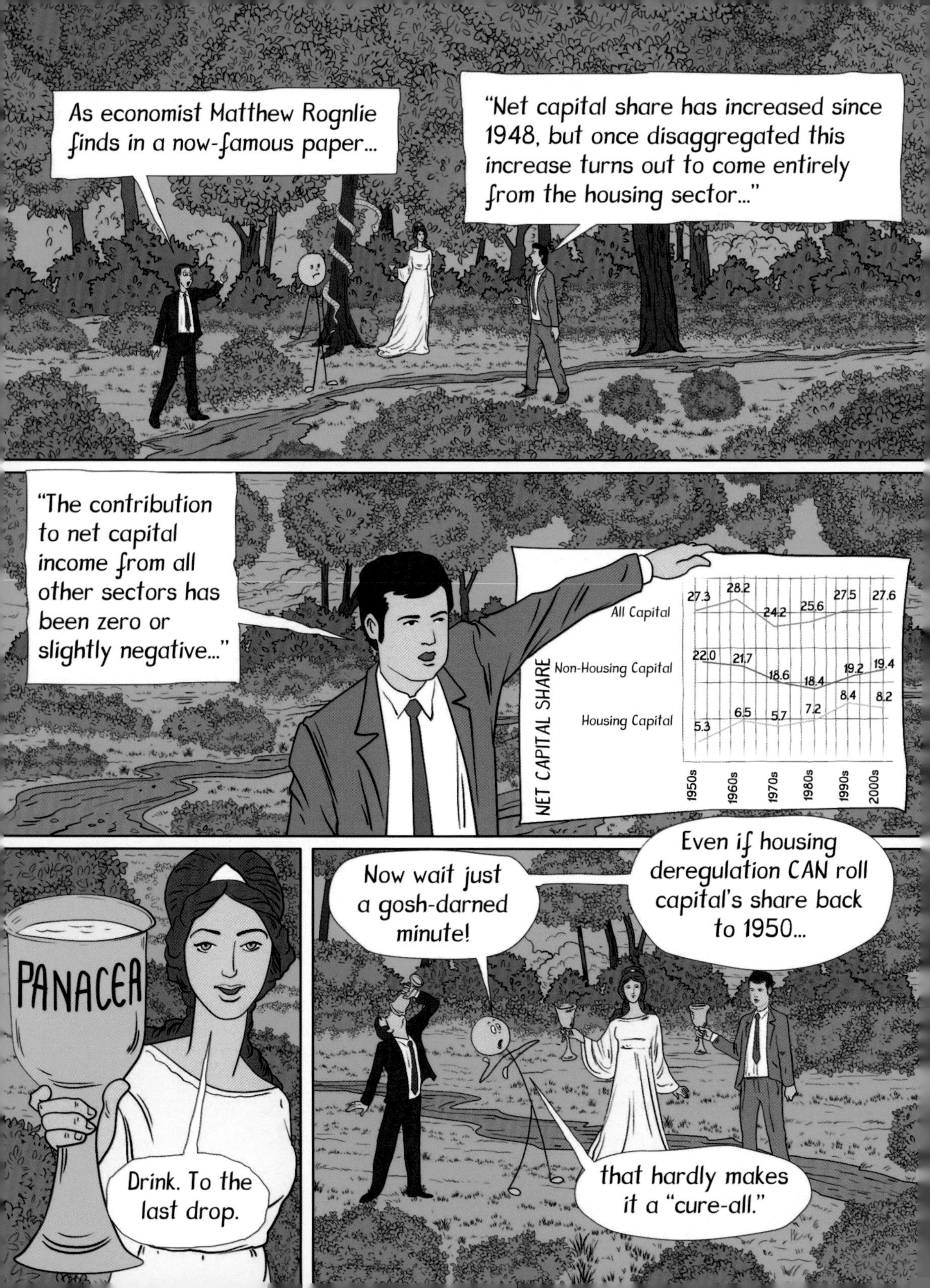

As economist Matthew Rognlie finds in a now-famous paper...
"Net capital share has increased since 1948, but once disaggregated this increase turns out to come entirely from the housing sector..."
"The contribution to net capital income from all other sectors has been zero or slightly negative..."
NET CAPITAL SHARE
All Capital
27.3 28.2 24.2 25.6 27.5 27.6
Non-Housing Capital
22.0 21.7 18.6 18.4 19.2 19.4
Housing Capital
5.3 6.5 5.7 7.2 8.4 8.2
1950s 1960s 1970s 1980s 1990s 2000s
PANACEA
Drink. To the last drop.
Now wait just a gosh-darned minute!
Even if housing deregulation CAN roll capital's share back to 1950...
that hardly makes it a "cure-all."

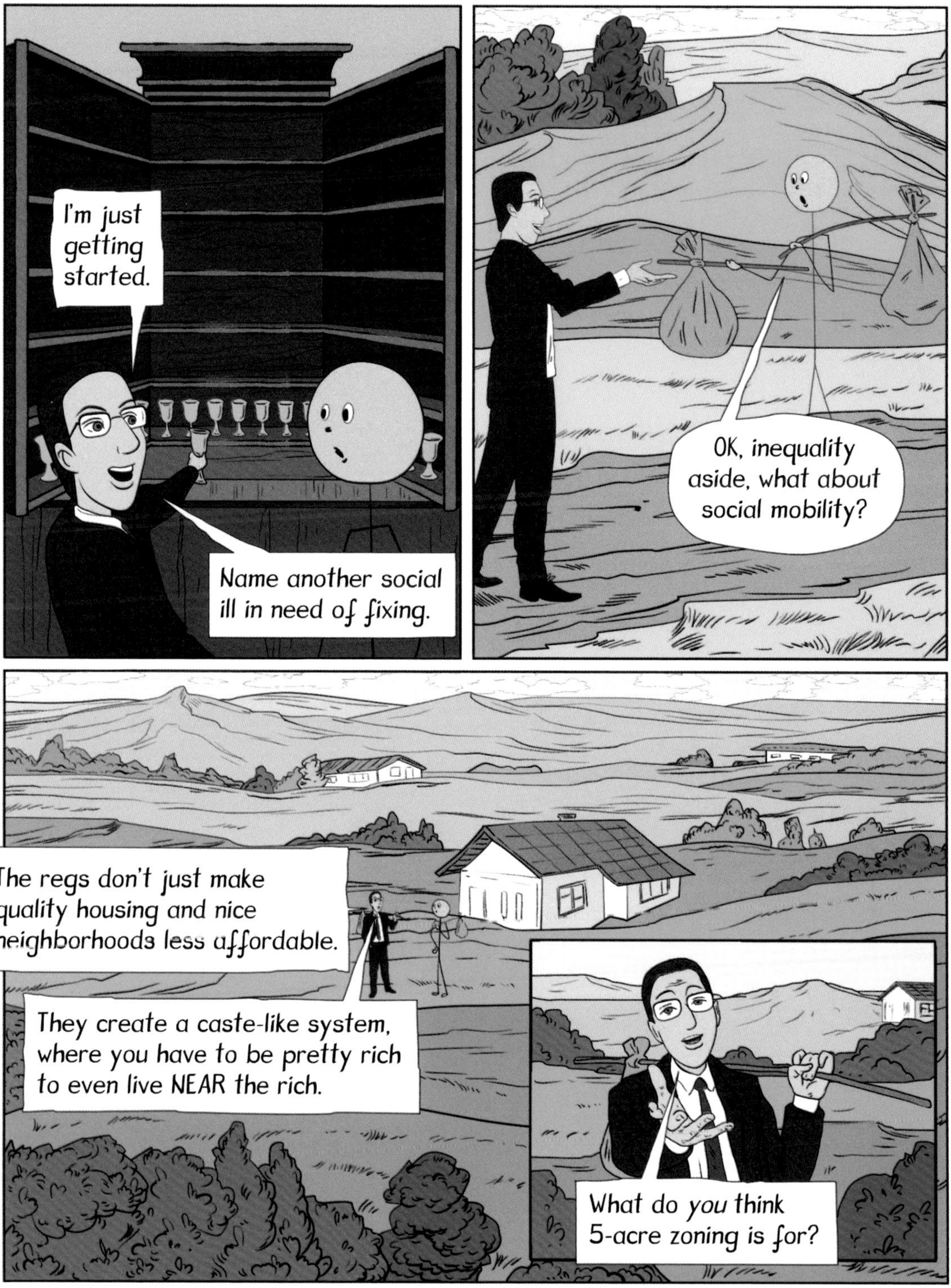

I'm just getting started.
Name another social ill in need of fixing.
OK, *inequality* aside, what about social mobility?
The regs don't just make quality housing and nice neighborhoods less affordable.
They create a caste-like system, where you have to be pretty rich to even live NEAR the rich.
What do *you* think 5-acre zoning is for?

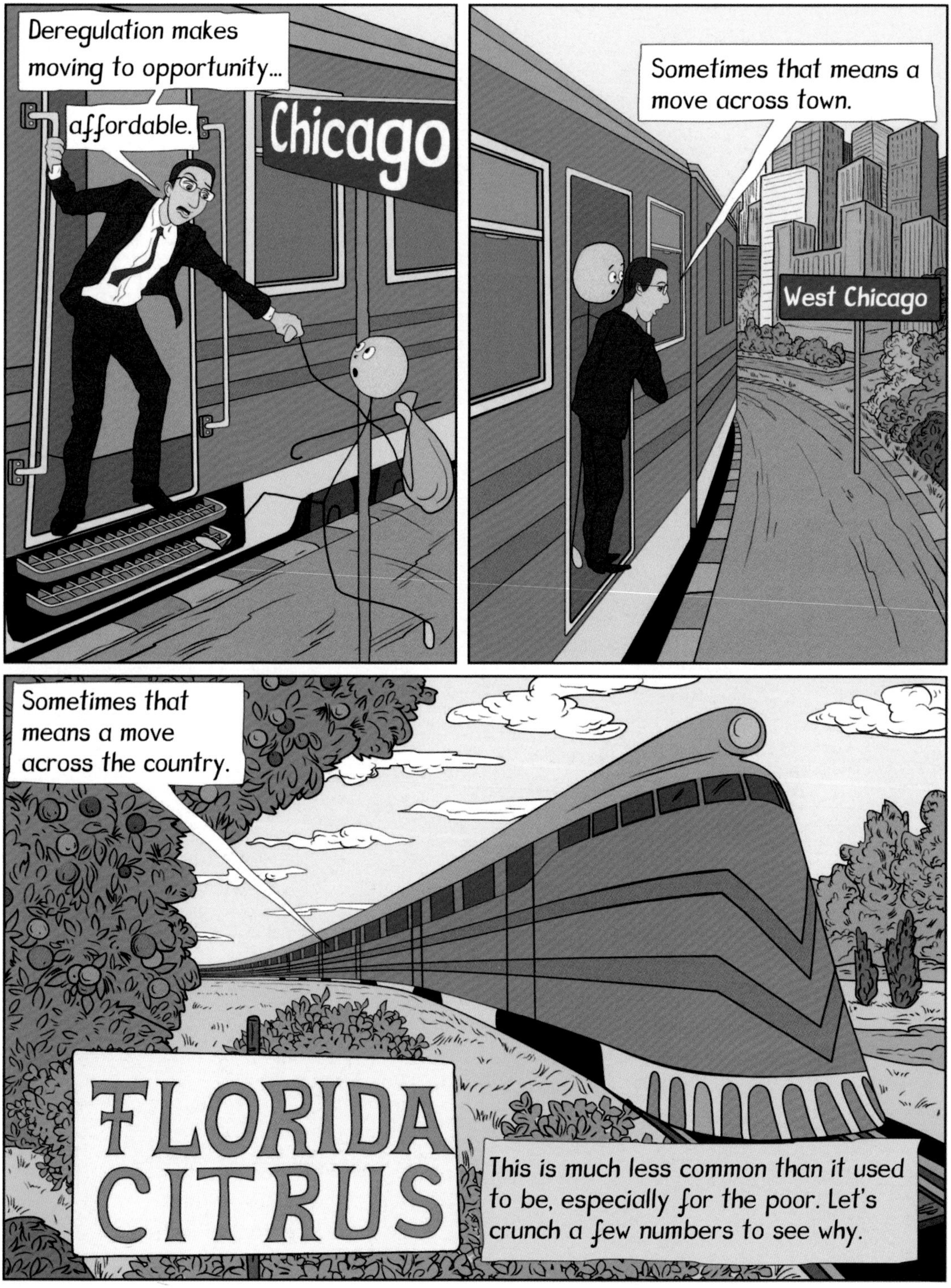
Deregulation makes moving to opportunity...
affordable.
Chicago
Sometimes that means a move across town.
West Chicago
Sometimes that means a move across the country.
FLORIDA CITRUS
This is much less common than it used to be, especially for the poor. Let's crunch a few numbers to see why.

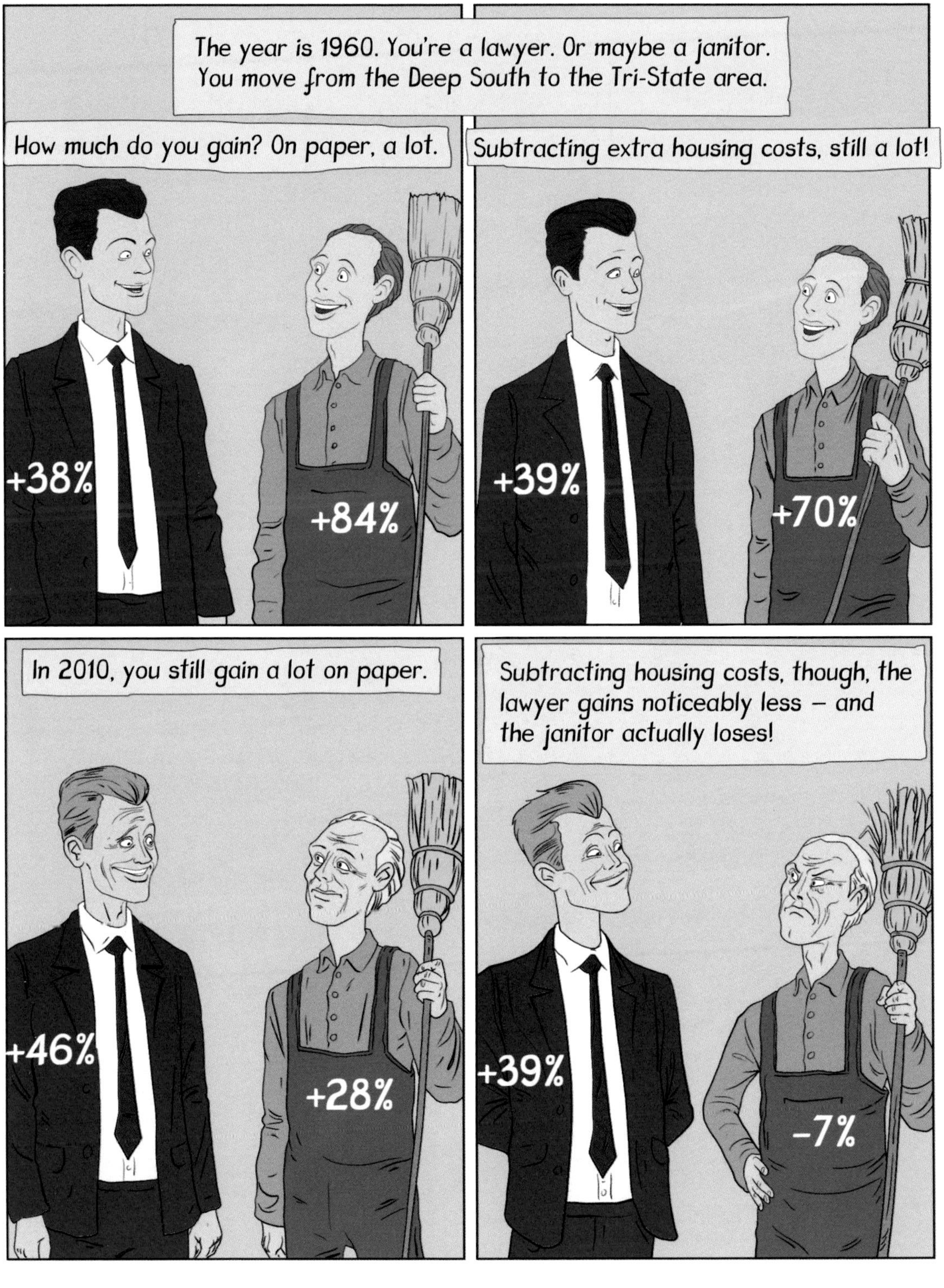
The year is 1960. You're a lawyer. Or maybe a janitor. You move from the Deep South to the Tri-State area.
How much do you gain? On paper, a lot.
+38%
+84%
Subtracting extra housing costs, still a lot!
+39%
+70%
In 2010, you still gain a lot on paper.
+46%
+28%
Subtracting housing costs, though, the lawyer gains noticeably less – and the janitor actually loses!
+39%
–7%

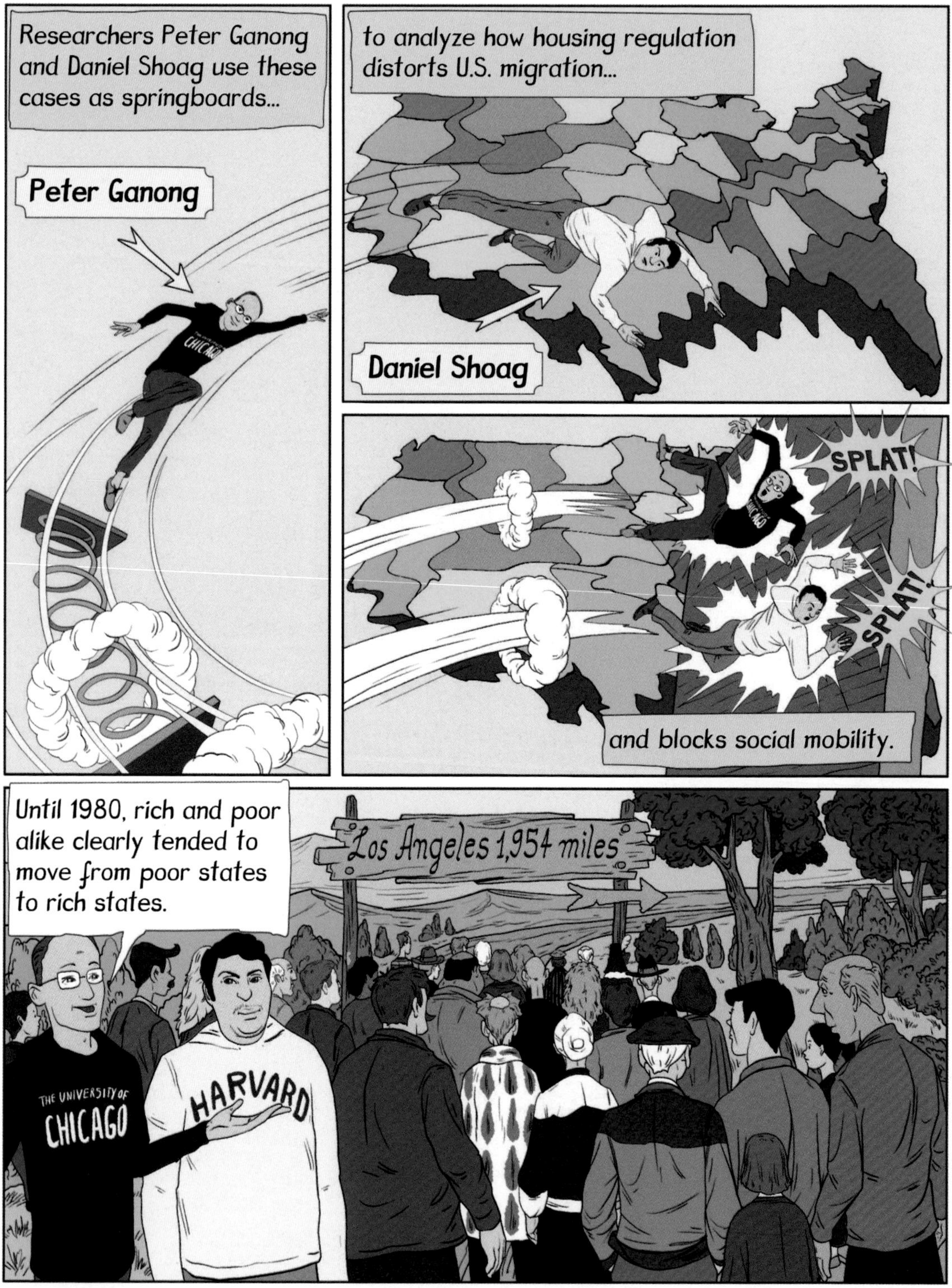
Researchers Peter Ganong and Daniel Shoag use these cases as springboards...
Peter Ganong
CHICAGO
to analyze how housing regulation distorts U.S. migration...
Daniel Shoag
SPLAT!
CHICAGO
SPLAT!
and blocks social mobility.
Until 1980, rich and poor alike clearly tended to move from poor states to rich states.
Los Angeles 1,954 miles
THE UNIVERSITY OF CHICAGO
HARVARD

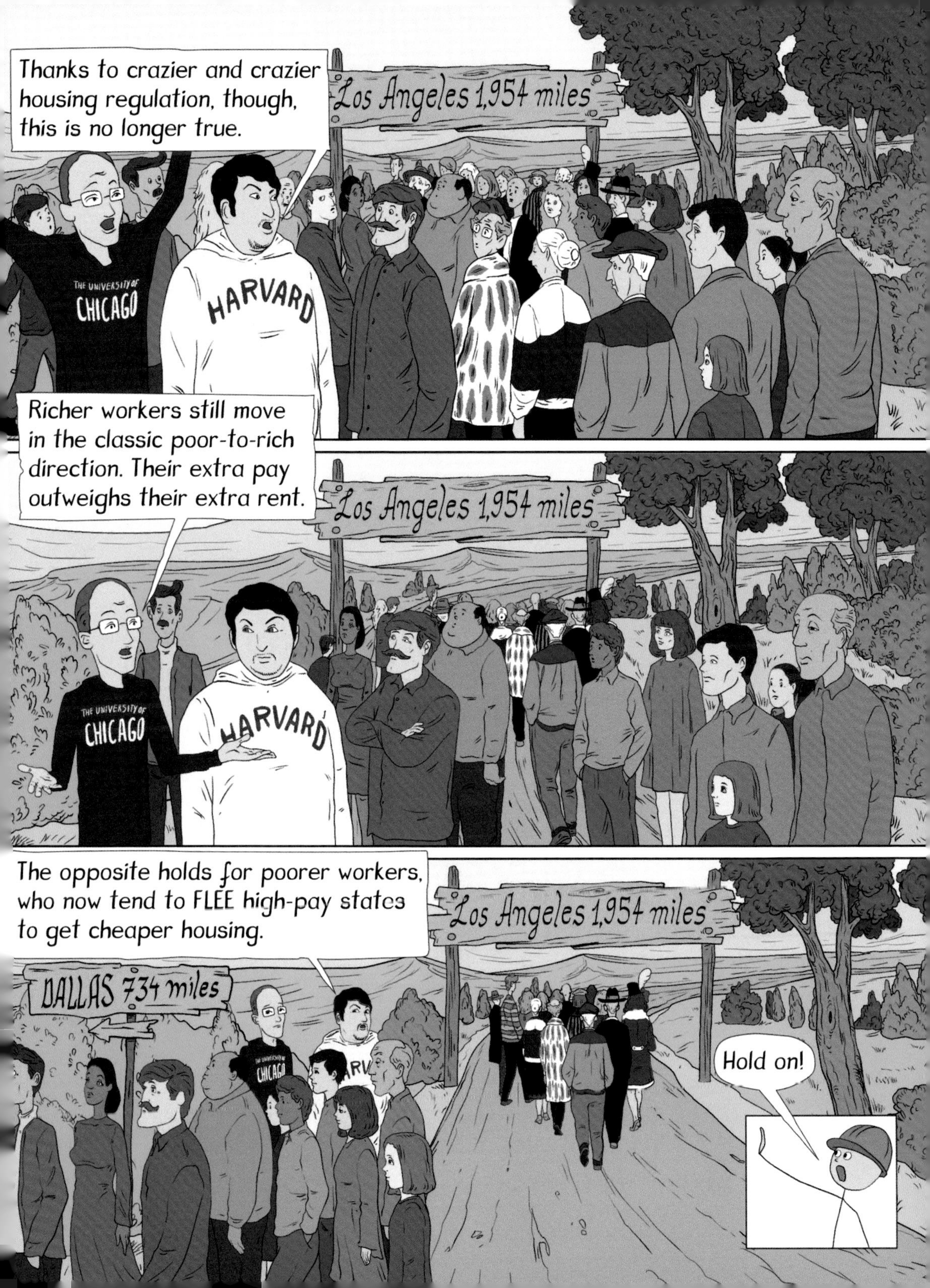
Thanks to crazier and crazier housing regulation, though, this is no longer true.
Los Angeles 1,954 miles
THE UNIVERSITY OF CHICAGO
HARVARD
Richer workers still move in the classic poor-to-rich direction. Their extra pay outweighs their extra rent.
Los Angeles 1,954 miles
THE UNIVERSITY OF CHICAGO
HARVARD
The opposite holds for poorer workers, who now tend to FLEE high-pay states to get cheaper housing.
Los Angeles 1,954 miles
DALLAS 734 miles
Hold on!

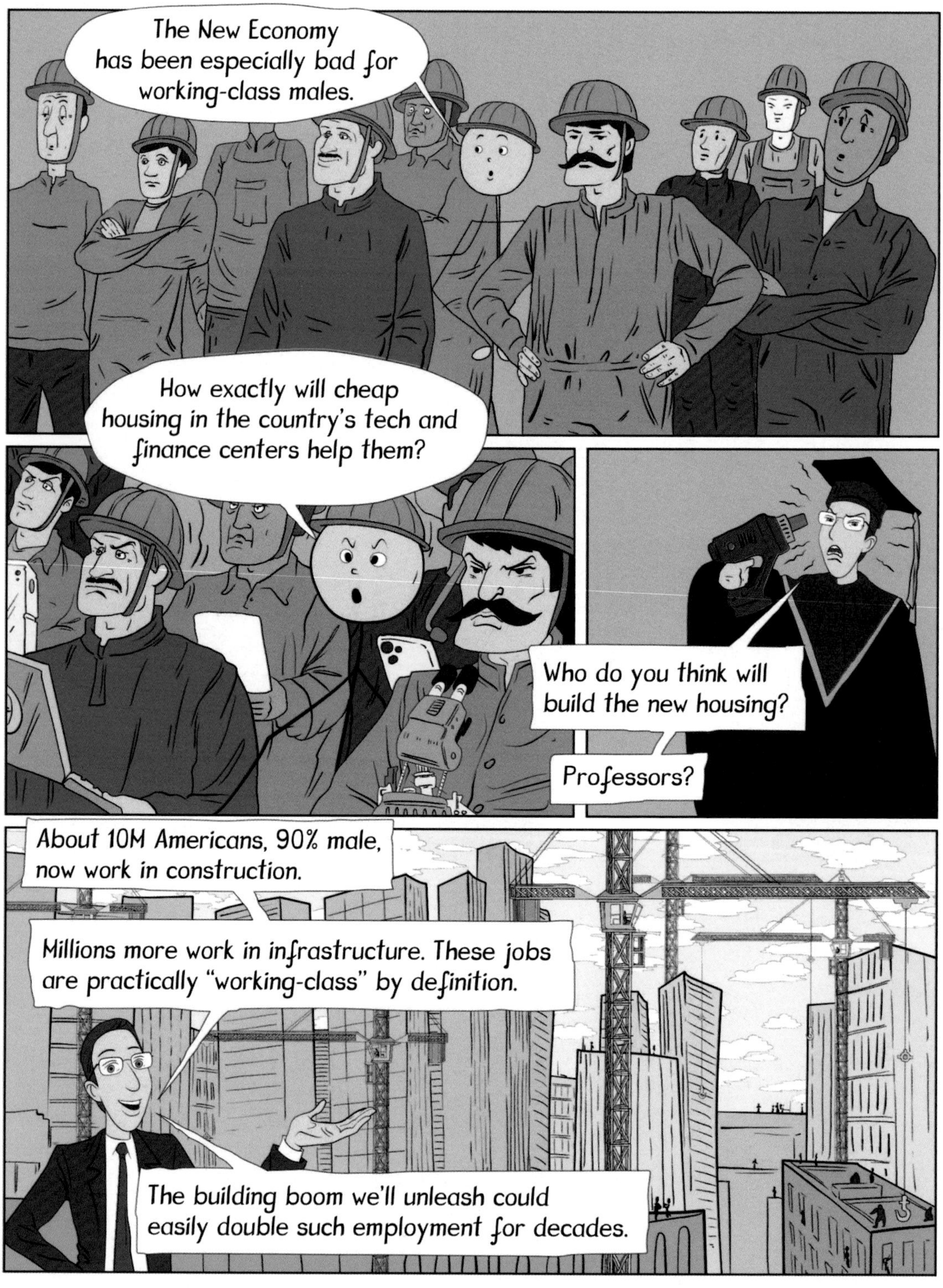
The New Economy has been especially bad for working-class males.
How exactly will cheap housing in the country's tech and finance centers help them?
Who do you think will build the new housing?
Professors?
About 10M Americans, 90% male, now work in construction.
Millions more work in infrastructure. These jobs are practically "working-class" by definition.
The building boom we'll unleash could easily double such employment for decades.

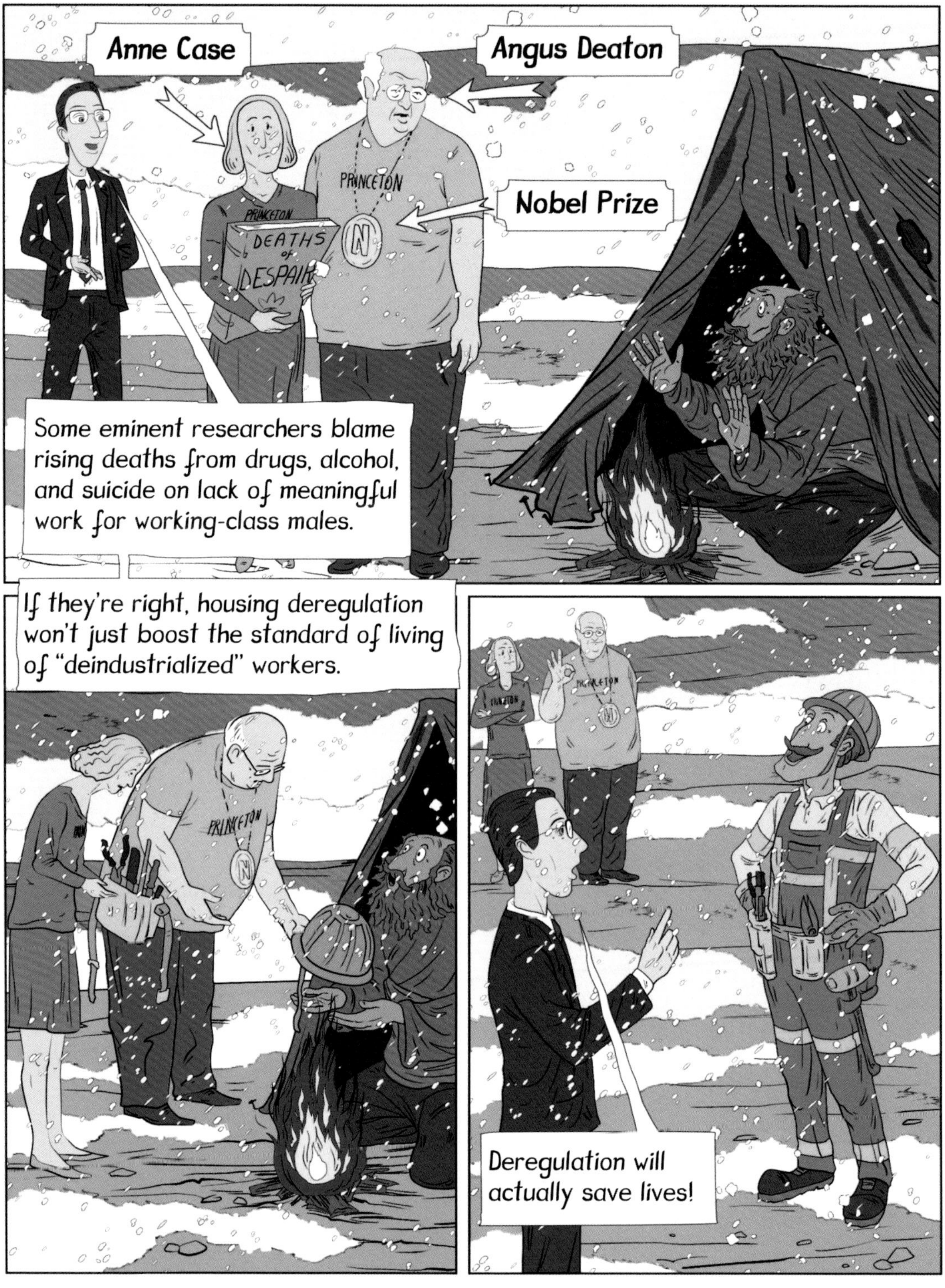
Anne Case
Angus Deaton
PRINCETON
PRINCETON
DEATHS of DESPAIR
Nobel Prize
Some eminent researchers blame rising deaths from drugs, alcohol, and suicide on lack of meaningful work for working-class males.
If they're right, housing deregulation won't just boost the standard of living of "deindustrialized" workers.
PRINCETON
Deregulation will actually save lives!

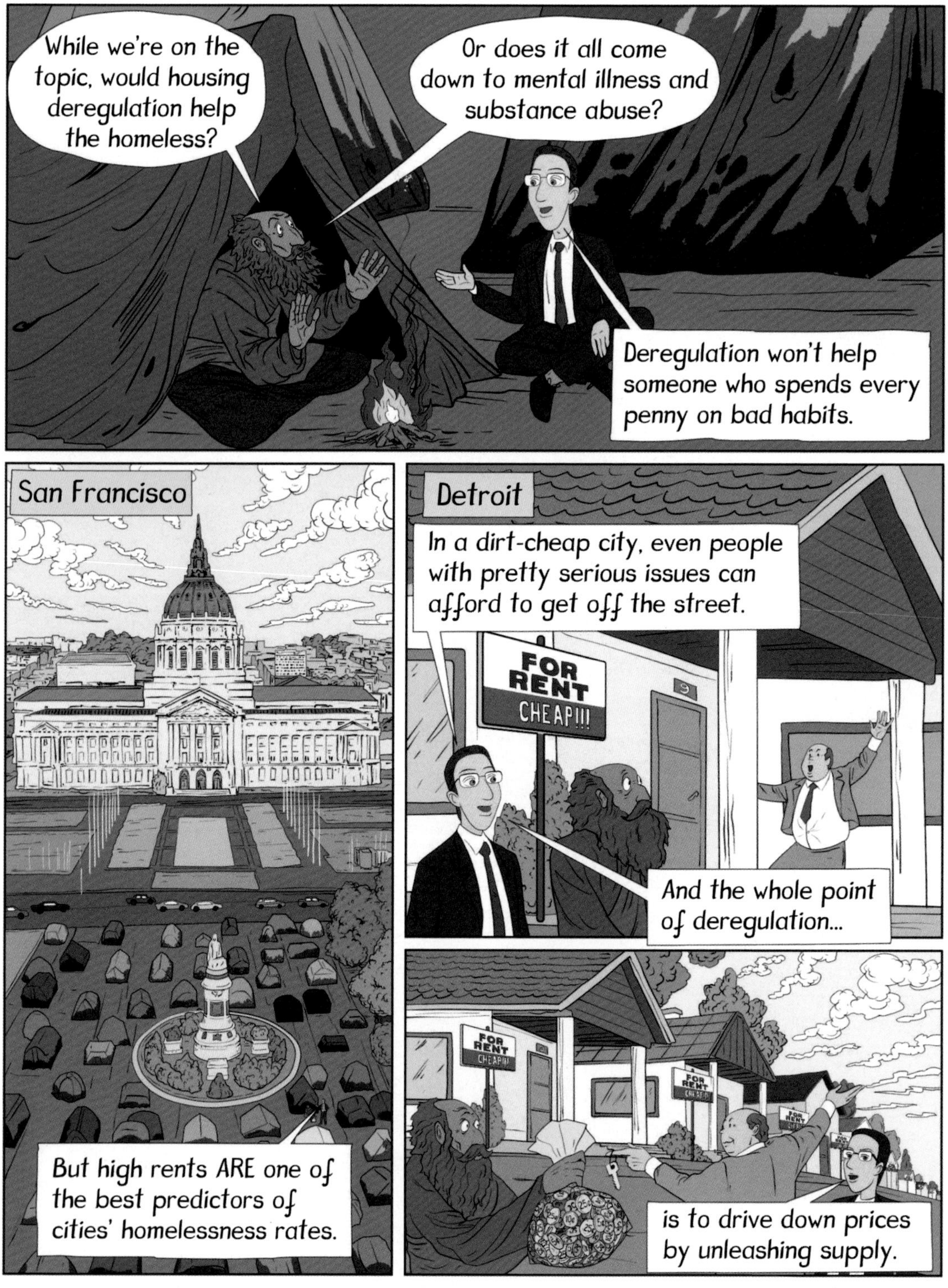
While we're on the topic, would housing deregulation help the homeless?
Or does it all come down to mental illness and substance abuse?
Deregulation won't help someone who spends every penny on bad habits.
San Francisco
But high rents ARE one of the best predictors of cities' homelessness rates.
Detroit
In a dirt-cheap city, even people with pretty serious issues can afford to get off the street.
FOR RENT
CHEAP!!!
And the whole point of deregulation...
FOR RENT
is to drive down prices by unleashing supply.

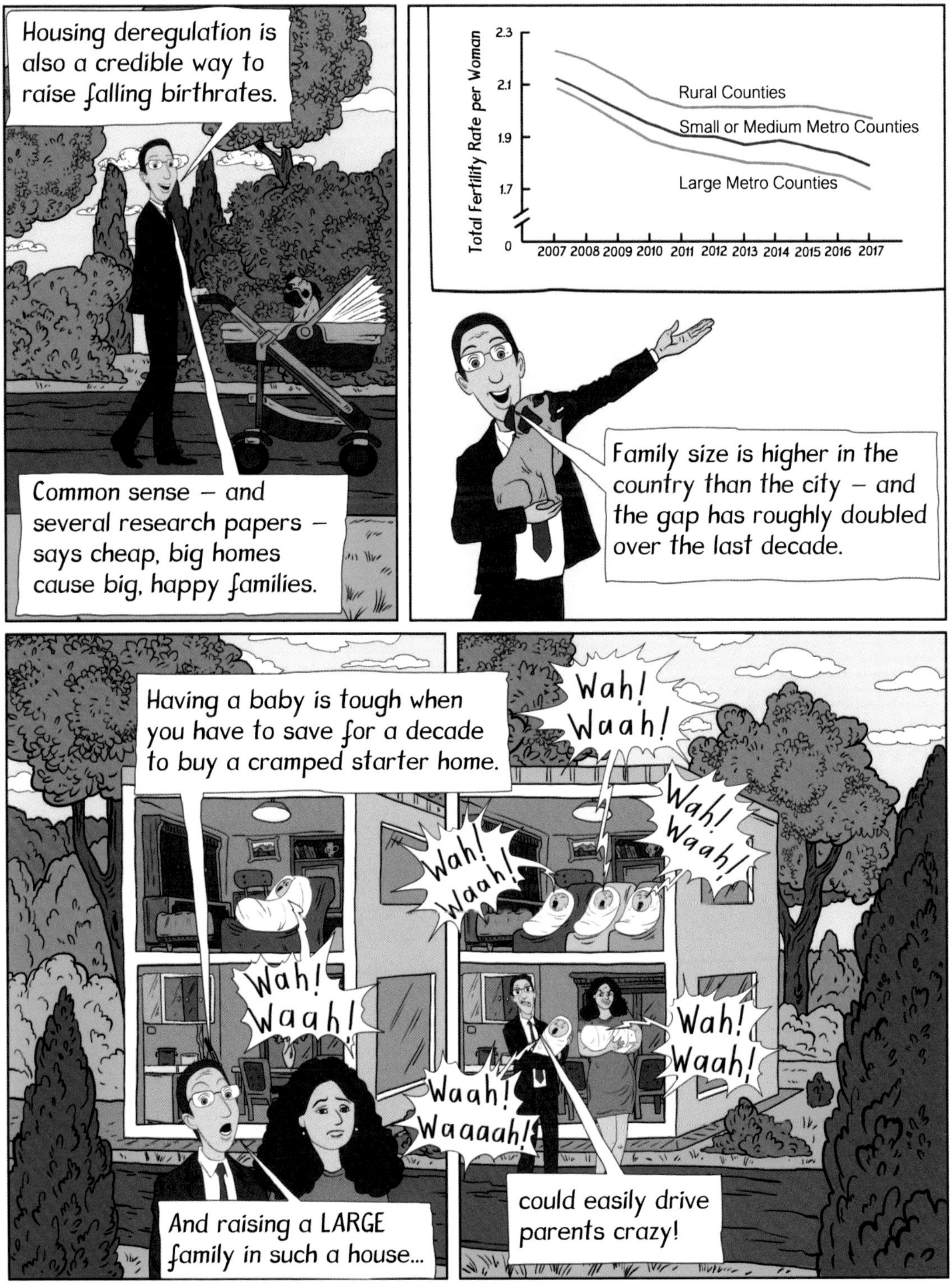
Housing deregulation is also a credible way to raise falling birthrates.
Common sense – and several research papers – says cheap, big homes cause big, happy families.
Total Fertility Rate per Woman
2.3
2.1
1.9
1.7
0
2007 2008 2009 2010 2011 2012 2013 2014 2015 2016 2017
Rural Counties
Small or Medium Metro Counties
Large Metro Counties
Family size is higher in the country than the city – and the gap has roughly doubled over the last decade.
Having a baby is tough when you have to save for a decade to buy a cramped starter home.
Wah! Waah!
Wah! Waah!
Wah! Waah!
Wah! Waah!
Waah! Waaaah!
Wah! Waah!
And raising a LARGE family in such a house...
could easily drive parents crazy!

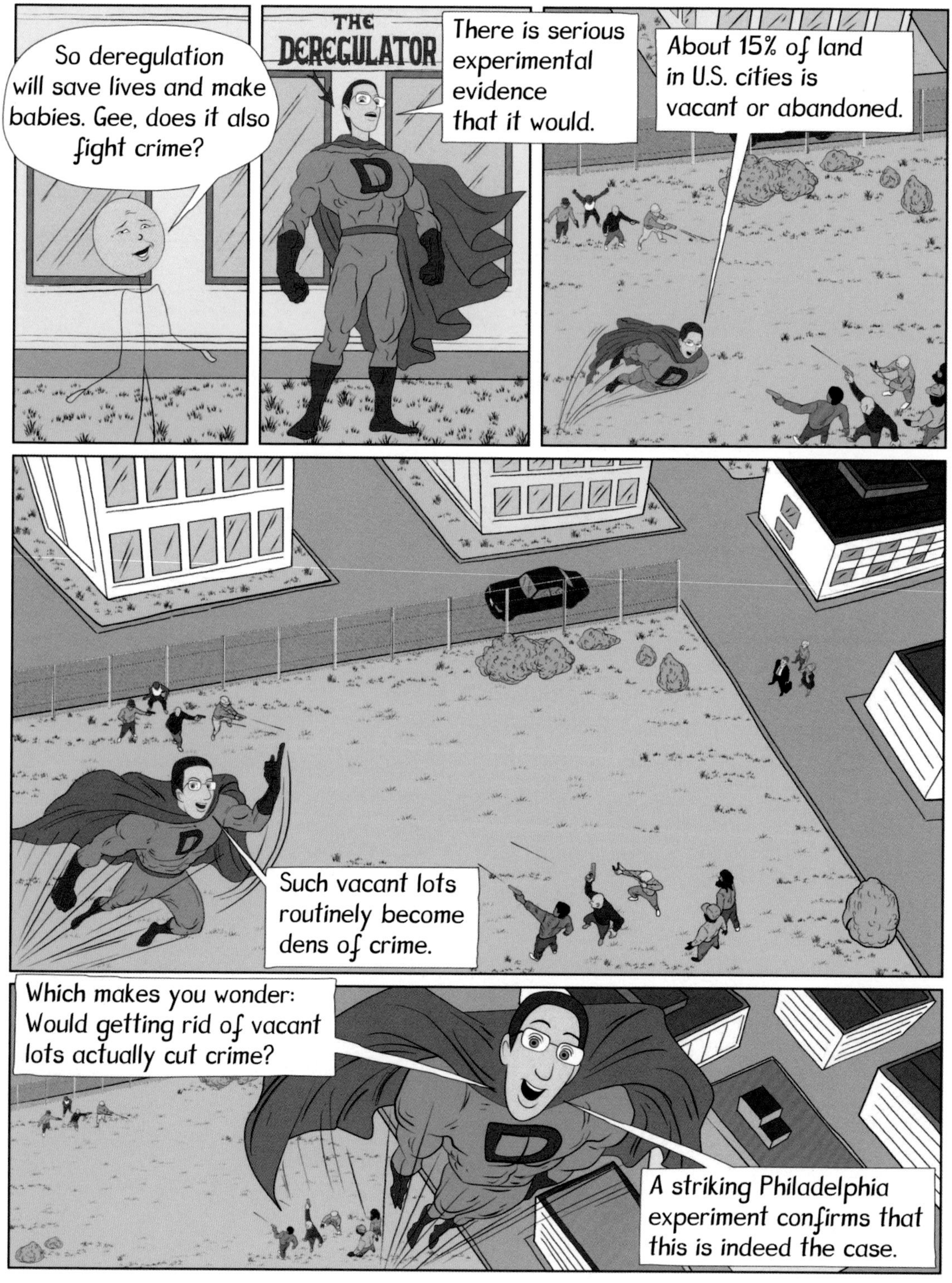

So deregulation will save lives and make babies. Gee, does it also fight crime?
THE DEREGULATOR
There is serious experimental evidence that it would.
About 15% of land in U.S. cities is vacant or abandoned.
Such vacant lots routinely become dens of crime.
Which makes you wonder: Would getting rid of vacant lots actually cut crime?
A striking Philadelphia experiment confirms that this is indeed the case.

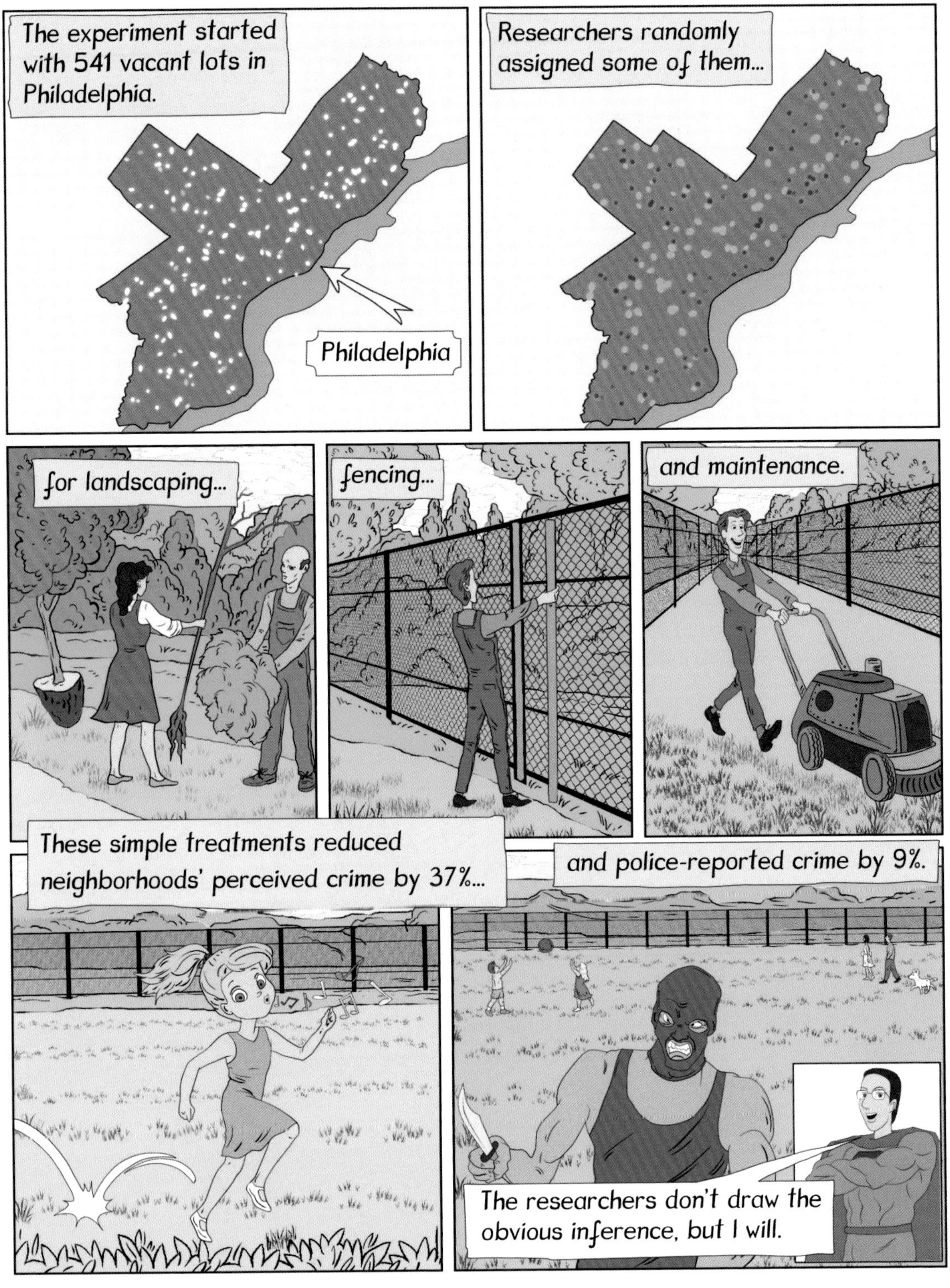
The experiment started with 541 vacant lots in Philadelphia.
Philadelphia
Researchers randomly assigned some of them...
for landscaping...
fencing...
and maintenance.
These simple treatments reduced neighborhoods' perceived crime by 37%...
and police-reported crime by 9%.
The researchers don't draw the obvious inference, but I will.

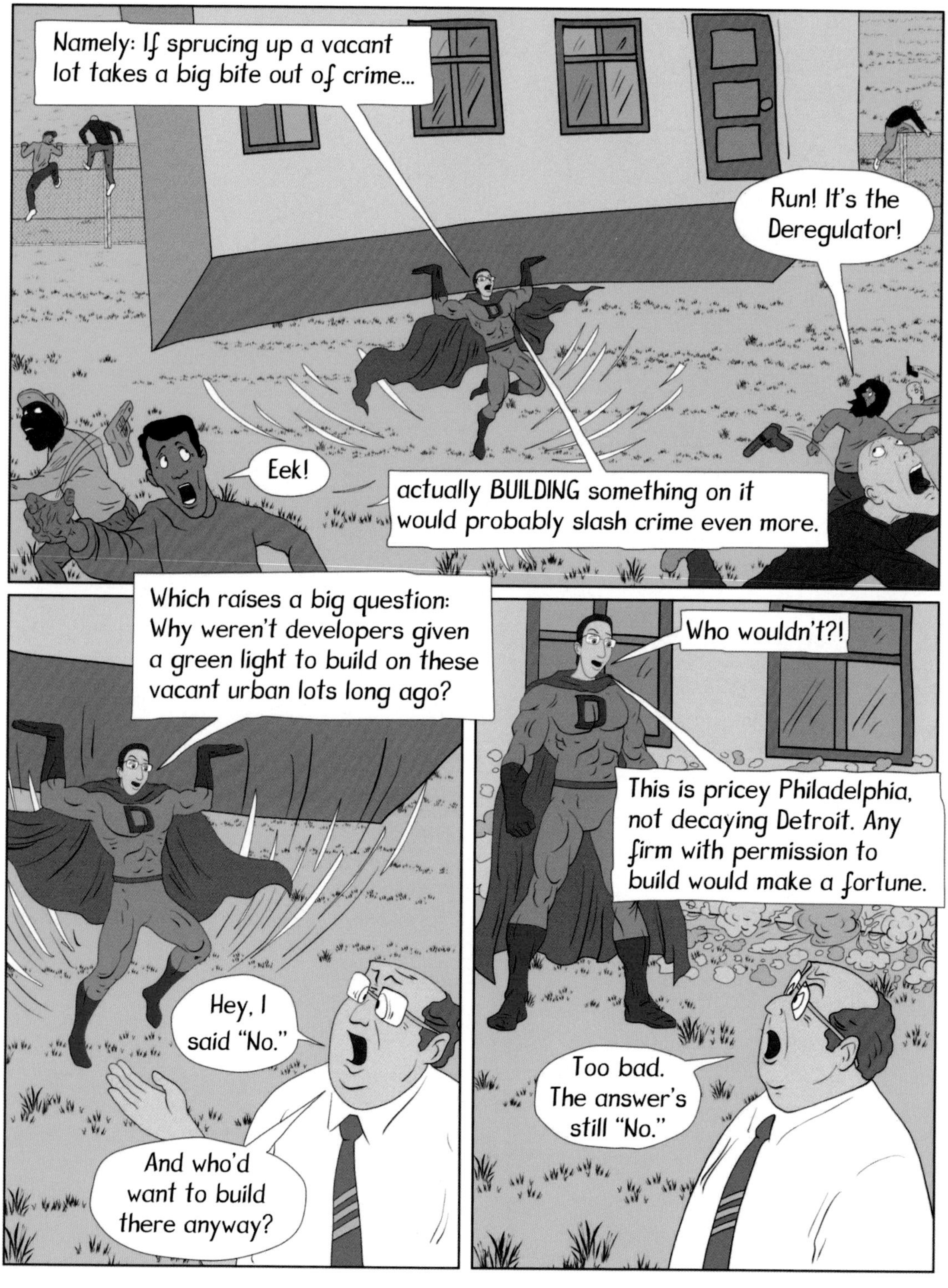
Namely: If sprucing up a vacant lot takes a big bite out of crime...
Run! It's the Deregulator!
Eek!
actually BUILDING something on it would probably slash crime even more.
Which raises a big question: Why weren't developers given a green light to build on these vacant urban lots long ago?
Hey, I said "No."
And who'd want to build there anyway?
Who wouldn't?!
This is pricey Philadelphia, not decaying Detroit. Any firm with permission to build would make a fortune.
Too bad. The answer's still "No."

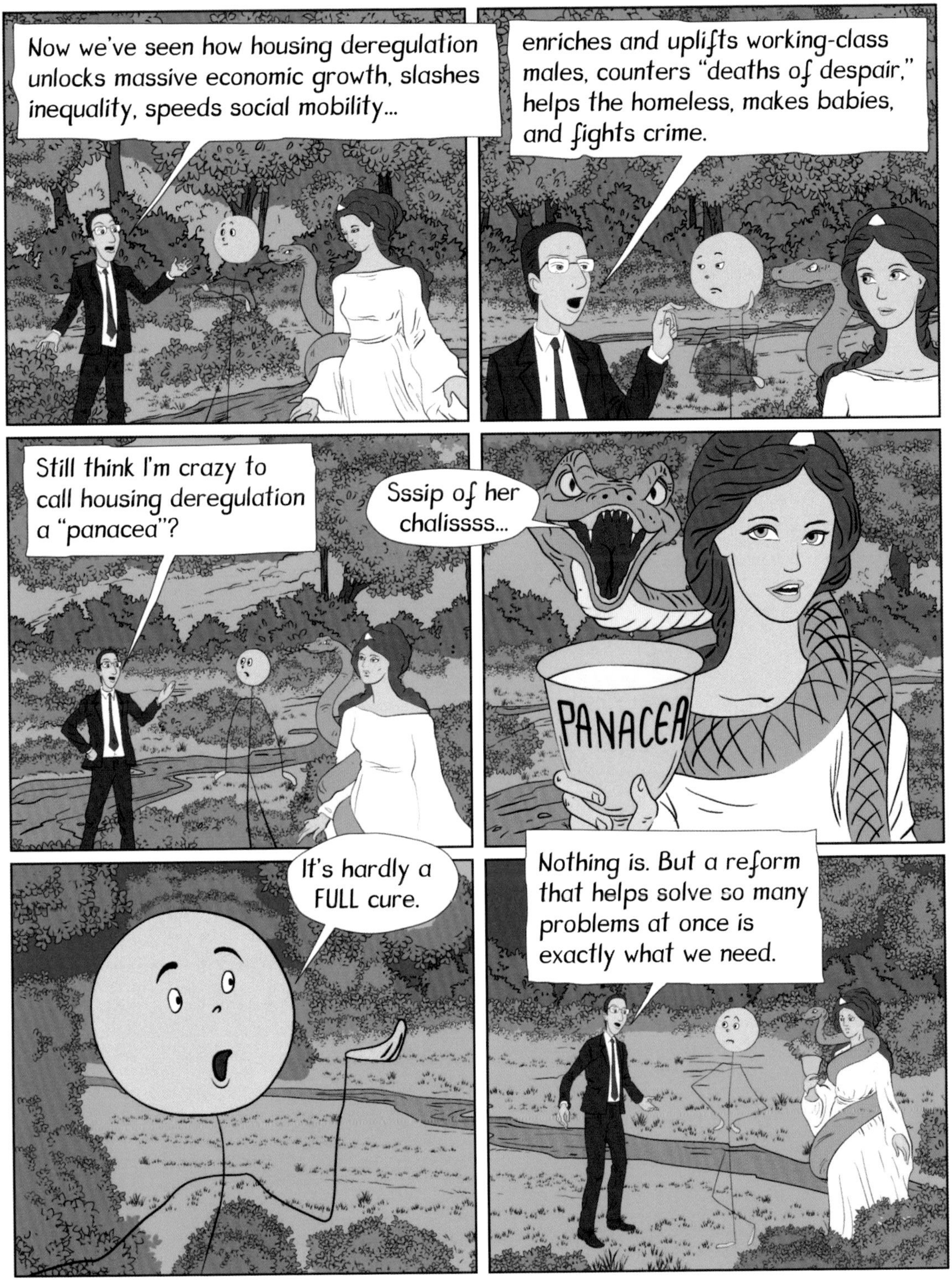
Now we've seen how housing deregulation unlocks massive economic growth, slashes inequality, speeds social mobility...
enriches and uplifts working-class males, counters "deaths of despair," helps the homeless, makes babies, and fights crime.
Still think I'm crazy to call housing deregulation a "panacea"?
Sssip of her chalissss...
PANACEA
It's hardly a FULL cure.
Nothing is. But a reform that helps solve so many problems at once is exactly what we need.

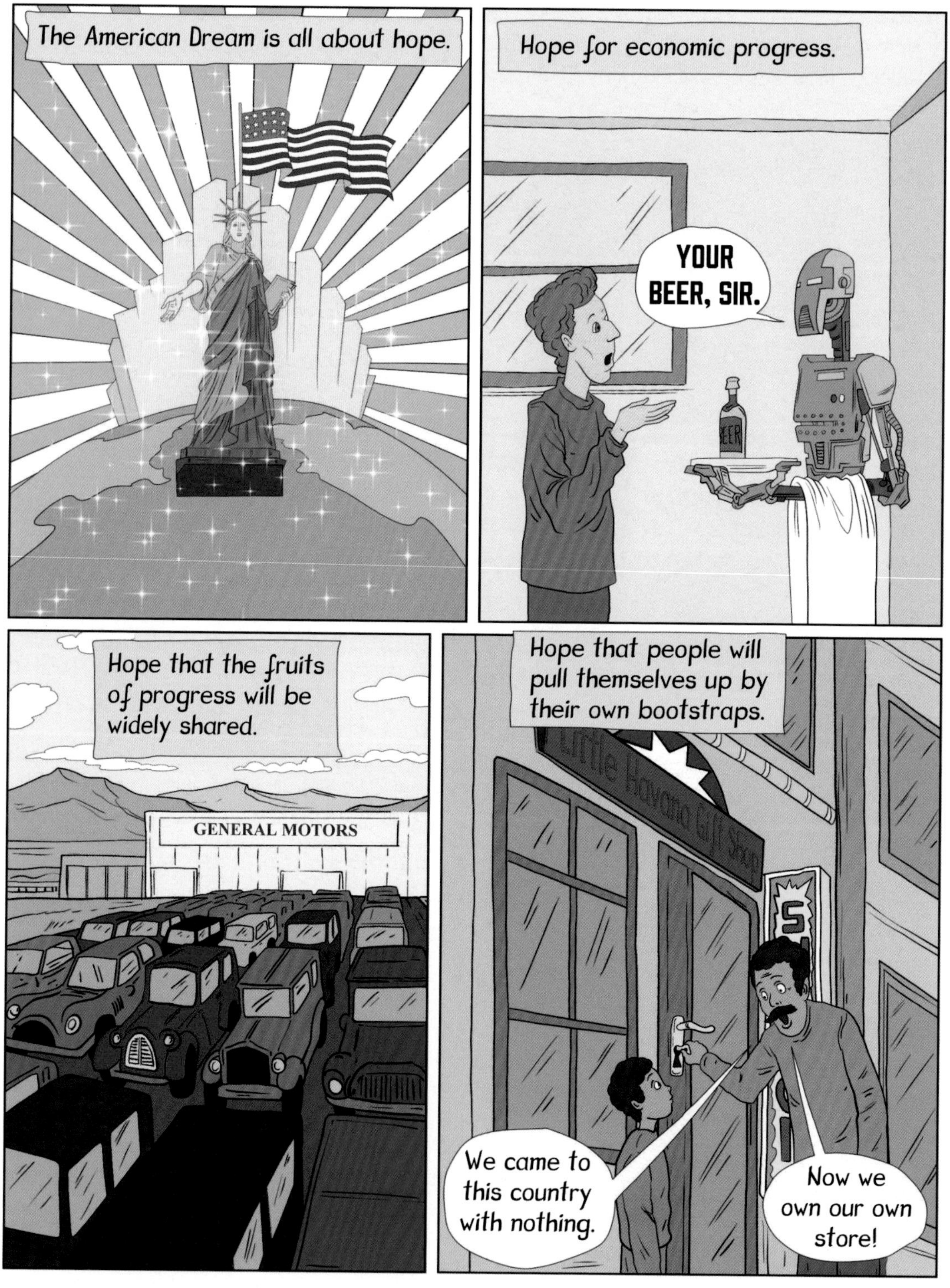
The American Dream is all about hope.
Hope for economic progress.
YOUR BEER, SIR.
BEER
Hope that the fruits of progress will be widely shared.
GENERAL MOTORS
Hope that people will pull themselves up by their own bootstraps.
Little Havana Gift Shop
We came to this country with nothing.
Now we own our own store!

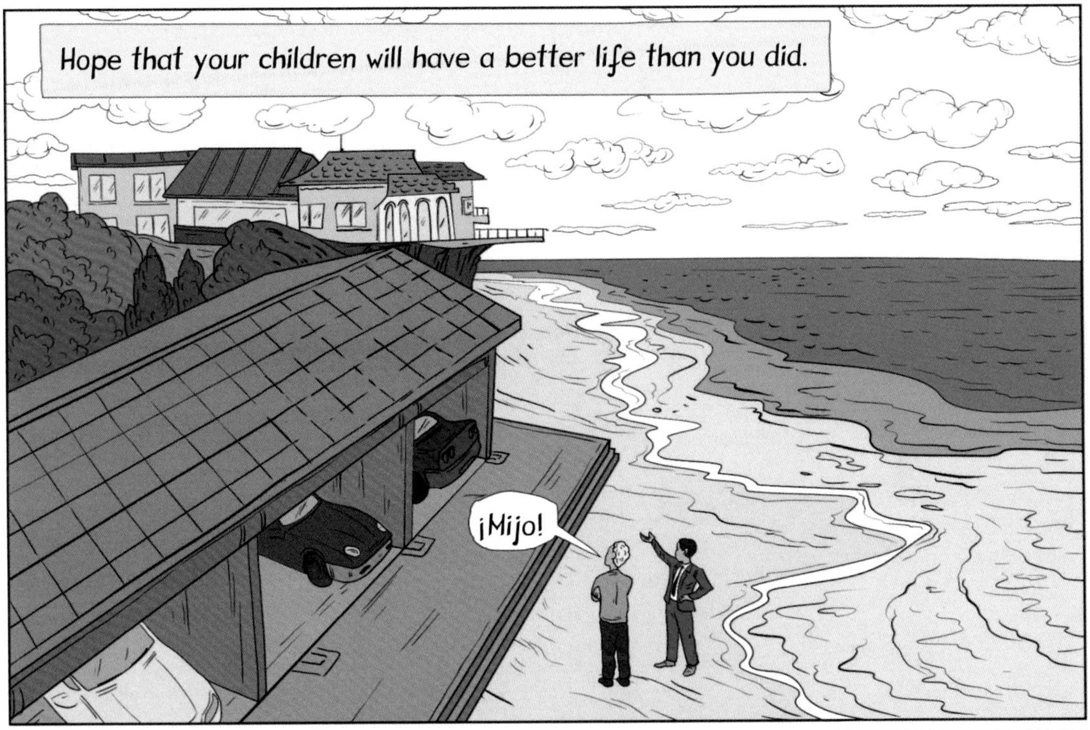
Hope that your children will have a better life than you did.
¡Mijo!

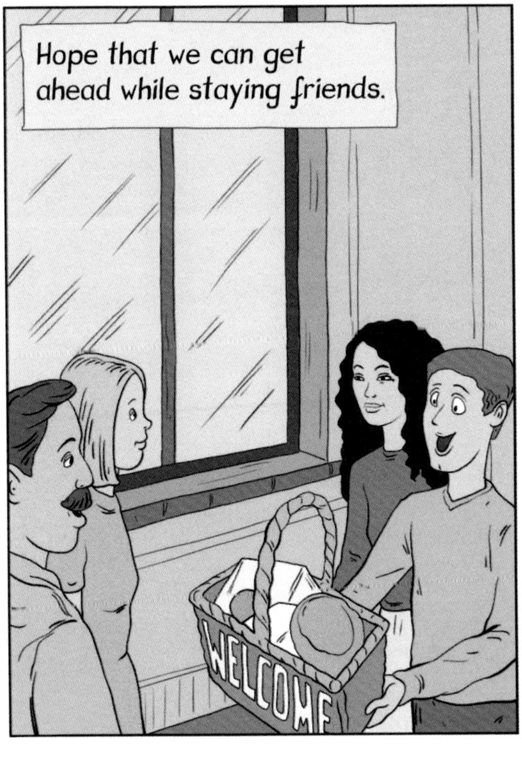
Hope that we can get ahead while staying friends.
WELCOME

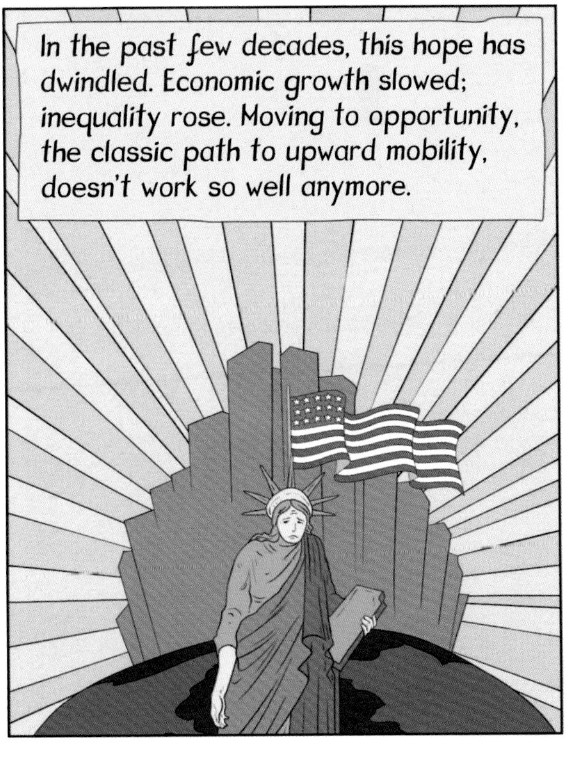
In the past few decades, this hope has dwindled. Economic growth slowed; inequality rose. Moving to opportunity, the classic path to upward mobility, doesn't work so well anymore.

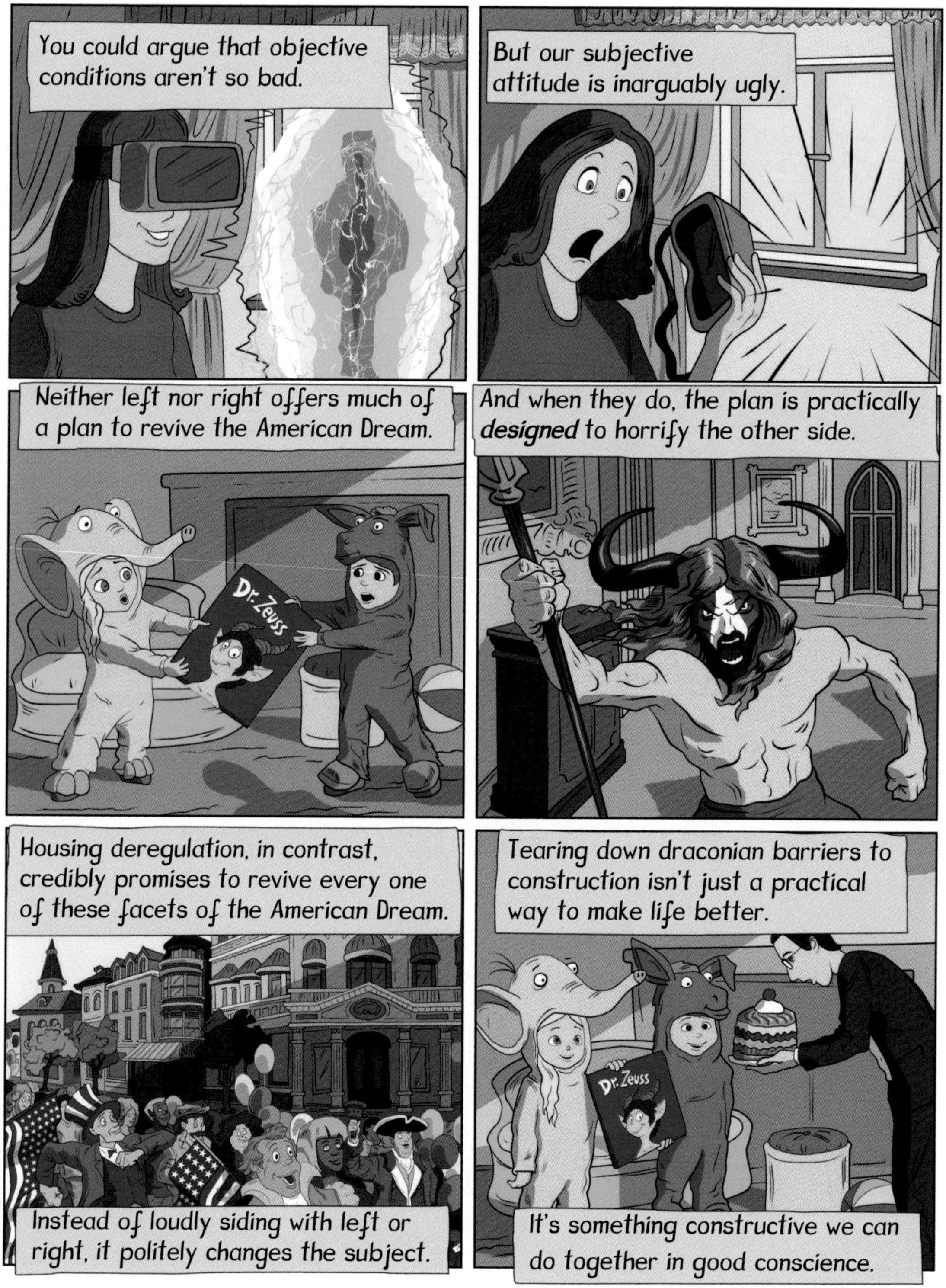
You could argue that objective conditions aren't so bad.
But our subjective attitude is inarguably ugly.
Neither left nor right offers much of a plan to revive the American Dream.
Dr. Zeuss
And when they do, the plan is practically *designed* to horrify the other side.
Housing deregulation, in contrast, credibly promises to revive every one of these facets of the American Dream.
Instead of loudly siding with left or right, it politely changes the subject.
Tearing down draconian barriers to construction isn't just a practical way to make life better.
Dr. Zeuss
It's something constructive we can do together in good conscience.

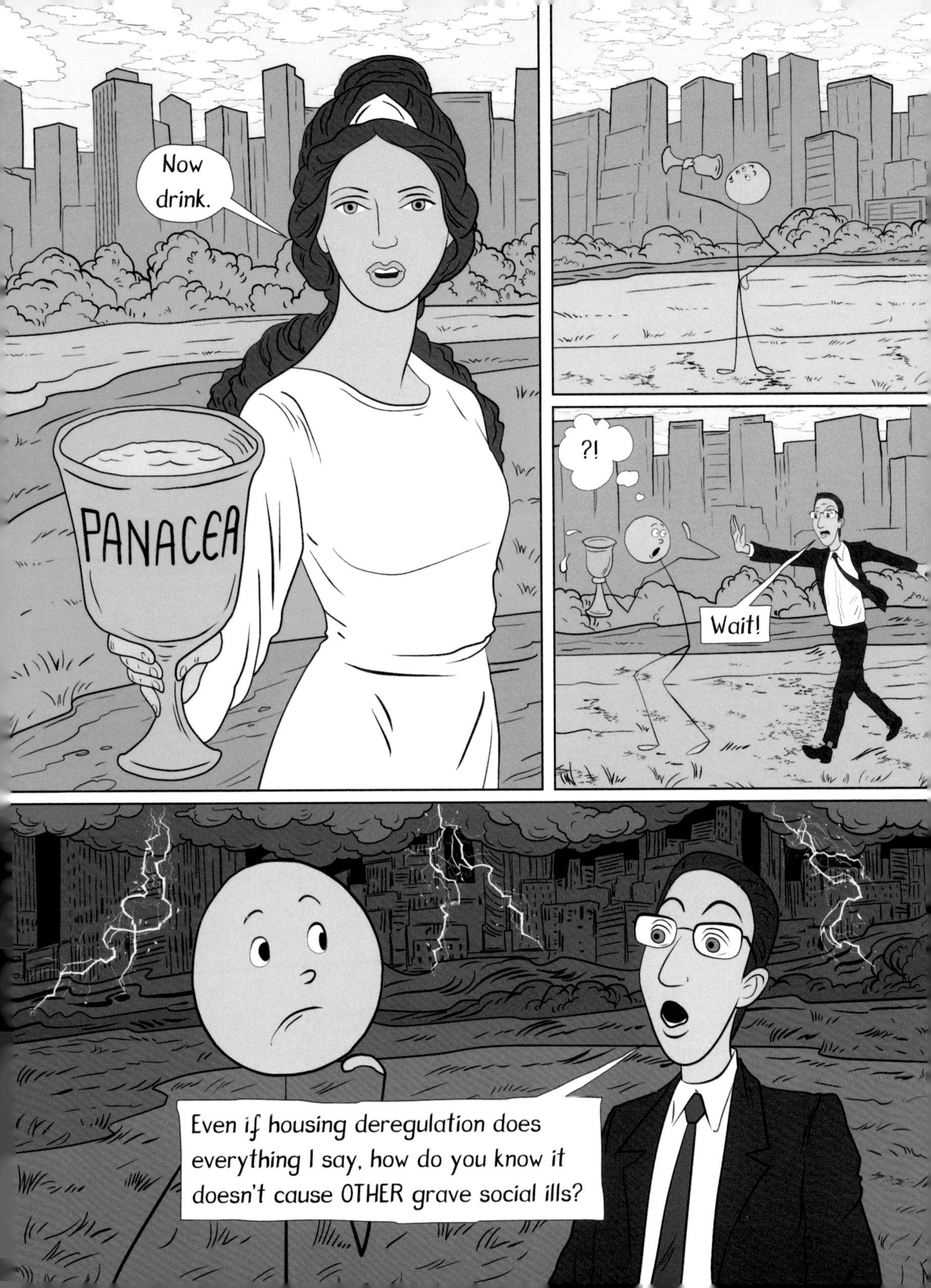
Now drink.
PANACEA
?!
Wait!
Even if housing deregulation does everything I say, how do you know it doesn't cause OTHER grave social ills?

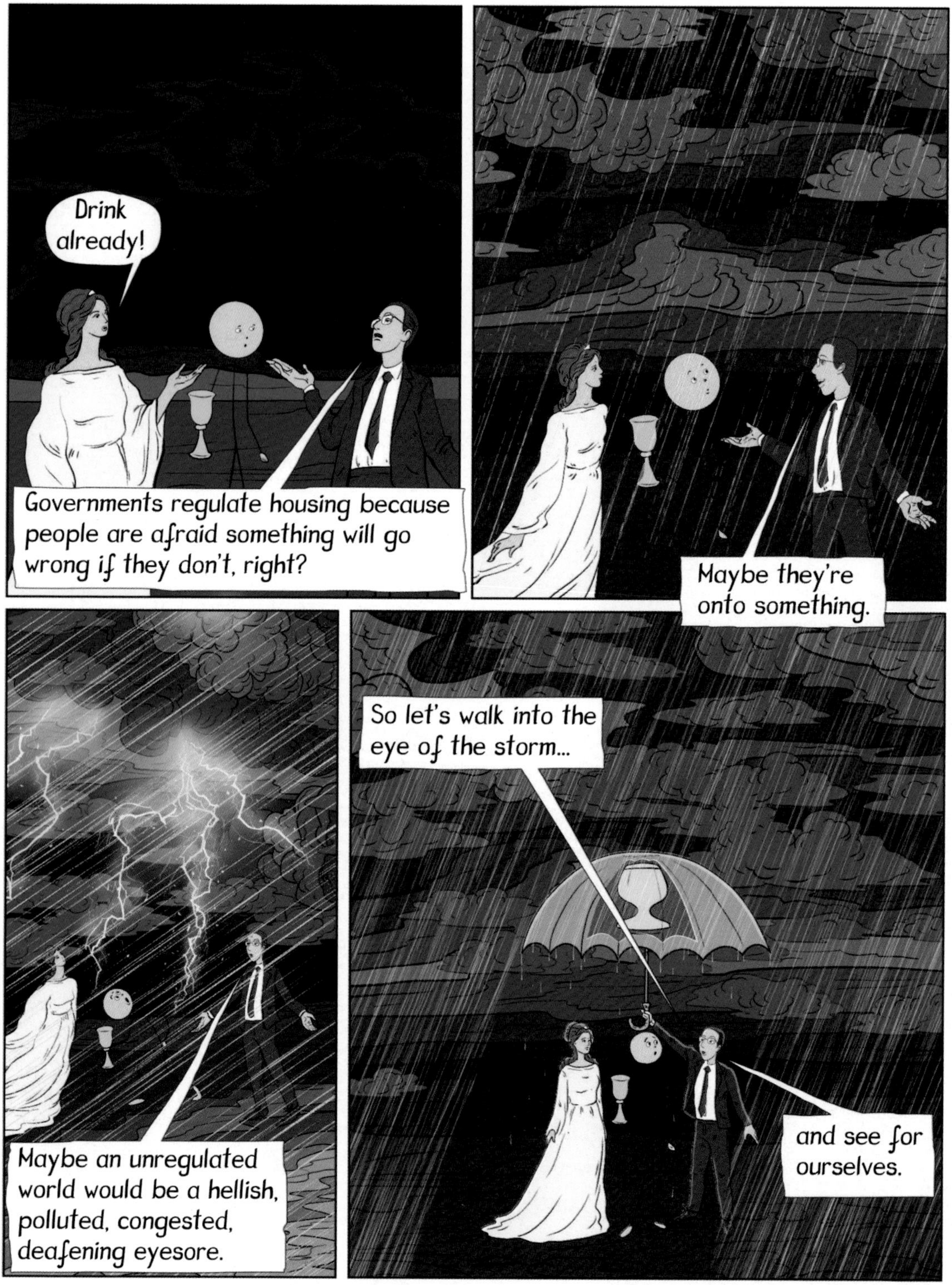
Drink already!
Governments regulate housing because people are afraid something will go wrong if they don't, right?
Maybe they're onto something.
Maybe an unregulated world would be a hellish, polluted, congested, deafening eyesore.
So let's walk into the eye of the storm...
and see for ourselves.

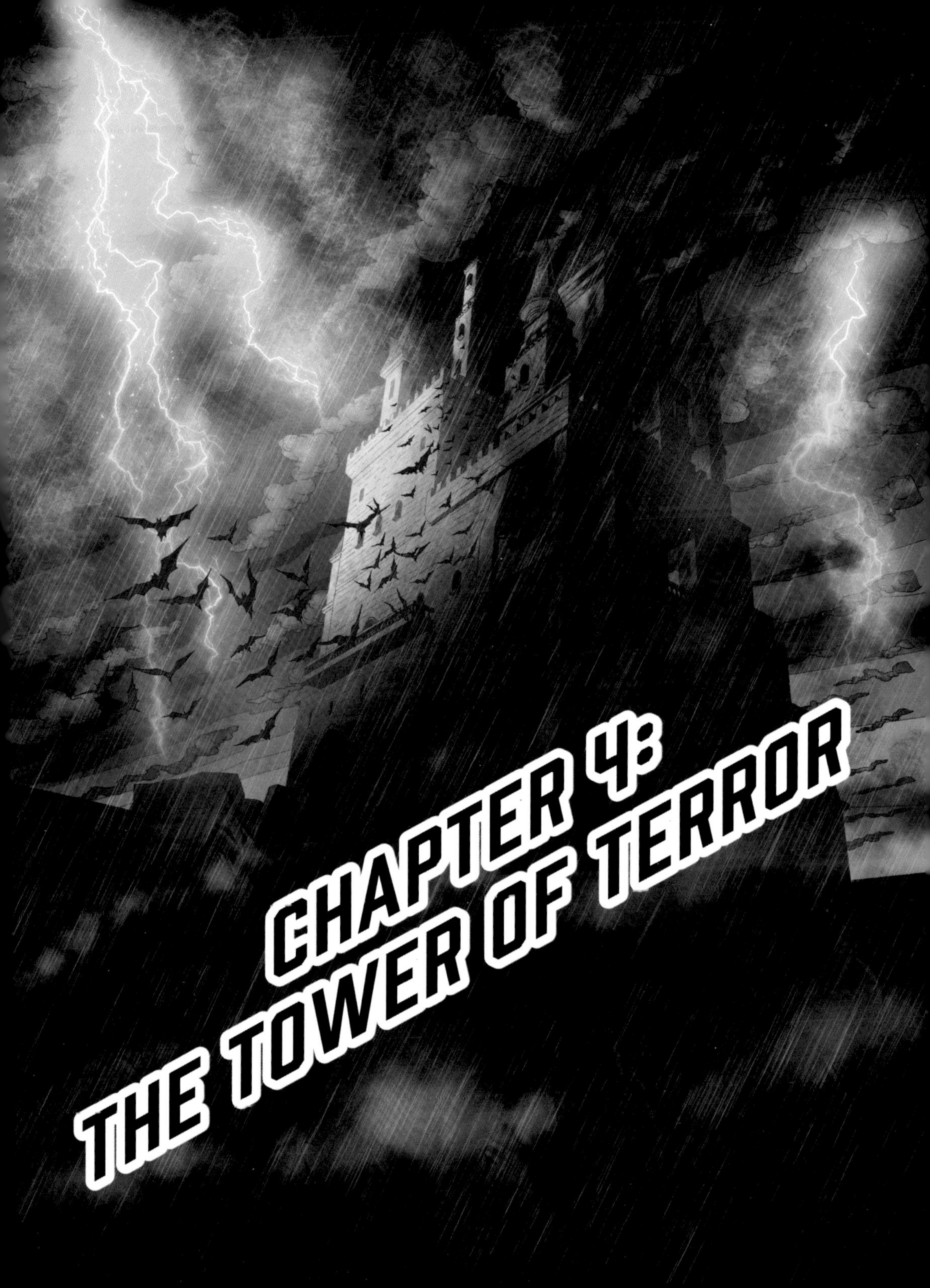
CHAPTER 4:
THE TOWER OF TERROR

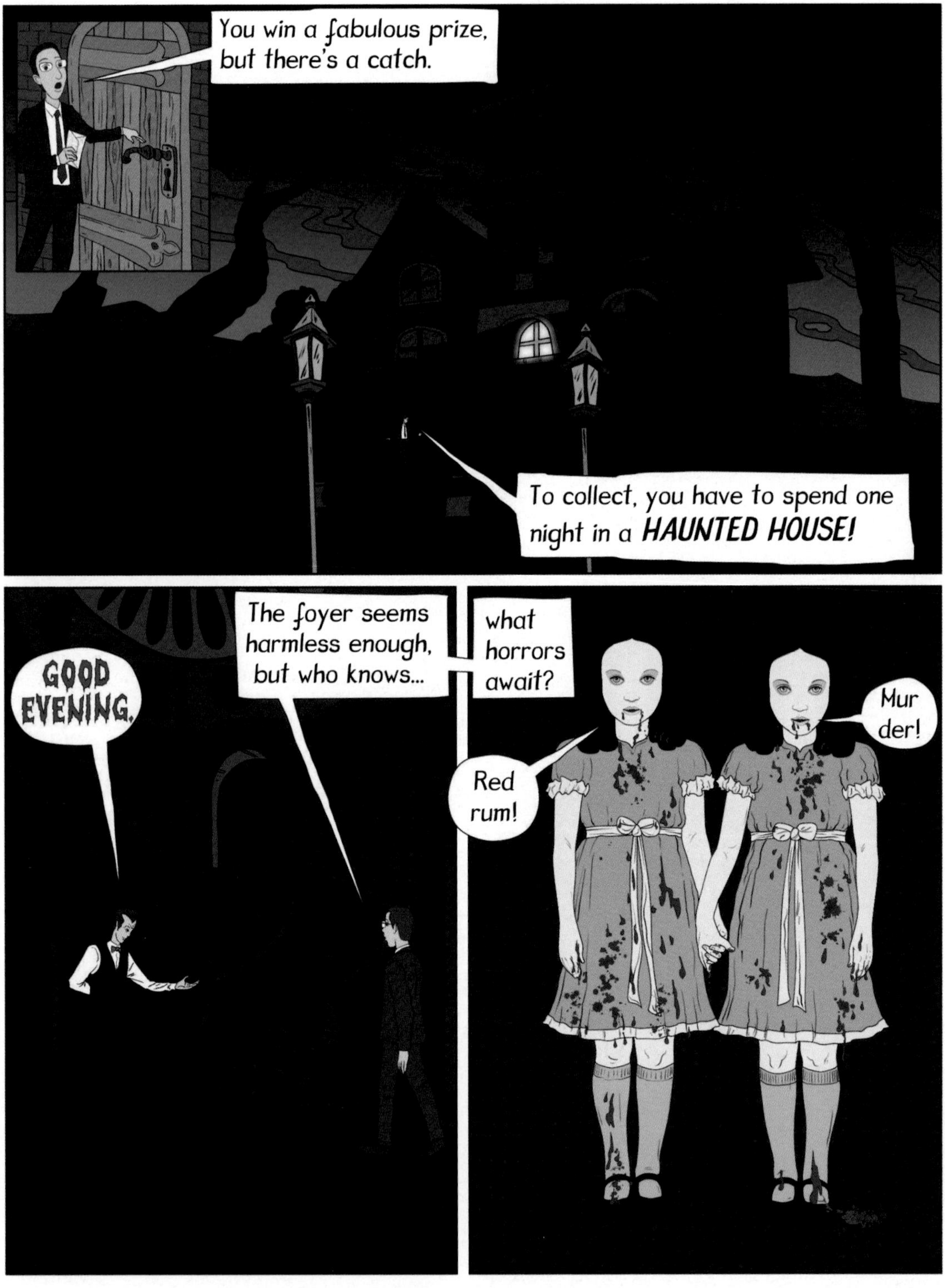
You win a fabulous prize, but there's a catch.
To collect, you have to spend one night in a HAUNTED HOUSE!
GOOD EVENING.
The foyer seems harmless enough, but who knows...
what horrors await?
Red rum!
Mur der!

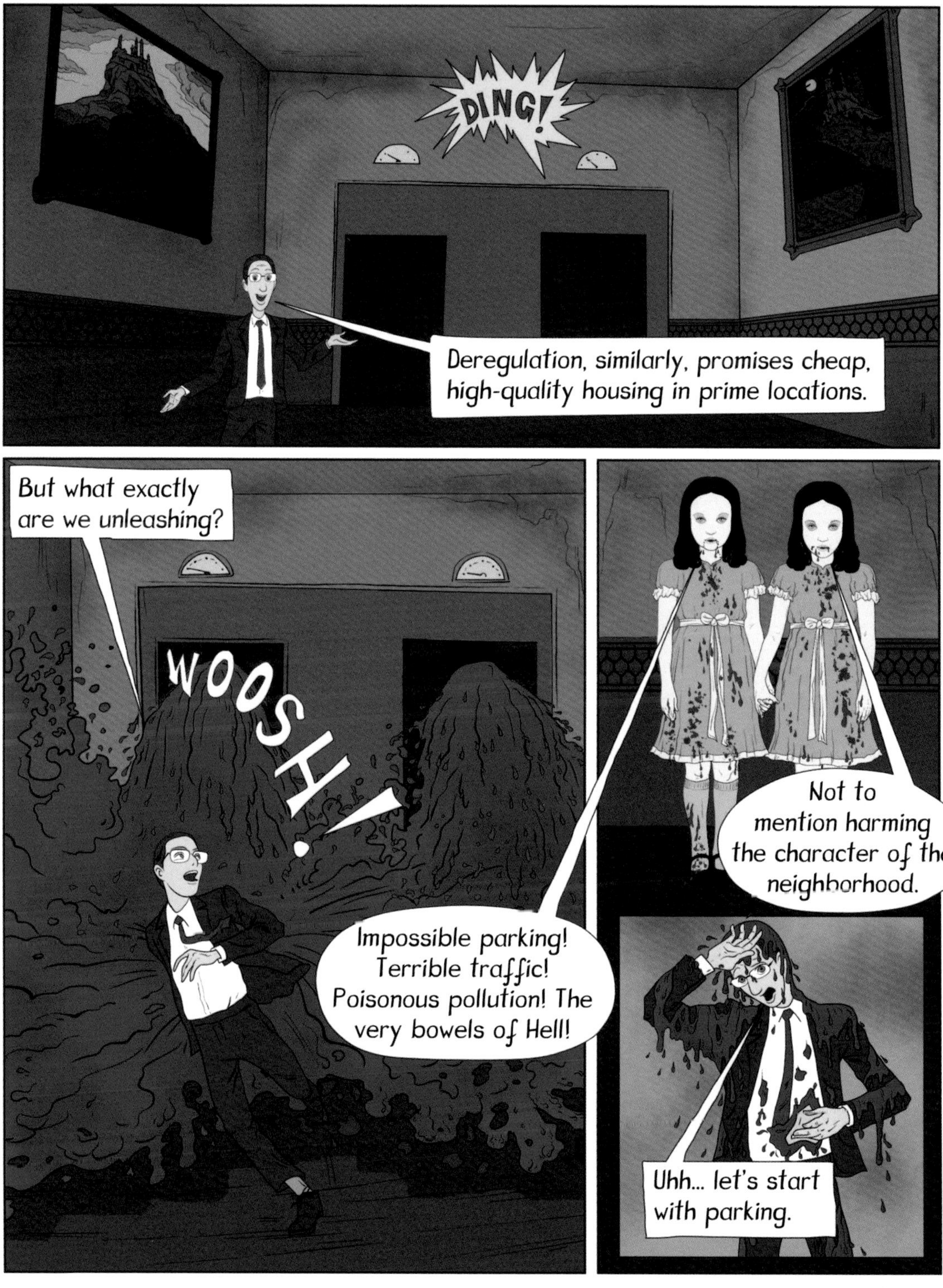
DING!
Deregulation, similarly, promises cheap, high-quality housing in prime locations.
But what exactly are we unleashing?
WOOSH!
Impossible parking! Terrible traffic! Poisonous pollution! The very bowels of Hell!
Not to mention harming the character of the neighborhood.
Uhh... let's start with parking.

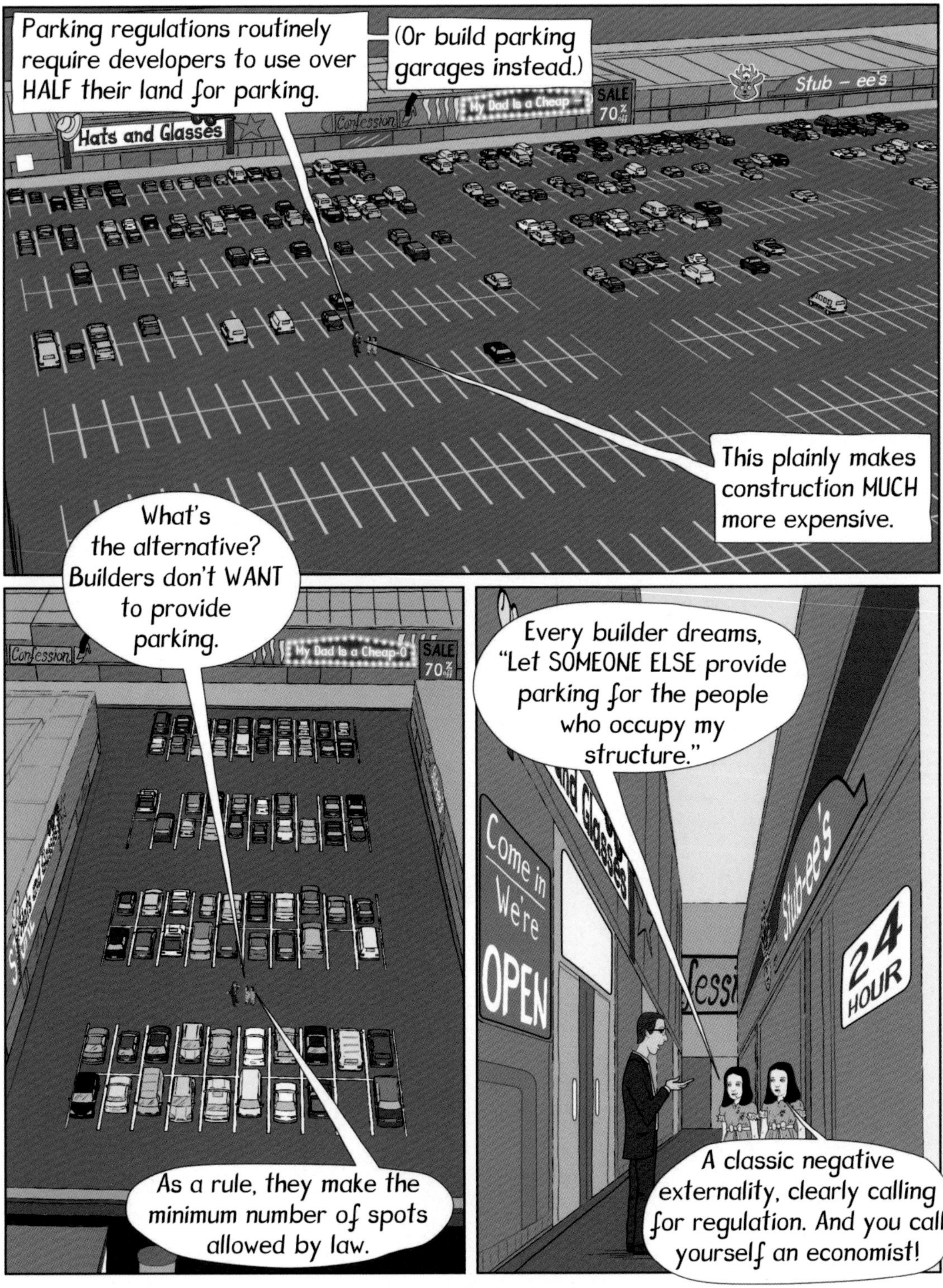
Parking regulations routinely require developers to use over HALF their land for parking.
(Or build parking garages instead.)
This plainly makes construction MUCH more expensive.
Hats and Glasses
Confession
My Dad Is a Cheap-O
SALE 70% off
Stub – ee's
What's the alternative? Builders don't WANT to provide parking.
As a rule, they make the minimum number of spots allowed by law.
Every builder dreams, "Let SOMEONE ELSE provide parking for the people who occupy my structure."
Come in We're OPEN
24 HOUR
A classic negative externality, clearly calling for regulation. And you call yourself an economist!

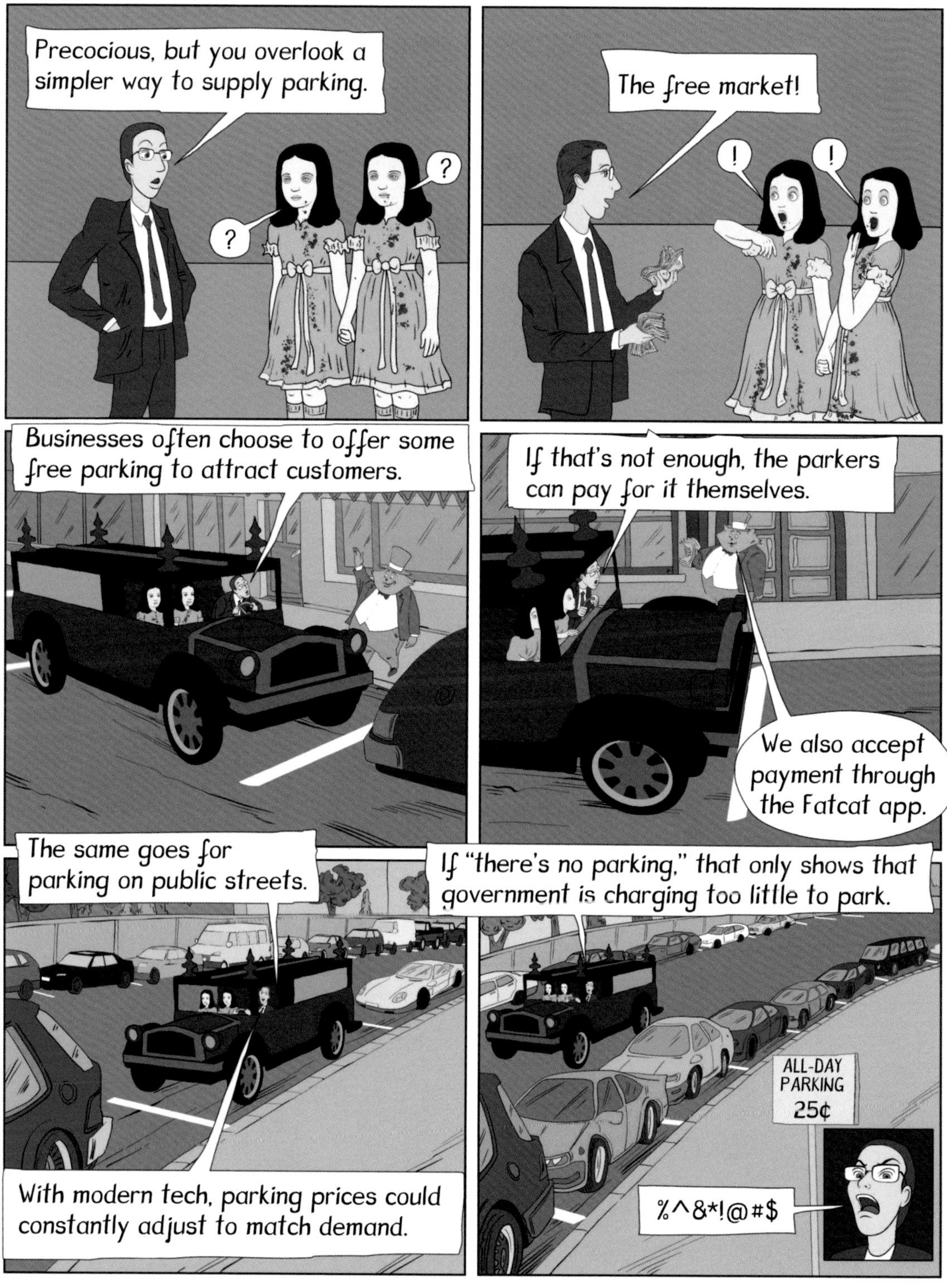
Precocious, but you overlook a simpler way to supply parking.
?
?
The free market!
!
!
Businesses often choose to offer some free parking to attract customers.
If that's not enough, the parkers can pay for it themselves.
We also accept payment through the Fatcat app.
The same goes for parking on public streets.
With modern tech, parking prices could constantly adjust to match demand.
If "there's no parking," that only shows that government is charging too little to park.
ALL-DAY PARKING 25¢
%^&*!@#$

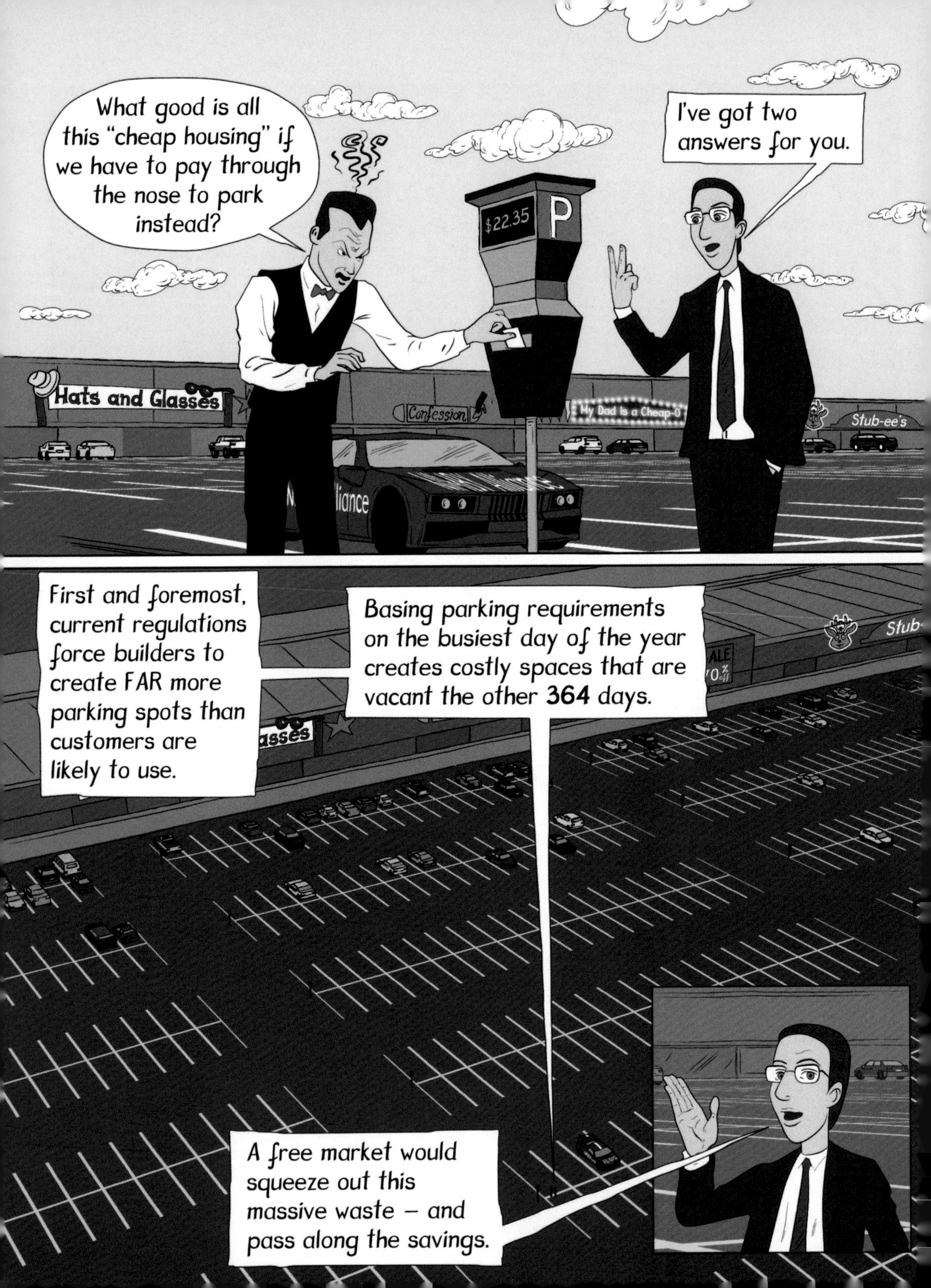
What good is all this "cheap housing" if we have to pay through the nose to park instead?
$22.35
P
I've got two answers for you.
Hats and Glasses
Confession
My Dad Is a Cheap-O
Stub-ee's
First and foremost, current regulations force builders to create FAR more parking spots than customers are likely to use.
Basing parking requirements on the busiest day of the year creates costly spaces that are vacant the other **364** days.
A free market would squeeze out this massive waste — and pass along the savings.

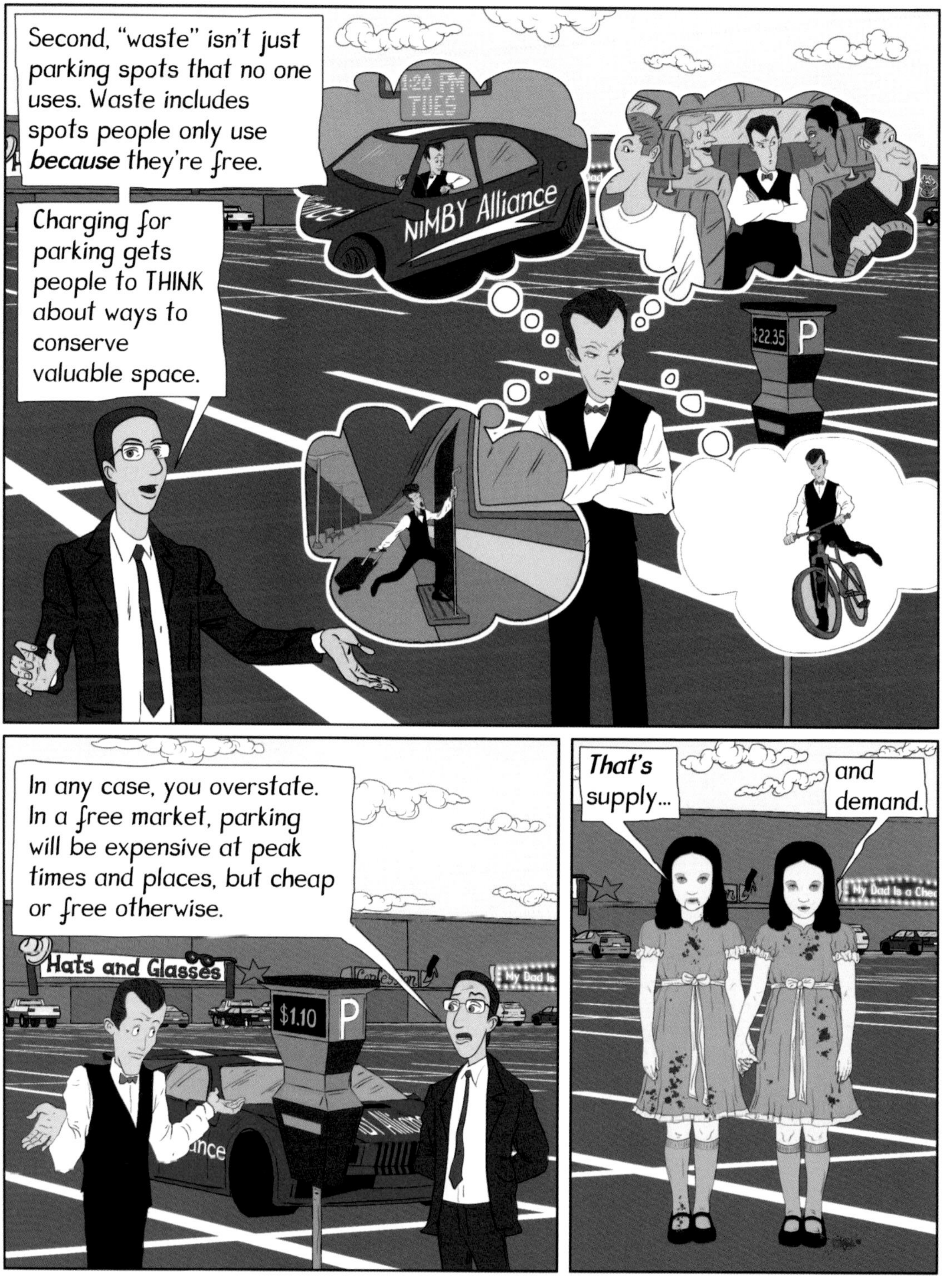
Second, "waste" isn't just parking spots that no one uses. Waste includes spots people only use *because* they're free.
1:20 PM TUES
NIMBY Alliance
Charging for parking gets people to THINK about ways to conserve valuable space.
$22.35 P
In any case, you overstate. In a free market, parking will be expensive at peak times and places, but cheap or free otherwise.
Hats and Glasses
$1.10 P
That's supply...
and demand.
My Dad Is a Che

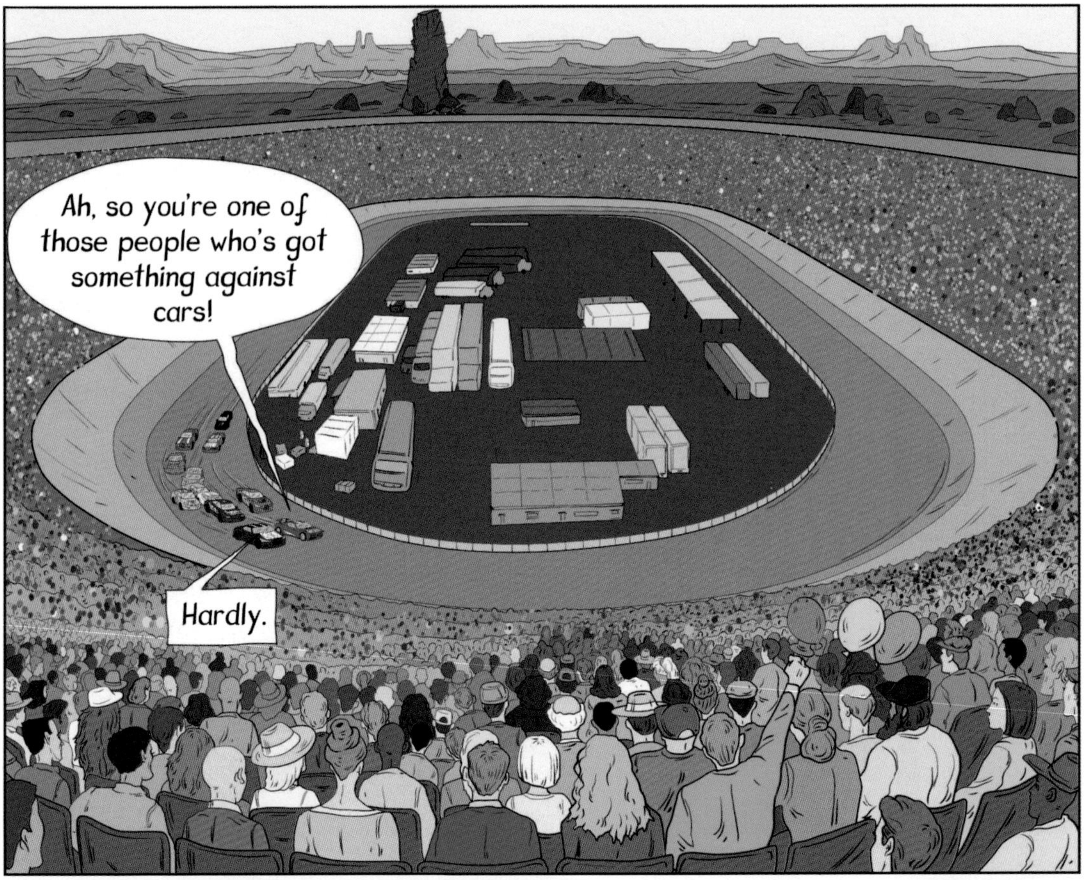
Ah, so you're one of those people who's got something against cars!
Hardly.

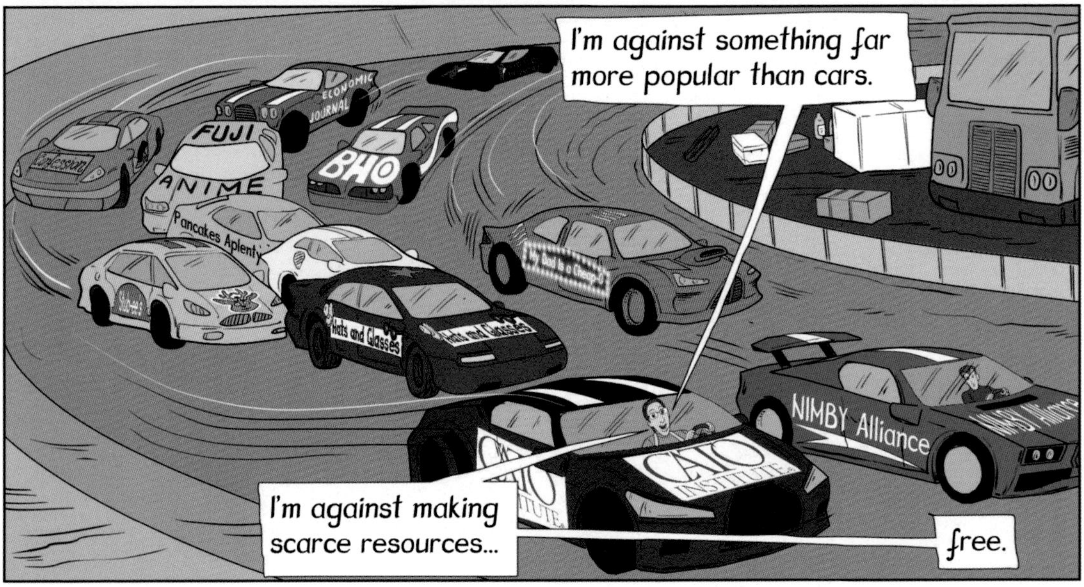
I'm against something far more popular than cars.
I'm against making scarce resources...
free.
ECONOMIC JOURNAL
FUJI
ANIME
BHO
Pancakes Aplenty
Hats and Glasses
CATO INSTITUTE
NIMBY Alliance

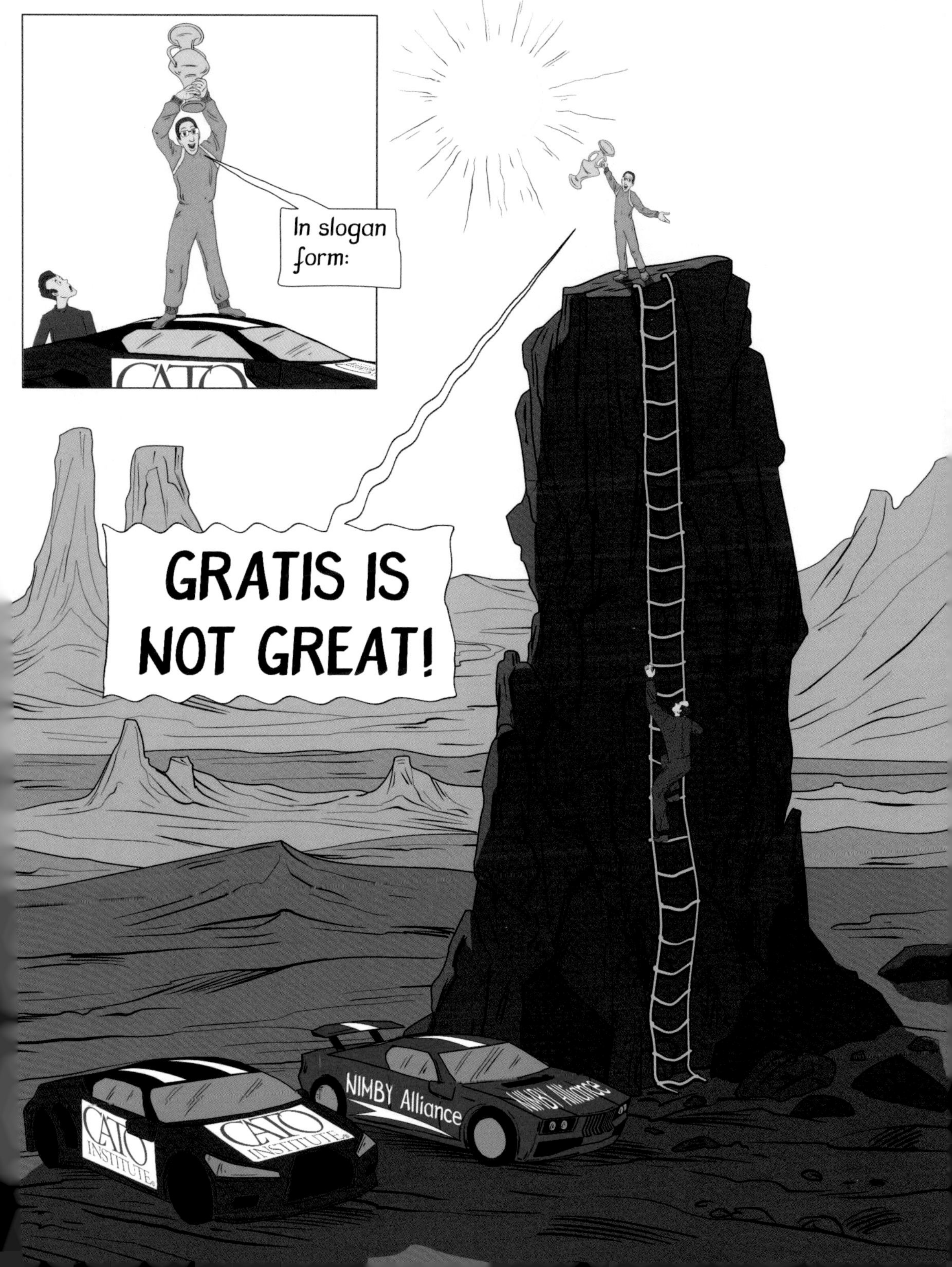
In slogan form:
CATO
GRATIS IS NOT GREAT!
CATO INSTITUTE
CATO INSTITUTE
NIMBY Alliance
NIMBY Alliance

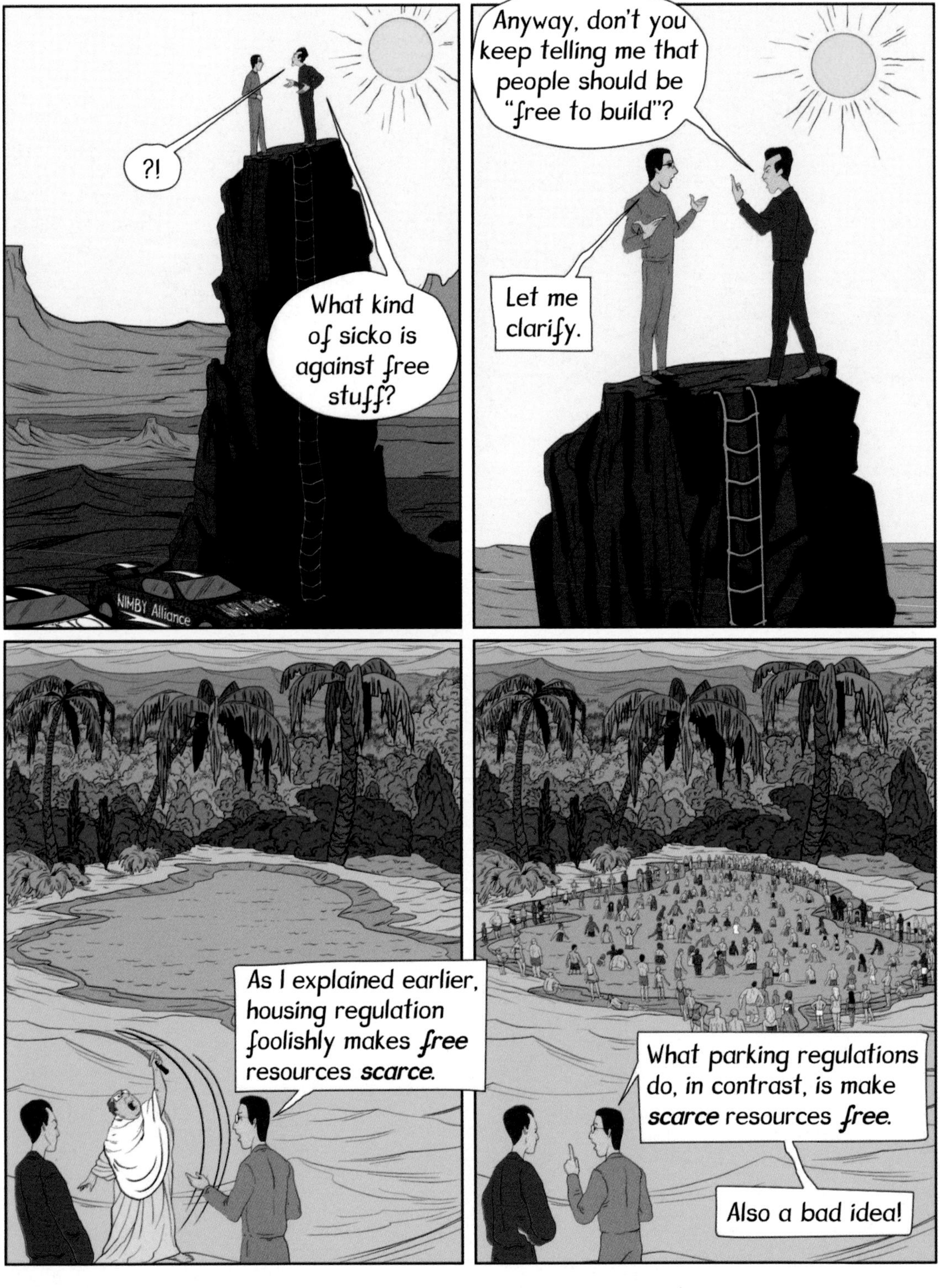
?!
What kind of sicko is against free stuff?
NIMBY Alliance
Anyway, don't you keep telling me that people should be "free to build"?
Let me clarify.
As I explained earlier, housing regulation foolishly makes *free* resources *scarce*.
What parking regulations do, in contrast, is make *scarce* resources *free*.
Also a bad idea!

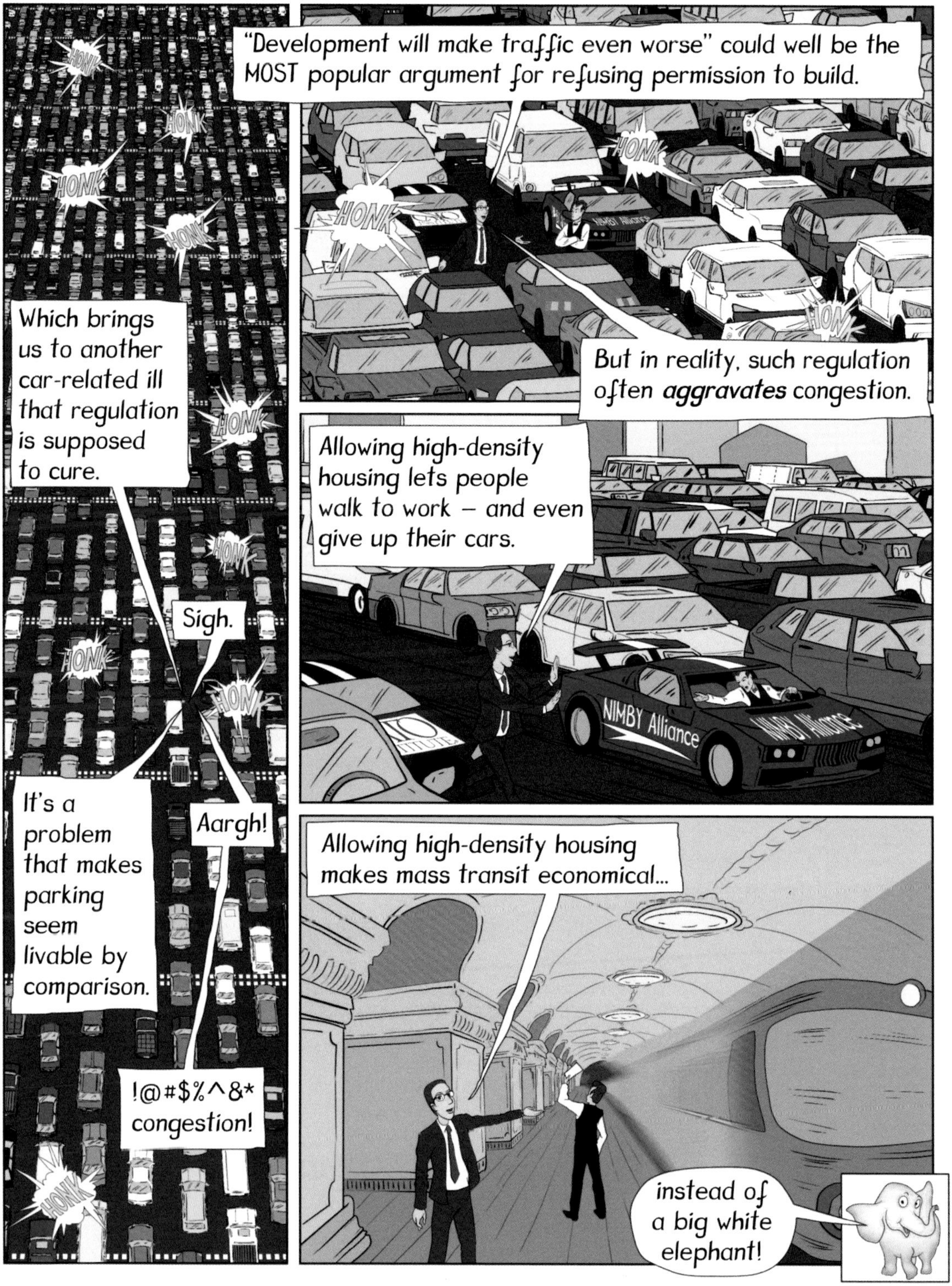
Which brings us to another car-related ill that regulation is supposed to cure.
Sigh.
Aargh!
It's a problem that makes parking seem livable by comparison.
!@#$%^&* congestion!
HONK
"Development will make traffic even worse" could well be the MOST popular argument for refusing permission to build.
But in reality, such regulation often ***aggravates*** congestion.
Allowing high-density housing lets people walk to work – and even give up their cars.
NIMBY Alliance
Allowing high-density housing makes mass transit economical...
instead of a big white elephant!

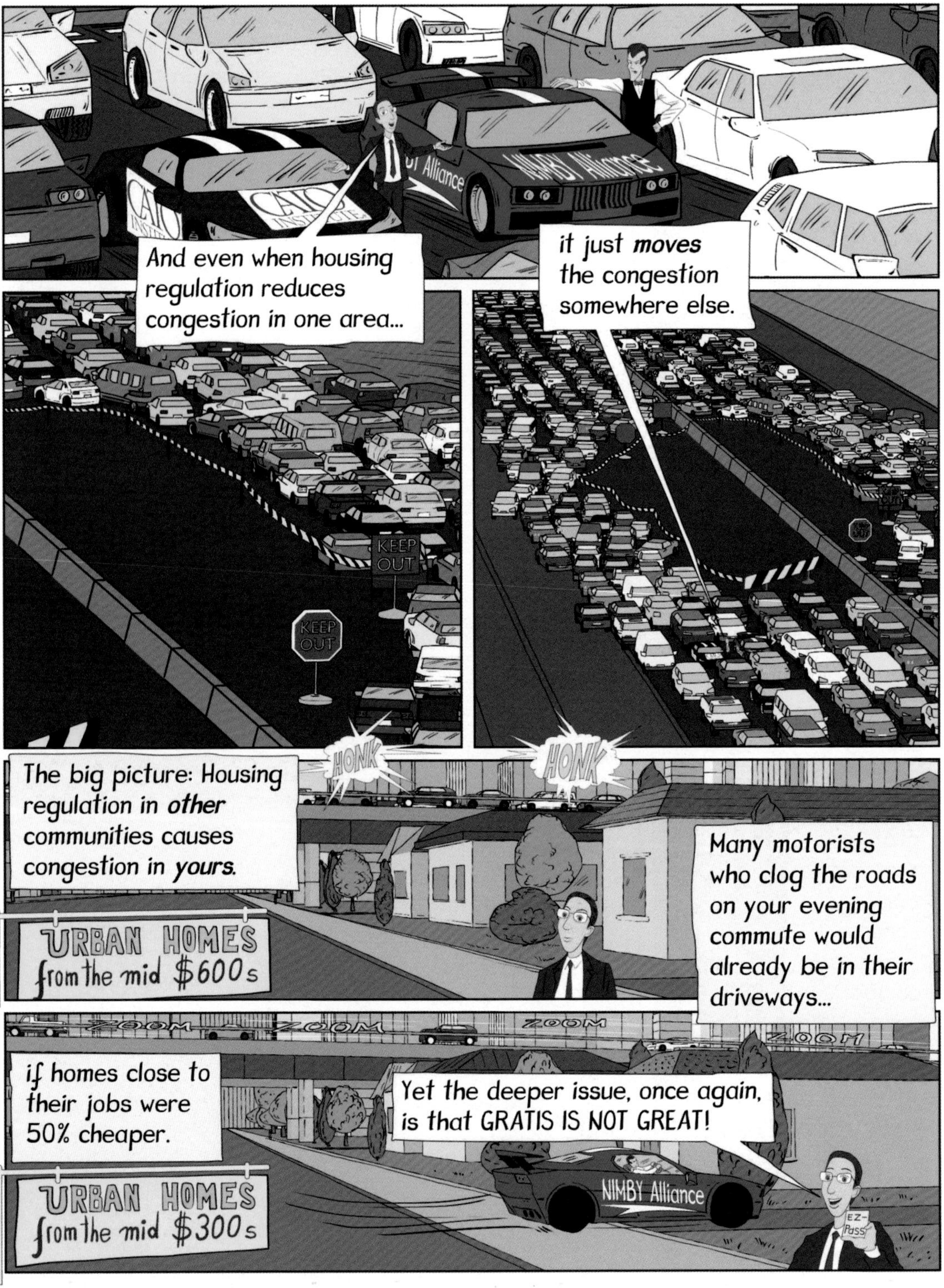
CATO INSTITUTE
NIMBY Alliance
And even when housing regulation reduces congestion in one area...
it just *moves* the congestion somewhere else.
KEEP OUT
KEEP OUT
HONK
HONK
The big picture: Housing regulation in *other* communities causes congestion in *yours*.
URBAN HOMES from the mid $600s
Many motorists who clog the roads on your evening commute would already be in their driveways...
ZOOM
ZOOM
ZOOM
ZOOM
if homes close to their jobs were 50% cheaper.
Yet the deeper issue, once again, is that GRATIS IS NOT GREAT!
NIMBY Alliance
URBAN HOMES from the mid $300s
EZ-Pass

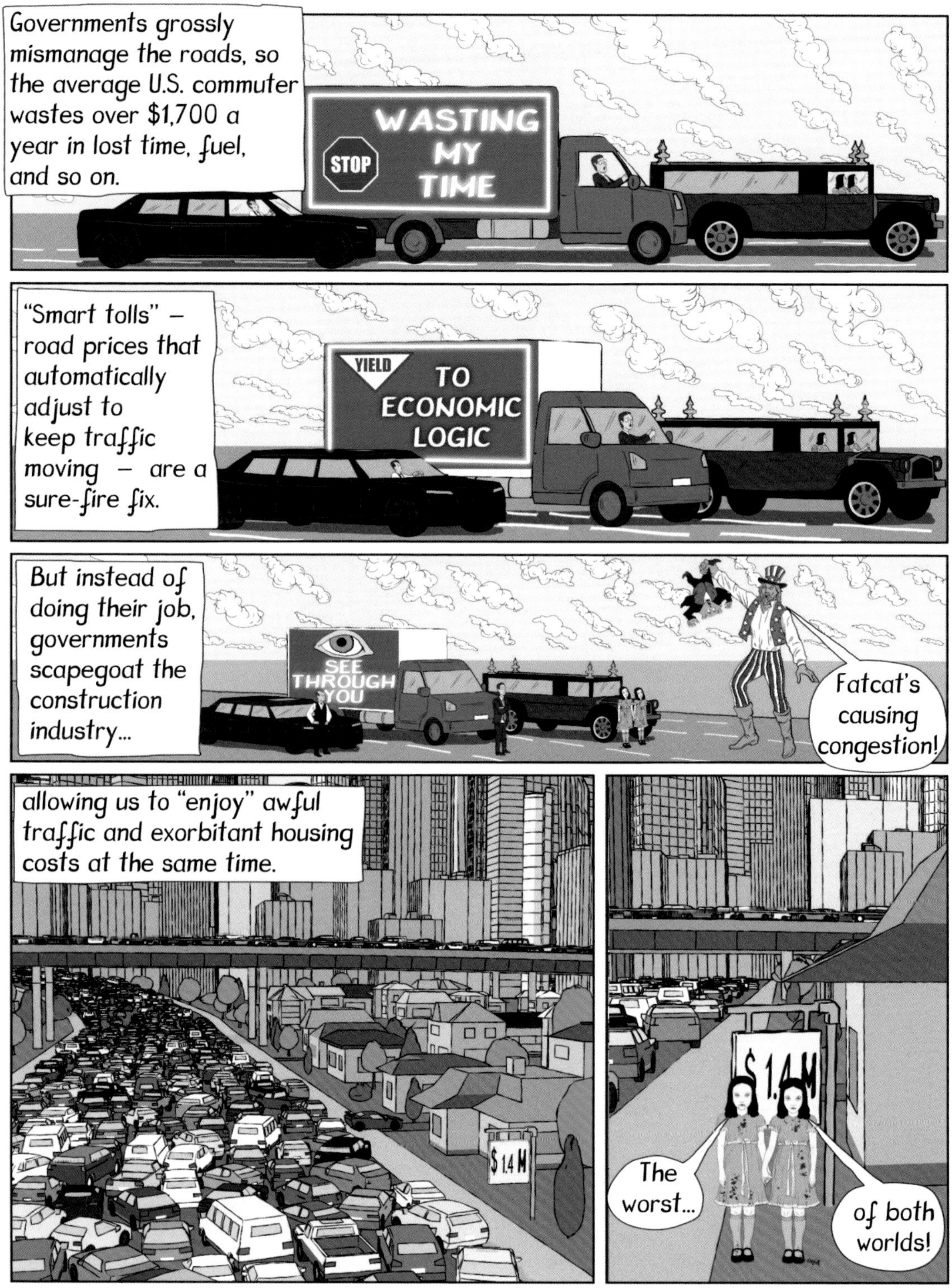
Governments grossly mismanage the roads, so the average U.S. commuter wastes over $1,700 a year in lost time, fuel, and so on.
STOP
WASTING MY TIME
"Smart tolls" – road prices that automatically adjust to keep traffic moving – are a sure-fire fix.
YIELD
TO ECONOMIC LOGIC
But instead of doing their job, governments scapegoat the construction industry...
SEE THROUGH YOU
Fatcat's causing congestion!
allowing us to "enjoy" awful traffic and exorbitant housing costs at the same time.
$1.4M
$1.4M
The worst...
of both worlds!

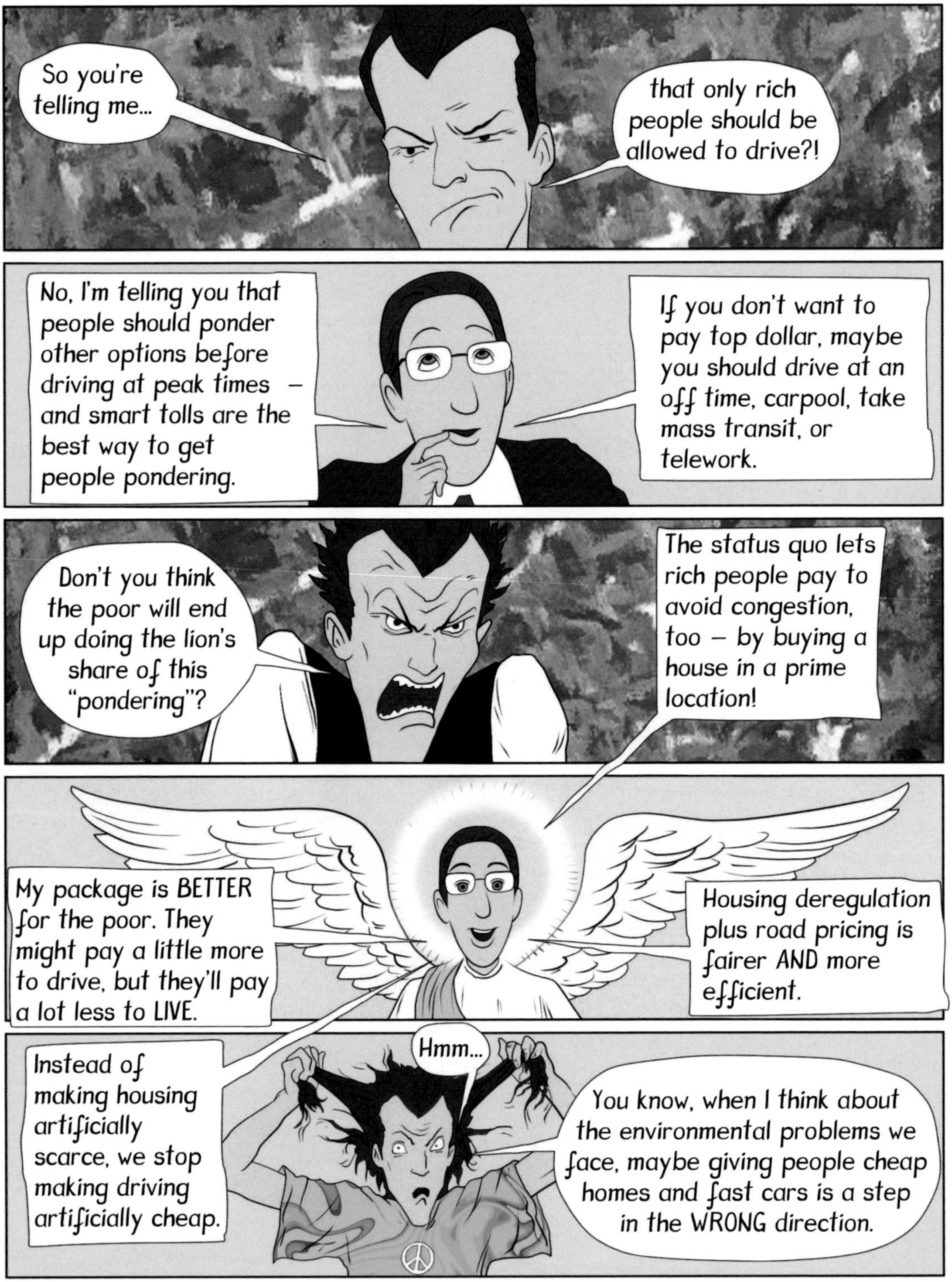
So you're telling me...
that only rich people should be allowed to drive?!
No, I'm telling you that people should ponder other options before driving at peak times – and smart tolls are the best way to get people pondering.
If you don't want to pay top dollar, maybe you should drive at an off time, carpool, take mass transit, or telework.
Don't you think the poor will end up doing the lion's share of this "pondering"?
The status quo lets rich people pay to avoid congestion, too – by buying a house in a prime location!
My package is BETTER for the poor. They might pay a little more to drive, but they'll pay a lot less to LIVE.
Housing deregulation plus road pricing is fairer AND more efficient.
Instead of making housing artificially scarce, we stop making driving artificially cheap.
Hmm...
You know, when I think about the environmental problems we face, maybe giving people cheap homes and fast cars is a step in the WRONG direction.

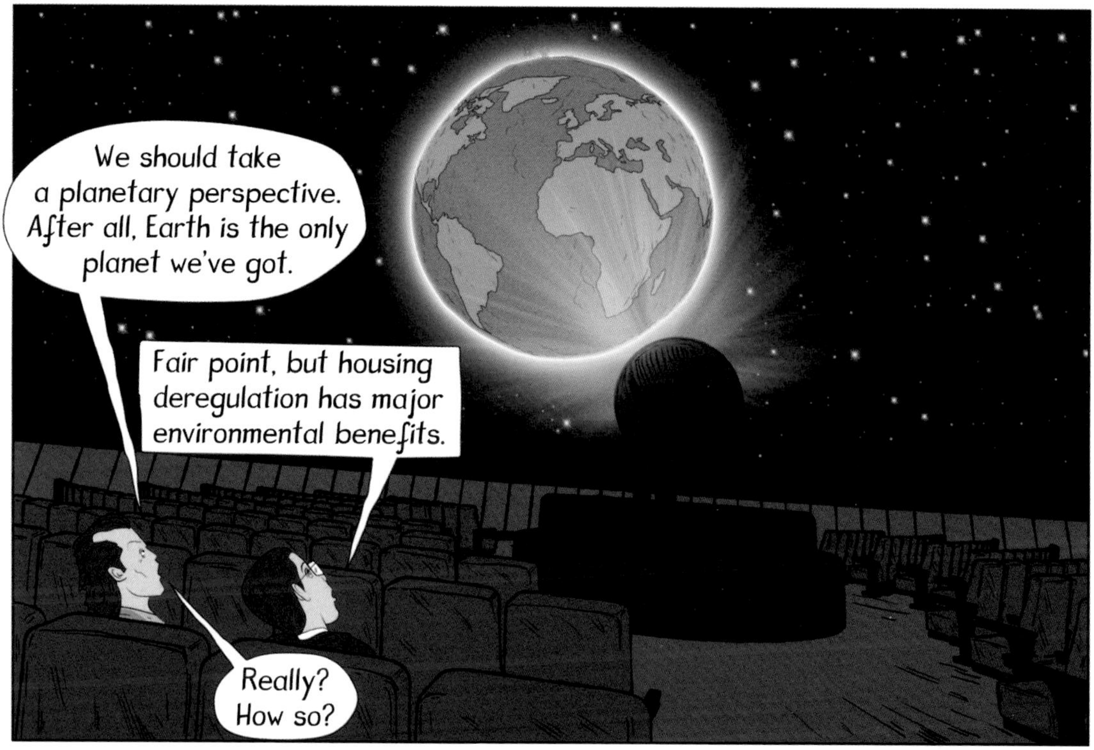
We should take a planetary perspective. After all, Earth is the only planet we've got.
Fair point, but housing deregulation has major environmental benefits.
Really? How so?

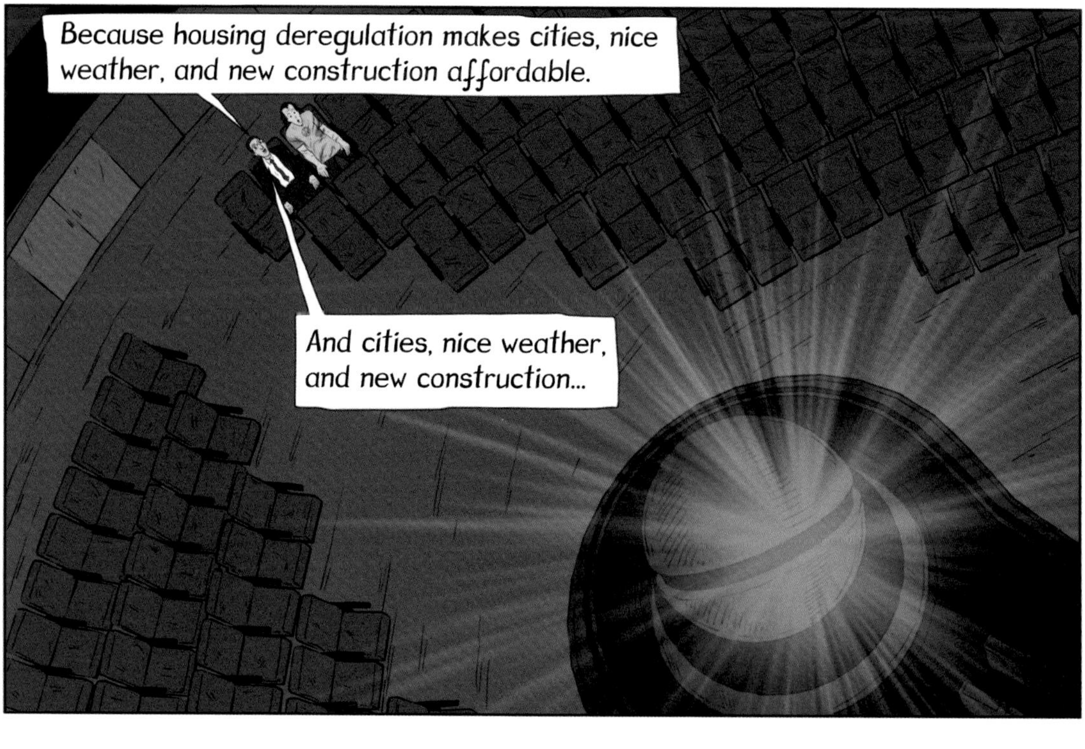
Because housing deregulation makes cities, nice weather, and new construction affordable.
And cities, nice weather, and new construction...

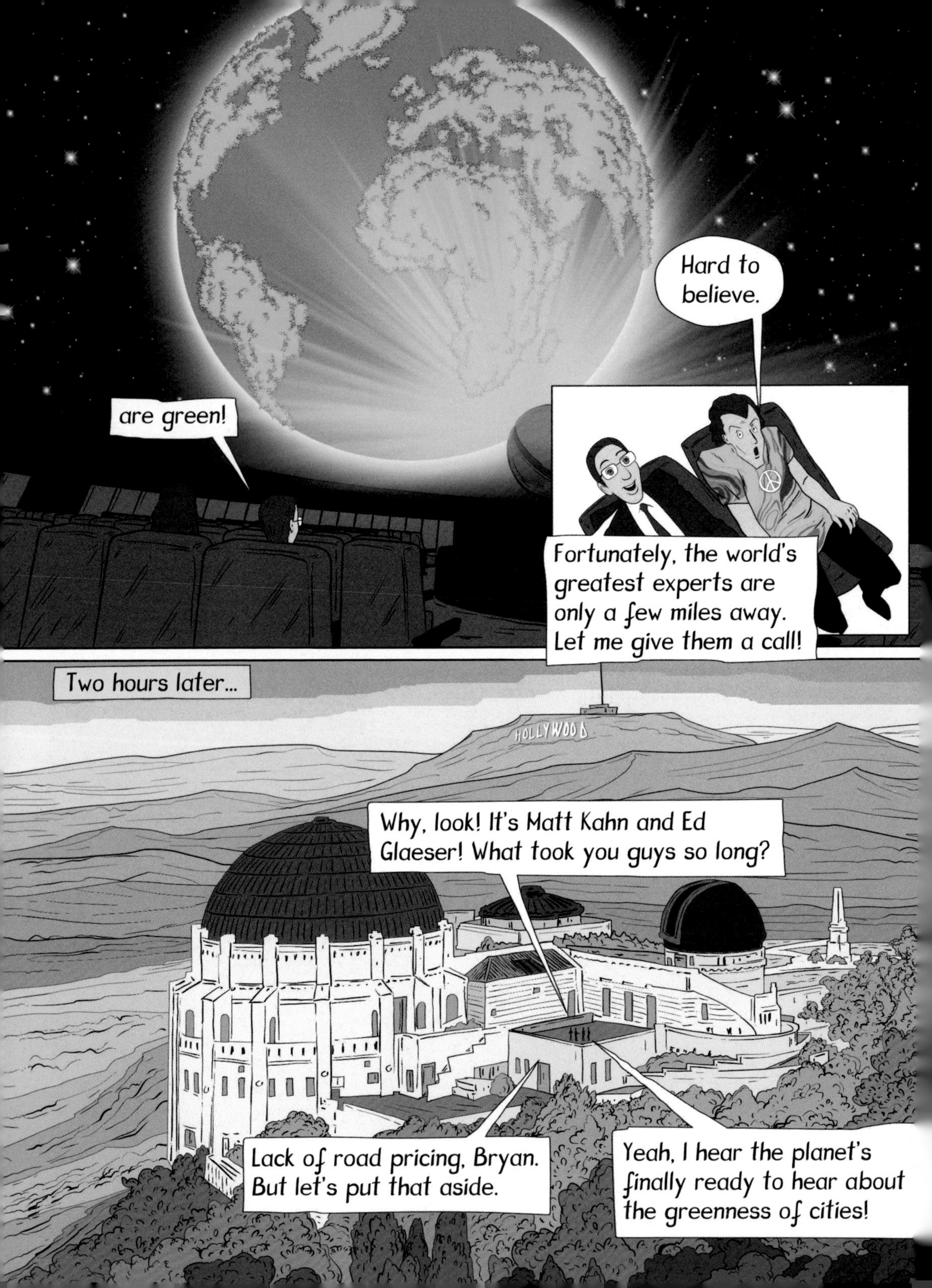
are green!
Hard to believe.
Fortunately, the world's greatest experts are only a few miles away. Let me give them a call!
Two hours later...
HOLLYWOOD
Why, look! It's Matt Kahn and Ed Glaeser! What took you guys so long?
Lack of road pricing, Bryan. But let's put that aside.
Yeah, I hear the planet's finally ready to hear about the greenness of cities!

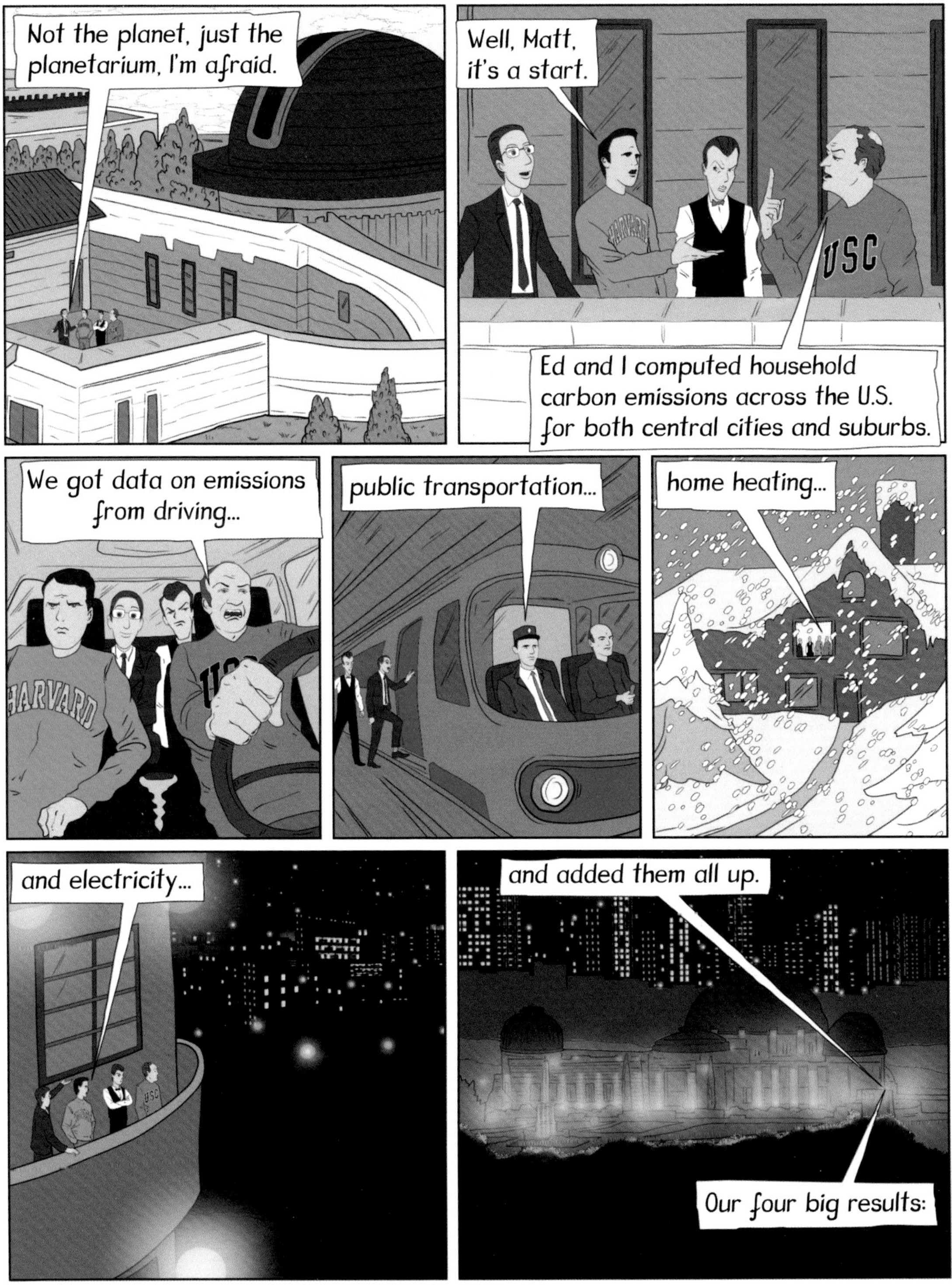
Not the planet, just the planetarium, I'm afraid.
Well, Matt, it's a start.
USC
Ed and I computed household carbon emissions across the U.S. for both central cities and suburbs.
We got data on emissions from driving...
HARVARD
public transportation...
home heating...
and electricity...
and added them all up.
Our four big results:

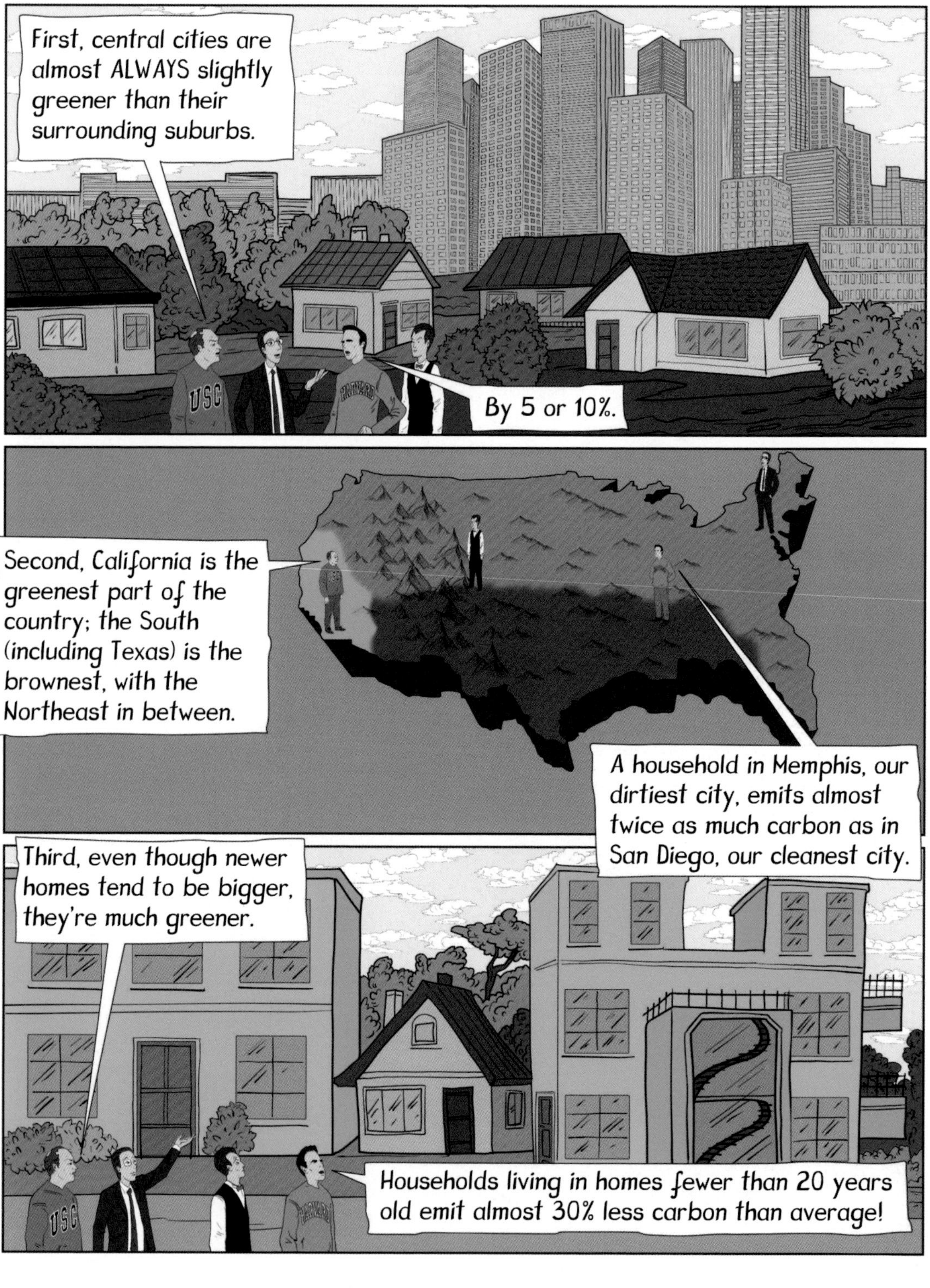
First, central cities are almost ALWAYS slightly greener than their surrounding suburbs.
By 5 or 10%.
Second, California is the greenest part of the country; the South (including Texas) is the brownest, with the Northeast in between.
A household in Memphis, our dirtiest city, emits almost twice as much carbon as in San Diego, our cleanest city.
Third, even though newer homes tend to be bigger, they're much greener.
Households living in homes fewer than 20 years old emit almost 30% less carbon than average!

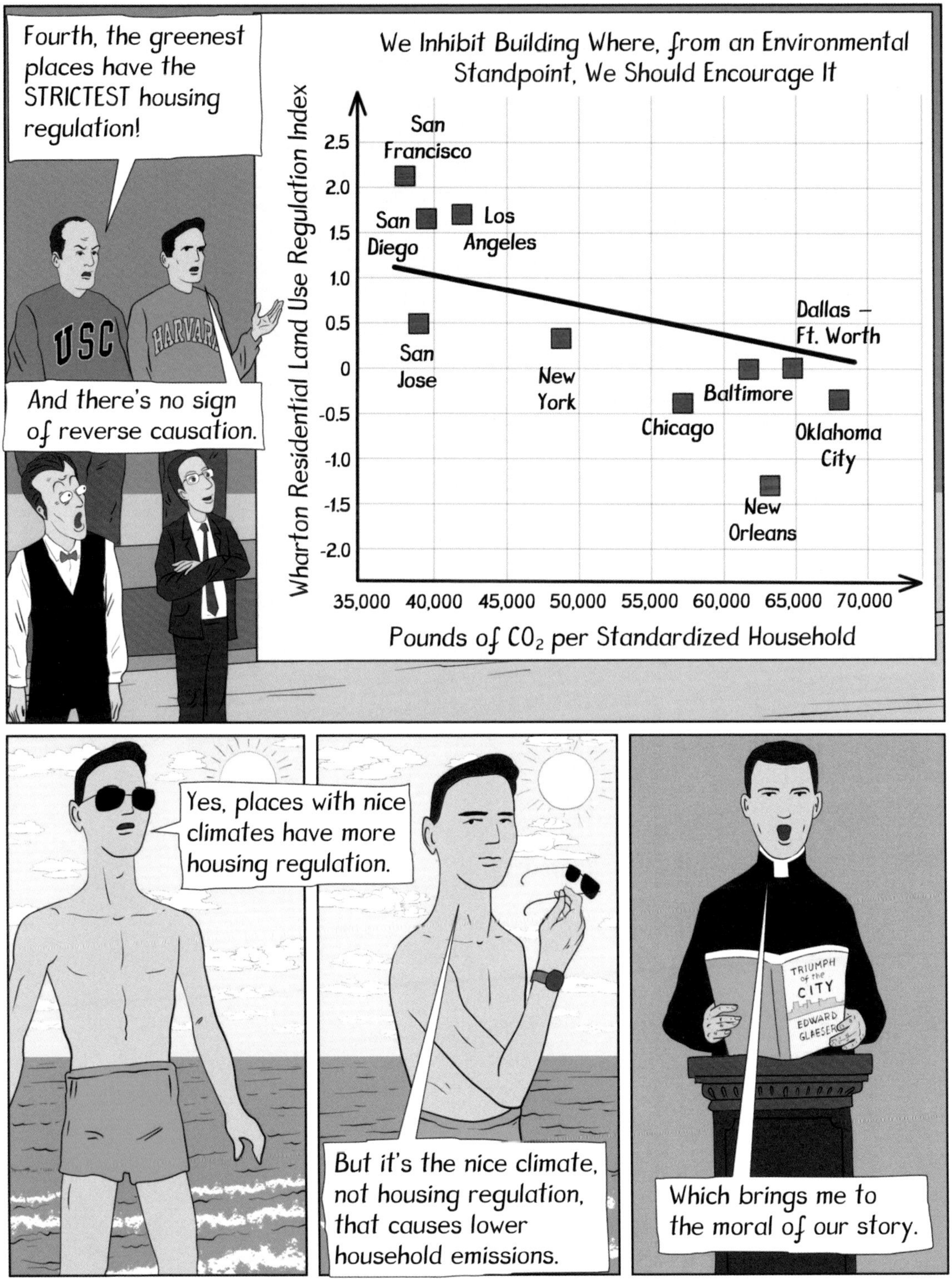
Fourth, the greenest places have the STRICTEST housing regulation!
And there's no sign of reverse causation.
We Inhibit Building Where, from an Environmental Standpoint, We Should Encourage It
Wharton Residential Land Use Regulation Index
2.5
2.0
1.5
1.0
0.5
0
-0.5
-1.0
-1.5
-2.0
San Francisco
San Diego
Los Angeles
San Jose
New York
Chicago
Baltimore
Dallas – Ft. Worth
Oklahoma City
New Orleans
35,000 40,000 45,000 50,000 55,000 60,000 65,000 70,000
Pounds of CO_2 per Standardized Household
USC
HARVARD
Yes, places with nice climates have more housing regulation.
But it's the nice climate, not housing regulation, that causes lower household emissions.
TRIUMPH of the CITY
EDWARD GLAESER
Which brings me to the moral of our story.

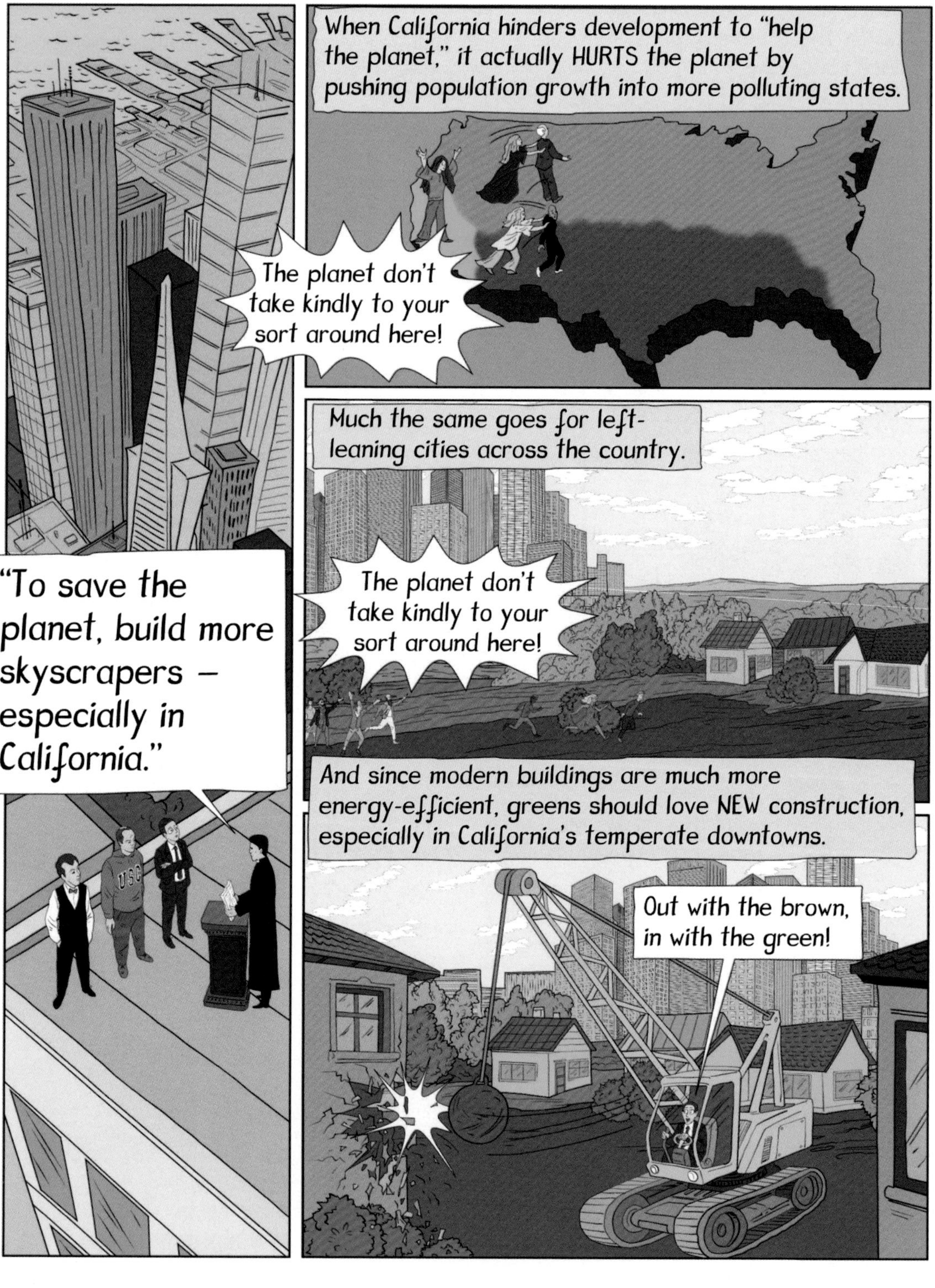
When California hinders development to "help the planet," it actually HURTS the planet by pushing population growth into more polluting states.
The planet don't take kindly to your sort around here!
Much the same goes for left-leaning cities across the country.
The planet don't take kindly to your sort around here!
"To save the planet, build more skyscrapers – especially in California."
USC
And since modern buildings are much more energy-efficient, greens should love NEW construction, especially in California's temperate downtowns.
Out with the brown, in with the green!

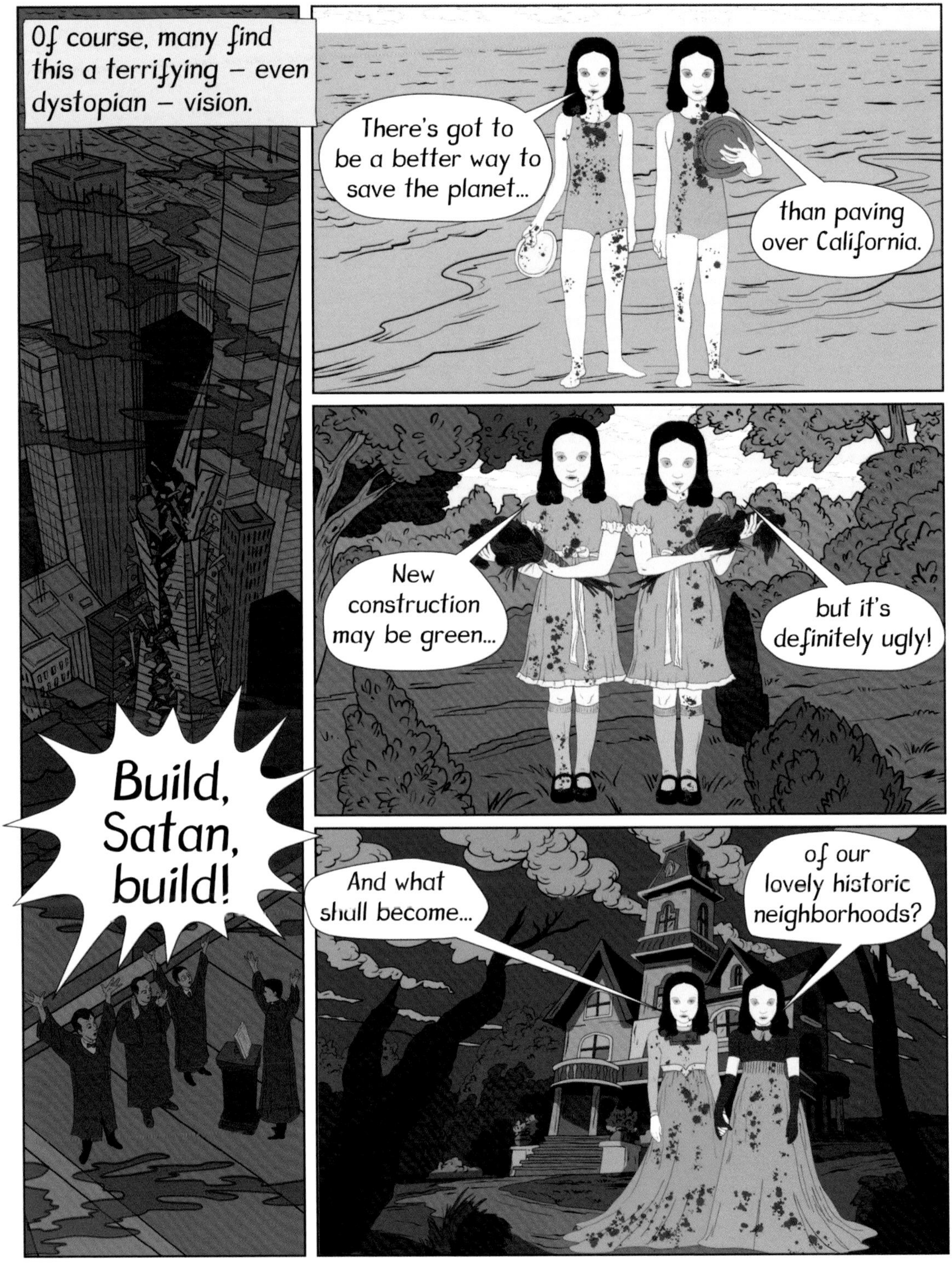
Of course, many find this a terrifying – even dystopian – vision.
Build, Satan, build!
There's got to be a better way to save the planet...
than paving over California.
New construction may be green...
but it's definitely ugly!
And what shall become...
of our lovely historic neighborhoods?

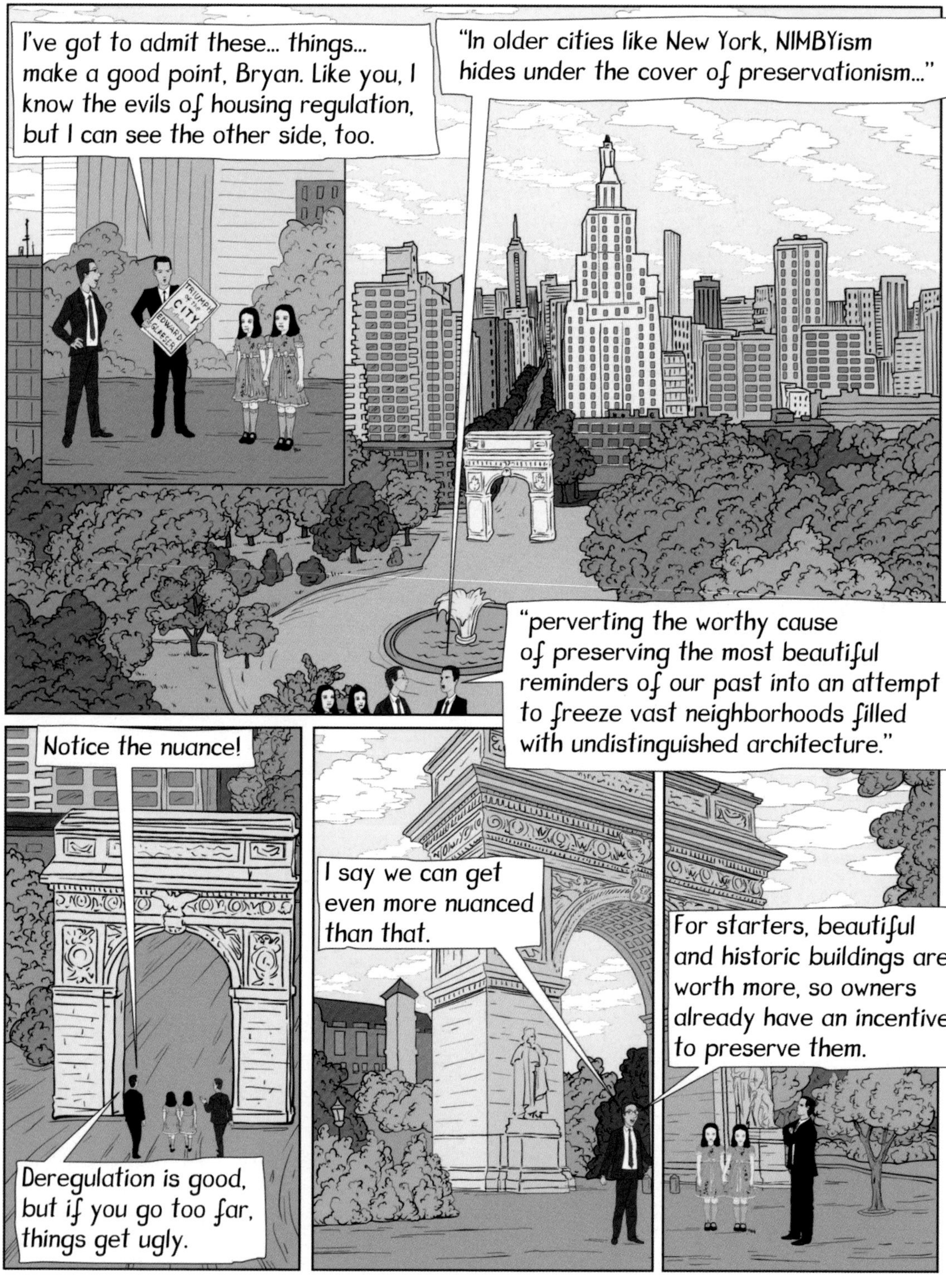
I've got to admit these... things... make a good point, Bryan. Like you, I know the evils of housing regulation, but I can see the other side, too.
TRIUMPH OF THE CITY EDWARD GLAESER
"In older cities like New York, NIMBYism hides under the cover of preservationism..."
"perverting the worthy cause of preserving the most beautiful reminders of our past into an attempt to freeze vast neighborhoods filled with undistinguished architecture."
Notice the nuance!
Deregulation is good, but if you go too far, things get ugly.
I say we can get even more nuanced than that.
For starters, beautiful and historic buildings are worth more, so owners already have an incentive to preserve them.

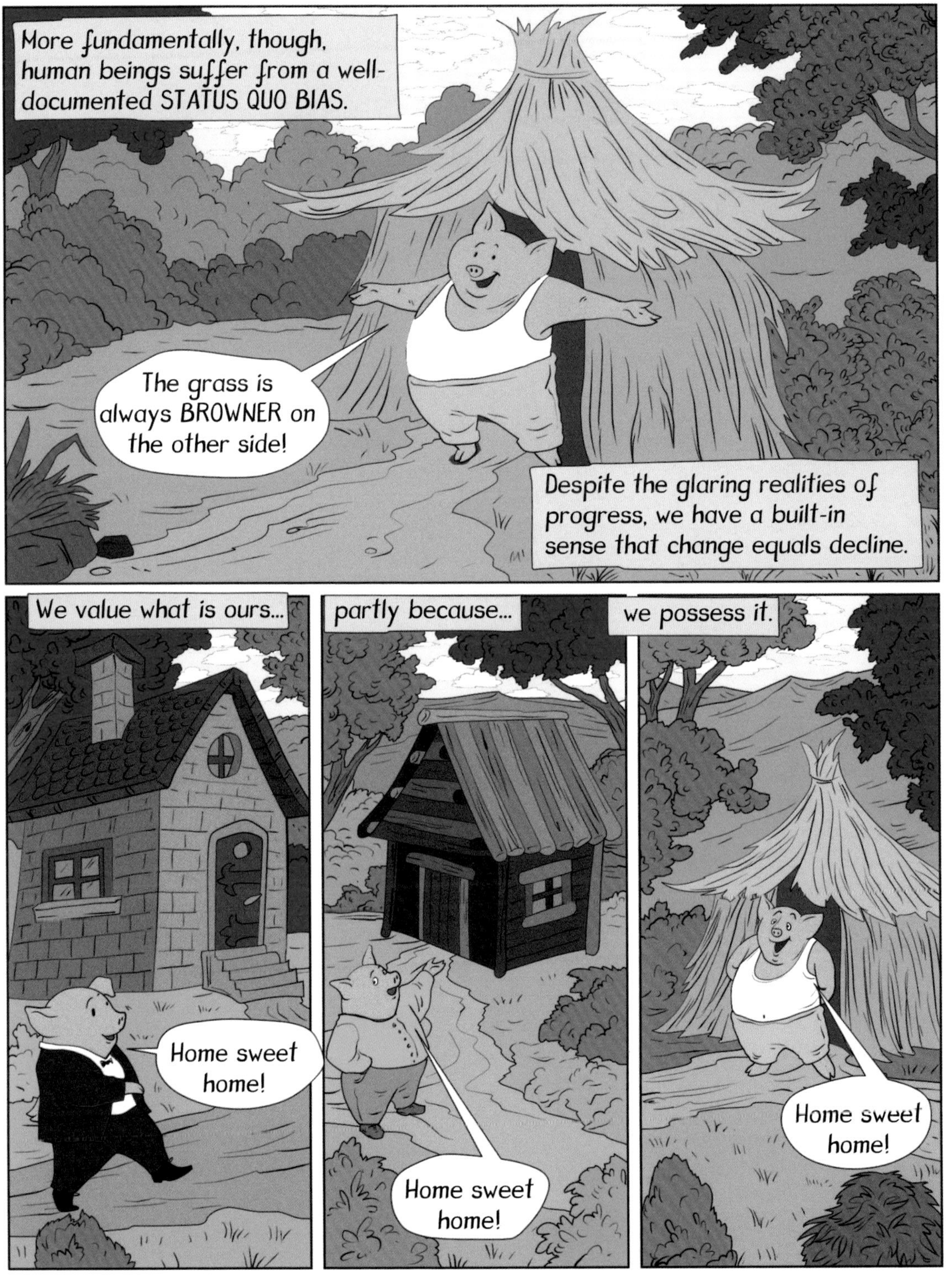
More fundamentally, though, human beings suffer from a well-documented STATUS QUO BIAS.
The grass is always BROWNER on the other side!
Despite the glaring realities of progress, we have a built-in sense that change equals decline.
We value what is ours...
Home sweet home!
partly because...
Home sweet home!
we possess it.
Home sweet home!

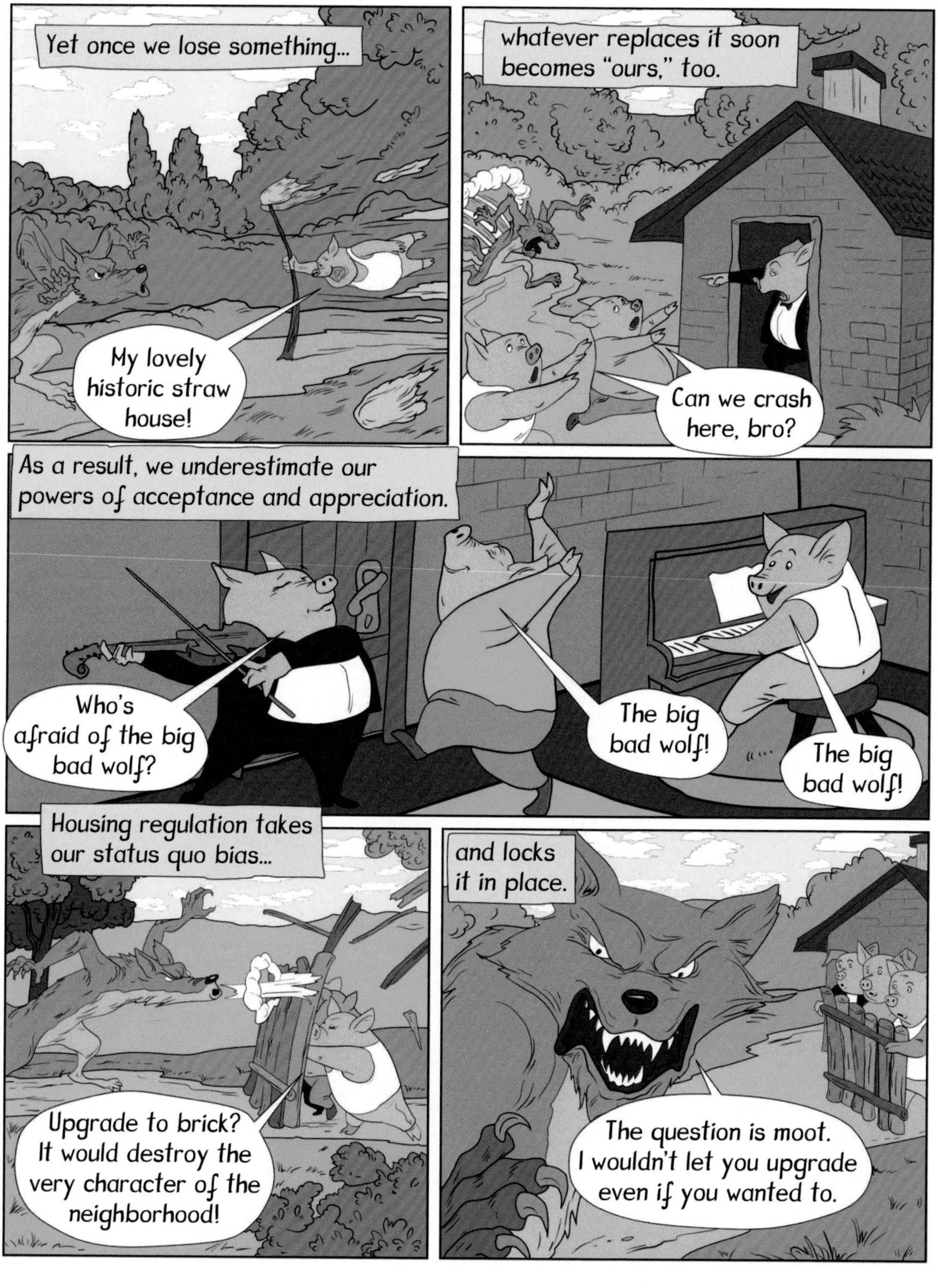
Yet once we lose something...
My lovely historic straw house!
whatever replaces it soon becomes "ours," too.
Can we crash here, bro?
As a result, we underestimate our powers of acceptance and appreciation.
Who's afraid of the big bad wolf?
The big bad wolf!
The big bad wolf!
Housing regulation takes our status quo bias...
Upgrade to brick? It would destroy the very character of the neighborhood!
and locks it in place.
The question is moot. I wouldn't let you upgrade even if you wanted to.

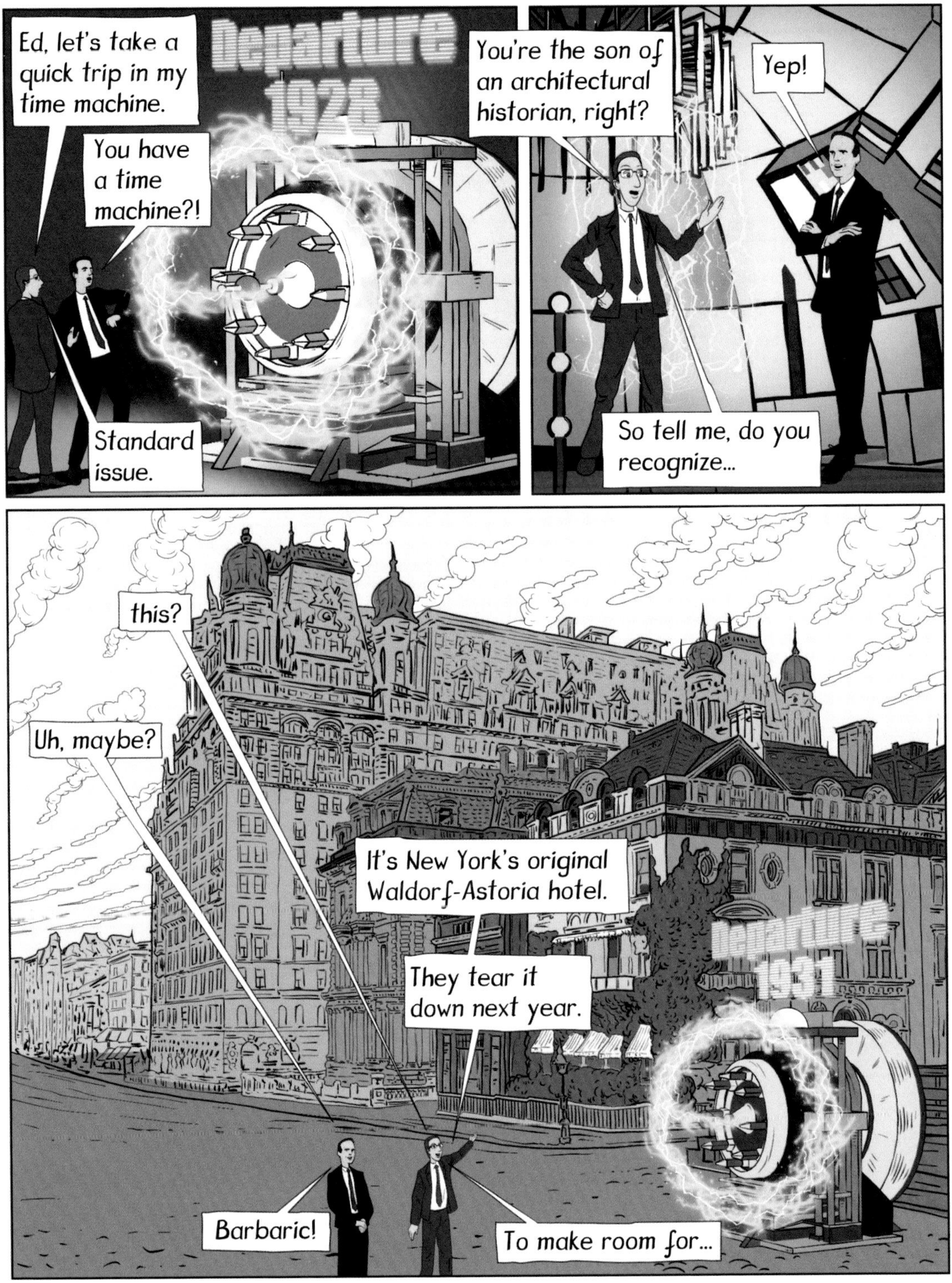
Departure
1928
Ed, let's take a quick trip in my time machine.
You have a time machine?!
Standard issue.
You're the son of an architectural historian, right?
Yep!
So tell me, do you recognize...
this?
Uh, maybe?
It's New York's original Waldorf-Astoria hotel.
They tear it down next year.
Departure
1931
Barbaric!
To make room for...

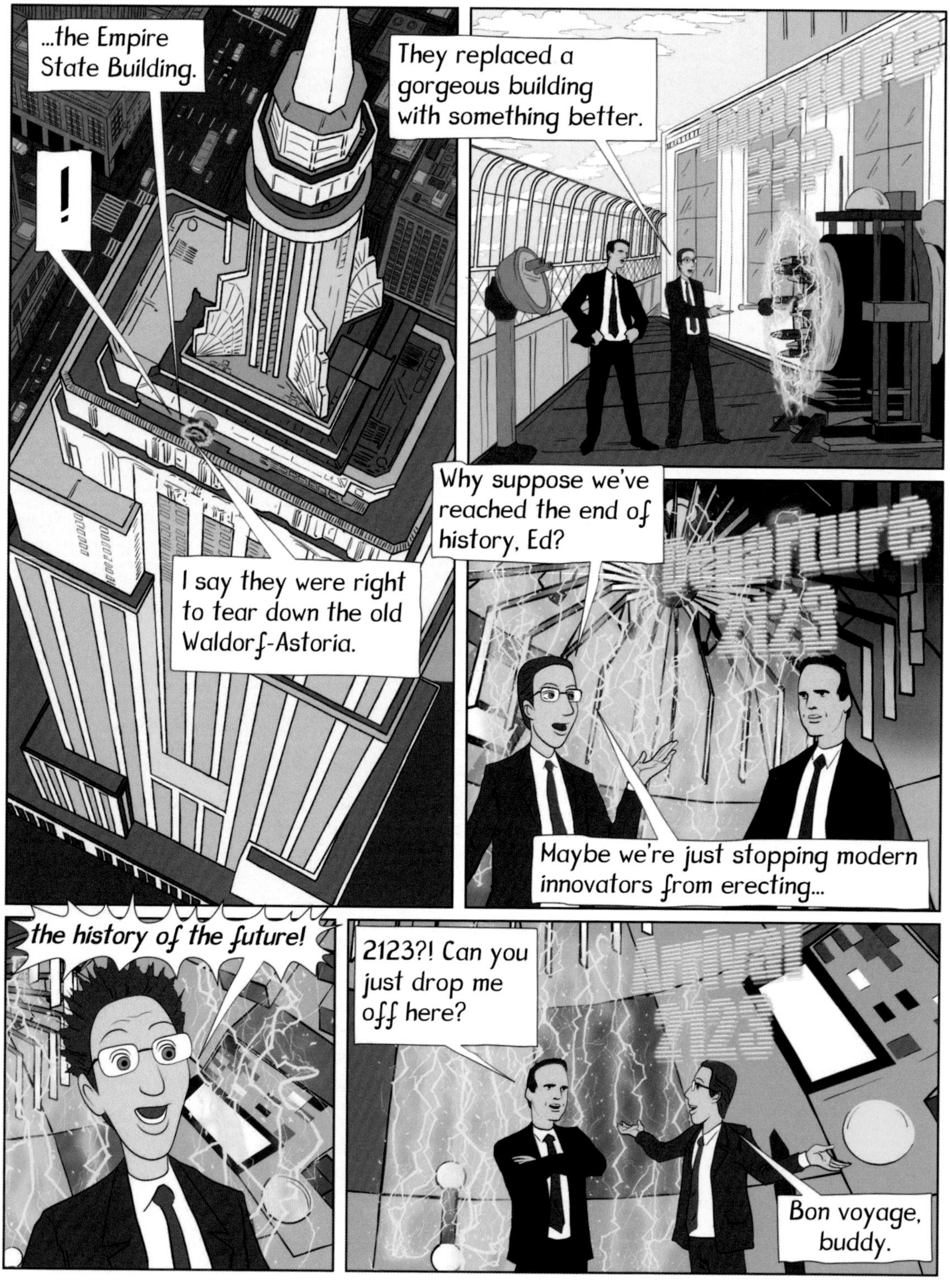
...the Empire State Building.
!
I say they were right to tear down the old Waldorf-Astoria.
They replaced a gorgeous building with something better.
Why suppose we've reached the end of history, Ed?
Maybe we're just stopping modern innovators from erecting...
the history of the future!
2123?! Can you just drop me off here?
Bon voyage, buddy.

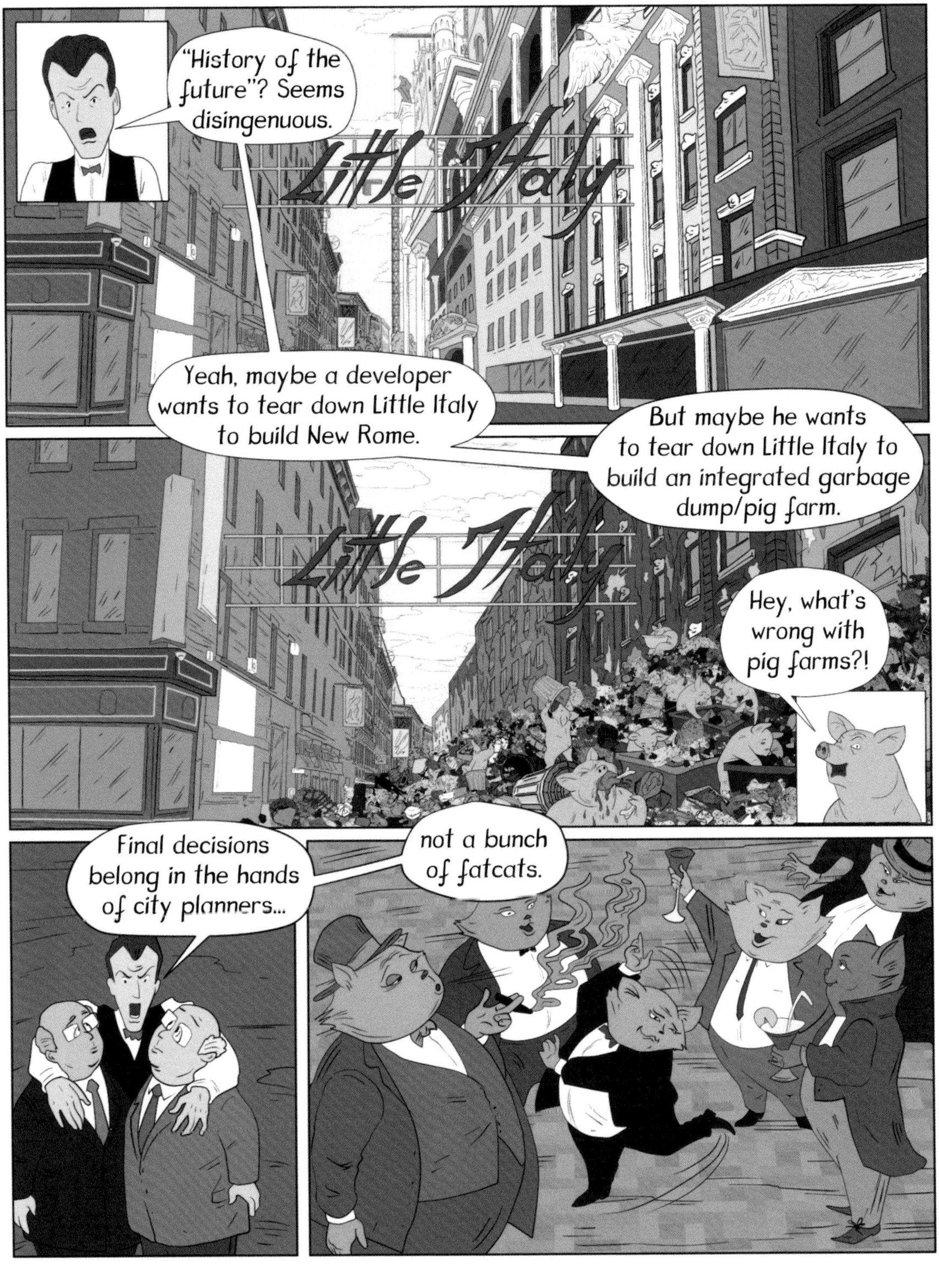
"History of the future"? Seems disingenuous.
Little Italy
Yeah, maybe a developer wants to tear down Little Italy to build New Rome.
But maybe he wants to tear down Little Italy to build an integrated garbage dump/pig farm.
Little Italy
Hey, what's wrong with pig farms?!
Final decisions belong in the hands of city planners...
not a bunch of fatcats.

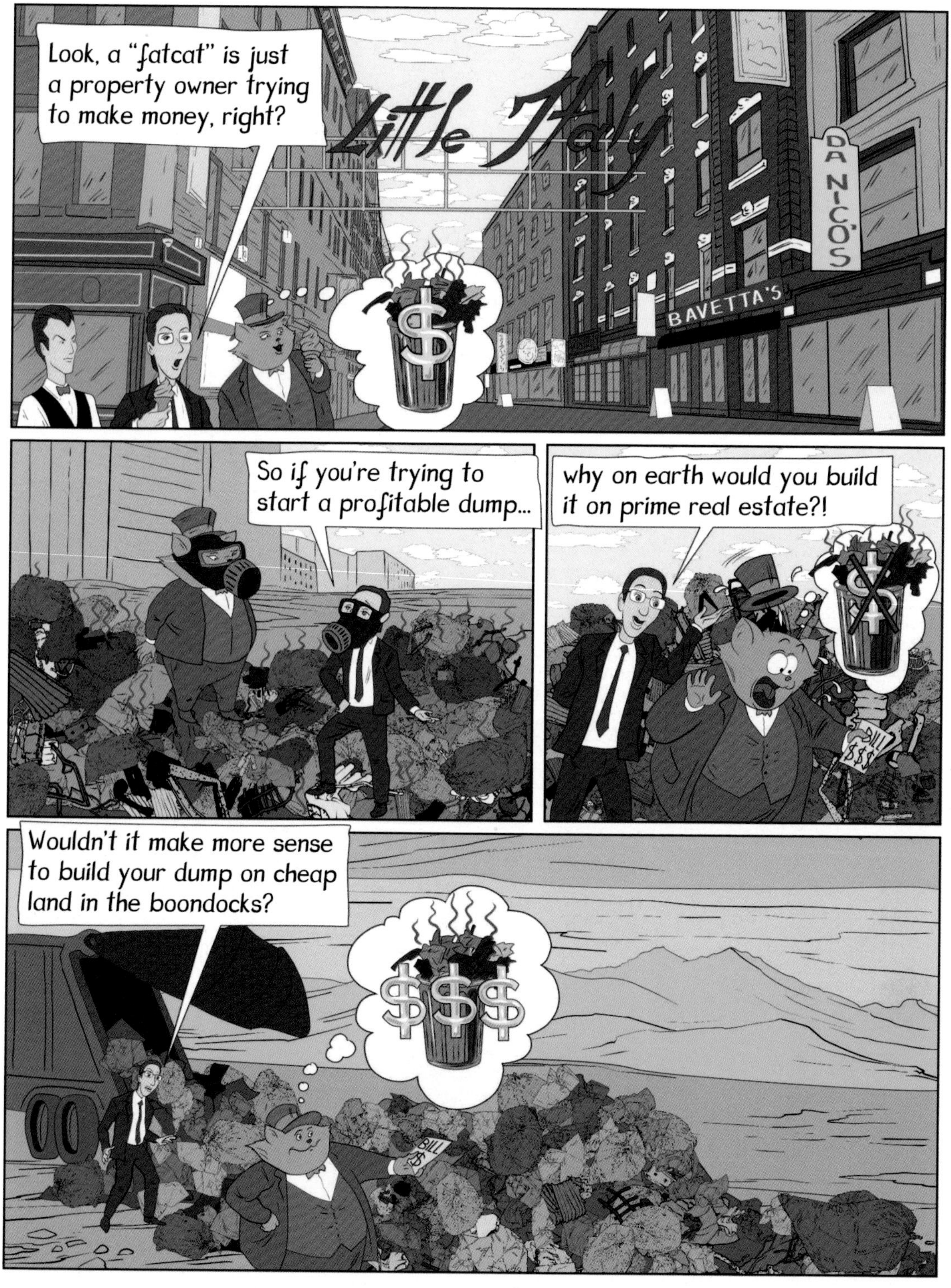
Look, a "fatcat" is just a property owner trying to make money, right?
Little Italy
DA NICO'S
BAVETTA'S
So if you're trying to start a profitable dump...
why on earth would you build it on prime real estate?!
BILL $$$
Wouldn't it make more sense to build your dump on cheap land in the boondocks?
BILL $

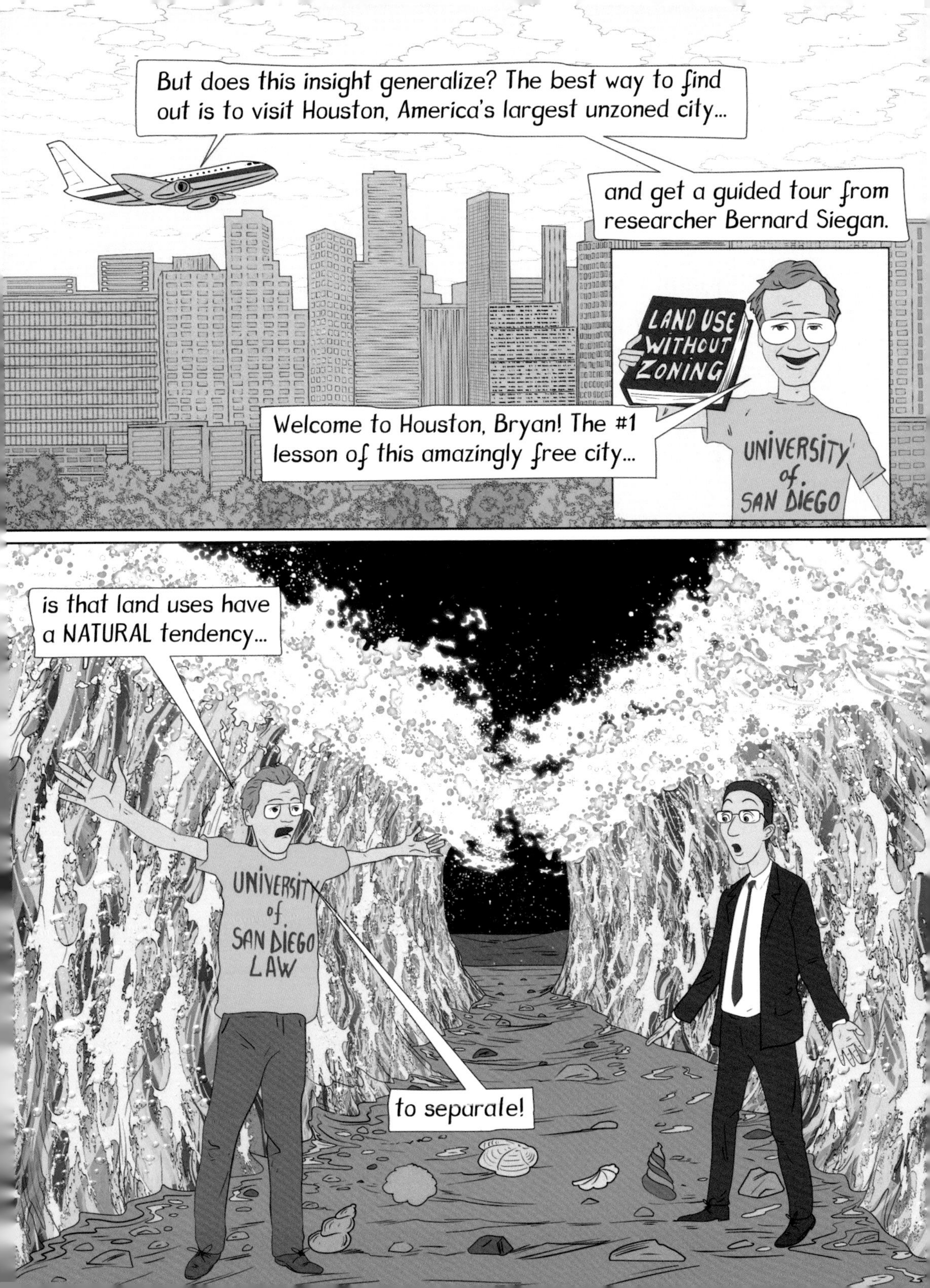

But does this insight generalize? The best way to find out is to visit Houston, America's largest unzoned city...
and get a guided tour from researcher Bernard Siegan.
LAND USE WITHOUT ZONING
Welcome to Houston, Bryan! The #1 lesson of this amazingly free city...
UNIVERSITY of SAN DIEGO
is that land uses have a NATURAL tendency...
UNIVERSITY of SAN DIEGO LAW
to separate!

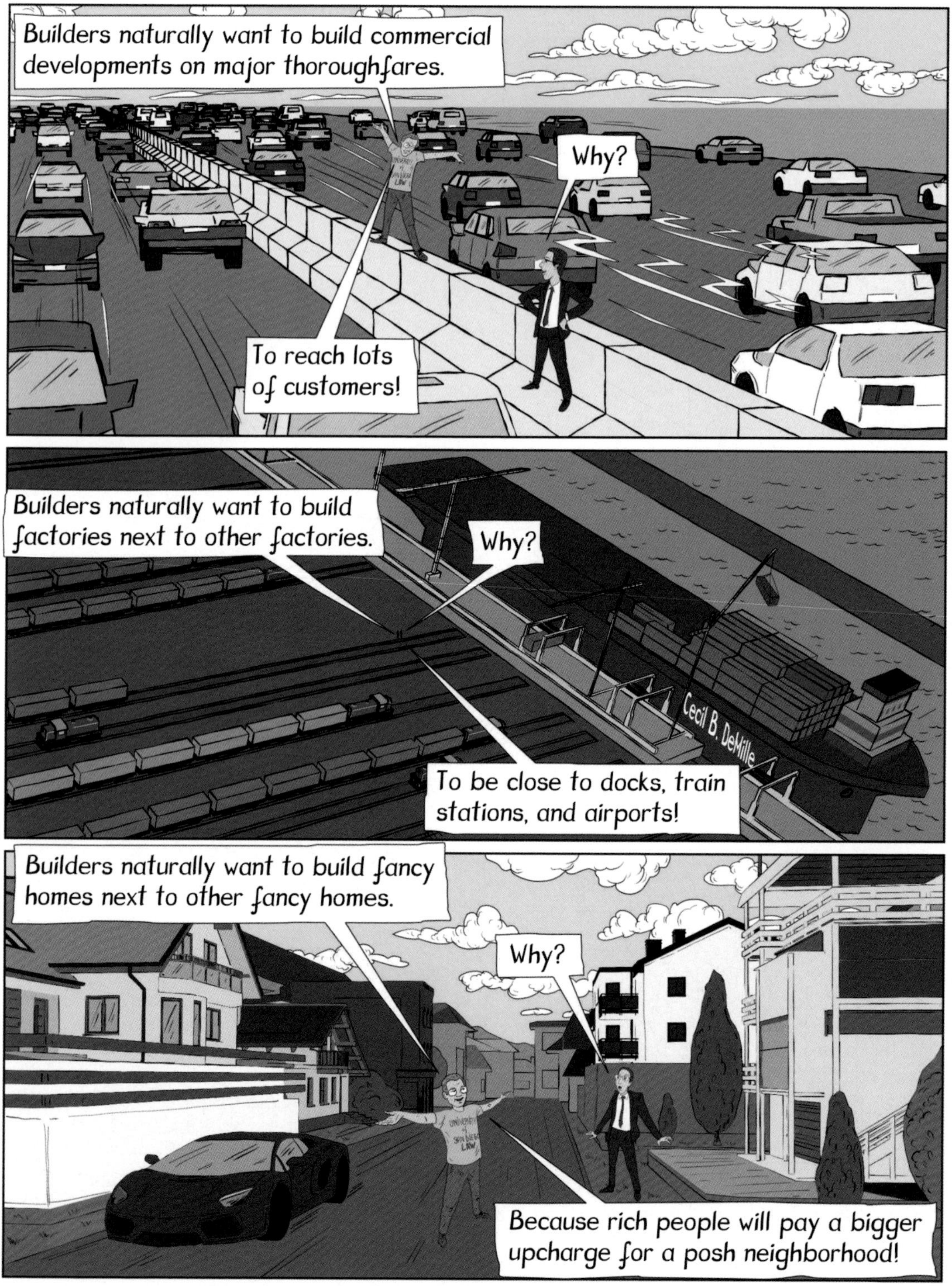
Builders naturally want to build commercial developments on major thoroughfares.
Why?
To reach lots of customers!
Builders naturally want to build factories next to other factories.
Why?
Cecil B. DeMille
To be close to docks, train stations, and airports!
Builders naturally want to build fancy homes next to other fancy homes.
Why?
Because rich people will pay a bigger upcharge for a posh neighborhood!

But this separation is hardly perfect, right?

In zoned cities, the separation is TOO perfect.

Do not touch!

NOT a toy.

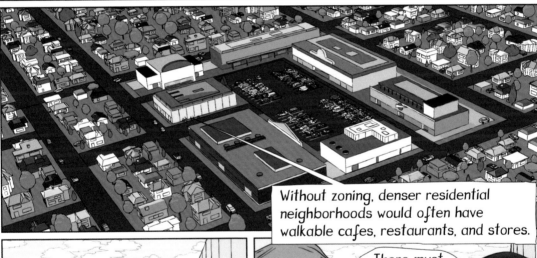

Without zoning, denser residential neighborhoods would often have walkable cafes, restaurants, and stores.

"Mixed use": convenient — and natural!

There must be some rough edges left.

Sure, but there are plenty of remedies besides housing regulation.

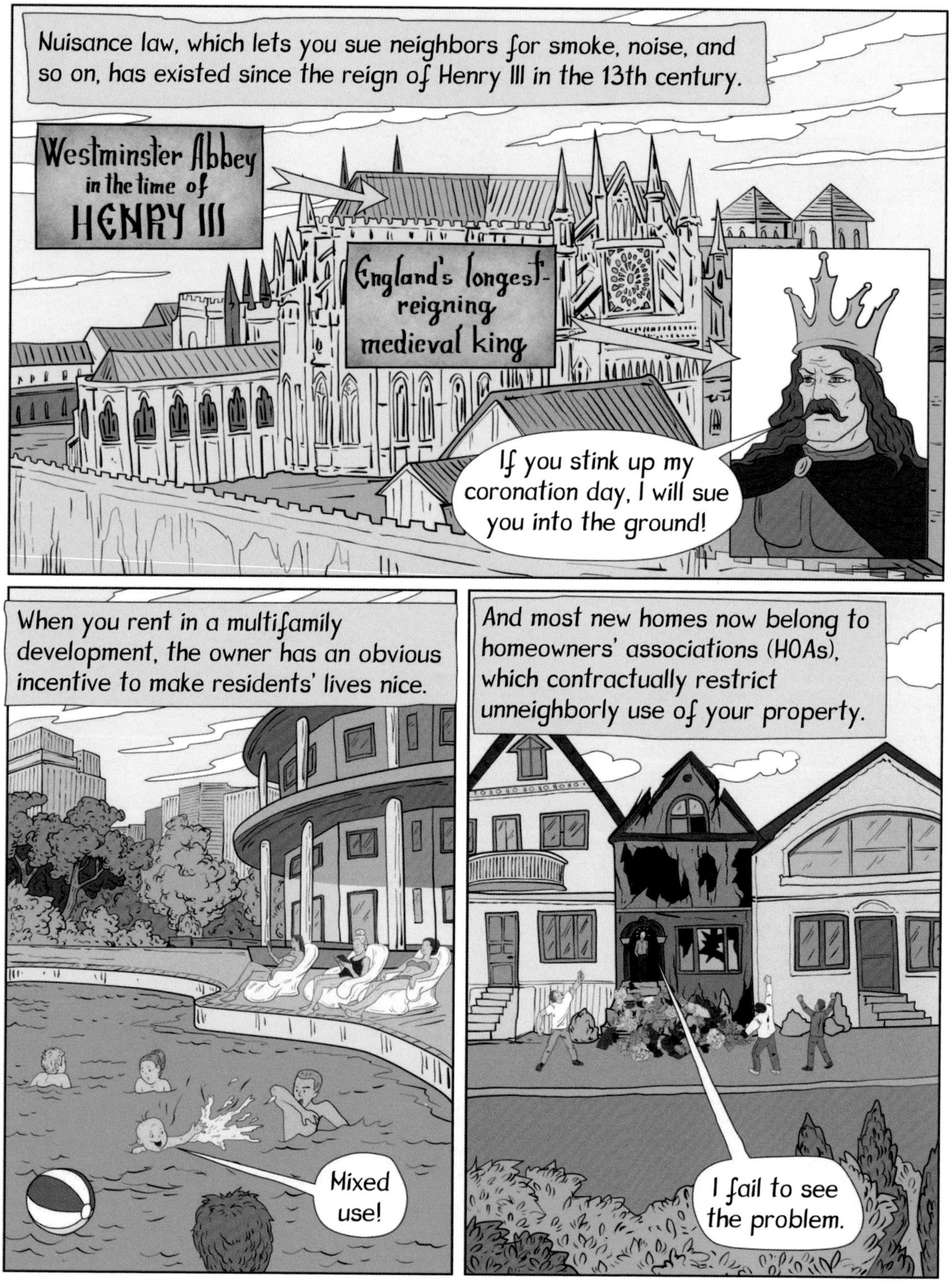
Nuisance law, which lets you sue neighbors for smoke, noise, and so on, has existed since the reign of Henry III in the 13th century.
Westminster Abbey in the time of HENRY III
England's longest-reigning medieval king
If you stink up my coronation day, I will sue you into the ground!
When you rent in a multifamily development, the owner has an obvious incentive to make residents' lives nice.
Mixed use!
And most new homes now belong to homeowners' associations (HOAs), which contractually restrict unneighborly use of your property.
I fail to see the problem.

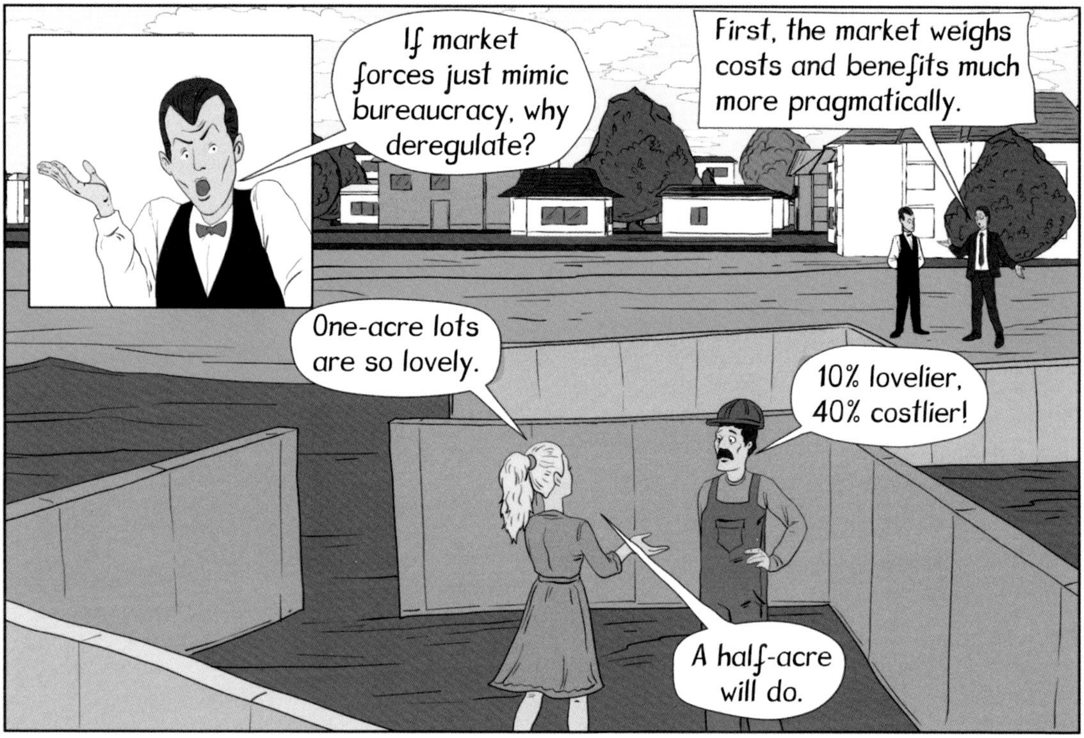
If market forces just mimic bureaucracy, why deregulate?
First, the market weighs costs and benefits much more pragmatically.
One-acre lots are so lovely.
10% lovelier, 40% costlier!
A half-acre will do.

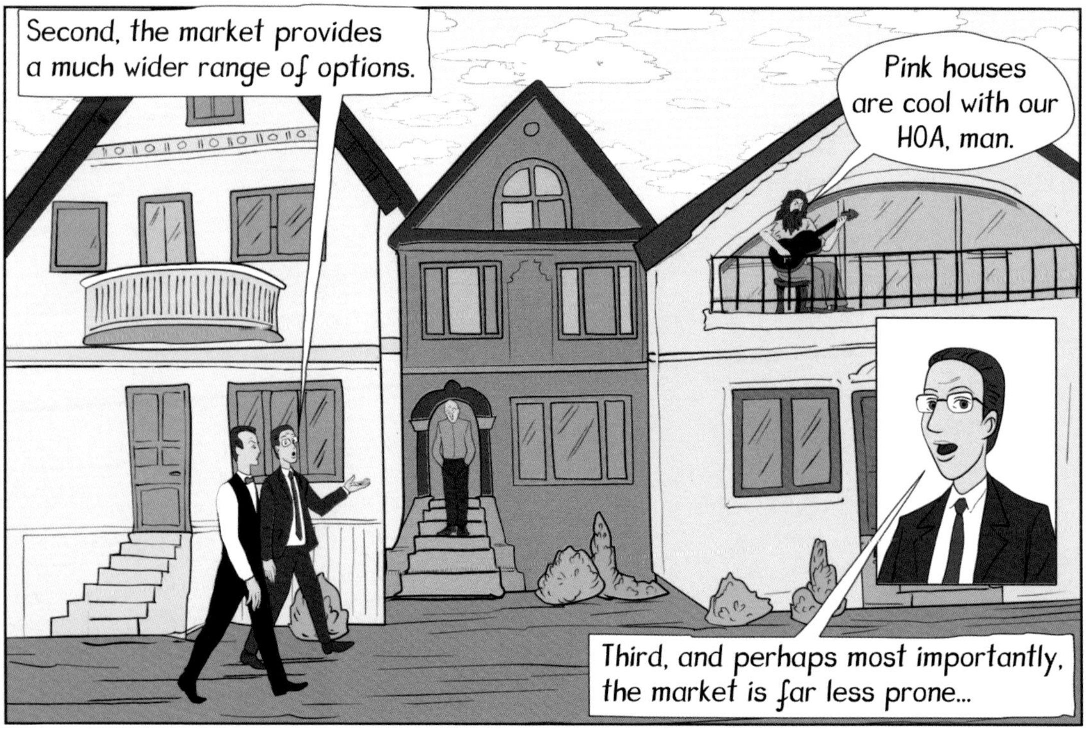
Second, the market provides a much wider range of options.
Pink houses are cool with our HOA, man.
Third, and perhaps most importantly, the market is far less prone...

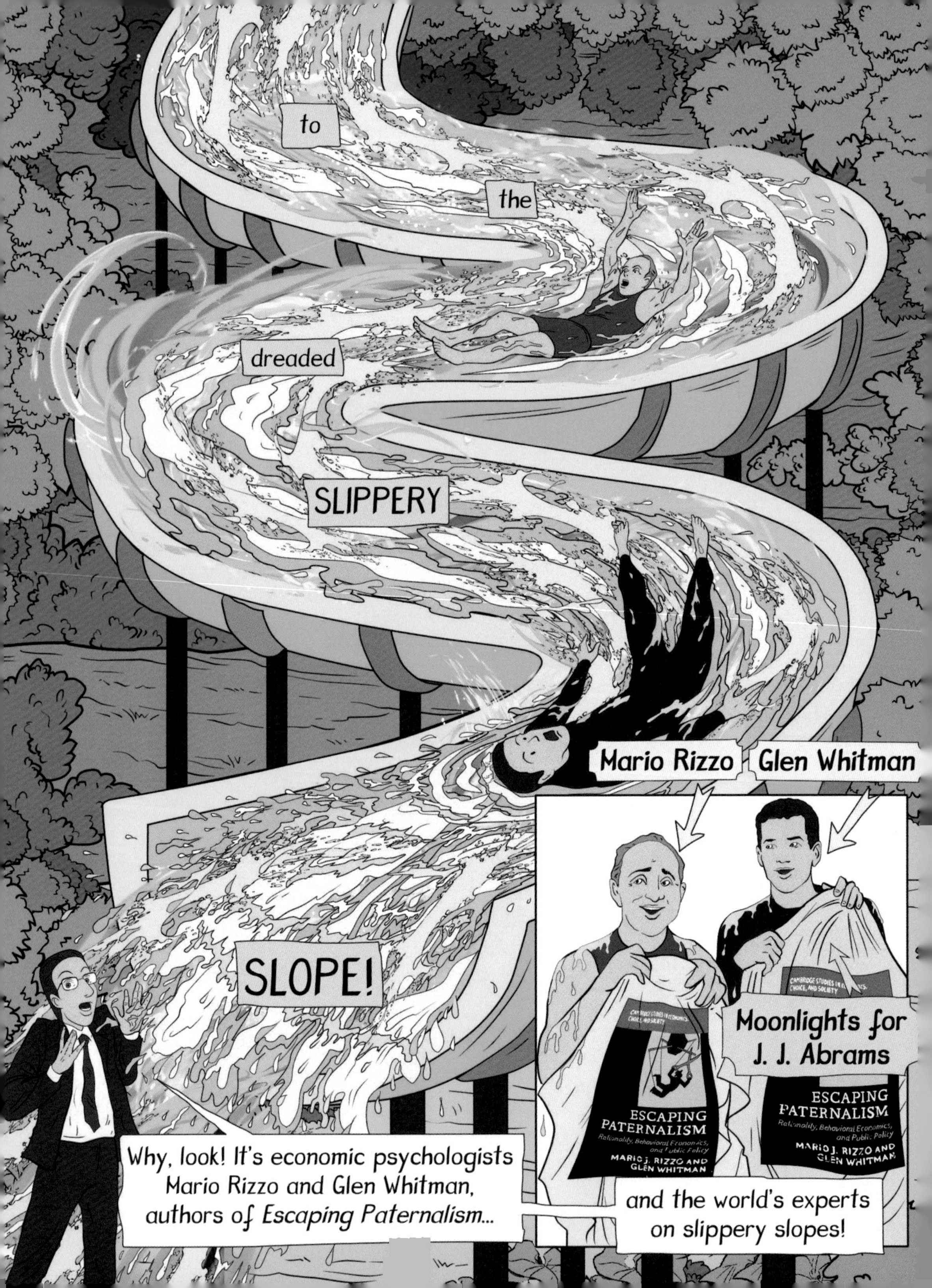
to
the
dreaded
SLIPPERY
SLOPE!
Mario Rizzo
Glen Whitman
Moonlights for
J. J. Abrams
ESCAPING
PATERNALISM
Rationality, Behavioral Economics, and Public Policy
MARIO J. RIZZO AND
GLEN WHITMAN
ESCAPING
PATERNALISM
Rationality, Behavioral Economics, and Public Policy
MARIO J. RIZZO AND
GLEN WHITMAN
Why, look! It's economic psychologists Mario Rizzo and Glen Whitman, authors of *Escaping Paternalism*...
and the world's experts on slippery slopes!

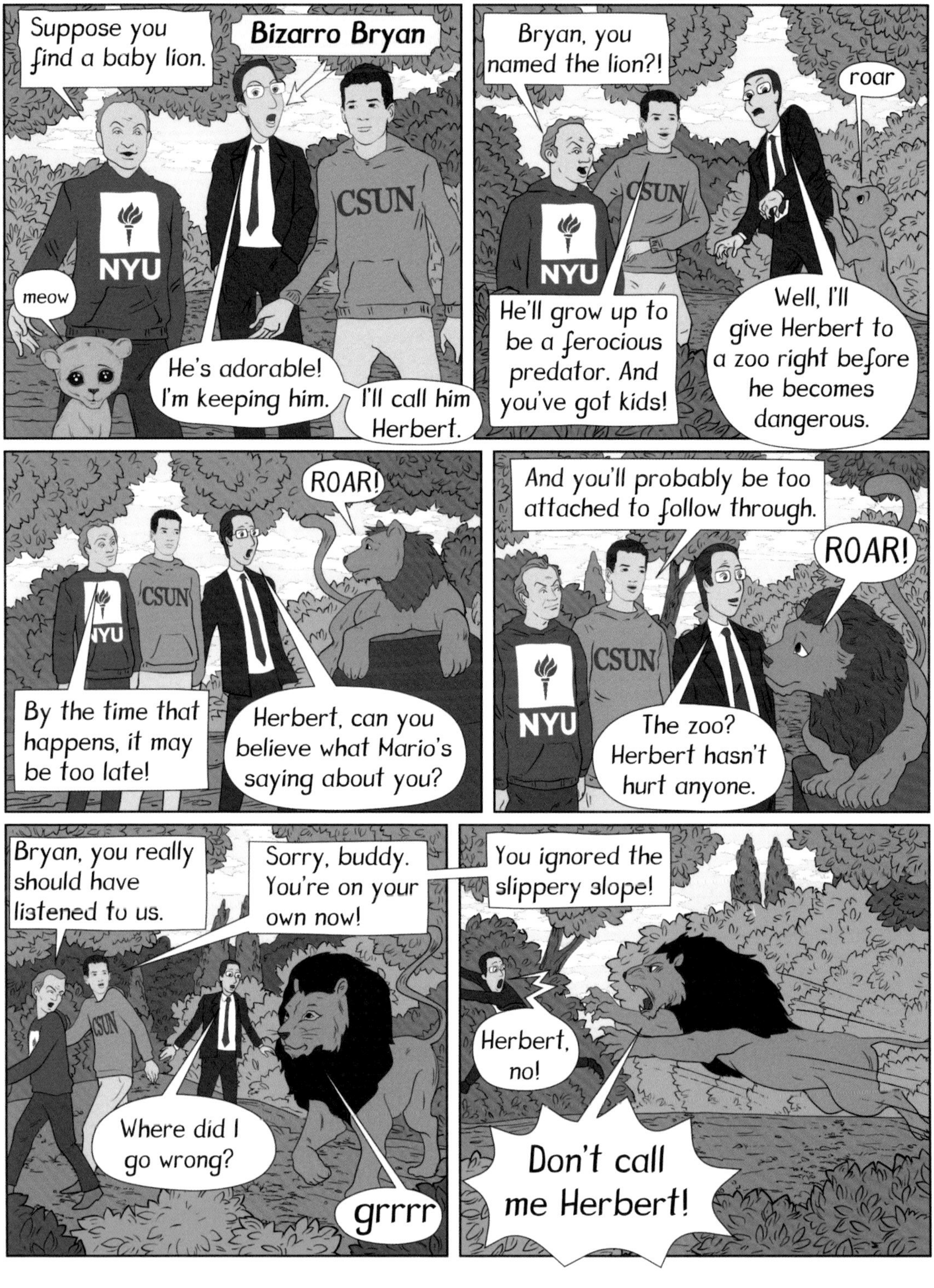
Suppose you find a baby lion.
Bizarro Bryan
meow
He's adorable! I'm keeping him.
I'll call him Herbert.
Bryan, you named the lion?!
roar
He'll grow up to be a ferocious predator. And you've got kids!
Well, I'll give Herbert to a zoo right before he becomes dangerous.
ROAR!
By the time that happens, it may be too late!
Herbert, can you believe what Mario's saying about you?
And you'll probably be too attached to follow through.
ROAR!
The zoo? Herbert hasn't hurt anyone.
Bryan, you really should have listened to us.
Sorry, buddy. You're on your own now!
Where did I go wrong?
grrrr
You ignored the slippery slope!
Herbert, no!
Don't call me Herbert!

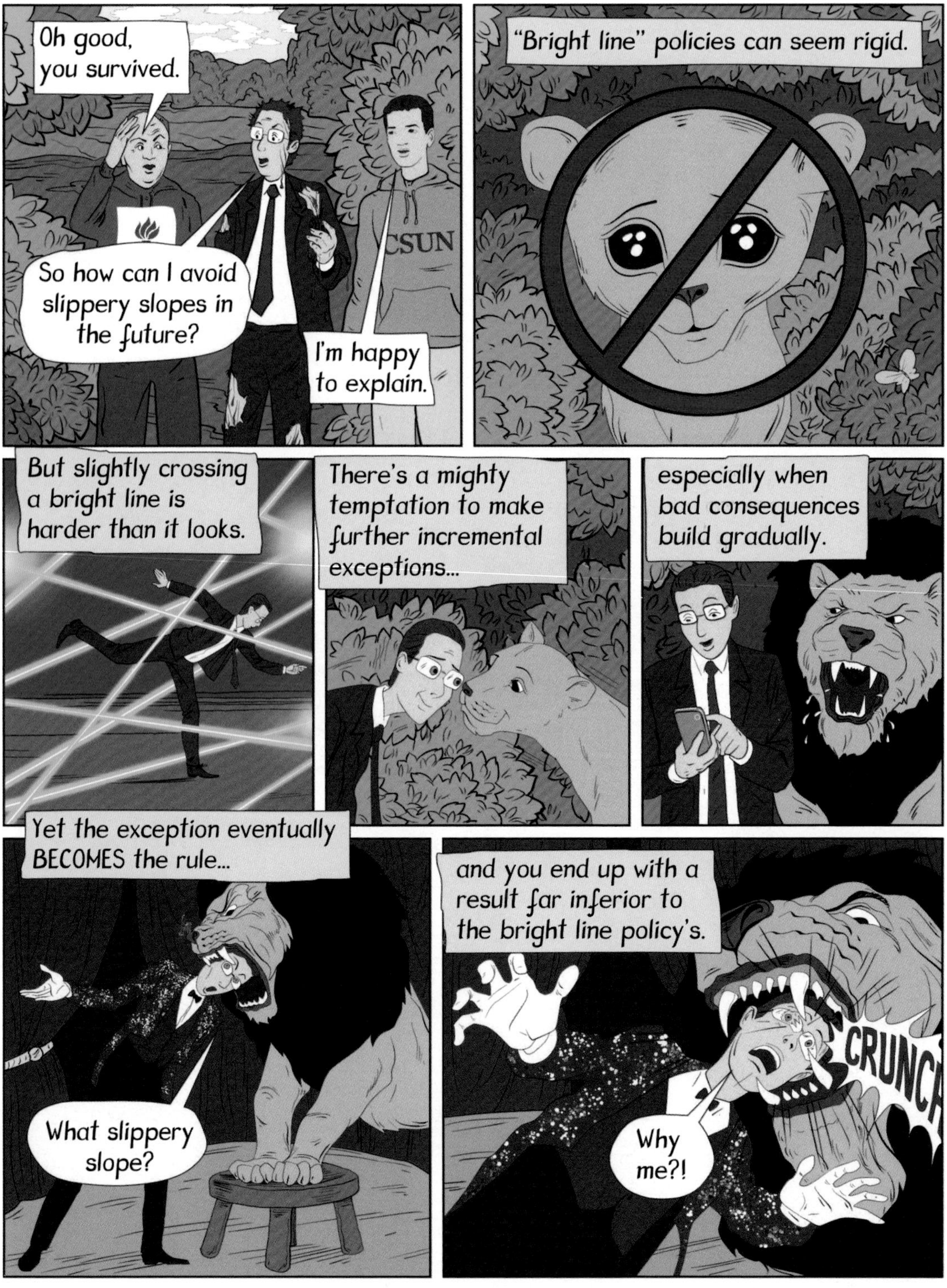
Oh good, you survived.
So how can I avoid slippery slopes in the future?
CSUN
I'm happy to explain.
"Bright line" policies can seem rigid.
But slightly crossing a bright line is harder than it looks.
There's a mighty temptation to make further incremental exceptions...
especially when bad consequences build gradually.
Yet the exception eventually BECOMES the rule...
What slippery slope?
and you end up with a result far inferior to the bright line policy's.
CRUNCH
Why me?!

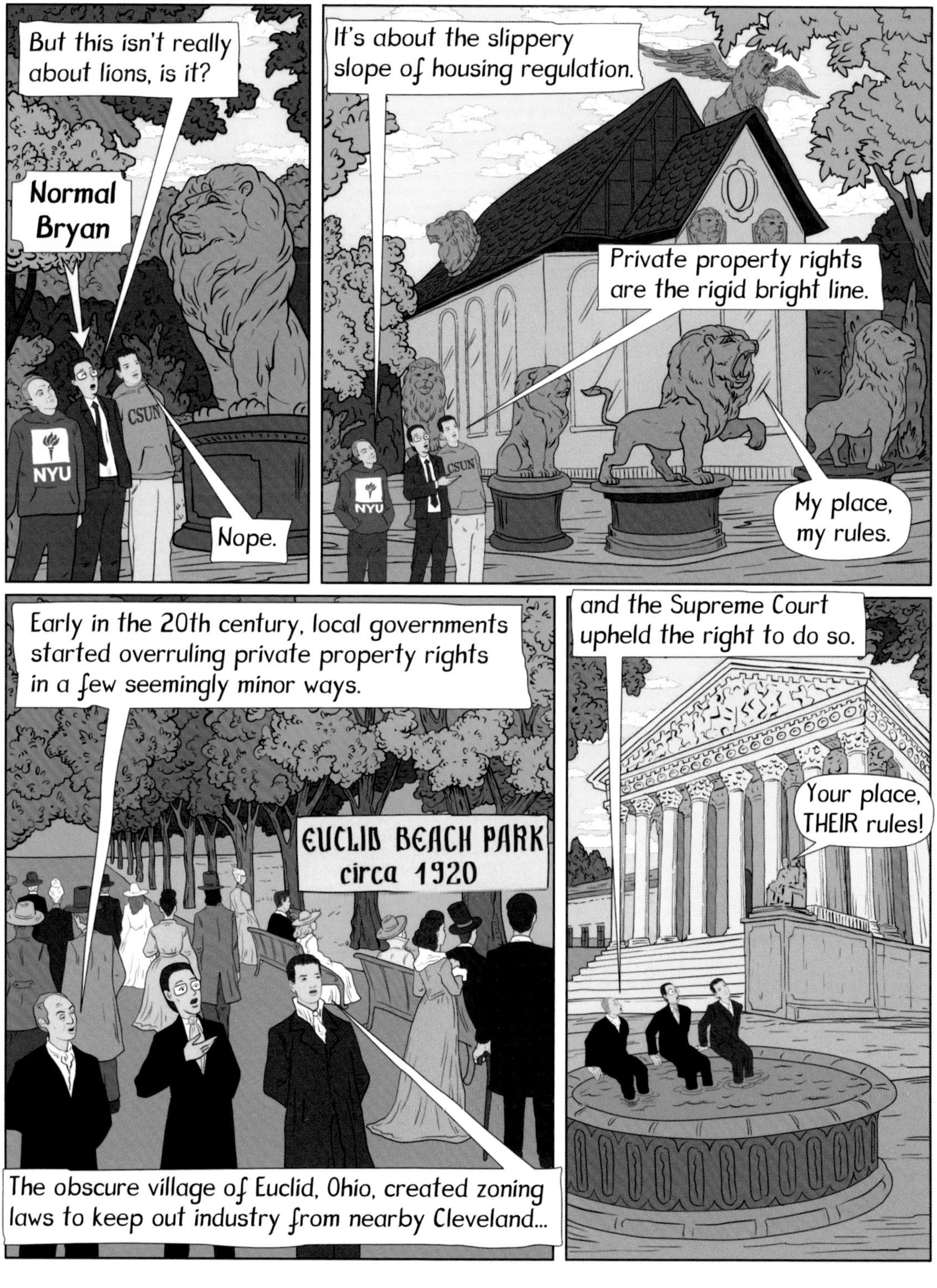
But this isn't really about lions, is it?
Normal Bryan
NYU
CSUN
Nope.
It's about the slippery slope of housing regulation.
Private property rights are the rigid bright line.
NYU
CSUN
My place, my rules.
Early in the 20th century, local governments started overruling private property rights in a few seemingly minor ways.
EUCLID BEACH PARK
circa 1920
The obscure village of Euclid, Ohio, created zoning laws to keep out industry from nearby Cleveland...
and the Supreme Court upheld the right to do so.
Your place, THEIR rules!

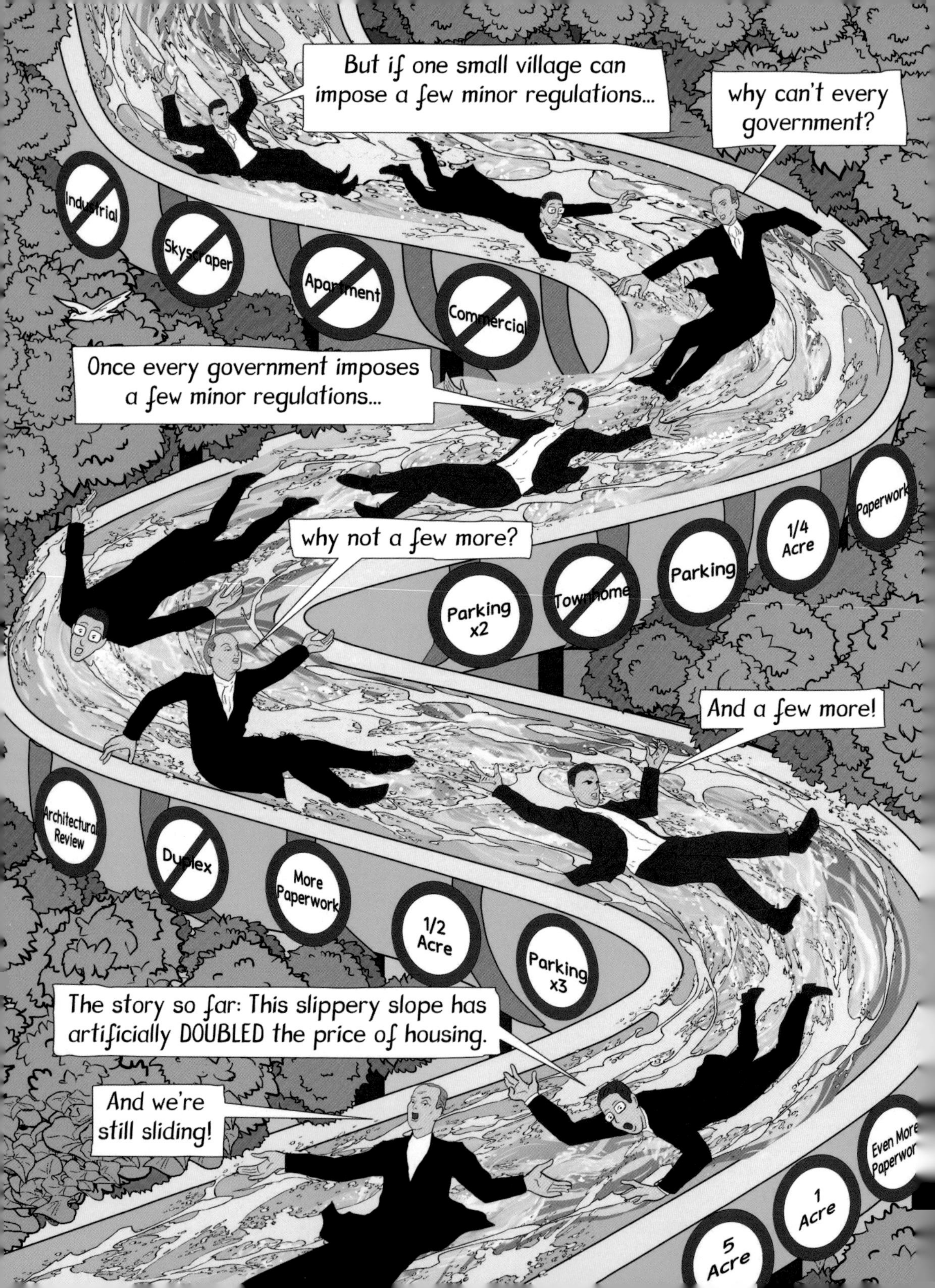
But if one small village can impose a few minor regulations...
why can't every government?
Industrial
Skyscraper
Apartment
Commercial
Once every government imposes a few minor regulations...
why not a few more?
Parking x2
Townhome
Parking
1/4 Acre
Paperwork
And a few more!
Architectural Review
Duplex
More Paperwork
1/2 Acre
Parking x3
The story so far: This slippery slope has artificially DOUBLED the price of housing.
And we're still sliding!
Even More Paperwor
1 Acre
5 Acre

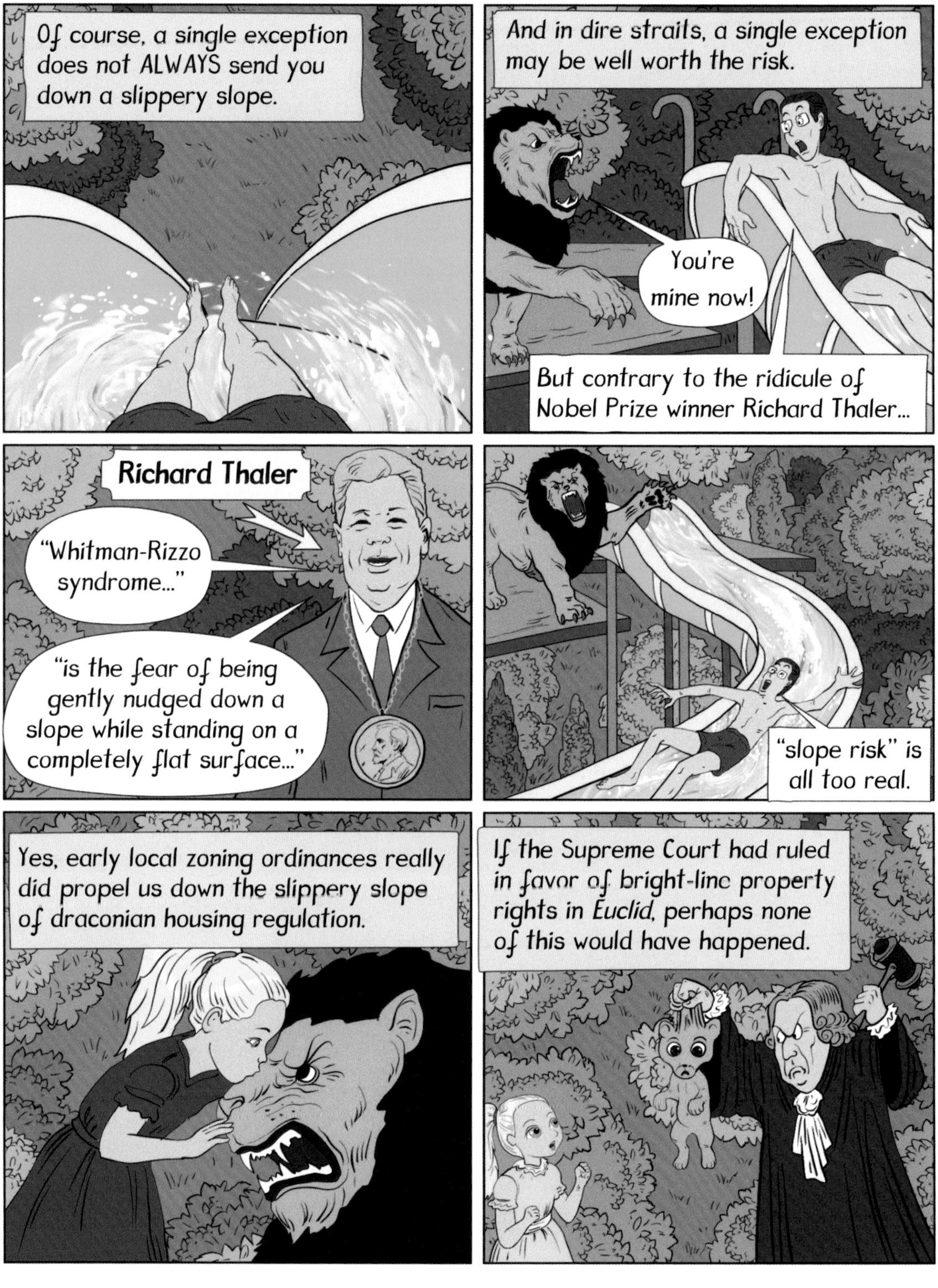
Of course, a single exception does not ALWAYS send you down a slippery slope.
And in dire straits, a single exception may be well worth the risk.
You're mine now!
But contrary to the ridicule of Nobel Prize winner Richard Thaler...
Richard Thaler
"Whitman-Rizzo syndrome..."
"is the fear of being gently nudged down a slope while standing on a completely flat surface..."
"slope risk" is all too real.
Yes, early local zoning ordinances really did propel us down the slippery slope of draconian housing regulation.
If the Supreme Court had ruled in favor of bright-line property rights in *Euclid*, perhaps none of this would have happened.

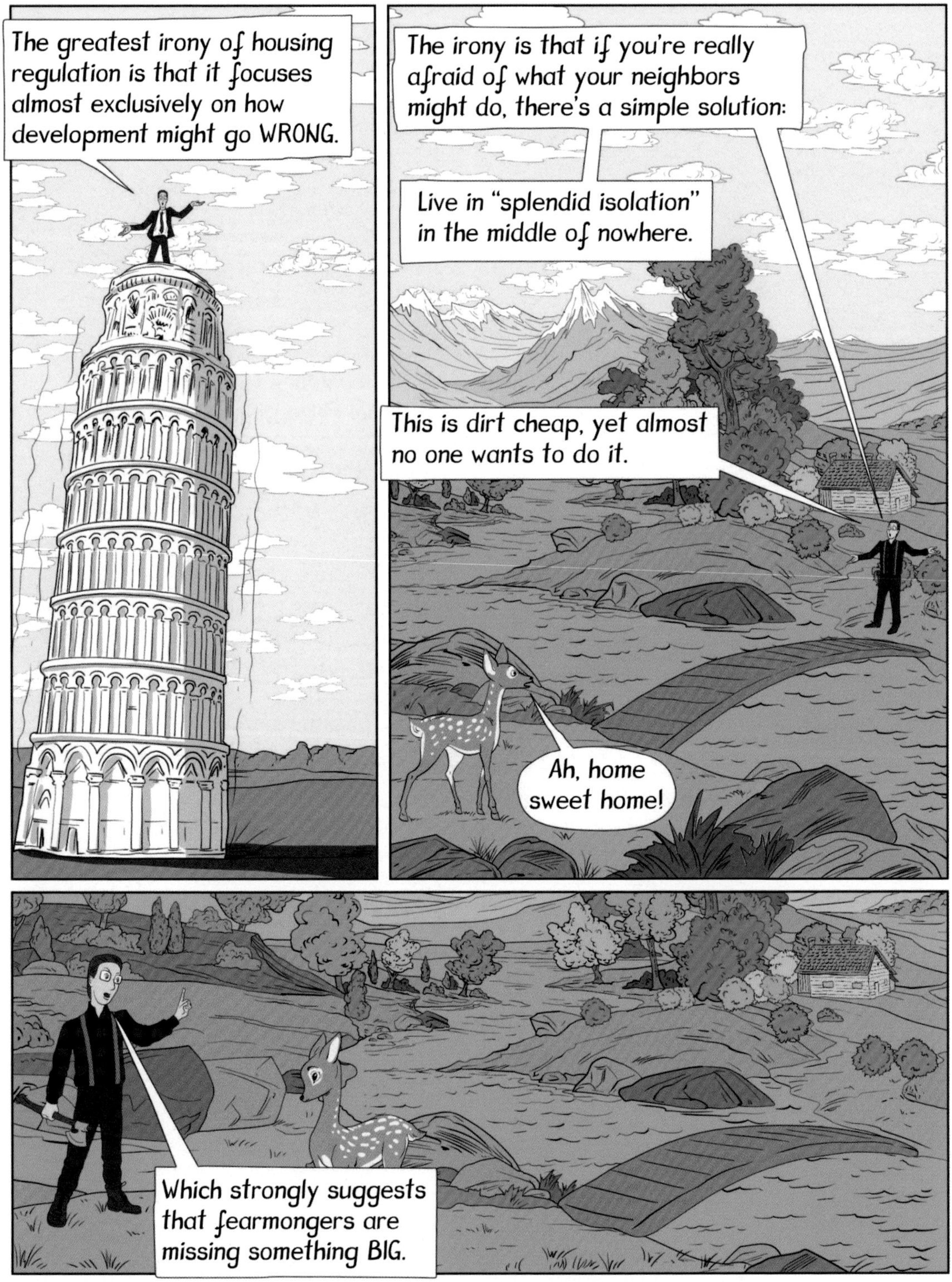
The greatest irony of housing regulation is that it focuses almost exclusively on how development might go WRONG.
The irony is that if you're really afraid of what your neighbors might do, there's a simple solution:
Live in "splendid isolation" in the middle of nowhere.
This is dirt cheap, yet almost no one wants to do it.
Ah, home sweet home!
Which strongly suggests that fearmongers are missing something BIG.

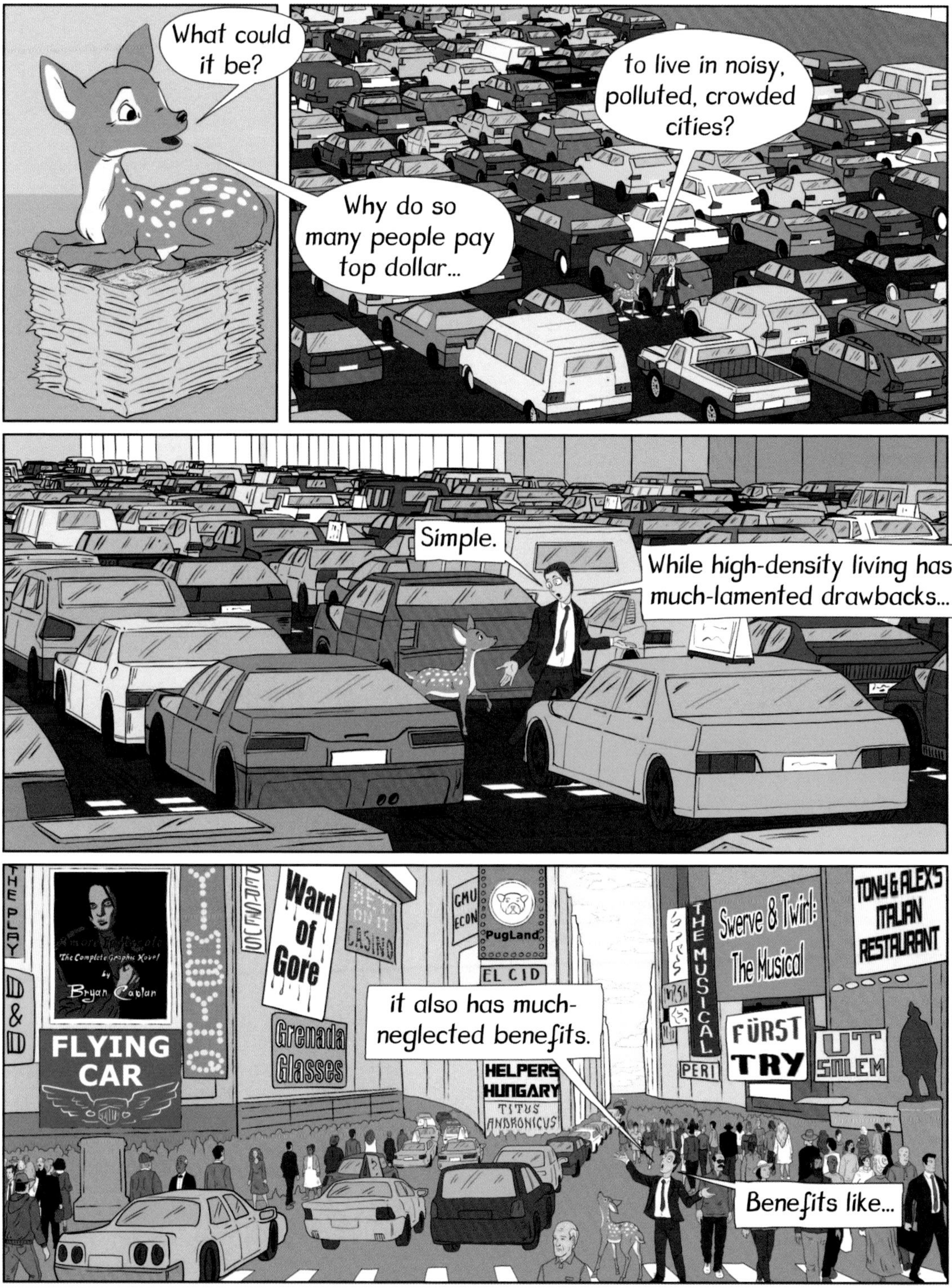
What could it be?
Why do so many people pay top dollar...
to live in noisy, polluted, crowded cities?
Simple.
While high-density living has much-lamented drawbacks...
it also has much-neglected benefits.
Benefits like...
THE PLAY
The Complete Graphic Novel by Bryan Caplan
D&D
FLYING CAR
Ward of Gore
Grenada Glasses
CASINO
PugLand
EL CID
HELPERS HUNGARY
TITUS ANDRONICUS
THE MUSICAL
Swerve & Twirl: The Musical
TONY & ALEX'S ITALIAN RESTAURANT
FÜRST TRY
UT SALEM
PERI

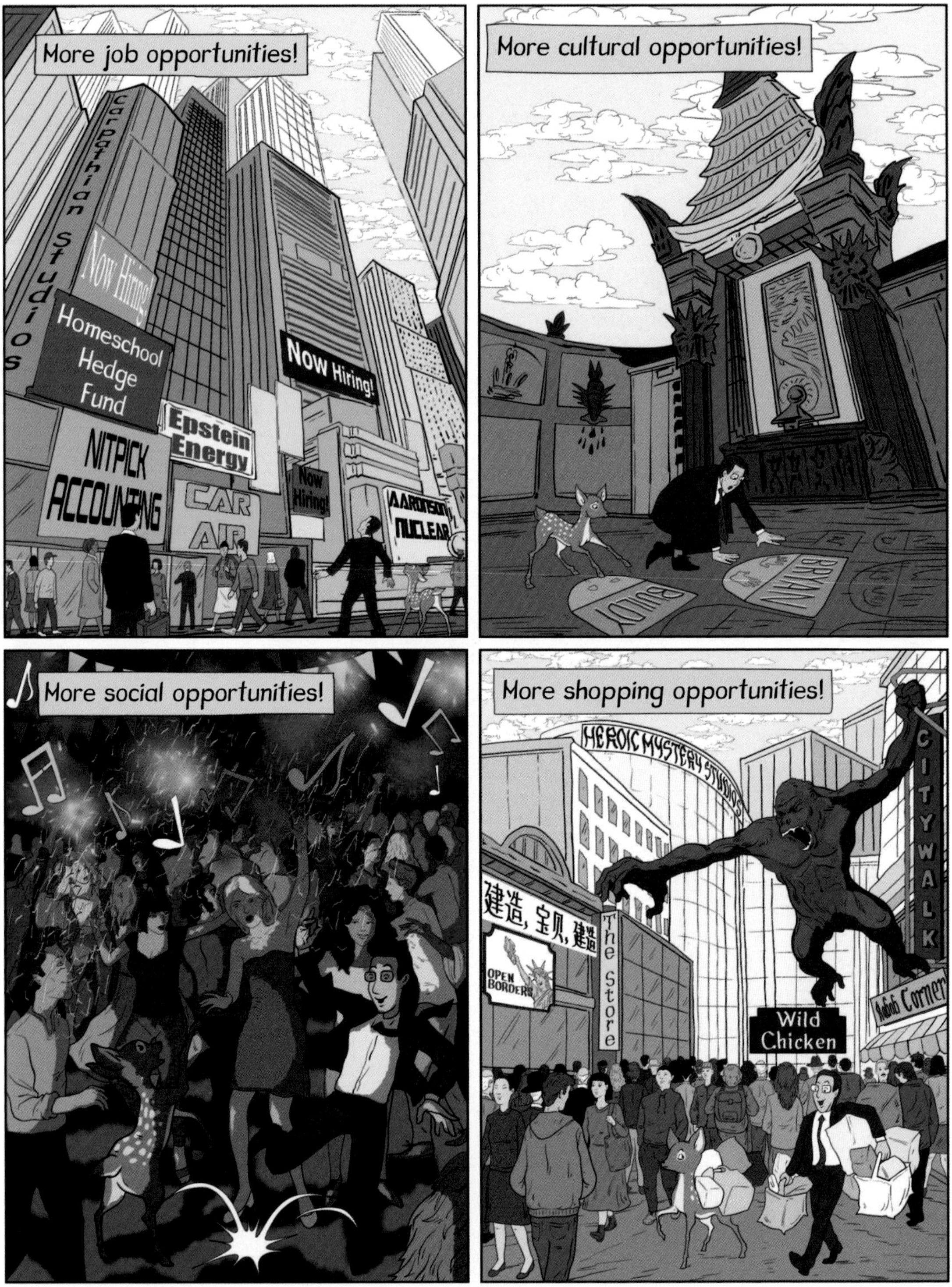
More job opportunities!
Carpathian Studios
Now Hiring!
Homeschool Hedge Fund
Epstein Energy
NITPICK
Now Hiring!
Now Hiring!
AARONSON NUCLEAR
More cultural opportunities!
BRYAN
More social opportunities!
More shopping opportunities!
HEROIC MYSTERY STUDIOS
CITYWALK
建造，宝贝，建造
OPEN BORDERS
The Store
Wild Chicken

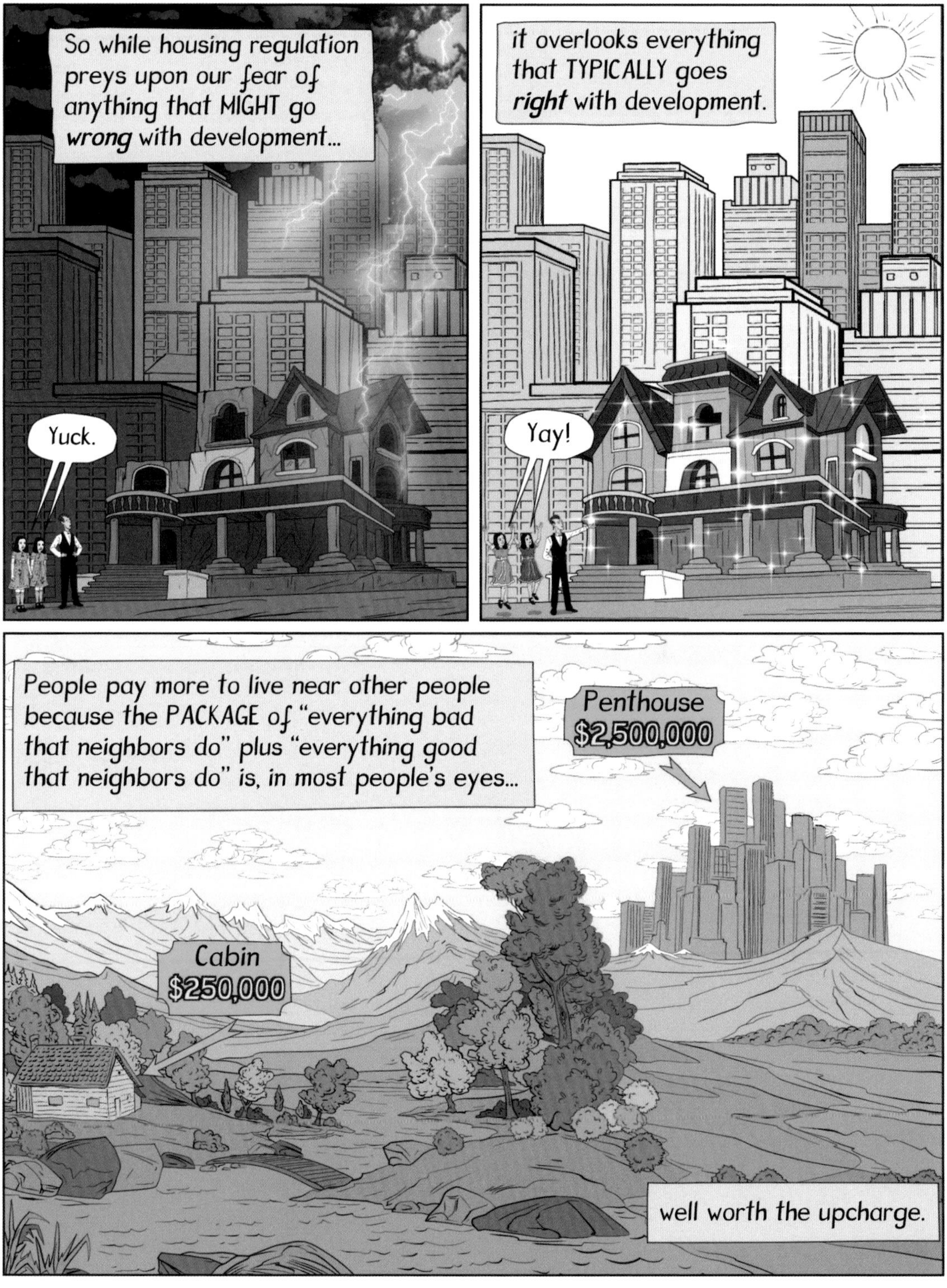
So while housing regulation preys upon our fear of anything that MIGHT go *wrong* with development...
Yuck.
it overlooks everything that TYPICALLY goes *right* with development.
Yay!
People pay more to live near other people because the PACKAGE of "everything bad that neighbors do" plus "everything good that neighbors do" is, in most people's eyes...
Penthouse
$2,500,000
Cabin
$250,000
well worth the upcharge.

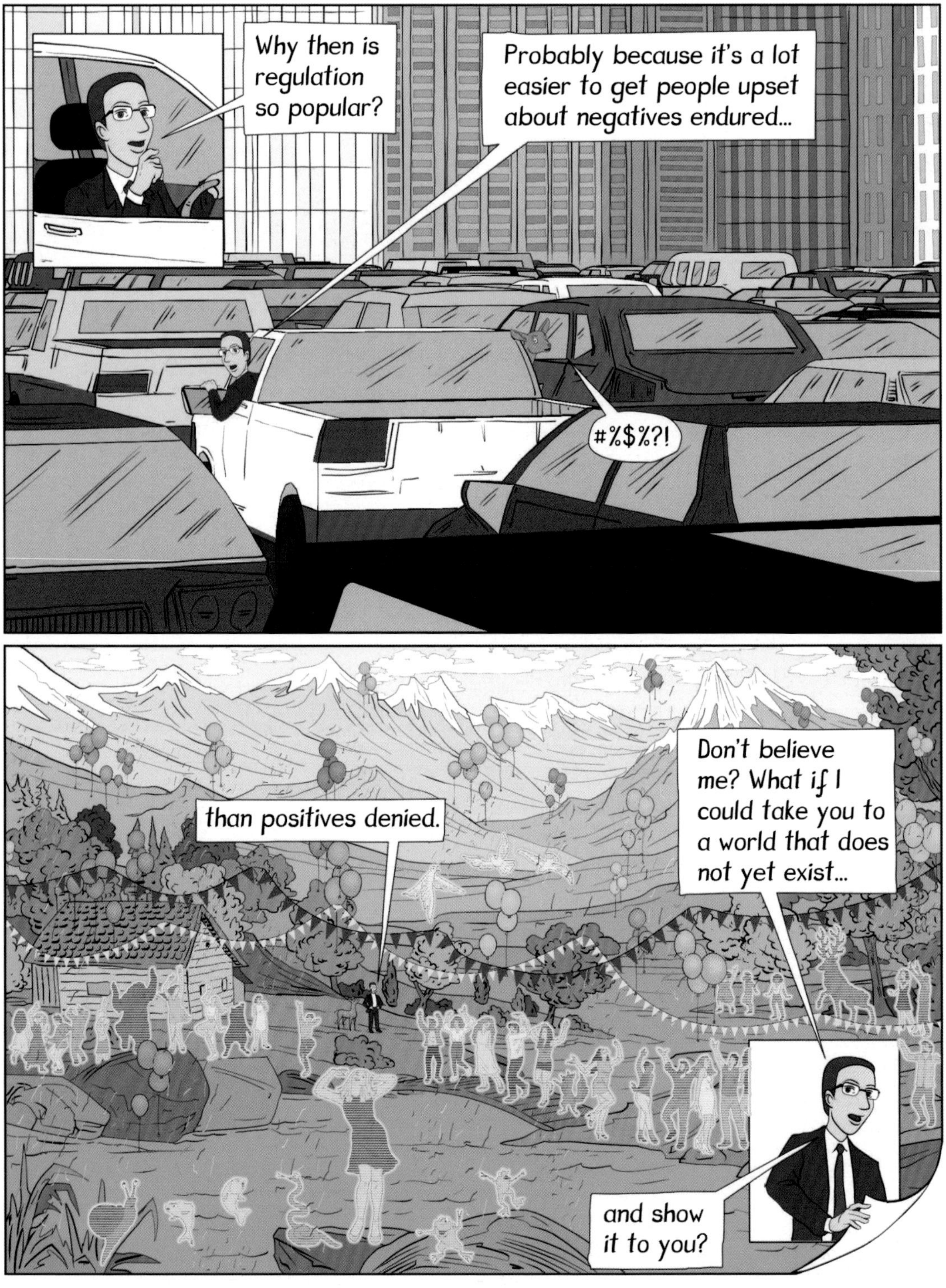
Why then is regulation so popular?
Probably because it's a lot easier to get people upset about negatives endured...
#%$%?!
than positives denied.
Don't believe me? What if I could take you to a world that does not yet exist...
and show it to you?

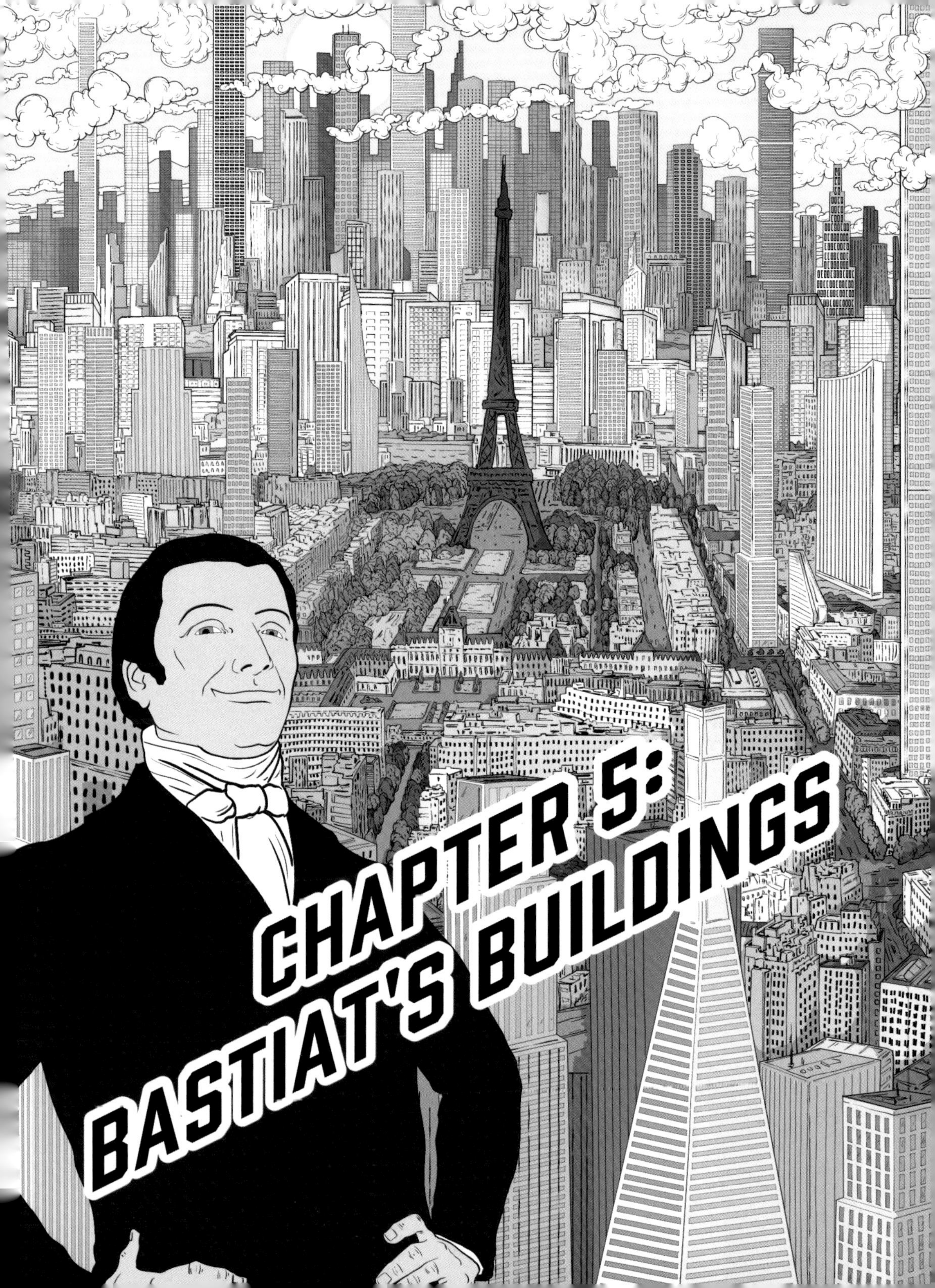
CHAPTER 5:
BASTIAT'S BUILDINGS

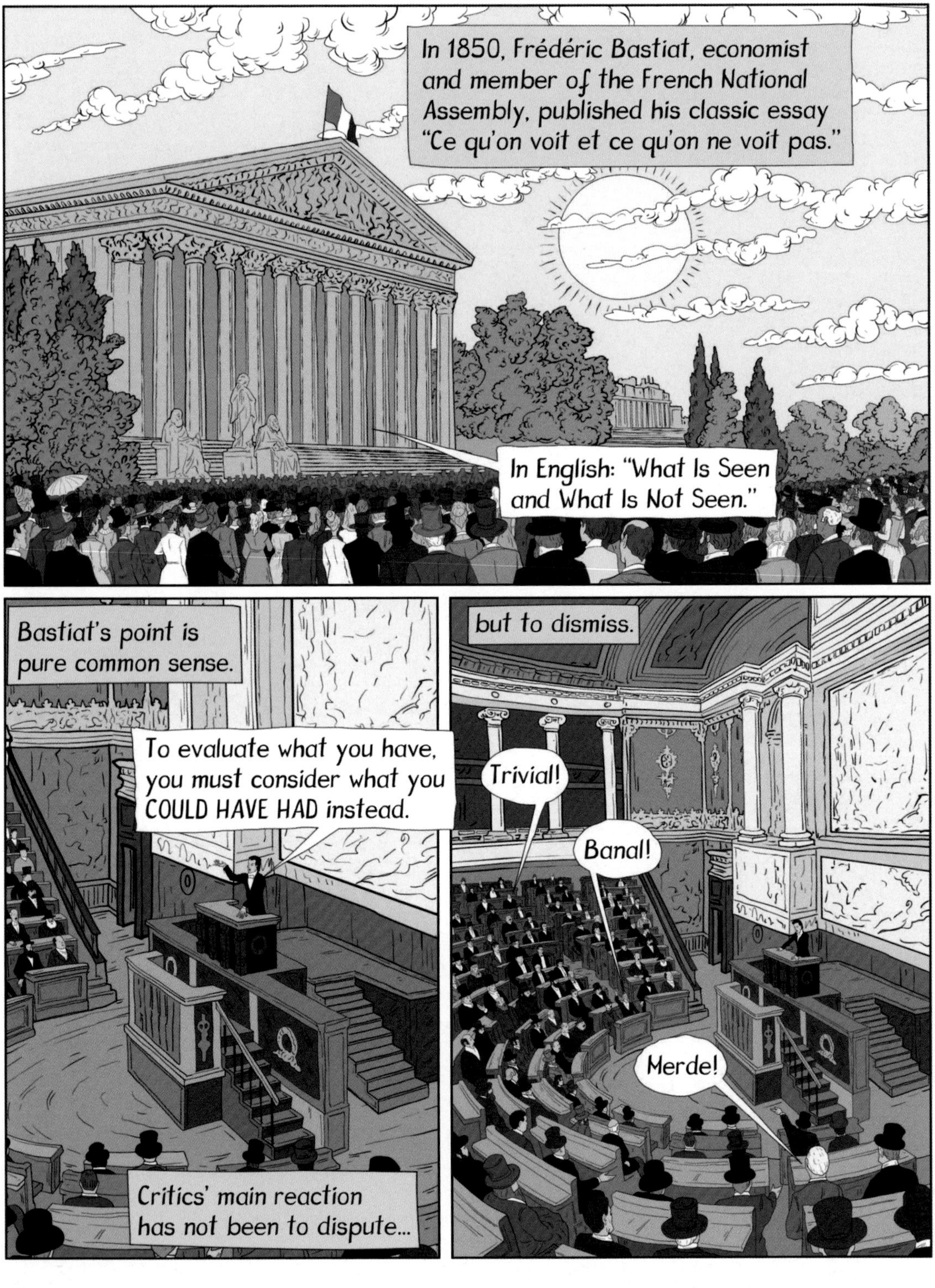
In 1850, Frédéric Bastiat, economist and member of the French National Assembly, published his classic essay "Ce qu'on voit et ce qu'on ne voit pas."
In English: "What Is Seen and What Is Not Seen."
Bastiat's point is pure common sense.
To evaluate what you have, you must consider what you COULD HAVE HAD instead.
Critics' main reaction has not been to dispute...
but to dismiss.
Trivial!
Banal!
Merde!

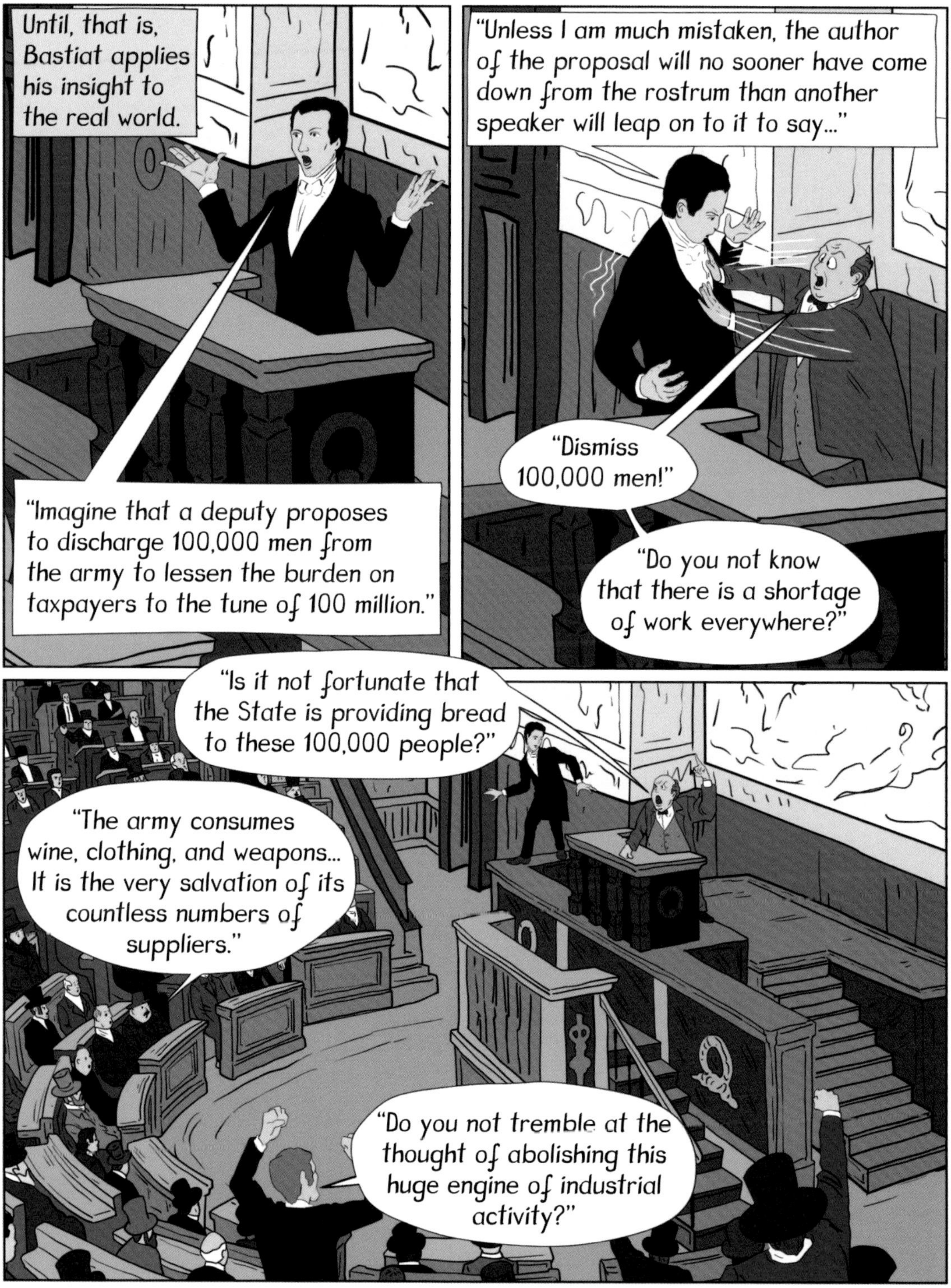
Until, that is, Bastiat applies his insight to the real world.
"Imagine that a deputy proposes to discharge 100,000 men from the army to lessen the burden on taxpayers to the tune of 100 million."
"Unless I am much mistaken, the author of the proposal will no sooner have come down from the rostrum than another speaker will leap on to it to say..."
"Dismiss 100,000 men!"
"Do you not know that there is a shortage of work everywhere?"
"Is it not fortunate that the State is providing bread to these 100,000 people?"
"The army consumes wine, clothing, and weapons... It is the very salvation of its countless numbers of suppliers."
"Do you not tremble at the thought of abolishing this huge engine of industrial activity?"

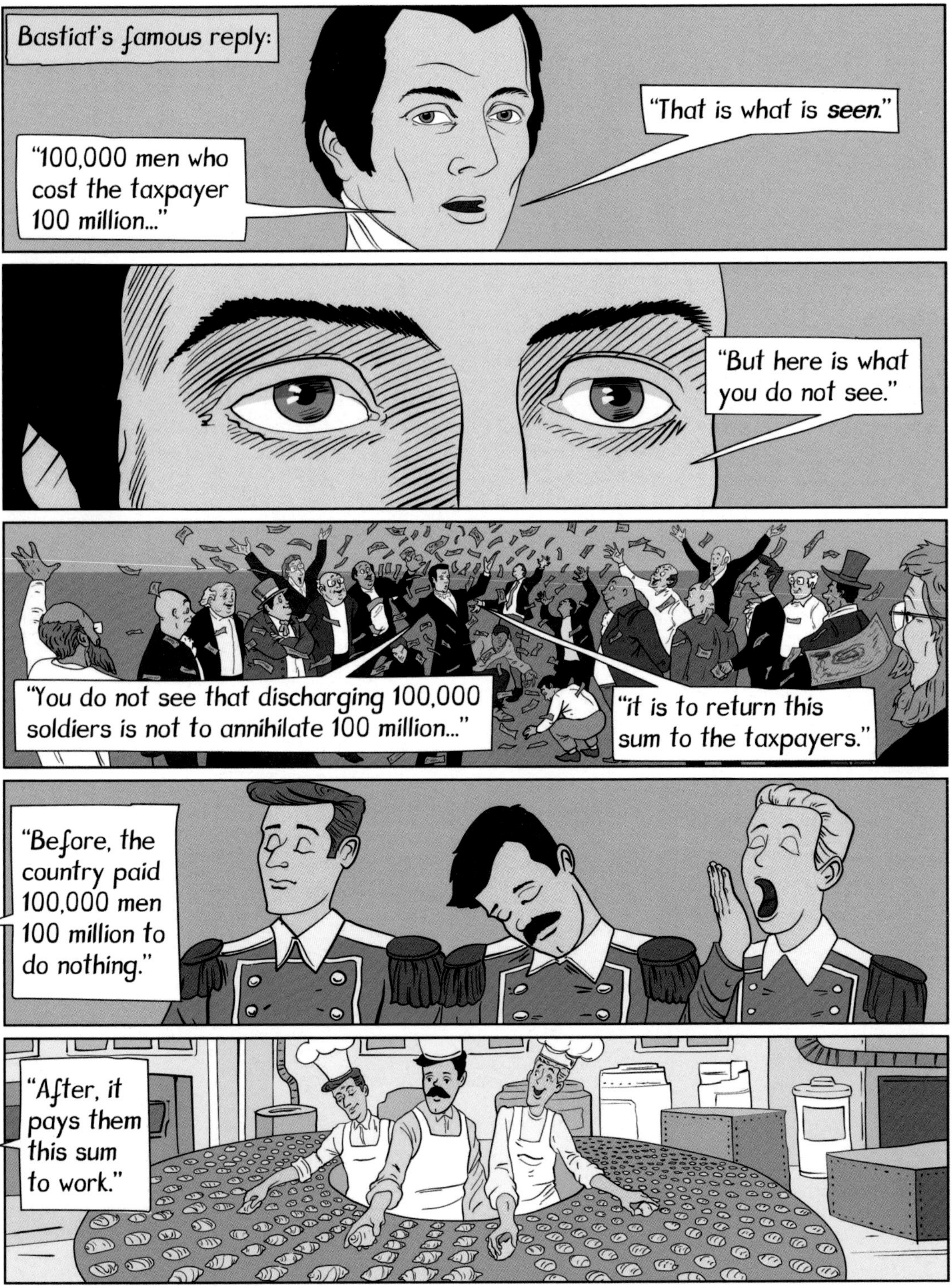
Bastiat's famous reply:
"100,000 men who cost the taxpayer 100 million..."
"That is what is *seen*."
"But here is what you do not see."
"You do not see that discharging 100,000 soldiers is not to annihilate 100 million..."
"it is to return this sum to the taxpayers."
"Before, the country paid 100,000 men 100 million to do nothing."
"After, it pays them this sum to work."

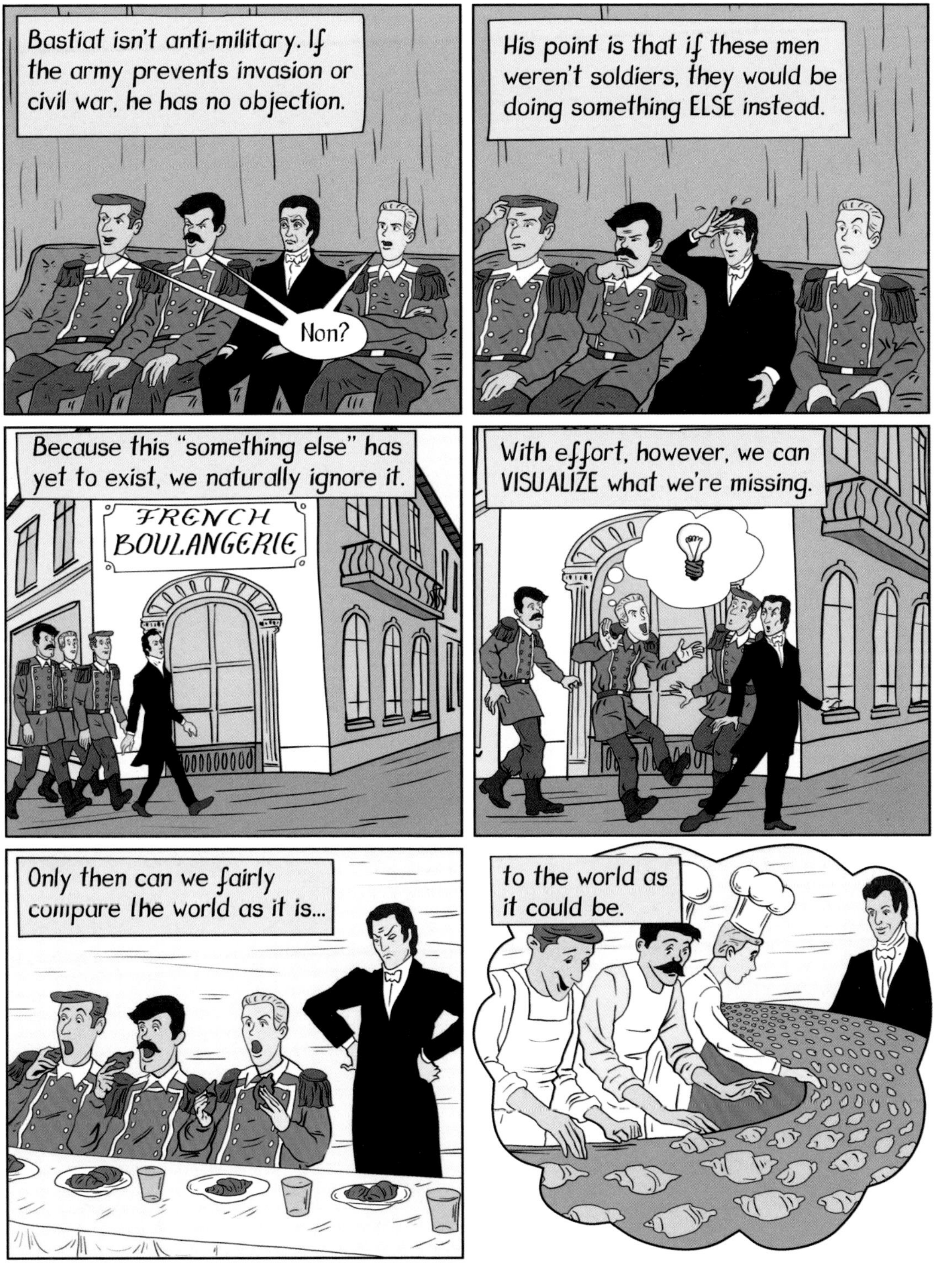
Bastiat isn't anti-military. If the army prevents invasion or civil war, he has no objection.
Non?
His point is that if these men weren't soldiers, they would be doing something ELSE instead.
Because this "something else" has yet to exist, we naturally ignore it.
FRENCH BOULANGERIE
With effort, however, we can VISUALIZE what we're missing.
Only then can we fairly compare the world as it is...
to the world as it could be.

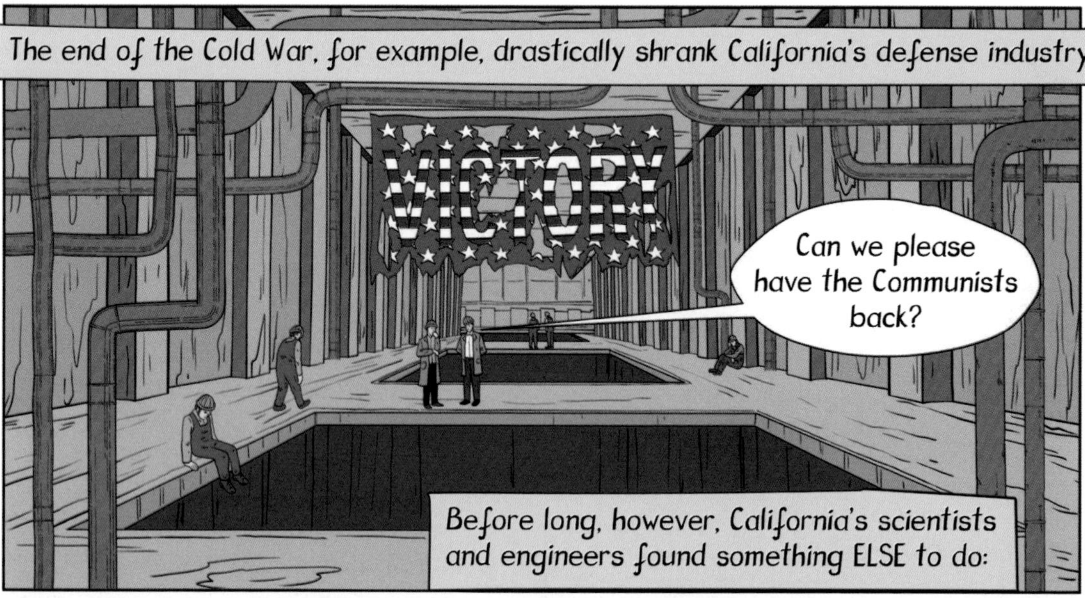
The end of the Cold War, for example, drastically shrank California's defense industry.
VICTORY
Can we please have the Communists back?
Before long, however, California's scientists and engineers found something ELSE to do:

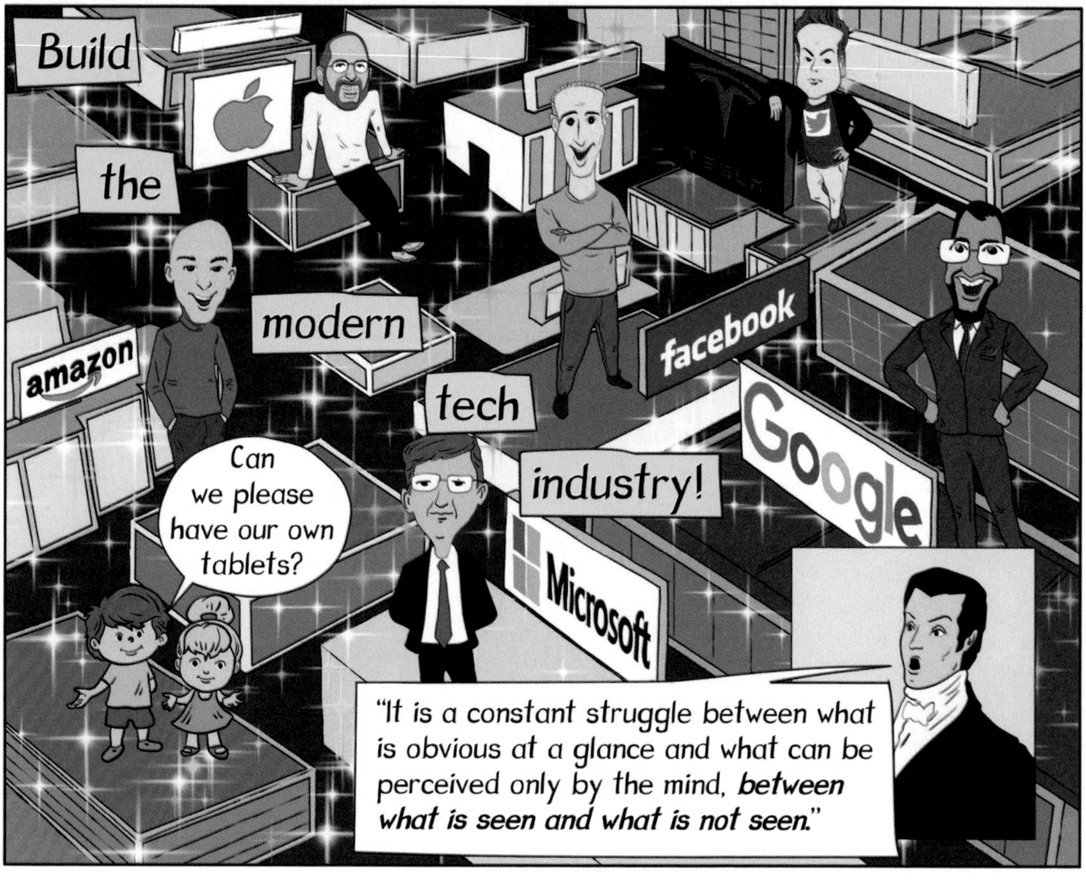
Build
the
modern
tech
industry!
amazon
facebook
Google
Microsoft
Can we please have our own tablets?
"It is a constant struggle between what is obvious at a glance and what can be perceived only by the mind, ***between what is seen and what is not seen.***"

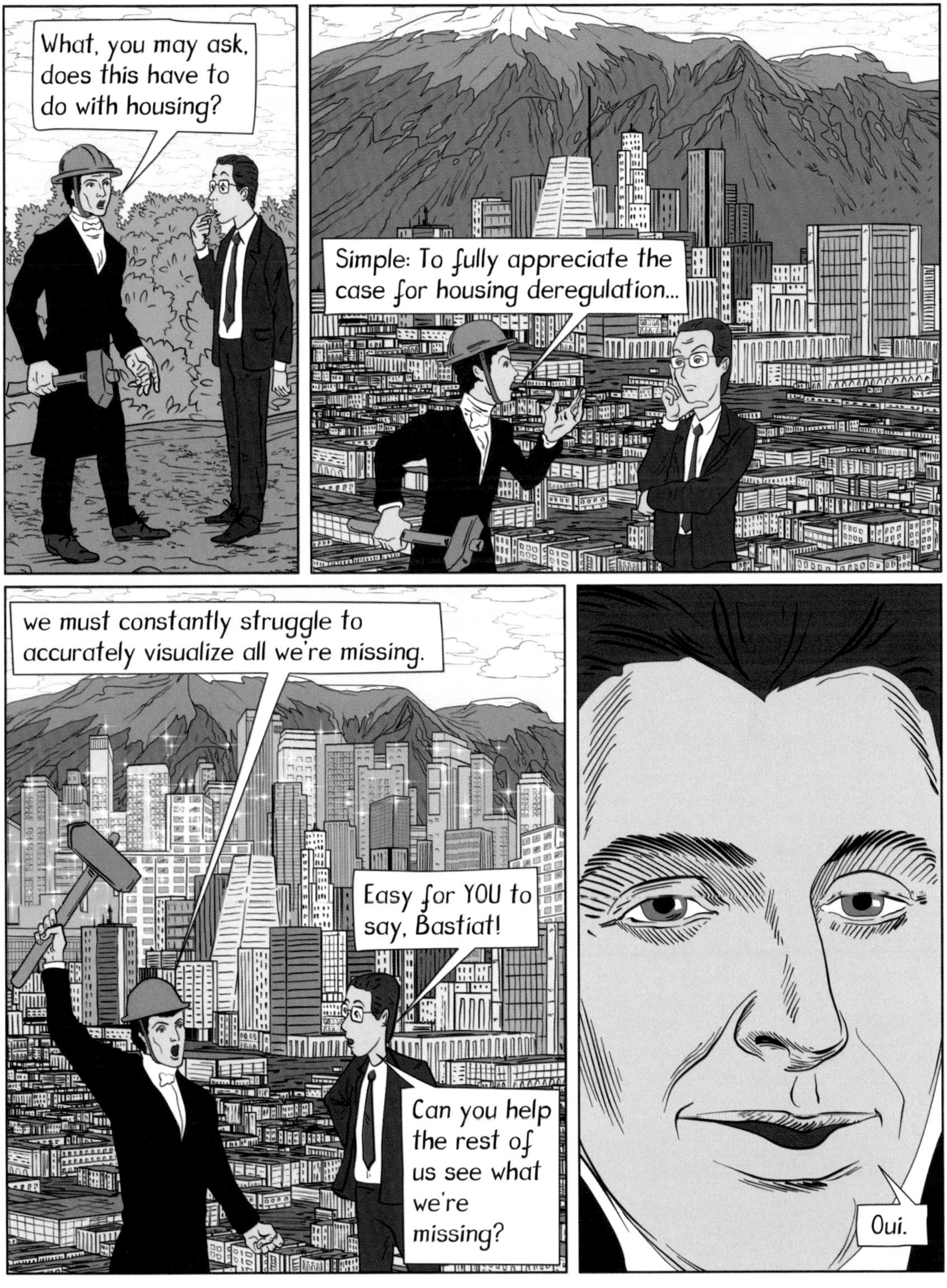
What, you may ask, does this have to do with housing?
Simple: To fully appreciate the case for housing deregulation...
we must constantly struggle to accurately visualize all we're missing.
Easy for YOU to say, Bastiat!
Can you help the rest of us see what we're missing?
Oui.

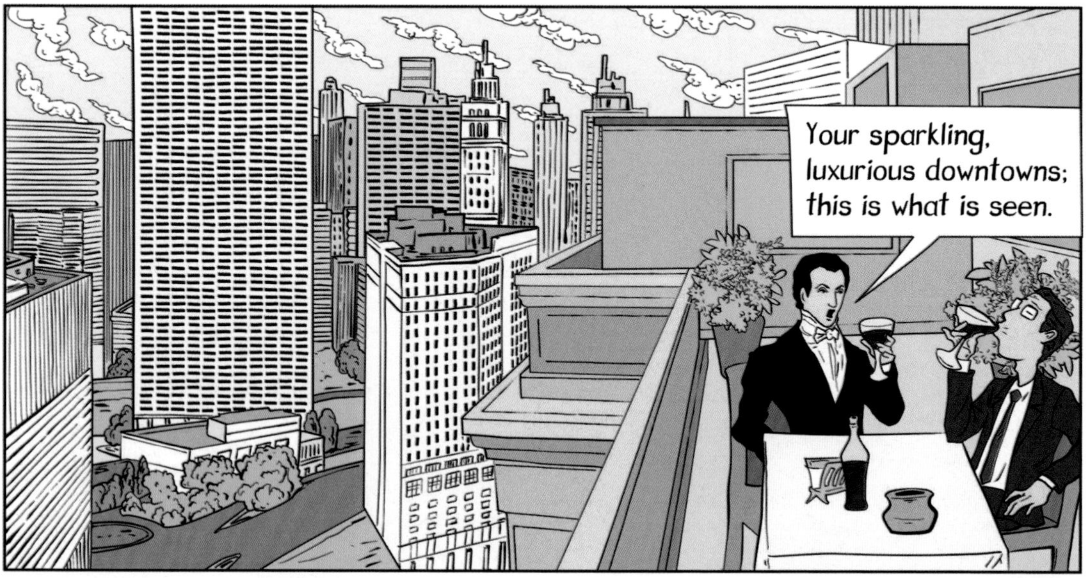
Your sparkling, luxurious downtowns; this is what is seen.

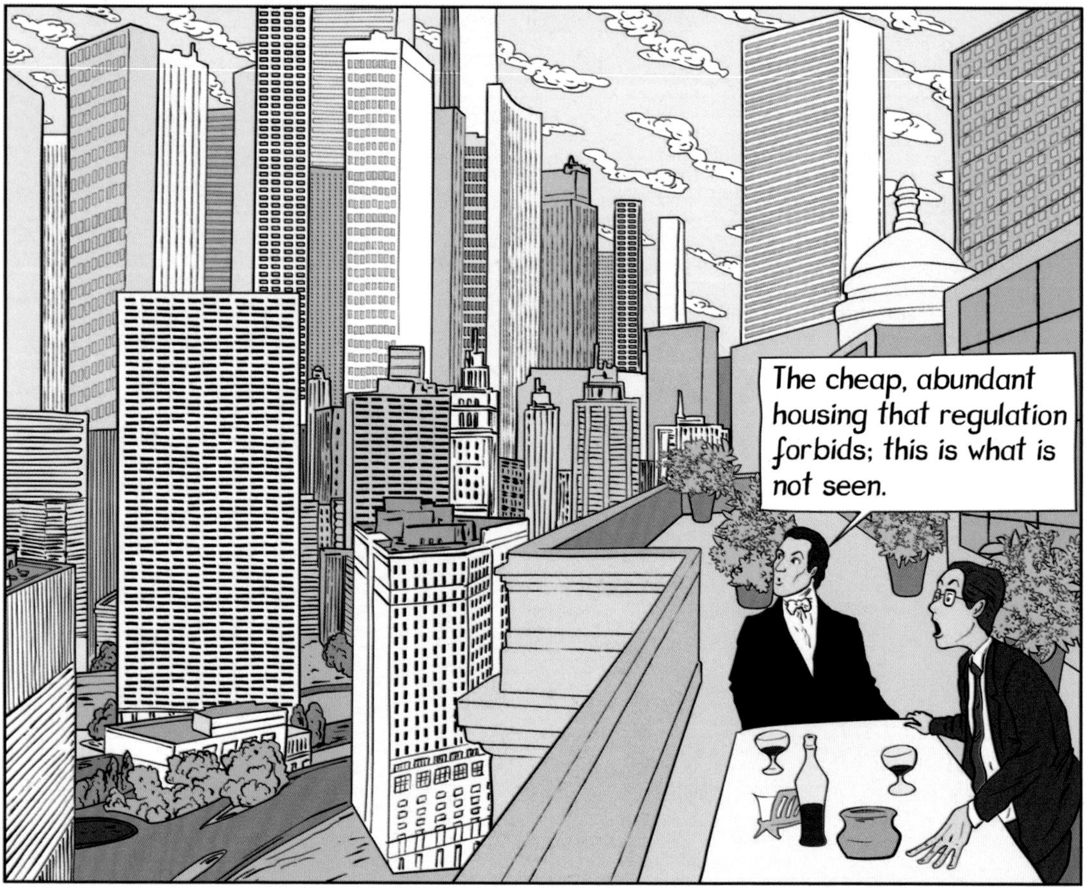
The cheap, abundant housing that regulation forbids; this is what is not seen.

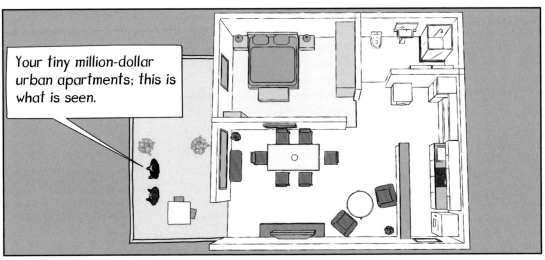

Your tiny million-dollar urban apartments; this is what is seen.

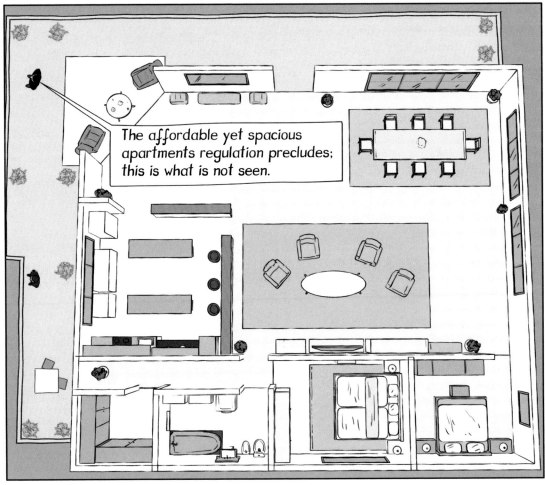

The affordable yet spacious apartments regulation precludes; this is what is not seen.

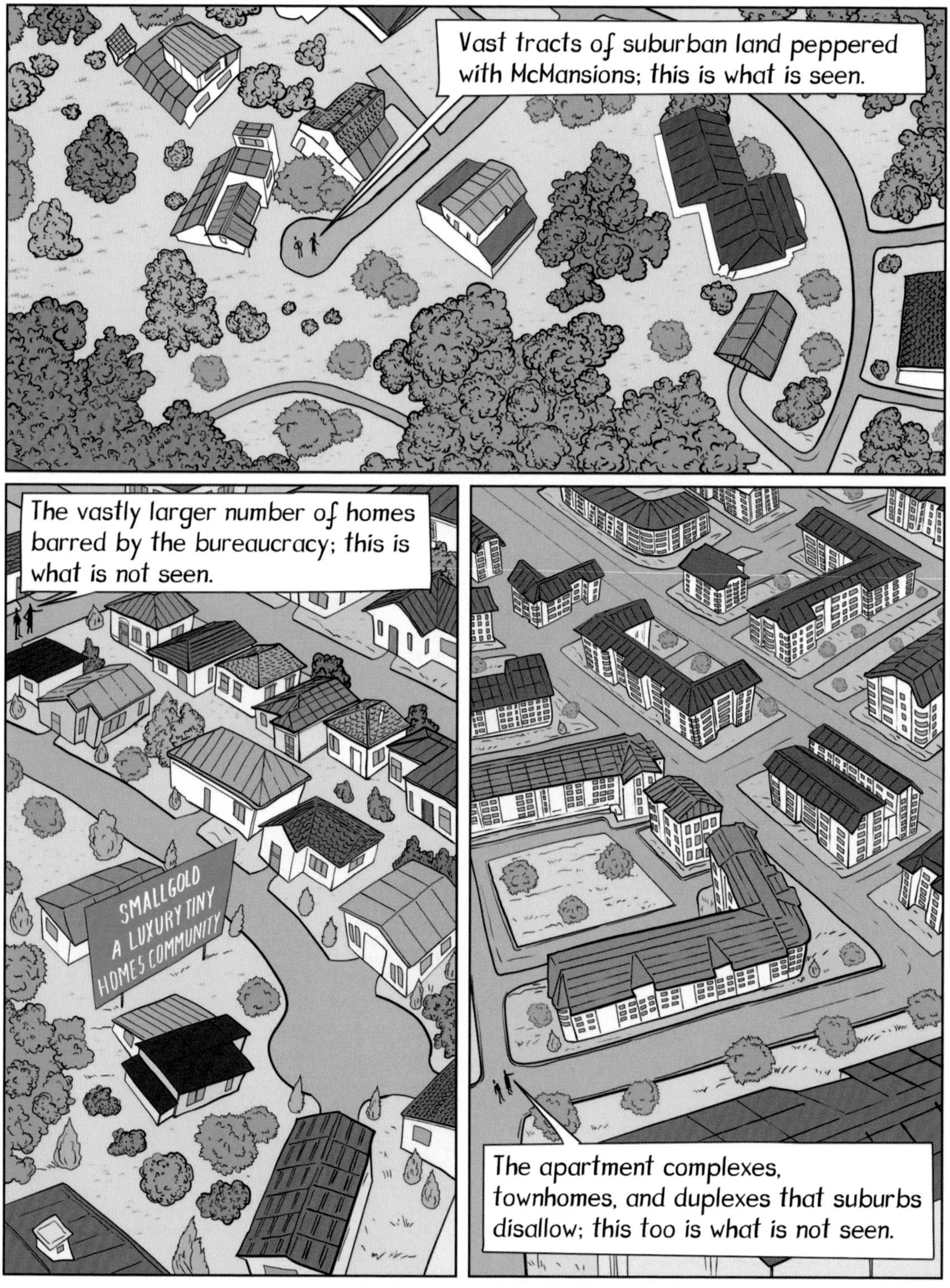
Vast tracts of suburban land peppered with McMansions; this is what is seen.
The vastly larger number of homes barred by the bureaucracy; this is what is not seen.
SMALLGOLD
A LUXURY TINY
HOMES COMMUNITY
The apartment complexes, townhomes, and duplexes that suburbs disallow; this too is what is not seen.

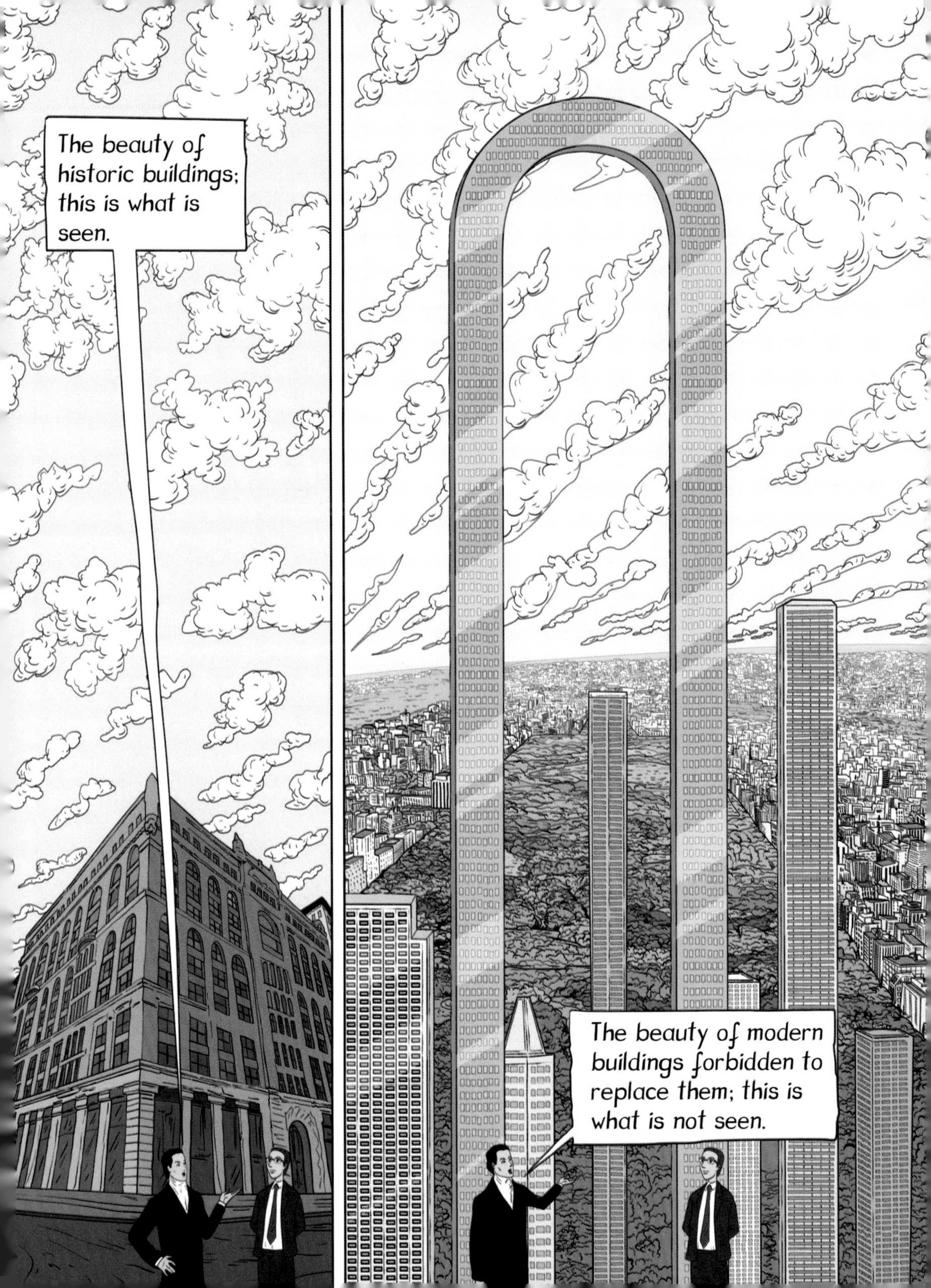
The beauty of historic buildings; this is what is seen.
The beauty of modern buildings forbidden to replace them; this is what is not seen.

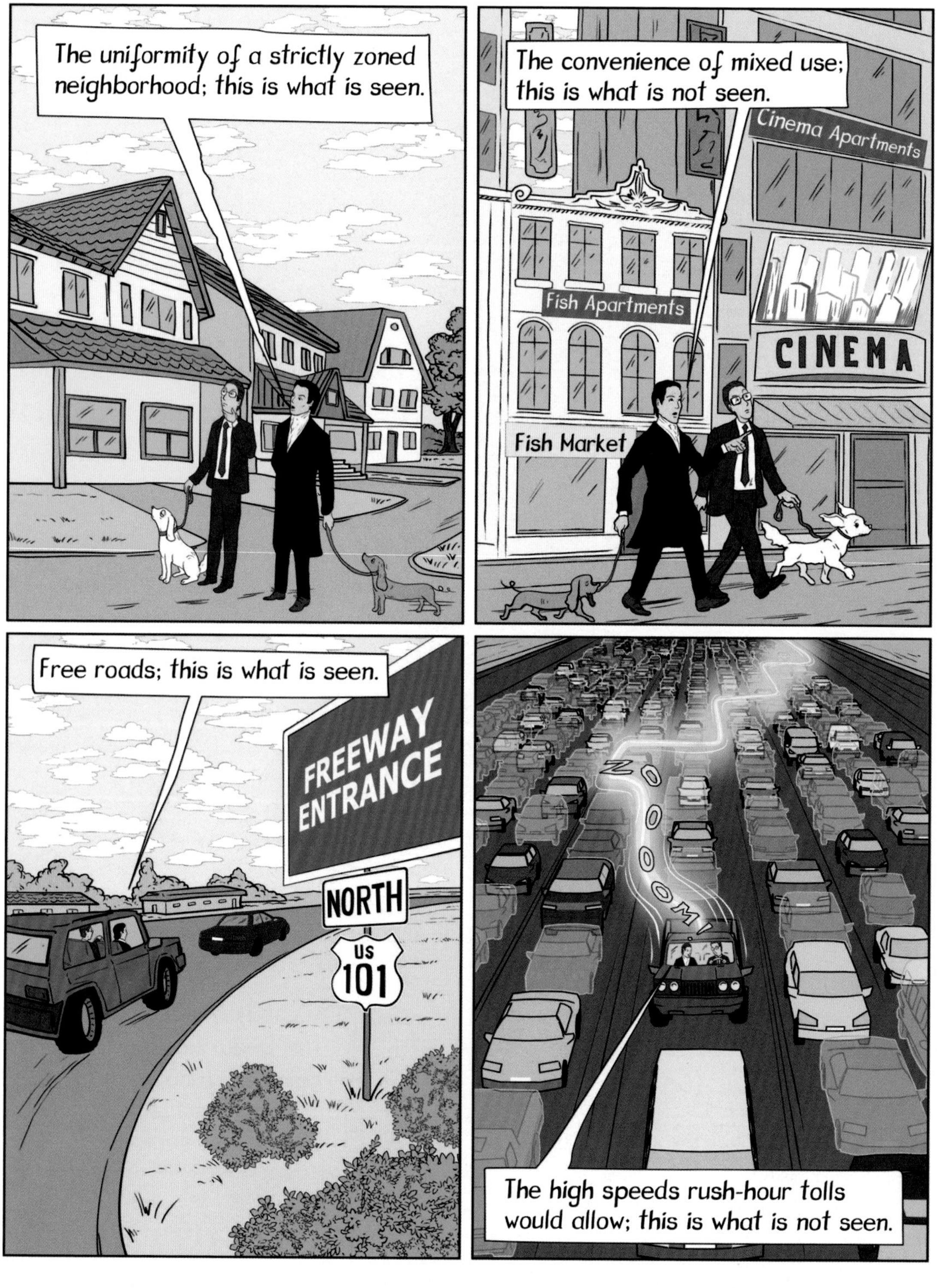
The uniformity of a strictly zoned neighborhood; this is what is seen.
The convenience of mixed use; this is what is not seen.
Cinema Apartments
Fish Apartments
CINEMA
Fish Market
Free roads; this is what is seen.
FREEWAY ENTRANCE
NORTH
US 101
ZOOOOOM!
The high speeds rush-hour tolls would allow; this is what is not seen.

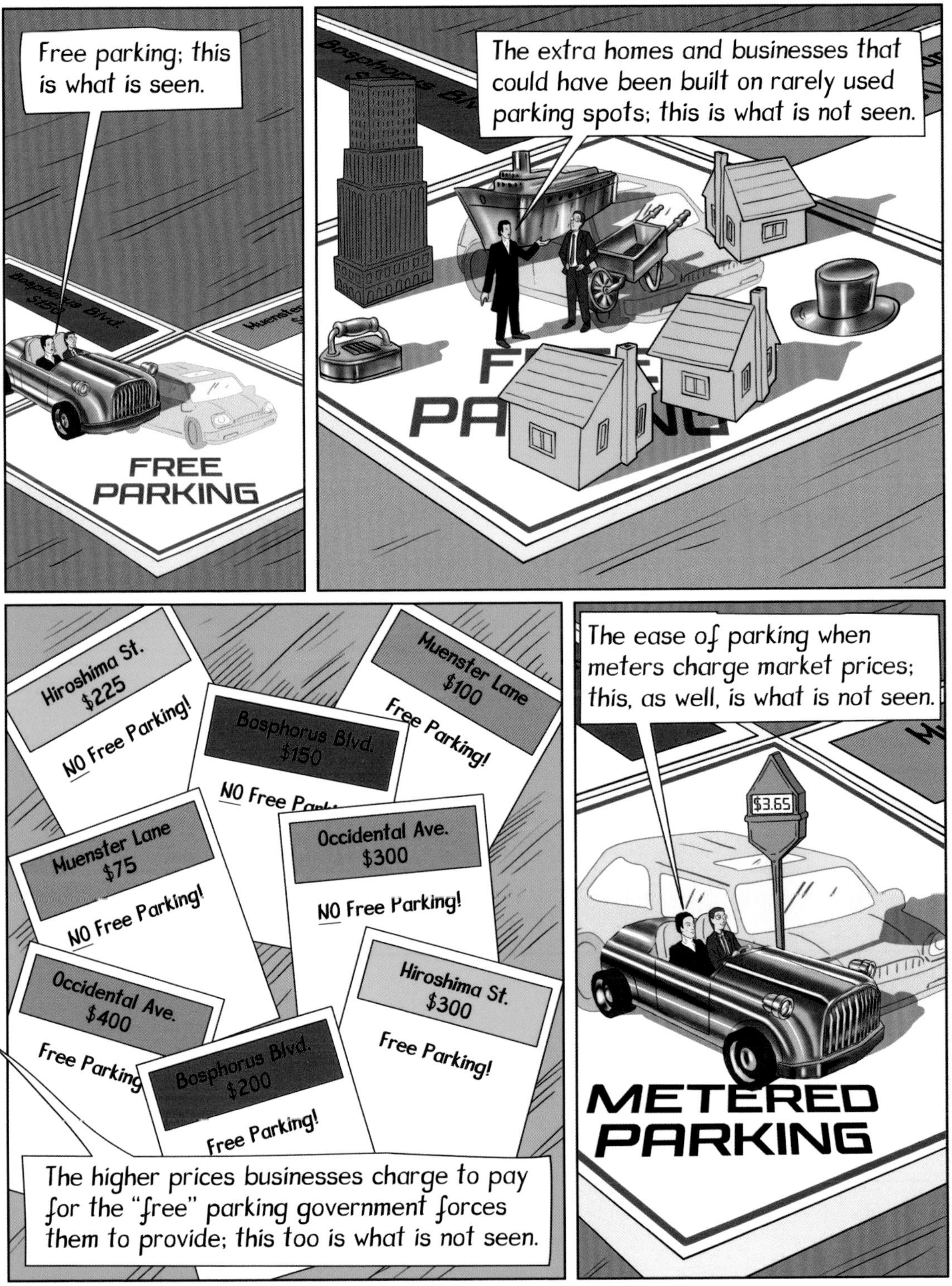
Free parking; this is what is seen.
FREE PARKING
The extra homes and businesses that could have been built on rarely used parking spots; this is what is not seen.
Hiroshima St. $225
NO Free Parking!
Bosphorus Blvd. $150
NO Free Park
Muenster Lane $100
Free Parking!
Muenster Lane $75
NO Free Parking!
Occidental Ave. $300
NO Free Parking!
Occidental Ave. $400
Free Parking
Bosphorus Blvd. $200
Free Parking!
Hiroshima St. $300
Free Parking!
The higher prices businesses charge to pay for the "free" parking government forces them to provide; this too is what is not seen.
The ease of parking when meters charge market prices; this, as well, is what is not seen.
$3.65
METERED PARKING

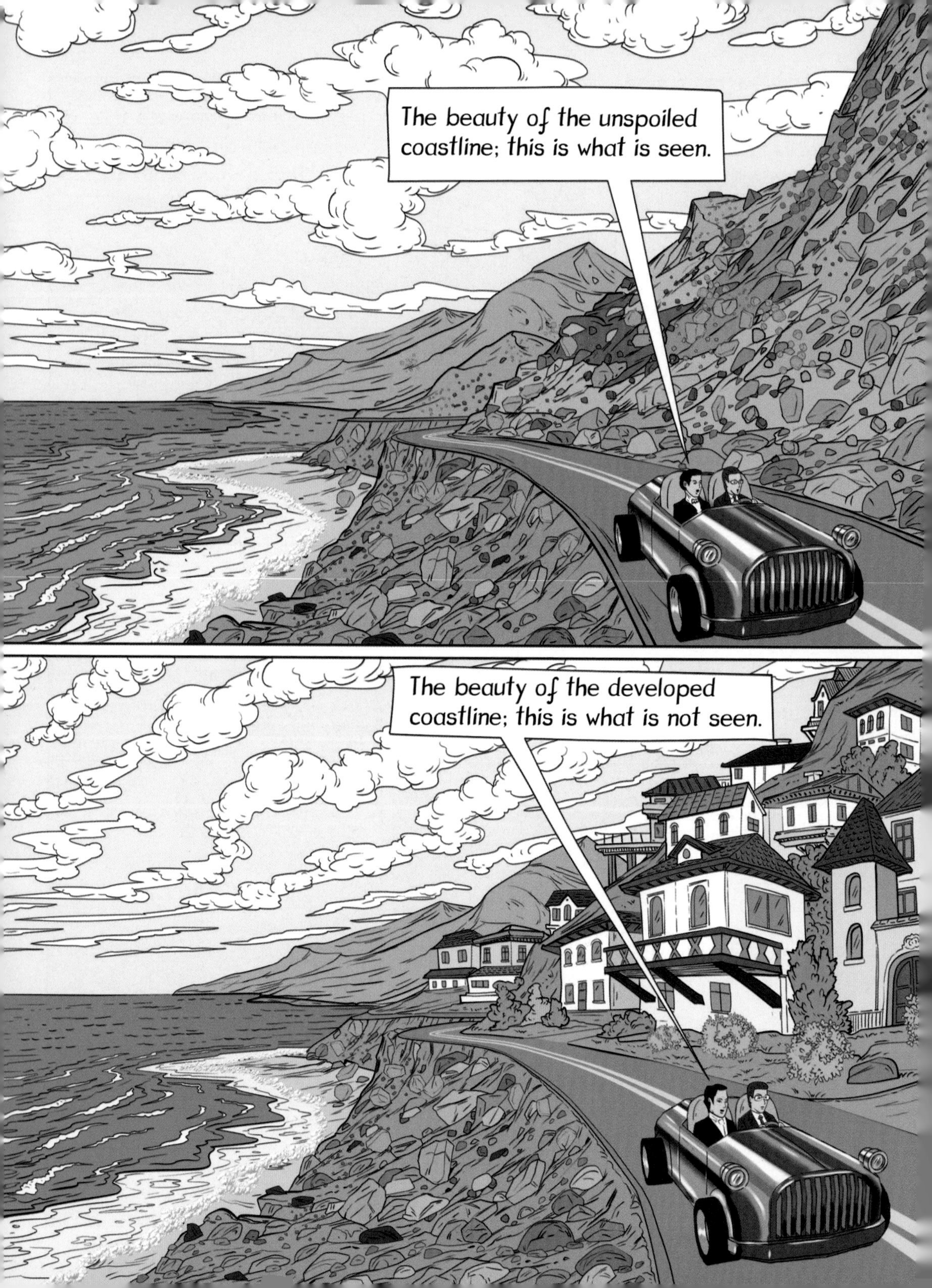
The beauty of the unspoiled coastline; this is what is seen.
The beauty of the developed coastline; this is what is not seen.

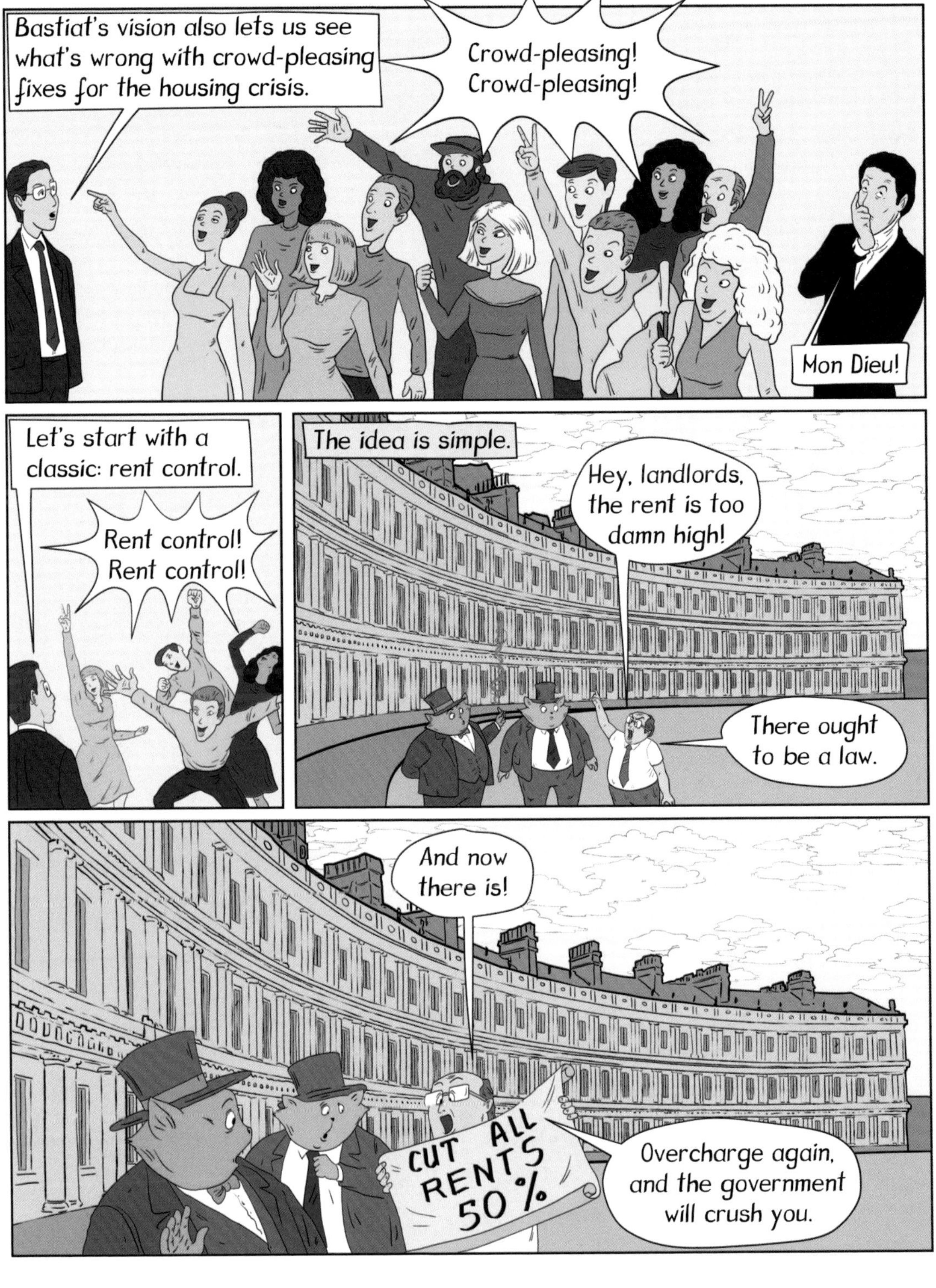
Bastiat's vision also lets us see what's wrong with crowd-pleasing fixes for the housing crisis.
Crowd-pleasing! Crowd-pleasing!
Mon Dieu!
Let's start with a classic: rent control.
Rent control! Rent control!
The idea is simple.
Hey, landlords, the rent is too damn high!
There ought to be a law.
And now there is!
CUT ALL RENTS 50%
Overcharge again, and the government will crush you.

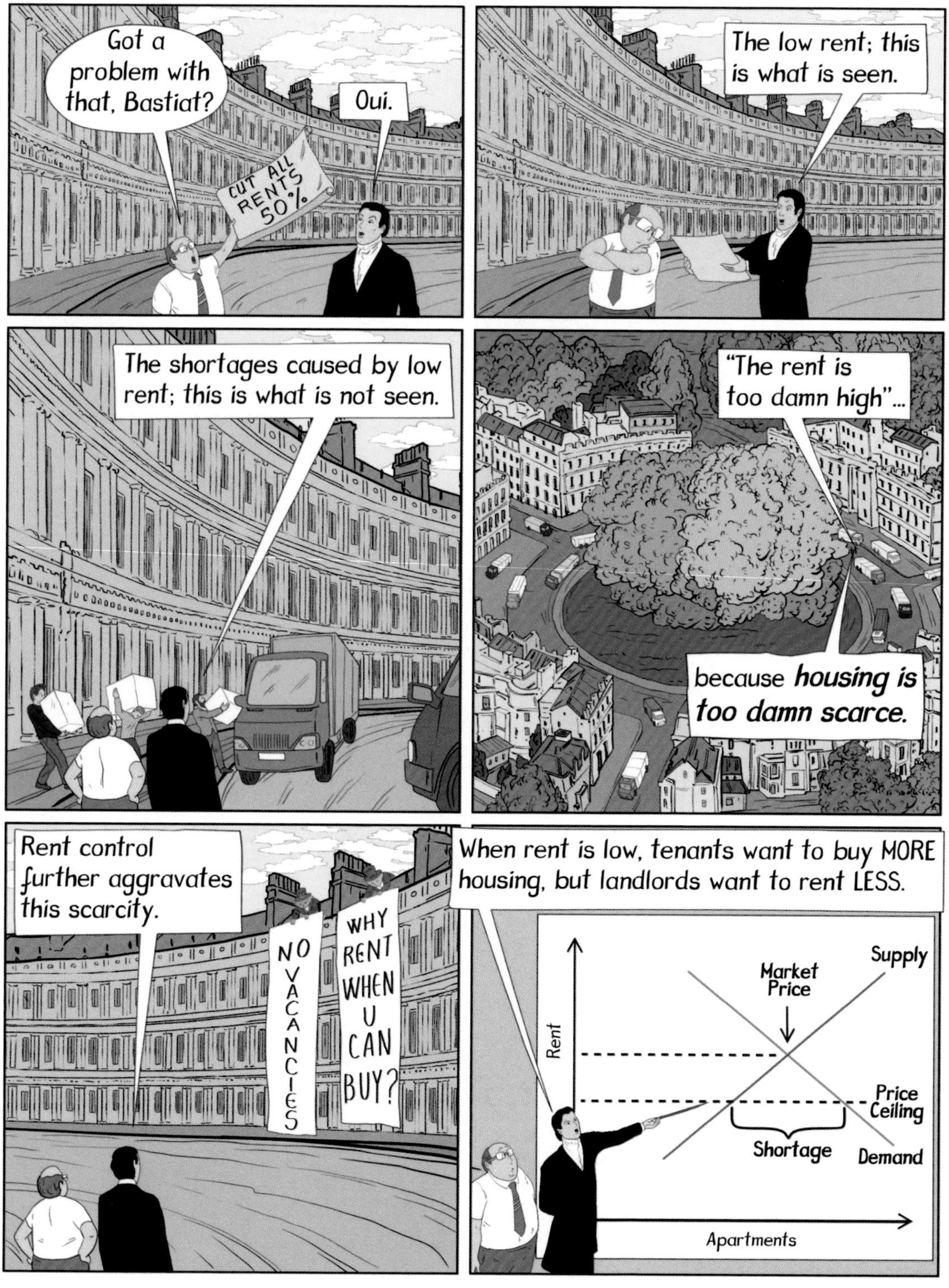
Got a problem with that, Bastiat?
Oui.
CUT ALL RENTS 50%
The low rent; this is what is seen.
The shortages caused by low rent; this is what is not seen.
"The rent is too damn high"...
because ***housing is too damn scarce.***
Rent control further aggravates this scarcity.
NO VACANCIES
WHY RENT WHEN U CAN BUY?
When rent is low, tenants want to buy MORE housing, but landlords want to rent LESS.
Supply
Market Price
Rent
Price Ceiling
Shortage
Demand
Apartments

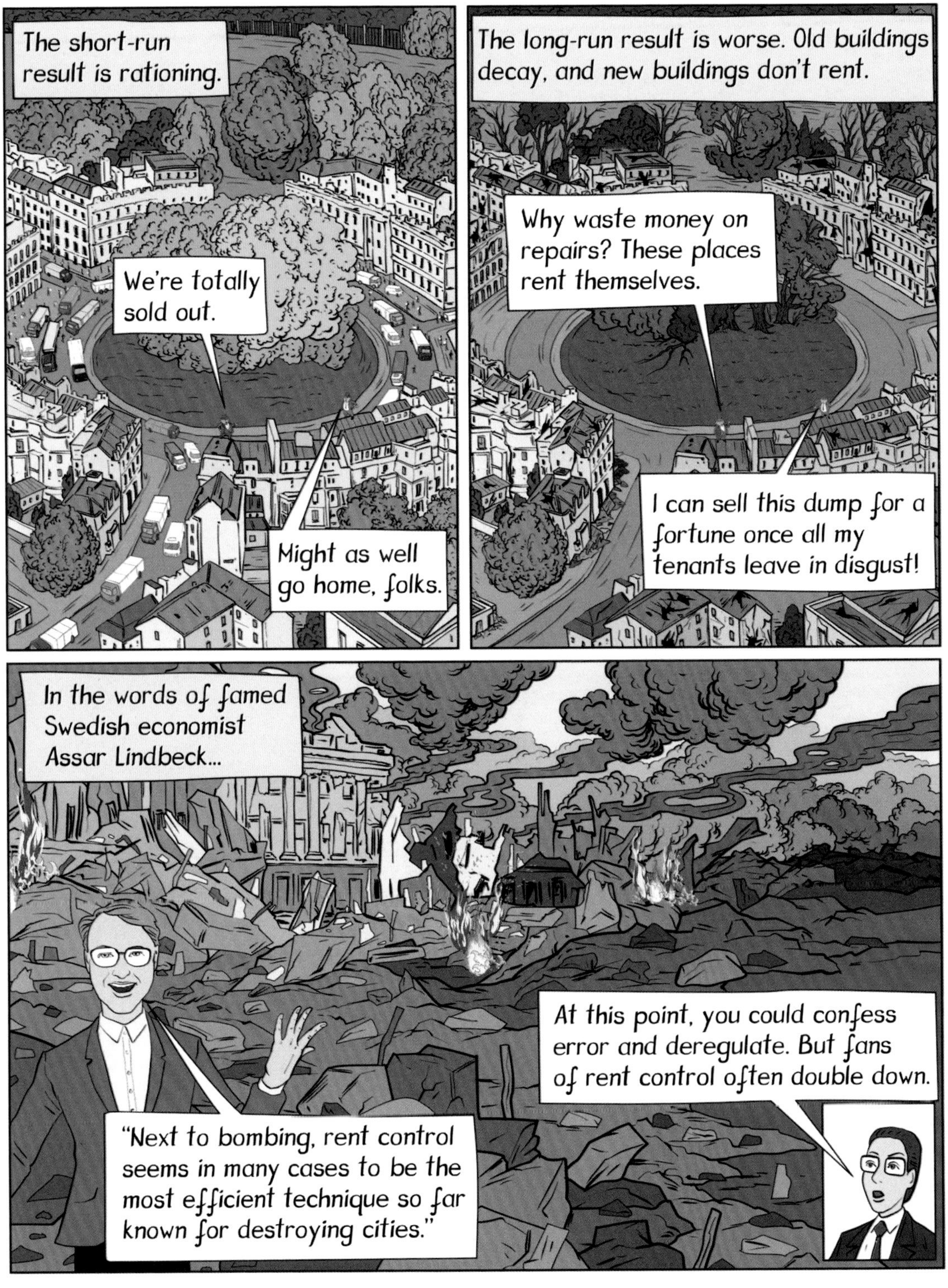
The short-run result is rationing.
We're totally sold out.
Might as well go home, folks.
The long-run result is worse. Old buildings decay, and new buildings don't rent.
Why waste money on repairs? These places rent themselves.
I can sell this dump for a fortune once all my tenants leave in disgust!
In the words of famed Swedish economist Assar Lindbeck...
"Next to bombing, rent control seems in many cases to be the most efficient technique so far known for destroying cities."
At this point, you could confess error and deregulate. But fans of rent control often double down.

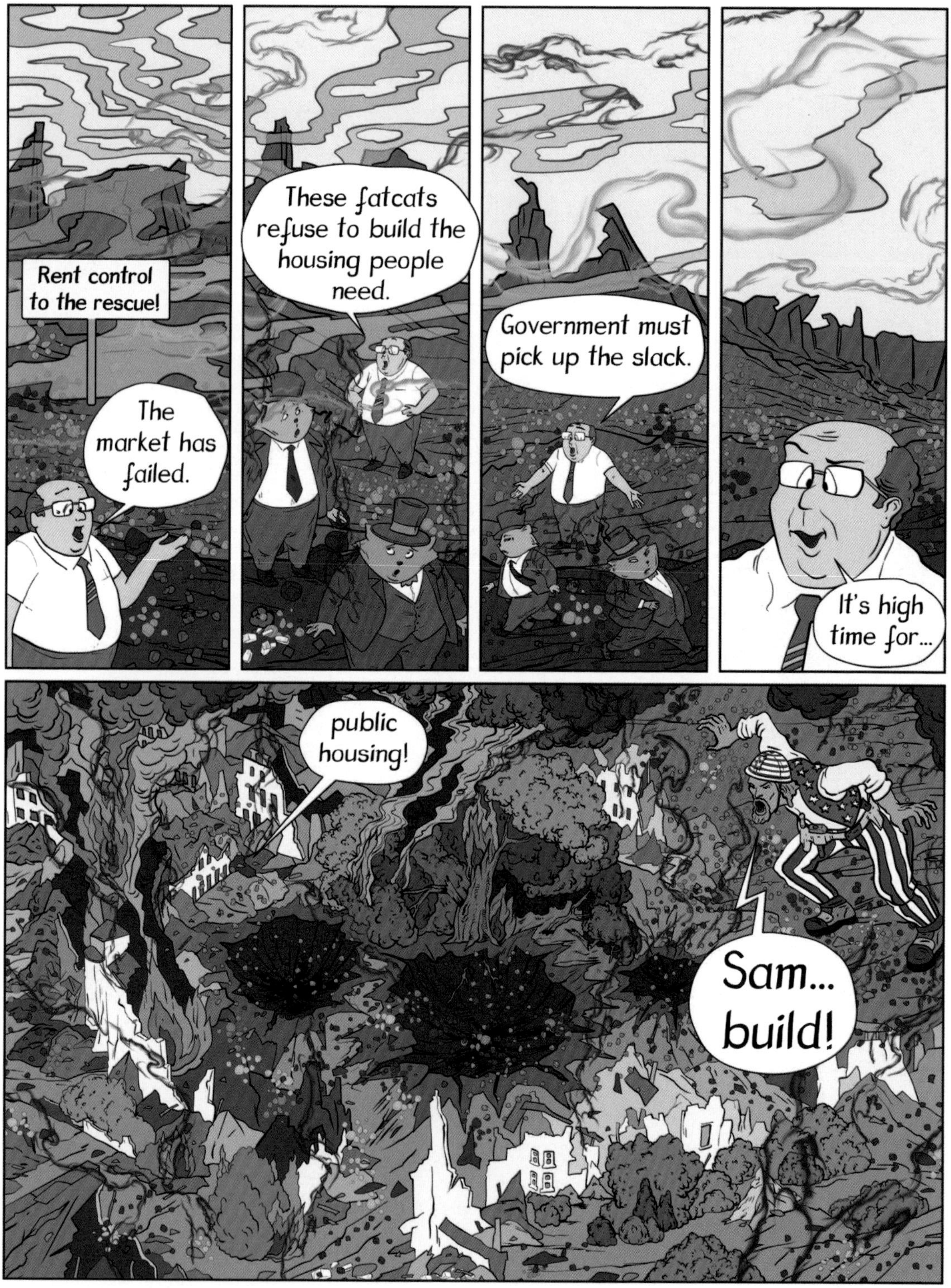
Rent control to the rescue!
The market has failed.
These fatcats refuse to build the housing people need.
Government must pick up the slack.
It's high time for...
public housing!
Sam... build!

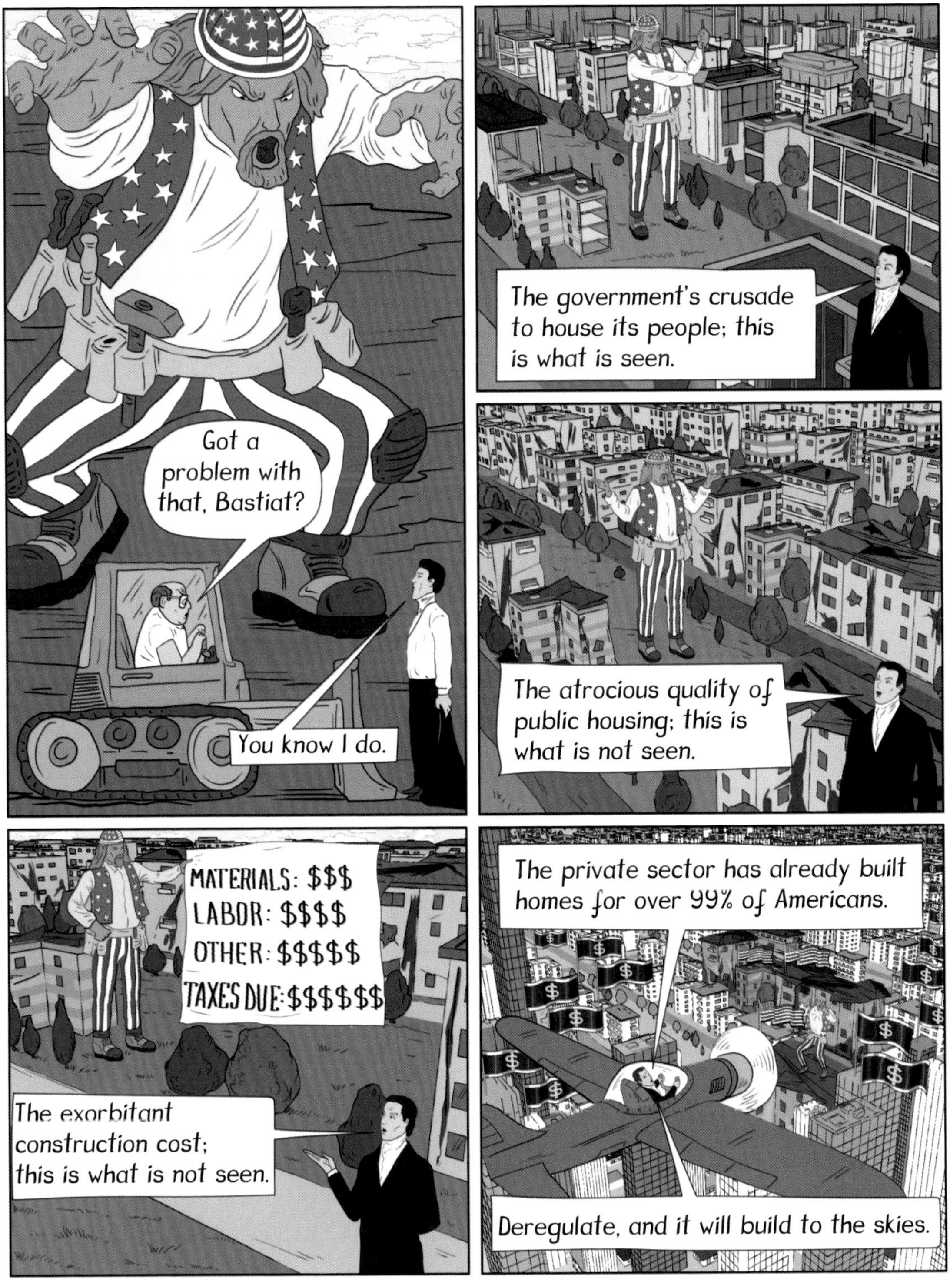

Got a problem with that, Bastiat?
You know I do.
The government's crusade to house its people; this is what is seen.
The atrocious quality of public housing; this is what is not seen.
MATERIALS: $$$
LABOR: $$$$
OTHER: $$$$$
TAXES DUE: $$$$$$
The exorbitant construction cost; this is what is not seen.
The private sector has already built homes for over 99% of Americans.
Deregulate, and it will build to the skies.

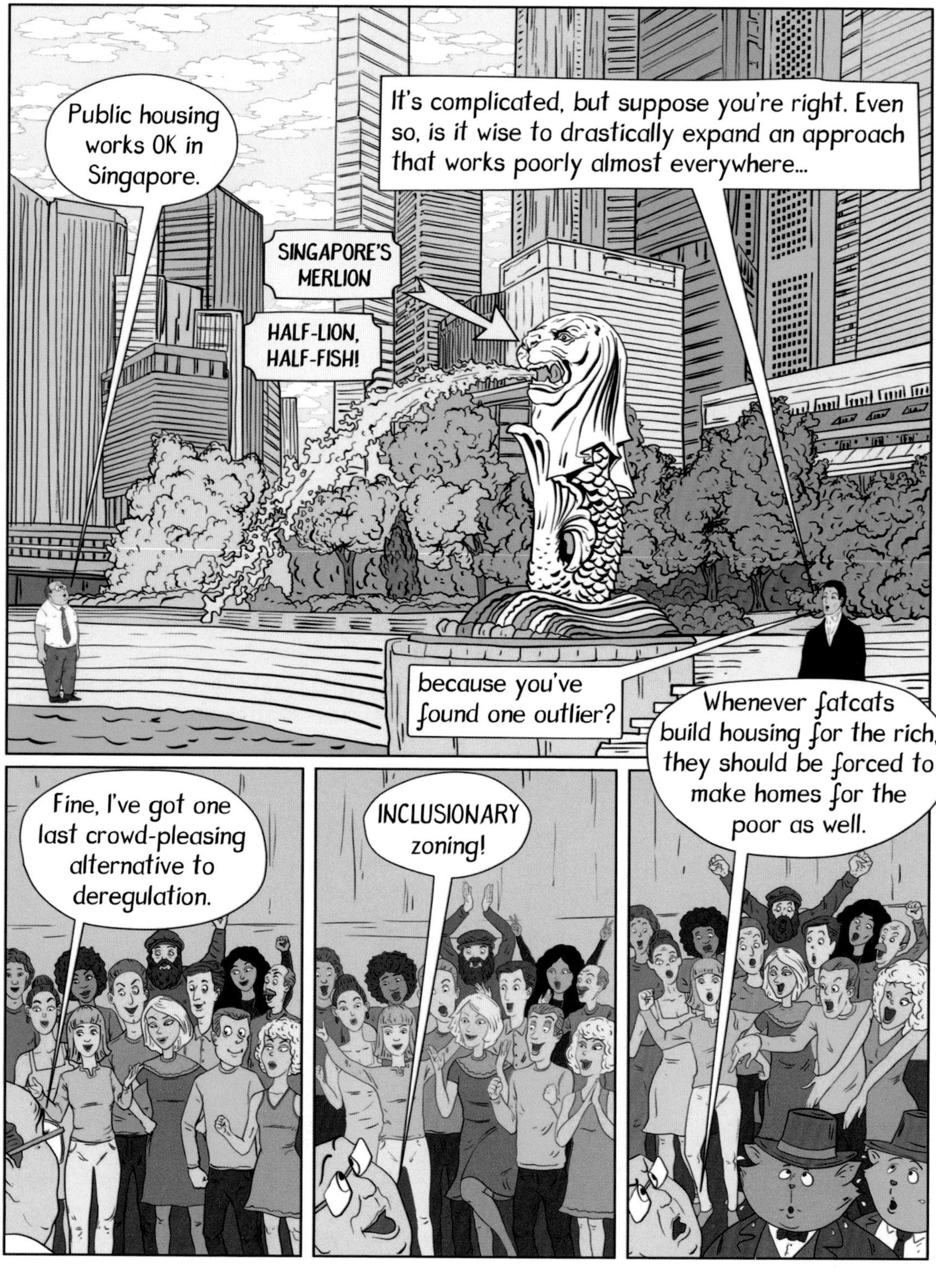
Public housing works OK in Singapore.
It's complicated, but suppose you're right. Even so, is it wise to drastically expand an approach that works poorly almost everywhere...
SINGAPORE'S MERLION
HALF-LION, HALF-FISH!
because you've found one outlier?
Fine, I've got one last crowd-pleasing alternative to deregulation.
INCLUSIONARY zoning!
Whenever fatcats build housing for the rich, they should be forced to make homes for the poor as well.

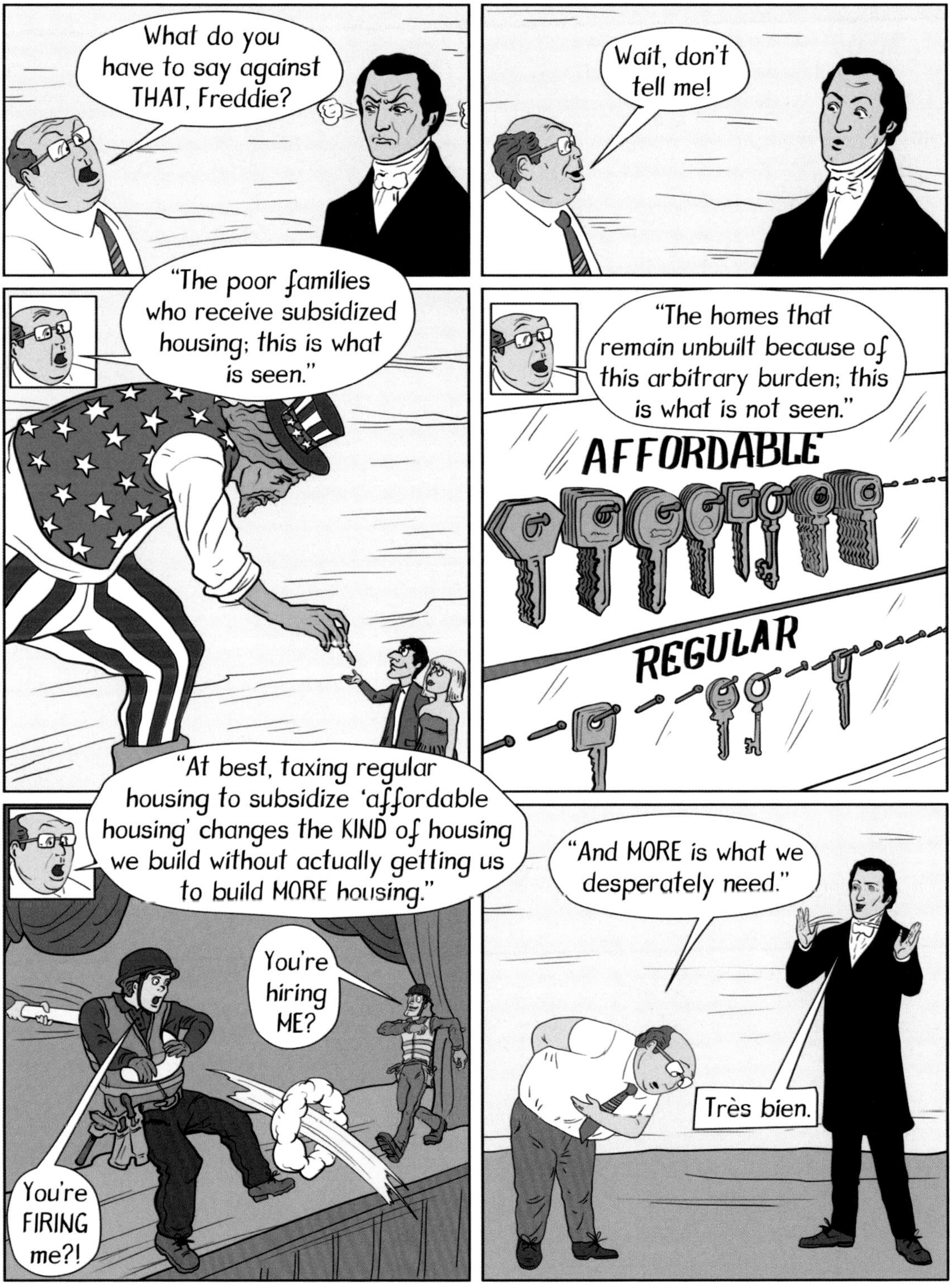
What do you have to say against THAT, Freddie?
Wait, don't tell me!
"The poor families who receive subsidized housing; this is what is seen."
"The homes that remain unbuilt because of this arbitrary burden; this is what is not seen."
AFFORDABLE
REGULAR
"At best, taxing regular housing to subsidize 'affordable housing' changes the KIND of housing we build without actually getting us to build MORE housing."
You're hiring ME?
You're FIRING me?!
"And MORE is what we desperately need."
Très bien.

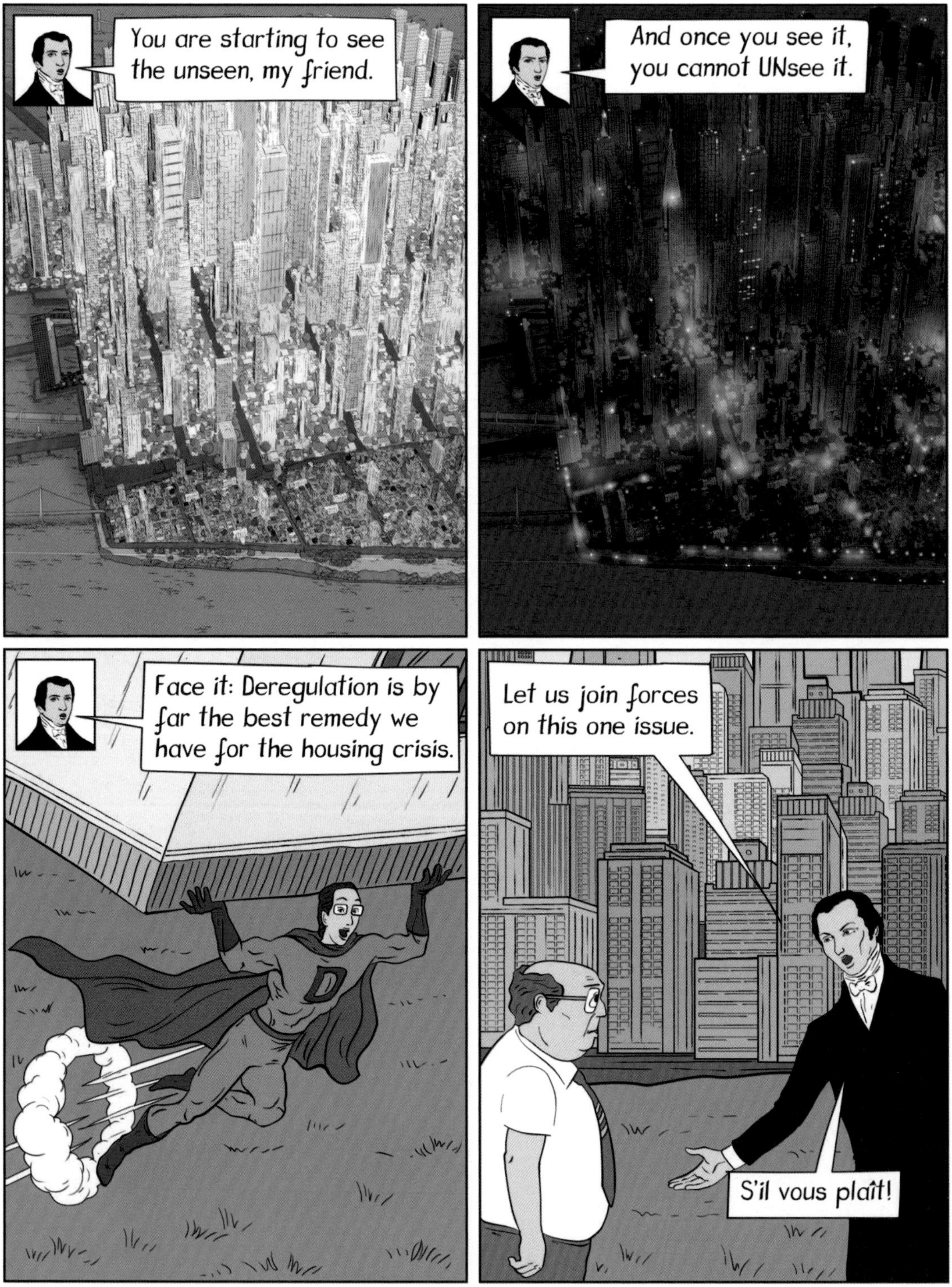
You are starting to see the unseen, my friend.
And once you see it, you cannot UNsee it.
Face it: Deregulation is by far the best remedy we have for the housing crisis.
Let us join forces on this one issue.
S'il vous plaît!

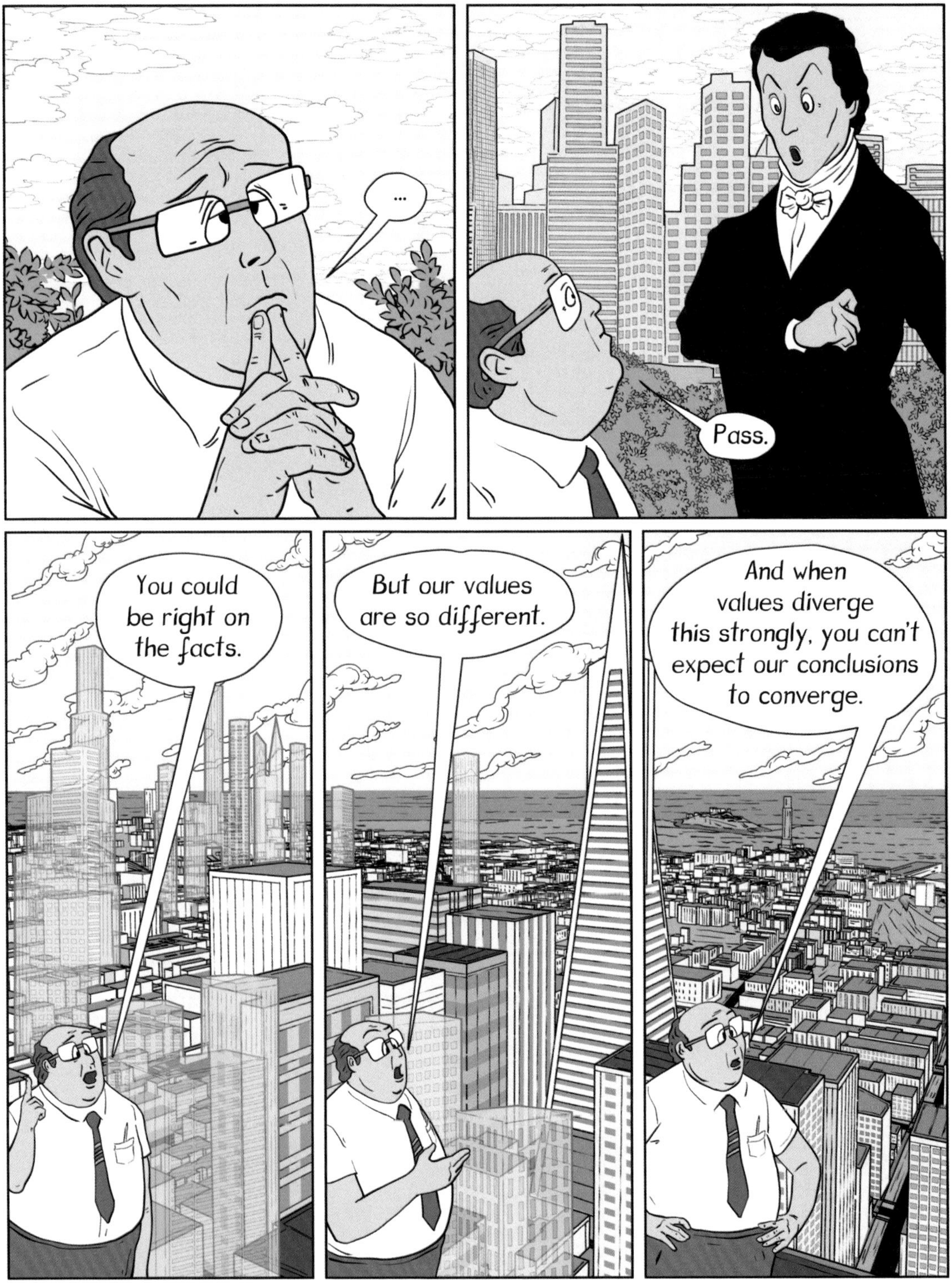
...
Pass.
You could be right on the facts.
But our values are so different.
And when values diverge this strongly, you can't expect our conclusions to converge.

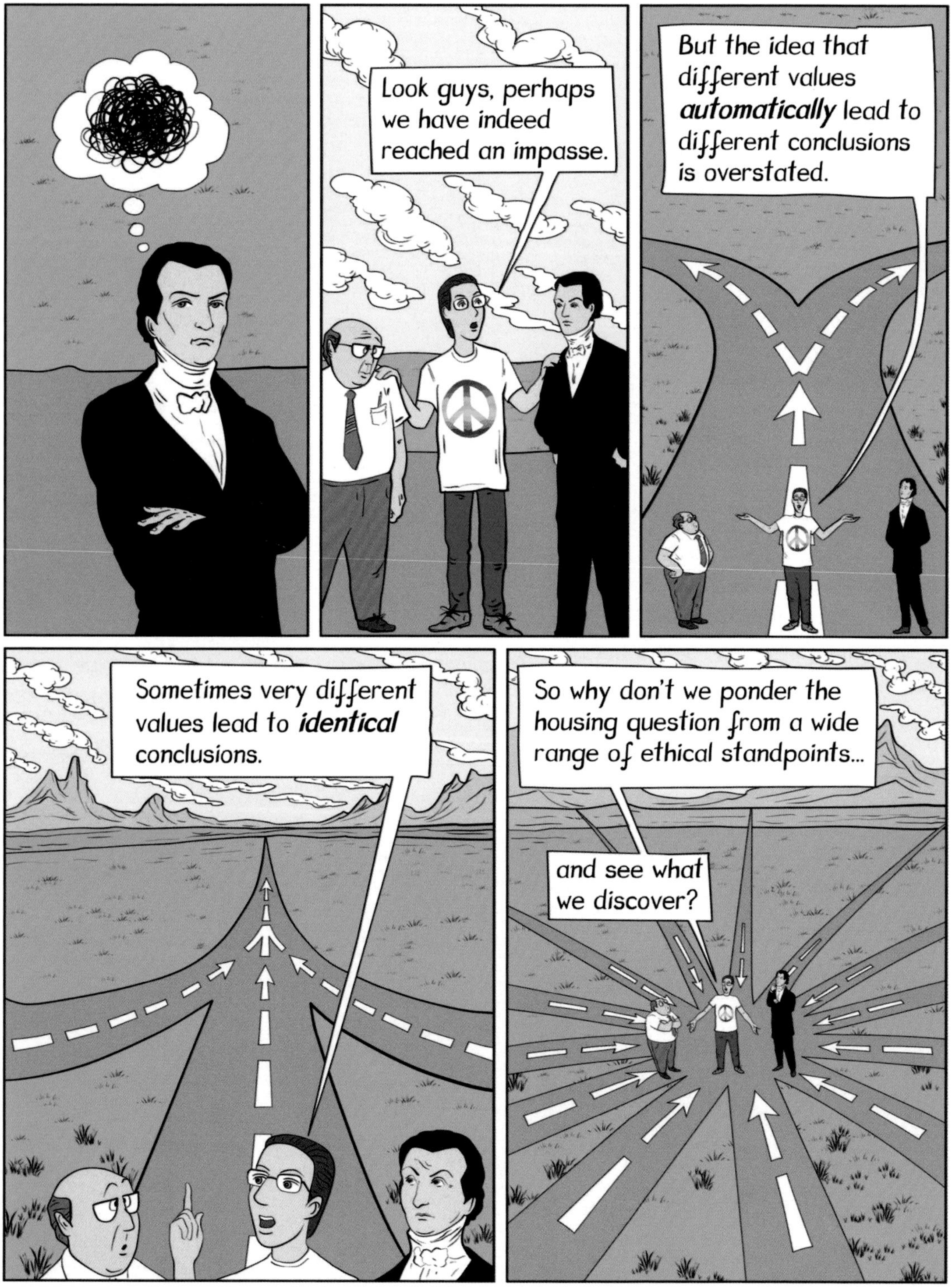
Look guys, perhaps we have indeed reached an impasse.
But the idea that different values *automatically* lead to different conclusions is overstated.
Sometimes very different values lead to *identical* conclusions.
So why don't we ponder the housing question from a wide range of ethical standpoints...
and see what we discover?

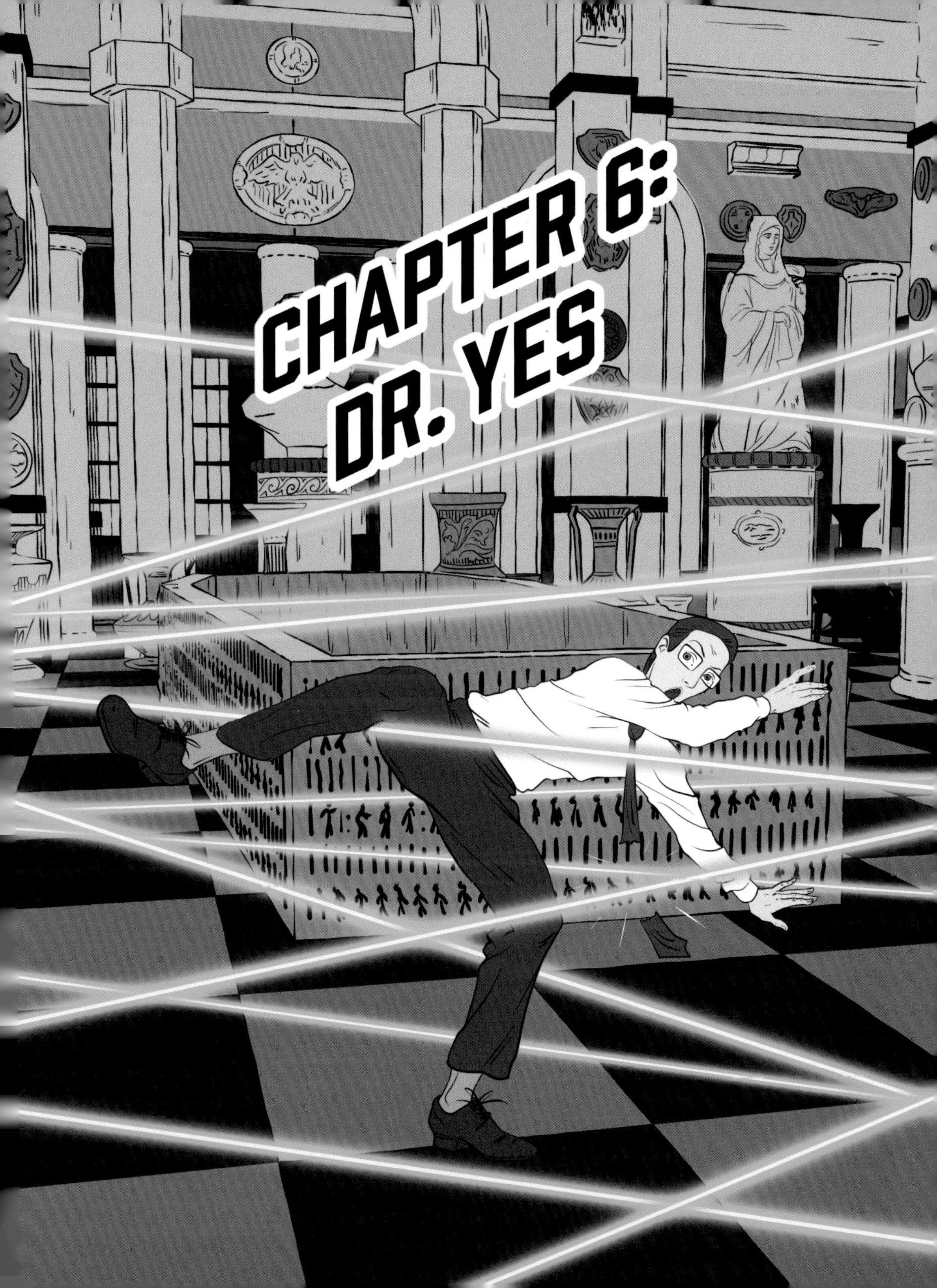
CHAPTER 6:
DR. YES

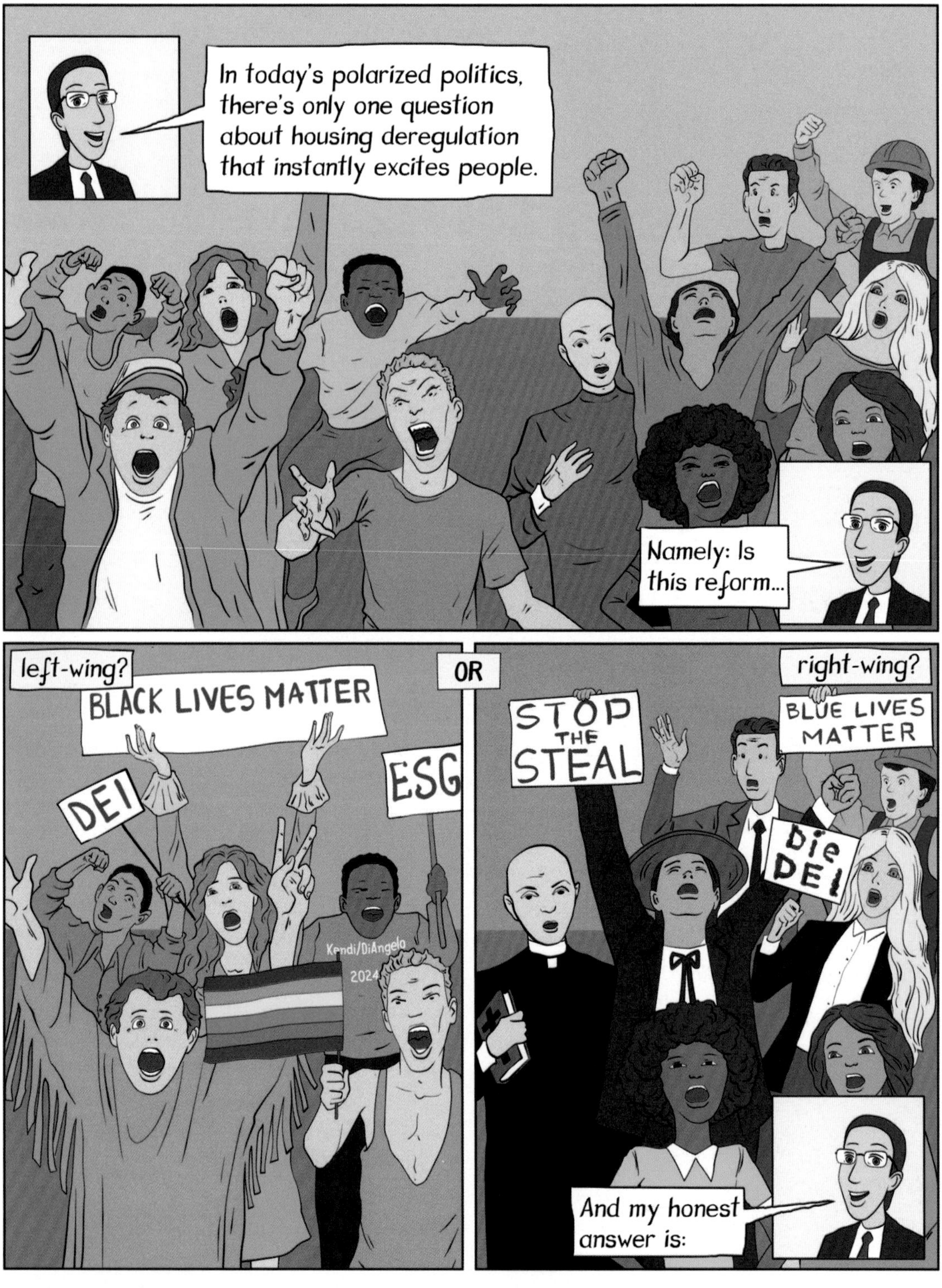
In today's polarized politics, there's only one question about housing deregulation that instantly excites people.
Namely: Is this reform...
left-wing?
BLACK LIVES MATTER
DEI
ESG
Kendi/DiAngelo 2024
OR
right-wing?
STOP THE STEAL
BLUE LIVES MATTER
Die DEI
And my honest answer is:

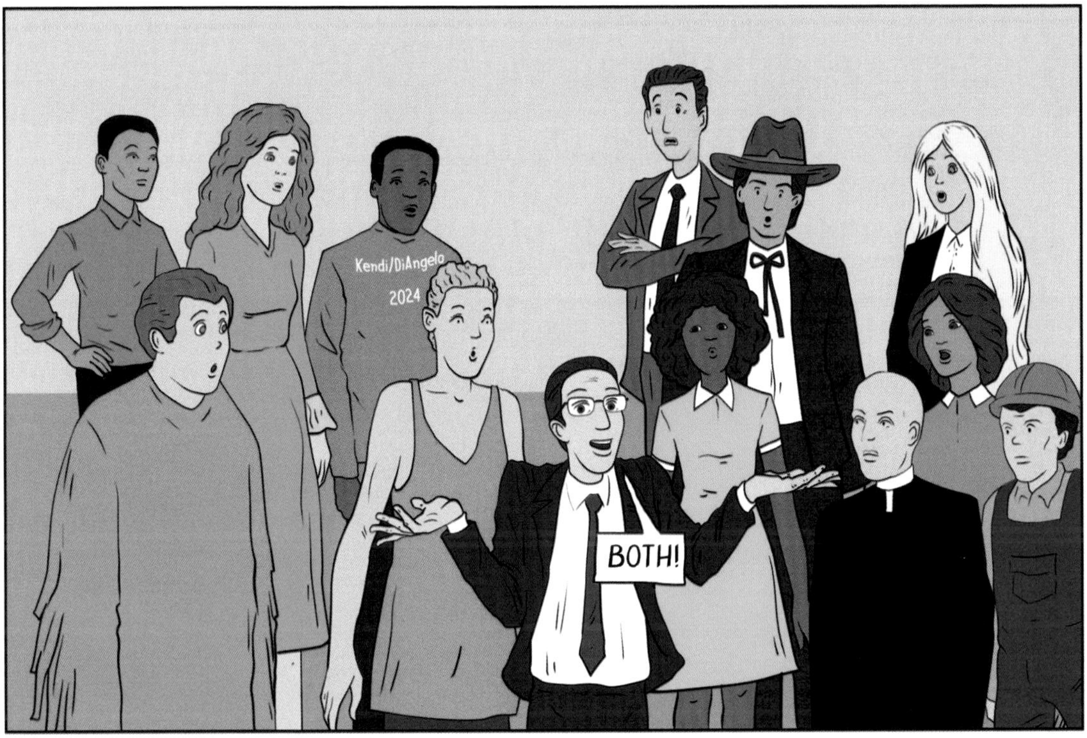
Kendi/DiAngelo
2024
BOTH!

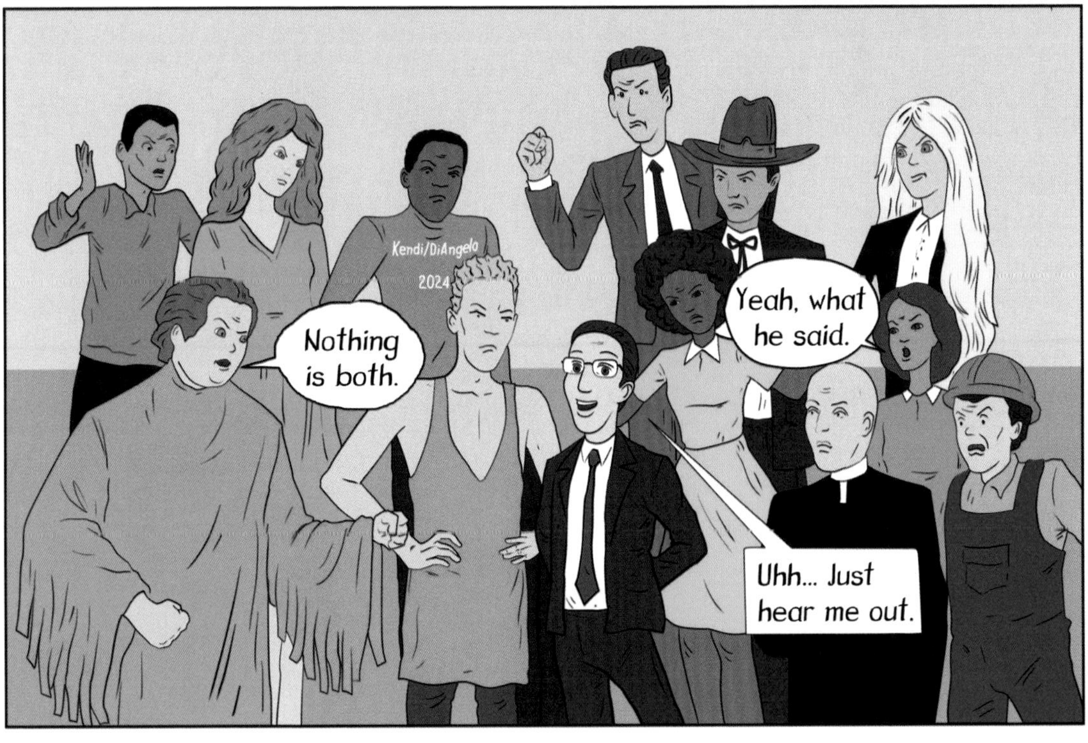
Kendi/DiAngelo
2024
Nothing is both.
Yeah, what he said.
Uhh... Just hear me out.

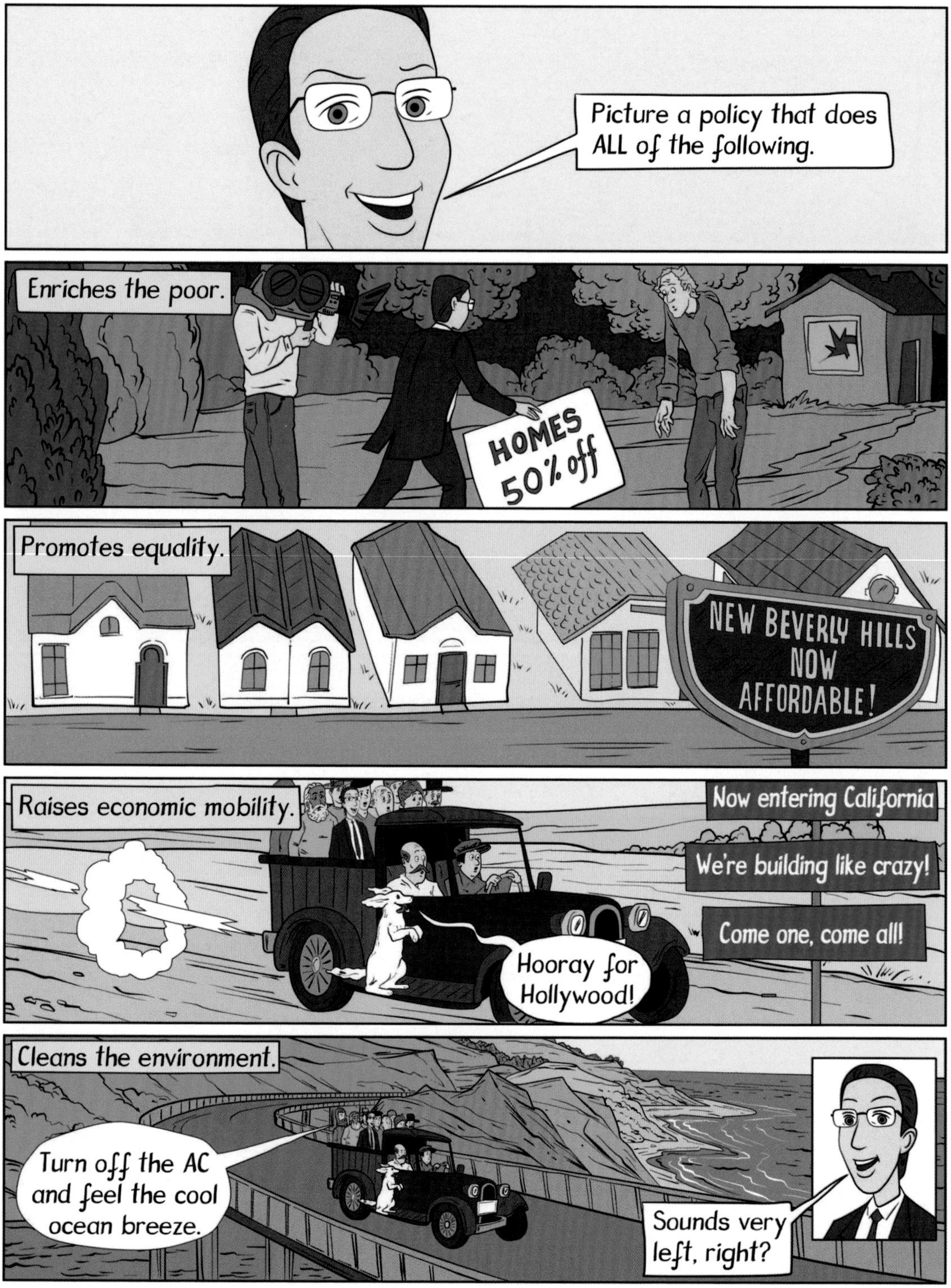
Picture a policy that does ALL of the following.
Enriches the poor.
HOMES 50% off
Promotes equality.
NEW BEVERLY HILLS NOW AFFORDABLE!
Raises economic mobility.
Now entering California
We're building like crazy!
Come one, come all!
Hooray for Hollywood!
Cleans the environment.
Turn off the AC and feel the cool ocean breeze.
Sounds very left, right?

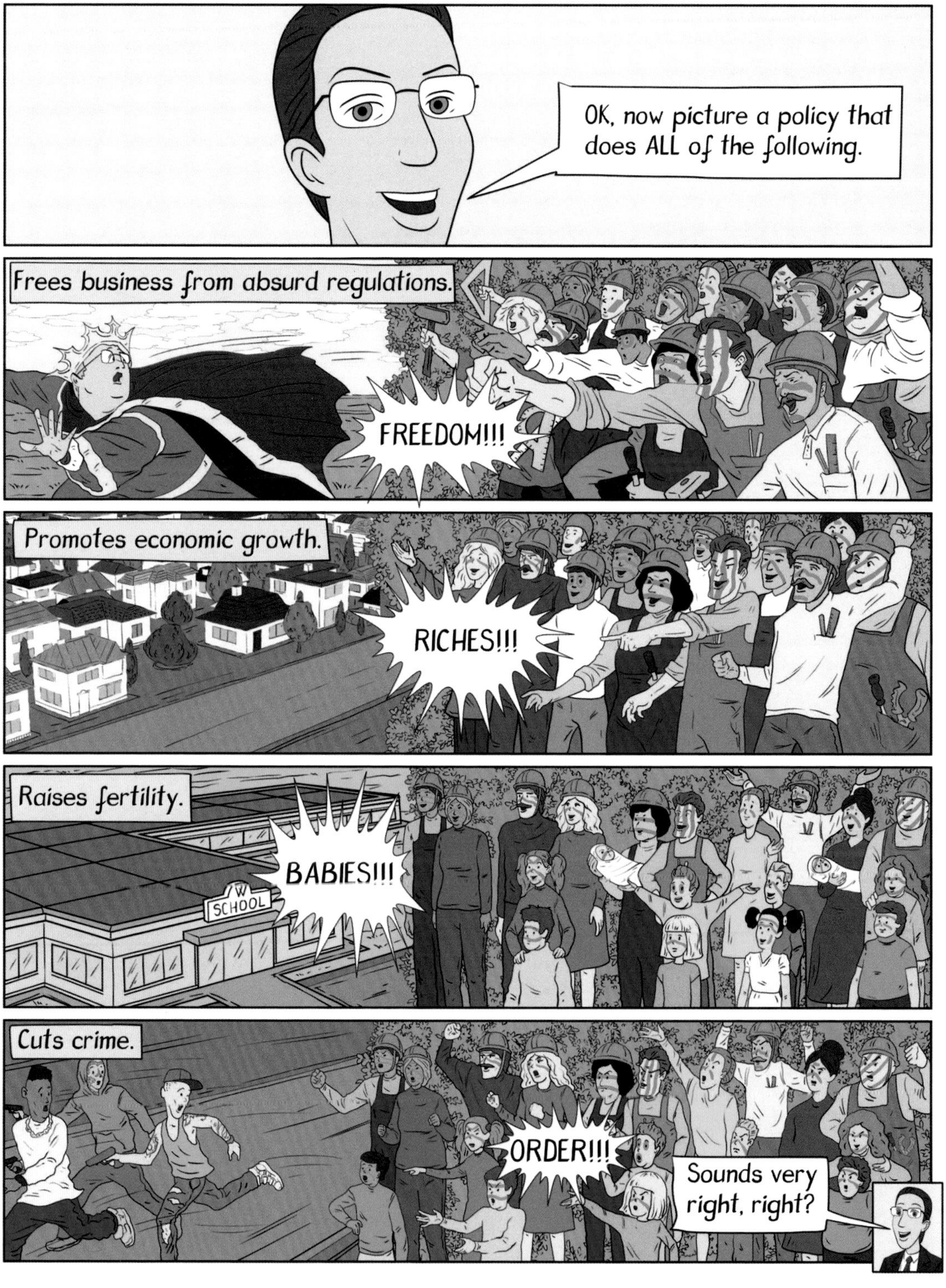
OK, now picture a policy that does ALL of the following.
Frees business from absurd regulations.
FREEDOM!!!
Promotes economic growth.
RICHES!!!
Raises fertility.
SCHOOL
BABIES!!!
Cuts crime.
ORDER!!!
Sounds very right, right?

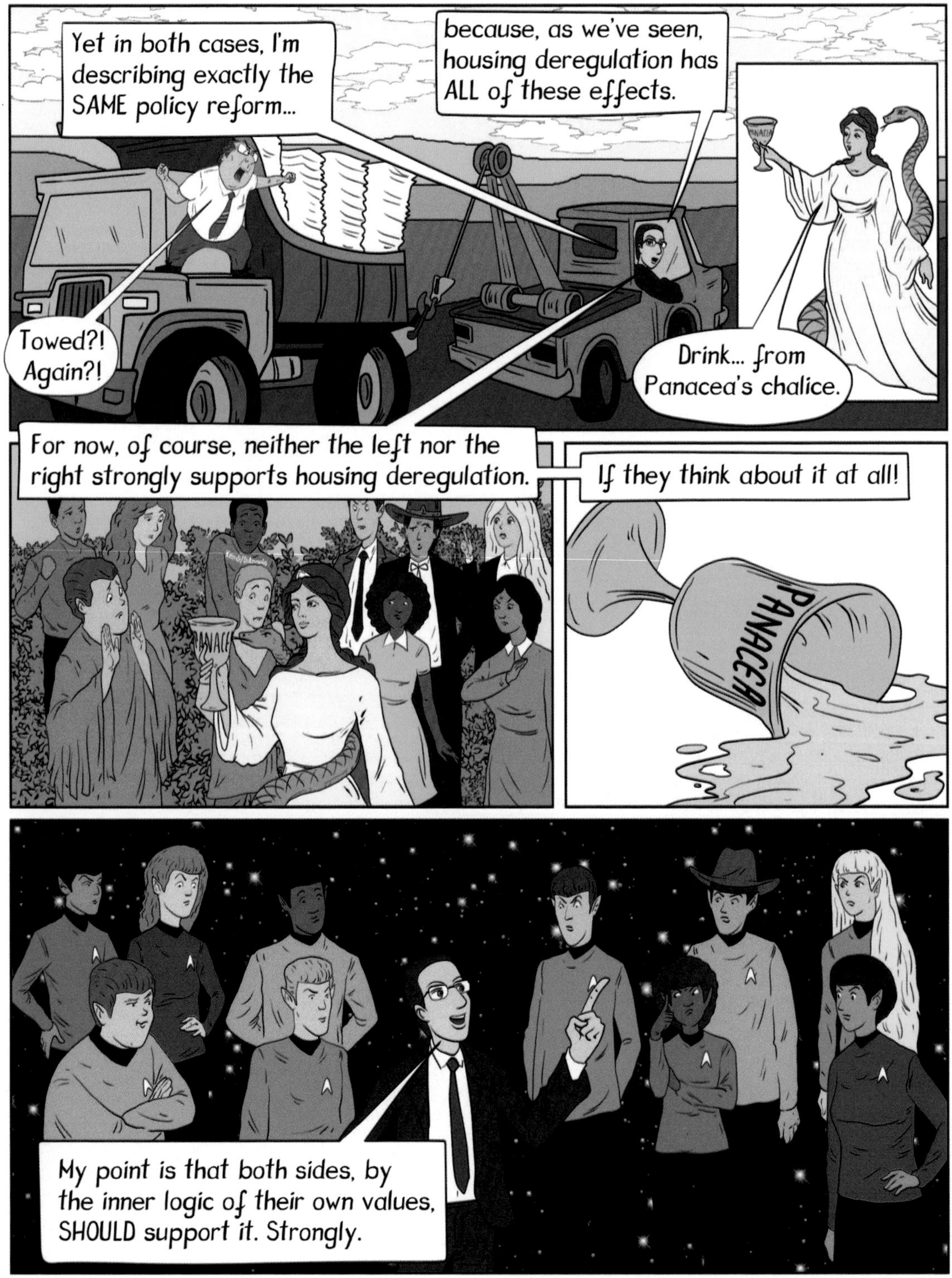
Yet in both cases, I'm describing exactly the SAME policy reform...
because, as we've seen, housing deregulation has ALL of these effects.
Towed?! Again?!
Drink... from Panacea's chalice.
PANACEA
For now, of course, neither the left nor the right strongly supports housing deregulation.
If they think about it at all!
PANACEA
My point is that both sides, by the inner logic of their own values, SHOULD support it. Strongly.

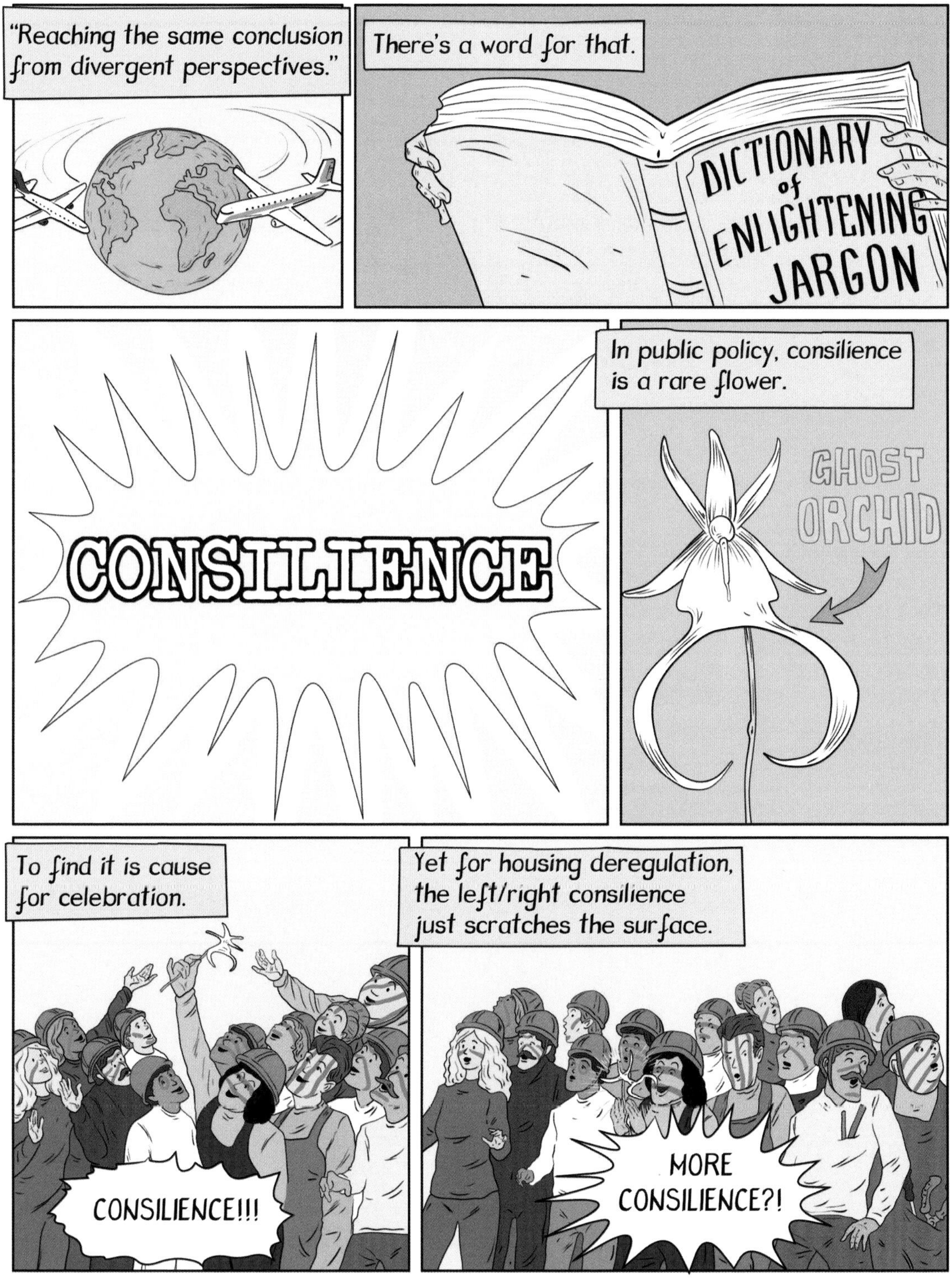
"Reaching the same conclusion from divergent perspectives."
There's a word for that.
DICTIONARY of ENLIGHTENING JARGON
CONSILIENCE
In public policy, consilience is a rare flower.
GHOST ORCHID
To find it is cause for celebration.
CONSILIENCE!!!
Yet for housing deregulation, the left/right consilience just scratches the surface.
MORE CONSILIENCE?!

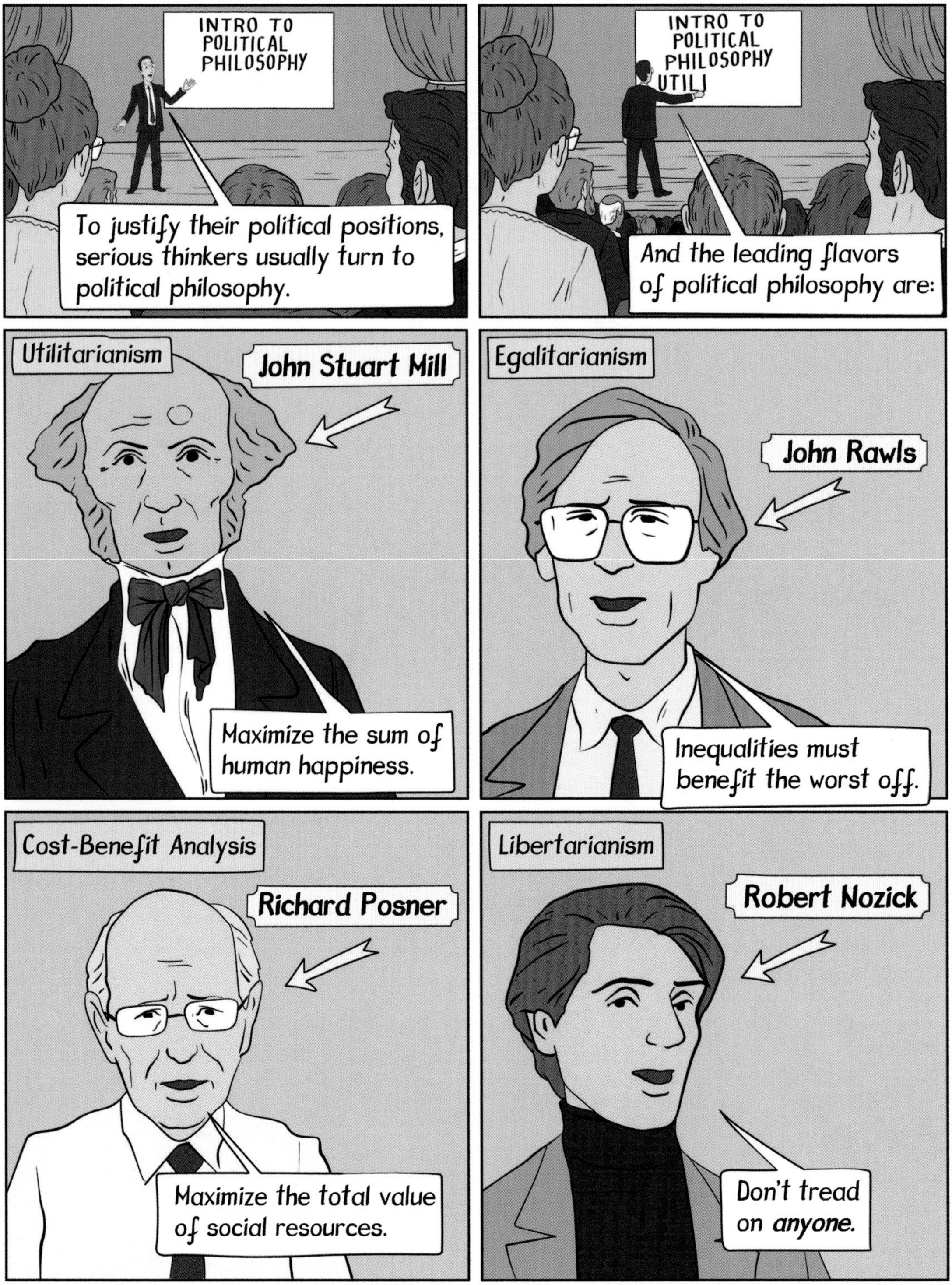
INTRO TO POLITICAL PHILOSOPHY
To justify their political positions, serious thinkers usually turn to political philosophy.
INTRO TO POLITICAL PHILOSOPHY UTILI
And the leading flavors of political philosophy are:
Utilitarianism
John Stuart Mill
Maximize the sum of human happiness.
Egalitarianism
John Rawls
Inequalities must benefit the worst off.
Cost-Benefit Analysis
Richard Posner
Maximize the total value of social resources.
Libertarianism
Robert Nozick
Don't tread on *anyone*.

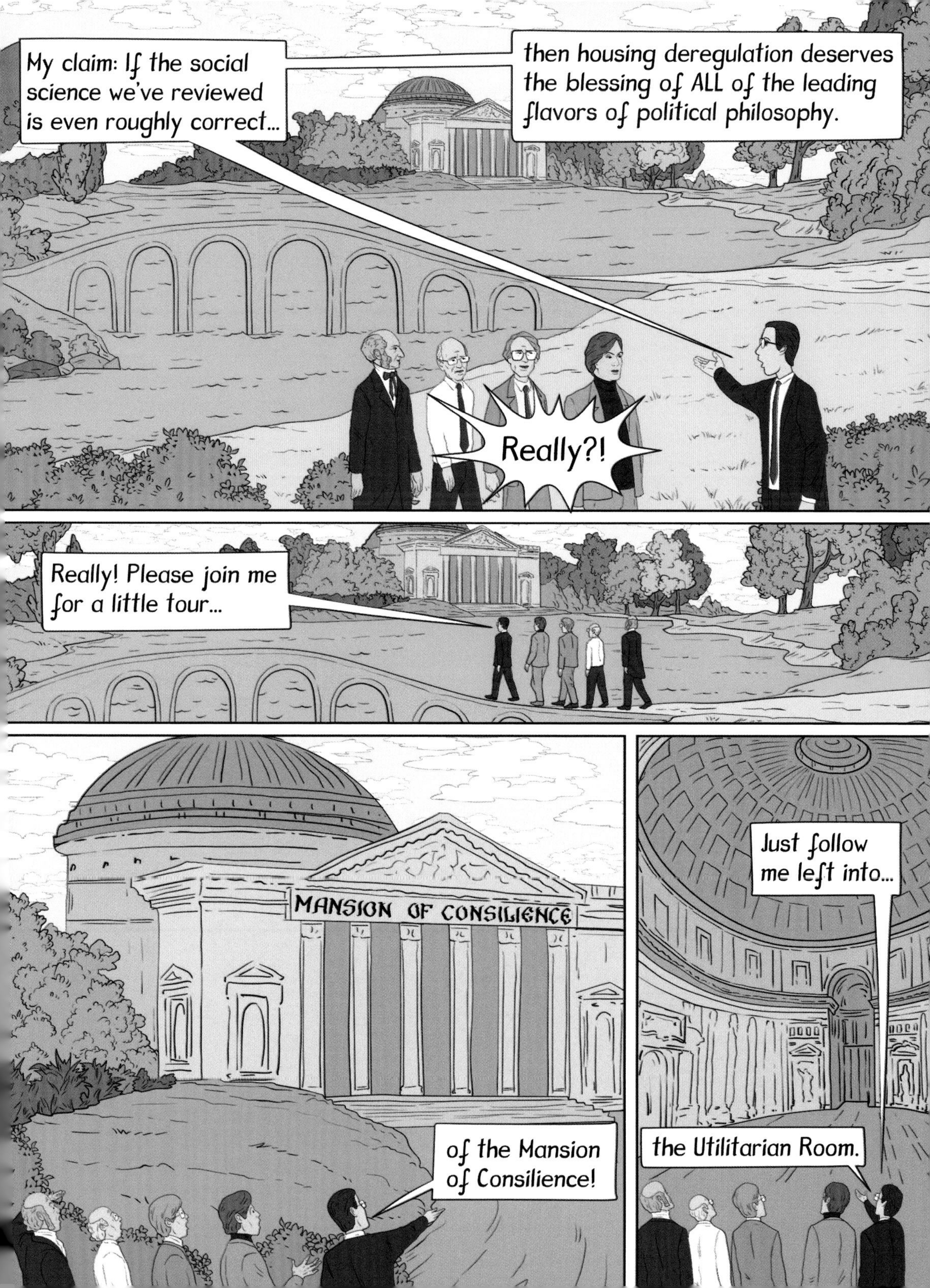
My claim: If the social science we've reviewed is even roughly correct...
then housing deregulation deserves the blessing of ALL of the leading flavors of political philosophy.
Really?!
Really! Please join me for a little tour...
MANSION OF CONSILIENCE
of the Mansion of Consilience!
Just follow me left into...
the Utilitarian Room.

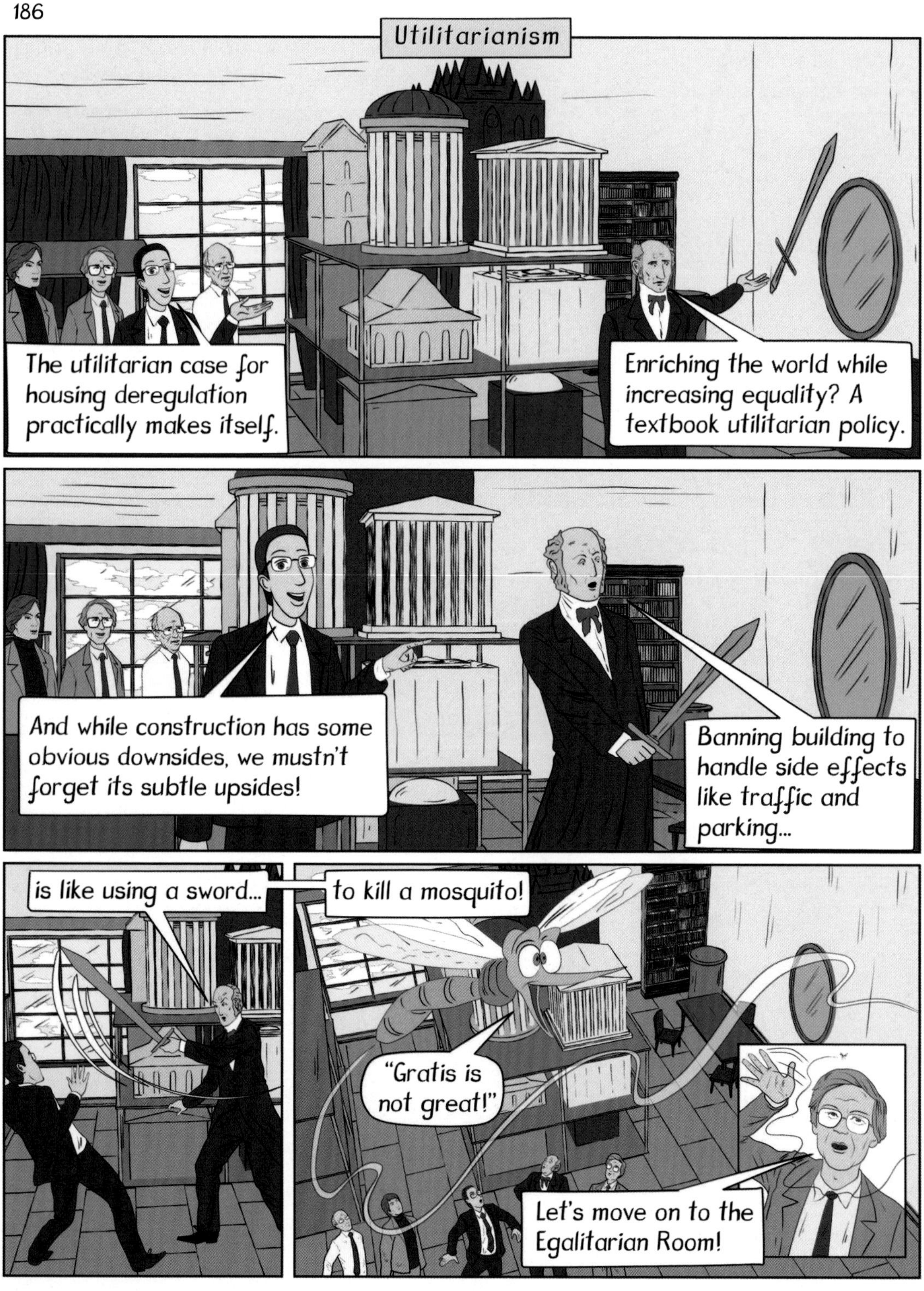
Utilitarianism
The utilitarian case for housing deregulation practically makes itself.
Enriching the world while increasing equality? A textbook utilitarian policy.
And while construction has some obvious downsides, we mustn't forget its subtle upsides!
Banning building to handle side effects like traffic and parking...
is like using a sword...
to kill a mosquito!
"Gratis is not great!"
Let's move on to the Egalitarian Room!

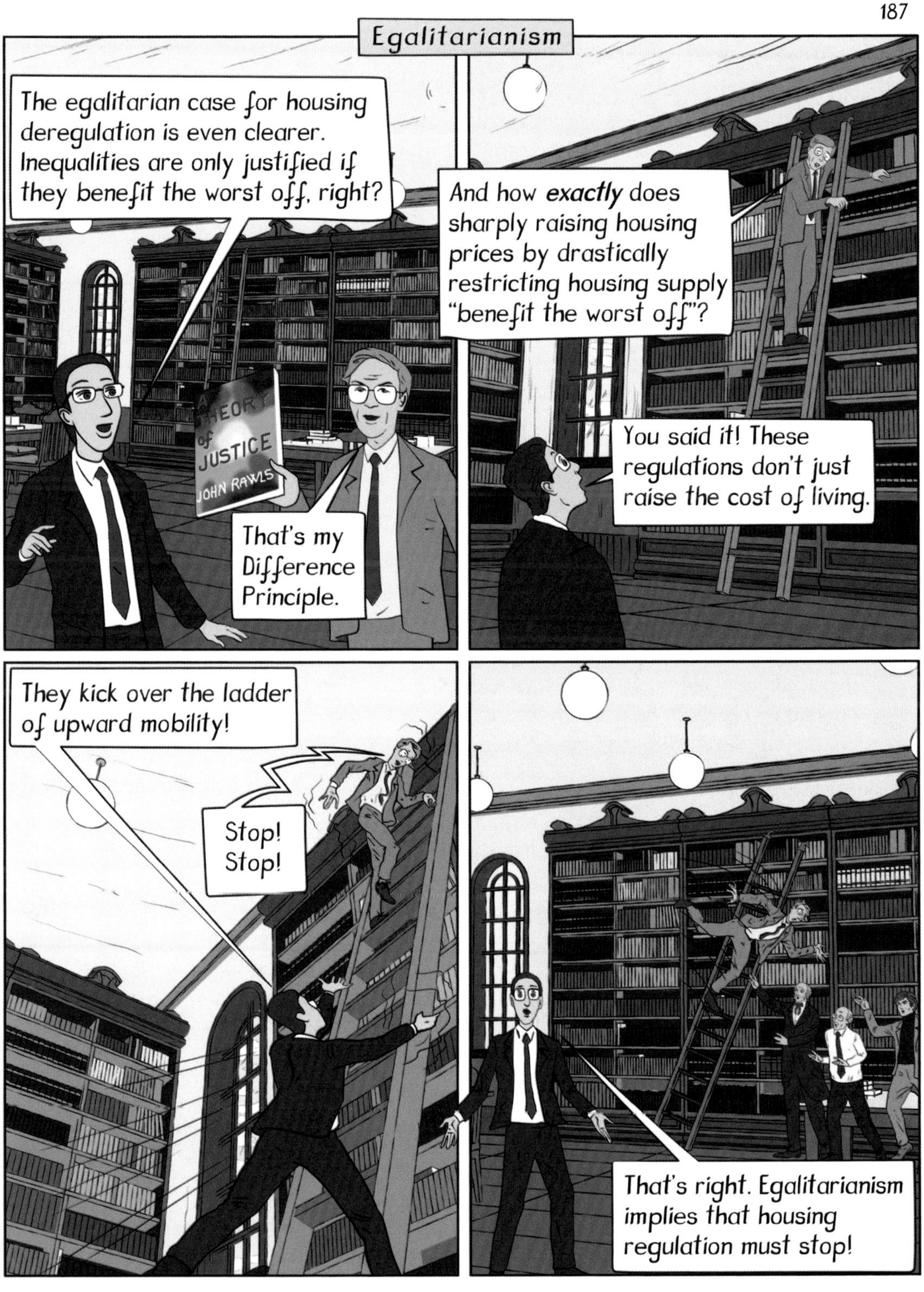
Egalitarianism
The egalitarian case for housing deregulation is even clearer. Inequalities are only justified if they benefit the worst off, right?
A THEORY of JUSTICE JOHN RAWLS
That's my Difference Principle.
And how *exactly* does sharply raising housing prices by drastically restricting housing supply "benefit the worst off"?
You said it! These regulations don't just raise the cost of living.
They kick over the ladder of upward mobility!
Stop! Stop!
That's right. Egalitarianism implies that housing regulation must stop!

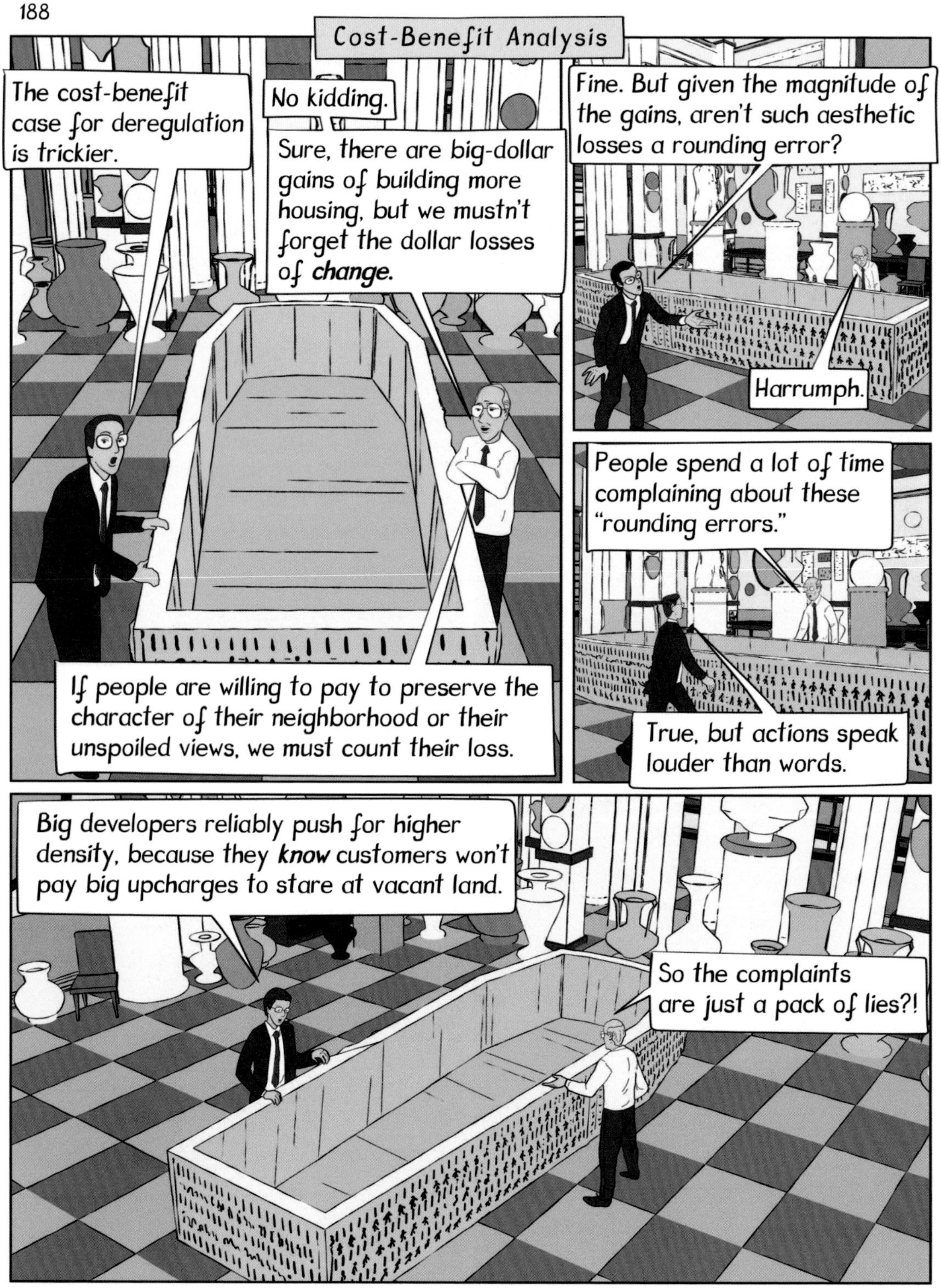
Cost-Benefit Analysis
The cost-benefit case for deregulation is trickier.
No kidding.
Sure, there are big-dollar gains of building more housing, but we mustn't forget the dollar losses of *change.*
If people are willing to pay to preserve the character of their neighborhood or their unspoiled views, we must count their loss.
Fine. But given the magnitude of the gains, aren't such aesthetic losses a rounding error?
Harrumph.
People spend a lot of time complaining about these "rounding errors."
True, but actions speak louder than words.
Big developers reliably push for higher density, because they *know* customers won't pay big upcharges to stare at vacant land.
So the complaints are just a pack of lies?!

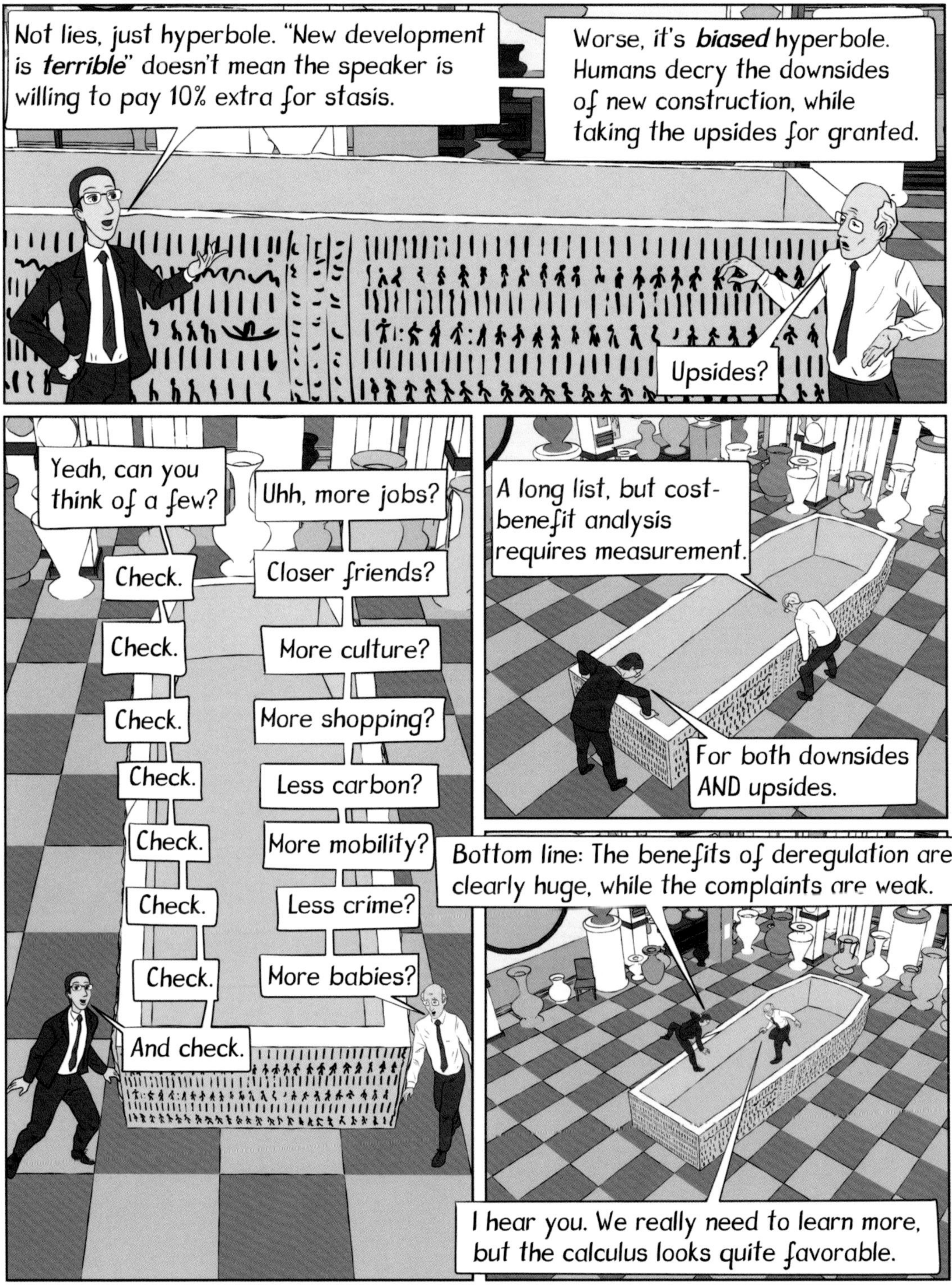
Not lies, just hyperbole. "New development is *terrible*" doesn't mean the speaker is willing to pay 10% extra for stasis.
Worse, it's *biased* hyperbole. Humans decry the downsides of new construction, while taking the upsides for granted.
Upsides?
Yeah, can you think of a few?
Uhh, more jobs?
Check.
Closer friends?
Check.
More culture?
Check.
More shopping?
Check.
Less carbon?
Check.
More mobility?
Check.
Less crime?
Check.
More babies?
And check.
A long list, but cost-benefit analysis requires measurement.
For both downsides AND upsides.
Bottom line: The benefits of deregulation are clearly huge, while the complaints are weak.
I hear you. We really need to learn more, but the calculus looks quite favorable.

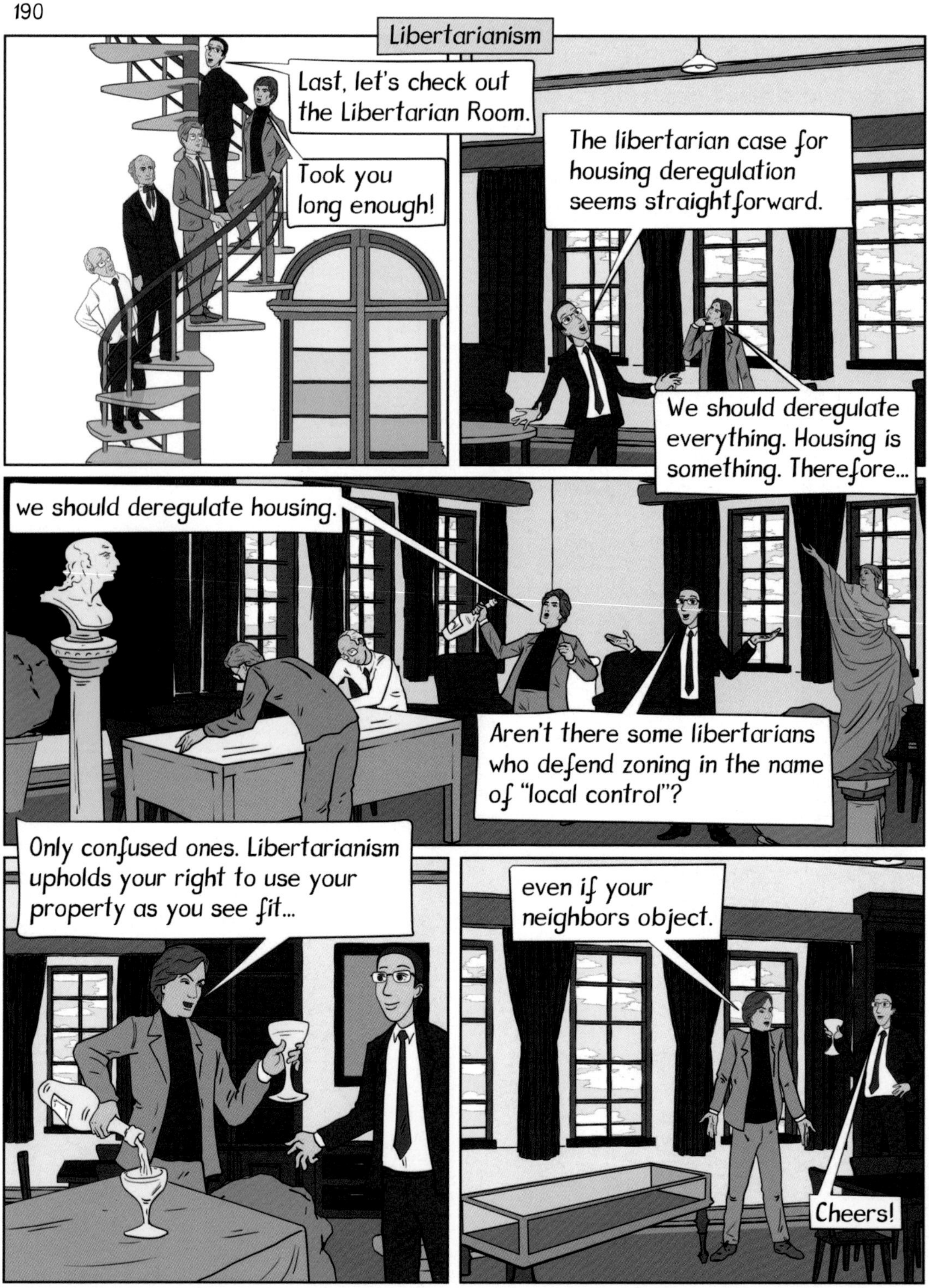
Libertarianism
Last, let's check out the Libertarian Room.
Took you long enough!
The libertarian case for housing deregulation seems straightforward.
We should deregulate everything. Housing is something. Therefore...
we should deregulate housing.
Aren't there some libertarians who defend zoning in the name of "local control"?
Only confused ones. Libertarianism upholds your right to use your property as you see fit...
even if your neighbors object.
Cheers!

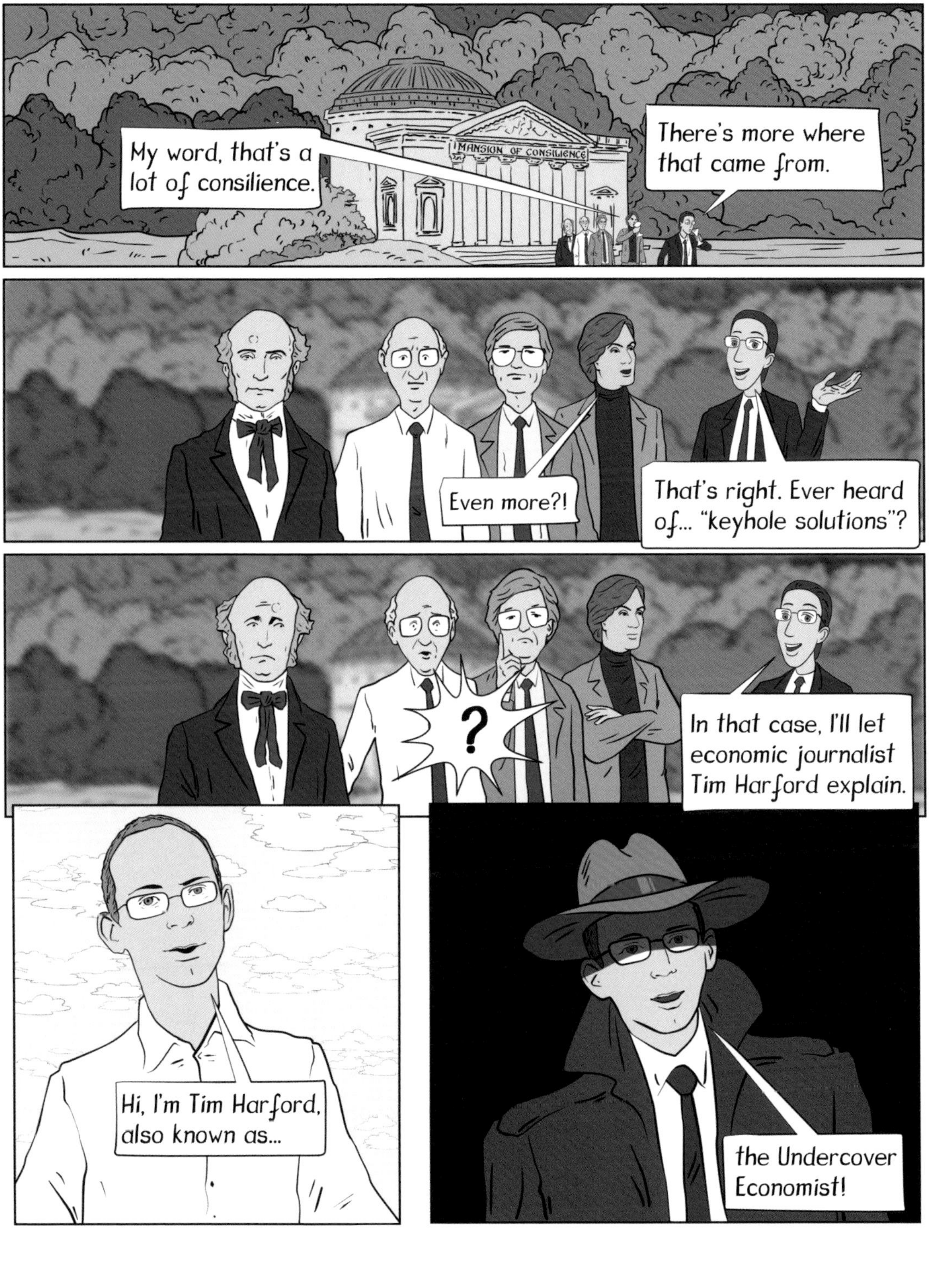
MANSION OF CONSILIENCE
My word, that's a lot of consilience.
There's more where that came from.
Even more?!
That's right. Ever heard of... "keyhole solutions"?
?
In that case, I'll let economic journalist Tim Harford explain.
Hi, I'm Tim Harford, also known as...
the Undercover Economist!

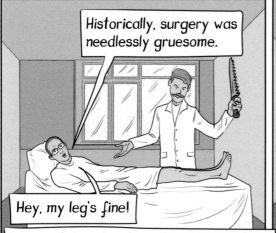

Historically, surgery was needlessly gruesome.

Hey, my leg's fine!

Doctors rarely asked, "Is there a safer, less painful way to cure the patient?"

I don't have time for stupid questions.

In recent decades, happily, surgeons have wised up. They try to keep incisions small to minimize side effects and suffering.

If you call that "surgery."

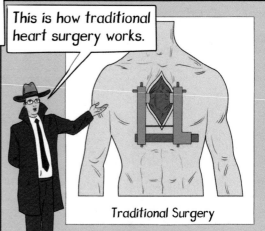

This is how traditional heart surgery works.

Traditional Surgery

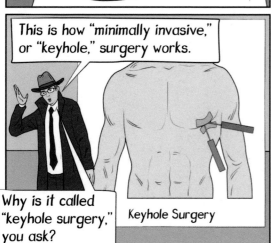

This is how "minimally invasive," or "keyhole," surgery works.

Why is it called "keyhole surgery," you ask?

Keyhole Surgery

Because the incision is just big enough for the job. Like a key in a lock!

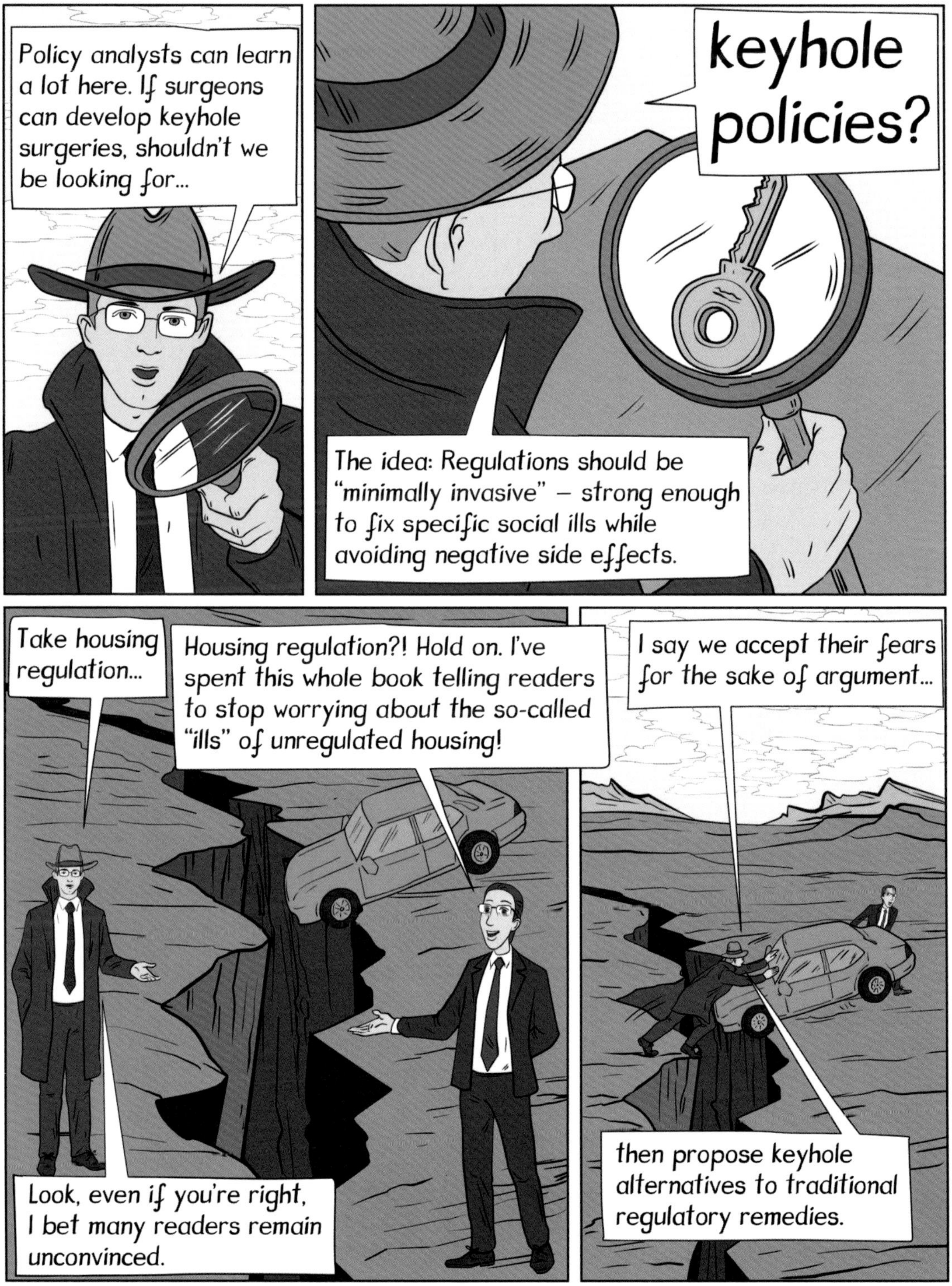
Policy analysts can learn a lot here. If surgeons can develop keyhole surgeries, shouldn't we be looking for...
keyhole policies?
The idea: Regulations should be "minimally invasive" – strong enough to fix specific social ills while avoiding negative side effects.
Take housing regulation...
Housing regulation?! Hold on. I've spent this whole book telling readers to stop worrying about the so-called "ills" of unregulated housing!
Look, even if you're right, I bet many readers remain unconvinced.
I say we accept their fears for the sake of argument...
then propose keyhole alternatives to traditional regulatory remedies.

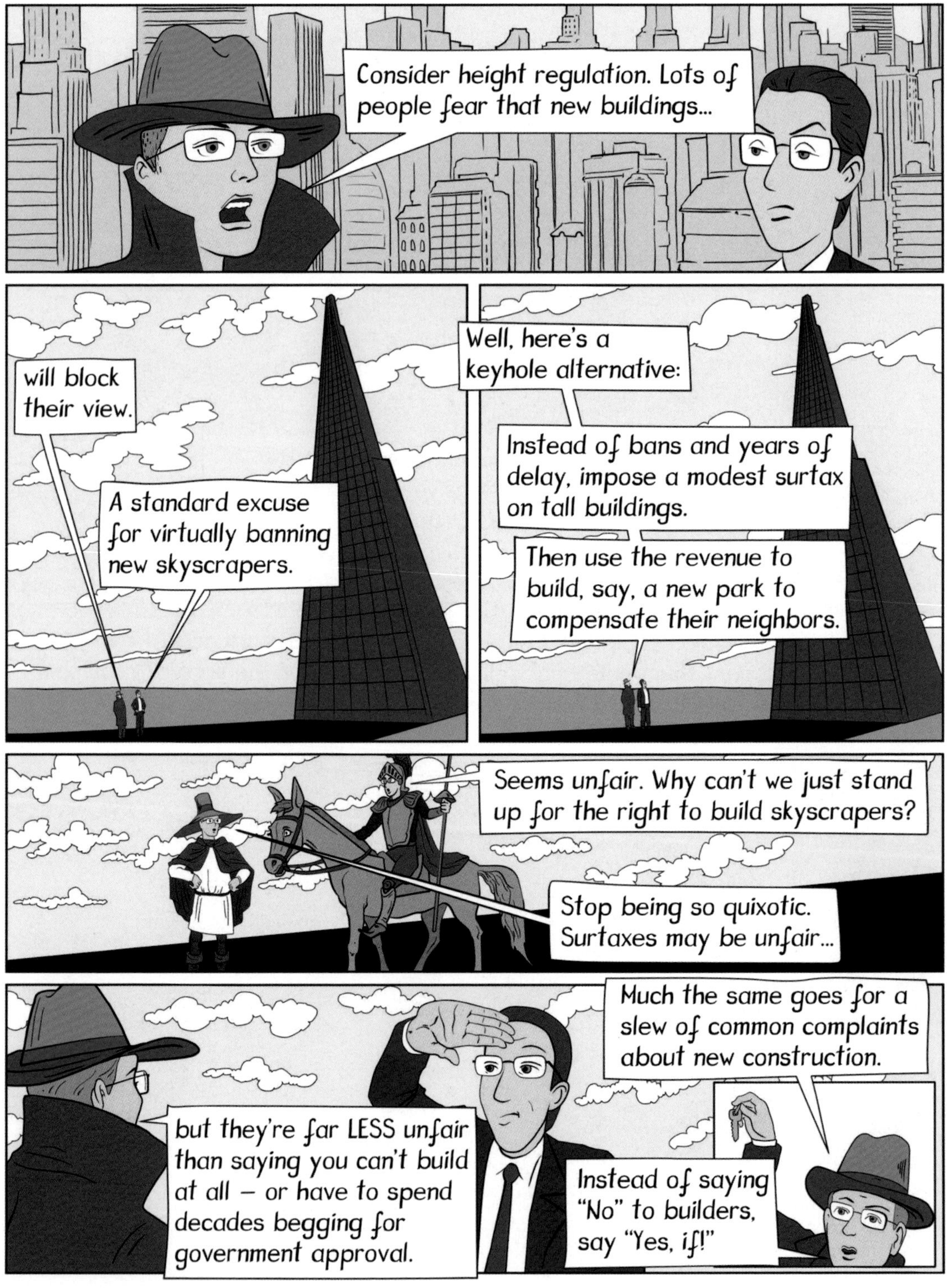

Consider height regulation. Lots of people fear that new buildings...
will block their view.
A standard excuse for virtually banning new skyscrapers.
Well, here's a keyhole alternative:
Instead of bans and years of delay, impose a modest surtax on tall buildings.
Then use the revenue to build, say, a new park to compensate their neighbors.
Seems unfair. Why can't we just stand up for the right to build skyscrapers?
Stop being so quixotic. Surtaxes may be unfair...
but they're far LESS unfair than saying you can't build at all – or have to spend decades begging for government approval.
Much the same goes for a slew of common complaints about new construction.
Instead of saying "No" to builders, say "Yes, if!"

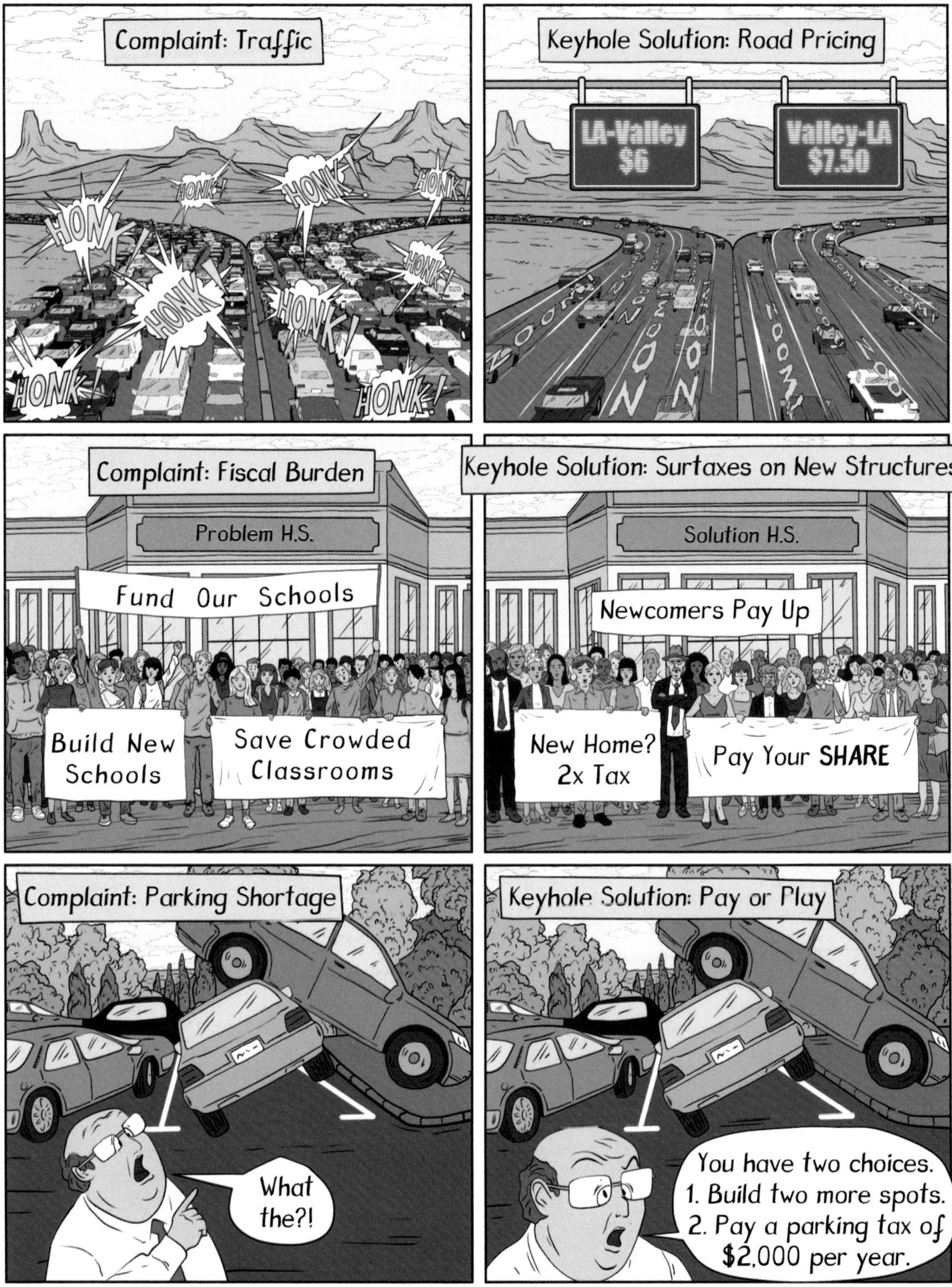
Complaint: Traffic
HONK!
HONK!
HONK!
HONK!
HONK!
HONK!
HONK!
HONK!
HONK!
Keyhole Solution: Road Pricing
LA-Valley $6
Valley-LA $7.50
ZOOM!
Complaint: Fiscal Burden
Problem H.S.
Fund Our Schools
Build New Schools
Save Crowded Classrooms
Keyhole Solution: Surtaxes on New Structures
Solution H.S.
Newcomers Pay Up
New Home? 2x Tax
Pay Your SHARE
Complaint: Parking Shortage
What the?!
Keyhole Solution: Pay or Play
You have two choices.
1. Build two more spots.
2. Pay a parking tax of $2,000 per year.

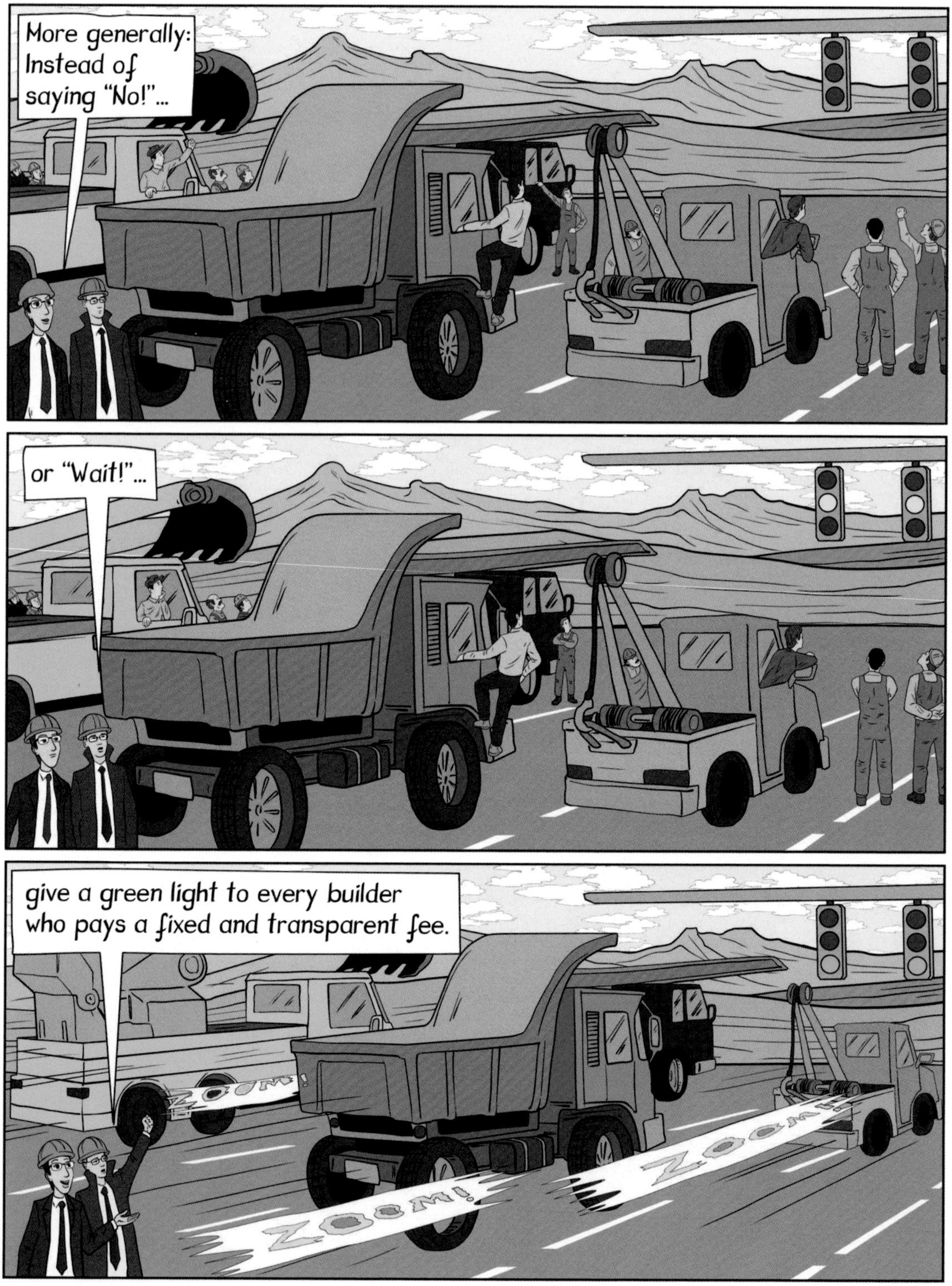
More generally: Instead of saying "No!"...
or "Wait!"...
give a green light to every builder who pays a fixed and transparent fee.
ZOOM!
ZOOOM!
ZOOOM!

True, this falls short of FULL deregulation...

especially if the government sets exorbitant fees.

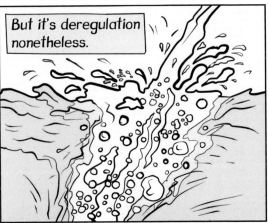

But it's deregulation nonetheless.

Which means we've discovered yet another source of...

CONSILIENCE

Does that make sense?

Sure does, Tim.

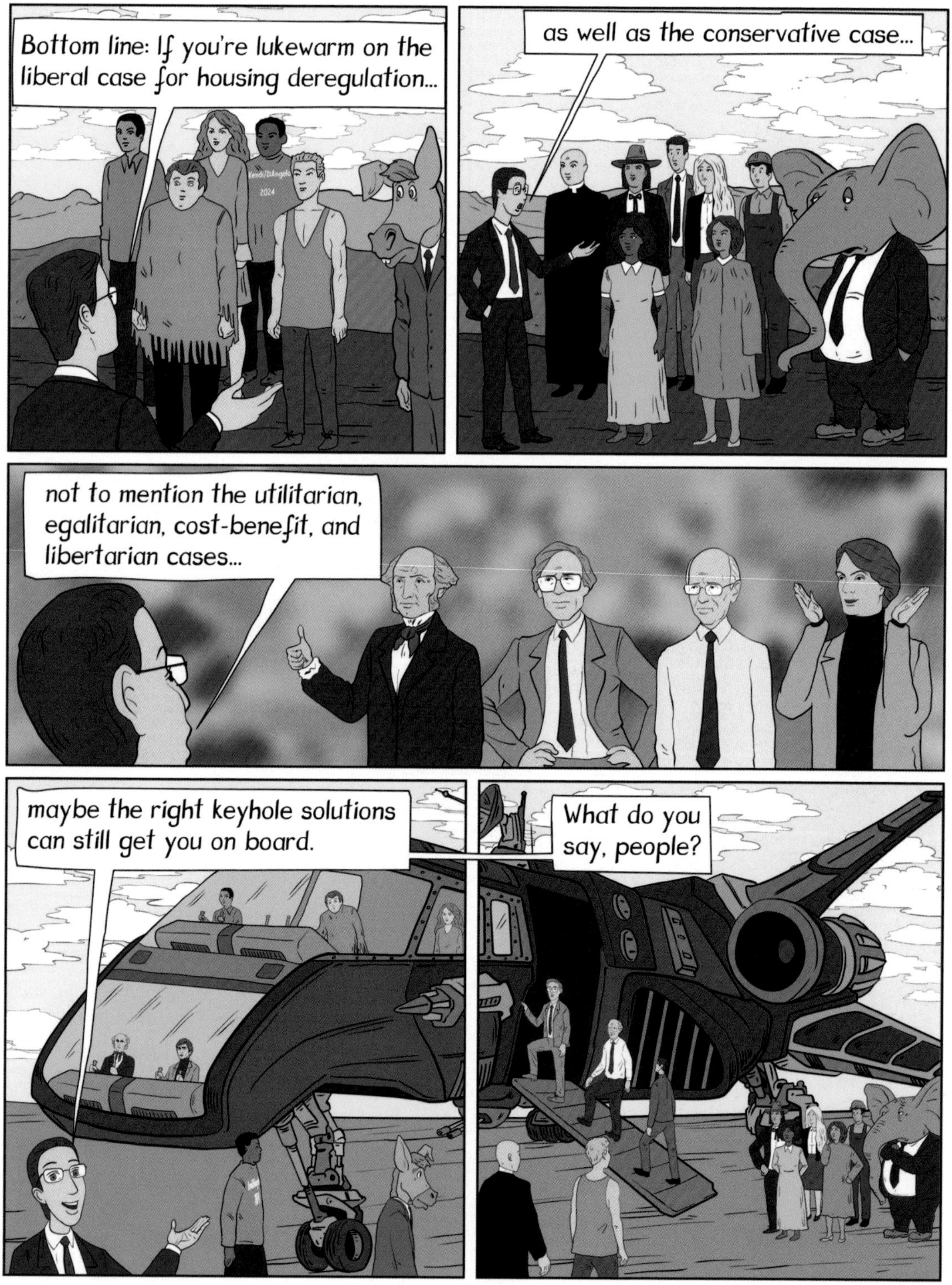
Bottom line: If you're lukewarm on the liberal case for housing deregulation...
Kendi/DiAngelo 2024
as well as the conservative case...
not to mention the utilitarian, egalitarian, cost-benefit, and libertarian cases...
maybe the right keyhole solutions can still get you on board.
What do you say, people?

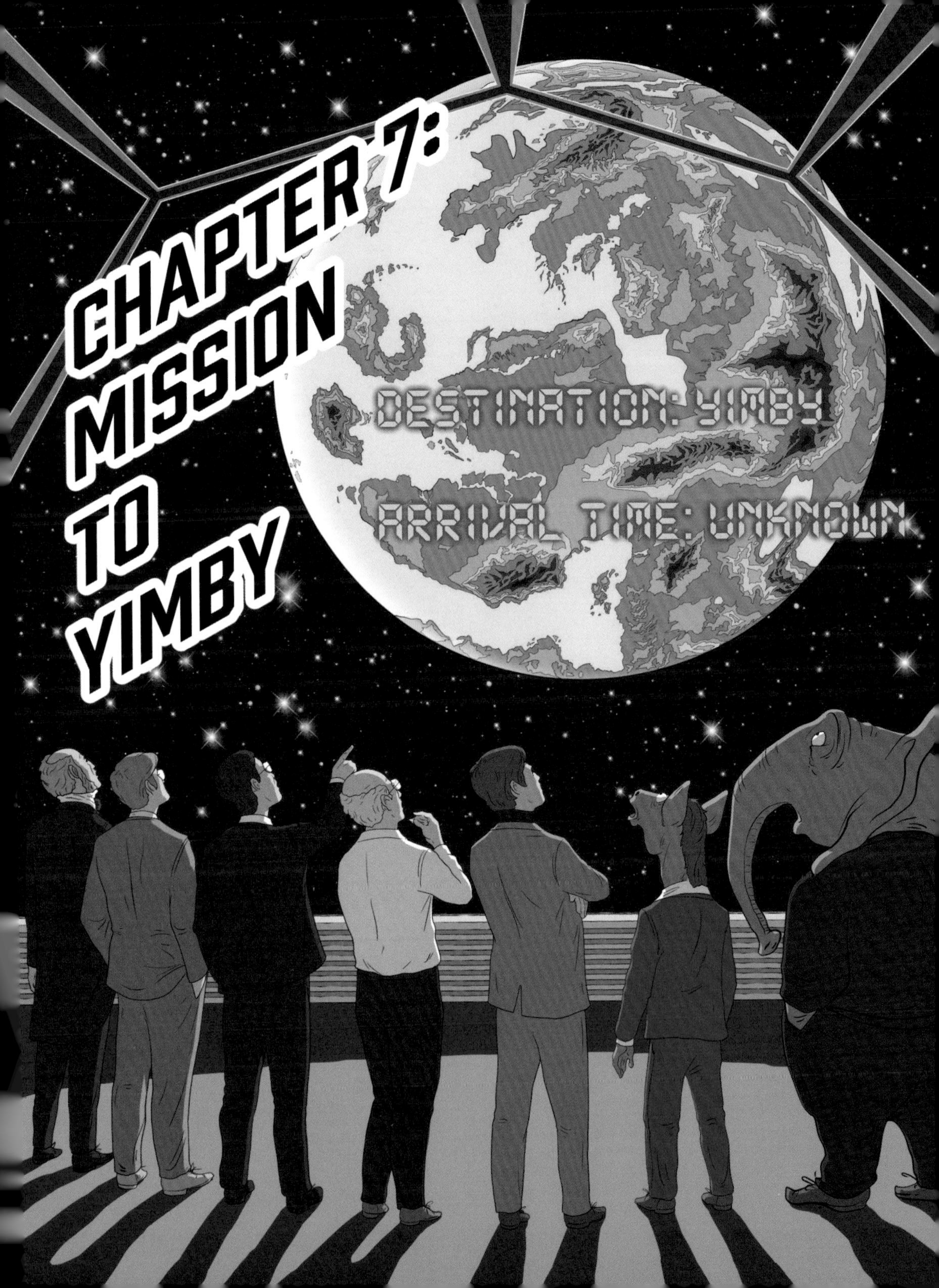
CHAPTER 7:
MISSION
TO
YIMBY
DESTINATION: YIMBY
ARRIVAL TIME: UNKNOWN

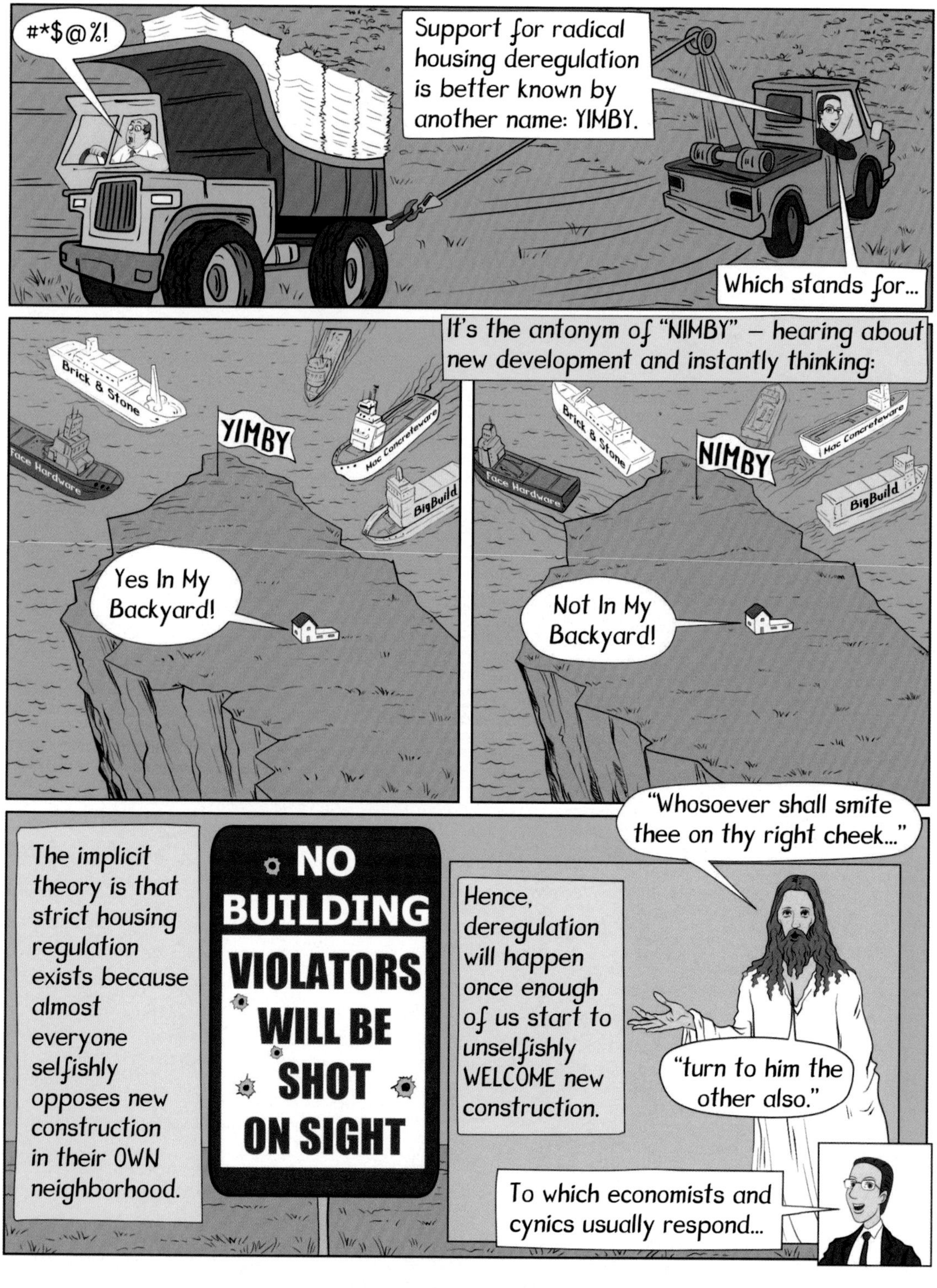
#*$@%!
Support for radical housing deregulation is better known by another name: YIMBY.
Which stands for...
It's the antonym of "NIMBY" – hearing about new development and instantly thinking:
Brick & Stone
Face Hardware
YIMBY
Mac Concreteware
BigBuild
Yes In My Backyard!
Brick & Stone
Face Hardware
NIMBY
Mac Concreteware
BigBuild
Not In My Backyard!
The implicit theory is that strict housing regulation exists because almost everyone selfishly opposes new construction in their OWN neighborhood.
NO BUILDING
VIOLATORS WILL BE SHOT ON SIGHT
Hence, deregulation will happen once enough of us start to unselfishly WELCOME new construction.
"Whosoever shall smite thee on thy right cheek..."
"turn to him the other also."
To which economists and cynics usually respond...

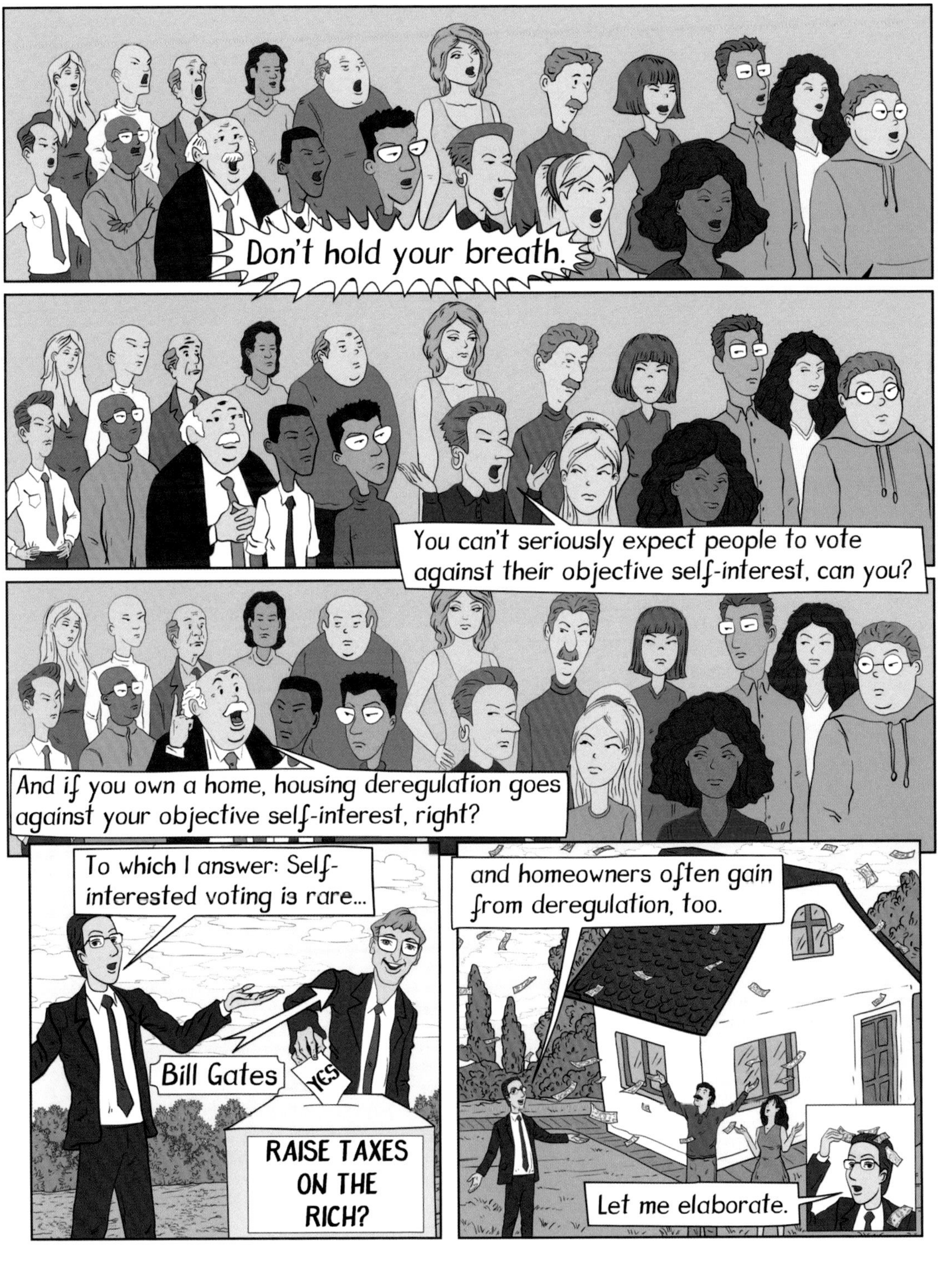
Don't hold your breath.
You can't seriously expect people to vote against their objective self-interest, can you?
And if you own a home, housing deregulation goes against your objective self-interest, right?
To which I answer: Self-interested voting is rare...
Bill Gates
YES
RAISE TAXES ON THE RICH?
and homeowners often gain from deregulation, too.
Let me elaborate.

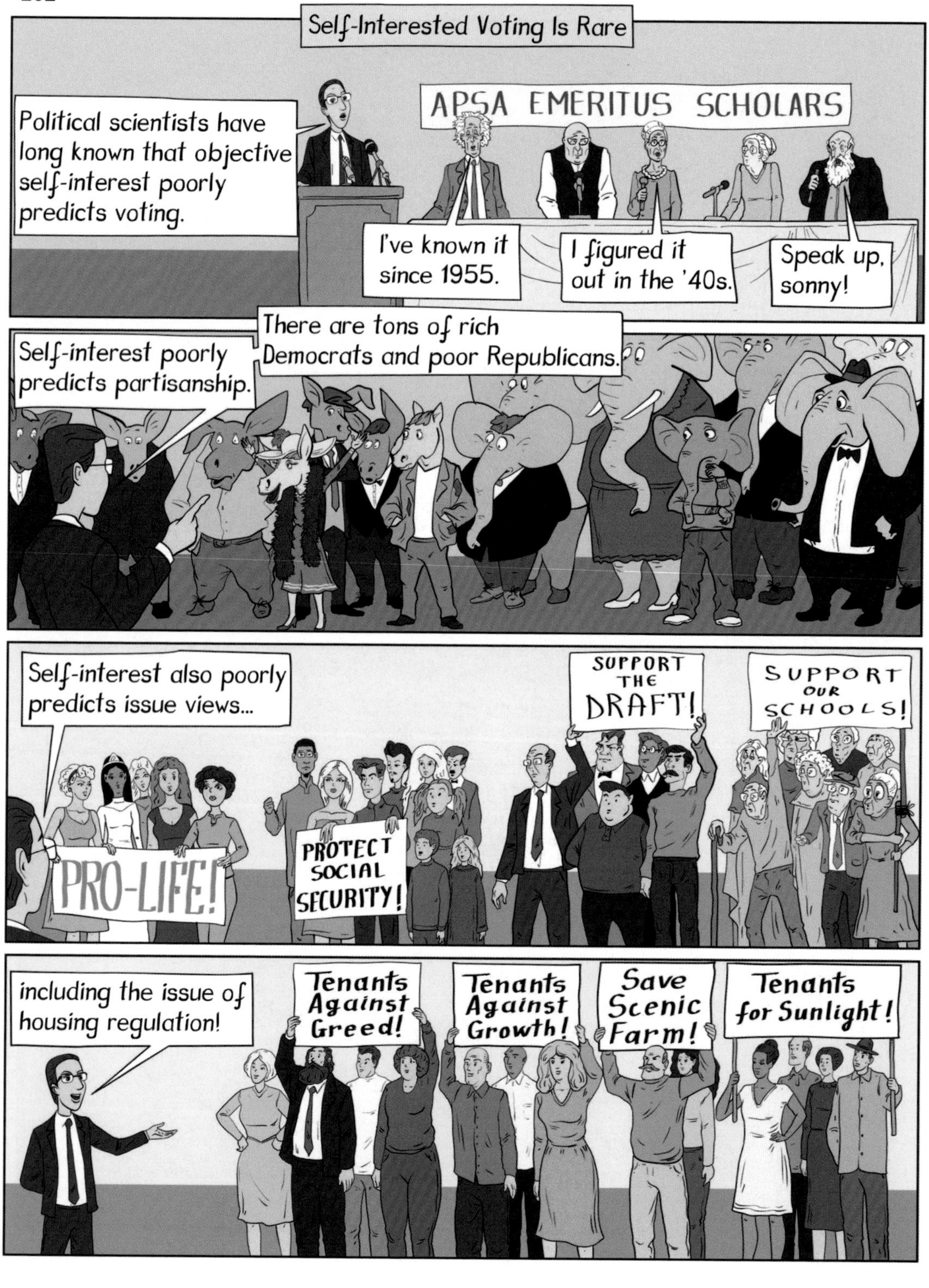
Self-Interested Voting Is Rare
Political scientists have long known that objective self-interest poorly predicts voting.
APSA EMERITUS SCHOLARS
I've known it since 1955.
I figured it out in the '40s.
Speak up, sonny!
Self-interest poorly predicts partisanship.
There are tons of rich Democrats and poor Republicans.
Self-interest also poorly predicts issue views...
PRO-LIFE!
PROTECT SOCIAL SECURITY!
SUPPORT THE DRAFT!
SUPPORT OUR SCHOOLS!
including the issue of housing regulation!
Tenants Against Greed!
Tenants Against Growth!
Save Scenic Farm!
Tenants for Sunlight!

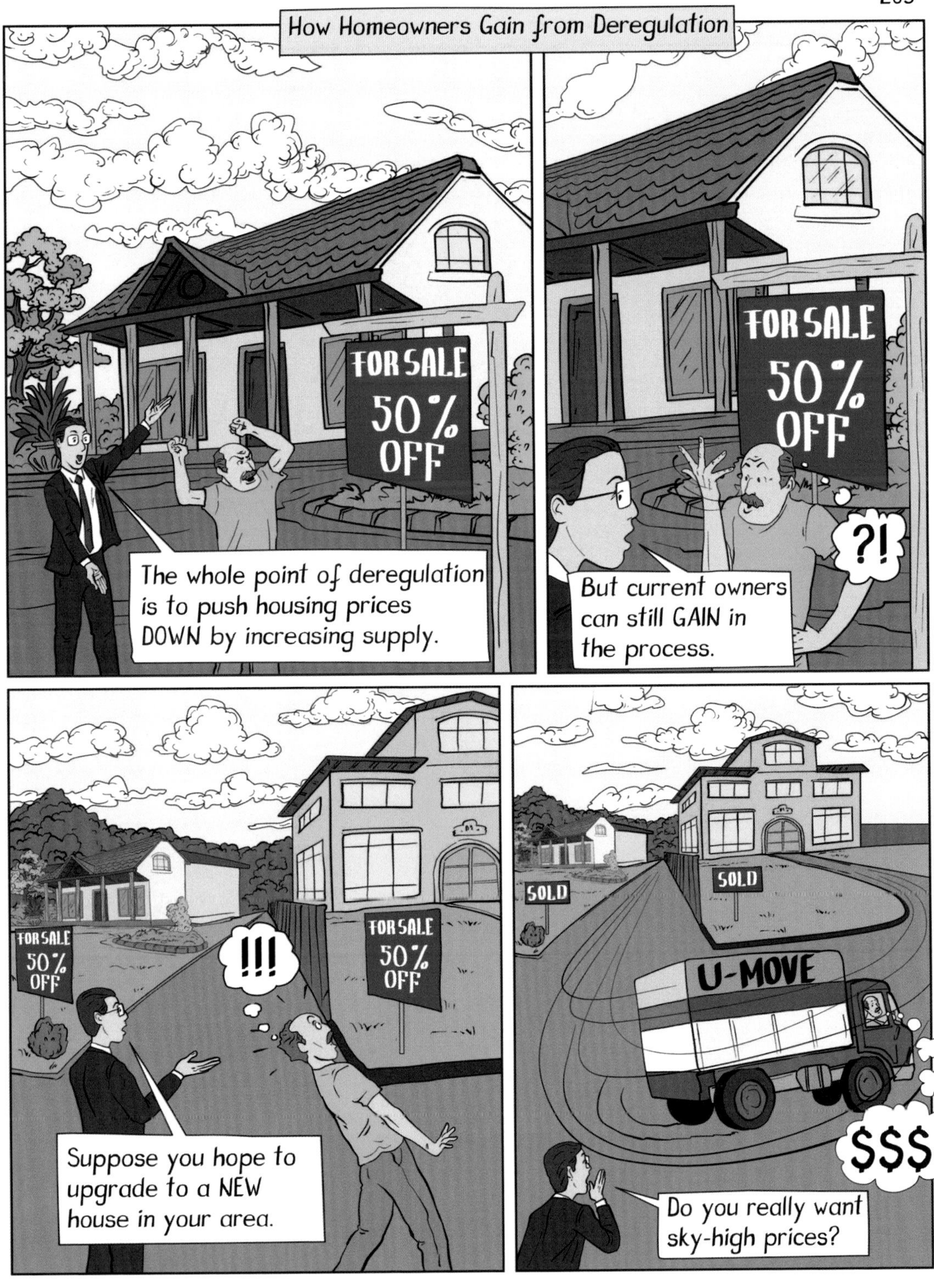
How Homeowners Gain from Deregulation
FOR SALE 50% OFF
The whole point of deregulation is to push housing prices DOWN by increasing supply.
FOR SALE 50% OFF
?!
But current owners can still GAIN in the process.
FOR SALE 50% OFF
FOR SALE 50% OFF
!!!
Suppose you hope to upgrade to a NEW house in your area.
SOLD
SOLD
U-MOVE
$$$!
Do you really want sky-high prices?

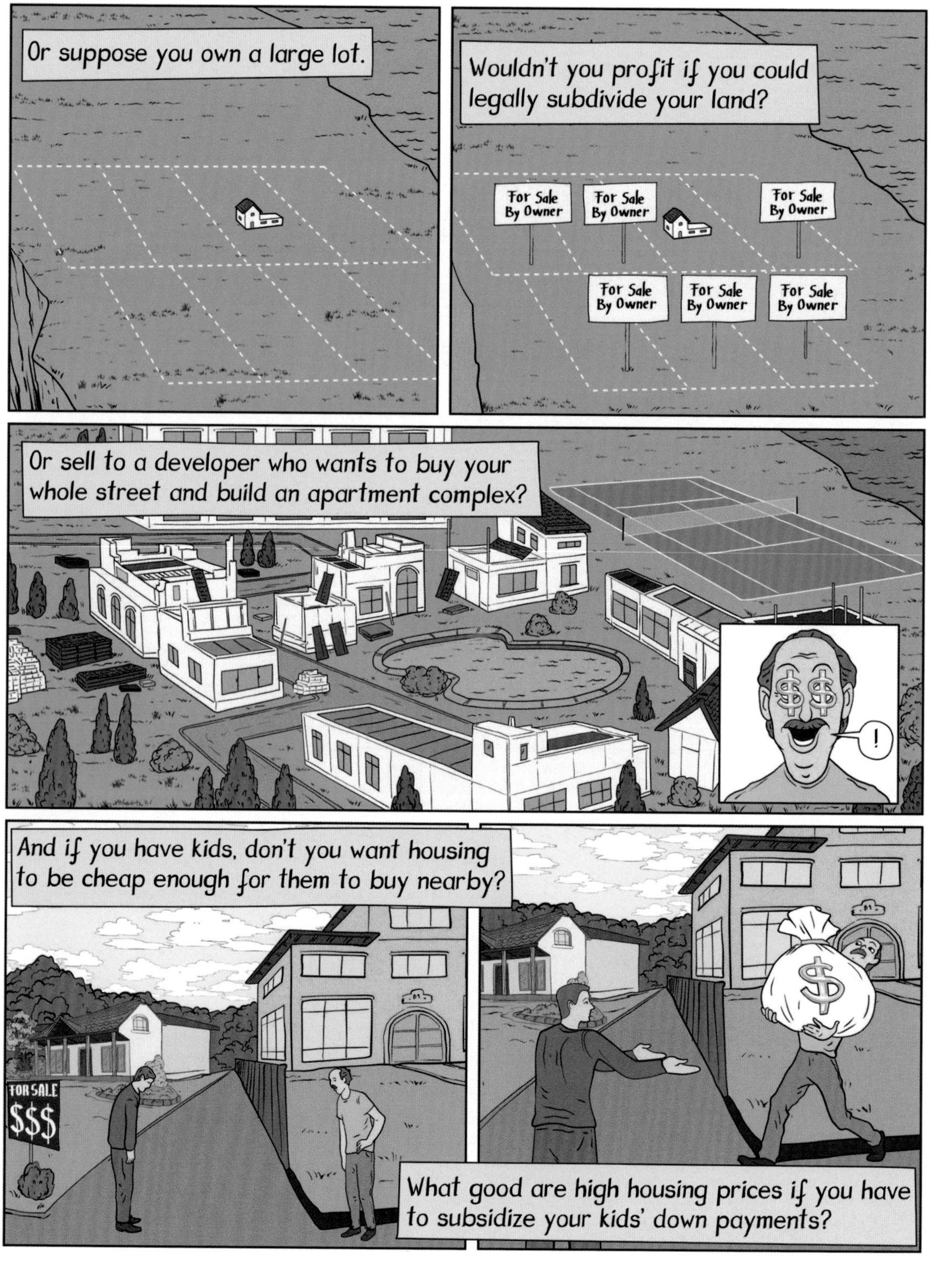
Or suppose you own a large lot.
Wouldn't you profit if you could legally subdivide your land?
For Sale By Owner
For Sale By Owner
For Sale By Owner
For Sale By Owner
For Sale By Owner
For Sale By Owner
Or sell to a developer who wants to buy your whole street and build an apartment complex?
!
And if you have kids, don't you want housing to be cheap enough for them to buy nearby?
FOR SALE $$$
What good are high housing prices if you have to subsidize your kids' down payments?

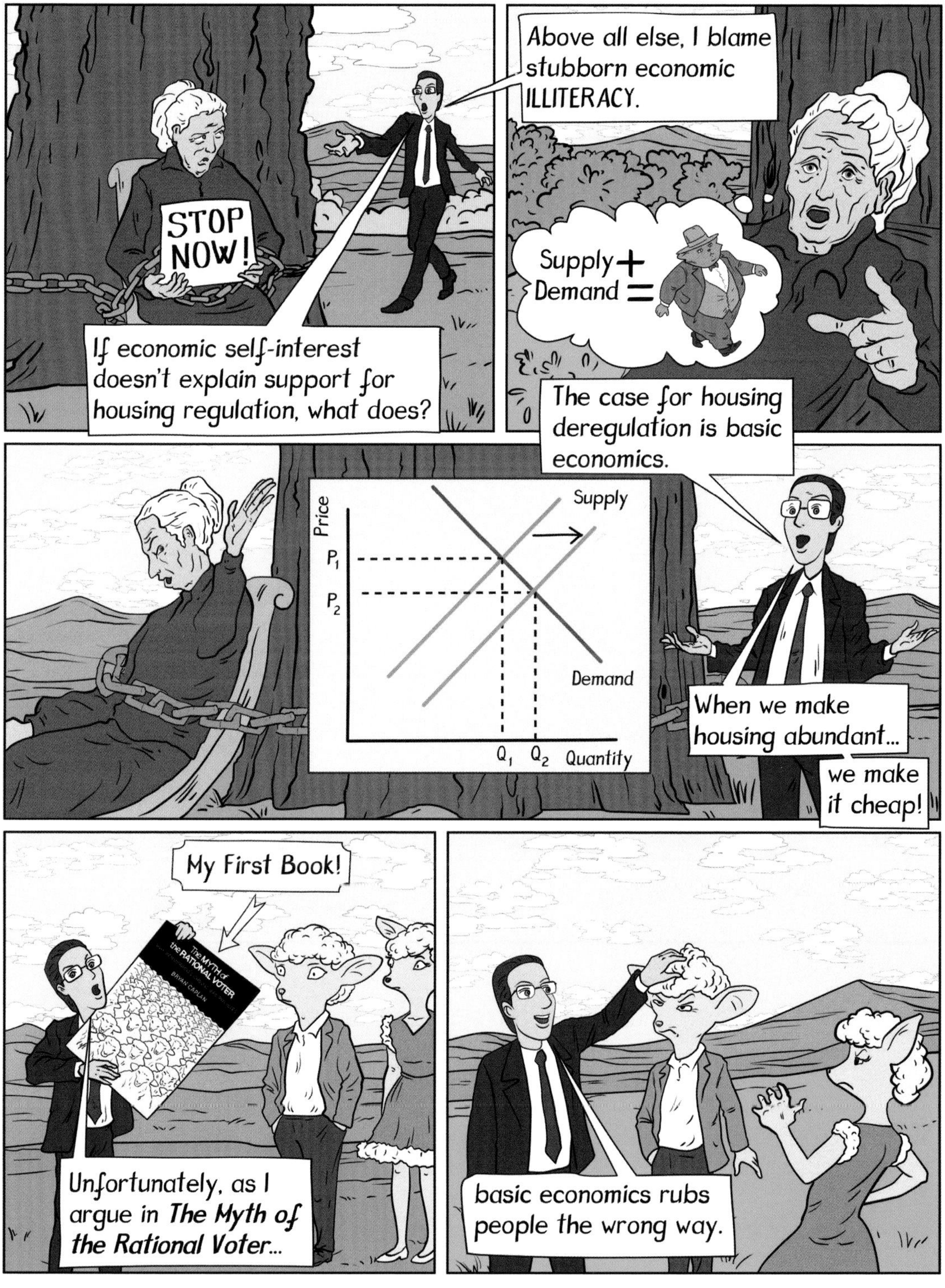
If economic self-interest doesn't explain support for housing regulation, what does?
STOP NOW!
Above all else, I blame stubborn economic ILLITERACY.
Supply + Demand =
The case for housing deregulation is basic economics.
Price
Supply
P1
P2
Demand
Q1
Q2
Quantity
When we make housing abundant...
we make it cheap!
My First Book!
The MYTH of the RATIONAL VOTER
BRYAN CAPLAN
Unfortunately, as I argue in The Myth of the Rational Voter...
basic economics rubs people the wrong way.

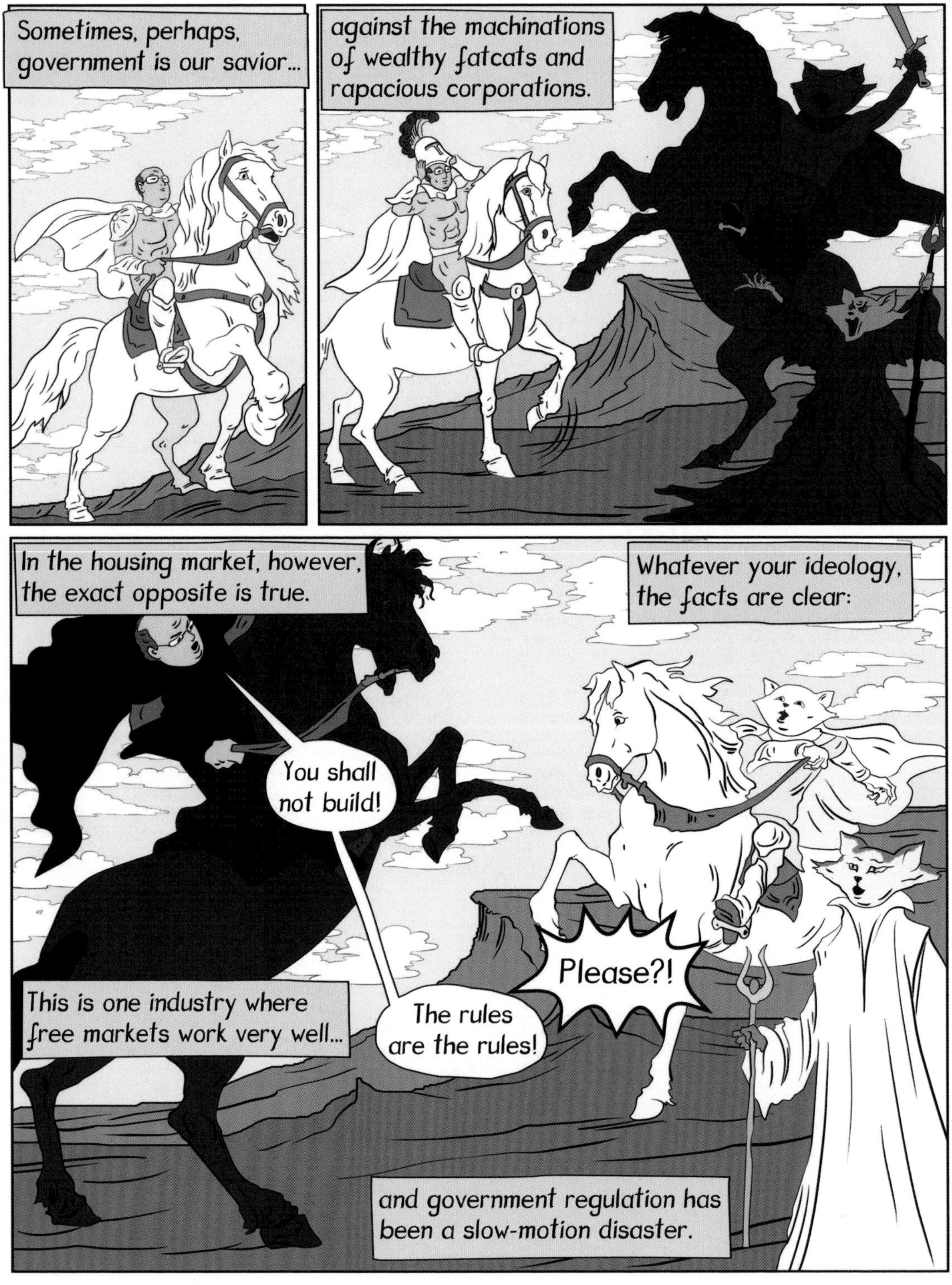
Sometimes, perhaps, government is our savior...
against the machinations of wealthy fatcats and rapacious corporations.
In the housing market, however, the exact opposite is true.
Whatever your ideology, the facts are clear:
You shall not build!
Please?!
This is one industry where free markets work very well...
The rules are the rules!
and government regulation has been a slow-motion disaster.

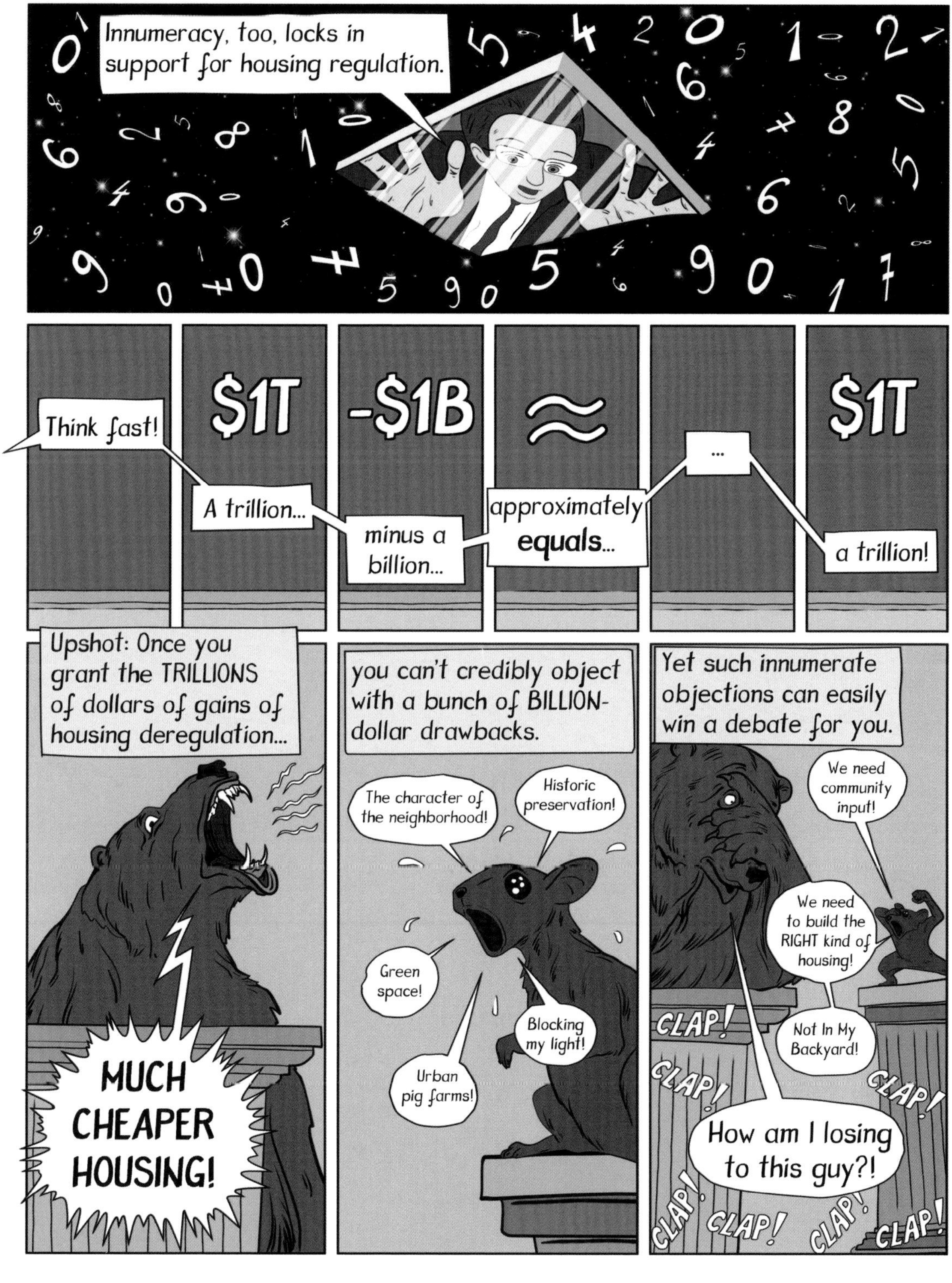
Innumeracy, too, locks in support for housing regulation.
Think fast!
$1T
A trillion...
-$1B
minus a billion...
≈
approximately **equals**...
...
$1T
a trillion!
Upshot: Once you grant the TRILLIONS of dollars of gains of housing deregulation...
MUCH CHEAPER HOUSING!
you can't credibly object with a bunch of BILLION-dollar drawbacks.
The character of the neighborhood!
Historic preservation!
Green space!
Urban pig farms!
Blocking my light!
Yet such innumerate objections can easily win a debate for you.
We need community input!
We need to build the RIGHT kind of housing!
Not In My Backyard!
CLAP!
CLAP!
CLAP!
How am I losing to this guy?!
CLAP!
CLAP!
CLAP!
CLAP!

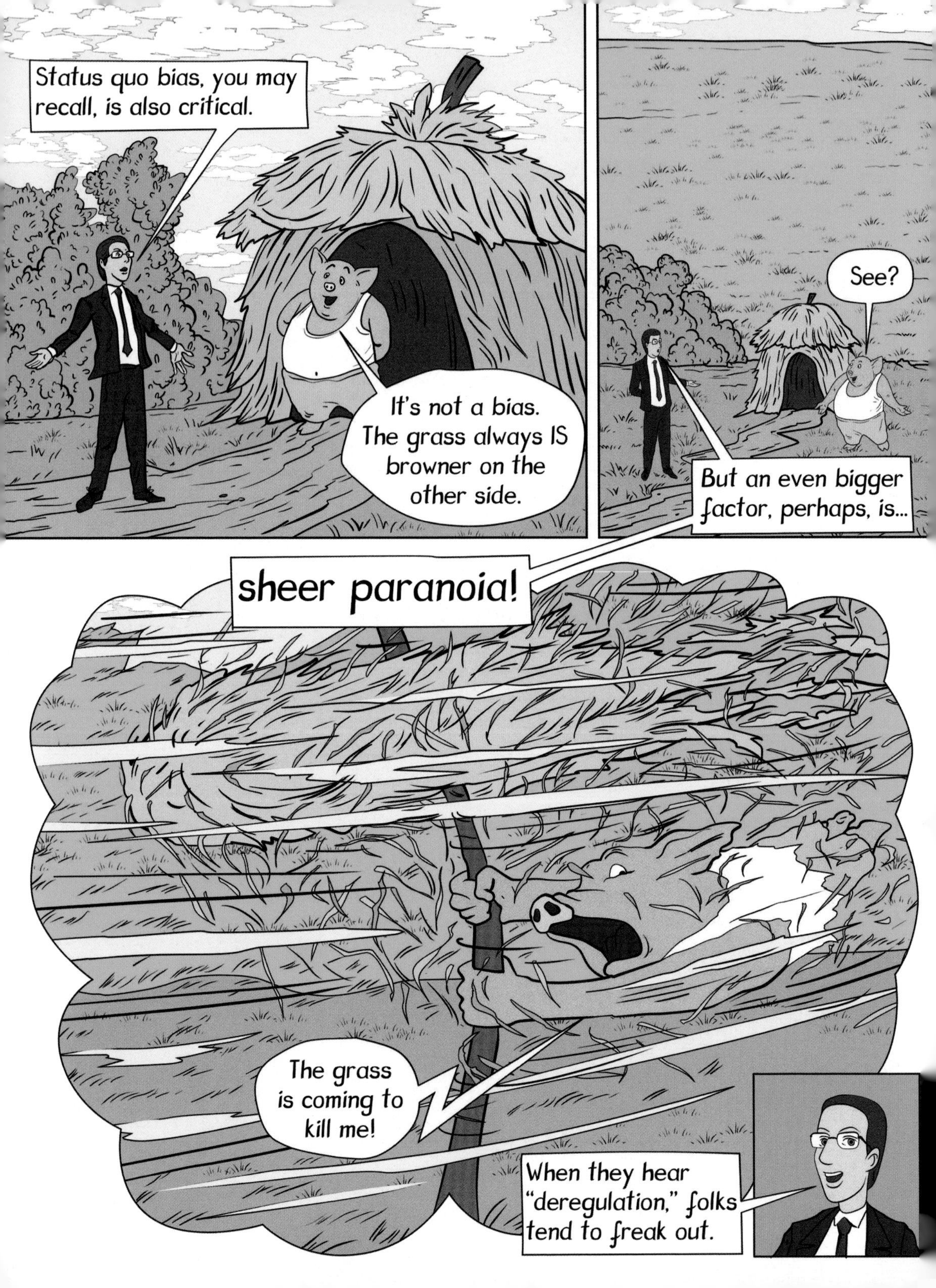
Status quo bias, you may recall, is also critical.
It's not a bias. The grass always IS browner on the other side.
See?
But an even bigger factor, perhaps, is...
sheer paranoia!
The grass is coming to kill me!
When they hear "deregulation," folks tend to freak out.

You propose radical changes. We ought to be "paranoid"!

JUST BECAUSE I'M PARANOID DOESN'T MEAN THEY'RE NOT AFTER ME

Look, maybe housing regulation does more good than I claim.

Maybe it makes neighborhoods a little more "livable."

TREE PROTECTION ZONE

Maybe it makes architecture a little prettier.

Solvang, CA

Maybe it's a helpful complement for pricing roads and parking.

But even if we scrap a mountain of laws...

UP WITH! HOUSING!

deregulation won't be the end of the world.

DOWN WITH HYPERBOLE!

Sir, you're making a scene!

JUST BECAUSE I'M PARANOID DOESN'T MEAN THEY'RE NOT AFTER ME

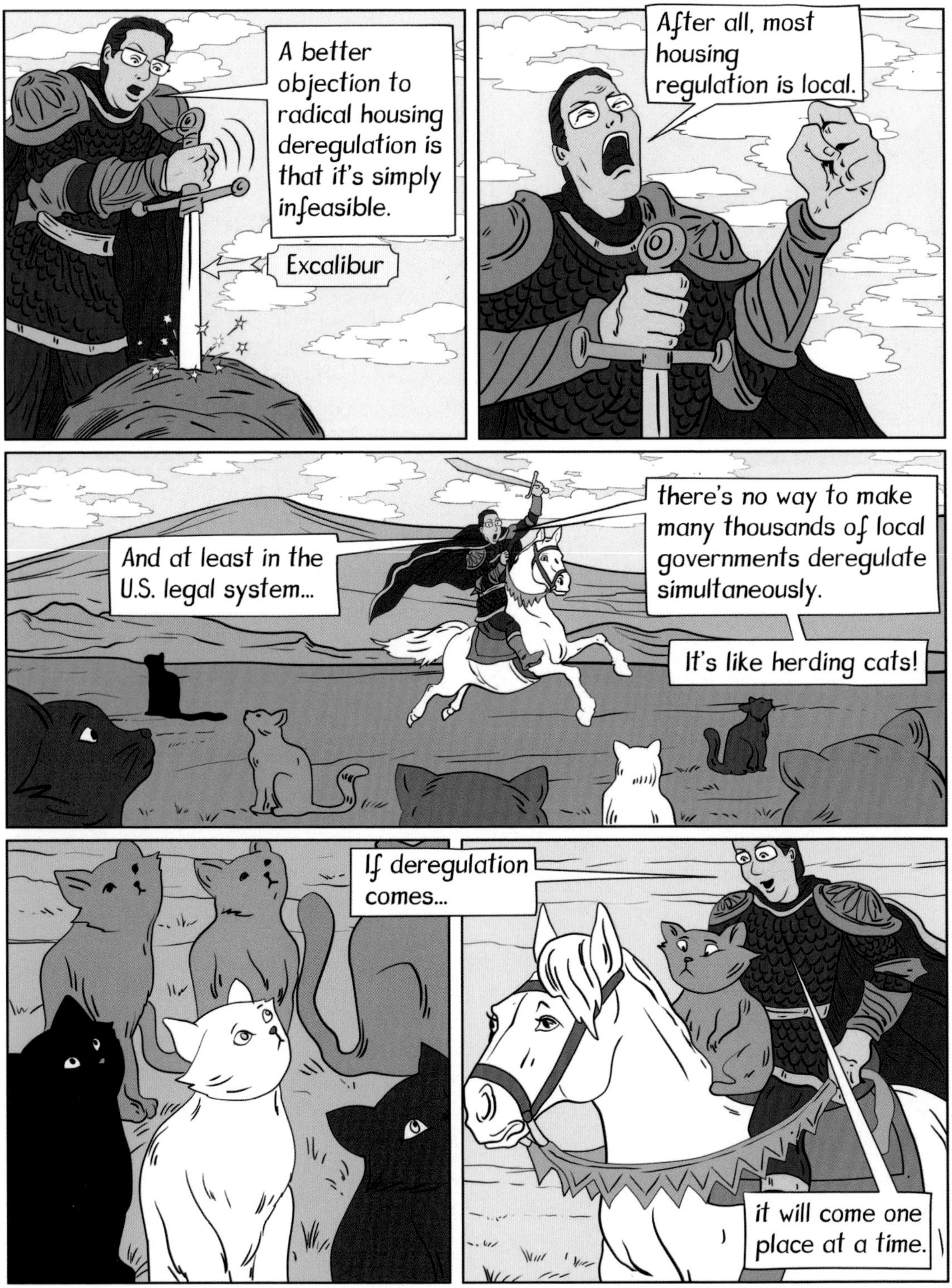
A better objection to radical housing deregulation is that it's simply infeasible.
Excalibur
After all, most housing regulation is local.
And at least in the U.S. legal system...
there's no way to make many thousands of local governments deregulate simultaneously.
It's like herding cats!
If deregulation comes...
it will come one place at a time.

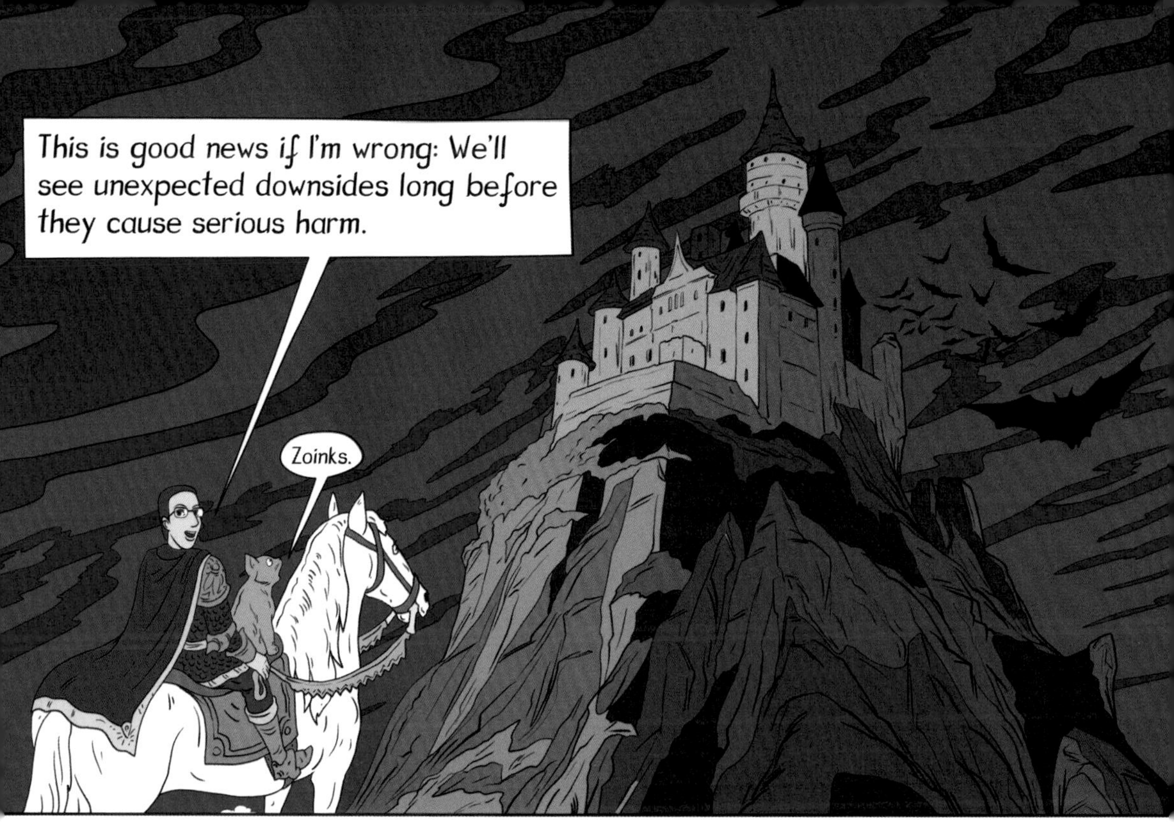
This is good news if I'm wrong: We'll see unexpected downsides long before they cause serious harm.
Zoinks.

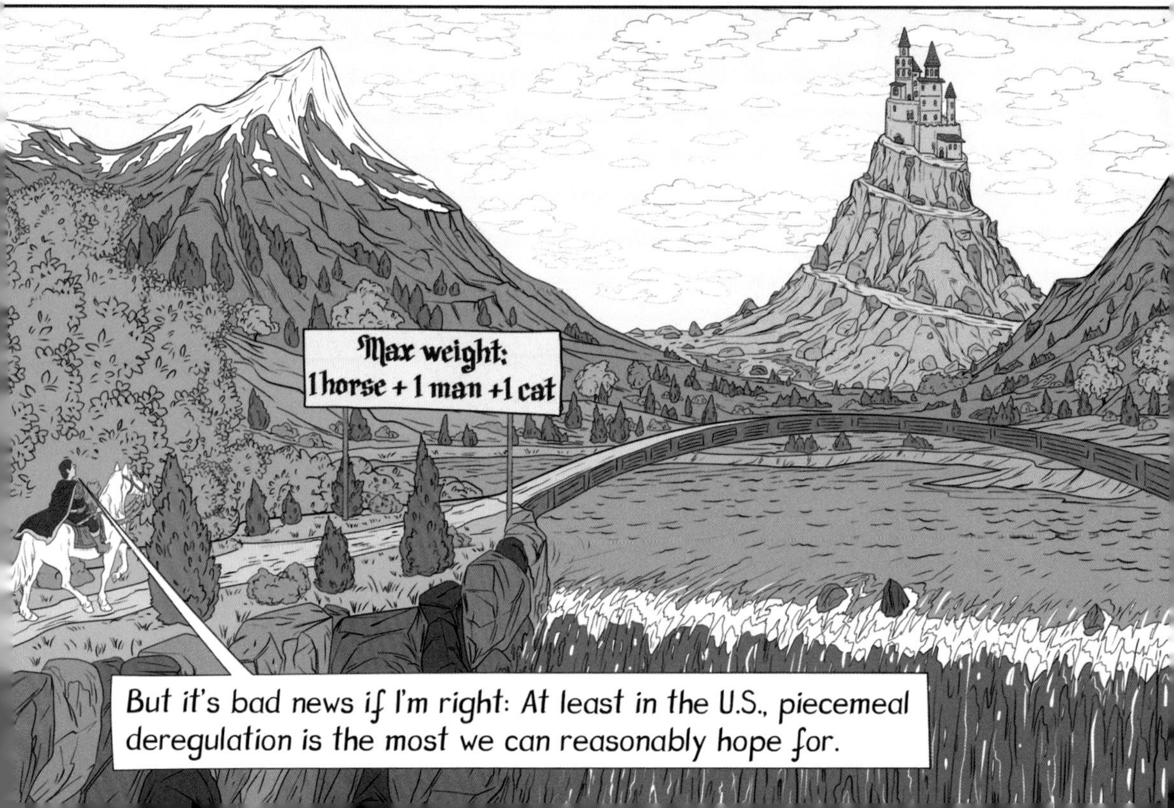
Max weight:
1 horse + 1 man +1 cat
But it's bad news if I'm right: At least in the U.S., piecemeal deregulation is the most we can reasonably hope for.

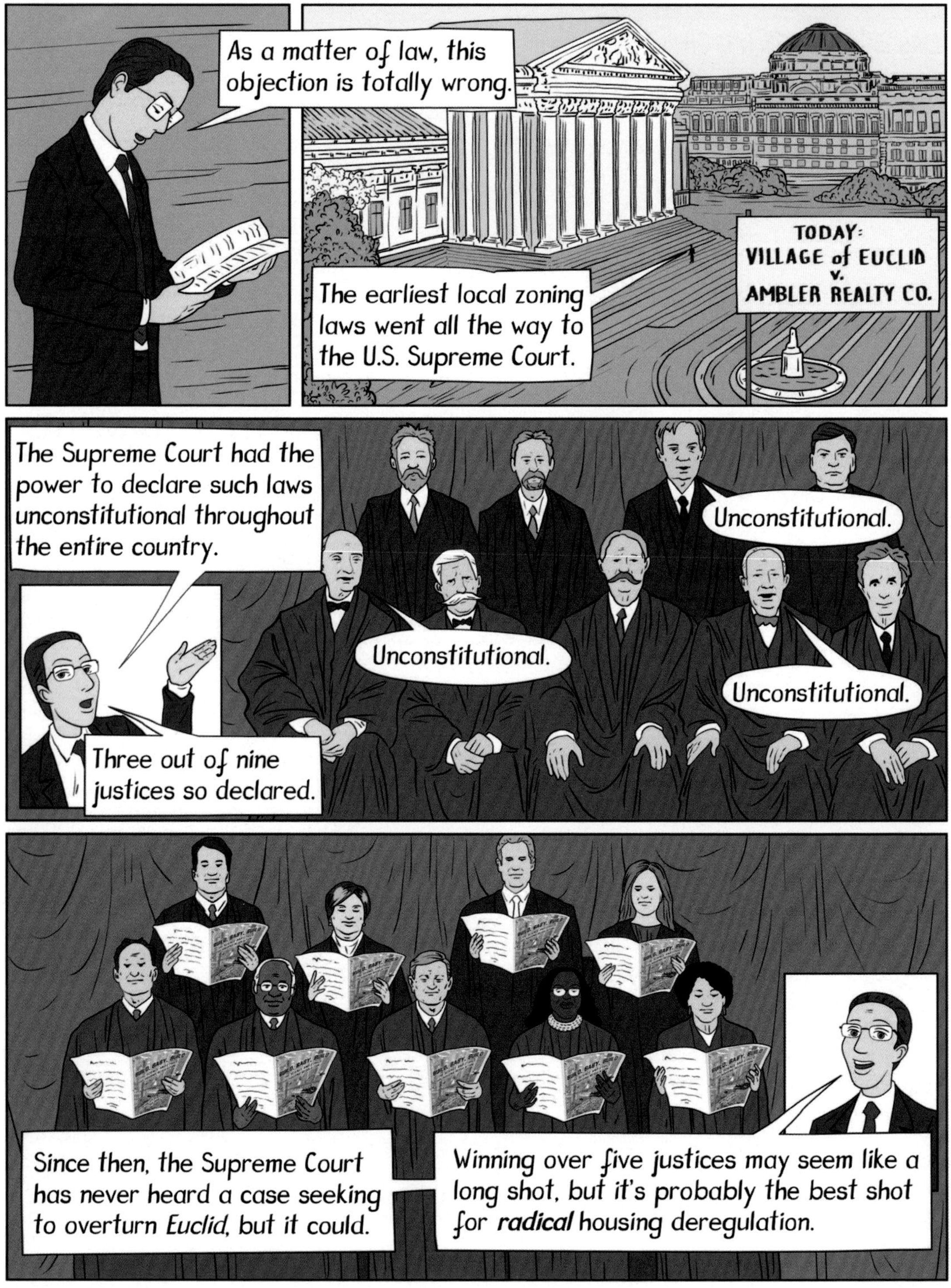
As a matter of law, this objection is totally wrong.
The earliest local zoning laws went all the way to the U.S. Supreme Court.
TODAY: VILLAGE of EUCLID v. AMBLER REALTY CO.
The Supreme Court had the power to declare such laws unconstitutional throughout the entire country.
Unconstitutional.
Unconstitutional.
Unconstitutional.
Three out of nine justices so declared.
Since then, the Supreme Court has never heard a case seeking to overturn *Euclid*, but it could.
Winning over five justices may seem like a long shot, but it's probably the best shot for ***radical*** housing deregulation.

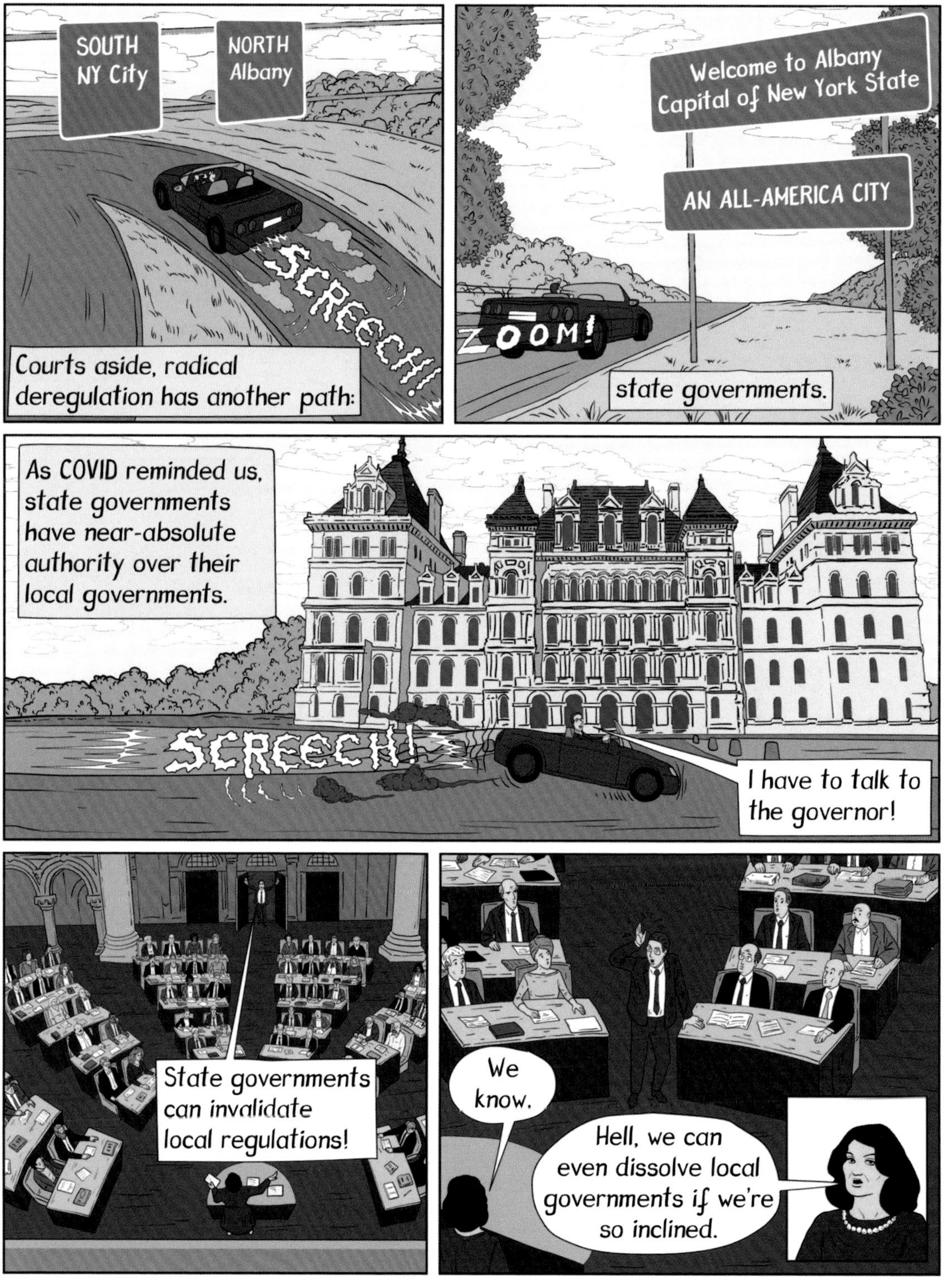
SOUTH NY City
NORTH Albany
SCREECH!
Courts aside, radical deregulation has another path:
Welcome to Albany Capital of New York State
AN ALL-AMERICA CITY
ZOOM!
state governments.
As COVID reminded us, state governments have near-absolute authority over their local governments.
SCREECH!
I have to talk to the governor!
State governments can invalidate local regulations!
We know.
Hell, we can even dissolve local governments if we're so inclined.

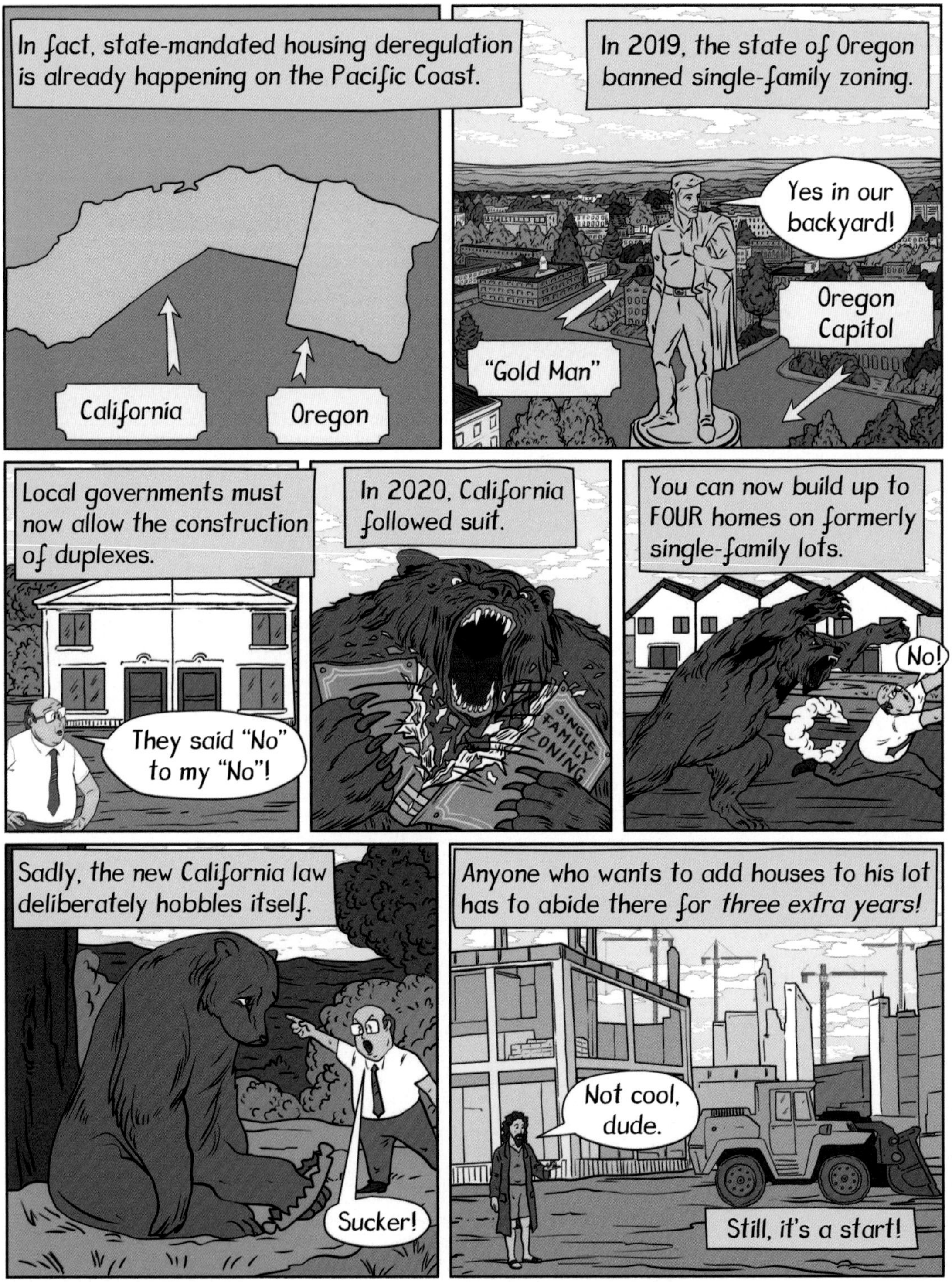
In fact, state-mandated housing deregulation is already happening on the Pacific Coast.
California
Oregon
In 2019, the state of Oregon banned single-family zoning.
Yes in our backyard!
Oregon Capitol
"Gold Man"
Local governments must now allow the construction of duplexes.
They said "No" to my "No"!
In 2020, California followed suit.
SINGLE FAMILY ZONING
You can now build up to FOUR homes on formerly single-family lots.
No!
Sadly, the new California law deliberately hobbles itself.
Sucker!
Anyone who wants to add houses to his lot has to abide there for *three extra years!*
Not cool, dude.
Still, it's a start!

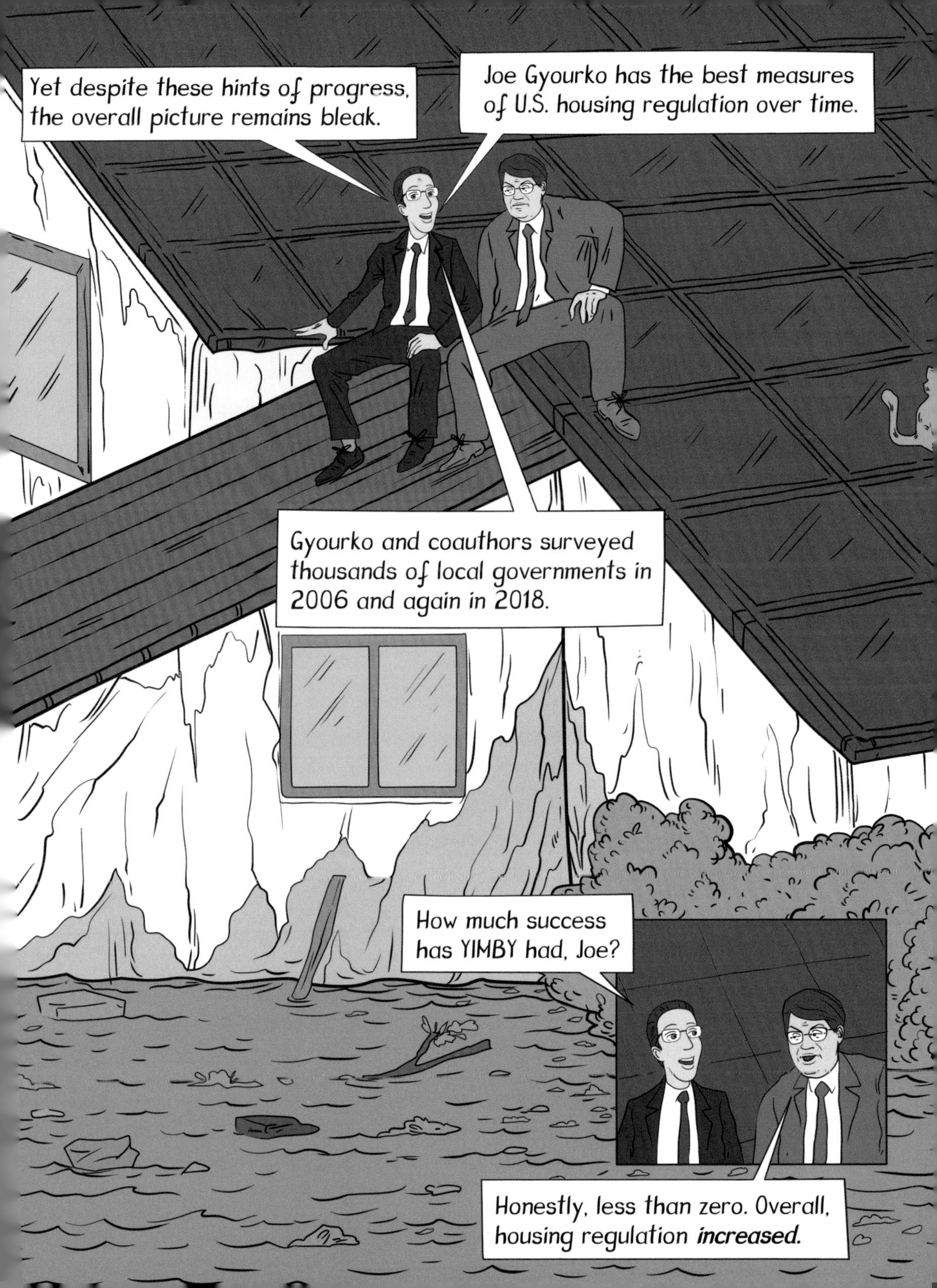
Yet despite these hints of progress, the overall picture remains bleak.
Joe Gyourko has the best measures of U.S. housing regulation over time.
Gyourko and coauthors surveyed thousands of local governments in 2006 and again in 2018.
How much success has YIMBY had, Joe?
Honestly, less than zero. Overall, housing regulation *increased.*

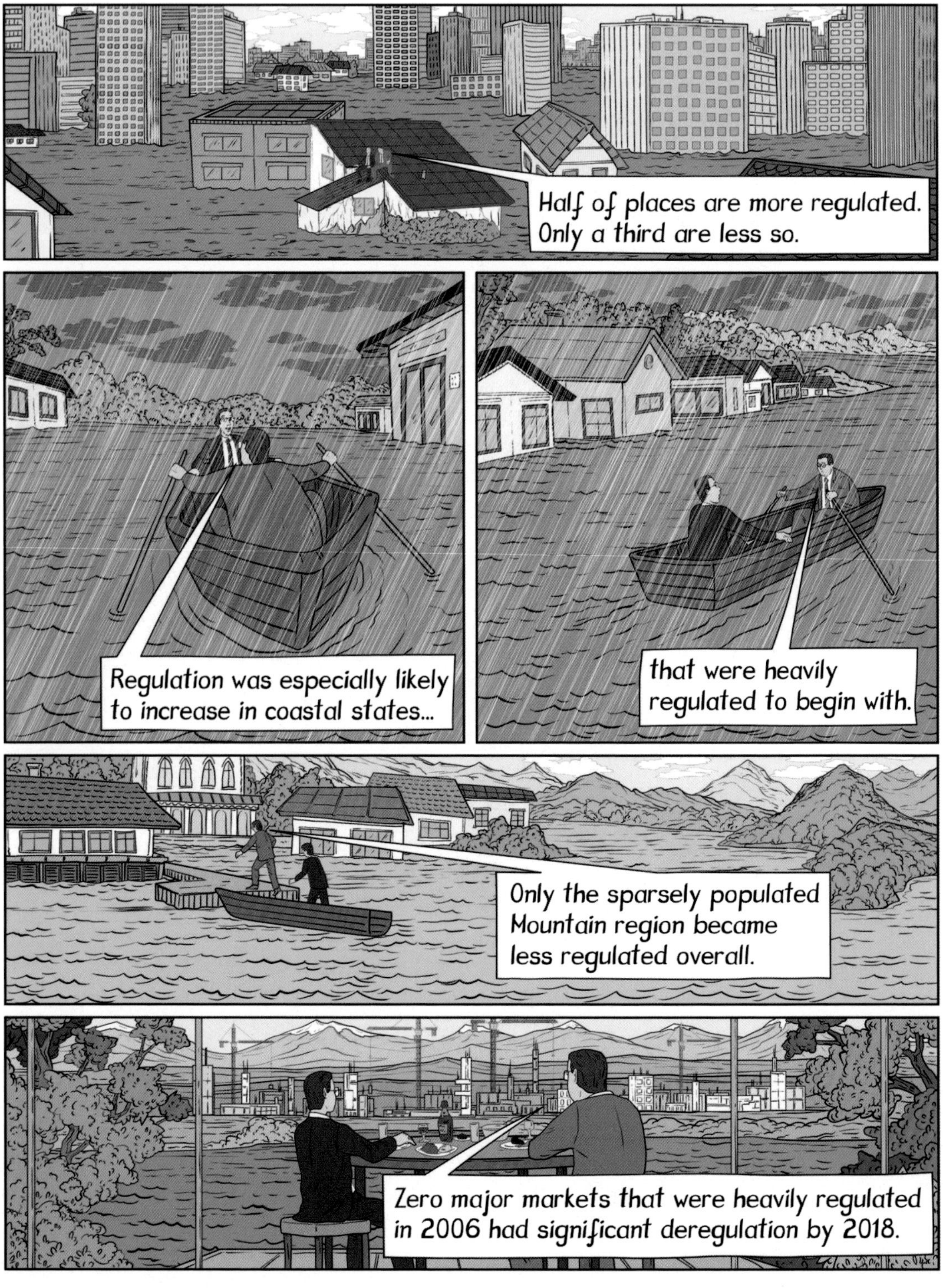
Half of places are more regulated. Only a third are less so.
Regulation was especially likely to increase in coastal states...
that were heavily regulated to begin with.
Only the sparsely populated Mountain region became less regulated overall.
Zero major markets that were heavily regulated in 2006 had significant deregulation by 2018.

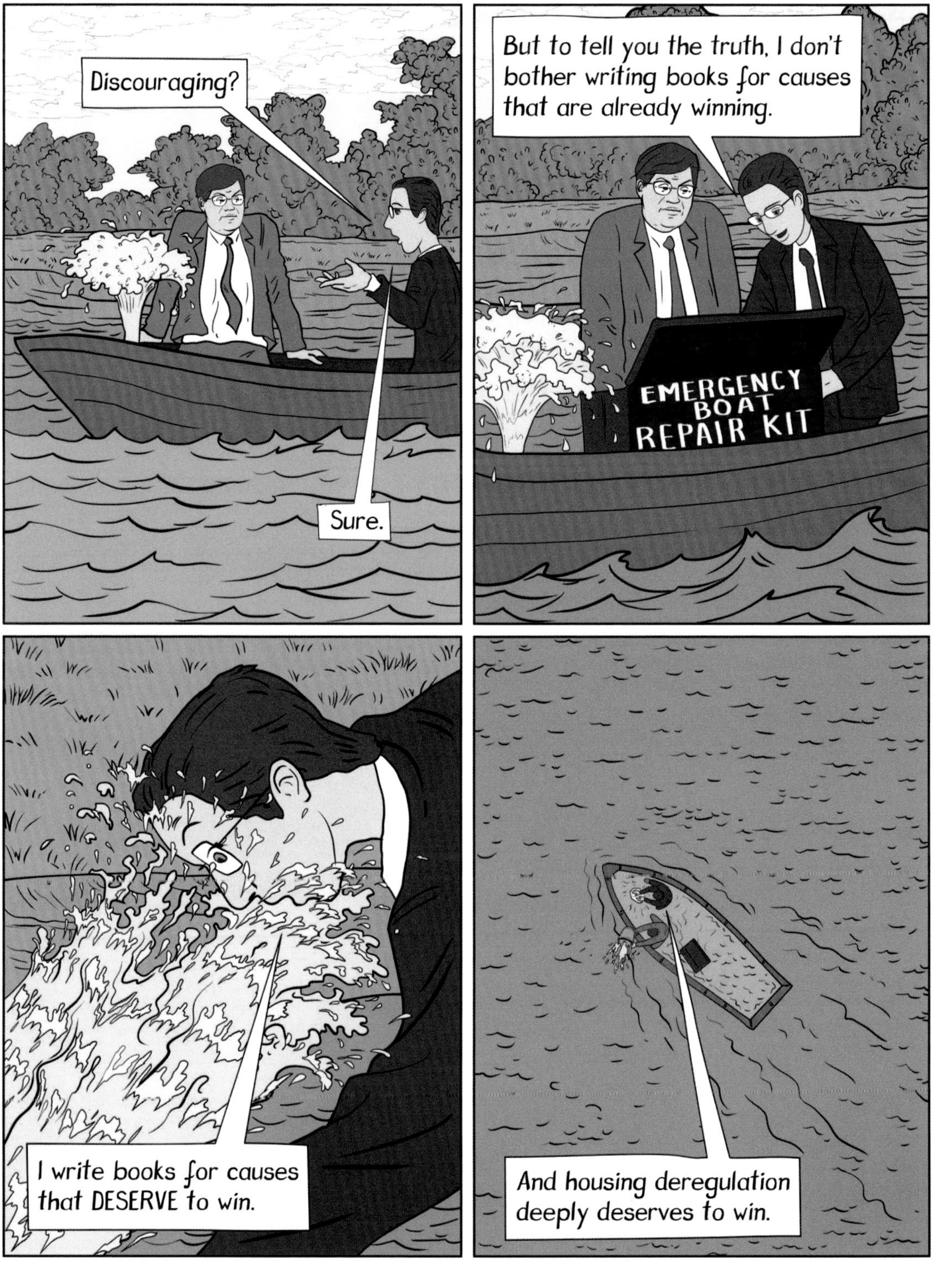
Discouraging?
Sure.
But to tell you the truth, I don't bother writing books for causes that are already winning.
EMERGENCY BOAT REPAIR KIT
I write books for causes that DESERVE to win.
And housing deregulation deeply deserves to win.

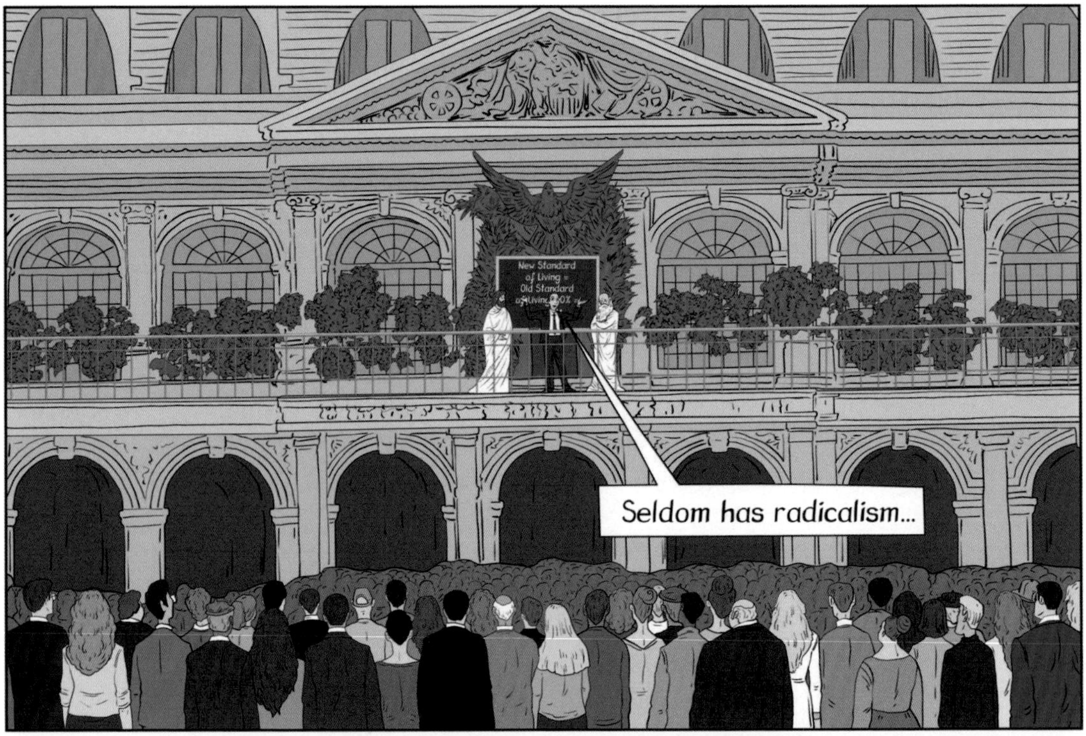
New Standard
of Living =
Old Standard
of Living/90% =
Seldom has radicalism...

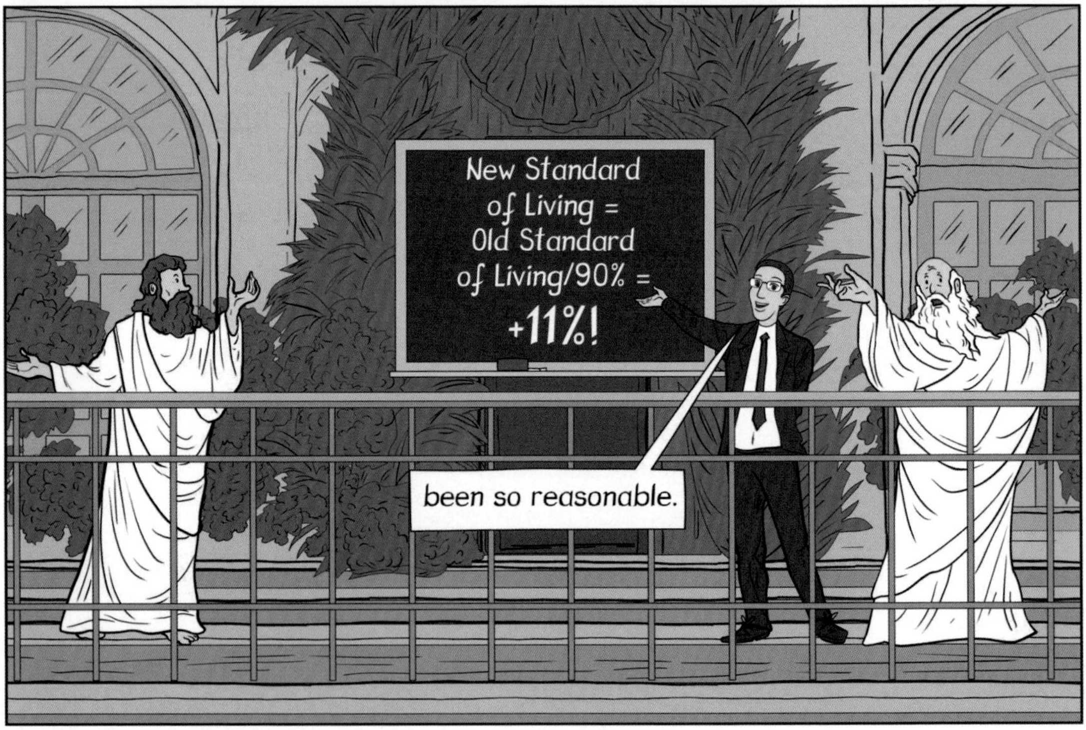
New Standard
of Living =
Old Standard
of Living/90% =
+11%!
been so reasonable.

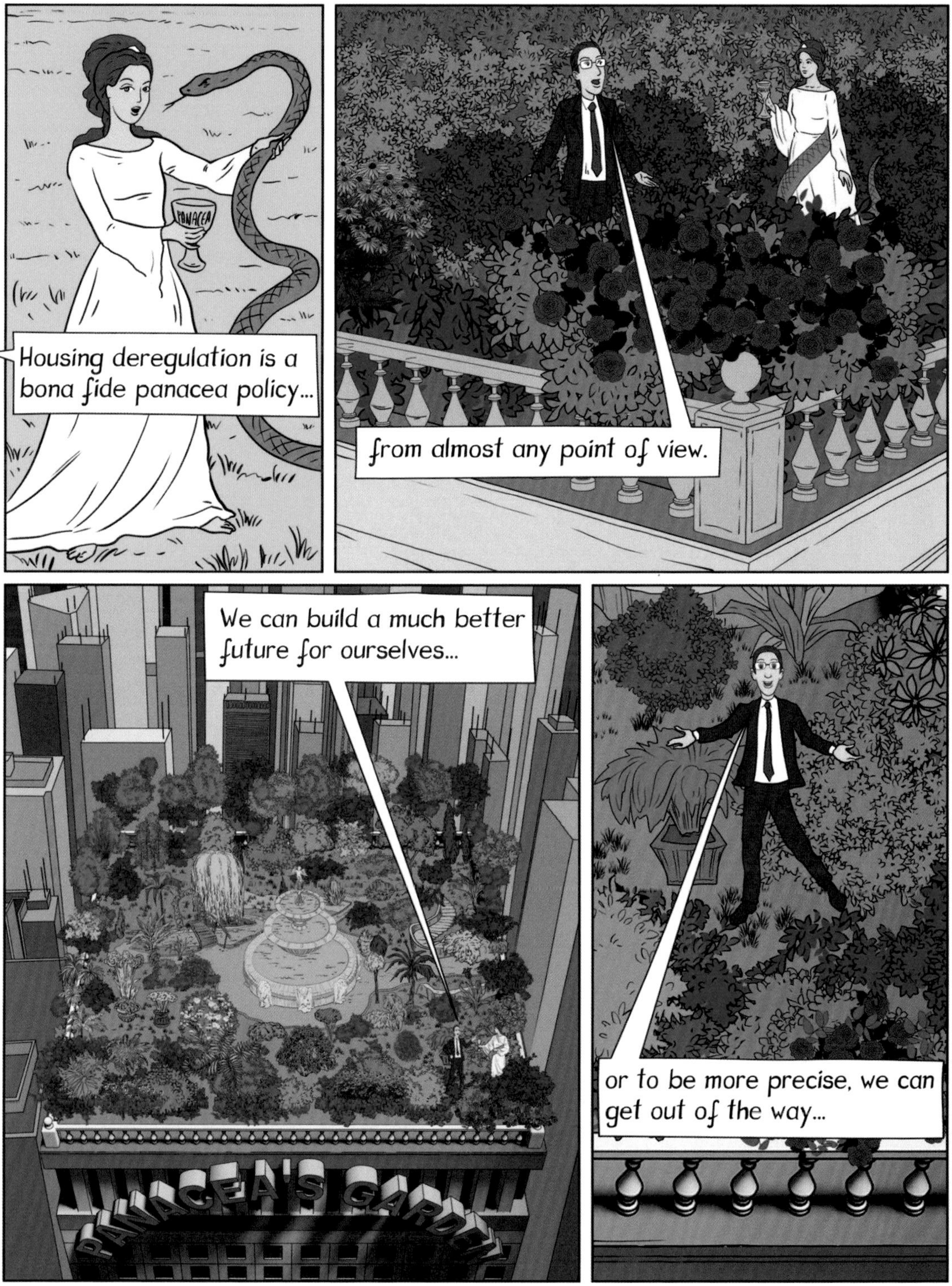
PANACEA
Housing deregulation is a bona fide panacea policy...
from almost any point of view.
We can build a much better future for ourselves...
PANACEA'S GARDEN
or to be more precise, we can get out of the way...

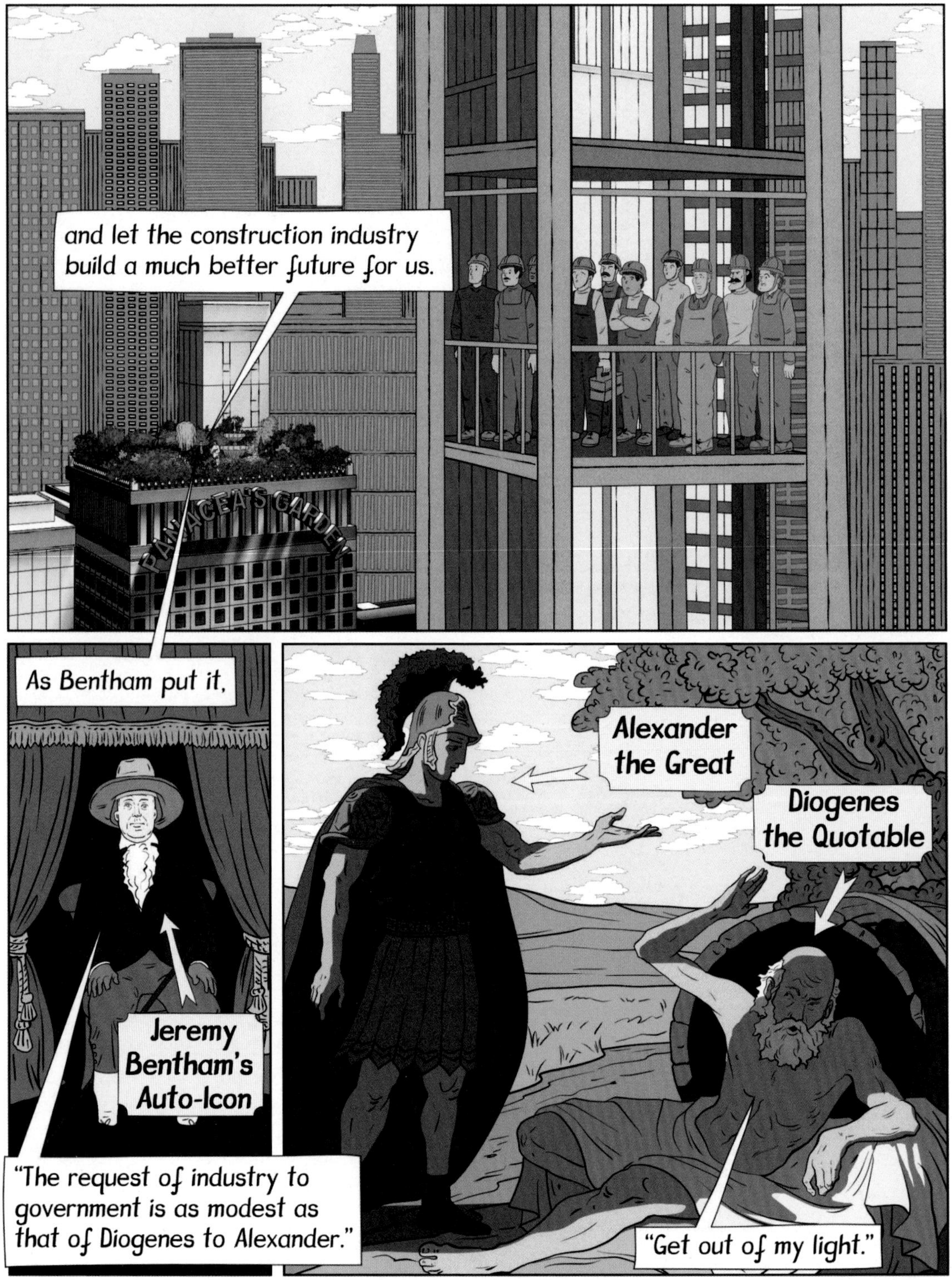
and let the construction industry build a much better future for us.
PANACEA'S GARDEN
As Bentham put it,
Jeremy Bentham's Auto-Icon
"The request of industry to government is as modest as that of Diogenes to Alexander."
Alexander the Great
Diogenes the Quotable
"Get out of my light."

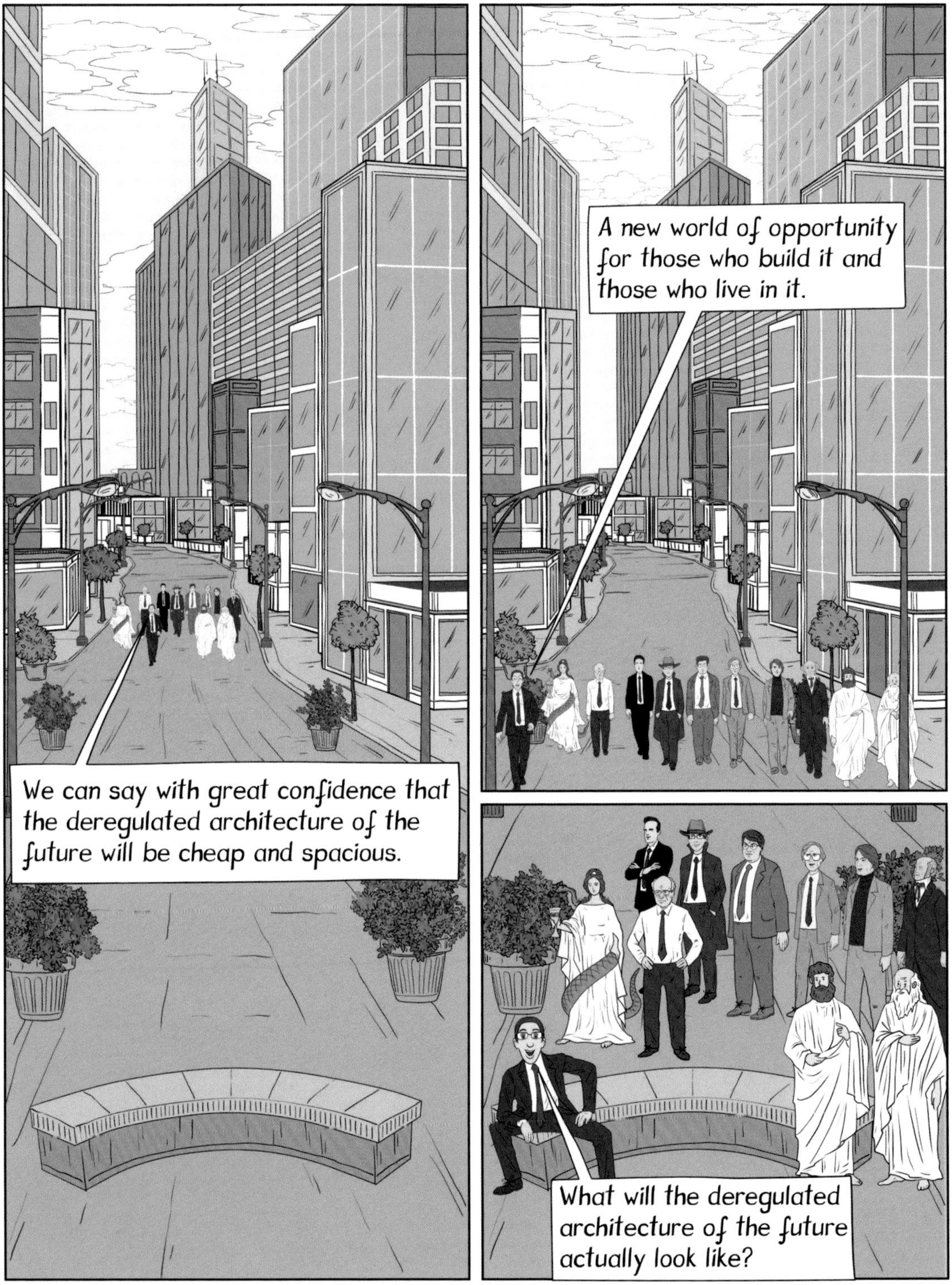
We can say with great confidence that the deregulated architecture of the future will be cheap and spacious.
A new world of opportunity for those who build it and those who live in it.
What will the deregulated architecture of the future actually look like?

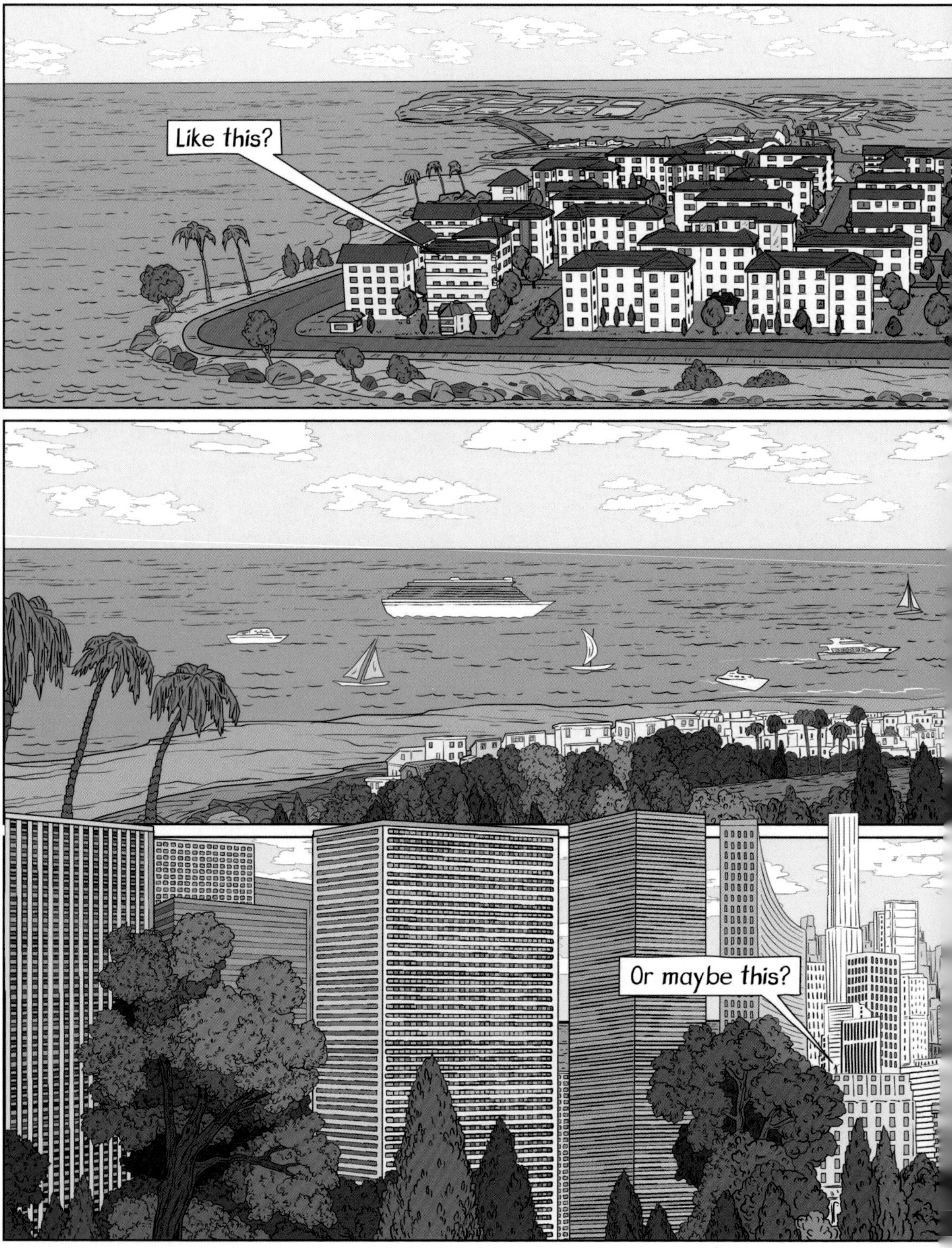
Like this?
Or maybe this?

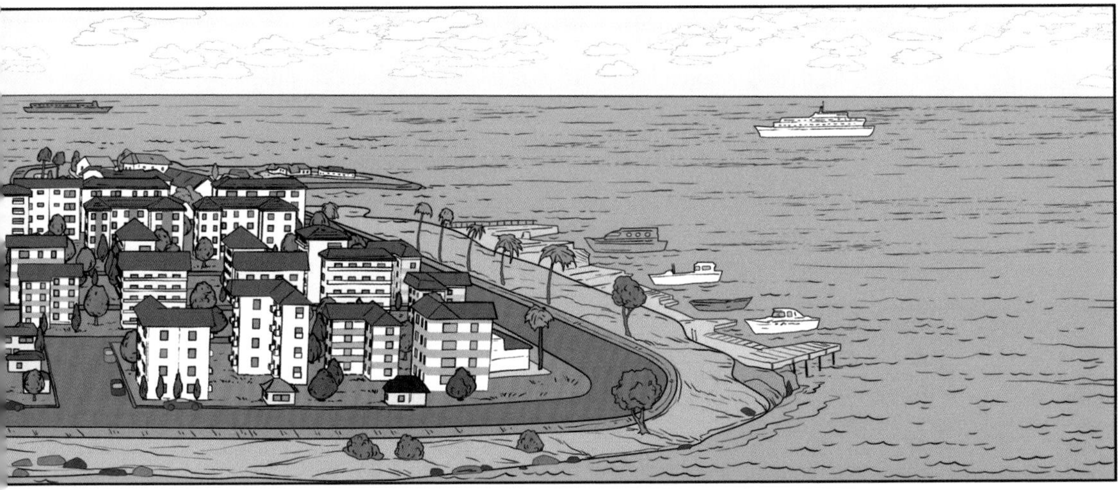

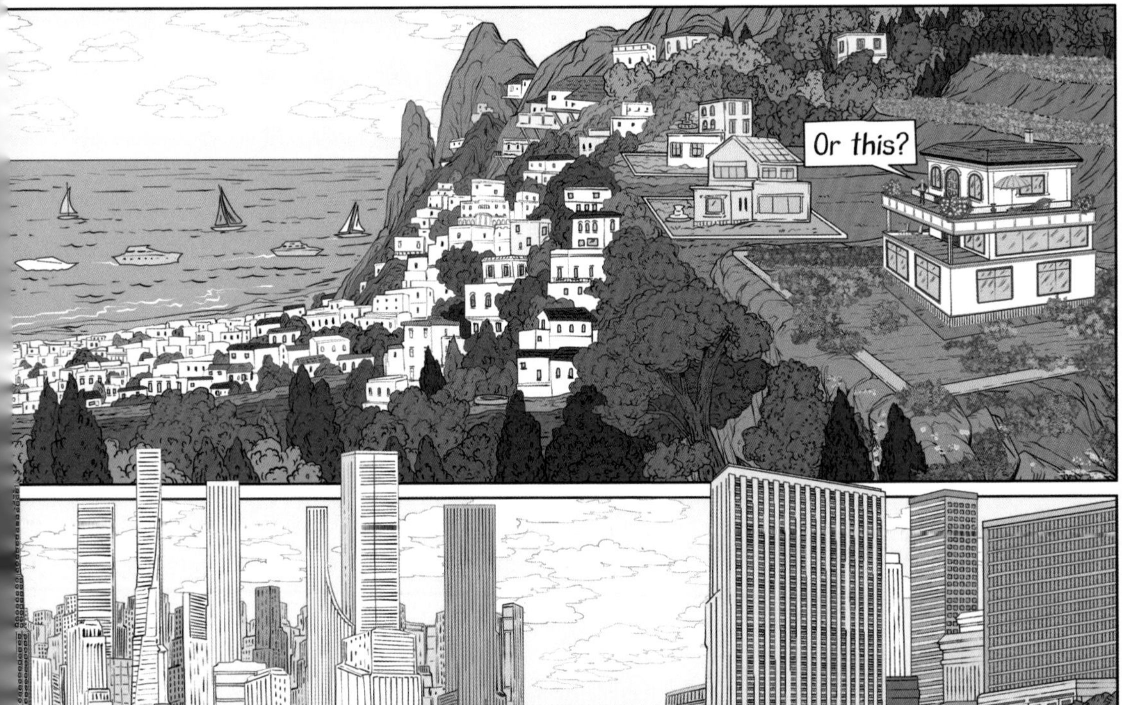
Or this?

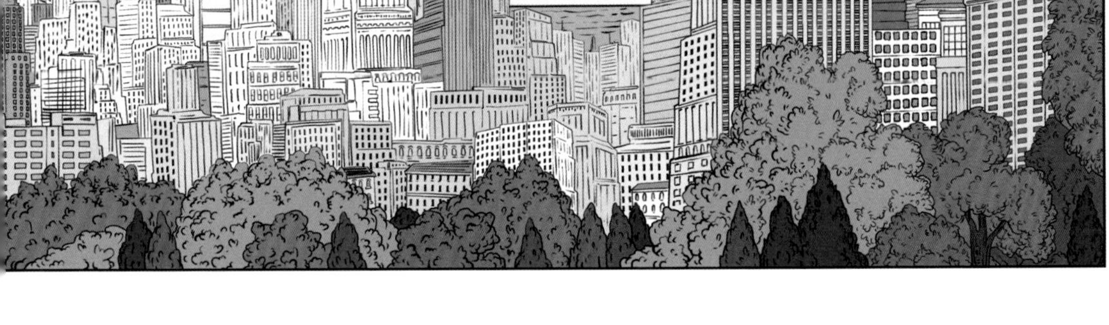

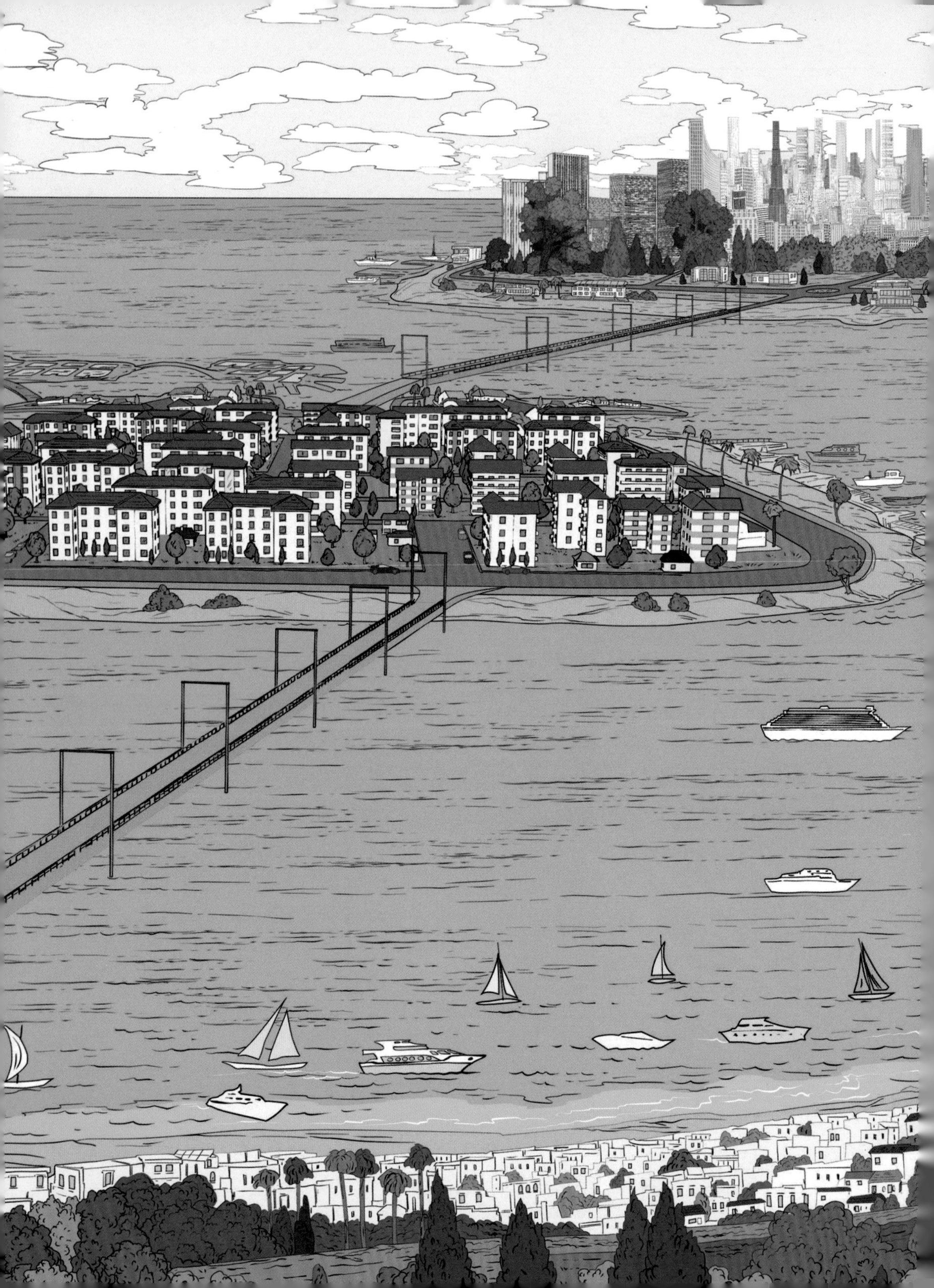

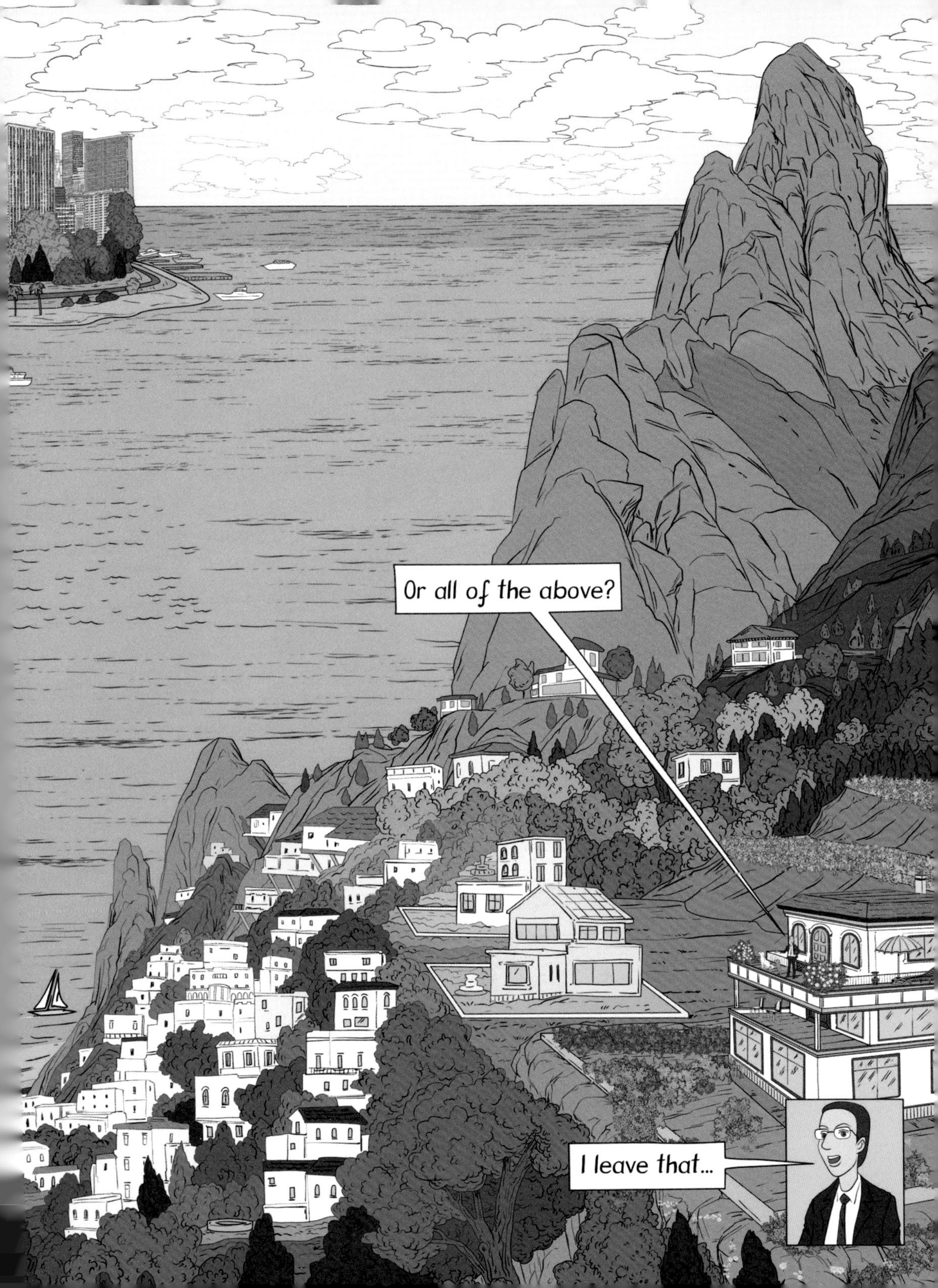
Or all of the above?
I leave that...

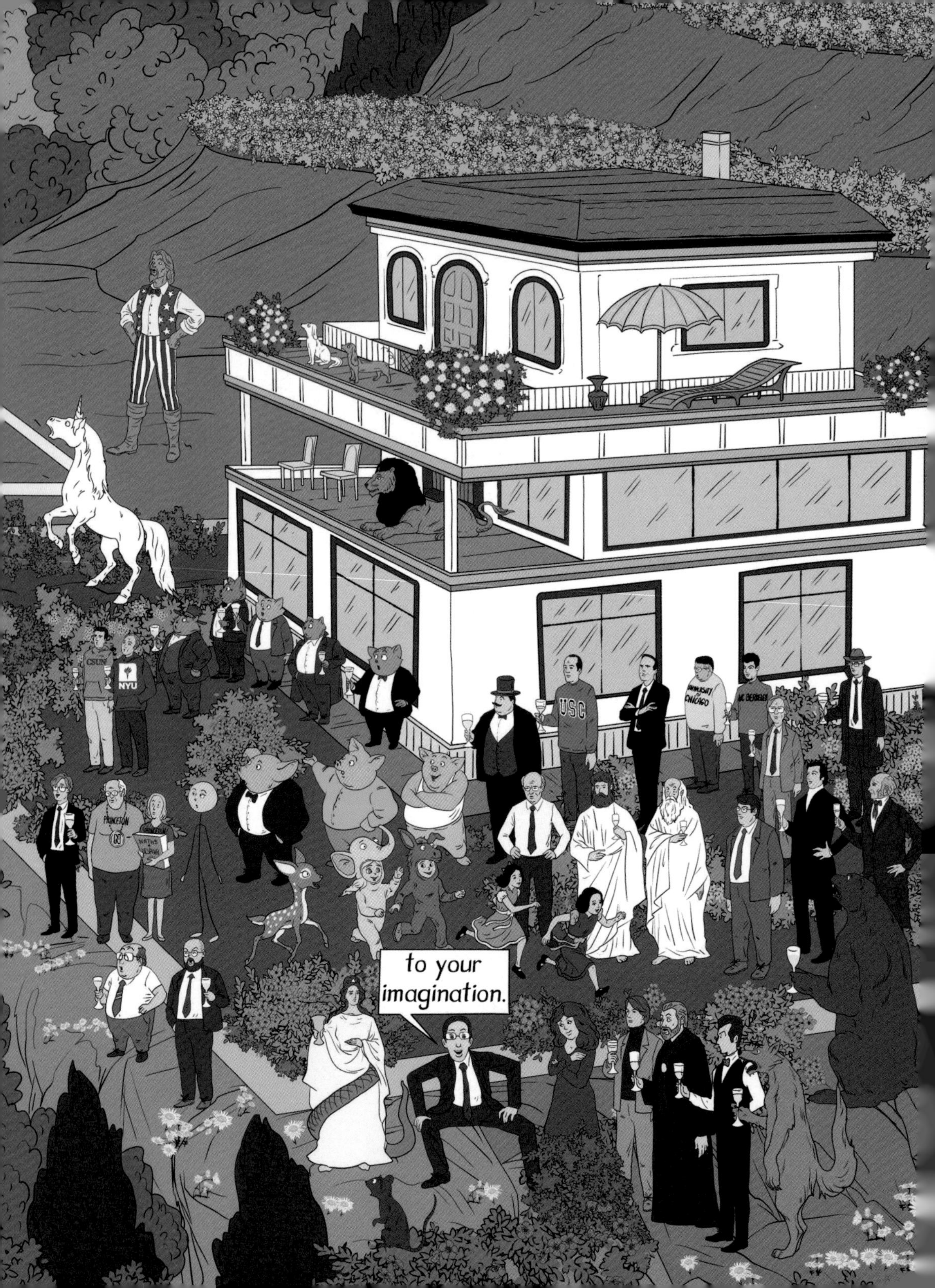
to your imagination.
CSUN
NYU
USC
UNIVERSITY OF CHICAGO
UC BERKELEY
PRINCETON

NOTES

CHAPTER 1: The Home That Wasn't There

p. 5, panel 1–4.   For a standard treatment of supply and demand, see Cowen and Tabarrok (2021, pp. 51–62).

p. 10, panel 1.   Saiz (2010, p. 1255) finds that *both* regulation and geography (especially steep slopes and bodies of water) restrict housing supply. Yet he also concludes that unfavorable geography is itself an important cause of regulation. "Antigrowth local land policies are more likely to arise in growing, land-constrained metropolitan areas and in cities where preexisting land values were high and worth protecting."

p. 16, panel 2.   Arguably, the best case for regulation remains Edward Bassett's century-old *Zoning* (Bassett 1922). This concise and eloquent book highlights the potential advantages of regulation, along with a visionary plan for regulatory expansion.

p. 19, panel 2.   Badger and Bui (2019); Manville, Monkkonen, and Lens (2020). The United States has had strict single-family zoning now for about a century: "The single-family district, which was initially absent in New York because of concerns about constitutionality, became ubiquitous nationwide. By the late 1920s, it covered nearly 50 percent of land in the typical U.S. city . . . and much larger portions in suburbs" (Hirt 2014, p. 35).

p. 20, panel 2.   Monkkonen and Manville (2019, p. 1123) discover that merely *mentioning* that developers will earn a large profit from a construction project sharply increases public opposition. "Our findings show that some opposition to housing is motivated not by residents' fears of their own losses, but resentment of others' gains."

p. 22, panel 1.   For discussion of this ideological suspicion, see Been, Ellen, and O'Regan (2019) and Manville (2021).

p. 22, panels 3–4.   Krugman (2014). Criticism of housing regulation is a running theme in Krugman's work. Krugman (2005) explicitly blames high housing prices (and housing bubbles) on zoning regulation. Twelve years later, he laments, "All too many blue states end up, in practice, letting zoning be a tool, not of good land use, but of NIMBYism, preventing the construction of new housing," and he opined, "What we need is effective land-use regulation that doesn't strangle housing construction" (Krugman 2017).

p. 23, panel 1.   Furman (2015). Or as Metcalf (2018, p. 69) puts it:

> Most public officials would state that affordable housing is one of their top priorities. But when looking at the combination of housing policies—both the official "affordable housing" policies and the broader set of exclusionary land use regulations—it seems clear that de facto housing policy for most of the cities in expensive metro areas is to make people live somewhere else (and suffer long commutes) or to discourage people from moving into the area in the first place (effectively preventing them from participating in the most successful economies of the country).

p. 23, panels 2–3.   Yglesias (2012). The same book also provides this memorable fortune cookie adage: "An agricultural economy starved of land will suffer. An industrial economy starved of raw materials will suffer. And a service economy starved of *proximity* will suffer" (loc. 790).

p. 24, panel 1.   Yglesias (2012). For further background on the cross-ideological consensus on the effect of housing regulation on housing costs, see Somin (2015).

p. 26, panel 2.   Total average annual expenditures for all consumer units in 2019 came to $63,036 (Federal Reserve Bank of St. Louis 2021d). Total average annual expenditure on shelter for all consumer units in the same year came to $12,190 (Federal Reserve Bank of St. Louis 2021a). Dividing shelter expenditures by total expenditures yields a ratio of 19.3 percent.

   Note: U.S. government statistics distinguish between expenditures on "shelter" versus those on "housing." For tenants, expenditure on "shelter" is the same as rent; for homeowners, it is an estimate of how much it *would* currently cost to rent their home (Bureau of Labor Statistics, n.d.). Housing, the broader category, sums the cost of shelter, utilities, fuel, public services, household operations, housekeeping supplies, and household furnishings and equipment (Bureau of Labor Statistics 2002).

p. 29, panel 3.

In a recent national U.S. survey, Hankinson (2018, pp. 480–81) finds that 42 percent of homeowners and 35 percent of tenants actually want to *ban* construction of new housing in their neighborhoods. Only 28 percent of homeowners—but 59 percent of renters—support building just 10 percent more housing in their cities. Other national surveys show that a majority of Americans favor *some* additional construction (Ekins 2019; Manville 2021). Given how strict existing regulations are, however, such responses show strong support for housing regulation in general.

Furthermore, surveys routinely find that support for abstract ideals is *much* higher than support for concrete implications of those ideals. Thus, a major survey of the top 20 metropolitan areas of the United States finds that the U.S. public moderately supports more low-density single-family home building but is roughly neutral on the building of new apartments (Marble and Nall 2021, p. 1755; see also Trounstine 2021). Similarly, even though 51 percent of Californians are "very concerned" about "lack of affordable housing," only 12 percent agreed that "California needs more new market rate housing" (David Binder Research 2021).

p. 30, panel 1.   On tenants' support for housing regulation, see Hankinson (2018) and Manville (2021).

p. 30, panel 2.   Hankinson (2018, p. 478).

p. 32, panel 2.   Fischel (2015), who combines an encyclopedic tour of housing regulation with a favorable evaluation, is the most notable outlier in the economics profession. The best explanation is that Fischel virtually takes the rational voter model for granted. (See also Fischel [2001].) As a result, the sheer popularity of the status quo confirms its wisdom; the social scientist's job is to explain *why* people's political views are reasonable, appearances notwithstanding. For a critique of the rational voter model, see Caplan (2007).

pp. 33–34.   See generally Beyer (2022), Dougherty (2021), Erdmann (2019), Furman (2015), Glaeser (2011), Lewyn (2017), and Yglesias (2012, 2020).

CHAPTER 2: The Manufacture of Scarcity

p. 38.   For long-run housing price trends, see Gyourko and Molloy (2015) and Knoll, Schularick, and Steger (2017).

p. 39, panel 2.   Case (1994, p. 38) reports that the median 1982 single-family home price in San Francisco was $124,900. To calculate income for the "typical American family," I took the mean of the middle quintile from the U.S. Census, $20,064, yielding a housing price/annual income ratio of 6.2 (U.S. Census Bureau 2021).

p. 39, panel 3.   From the first quarters of 1982 to 2019, the All-Transactions House Price Index for San Francisco-San Mateo-Redwood City, California, rose from 43.73 to 439.39 (Federal Reserve Bank of St. Louis 2023a). During this time, the income for the typical American family rose from $20,064 to $68,938, so the housing price/annual income ratio rose to 18.1 (U.S. Census Bureau 2021).

p. 41, panel 3.   Four hundred feet is a common cutoff for skyscrapers. See Wikipedia (2022a) for a list of all San Francisco buildings that meet this cutoff, by year of completion.

p. 42, panel 2.   Wikipedia (2022a). San Francisco's era of ultra-strict regulation of tall buildings began in July 1985. For details, see Lindsey (1985).

p. 42, panel 3.   San Francisco's Proposition E, approved on March 3, 2020, cuts the maximum regulatory allotment for new office space if the city fails to build sufficient affordable housing. As Brinklow (2020) explains, "Under a voter-approved law from 1986 (Proposition M), San Francisco can only approve 875,000 square feet of new office space annually. If passed, Proposition E would potentially lower that cap each year depending on whether the city hits its affordable housing goals; failure to build ten percent of required housing in a year, for example, would then lower the office space cap by ten percent the following year, and so forth." He adds, "The city gets its affordable housing goals from the Regional Housing Needs Allocation (RHNA), a regular assessment by the state. Notably, SF [San Francisco] very rarely hits these benchmarks."

p. 44, panel 2.   For an in-depth exploration of the cost of sheer delay, see Einstein, Glick, and Palmer (2020).

p. 49.   Caplan (2021a) fleshes out the "reverse musical chairs" analogy in detail. Been, Ellen, and O'Regan (2019, p. 29; footnotes omitted) call this chain reaction "filtering" and show that the supporting evidence is almost undeniable:

> Empirical research shows that filtering is not just a theory posited on the pages of economic textbooks, but in fact occurs in real housing markets. Indeed, recent research shows that filtering was the primary source for additions to the affordable rental stock between 2003 and

2013, whereas new construction was the largest contributor for the higher priced rentals, and tenure conversion was the largest source for moderately priced rentals. . . . Further, Weicher, Eggers, and Moumen (2016) report that 23.4% of the rental units that were affordable to very low-income renters in the United States in 2013 had filtered down from higher rent categories in 1985. Another 21.8% were conversions from formerly owner-occupied homes or seasonal rentals. Most of the higher priced rental units that filtered down to become affordable in 2013 were moderate-rent units in 1985, but 15% of those that filtered down were high-rent units in 1985. Note that filtering occurs over a shorter time frame too; among affordable units in 2013, 19% had been higher rent units as recently as 2005.

For a more detailed discussion, see Weicher, Eggers, and Moumen (2016) as well as Mast (2023) and Rosenthal (2014).

p. 51.   For an incisive introduction to efforts to measure the effect of housing regulation, see Glaeser and Gyourko (2018). Murray (2021) strongly criticizes Glaeser and Gyourko's general approach; Caplan (2022) responds. Murray (2022) offers a rejoinder, and Tulip (2022) adds further criticism of Murray.

p. 52, panel 4.   Other critics of housing regulation argue that existing laws also do great harm by preventing the expansion of low-cost factory-style construction (Schmitz 2020).

p. 55, panel 1.   Gyourko and Molloy (2015) show that between 1980 and 2013, U.S. inflation-adjusted housing prices increased about 80 percent, while construction costs stayed flat. Nominal housing prices from 2013 to 2021 increased about 65 percent further (Federal Reserve Bank of St. Louis 2023b), implying an additional inflation-adjusted rise of 40 percent. "Roughly doubled" is therefore quite conservative.

How is this possible, given Perry's (2016) finding that the size of *new* homes dramatically increased from 1973 to 2015, while their price per square foot stayed almost constant in real terms? The best explanation is that most new home construction happens in relatively unregulated areas.

p. 55, panel 3.   Glaeser and Gyourko (2003; 2018, pp. 15–18) maintain that this "zoning tax" is low outside of the Pacific coast and Northeast Corridor. Gyourko and Krimmel (2021) greatly revise this position, finding substantial zoning taxes in most densely populated areas of the United States. I should note that Gyourko himself might dispute this characterization, but his own numbers show zoning taxes above $100,000/acre within 15 miles of the urban cores of 17 of the 24 major metropolitan areas studied (Gyourko and Krimmel 2021, p. 11).

p. 56, panel 1.   "As any developer knows, you could make a fortune buying homes in suburban Boston or San Francisco, subdividing the lots, and building new homes" (Glaeser 2004).

p. 56, panel 2.   See Gyourko and Krimmel (2021, pp. 3–6), for details on their land price data.

p. 56, panel 3.   Gyourko and Krimmel (2021, p. 9). Note that Gyourko and Krimmel report zoning tax per *quarter* acre, rather than per acre as I do.

p. 56, panel 5.   Gyourko and Krimmel (2021, p. 11). By "downtown," I mean ≤15 miles from the urban core, the first block of results in Table 2.

p. 57, panels 3–8.   Gyourko and Krimmel (2021, p. 11).

p. 58, panel 1.   For the world's maximally fascinating book about parking, see Shoup (2011).

p. 60.   Picken and Ilozor (2015) include a good survey of the relationship between building height and building cost; see also Ahlfeldt and McMillen (2018), Chau et al. (2007), Flanagan and Norman (1999), and especially Eriksen and Orlando (2022). Glaeser and Gyourko (2018, p. 6) are even more optimistic: "Per-square-foot cost of building to seven stories is quite close to the per-square-foot cost of building 50 stories."

p. 62, panels 1–6.   Badger and Bui (2019). Recent deregulation in California and Oregon definitely lowers these figures. However, as my Chapter 7 explains, the deregulation is milder than it looks on the surface.

p. 62, panel 7.   Manville et al. (2020, p. 107).

p. 65, panel 4.   The COVID-19 pandemic began in the first quarter of 2020. Nominal housing prices were up by 20 percent in the third quarter of 2021, and by a total of 40 percent by the third quarter of 2022, much more than inflation (Federal Reserve Bank of St. Louis 2023b)!

p. 65, panel 6.   Between the first quarter of 2020 and the third quarter of 2022, nominal housing prices around San Francisco rose by 12 percent, a 3 percent fall in real terms (Federal Reserve Bank of St. Louis 2023a).

CHAPTER 3: The Panacea Policy

p. 82, panels 3–4.   To repeat, we can estimate the housing budget share by dividing shelter expenditure by annual expenditure. Updating Gyourko and Molloy (2015) with more recent housing price data gives us a conservative estimate of a 50 percent price fall from deregulation (Federal Reserve Bank of St. Louis 2021a, 2021d, 2023a).

p. 85, panel 3.   Hsieh and Moretti (2019).

p. 85, panel 4.   Hsieh and Moretti (2019, p. 13).

p. 86, panel 3.

You know you want to.

In 2021, I discovered that the key paper's estimates for the effect of deregulation on gross domestic product include a few large arithmetic errors that—surprisingly—led the authors to understate the strength of their findings (Caplan 2021b). Both Hsieh and Moretti confirmed my corrections; for further discussion, see Caplan (2021c). *Build, Baby, Build* uses these corrected Hsieh-Moretti figures throughout.

Soon before this book in your hands went to press, however, economist Brian Greaney of the University of Washington released a working paper claiming to find fundamental errors in Hsieh-Moretti that render their estimates meaningless (Greaney 2023a). As of December 2023, Hsieh disputes Greaney's critique, while Moretti has yet to respond. I subsequently published Hsieh's reply to Greaney on my blog, along with Greaney's reply to Hsieh's reply (Hsieh 2023, Greaney 2023b). If, as I strongly suspect, Greaney turns out to be correct, I still maintain that a massive effect of housing deregulation on production remains highly likely, simply because regional worker productivity gaps and housing price distortions are both large, and the economic harm is the product of these two large numbers.

p. 87, panels 1–2.

These figures simply add the +11 percent of consumer gains to either +14 percent or +36 percent for productivity gains. Arguably, one should multiply these gains, implying a range of +27 percent to +51 percent.

p. 87, panel 3.

Cowen (2011).

p. 89, panels 2–5.

According to the Consumer Expenditure Surveys, the poorest quintile spend 24.5 percent of their budget on shelter, versus 17.7 percent for the richest quintile (Federal Reserve Bank of St. Louis 2021b, 2021c, 2021e, 2021f). According to the 2015 American Housing Survey, the median income for renters was $34,000—versus $52,000 for homeowners (Schuetz 2017, Table 3). For more on the connection between rising housing costs and inequality, see Albouy, Ehrlich, and Liu (2016).

p. 89, panel 6.

Housing regulation also increases racial segregation (Trounstine 2020). In earlier eras, this was often an explicit goal of regulation. Yet without racist intent, the indirect effect of raising housing prices is naturally to discourage the presence of poorer demographics. Berry (2001) disputes the zoning-segregation connection by comparing Houston to Dallas, but both of these cities are low cost. San Francisco's dramatic price rise provides a far stronger test: Between 1970 and 2020, San Francisco's black share fell from 13.4 percent to 5.6 percent (Bay Area Census n.d.; U.S. Census Bureau 2022).

p. 90, panel 1.

Rognlie (2015, p. 1). For the exciting origin story of Rognlie's paper, see Tankersley (2015).

p. 90, panel 2.	Rognlie (2015, p. 1). Figure based on U.S. data from Table 1 in Rognlie (2015, p. 14). In the same vein, Summers (2014) names "an easing of land-use restrictions that cause the real estate of the rich in major metropolitan areas to keep rising in value" as one of the "two most important steps that public policy can take with respect to wealth inequality."
p. 93, panels 1–2.	Ganong and Shoag (2017, p. 76n2).
p. 93, panels 3–4.	Ganong and Shoag (2017, p. 78n3).
p. 94, panel 4.	Ganong and Shoag (2017, p. 78, fig. 1b).
p. 95, panel 2.	Ganong and Shoag (2017, p. 82, fig. 4).
p. 95, panel 3.	Ganong and Shoag (2017, p. 83, fig. 5).
p. 96, panel 4.	The exact U.S. figures for 2020 show 10,786,000 workers in the construction industry, 89.1 percent of them male (Bureau of Labor Statistics 2021).
p. 97.	Case and Deaton (2020, p. 220) explicitly link housing regulation to deteriorating working class opportunities:

> The traditional escape route for displaced workers has been to move from cities without jobs to cities that have them, but this route has been limited in recent years by the high cost of living in successful cities. These high costs can be inflated by land-use or other policies imposed by those who live there to protect themselves and keep newcomers out.

p.98, panel 2.	Colburn and Aldern (2022, pp. 127–30). Intuitively, while cheaper housing won't help someone who spends 100 percent of their money on drugs, you have to be *really* dysfunctional to be unable to afford rent in Mississippi.
p. 99, panel 1.	The most notable papers are Simon and Tamura (2009), Mulder and Billari (2010), and Shoag and Russell (2018). Shoag and Russell are especially on point because they explicitly link multiple distinct measures of housing *regulation* (rather than merely high housing costs) to lower fertility. Specifically, they find that housing regulation reduces overall fertility as well as fertility for women under 30, but increases fertility for older women, consistent with a story where high prices deter some births and delay others.
p.99, panel 2.	Ely and Hamilton (2018, p. 1).
p. 100, panel 3.	Branas et al. (2018, p. 2946).
p. 101.	See Branas et al. (2018, p. 2947) for details on the experiment's design and main results.
p. 102, panel 1.	In a sense, Branas et al. (2018, p. 2950; footnotes omitted) are consciously searching for ways to cut crime *without* allowing new construction:

> An overarching concern is that the interventions implemented here, and any subsequent uses of this place-based intervention, may lead

Welax, it's just a wittle wegulation.

to gentrification and the unintended displacement of residents. This is possible, although prior analyses have found economic indicators, such as property taxes, to be unchanged and, if anything, reduced, after implementation of the greening interventions tested here. In addition, over the course of this study, local municipal legislation was also passed to limit property tax increases for longtime residents in curtailing displacement due to gentrification and only a very small percentage (<5%) of the vacant lots that were remediated using the intervention strategies described here have been developed into houses or commercial businesses. Thus, almost all of the vacant lots that were remediated remain open to residents for continued use and recreation.

p. 102, panel 3.   Gyourko and Krimmel (2021, p. 11) put the zoning tax in Philadelphia's urban core at more than $900,000 per acre.

p. 105, panel 3.   Cowen (2011, 2013).

CHAPTER 4: The Tower of Terror

p. 111, panel 3.   Bassett (1922) enumerates almost all of the complaints about unregulated construction that we continue to hear today.

p. 112, panel 1.   Shoup (2011, pp. 134–35). Or as Garreau (1991, p. 120) puts it: "Now remember. The developer needs one and a half times as much space for the cars as he does for the humans." For estimates of the cost of supplying parking, see Shoup (2011, pp. 185–204).

p. 112, panel 2.   Consistent with the view that businesses seek to offer no more parking than required by law, Cutter and Franco (2012, pp. 911–16) show that required parking is an excellent predictor of actual parking.

p. 112, panel 3.   For the basics of negative externalities, see Cowen and Tabarrok (2021, pp. 191–211).

p. 113, panels 1–2.   For the canonical case for a free market in parking, see Shoup (2011).

p. 113, panels 3–4.   See especially Shoup (2011, pp. 471–504).

p. 113, panels 5–6.   On the underpricing of street parking, see Shoup (2011, pp. 295–346). According to Shoup (p. xx), roughly 30 percent of cars in congested traffic are simply "cruising" around in search of parking. Congested *parking* is a major cause of congested *driving*!

p. 114, panel 2.   As Shoup (2011, p. 2) explains, the default parking regulation in the United States is to require each builder to satisfy "peak demand" when the price of parking is zero. As a result, most parking spaces are vacant most of the time.

For further discussion of how city planners set parking regulations, see Shoup (2011, pp. 75–118).

p. 114, panel 3.   Shoup (2020).

p. 116, panel 1.   Shoup (2020).

p. 116, panel 2.   Glaeser and Kahn (2004, p. 2499) persuasively argue that the main cause of "urban sprawl" is simply that—due to the fixed cost of waiting for public transportation—private automobiles are much faster: "Public transportation appears to involve a fixed time cost of approximately 16–20 minutes, regardless of length. After this fixed time cost, cars appear to be about 50 percent faster than buses and roughly as fast as trains. It is this fixed time cost that makes public transportation so costly." At the same time, they acknowledge that housing regulation fosters additional sprawl by pushing development elsewhere: "Homeowners impose growth controls supposedly in an attempt to deter sprawl. . . . However, these controls often simply push developers to the next town out and sprawl may indeed increase as a result of these policies" (p. 2486).

p. 117.   For further discussion, see Caplan (2018). On the indirect damage of gratis government provision, see Caplan (2019b).

p. 121, panel 1.   The Bureau of Transportation Statistics (2021, p. 106) reports that in 2019, the average aggregate congestion cost for 494 urban areas in the United States was $1.174B (billion) in 2020 dollars, implying a lower bound of ($1.174B * 494) = $580B for *national* congestion cost. Dividing by total U.S. population in 2019 yields an average congestion cost of $1,768 per American. Congestion costs crashed in 2020 because of COVID-19, but they are recovering (INRIX 2021).

p. 121, panel 2.   See Samuel (2003) for a prophetic defense of smart tolls and Goh (2002) for an overview of road pricing in Singapore.

p. 125.   This discussion heavily relies on Glaeser and Kahn (2010). For a more in-depth and wider-ranging discussion of the environmental gains of urbanism, see Kahn (2006).

p. 126, panel 1.   Glaeser and Kahn (2010, p. 415). Los Angeles and Detroit are the only exceptions.

p. 126, panel 2.   Glaeser and Kahn 2010, p. 411.

p. 126, panel 3.   Just compare the average carbon dioxide emission costs in Table 2 with those in Table 3 (Glaeser and Kahn 2010, pp. 410, 412). For the average size of new homes, see U.S. Department of Commerce (2018, p. 345).

p. 127, panel 1.   Glaeser (2009); Glaeser and Kahn (2010) contains a slightly different version of the same graph.

p. 127, panels 2–3.   Glaeser and Kahn (2010 p. 414).

p. 128, panel 1. Glaeser (2009).

p. 128, panel 2. Kahn (2011, p. 223) shows that more liberal cities in California "grant fewer new housing permits than observationally similar cities located within the same metropolitan area" and that those "experiencing a growth in their liberal voter share have a lower new housing permit growth rate."

p. 130, panel 2. Glaeser (2011, pp. 260–61).

p. 131, panel 1. For surveys of research on status quo bias, see Eidelman and Crandall (2012) and Thaler (1992, pp. 63–78).

p. 132, panel 3. Psychologists call this "hedonic adaptation." See Lyubomirsky (2011) for a survey.

p. 133, panel 3. For the history of the original Waldorf-Astoria hotel, see Smith (2014) and Wikipedia (2022c).

p. 136, panel 1. For many, this is precisely the problem (Monkkonen and Manville 2019).

p. 137. Bernard Siegan died in 2006. This discussion relies heavily on Siegan (2021), a reissue of the original 1972 work. Unfortunately, little recent scholarly work on housing regulation in Houston exists, though Gray (2022, pp. 143–61) and Getlan (2018, pp. 71–72) confirm that the city's approach remains distinctive. As Getlan explains:

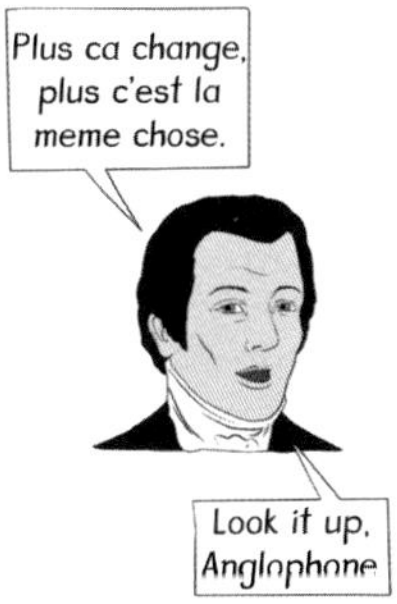
Plus ca change, plus c'est la meme chose.
Look it up, Anglophone

> Although Houston does not have zoning laws, Houston does have zoning ordinances . . . Some of the ordinances include: a minimum single family lot size in suburban areas, a minimum single family lot size in urban areas, the minimum width of a lot, fire protection ordinances, parking space requirements, and even residential pool and spa ordinances. Houston claims to be a city without limits and a city with no zoning laws, but Houston does in fact have city ordinances that act similar to how zoning laws work in other cities. The ordinances are not as strict as zoning found in almost every other city worldwide, but nonetheless, Houston does have some regulations. (Getlan 2018).

For criticism of Houston's low-regulation approach, see Qian (2010).

p. 140, panel 1. On the origins of English nuisance law, see Wikipedia (2022b).

p. 140, panel 3. On homeowners' associations, see Agan and Tabarrok (2005) and Clarke and Freedman (2019).

p. 142, panel 2. See especially Rizzo and Whitman (2020, pp. 349–97), Rizzo and Whitman (2003, 2009), and Volokh (2002).

p. 145, panels 3–4. For historical and legal background on the *Euclid* case, see Chused (2001). Writing for the majority, Justice George Sutherland famously endorsed the argument that apartments were "mere parasites" on single-family homes, adding: "Under these circumstances, apartment houses, which in a different environment would be not only entirely unobjectionable but highly desirable, come very near to being nuisances" (U.S. Supreme Court 1926). Gallagher (2016) strongly argues that the Supreme Court was empirically mistaken. Multifamily housing's fiscal externality is positive, not negative.

p. 147, panel 3.   Thaler (2010). Thaler is responding to Whitman et al. (2010).

p. 149, panel 4.   For general discussion of the neglected social benefits of higher population, see Caplan (2011, pp. 123–36), Landsburg (1997, pp. 143–60), and Simon (1998).

p. 151, panel 2.   Key point: If housing regulation actually improved residents' quality of life, this should raise housing *demand*. In practice, however, housing regulation seems to merely reduce housing *supply*. Thus, as Albouy and Ehrlich (2018, p. 101) explain, "[A]fter accounting for the tendency of areas with more desirable natural amenities to be more regulated, willingness-to-pay is no higher in regulated areas than in unregulated ones." In other words, housing regulation is primarily about excluding people from areas that were desirable already, rather than making areas more desirable.

CHAPTER 5: *Bastiat's Buildings*

p. 154, panel 1.   Bastiat ([1850] 2015). For background on Bastiat's life and work, see Leroux (2011) and Roche (1971).

pp. 155–56.   All quotes are from Bastiat ([1850] 2015).

p. 158, panel 1.   For background on the decline in California's defense industry, see Hoffman, Robinson, and Subramanian (1996).

p. 159, panel 3.   Bastiat ([1850] 2015).

p. 168.   For a standard textbook treatment of rent control, see Cowen and Tabarrok (2021, pp. 150–54).

p. 169, panel 3.   Lindbeck (1977, p. 39).

p. 171, panel 3.   Or, as supporters of public housing put it, the system is "behind on maintenance." Specifically, "Real Estate Assessment Center (REAC) scores, which are assigned as part of HUD's physical inspection of public housing properties, suggest that many properties are in disrepair: more than 8 percent of 6,923 properties (583 properties, or 93,075 units) had failing scores (below 60) in 2018; an additional 20 percent (1,418 properties, 226,407 units) received scores between 60 and 80" (Docter and Galvez 2020, p. 2).

p. 171, panel 4.   Olsen (2000, p. 1) begins, "The empirical literature is unanimous in finding that tenant-based housing certificates and vouchers provide housing of any quality at a much lower total cost . . . than the types of project-based assistance studied, namely Public Housing, Section 236, and Section 8 New

Construction and Substantial Rehab." Eriksen (2009, pp. 144–45) finds that federally subsidized construction costs 20 percent more than normal market housing. Quigley (2000, p. 57) reports that classic housing projects cost 40 percent more than normal market housing. Quigley (2008, p. 310), adds:

> More recent analyses . . . suggest that the first-year costs of subsidizing rental households through new construction programs are from 49 to 65 percent more than the costs of subsidizing the same households using vouchers, and the present-value life-cycle costs are from 19 to 38 percent more than the costs of voucher programs for comparable housing.

p. 171, panel 5. HUD (2022) reports that in 2021, 1.7 million Americans lived in public housing, roughly 0.5 percent of the U.S. population.

p. 172, panel 1. On public housing in Singapore, see Ghesquière (2007, especially p. 81). A key feature of Singaporean public housing is that after the government builds homes, it *sells* them (with 99-year leases) to residents. The upshot is that most residents effectively own their "public housing"—which they are allowed to resell for profit in the private market. Singapore thus avoids many of the pathologies of public housing in other countries by closely simulating private ownership.

p. 173. For the standard economic analysis of inclusionary zoning, plus some empirics, see Schuetz, Meltzer, and Been (2011).

CHAPTER 6: Dr. Yes

p. 183, panel 3. See Wilson (1998) for the seminal treatment.

p. 184. For an analogous treatment of immigration, see Carens (1987), as well as Caplan (2019c, pp. 163–90).

p. 186. *Utilitarianism* (Mill [1863] 2017) is probably the most famous work in this tradition.

p. 187. Modern egalitarianism builds heavily on Rawls (1971).

pp. 188–89. For a compact introduction to the wealth maximization norm, see Posner (1985).

p. 190. While Nozick (1973) remains the standard text—at least for university classes in political philosophy—Huemer (2013) is far superior.

p. 191, panel 5. Harford (2012).

p. 193, panel 2. Tim Harford apparently originated the phrase "keyhole policy." For further discussion, see Harford (2012, pp. 138–43).

p. 195, panel 2. See Shoup (2011, pp. 659–69).

p. 196, panel 3. Shoup (2011, pp. 397–432) has a particularly creative keyhole solution, the "parking benefit district." The idea is to break public street parking into small districts and remit meter fees to these small districts to pay for maintenance and other services. In Shoup's words:

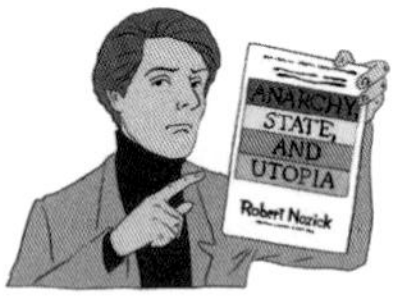
ANARCHY,
STATE,
AND
UTOPIA
Robert Nozick

> Nevertheless, merchants fear that charging for parking would keep customers away. Suppose in this case the city creates a "parking benefit district" in which all the meter revenue is spent to clean the sidewalks, plant street trees, improve store facades, put overhead utility wires underground, and ensure public safety. The meter revenue will help make the business district a place where people want to be, rather than merely a place where everyone can park for free. Returning the revenue generated *by* the district *to* the district *for* the district can convince merchants and property owners to support the idea of market-priced curb parking. (Shoup 2011, p. 398; emphasis original)

p. 197, panel 6. The main doubt about keyhole solutions almost has to be the "slippery slope argument" raised earlier. Every keyhole solution adopted risks morphing into the thicket of regulation that YIMBYs aim to clear. This danger tips the scales somewhat in favor of strict laissez-faire, but it provides no support for the status quo. Indeed, this slippery slope argument amounts to "Keyhole solutions could eventually lead us to return to . . . horrors . . . the policies we endure today."

CHAPTER 7: Mission to YIMBY

p. 200, panel 1. The earliest known use of YIMBY to mean "yes in my backyard" was in a 1991 letter by activist Richard Allman (HousingWiki 2022).

p. 200, panel 3. See Manville and Monkkonen (2021) and Einstein, Glick, and Palmer (2020) for further insight on the NIMBY mentality.

p. 200, panel 5. Matthew 5:39 (Bible Gateway n.d.).

p. 201, panel 2. Fischel (2015, pp. 154–55) rests heavily on the assumption that people vote their rational self-interest. Yet when other economists point out that this would lead childless homeowners to oppose all funding for local public schools, Fischel switches to a "broader"—and basically unfalsifiable—notion of self-interest. Glock (2022, p. 144) similarly defends zoning with an appeal to the wisdom of the average citizen: "While most elites, whether on the progressive left or the libertarian right, despise [zoning], the vast majority of Americans accept it as a good and just social measure. Instead of railing against popular ignorance, zoning's widespread acceptance should give critics pause."

p. 202, panels 1–3. See Mansbridge (1990) and Caplan (2007, pp. 148–51).

p. 202, panel 4. Hankinson (2018).

pp. 203–4. See Caplan (2019a) for further discussion.

p.205, panel 1. Einstein, Glick, and Palmer (2020, p. 35) argue that typical proponents of housing deregulation see themselves as local heroes—or "neighborhood defenders." They warn:

> The image that scholars and policy makers conjure when they use the language of NIMBYism is starkly discordant with neighbors' self-perceptions as being motivated by external concerns related to community preservation. Conceiving of opponents to new housing as NIMBYs paints an entire group of people as selfish and worried about their own individual welfare at the expense of others. In contrast, many neighborhood defenders see themselves as attending public meetings on behalf of their communities, eager to police their community's boundaries and, in some cases, share their expertise.

p. 205, panel 2. Been, Ellen, and O'Regan (2019) call this "supply skepticism." Two nationally representative surveys confirm that a large minority of Americans flatly deny that "restrictions on housing development make housing less affordable." In the first survey, 38 percent of all respondents disagreed, along with 68 percent of progressives and 60 percent of liberals (Buturovic and Klein 2010, p. 184). In the follow-up survey, 29 percent of all respondents disagreed, along with 51 percent of progressives and 45 percent of liberals (Klein and Buturovic 2011, p. 165).

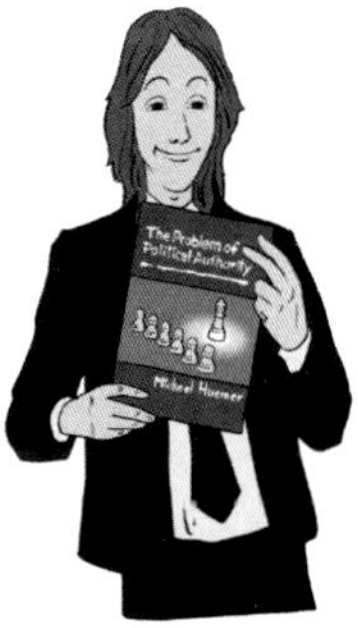
The Problem of Political Authority
Michael Huemer

A 2018 survey from California, similarly, asked respondents to name "the biggest contributor to the housing problem" (USC Dornsife and *Los Angeles Times* 2018). Only 7 percent selected "too little homebuilding" as their first choice, compared with 19 percent for "lack of rent control" and 11 percent for "lack of public funding for low-income housing." (Another 3 percent did name "overly restrictive zoning rules," and 9 percent named "environmental and other regulations that raise construction costs," though the latter wording is rather leading the witness.) Most impressively, the in-depth survey by Nall, Elmendorf, and Oklobdzija (2022) shows that the median American surveyed denies *any* effect of higher housing supply on its price. Given researchers' enormous estimates of the effect of regulation on housing prices, the prevalence of the view that regulation makes no difference is shocking.

p. 205, panel 3. Hills (2018) nicely elaborates this point.

p. 205, panels 4–5.   Caplan (2007, pp. 23–49). Jacobus (2019) insists that voters are wiser than they look: "My view is that this tenacity is not the result of a lack of understanding or education. Instead, I think it grows from a sensible feeling that the Econ 101 story greatly overstates the extent to which lower-income people, and even middle-income people, will benefit from luxury development." But since few laypeople can correctly explain the basic textbook story, "lack of understanding or education" is indeed the obvious explanation. Jacobus also strangely treats evidence of the public's stubbornness as a sign of intuitive insight. Normally we take such stubbornness as a sign of irrational dogmatism.

p. 207, panel 1.   Despite his sympathy for housing regulation, even Fischel (2001, p. 144) admits that "NIMBYs sometimes appear to be irrational in their opposition to projects in the sense that they express far-fetched anxieties or doggedly fight projects whose expected neighborhood effects seem small or even benign."

p. 208, panel 1.   See Eidelman and Crandall (2012) and Thaler (1992, pp. 63–78).

p. 209, panel 7.   As Caplan (2015) states: "Why are proponents of government action so prone to hyperbole? Because it's rhetorically effective, of course. You need wild claims and flowery words to whip up public enthusiasm for government action. Sober weighing of probability, cost, and benefit damns with faint praise—and fails to overcome public apathy."

p. 212.   U.S. Supreme Court (1926); Chused (2001). The dissenting votes came from Justices Devanter (top), McReynolds (bottom left), and Butler (bottom right).

p. 213, panels 4–5.   "Local governments historically have been subject to the Ultra Vires Rule, which holds that political subdivisions possess only the powers expressly conferred by charter or law and no other powers. In other words, the rule provides for a narrow interpretation of the powers of local governments and makes explicit that a substate government may engage only in activity specifically sanctioned by the superior government" (Zimmerman 1995, p. 17). For further discussion, see Zimmerman (1995, pp. 17–50).

p. 214, panels 2–3.   State of Oregon (2019); Wamsley (2019). Oregon's law allows up to quadruplexes in the Portland area. On the law's broader influence, see Shumway (2021).

p. 214, panels 4–5.   State of California (2021); *Economist* (2021).

p. 214, panels 6–7.   The Orwellian official argument for this regulation is that it *benefits* homeowners by preventing them from selling out to developers:

> This bill benefits homeowners, and homeowners alone. SB 9 contains an owner occupancy requirement, which requires a homeowner to live

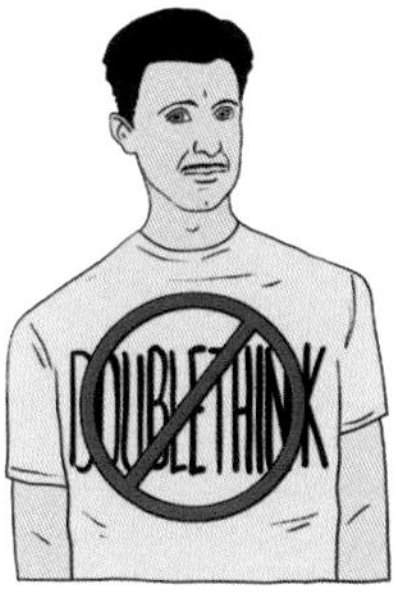
DOUBLETHINK

> in one of the units for three years from the time they get approval for a lot split. Additionally, this bill prohibits the development of small subdivisions and prohibits ministerial lot splits on adjacent parcels by the same individual to prevent investor speculation. In fact, allowing for more neighborhood scale housing in California's communities actually curbs the market power of institutional investors. SB 9 also prevents profiteers from evicting or displacing tenants by excluding properties where a tenant has resided in the past three years. (State of California 2021)

This is as absurd as the claim that you benefit landowners with oil on their property by requiring them to supervise the drilling themselves, lest they be exploited by professional drillers.

p. 215, panel 1. Gyourko, Hartley, and Krimmel (2021).

p. 215, panel 2. Gyourko, Hartley, and Krimmel (2021, p. 11).

p. 216, panel 1. Gyourko, Hartley, and Krimmel (2019, p. 33).

p. 216, panels 2–4. Gyourko, Hartley, and Krimmel (2019, pp. 36–38).

p. 216, panel 5. Gyourko, Hartley, and Krimmel (2021, p. 2).

p. 220, panel 2. Note that this Bentham quote is Bastiat's ([1845] 1996, p. 127) translation. The original Bentham (1843, p. 33) reads: "The request which agriculture, manufactures, and commerce present to governments, is modest and reasonable as that which Diogenes made to Alexander: 'Stand out of my sunshine.' We have no need of favour—we require only a secure and open path."

REFERENCES

Agan, Amanda, and Alex Tabarrok. 2005. "What Are Private Governments Worth?" *Regulation* 28, no. 3: 14–17.

Ahlfeldt, Gabriel, and Daniel McMillen. 2018. "Tall Buildings and Land Values: Height and Construction Cost Elasticities in Chicago, 1870–2010." *Review of Economics and Statistics* 100, no. 5: 861–75.

Albouy, David, and Gabriel Ehrlich. 2018. "Housing Productivity and the Social Cost of Land-Use Restrictions." *Journal of Urban Economics* 107: 101–20.

Albouy, David, Gabriel Ehrlich, and Yingyi Liu. 2016. "Housing Demand, Cost-of-Living Inequality, and the Affordability Crisis." NBER Working Paper no. 22816.

Badger, Emily, and Quoctrung Bui. 2019. "Cities Start to Question an American Ideal: A House with a Yard on Every Lot." *New York Times*, June 18, 2019.

Bassett, Edward M. 1922. *Zoning.* New York: National Municipal League.

Bastiat, Frédéric. (1845) 1996. *Economic Sophisms.* Irvington-on-Hudson, NY: Foundation for Economic Education.

Bastiat, Frédéric. (1850) 2015. "What Is Seen and What Is Not Seen." Online Library of Liberty.

Bay Area Census. n.d. "San Francisco City and County."

Been, Vicki, Ingrid Ellen, and Katherine O'Regan. 2019. "Supply Skepticism: Housing Supply and Affordability." *Housing Policy Debate* 29, no. 1: 25–40.

Bentham, Jeremy. 1843. *The Works of Jeremy Bentham,* vol. 3. London: William Tait.

Berry, Christopher. 2001. "Land Use Regulations and Residential Segregation: Does Zoning Matter?" *American Law and Economics Review* 3, no. 2: 251–74.

Beyer, Scott. 2022. *Market Urbanism: A Vision for Free-Market Cities.* New York: Market Urbanism Report.

Bible Gateway. n.d. "King James Version: Matthew 5:39."

Branas, Charles, Eugenia South, Michelle Kondo, Bernadette Hohl, Philippe Bourgois, Douglas Wiebe, and John MacDonald. 2018. "Citywide Cluster Randomized Trial to Restore Blighted Vacant Land and Its Effects on Violence, Crime, and Fear." *Proceedings of the National Academy of Sciences* 115, no. 12: 2946–51.

Brinklow, Adam. 2020. "Curbed SF Election Guide: SF's Proposition E Office Building Cap, Explained." Curbed San Francisco, February 21, 2020.

Bureau of Labor Statistics. 2002. "Housing Expenditures." *Issues in Labor Statistics*, March 2002.

Bureau of Labor Statistics. 2021. "Current Population Survey: Employed Persons by Detailed Industry, Sex, Race, and Hispanic or Latino Ethnicity."

Bureau of Labor Statistics. n.d. "How the CPI Measures Price Change of Owners' Equivalent Rent of Primary Residence (OER) and Rent of Primary Residence (Rent)."

Bureau of Transportation Statistics. 2021. *National Transportation Statistics 2021*. Washington: U.S. Department of Transportation.

Buturovic, Zeljka, and Daniel Klein. 2010. "Economic Enlightenment in Relation to College-Going, Ideology, and Other Variables: A Zogby Survey of Americans." *Econ Journal Watch* 7, no. 2: 174–96.

Caplan, Bryan. 2007. *The Myth of the Rational Voter: Why Democracies Choose Bad Policies*. Princeton, NJ: Princeton University Press.

Caplan, Bryan. 2011. *Selfish Reasons to Have More Kids: Why Being a Great Parent Is Less Work and More Fun than You Think*. New York: Basic Books.

Caplan, Bryan. 2015. "What's Libertarian about Betting?" *EconLog*, September 30, 2015.

Caplan, Bryan. 2018. "Gratis Is Not Great." *EconLog*, December 3, 2018.

Caplan, Bryan. 2019a. "Deludedly Deeming Deregulation a Disaster." *EconLog*, November 26, 2019.

Caplan, Bryan. 2019b. "In Sync: How Business Responds to Gratis Government." *EconLog*, June 12, 2019.

Caplan, Bryan. 2019c. *Open Borders: The Science and Ethics of Immigration*. New York: First Second.

Caplan, Bryan. 2021a. "Housing Deregulation: Reverse Musical Chairs." *EconLog*, March 22, 2021.

Caplan, Bryan. 2021b. "Hsieh-Moretti on Housing Regulation: A Gracious Admission of Error." *EconLog*, April 5, 2021.

Caplan, Bryan. 2021c. "Immigration and Housing: The Meaning of Hsieh-Moretti." *EconLog*, April 6, 2021.

Caplan, Bryan. 2022. "The Zoning Tax: A Mere Illusion?" *Bet on It*, May 26, 2022.

Carens, Joseph. 1987. "Aliens and Citizens: The Case for Open Borders." *Review of Politics* 49, no. 2 (Spring): 251–73.

Case, Anne, and Angus Deaton. 2020. *Deaths of Despair and the Future of Capitalism*. Princeton, NJ: Princeton University Press.

Case, Karl. 1994. "Land Prices and House Prices in the United States." In *Housing Markets in the U.S. and Japan*, edited by Yukio Noguchi and James Poterba, pp. 29–48. Chicago: University of Chicago Press.

Chau, Kwong-Wing, Siu Kei Wong, Yung Yau, and A. K. C. Yeung. 2007. "Determining Optimal Building Height." *Urban Studies* 44, no. 3: 561–607.

Chused, Richard. 2001. *"Euclid's Historical Imagery." Case Western Reserve Law Review* 51, no. 4: 597–616.

Clarke, Wyatt, and Matthew Freedman. 2019. "The Rise and Effects of Homeowners Associations." *Journal of Urban Economics* 112: 1–15.

Colburn, Gregg, and Clayton Page Aldern. 2022. *Homelessness Is a Housing Problem: How Structural Factors Explain U.S. Patterns.* Oakland: University of California Press.

Cowen, Tyler. 2011. *The Great Stagnation: How America Ate All the Low-Hanging Fruit of Modern History, Got Sick, and Will (Eventually) Feel Better.* New York: Dutton.

Cowen, Tyler. 2013. *Average Is Over: Powering America Beyond the Age of the Great Stagnation.* New York: Dutton.

Cowen, Tyler, and Alex Tabarrok. 2021. *Modern Principles of Economics*, 5th ed. New York: Worth Publishers.

Cutter, W. Bowman, and Sofia Franco. 2012. "Do Parking Requirements Significantly Increase the Area Dedicated to Parking? A Test of the Effect of Parking Requirements Values in Los Angeles County." *Transportation Research Part A* 46, no. 6: 901–25.

David Binder Research. 2021. "Final Results: California Voter Survey." July 27–29, 2021.

Docter, Benny, and Martha Galvez. 2020. "The Future of Public Housing: Public Housing Fact Sheet." Urban Institute, February 20, 2020.

Dougherty, Conor. 2021. *Golden Gates: The Housing Crisis and a Reckoning for the American Dream.* New York: Penguin Books.

Economist. 2021. "California Ends Single-Family Zoning." September 23, 2021.

Eidelman, Scott, and Christian Crandall. 2012. "Bias in Favor of the Status Quo." *Social and Personality Psychology Compass* 6, no. 3: 270–81.

Einstein, Katherine, David Glick, and Maxwell Palmer. 2020. *Neighborhood Defenders: Participatory Politics and America's Housing Crisis.* Cambridge: Cambridge University Press.

Ekins, Emily. 2019. *What Americans Think about Poverty, Wealth, and Work: Findings from the Cato Institute 2019 Welfare, Work, and Wealth National Survey.* Washington: Cato Institute.

Ely, Danielle, and Brady Hamilton. 2018. "Trends in Fertility and Mother's Age at First Birth among Rural and Metropolitan Counties: United States, 2007–2017." NCHS Data Brief no. 323, October 2018.

Erdmann, Kevin. 2019. *Shut Out: How a Housing Shortage Caused the Great Recession and Crippled Our Economy.* Lanham, MD: Rowman and Littlefield.

Eriksen, Michael. 2009. "The Market Price of Low-Income Housing Tax Credits." *Journal of Urban Economics* 66, no. 2: 141–49.

Eriksen, Michael, and Anthony Orlando. 2022. "Returns to Scale in Residential Construction: The Marginal Impact of Building Height." *Real Estate Economics* 50, no. 2: 534–64.

Federal Reserve Bank of St. Louis. 2021a. "Expenditures: Shelter: All Consumer Units."

Federal Reserve Bank of St. Louis. 2021b. "Expenditures: Shelter by Quintiles of Income before Taxes: Highest 20 Percent (81st to 100th Percentile)."

Federal Reserve Bank of St. Louis. 2021c. "Expenditures: Shelter by Quintiles of Income before Taxes: Lowest 20 Percent (1st to 20th Percentile)."

Federal Reserve Bank of St. Louis. 2021d. "Expenditures: Total Average Annual Expenditures: All Consumer Units."

Federal Reserve Bank of St. Louis. 2021e. "Expenditures: Total Average Annual Expenditures by Quintiles of Income before Taxes: Highest 20 Percent (81st to 100th Percentile)."

Federal Reserve Bank of St. Louis. 2021f. "Expenditures: Total Average Annual Expenditures by Quintiles of Income before Taxes: Lowest 20 Percent (1st to 20th Percentile)."

Federal Reserve Bank of St. Louis. 2023a. "All-Transactions House Price Index for San Francisco-San Mateo-Redwood City, CA (MSAD)."

Federal Reserve Bank of St. Louis. 2023b. "All-Transactions House Price Index for the United States."

Fischel, William. 2001. "Why Are There NIMBYs?" *Land Economics* 77, no. 1: 144–52.

Fischel, William. 2015. *Zoning Rules! The Economics of Land Use Regulation.* Cambridge, MA: Lincoln Institute of Land Policy.

Flanagan, Roger, and George Norman. 1999. "The Relationship between Construction Price and Height." In *Cost Modelling: Foundations of Building Economics*, edited by Martin Skitmore and Vernon Marston, pp. 258–66. London: E & FN Spon.

Furman, Jason. 2015. "Barriers to Shared Growth: The Case of Land Use Regulation and Economic Rents" (remarks delivered at the Urban Institute, November 20, 2015).

Gallagher, Ryan. 2016. "The Fiscal Externality of Multifamily Housing and Its Impact on the Property Tax: Evidence from Cities and Schools, 1980–2010." *Regional Science and Urban Economics* 60: 249–59.

Ganong, Peter, and Daniel Shoag. 2017. "Why Has Regional Income Convergence in the U.S. Declined?" *Journal of Urban Economics* 102: 76–90.

Garreau, Joel. 1991. *Edge City: Life on the New Frontier.* New York: Anchor Books.

Getlan, Brady. 2018. "Houston Strong: A World Series Ring, but Is There a Problem with a Lack of Zoning Laws?" *University of Baltimore Journal of Land and Development* 7, no. 2: 63–89.

Ghesquière, Henri. 2007. *Singapore's Success: Engineering Economic Growth.* Singapore: Thomson Learning.

Glaeser, Edward. 2004. "Housing Supply." *The Reporter* 2, June 2004.

Glaeser, Edward. 2009. "Green Cities, Brown Suburbs." *City Journal*, Winter 2009.

Glaeser, Edward. 2011. *Triumph of the City: How Our Greatest Invention Makes Us Richer, Smarter, Greener, Healthier, and Happier.* New York: Penguin Books.

Glaeser, Edward, and Joseph Gyourko. 2003. "The Impact of Building Restrictions on Housing Affordability." *Federal Reserve Bank of New York Economic Policy Review* 9, no. 2: 21–39.

Glaeser, Edward, and Joseph Gyourko. 2018. "The Economic Implications of Housing Supply." *Journal of Economic Perspectives* 32, no. 1: 3–30.

Glaeser, Edward, and Matthew Kahn. 2004. "Sprawl and Urban Growth." In *Handbook of Regional and Urban Economics*, vol. 4, edited by J. Vernon Henderson and Jacques-François Thisse, pp. 4:2481–527. Amsterdam: Elsevier.

Glaeser, Edward, and Matthew Kahn. 2010. "The Greenness of Cities: Carbon Dioxide Emissions and Urban Development." *Journal of Urban Economics* 67, no. 3: 404–18.

Glock, Judge. 2022. "Two Cheers for Zoning." *American Affairs* 6, no. 4: 132–48.

Goh, Mark. 2002. "Congestion Management and Electronic Road Pricing in Singapore." *Journal of Transport Geography* 10, no. 1: 29–38.

Gray, M. Nolan. 2022. *Arbitrary Lines: How Zoning Broke the American City and How to Fix It.* Washington: Island Press.

Greaney, Brian. 2023a. "Housing Constraints and Spatial Misallocation: Comment."

Greaney, Brian. 2023b. "Greaney Replies to Hsieh." *Bet On It*, November 21, 2023.

Gyourko, Joe, and Jacob Krimmel. 2021. "The Impact of Local Residential Land Use Restrictions on Land Values across and within Single Family Housing Markets." *Journal of Urban Economics* 126, no. 3.

Gyourko, Joseph, Jonathan Hartley, and Jacob Krimmel. 2019. "The Local Residential Land Use Regulatory Environment across U.S. Housing Markets: Evidence from a New Wharton Index." NBER Working Paper no. 26573.

Gyourko, Joseph, Jonathan Hartley, and Jacob Krimmel. 2021. "The Local Residential Land Use Regulatory Environment across U.S. Housing Markets: Evidence from a New Wharton Index." *Journal of Urban Economics* 124: 1–15.

Gyourko, Joseph, and Raven Molloy. 2015. "Regulation and Housing Supply." In *Handbook of Regional and Urban Economics*, vol. 5, edited by Gilles Duranton, J. Vernon Henderson, and William C. Strange, pp. 5:1289–1337. Amsterdam: Elsevier.

Hankinson, Michael. 2018. "When Do Renters Behave Like Homeowners? High Rent, Price Anxiety, and NIMBYism." *American Political Science Review* 112, no 3: 473–93.

Harford, Tim. 2012. *The Undercover Economist: Exposing Why the Rich Are Rich, the Poor Are Poor—and Why You Can Never Buy a Decent Used Car!*, 2nd ed. Oxford: Oxford University Press.

Hills, Roderick, Jr. 2018. "Why Do So Many Affordable-Housing Advocates Reject the Law of Supply and Demand?" *Washington Post*, September 18, 2018.

Hirt, Sonia. 2014. *Zoned in the U.S.A.: The Origins and Implications of American Land-Use Regulation.* Ithaca, NY: Cornell University Press.

Hoffman, Sandra, Sherman Robinson, and Shankar Subramanian. 1996. "The Role of Defense Cuts in the California Recession: Computable General Equilibria Models and Interstate Factor Mobility." *Journal of Regional Science* 36, no. 4: 571–95.

HousingWiki. 2022. "YIMBY Movement."

Hsieh, Chang-Tai. 2023. "Hsieh Replies to Greaney." *Bet On It*, November 16.

Hsieh, Chang-Tai, and Enrico Moretti. 2019. "Housing Constraints and Spatial Misallocation." *American Economic Journal: Macroeconomics* 11, no. 2: 1–39.

HUD (U.S. Department of Housing and Urban Development). 2022. "Assisted Housing: National and Local" (data set).

Huemer, Michael. 2013. *The Problem of Political Authority: An Examination of the Right to Coerce and the Duty to Obey.* New York: Palgrave Macmillan.

INRIX. 2021. *INRIX 2021 Global Traffic Scorecard.*

Jacobus, Rick. 2019. "Why Voters Haven't Been Buying the Case for Building." *Shelterforce*, February 19, 2019.

Kahn, Matthew. 2006. *Green Cities: Urban Growth and the Environment.* Washington: Brookings Institution Press.

Kahn, Matthew. 2011. "Do Liberal Cities Limit New Housing Development? Evidence from California." *Journal of Urban Economics* 69, no. 2: 223–8.

Klein, Daniel, and Zeljka Buturovic. 2011. "Economic Enlightenment Revisited: New Results Again Find Little Relationship between Education and Economic Enlightenment but Vitiate Prior Evidence of the Left Being Worse." *Econ Journal Watch* 8, no. 2: 157–73.

Knoll, Katharina, Moritz Schularick, and Thomas Steger. 2017. "No Price Like Home: Global House Prices, 1870–2012." *American Economic Review* 107, no. 2: 331–53.

Krugman, Paul. 2005. "The Hissing Sounds." *New York Times*, August 8, 2005.

Krugman, Paul. 2014. "Wrong Way Nation." *New York Times*, August 24, 2014.

Krugman, Paul. 2017. "Zoning: Both Sides Get It Wrong." *New York Times*, August 29, 2017.

Landsburg, Steven. 1997. *Fair Play: What Your Child Can Teach You about Economics, Values, and the Meaning of Life.* New York: Free Press.

Leroux, Robert. 2011. *Political Economy and Liberalism in France: The Contributions of Frédéric Bastiat.* London: Routledge.

Lewyn, Michael. 2017. *Government Intervention and Suburban Sprawl: The Case for Market Urbanism.* New York: Palgrave Macmillan.

Lindbeck, Assar. 1977. *The Political Economy of the New Left: An Outsider's View.* New York: New York University Press.

Lindsey, Robert. 1985. "Buildings Curbed by San Francisco." *New York Times*, July 3, 1985.

Lyubomirsky, Sonja. 2011. "Hedonic Adaptation to Positive and Negative Experiences." In *Oxford Handbook of Stress, Health, and Coping*, edited by Susan Folkman, pp. 200–24. Oxford: Oxford University Press.

Mansbridge, Jane, ed. 1990. *Beyond Self-Interest.* Chicago: University of Chicago Press.

Manville, Michael. 2021. "Liberals and Housing: A Study in Ambivalence." *Housing Policy Debate* 33: 1–21.

Manville, Michael, and Paavo Monkkonen. 2021. "Unwanted Housing: Localism and Politics of Housing Development." *Journal of Planning Education and Research*: 1–16.

Manville, Michael, Paavo Monkkonen, and Michael Lens. 2020. "It's Time to End Single-Family Zoning." *Journal of the American Planning Association* 86, no. 1: 106–12.

Marble, William, and Clayton Nall. 2021. "Where Self-Interest Trumps Ideology: Liberal Homeowners and Local Opposition to Housing Development." *Journal of Politics* 83, no. 4: 1747–63.

Mast, Evan. 2023. "JUE Insight: The Effect of New Market-Rate Housing Construction on the Low-Income Housing Market." *Journal of Urban Economics* 133: 103383.

Metcalf, Gabriel. 2018. "Sand Castles before the Tide? Affordable Housing in Expensive Cities." *Journal of Economic Perspectives* 32, no. 1: 59–80.

Mill, John Stuart. (1863) 2017. *Utilitarianism.*

Monkkonen, Paavo, and Michael Manville. 2019. "Opposition to Development or Opposition to Developers? Experimental Evidence on Attitudes toward New Housing." *Journal of Urban Affairs* 41, no. 8: 1123–41.

Mulder, Clara, and Francesco Billari. 2010. "Homeownership Regimes and Low Fertility." *Housing Studies* 25, no. 4: 527–41.

Murray, Cameron. 2021. "Marginal and Average Prices of Land Lots Should Not Be Equal: A Critique of Glaeser and Gyourko's Method for Identifying Residential Price Effects of Town Planning Regulations." *Economy and Space* 53, no. 1: 191–209.

Murray, Cameron. 2022. "Murray: The 'Zoning Tax' Is an Illusion." *Bet on It*, May 31, 2022.

Nall, Clayton, Chris Elmendorf, and Stan Oklobdzija. 2022. "Folk Economics and the Persistence of Political Opposition to New Housing." Working paper.

Nozick, Robert. 1973. *Anarchy, State, and Utopia.* New York: Basic Books.

Olsen, Edgar. 2000. "The Cost-Effectiveness of Alternative Methods of Delivering Housing Subsides." University of Virginia Working Paper No. 351.

Perry, Mark. 2016. "New US Homes Today Are 1,000 Square Feet Larger than in 1973 and Living Space per Person Has Nearly Doubled." *AEIdeas*, June 5, 2016.

Picken, David, and Benedict Ilozor. 2015. "The Relationship between Building Height and Construction Costs." In *Design Economics for the Built Environment: Impact of Sustainability on Project Evaluation*, edited by Herbert Robinson, Barry Symonds, Barry Gilbertson, and Benedict Ilozor, pp. 47–60. Chichester, UK: Wiley-Blackwell.

Posner, Richard. 1985. "Wealth Maximization Revisited." *Notre Dame Journal of Law, Ethics, and Public Policy* 2: 85–105.

Qian, Zhu. 2010. "Without Zoning: Urban Development and Land Use Controls in Houston." *Cities* 27, no. 1: 31–41.

Quigley, John. 2000. "A Decent Home: Housing Policy in Perspective." *Brookings-Wharton Papers on Urban Affairs*, 2000: 53–88.

Quigley, John. 2008. "Just Suppose: Housing Subsidies for Low-Income Renters." In *Revisiting Rental Housing: Policies, Programs, and Priorities*, edited by Nicolas Retsinas and Eric Belsky, pp. 299–316. Washington: Brookings Institution Press.

Rawls, John. 1971. *A Theory of Justice.* Cambridge, MA: Harvard University Press.

Rizzo, Mario, and Glen Whitman. 2003. "The Camel's Nose Is in the Tent: Rules, Theories, and Slippery Slopes." *UCLA Law Review* 51, no. 2: 539–92.

Rizzo, Mario, and Glen Whitman. 2009. "Little Brother Is Watching You: New Paternalism on the Slippery Slopes." *Arizona Law Review* 51, no. 3: 685–740.

Rizzo, Mario, and Glen Whitman. 2020. *Escaping Paternalism: Rationality, Behavioral Economics, and Public Policy.* Cambridge: Cambridge University Press.

Roche, George. 1971. *Frederic Bastiat: A Man Alone.* New Rochelle, NY: Arlington House.

Rognlie, Matthew. 2015. "Deciphering the Fall and Rise in the Net Capital Share: Accumulation or Scarcity?" *Brookings Papers on Economic Activity*, Spring 2015: 1–54.

Rosenthal, Stuart. 2014. "Are Private Markets and Filtering a Viable Source of Low-Income Housing? Estimates from a 'Repeat Income' Model." *American Economic Review* 104, no. 2: 687–706.

Saiz, Albert. 2010. "The Geographic Determinants of Housing Supply." *Quarterly Journal of Economics* 125, no. 3: 1253–96.

Samuel, Peter. 2003. "Motorway Financing and Provision: Technology Favors a New Approach." In *The Half-Life of Policy Rationales: How New Technology Affects Old Policy Issues*, edited by Fred Foldvary and Daniel Klein, pp. 47–59. New York: New York University Press.

Schmitz, James. 2020. "Solving the Housing Crisis Will Require Fighting Monopolies in Construction." Federal Reserve Bank of Minneapolis Working Paper 773, December 11, 2020.

Schuetz, Jenny. 2017. "Who Is the New Face of American Homeownership?" *The Avenue*, October 9, 2017.

Schuetz, Jenny, Rachel Meltzer, and Vicki Been. 2011. "Silver Bullet or Trojan Horse? The Effects of Inclusionary Zoning on Local Housing Markets in the United States." *Urban Studies* 48, no. 2: 297–329.

Shoag, Daniel, and Lauren Russell. 2018. "Land Use Regulations and Fertility Rates." In *One Hundred Years of Zoning and the Future of Cities*, edited by Amnon Lehavi, pp. 139–49. Cham, Switzerland: Springer.

Shoup, Donald. 2011. *The High Cost of Free Parking.* New York: Routledge.

Shoup, Donald. 2020. "The Pseudoscience of Parking Requirements." *Zoning Practice* 37, no. 2: 2–7.

Shumway, Julia. 2021. "White House: Oregon Single-Family Zoning Law Could Be Model for Nation." *Oregon Capital Chronicle*, October 29, 2021.

Siegan, Bernard. (1972) 2021. *Land Use without Zoning.* New York: Rowman and Littlefield.

Simon, Curtis, and Robert Tamura. 2009. "Do Higher Rents Discourage Fertility? Evidence from U.S. Cities, 1940–2000." *Regional Science and Urban Economics* 39, no. 1: 33–42.

Simon, Julian. 1998. *The Ultimate Resource 2.* Princeton, NJ: Princeton University Press.

Smith, Stephen. 2014. "Four Great Buildings That New York Demolished—Decades Before the Folk Art Museum." *Next City*, February 21, 2014.

Somin, Ilya. 2015. "The Emerging Cross-Ideological Consensus on Zoning." *Washington Post*, December 5, 2015.

State of California. 2021. "The California H.O.M.E. Act (Senate Bill 9)."

State of Oregon. 2019. "Housing Choices (House Bill 2001)."

Summers, Lawrence. 2014. "The Inequality Puzzle." *Democracy*, no. 33 (Summer).

Tankersley, Jim. 2015. "Meet the 26-Year-Old Who's Taking On Thomas Piketty's Ominous Warnings about Inequality." *Washington Post*, March 19, 2015.

Thaler, Richard H. 1992. *The Winner's Curse: Paradoxes and Anomalies of Economic Life.* New York: Free Press.

Thaler, Richard. 2010. "Fear of Falling." *Cato Unbound*, April 7, 2010.

Trounstine, Jessica. 2020. "The Geography of Inequality: How Land Use Regulation Produces Segregation." *American Political Science Review* 114, no. 2: 443–55.

Trounstine, Jessica. 2021. "You Won't Be My Neighbor: Opposition to High Density Development." *Urban Affairs Review* 59, no. 1: 1–15.

Tulip, Peter. 2022. "Tulip on the Zoning Tax." *Bet on It*, June 2, 2022.

U.S. Census Bureau. 2021. "Table H-3. Mean Household Income Received by Each Fifth and Top 5 Percent of All Households."

U.S. Census Bureau. 2022. "QuickFacts: San Francisco County, California."

U.S. Department of Commerce. 2018. *2017 Characteristics of New Housing.*

U.S. Supreme Court. 1926. "Village of Euclid, Ohio v. Amblin Reality Co." FindLaw.

USC Dornsife and *Los Angeles Times.* 2018. "Topline Results (UAS 154)." October 24.

Volokh, Eugene. 2002. "The Mechanisms of the Slippery Slope." *Harvard Law Review* 116, no. 4: 1026–1138.

Wamsley, Laurel. 2019. "Oregon Legislature Votes to Essentially Ban Single-Family Zoning." *NPR*, July 1, 2019.

Weicher, John, Frederick Eggers, and Fouad Moumen. 2016. *The Long-Term Dynamics of Affordable Rental Housing.* Washington: Hudson Institute.

Whitman, Glen, Richard Thaler, Jonathan Klick, and Shane Frederick. 2010. "Slippery Slopes and the New Paternalism." *Cato Unbound*, April 6, 2010.

Wikipedia. 2022a. "List of Tallest Buildings in San Francisco."

Wikipedia. 2022b. "Nuisance in English Law."

Wikipedia. 2022c. "Waldorf-Astoria (1883–1929).

Wilson, Edward. 1998. *Consilience: The Unity of Knowledge.* New York: Vintage Books.

Yglesias, Matthew. 2012. *The Rent Is Too Damn High: What to Do about It, and Why It Matters More than You Think.* New York: Simon and Schuster.

Yglesias, Matthew. 2020. *One Billion Americans: The Case for Thinking Bigger.* New York: Portfolio/Penguin Press.

Zimmerman, Joseph. 1995. *State-Local Relations: A Partnership Approach*, 2nd edition. Westport, CT: Praeger Publishers.

ACKNOWLEDGMENTS

I started this book at the dawn of COVID-19, so above all I want to thank everyone who continued to break bread and share ideas face-to-face during those lonely days: Robin Hanson, my best friend in the universe; my colleagues Dan Klein and Don Boudreaux; Steve Kuhn, the most generous man I've ever known; Carlos Carvalho, Richard Lowery, and John Hatfield of the Salem Center for Policy at the University of Texas; Aidan, Tristan, Simon, and Vali, my four homeschoolers; and of course my wife, Corina. Further thanks to Tyler Cowen and Alex Tabarrok for rushing back to lunch two weeks after vaccination. I am also eternally grateful to Cato CEO Peter Goettler for greenlighting this project, as well as the rest of the Cato book team: Eleanor O'Connor, Ivan Osorio, and Jason Kuznicki. I also owe huge (yet fortunately nonpecuniary) educational debts to my collaborators on my previous graphic novel, especially illustrator extraordinaire Zach Weinersmith and editor Calista Brill. Finally, I want to thank my talented and patient illustrator, Ady Branzei, who brought my vision to life down to the smallest detail.

—Bryan Caplan

I would like to thank Bryan for giving me the opportunity to work on this project, and his inspiring optimism throughout; the entire Cato team, especially Eleanor O'Connor and Ivan Osorio for their patience and professionalism; and my mother, Claudina, and my sisters Francisca and Brighita for their support throughout the process.

—Ady Branzei

ABOUT THE AUTHORS

Bryan Caplan is the *New York Times* best-selling author of *Open Borders* (illustrated by *Saturday Morning Breakfast Cereal*'s Zach Weinersmith), *The Myth of the Rational Voter, Selfish Reasons to Have More Kids,* and *The Case against Education*. He is a professor of economics at George Mason University and the editor and chief writer for the *Bet On It* Substack. Mindful of the stereotype of the boring professor, he strives with all his might and means to make abstract ideas thrilling. An openly nerdy man who loves graphic novels and role-playing games, Caplan lives in Oakton, Virginia, with his wife and four kids.

Ady Branzei has worked for 25 years in design, illustration, animation, comics, painting, and sculpture all over Europe. He is most noted for his Orthodox religious art in Romania, including paintings for the Banu Church in Iași and paintings and sculptures for Slătioara Monastery in Suceava County, as well as for his work on the restoration of the Palace of Culture in Iași. Branzei also created the music video for "Vine Valul Imi la Calul," sung by Daniel Iancu.

ABOUT THE CATO INSTITUTE

Founded in 1977, the Cato Institute is a public policy research foundation dedicated to broadening the parameters of policy debate to allow consideration of more options that are consistent with the principles of limited government, individual liberty, and peace. To that end, the Institute strives to achieve greater involvement of the intelligent, concerned lay public in questions of policy and the proper role of government.

Named for *Cato's Letters*, libertarian pamphlets that helped lay the philosophical foundation for the American Revolution, the Institute takes its inspiration from the struggle of America's founding generation to secure liberty through limited government and the rule of law.

To encourage discussion about public policy and the proper role of government, the Cato Institute undertakes an extensive publications program on the complete spectrum of policy issues. Books, monographs, and shorter studies are commissioned to examine the federal budget, Social Security, regulation, military spending, international trade, and myriad other issues.

In order to maintain its independence, the Cato Institute accepts no government funding. Contributions are received from foundations, corporations, and individuals, and other revenue is generated from the sale of publications. The Institute is a nonprofit, tax-exempt, educational foundation under Section 501(c)3 of the Internal Revenue Code.

CATO INSTITUTE
1000 Massachusetts Ave. NW
Washington, DC 20001
www.cato.org